The *E*ditor

PHILIP APPLEMAN is Distinguished Professor Emeritus at Indiana University, where he was a founding editor of *Victorian Studies,* national committee chairman for English Section II of the Modern Language Association, and member of the national council of the American Association of University Professors. He is the author of a book on overpopulation, *The Silent Explosion;* coeditor of *1859: Entering an Age of Crisis;* editor of Thomas Malthus's *An Essay on the Principle of Population*: A Norton Critical Edition, and of the W. W. Norton abridged edition of Charles Darwin's *The Origin of Species;* and author of several award-winning volumes of poetry, including *Darwin's Ark* and *New and Selected Poems: 1956–1996,* as well as three novels, including *Apes and Angels.*

Norton Critical Editions in the History of Ideas

AQUINAS • St. Thomas Aquinas on Politics and Ethics
translated and edited by Paul E. Sigmund

DARWIN • Darwin
selected and edited by Philip Appleman (Third Edition)

ERASMUS • The Praise of Folly and Other Writings
translated and edited by Robert M. Adams

HERODOTUS • The Histories
*translated by Walter E. Blanco, edited by Walter E.
Blanco and Jennifer Tolbert Roberts*

HOBBES • Leviathan
edited by Richard E. Flathman and David Johnston

MACHIAVELLI • The Prince
translated and edited by Robert M. Adams (Second Edition)

MALTHUS • An Essay on the Principle of Population
edited by Philip Appleman

MARX • The Communist Manifesto
edited by Frederic L. Bender

MILL • Mill: The Spirit of the Age, On Liberty,
The Subjection of Women
edited by Alan Ryan

MORE • Utopia
translated and edited by Robert M. Adams (Second Edition)

NEWMAN • Apologia Pro Vita Sua
edited by David J. DeLaura

NEWTON • Newton
selected and edited by I. Bernard Cohen and Richard S. Westfall

ROUSSEAU • Rousseau's Political Writings
translated by Julia Conaway Bondanella, edited by Alan Ritter

ST. PAUL • The Writings of St. Paul
edited by Wayne A. Meeks

THOREAU • Walden and Resistance to Civil Government
edited by William Rossi (Second Edition)

THUCYDIDES • The Peloponnesian War
*translated by Walter E. Blanco, edited by Walter E. Blanco
and Jennifer Tolbert Roberts*

WATSON • The Double Helix: A Personal Account
of the Discovery of the Structure of DNA
edited by Gunther S. Stent

WOLLSTONECRAFT • A Vindication of the Rights of Woman
edited by Carol H. Poston (Second Edition)

For a complete list of Norton Critical Editions, visit
www.wwnorton.com/college/english/nce.welcome.htm

DARWIN

A NORTON CRITICAL EDITION

Third Edition

A NORTON CRITICAL EDITION

DARWIN

TEXTS

COMMENTARY

Third Edition

Selected and Edited by

PHILIP APPLEMAN

INDIANA UNIVERSITY

W • W • NORTON & COMPANY • *New York* • *London*

The text of this book is composed in Electra
with the display set in Bernhard Modern.
Composition by PennSet, Inc.
Manufacturing by Courier Companies, Inc.
Book design by Antonina Krass.

Library of Congress Cataloging-in-Publication Data

Darwin / selected and edited by Philip Appleman. — 3rd ed.
    p. cm — (Norton critical edition)
Includes bibliographical references (p.).

ISBN 0-393-95849-3 (pbk.)

1. Evolution (Biology) — History. 2. Darwin, Charles, 1809–1882. 3. Naturalists
— Great Britain — Biography. I. Appleman, Philip, 1926– II. Series.

QH365.Z9 A7 2000
576.8'092 — dc21
[B]   00-058240

W. W. Norton & Company, Inc., 500 Fifth Avenue, New York, N.Y. 10110
www.wwnorton.com

W. W. Norton & Company Ltd., Castle House, 75/76 Wells Street,
London W1T 3QT

4 5 6 7 8 9 0

For Margie, with love

Contents

Part V: Darwin's Influence on Science   255

Part VI: Darwinian Patterns in Social Thought

Part VII: Darwinian Influences in Philosophy and Ethics

Part VIII: Evolutionary Theory and Religious Theory

Preface

The Norton Critical Edition of *Darwin*, in its two previous editions and thirty-five printings, has helped to inform a multitude of readers about the importance, and enduring relevance, of Darwin and evolution. It is hoped that it will continue to do so in this third edition, the first one of the twenty-first century.

There is a great deal of new material in this edition, indicating the voluminous scientific research and scholarly analysis that is being done in every field of evolutionary study. The book now has nine parts, beginning with an expanded and updated Introduction as Part I; more biographical detail about Darwin in Part II, "Darwin's Life"; and more selections from his scientific predecessors in Part III, "Scientific Thought: Just before Darwin"; as well as more of Darwin's own works, and longer excerpts from them, in Part IV.

Part V, "Darwin's Influence on Science," includes selections both from Darwin's contemporary supporters and from his contemporary critics. Updated and more detailed, this part also explains why the scientific method is so persuasive and how it confirms the validity and significance of evolution. In addition, Part V shows how much the knowledge of our primate heritage has grown in recent years, how biological classification and the pace of evolution are being re-evaluated, and how natural selection itself can be convincingly witnessed in real time.

Part VI, "Darwinian Patterns in Social Thought," explores the implications of biological cooperation as well as biological competition; scrutinizes the recent studies of genetic influences on human behavior; and examines the implications of evolution as regards gender, psychology, language, and medicine.

Part VII, "Darwinian Influences in Philosophy and Ethics," is more current and more diverse and is now set apart from theology (which is the subject of Part VIII). Darwinian epistemology and the origins and premises of ethical thinking are shown to be the absorbing interests of contemporary scholars.

Part VIII, "Evolutionary Theory and Religious Theory," has been greatly expanded, partly to illustrate the current broad approval of evolution by mainstream religions; partly to show the varieties of antievolutionary, creationist opinions; and partly to give both the scientific and the religious critiques of creationism.

Part IX, "Darwin and Literature," explores more thoroughly Darwin's own literary sensibility; the several kinds of interplay between Darwin as scientist and Darwin as writer; and his literary influence on other writers, from his own time until the present.

I should add that, although this volume is substantially longer than the previous edition, it is not exhaustive. In the preface to another anthology, the Norton Critical Edition of Malthus's *Essay on the Principle of Population*, I commented editorially on the difficulty of attempting to represent the rich productivity of the scientific, scholarly, and literary world within the limited scope of a single book. That difficulty remains. Although I have tried here to choose central and succinct passages, they are necessarily excerpts from longer, more detailed studies; and they were selected from a vast array of other important books and articles that might also have been used. I regret that for want of space, the work of many significant scientists, scholars, and writers could not be included. Some of them are listed in the Selected Readings (p. 683), although that section also had to be limited in scope.

The editor of any wide-ranging anthology is certain to need a lot of help. I am pleased to be able to acknowledge the many scholars and friends who have advised me so carefully and so generously. My sincere thanks to David Baker, Charles Blinderman, William Burgan, Peter Busher, Fran Castan, Bette Chambers, Frederick B. Churchill, Kay Dinsmoor, Edd Doerr, Taner Edis, Dennis Flanagan, Antony Flew, Stephen Jay Gould, Loren Graham, Quentin Hope, Karl Jaeger, James R. Kincaid, Noretta Koertge, Richard A. Levine, Laurence Lockridge, Molleen Matsumura, Betty McCollister, Thomas McIver, Craig Nelson, Kevin Padian, Warren Schmaus, Eugenie C. Scott, George Stade, Claire Szego, Charles E. Taylor, John Van Sickle, and John Woodcock. Special thanks to my previous W. W. Norton editor, James L. Mairs; to my current editor, Carol Bemis; and to the editorial assistants, Ben Reynolds, Christa Grenawalt, and Brian Baker; as well as to William A. Madden, Michael Wolff, Donald Gray, and George Levine, good friends and my co-founders and editorial colleagues throughout the challenging and rewarding early years of the interdisciplinary journal, *Victorian Studies*.

I also want to reaffirm here my profound gratitude and love to my lifelong partner, Margie—playwright and poet, who was for this book, as for all my others, the indispensable and tireless in-house editor.

Philip Appleman

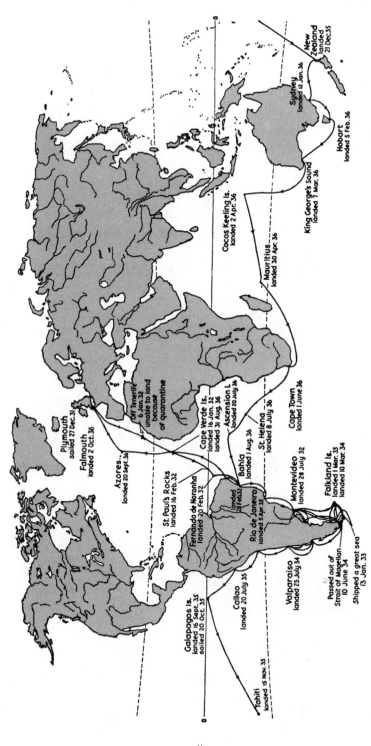

Plymouth
sailed 27 Dec.31
Falmouth
landed 2 Oct. 36

Off Tenerife
6 Jan. 32
unable to land
because
of quarantine

Azores
landed 20 Sept. 36

St. Paul's Rocks
landed 16 Feb. 32

Cape Verde Is.
landed 16 Jan. 32
sailed 31 Aug. 36

Ascension I.
landed 20 July 36

Fernando de Noronha
landed 20 Feb. 32

Bahia
landed 1 Aug. 36

St. Helena
landed 8 July 36

Cape Town
landed 1 June 36

Montevideo
landed 28 July 32

Falkland Is.
landed 1 Mar. 33
landed 10 Mar. 34

Rio de Janeiro
landed 4 Apr. 32
landed 28 Feb.32

Passed out of
Strait of Magellan
10 June 34

Shipped a great sea
13 Jan. 33

Valparaiso
landed 23 July 34

Callao
landed 20 July 35

Galapagos Is.
landed 16 Sept. 35
sailed 20 Oct. 35

Tahiti
landed 15 Nov. 35

Cocos Keeling Is.
landed 2 Apr. 36

Mauritius
landed 30 Apr. 36

King George's Sound
landed 7 Mar. 36

Sydney
landed 12 Jan. 36

Hobart
landed 5 Feb. 36

New
Zealand
landed
21 Dec.35

The Voyage of the *Beagle* 1831–1836

xvii

PART I
INTRODUCTION

There is grandeur in this view of life, with its several powers, having been originally breathed into a few forms or into one; and that, whilst this planet has gone cycling on according to the fixed law of gravity, from so simple a beginning endless forms most beautiful and most wonderful have been, and are being, evolved.

—Charles Darwin, 1859

THE SKELETONS OF DREAMS†

He found giants
in the earth: mastodon,
Mylodon, thigh bones
like tree trunks, Megatherium, skulls
big as boulders—once,
in this savage country, treetops
trembled at their passing.
But their passing was silent as snails,
silent as rabbits. Nothing at all recorded
the day when the last of them came
crashing through creepers and ferns,
shaking the earth a final time,
leaving behind them crickets,
monkeys, and mice.
For think: at last it is nothing
to be a giant—the dream
of an ending haunts tortoise and Toxodon,
troubles the sleep of the woodchuck
and the bear.

Back home in his English garden,
Darwin paused in his pacing,
writing it down in italics
in the book at the back of his mind:
When a species has vanished
from the face of the earth,
the same form never reappears . . .
So after our millions of years
of inventing a thumb and a cortex,
and after the long pain
of writing our clumsy epic,
we know we are mortal as mammoths,
we know the last lines of our poem.
And somewhere in curving space
beyond our constellations,
nebulae burn in their universal law:
nothing out there ever knew
that on one sky-blue planet
we dreamed that terrible dream.
Blazing along through black nothing
to nowhere at all, mastodons of heaven,
the stars do not need our small ruin.

—Philip Appleman, 1984

---

† From *New and Selected Poems, 1956–1996*, by Philip Appleman. Reprinted by permission of The University of Arkansas Press. Copyright © 1996 by Philip Appleman.

2

PHILIP APPLEMAN

Darwin: On Changing the Mind (2000)†

1

Born on February 12, 1809, Charles Darwin grew up in the comfort and security of the well-to-do Darwin and Wedgwood families. His mother was a Wedgwood, and he himself was to marry another, his cousin Emma. The son and grandson of prosperous physicians, he tried medical training himself but found the studies dull, and surgery (before anesthesia) too ghastly even to watch. So he followed the advice of his formidable father (six feet, 2 inches; 336 pounds; domineering in temperament) and went up to Cambridge to study for the ministry.

Darwin, however, was less interested in theology than in entomology; since childhood he had taken great pleasure in the popular Victorian hobby of collecting and studying beetles. To obtain his degree, he some-what impatiently went through the requisite three years of courses in classics, mathematics, and philosophy. At the same time, though, he was also able to study not only insects but the natural sciences in general, with learned professors like the botanist John Stevens Henslow, the geologist Adam Sedgwick, and the philosopher of science William Whewell. He also read John Herschel's impressive new book on scientific method and William Paley's arguments for design in nature. After a substantial education in a broad spectrum of scientific work, Darwin took his B.A. at Cambridge in 1831.

Then a remarkable turn of events saved him from a country parsonage. Professor Henslow unexpectedly arranged for Darwin the invitation to join H.M.S. *Beagle* during a long voyage of exploration. The British government—in the wake of the Napoleonic wars and on the brink of a great commercial expansion—had undertaken the ambitious task of mapping the ports and coastlines of the world. British naval ships were being sent to remote destinations, many of them carrying along naturalists, who were expected to make their collections and observations while the mapping expeditions were carried out. Justifying his nomination of so young a man for such a position, Henslow wrote to Darwin that although he was not "a *finished* naturalist," he was already "amply qualified for collecting, observing, and noting anything worthy to be noted in Natural History." So on December 27, 1831, at the age of twenty-two, Darwin left England for what became a five-year journey around the globe; it turned out to be not only a crucial experience for Darwin himself but a passage of consequence for the whole world.

During the voyage of the *Beagle*, Darwin resolutely transformed himself into a "finished naturalist"—an industrious collector, a keen observer, a canny theorist. And he took up the momentous problem that he would grapple with for more than twenty years: what he called the "mystery of

---

† First published in this Norton Critical Edition.

mysteries"—the origin of species. In the years after his extraordinary journey on the *Beagle*, however, Darwin's adventures were mostly intellectual,
his life deliberately domestic, primarily because he was chronically ill for
much of his later life with a mysterious, undiagnosable ailment. He suffered from heart palpitations and an almost daily debilitating nausea, the
cause of which is still not certain. So he lived quietly in his country house[1]
with his beloved and devoted wife, Emma, who managed their large
household of children, servants, and pets. Emma attended her husband
assiduously through his chronic sickness, while caring for their ten children; and she sustained him in his work, asking him challenging questions,
writing countless letters at his dictation, and helping correct the proofs of
his weighty books.

Despite his continuing ill health, Darwin worked hard almost every day,
and his industrious life was studded with solid contributions to science:
The Voyage of the Beagle (1845), *The Origin of Species* (1859), *The Variation of Animals and Plants under Domestication* (1868), *The Descent of
Man* (1871), *The Expression of the Emotions in Man and Animals* (1872),
The Formation of Vegetable Mould through the Action of Earthworms
(1881), and so on—as well as an autobiography and a voluminous worldwide correspondence on scientific matters. (See Selected Readings, p. 683.)

There was something paradoxical but eminently admirable about both
Darwin's character and his devotion to his task. Intellectually he was a
revolutionary, but the gentlest of revolutionaries. He lived the life of a
respectable and conventional country gentleman, but he gradually developed some very unconventional ideas and, as he wrote in his autobiography, ultimately rejected the "brutal" religion that threatened to condemn
his freethinking father, brother, and best friends to everlasting punishment
("a damnable doctrine"). He became, in T. H. Huxley's new terminology,
an agnostic; and like many another Victorian agnostic, he exemplified in
his life and work a high-minded benevolence, kindness, and generosity not
only to other people but to all creatures. So he continued to write about
the "grandeur" of "beautiful" and "wonderful" forms of life, and of humanity's high "destiny" in the future.

When he died in 1882 at age seventy-three, the man whose sacrilegious
ideas had once been publicly assailed by a multitude of critics was accorded the rare national honor of burial in Westminster Abbey, a few feet
from the grave of the other eminence among British scientists, Isaac
Newton.

2

It is not easy, a century and a half later, to enter fully into the mind-set
of the early Victorians, in which both religion and science presupposed
the glory of God to be manifested in nature. Nor is it easy to comprehend
the intensity of their commitment to the fixity of species, or to imagine the
intellectual and emotional upheaval that Darwin's work would cause. And

---

1. Down House, about fifteen miles southeast of London, near the village of Downe, in Kent; now
   a Darwin museum open to the public.

it is difficult to give sufficient credit to Darwin's boldness and originality, unless it is kept in mind that he had boarded H.M.S. *Beagle* young, as yet unseasoned in science, and still a believer in Genesis.

We need to picture him then, just out of Cambridge, carrying in his small shipboard library the first volume of Charles Lyell's revisionary new work, the *Principles of Geology* (see p. 49), but warned by his respected professor Henslow against its novel uniformitarian ideas. He also carried in his mental baggage the pious lessons of William Paley's *Natural Theology* (see p. 41), which he had studied at Cambridge so carefully that he later wrote in his autobiography, "I could almost formerly have said it by heart." And it was Paley more than anyone else who had already persuaded a generation of readers that in the Deity's neatly contructed universe, "the marks of [God's] *design* are too strong to be gotten over."

Darwin also kept in mind the ideas and opinions of the Cambridge professor William Whewell—"next to Sir J. Mackintosh," Darwin wrote, "the best converser on grave subjects to whom I ever listened." By an ironic trick of history, it was during the five years of Darwin's *Beagle* voyage that the British citadel of science, the Royal Society, was administering the publication of the Bridgewater Treatises, a series of books by notable scientists and moralists, including Whewell, who were commissioned specifically to demonstrate "the power, wisdom, and goodness of God as manifested in the Creation." So, while Darwin was in South America painstakingly examining plants and animals—assembling the physical evidence that would one day support his radical new theory—Whewell, in his Cambridge study, was writing for his treatise:

> If there be, in the administration of the universe, intelligence and benevolence, superintendence and foresight, grounds for love and hope, such qualities may be expected to appear in the . . . fundamental regulations by which the course of nature is . . . made to be what it is (see p. 58).

It is an awesome distance from that kind of thinking to Darwin's in *The Origin of Species*, which, a quarter of a century later, would turn Whewell's divinely planned, benevolent world topsy-turvy:

> Thus, from the war of nature, from famine and death, the most exalted object which we are capable of conceiving, namely, the production of the higher animals, directly follows (see p. 174).

Charles Darwin—cautious, skeptical, compulsively industrious, distrustful of his own talents, and never daring to suspect himself of the genius we now acknowledge—did not make that awesome voyage in a day.

As a modest young scientist, Darwin was understandably reluctant to reveal his revolutionary theory of the transmutation of species and thus set himself single-handedly against the massive forces of conventional scientific and religious opinion, both of which were committed to the ancient and sanctified belief in the fixity of species. He knew about Lamarck's bitter experience: Lamarck had tried to challenge that conventional opinion with an unconvincing evolutionary hypothesis and had been systematically attacked and ridiculed by virtually the entire scientific establishment. Other scientists, philosophers, and writers (including Darwin's own grandfather, Erasmus Darwin) had also speculated about the transmutation of species, but, like Lamarck's, their work was never taken seriously either; it was too hypothetical or too superficial to threaten in any serious way the established scientific and religious belief in the fixity of species.

Faced with such daunting odds, Darwin wisely avoided publishing anything about evolution, but he continued to build the evidence for his developing theory. Even as a young man, he had been a tenacious empiricist, a tireless gatherer of facts. During the *Beagle* voyage, for five years, from one exotic locale to another, he had explored riverbeds and coral reefs, hiked pampas and climbed mountains; he had recorded stratifications of rocks and soil and examined the earth with lens, compass, clinometer, penknife, blowpipe, and acids; he had discovered fossils of conifers and shellfish, of Megatherium and mastodon. During those five industrious years, he had collected and continuously shipped to England vast numbers of plants, birds, insects, reptiles, and fossils. And during those five early years he had also become a subtle theorist, pondering the causes of the elevation and subsidence of volcanic strata, of the earthquakes he had experienced, and of the formation of coral reefs.

After the *Beagle* voyage, the maturing Darwin, now widely respected as a naturalist, spent the next twenty years in a dogged pursuit of his evolutionary hypothesis—examining the many breeds of domestic pigeons, the skeletons of rabbits, the wings of ducks, the variations in ten thousand specimens of barnacles; keeping notebooks on "transmutation"; and discreetly discussing the "species question" with Charles Lyell and other close scientific friends. Finally, in middle age, he dared to begin to write the ambitious book that he intended to call "Natural Selection."

But even then—after five years of exploration on the *Beagle*; twenty years of patient study, careful observation, and cautious speculation; and then two more years of exhausting work on the steadily growing manuscript of "Natural Selection"—even after all that hard labor and deep thought, Darwin was still reluctant to publish his challenge to the scientific and religious establishment.

Then, on June 18, 1858, everything changed. On that day, Darwin received the momentous letter from Alfred Russel Wallace, describing Wallace's own recent discovery of the principle of natural selection. Darwin immediately wrote to Lyell: "Your words have come true with a vengeance—that I should be forestalled." But his dismay was temporary. Lyell and Joseph Hooker, the botanist, arranged a joint presentation of short papers by both Wallace and Darwin at the Linnean Society in London in July 1858; so their names became permanently linked as co-discoverers of the principle of natural selection. Wallace, however, was always modest about his contribution, because, as he said, compared to Darwin's, it was as two weeks are to twenty years.

After Wallace's unintentional prompting, Darwin realized that he should finish and publish his lengthy manuscript expeditiously; but to do so, he would have to restrict its size. So he condensed the project into what he called an "abstract" of his work, and by March 1859, he had completed *The Origin of Species*. It was published on November 24 of that year. The effects of that publication were immediate, extensive, and profound. Hardly any kind of thought—scientific, philosophical, religious, social, literary, or historical—remained long unchanged by the radical implications of the *Origin*. That extraordinary, continuing, and worldwide transformation is the subject of this volume.

3

There were various reasons for the remarkably swift spread of evolutionary thought after the publication of the *Origin*, and one of the most important was the Victorians' fascination with science in general. Thomas Henry Huxley wrote in 1873, "We are in the midst of a gigantic movement, greater than that which preceded and produced the Reformation." He was referring to the persuasiveness of the scientific method, so clearly burgeoning at the time.

However, for most people, then as now, what was meant by "science" was not the scientific method—a way of organizing data, hypothesizing about them, and generalizing from them—but rather applied science, that is, technology. During the long reign of Queen Victoria, from 1837 until her death in 1901, scientific technology transformed many of the conditions of people's lives. The first railroad was built in England in 1825, when Victoria was a little girl. Before that, the maximum speed of land travel was—for up-to-date Britons as it had been for Caesars and pharaohs—the speed of the horse. But by the time the venerable queen died, almost all of Britain's extensive railway system had been built. "Science" had liberated travel from animal muscle and had begun that acceleration toward inconceivable velocities, which is so characteristic of our own age and is as impressive to us as it was to the Victorians.

Impressive: "science" was *doing* things, making things *work*. While Victoria was still on the throne, transatlantic steamship service began, power-driven machines revolutionized industry, the telegraph and telephone were developed, and many other new inventions were put into use, from the electric light to the automobile. In 1851, eight years before *The Origin of Species*, the Victorians celebrated Progress at the first World's Fair in London—the Great Exhibition of the Industry of All Nations—in the splendid Crystal Palace, where it was abundantly demonstrated that "science" was indeed making things happen; it seemed, to many at the time, both fascinating and dependable.

Unlike philosophy or theology or literature, science compels rational assent. And ever since Copernicus shunted people off from the center of the universe, no scientific discovery had been as staggering as Darwin's. One could not simultaneously accept his evidence and the literal words of Genesis. No reconciliation was possible, T. H. Huxley insisted, "between free thought and traditional authority. One or the other will have to succumb."

What was at stake was no less than a worldview. In the seventeenth century, ecclesiastics had calculated that God created man at 9:00 A.M. on October 23 in the year 4004 B.C.E.—a year still cited in some annotated

King James Bibles. And Paley had argued confidently in 1802 that the universe was carefully designed by a provident Creator. However, natural selection functions not by design but by incessant opportunism, and it is an extremely time-consuming process: six thousand years are a mere instant on the evolutionary time scale. Paley's view of the world was familiar, pious, and comforting. Darwin's view of the world was revolutionary, disturbing—and persuasive.

Because it was so persuasive, *evolution* became a watchword for the late Victorians. By the end of the nineteenth century hardly any field of thought remained unchanged by the exciting new concept. Historians began looking at the past as a living, changing organism; legal theorists studied the law as a developing social institution; critics examined the evolution of literary types; anthropologists and sociologists invoked natural selection in their studies of social forms; apologists for the wealthy showed how the poor are the "unfit" and how progress, under the leadership of the "fit," was inevitable; novelists "observed" their characters as they "evolved" in an "empirical" way; and poets invoked an evolutionary life force. In 1800 the word evolution had been used only to signify the development of organisms from their immature to their mature state; but in the half century following the publication of *The Origin of Species*, evolution seemed capable of explaining anything and everything. The titles of ponderous books of the period indicate how religion itself was being reconsidered: *The Evolution of Morality* (1878), *The Evolution of Religion* (1894), *The Evolution of Immortality* (1901), *The Evolution of the Soul* (1904).

4

Science is not a single enterprise but a host of different activities, all having in common a special "way of knowing" that was stimulated by a new emphasis on inductive reasoning in the seventeenth century, and has been constantly examined and amended ever since. Its characteristic procedures—observation, hypothesis, testing, and then confirmation or rejection—are discussed in Part V ("Darwin's Influence on Science," p. 255).

Part V also shows how Charles Darwin's scientific work not only was a major contribution to knowledge in and of itself but also has been seminal for later biologists. Now, a century and a half after *The Origin of Species*, generations of dedicated scientists have labored to refine and augment Darwin's groundbreaking idea: discovering new evidence, developing new fields of study, changing emphases, and working out the thousand details of what Ashley Montagu called "the gigantic complex jigsaw puzzle that is evolution." Fitting together the pieces of that puzzle has required innumerable contributions from astronomy, biology, chemistry, biochemistry, physics, paleontology, geology, genetics, developmental biology, ecology, anthropology, geochemistry, geophysics, and other disciplines—as the following examples indicate.

- Paleontologists are revealing countless new facts about the human genealogy; about our evolutionary origins in Africa; and about our prehistoric incursions into Asia, Europe, and the rest of the world.
- At the announcement of the sequencing of the human genome in June 2000, geneticist Jon Seger pointed out that the genome is "evolution laid out for all to see." And Nobel laureate David Baltimore added, "The genome shows that we are all descended from the same humble beginnings and that the connections are written in our genes."
- Molecular biologists continue to inform us authoritatively about the close relationship of humans with other animals, especially, of course, with the other primates—for instance, our more than 98 percent genetic identity with chimpanzees.
- Collaterally, primatologists are generating voluminous new information about the intelligence of the great apes—and even, in the case of chimps, about their culture—which is causing us to rethink our attitudes, and our obligations, to our close biological cousins.
- Taxonomists are now working with the relatively new method of biological classification called cladistics—a method that focuses closely on genealogy and evolutionary "branching order"—which has altered some older classifications and has, among other things, helped sort out our own recent biological forebears.
- Naturalists in the Galapagos have painstakingly observed Darwin's finches, establishing the fact of natural selection operating in real time—that is, in the biologically brief period of a few decades. This is one of many recent studies in which natural selection has been subject to human observation.

As these and other important developments continue to demonstrate, natural selection remains fundamental to all fields of biological research; and biologists universally acknowledge and respect Darwin as the architect of modern biology.

5

As is shown in Part VI ("Darwinian Patterns in Social Thought," p. 387), discussions of Darwinism sometimes become analogical rather than analytical, "Darwinistic" rather than Darwinian. Morse Peckham made this useful distinction:

> Darwinism is a scientific theory about the origin of biological species from pre-existent species. . . . Darwinisticism can be an evolutionary metaphysic about the nature of reality and the universe . . . an economic theory, or a moral theory, or an aesthetic theory, or a psychological theory.[2]

Having been for years scrupulously careful and objective in his explorations of scientific matters, Darwin grew more and more willing, as time went by and his interests broadened, to speculate daringly on the basis of

2. Morse Peckham, "Darwinism and Darwinisticism," *Victorian Studies* 3 (1959), 32.

what he considered the best available knowledge. When writing *The Origin of Species*, Darwin characteristically exhibited a scientist's proper caution in language like this:

- "We must not overrate the accuracy of . . ."
- "We must be cautious in attempting . . ."
- "Judging from the past, we may safely infer that . . ."
- "We may look with some confidence to . . ."

And so on. As Alfred North Whitehead observed, "Darwin's own writings are for all time a model of refusal to go beyond the direct evidence, and of careful retention of every hypothesis."[3]

Twelve years later, in *The Descent of Man*, a more mature and experienced Darwin continued to exercise that same caution in discussing human bodily structure, embryonic development, and rudimentary organs. However, when he turned his attention to mental and moral qualities, he had less tangible, physical evidence at hand and had to rely more on anecdote and speculation, both of which are, of course, subject to cultural distortion. Darwin could not completely overcome this disadvantage; like everyone else, he was a product of his times, although he was often ahead of them. Having settled down to a conventional life in a rural village, he undertook the responsibilities of a respectable landowner and accepted without any serious question the gender roles of the society that had so generously nurtured him. Consequently, he was sometimes guilty himself of straying from Darwinism into some Darwinisticism or other, including what we are now accustomed to calling a sexist denigration of the intellectual abilities of women. But as Evelleen Richards points out,

> Darwin cannot be personally judged by twentieth-century yardsticks any more than his work can be assessed by twentieth-century standards and concepts. To label him a sexist may be technically correct . . . but is mere rhetoric in the context of a society in which almost everyone . . . held discriminatory views of woman's nature and social role (see p. 443).

But if Darwin strayed innocently into an occasional Darwinisticism, others took that step knowingly and intentionally. Some people saw an opportunity to take over his new concepts and exploit them as self-serving rationalizations. Social Darwinism, the most obvious example of this distortion, is the spurious claim that Darwinian competition in nature constitutes a proper model for the "survival of the fittest" in human society—in which everyone competes to survive, but only the wealthy have proven themselves "fit."

The publication of *The Origin of Species* and the American Civil War were almost coincident, and in the years following that war, the United States, like other Western nations, was industrializing very rapidly. The late nineteenth century became the pre-eminent period of the rugged individualists, the robber barons, the captains of industry, the accumulators of great wealth. However, it was also a harsh period for ordinary working

3. Alfred North Whitehead, *Science and the Modern World* (New York, 1925), 158.

people: a time of sweatshops, union busting, goon squads and strike-breaking massacres, dollar-a-day wages, tenements without sanitation, and widespread malnutrition.

It was not easy, in a "Christian" society, to reconcile such glaring contradictions. Ever since the beginnings of the industrial revolution, the economic establishment had been casting about for rationalizations, for self-justification. Free-market political economy had been just such a sanction, emphasizing as it did the necessity for untrammeled individual enterprise, for "enlightened self-interest," and for the "iron laws" of economics. Andrew Carnegie once said, "There is no more possibility of defeating the operation of these laws than there is of thwarting the laws of nature which determine the humidity of the atmosphere or the revolution of the earth upon its axis."[4]

Oddly enough, there were also religious sanctions for Social Darwinism—for had not the clergy always warned that material things were corrupting to people, and was it not therefore self-evident that the "lower classes" should be kept poor to be kept virtuous? And, paradoxically, could not the virtuous and industrious among the poor expect to be rewarded, even in this world? Ben Franklin had declared:

> He that gets all that he can honestly, and saves all he gets will certainly become rich, if that Being who governs the world, to whom all should look for a blessing on their endeavors, doth not, in His wise providence, otherwise determine.

Finally, as always in the nineteenth century, there was that court of last resort, the sanction of progress, in whose name all contradictions were resolved—or ignored.

Such rationalizations had always been welcomed by the economic establishment; but after 1859, it found in natural selection a universal sanction that gathered into one grand synthesis all of the previous ones and added to them its own scientific prestige. Natural selection and the struggle for existence lent authority to laissez-faire economics: the celebrated Social Darwinist, Herbert Spencer, insisted that the state should refrain from action calculated to interfere with the struggle for existence in the industrial field. Natural selection also reinforced the older religious sanctions: one economist said that the "laws" of natural selection were "merely God's regular methods of expressing his choice and approval."[5] And evolution seemed to make progress inevitable, ending, Spencer predicted, in "the establishment of the greatest perfection and the most complete happiness." In his opinion, progress was "not an accident, but a necessity."[6]

The captains of industry were quick to pick up this Darwinistic vocabulary. John D. Rockefeller told a Sunday-school class that

> The growth of a large business is merely a survival of the fittest. . . . The American Beauty rose can be produced in the splendor and fragrance which bring cheer to the beholder only by sacrificing the

4. Andrew Carnegie, *The Empire of Business* (London, 1907), 67.
5. Thomas Nixon Carver, quoted in Richard Hofstadter, *Social Darwinism in American Thought* (Boston, 1955), 40.
6. Hofstadter, *Social Darwinism*, 40.

early buds which grow up around it. This is not an evil tendency in business. It is merely the working-out of a law of nature and of God.[7]

Richard Tawney once argued that the true character of a social philosophy is defined most clearly by how it regards the misfortunes of those of its members who fall by the wayside. Those who fell by the wayside in late-nineteenth-century America were assured by the conservative apologists that this was their natural lot, that science "proved" that they were the unavoidable by-products of an ultimately beneficent struggle for existence, without which there could be no progress.

However, some people would not accept such a callous doctrine, and questioned whether the implications of evolution were really as somberly deterministic as was being alleged. As early as the 1870s, some naturalists had been investigating instances of cooperation, in addition to competition, in the natural world. In 1902 Peter Kropotkin published his book *Mutual Aid*, revealing that he had

> failed to find—although I was eagerly looking for it—that bitter struggle for the means of existence, *among animals belonging to the same species*, which was considered by most Darwinists (though not always by Darwin himself) as the dominant characteristic of the struggle for life, and the main factor of evolution. . . . On the other hand, wherever I saw animal life in abundance . . . I saw Mutual Aid and Mutual Support carried on to an extent which made me suspect in it a feature of the greatest importance for the maintenance of life, the preservation of each species, and its further evolution (see p. 398).

Thomas Henry Huxley had already made the famous distinction, in a notable lecture of 1893, that

> social progress means a checking of the cosmic process at every step and the substitution for it of another, which may be called the ethical process; the end of which is not the survival of those who may happen to be the fittest . . . but of those who are ethically the best (see p. 502).

By the end of the nineteenth century, then, some naturalists were broadening the evolutionary view of life to show that nature was not always, or not simply, competitive. And social and ethical thinkers were attempting to demonstrate that even though fierce competition does exist in nature, it does not necessarily follow that it is a proper pattern for human behavior.[8]

As the essays in Part VI show, the twentieth century inherited these controversial nineteenth-century issues, and they are still being debated, albeit in altered contexts. Scientists now discuss the extent of genetic in-

---

7. Quoted in J. Ghent, *Our Benevolent Feudalism* (New York, 1902), 29.
8. Ironically, communism and national socialism, like capitalism, had also been searching for "scientific" sanctions in Darwinism. Karl Marx read into *The Origin of Species* his own preoccupation with class struggle and historical patterns of social change. Later on, Adolf Hitler, too, rationalized the ruthless Nazi social plans as "Darwinian." All three examples—capitalist, communist, national-socialist—demonstrate how seductive Darwinistic pretentions can be, and (by their mutual contradictions and untrustworthy analogies) how unreliable they are. [Editor]

fluences on both altruistic and selfish behavior. They also consider the role that gender has played in the development of the various human cultures. And they argue about the extension of biological principles, not only into the study of modern psychology and medicine but also into the social sciences, and potentially even into the humanities.

6

A nineteenth-century adage proposed that it is the fate of all great scientific discoveries to pass through three stages. In the first stage, people say, "It's absurd"; in the second, "It's contrary to the Bible"; and in the third, "Oh, we've known *that* all along." Evolution passed through all three stages so rapidly that in the last edition of the *Origin* in Darwin's lifetime (1872), he could write:

> As a record of a former state of things, I have retained in the foregoing paragraphs, and elsewhere, several sentences which imply that naturalists believe in the separate creation of species, and I have been much censured for having thus expressed myself. But undoubtedly this was the general belief when the first edition of the present work appeared. I formerly spoke to very many naturalists on the subject of evolution, and never once met with any sympathetic agreement. . . . Now things are wholly changed, and almost every naturalist admits the great principle of evolution.

Scientific revolutions depend on, among other things, the insight and the determination—and sometimes the aggressiveness—of their protagonists. Darwin had the insight to discover natural selection, and he had the determination to fill hundreds of pages with minutely observed facts and close reasoning in support of it. Friends, when necessary, supplied the aggressiveness—and the world was changed: converted, in a very few years, from an almost total belief in the fixity of species to a widespread understanding of the transmutation of species.[9]

That in itself was a remarkable conversion, but the Darwinian revolution did not stop there; it also required a basic change in thinking about all ideas, all phenomena. To the conventionally religious, the most threatening thing about Darwinism was the implication that nothing was sacrosanct: evolution was becoming not only the science of sciences but, even more disturbing, the philosophy of philosophies.

For those hostile to such change, the impact was shocking, and counterattacks from the faithful were swift and fierce. In the pages of sectarian periodicals, where alleged scientific experts could flourish in protective anonymity, priests, parsons, and bishops defended not only their own faith

9. Although the *principle* of evolution was, as Darwin wrote, widely accepted in his own lifetime, scientists continued to debate the *mechanism* of evolution for decades—disputes that could not be resolved until the rediscovery of Mendelian genetics in 1900 and the mathematical work of Ronald Fisher in 1930, which led quickly to the modern neo-Darwinian synthesis (see p. 319) and the confirmation of natural selection as the primary agent in evolutionary change. [Editor]

but also "true Baconian induction." A truculent contributor to the *Catholic World* wrote:

> The theory of evolution has no scientific character, is irreconcilable with the conclusions of natural history, and has no ground to stand upon except the worn-out fallacies of a perverted logic.[1]

The aging Anglican sage Dr. Pusey sternly rejected Darwinism:

> Never probably was any system built upon so many 'perhaps,' 'probably,' 'possibly,' 'it may be,' 'it seems to be' . . . as that mythological account of the origin of all which has life, and, at last of ourselves, which is now being everywhere or widely acknowledged by unscientific minds as if it were axiomatic truth.[2]

Pope Pius IX, writing to a French anti-Darwinian author, was also thoroughly contemptuous:

> We have received with pleasure, dear son, the work in which you refute so well the aberrations of Darwinism. A system which is repudiated by history, by the traditions of all peoples, by exact science, by the observation of facts, and even by reason itself, would seem to have no need at all of refutation . . . . [But] such dreamings, absurd as they are, since they wear the mask of science, [must] be refuted by true science.[3]

It need hardly be pointed out that the concern of theologians for "true science" was not wholly disinterested. They worried because they saw, perhaps more clearly than others, the philosophical implications of post-Darwinian thought. It was not just that Darwin had undermined the Book of Genesis, or even that he had given scientific authority to the nineteenth-century affinity for endless continuities rather than eternal verities, or that the evolutionary orientation stressed context and complexity—although all such ideas threatened established religion. The most dangerous idea of all was that Darwin's universe operated not by design but by natural selection, a self-regulating mechanism. "Paley's divine watchmaker was unemployed," Gavin de Beer wrote in 1964, "because the wonderful property of organisms is that they make and mar themselves." Natural selection pictured the world in a constant process of change, but without any apparent prior intention of going anywhere in particular or of becoming anything in particular.

That was a devastating proposition for conventional believers—more so, perhaps, than the Copernican theory had been, because it struck even closer to home. Science, with all its impressiveness of fact and achievement, was moving in on the theologians, *taking over*—constantly enlarging the domain of fact and consequently reducing the domain of speculation. Given objective knowledge, most people tend (it was already clear) to give up the guessing games of ignorance—such as conjecture about which of

1. "Dr. Draper and Evolution," *Catholic World* 26 (1878), 775.
2. Edward Bouverie Pusey, *Un-Science, Not Science, Adverse to Faith* (London, 1879), 32.
3. Quoted in Constantin James, *L'Hypnotism expliqué et Mes Entretiens avec S.M. l'Empéreur Don Pedro sur le Darwinism* (Paris, 1888), 84–85.

the "humors" is overbalanced in a person whose blood pressure is abnormal or whether or not Adam and Eve had navels or what influence the planets have on our destinies. So it *made a difference* that humans had not only evolved but had evolved by natural selection rather than by an imaginary vital force or hypothetical cosmic urge. Darwinism was uncompromisingly nonteleological and nonvitalist, and that basic fact was anathema to theologians. Of course, theologians had always seen human beings as a part of nature, but usually as a much grander part: as the crowning achievement of God's universe, only a little below the angels. It was the Darwinian challenge to that lofty assumption that caused tremors among the reverential and the orthodox, who then repeatedly denounced the new heresy.

But with the passing of decades, direct opposition to Darwin gradually made way for accommodation. The opposition was still active in 1909, when the first edition of the *Catholic Encyclopedia* said of natural selection that

> As a theory it is scientifically inadequate. . . . The third signification of the term *Darwinism* arose from the application of the theory of selection to man, which is likewise impossible of acceptance.

However, by 1967, the *New Catholic Encyclopedia* was looking at these things more realistically:

> Today, with a much better understanding of both the theological sources of the Judeo-Christian revelation and of evolutionary theory, the compatibility of God's creative and directive action is more easily comprehended. . . . The solution of the basic difficulties [with Darwinism] was soon found to lie in Biblical research and scholarship and not in the rejection of the new theory. In his encyclical *Humani generis* [1950], Pope Pius [asserted] that general evolution, even of the body of man (and woman) should be professionally studied by both anthropologist and theologian.

Part VIII ("Evolutionary Theory and Religious Theory," p. 525) records the movement of theological opinion toward the acceptance of evolution, not only by Catholics but by Jewish groups and by mainstream Protestant denominations, such as Presbyterians, Lutherans, Episcopalians, and others.

Part VIII also examines the flagrant oxymoron "scientific creationism," which is being promoted by a vocal minority of fundamentalist Protestants; and it analyzes the motives and methods of two "new critics" of Darwin, religious believers who put their legal and scientific experience at the service of their theology. Finally, in Part VIII, these disputes are set in the context of the strong approval of evolution by genuine biologists; and it also shows how emphatically they disapprove of teaching the unscientific (and in fact antiscientific) notion of creationism in science classrooms.

Although the arguments of the creationists are intellectually frivolous, they are being promoted with evangelical fervor and often have serious political and educational consequences. One concrete way of illustrating this point is to recount my own personal experiences in learning about Darwin and evolution.

In the preface to one of my books of poetry, *Darwin's Ark*, I noted some ironic personal coincidences. For instance, I happened to be conceived in the same month in 1925 that John Thomas Scopes was indicted for the crime of teaching evolution to the schoolchildren of Dayton, Tennessee. (Scopes was targeted by a prohibitory law instigated by religious fundamentalists; see p. 542.) In due course, I was born in the same month that the legislature of the state of Mississippi, also under pressure from fundamentalists, passed an antievolution law similar to the one in Tennessee. Also in the year of my birth, the famous evangelist Aimee Semple McPherson, concocting an alibi for an extended rendezvous with her lover, claimed to have been kidnapped by "gamblers, dope peddlers, and *evolutionists.*" Then, a year after my birth, the American Anti-Evolution Association was founded, declaring itself open to all citizens except "Negroes, Atheists, Infidels, Agnostics, *Evolutionists,* and habitual drunkards."

By the time I started school, the fundamentalists, continuing their non-stop crusade against science, had caused antievolutionary laws to be passed in Arkansas and in Florida, and were agitating for similar laws in other states. Meanwhile, they also contrived to get high school and college teachers fired for discussing evolution in the classroom. At the same time that my classmates and I were learning to read, textbook publishers, fearing a loss of sales in the Bible Belt, were busy deleting any reference to Darwin or evolution from virtually all public school textbooks in this country. That boycott continued for decades—partly by laws devised by the fundamentalists, partly by collaborating or intimidated school boards, and partly by the publishers' ongoing self-censorship.

So in twelve years of education, including a high school course in biology, I never once heard the name of Darwin or the word evolution. Like millions of other students around the country, my classmates and I graduated from high school totally ignorant of one of the most basic facts of nature: the perpetual functioning of organic evolution. The fundamentalists had actually managed to abolish a natural law from the schools. It was an astonishing feat—the educational equivalent of, say, the Flat Earth Society abolishing gravity.

It would be gratifying if all that were now changed; but unfortunately, the creationist political lobbying is continuing and intensifying. As a result, even today in many American high school biology courses, evolution is still frequently ignored, diluted, or forbidden. The deplorable consequence is that many adults are not able to understand the science of evolution. Worse still, they are uninformed or misinformed about modern science in general—about its reliable methodology and its impressive intellectual achievements. Compounding their misfortune, these educationally deprived people often become the easy victims of assorted charlatans—astrologers, psychics, self-proclaimed prophets, Bermuda Triangle occultists, parapsychologists, UFO visionaries, New Age mystics, numerologists, faith healers, channelers, pyramidologists, fortune tellers—and creationists. Obviously, the scientific and educational community needs to maintain constant vigilance and a vigorous program of public information and public advocacy, if factual knowledge and common sense are to prevail over ignorance and superstition.

I finally did get around to reading Darwin, almost by accident. I had been in the Army Air Corps during World War II, and after the war, started college on the G.I. Bill. Two years later, to help pay tuition and expenses, I joined the Merchant Marine, and periodically spent many months at sea—a good place for earning money while also keeping up with my studies, because there was time for reading in the long hours off-watch. On one extended voyage to the Mediterranean in 1948, I happened to pack in my seabag, along with many other books, the Modern Library Giant edition of *The Origin of Species* and *The Descent of Man*, both in one thick volume: exactly one thousand pages of small print. (I still have that book, a bit dog-eared, its text underlined and annotated with a smudgy ball-point pen.) I was twenty-two—the same age as Charles Darwin when he set out on the *Beagle*—and because of his book, my trip, too, was a voyage of discovery. I remember that experience vividly: the exhilaration I felt, reading Darwin's clear and persuasive observations; the relief at being finally released from a constrained childhood allegiance to the primitive creationist myths of Genesis; the profound satisfaction of understanding the facts of biological evolution and knowing that I was truly and altogether a part of nature.

When I got back to college, I went on reading Darwin, and I have been reading him ever since—*The Voyage of the Beagle*; *The Expression of the Emotions in Man and Animals*; his books on barnacles, on earthworms, on orchids; and his journals, notebooks, letters, and autobiography—his whole prodigious labor of love. And I have also been reading *about* Darwin ever since, and writing about him: a doctoral dissertation, an abridged Norton edition of *The Origin of Species*, articles, lectures, chapters, reviews, novels, and poetry—particularly the novel *Apes and Angels* and the poems in *Darwin's Ark*, some of which are epigraphs in this volume—and, of course, the two previous editions of this book itself. So my own adventure with Darwin has ended happily; but the sad fact is that many thousands of young people, even today, are still being denied a sound education in biology as a result of creationist political pressures.

7

Ever since the seventeenth century, literature has been responsive to developments in science—astronomy, physics, and geology. And as is shown in Part IX ("Darwin and the Literary Mind," p. 631), nineteenth-century writers quickly began to assimilate evolutionary ideas into their work. Tennyson and Browning both wrote about evolution throughout their long careers; and evolution was also cited, discussed, and absorbed in the novels of George Eliot, Bulwer-Lytton, Charles Reade, Mrs. Humphry Ward, George Gissing, and Charles Kingsley, among many others. The writers most influenced by evolution include George Meredith, Thomas Hardy, and A. C. Swinburne, who tended to see the end result of human tribulations as true progress, even in a world that is red in tooth and claw. Meredith built a "philosophy of earth" around this belief, although at times he, like Tennyson, only "faintly trusted the larger hope [that] somehow good will be the final goal of ill." Somewhat later, Samuel Butler, H. G. Wells, George Bernard Shaw, and others also used evolutionary themes in their writing.

Not surprisingly, the philosophical and religious controversies over Darwinism continued to have significant literary consequences in the twentieth century. In one debate, for instance, it was alleged that Darwin's materialistic science eroded human values, and therefore destroyed high tragedy. However, that allegation conveniently ignored the dearth of tragedy in the century before Darwin. In fact, high tragedy at any time is rare; every age does not produce a Sophocles or a Shakespeare.

More to the point, why should it be assumed that a physically comprehensible world is necessarily a morally valueless one? Those who assert that it is seem unable to accept the fact that evolution is a natural and understandable process, preferring to believe in some hypothetical outside force that mysteriously guides human development. But since 1859, such unsupported assumptions have become increasingly untenable; nature simply does not reveal meaningful patterns of change toward a predestined goal.

In recent decades, many ethical thinkers have rejected the notion that Darwinism undermines human values (and therefore precludes great and tragic art in our time). On the contrary, they argue that, since Darwin, we have been compelled, in art as in life, to mature to finiteness—that is, not simply to realize that there are no credible absolutes in our moral experience (because that mere realization is still a kind of philosophical adolescence) but to accept our finiteness, to rely on our personal resources, and to determine for ourselves our own best values.

After all, Oedipus, Antigone, and Lear are great tragic figures not because they stand in relation to the gods as flies to wanton boys but because of their own decisions and actions—their own impressive humanity. And evolution has not destroyed our wonder at the special value of our own existence; quite the contrary. We are "the most exalted object which we are capable of conceiving," Darwin wrote, adding, "there is grandeur in this view of life."

If we now consider ourselves special because of our highly developed, highly specialized brain, rather than because of some traditional myth—and if we choose scientific fact in preference to superstition—our place in the world nevertheless remains important to us. Modern literature, despite its concern with absurdity, disillusion, black humor, antiheroism, and existential angst, remains human-centered and human-valued. Most recent writers have kept human aspiration as the tacit theme of their work, so that even when they record the bleak tale of our diverse failings, they also limn the ghostly negative of an implicitly positive picture.

A century and a half after *The Origin of Species*, Darwin himself continues to intrigue writers. And his literary experiences—the kinds of things he read, the ways he chose to write—retain an active fascination for scholars. As the final essay in Part IX shows, his books and ideas still inspire writers in all genres. Contemporary literature, like other current disciplines, has welcomed the larger perspectives and the sharpened perceptions that come from a clear understanding of Darwin's hard-earned reality.

8

We are perpetually moralists, Samuel Johnson said, but only occasionally geometricians. As is shown in Part VII ("Darwinian Influences in Philosophy and Ethics," p. 481), scientists and philosophers of science continue to ponder the origins of our communal ethics. Darwin, as usual, had anticipated them, and his ideas on the subject are still valuable. In *The Descent of Man*, Darwin speculated about our moral as well as our physical origins. He realized, better perhaps than anyone, that at all levels of animal life, the first necessity is self-preservation; but he also recognized that self-preservation sometimes means extending our survival tactics beyond the individual. Even at primitive levels of social organization, human beings have recognized that to live together in communities—as people must, to survive at all—we have to have some basic mutual agreements, some ground rules that we try to abide by. As Darwin observed, these can often be reduced to a kind of "golden rule": treat others as you would like to be treated. The golden rule principle undoubtedly evolved over time as a social necessity, a practical understanding; and its worldwide acknowledgment indicates that it is a general human concept, not the unique property of any one culture or religion.

Contemplating our social ground rules, Darwin surmised that after millions of years of living together in communities, our social behavior might to some extent be inherited. Darwin called that biological legacy "social instinct," the inheritance from our long past not only of the self-preservation imperative (the so-called animalistic urges that often cause people to be extraordinarily selfish and sometimes unscrupulous) but also our tendencies for "good" social behavior—that is, showing respect for others, fair dealing, honesty, and by a natural extension, kindness and charitableness.

It is commonly assumed that science, as such, has no ethics, that the gap between what "is" and what "ought to be" is broad and unbridgeable. However, scientific knowledge and understanding often do inform our ethical choices. For one thing, scientific knowledge has an important ethical role in identifying false issues that we can and should ignore—such as imagined astrological influences on our moral decisions. Such identification of error is obviously in itself a valuable service.

Beyond that, the growth of scientific knowledge has tended to have socially progressive effects. On the whole, factual knowledge of the physical world has been a far better basis for human understanding, human solidarity, and human sympathy than were folklore or superstition. The old myths of tribal and racial superiority, for instance, have now been thoroughly discredited by the biological understanding that we are one people, one species, in one world.

Moreover, it is the objective scientists who are actually now in the vanguard of ethical thought. In fact, some of the wisest thinkers who have reflected on the human condition over the last century have been biologists. Part VII traces the ethical preoccupations of scientists, from Darwin's friend T. H. Huxley a century ago, to the many present-day zoologists, philosophers, ethologists, and other thinkers who continue to grapple with the complexities of ethical theory and practice, frequently illuminated by the new perspectives of our increasing scientific knowledge.

In his groundbreaking book *The Expression of the Emotions in Man and Animals*, Darwin demonstrated that we share not only our flesh and blood with our fellow creatures but, in varying degrees, our emotional lives as well. With this knowledge, Darwin helped us understand the true wonder and significance of being human—an understanding that has since been broadened and deepened by thousands of hardworking biologists and anthropologists, who continue to examine the real world on our behalf. Thanks to all of them, as well as to Darwin, we now know the true story of our physical and emotional history, which reaches back through the millions of years of human and protohuman development, and even back to our animal ancestry—a history that is implicit in the ancient bones that the paleontologists are constantly bringing forth, and in the genes of every cell of every person on earth.

These basic and essential understandings have been achieved only because biology is a science thoroughly unified by the principle of evolution—and that unification we owe to Charles Darwin. In 1834, when the polymath Samuel Taylor Coleridge died, he believed that the science of zoology was in danger of falling apart because of its huge mass of uncoordinated factual information. That was just four years before Darwin picked up Malthus's *Essay on the Principle of Population* and discovered the clue to natural selection, and thus to the great organizing principle of evolution that would for the first time make a mature and coherent science of biology. Evolution by natural selection continues to serve biologists well in their professional work and in their ongoing explorations of our place in the universe. As Darwin wrote in *The Descent of Man*:

> The moral faculties are generally and justly esteemed as of higher value than the intellectual powers. But . . . the activity of the mind in vividly recalling past impressions is one of the . . . bases of conscience. This affords the strongest argument for educating and stimulating in all possible ways the intellectual faculties of every human being" (see p. 254).

The future is by definition obscure and risky, and admonitions about it notoriously fallible. But Darwin's sensible advice—"educating and stimulating in all possible ways the intellectual faculties of every human being"—probably gives us our best chance at what he himself called a "higher destiny in the distant future."

PART II
DARWIN'S LIFE

It was characteristic of Darwin on his journeys that when he saw a mountain he always tried to climb it.

—Gavin de Beer, 1964

ON THE *BEAGLE*†

Some people hold the world
in their fingertips, and
are part of what they hold.

The *Beagle* set sail
to easy summer—five years on
   sea
and land the watchful man
from Cambridge put
his fingers on a universe
of cuttlefish, sea-slugs, condors,
the ancient monsters' bones,
Megatherium, mastodon: all
fixed forever in immutable
   forms, creatures
of a benign Intelligence.
It was written.

But the young man put his
   fingers on
the pulse of rivers, coral reefs,
pampas and mountains,
the flotsam of earthquakes—and
on futures of learning, from
pigeons' plumage, the beaks of
   finches, bones
of rabbits and ducks—decades
of learning,
dissecting ten thousand
barnacles—pondering:
"If we choose to let
conjecture run wild, then
   animals—
our fellow brethren in pain,
disease, death, suffering, and
   famine—
may partake from our origin

in one common ancestor:
we may be all
netted together."

The *Beagle* labored on: in the
   winter
of Cape Horn,
twenty-three days of beating
against the icy bluster
came to broken boats
and spoiled collections.
The good ship rode to shelter—
and there on a rocky point
of Tierra del Fuego, naked
in snow, a mother
suckled her child
("whilst the sleet fell and thawed
on her naked bosom, and on the
   skin
of her naked baby")—there, in a
   little band,
stood
"man in his primitive wildness,"
ringed by the dark beech forest:
"As they threw their arms wildly
around their heads,
their long hair streaming,
they seemed the troubled spirits
of another world."
There
in the Bay of Good Success,
Charles Darwin, on the foredeck
   of the *Beagle*,
our future in his freezing
   fingertips,
stared into the faces
of our past.

—Philip Appleman, 1984

† From *New and Selected Poems, 1956–1996*, by Philip Appleman. Reprinted by permission of The University of Arkansas Press. Copyright © 1996 by Philip Appleman.

ERNST MAYR

Who Is Darwin? (1991)†

Historical periods are dominated by distinct sets of ideas which, taken together, form a well-defined *Zeitgeist*. Greek philosophy, Christianity, Renaissance thought, the Scientific Revolution, and the Enlightenment are examples of sets of ideas that dominated their historical period. The changes from one period to the next are usually rather gradual; other changes—more abrupt—are often referred to as revolutions. The most far-reaching of all these intellectual upheavals was the Darwinian revolution. The worldview formed by any thinking person in the Western world after 1859, when *On the Origin of Species* was published, was by necessity quite different from a worldview formed prior to 1859. It is almost impossible for a modern person to project back to the early half of the nineteenth century and reconstruct the thinking of this pre-Darwinian period, so great has been the impact of Darwinism on our views.

The intellectual revolution generated by Darwin went far beyond the confines of biology, causing the overthrow of some of the most basic beliefs of his age. For example, Darwin refuted the belief in the individual creation of each species, establishing in its place the concept that all of life descended from a common ancestor. By extension, he introduced the idea that humans were not the special products of creation but evolved according to principles that operate everywhere else in the living world. Darwin upset current notions of a perfectly designed, benign natural world and substituted in their place the concept of a struggle for survival. Victorian notions of progress and perfectibility were seriously undermined by Darwin's demonstration that evolution brings about change and adaptation, but it does not necessarily lead to progress, and it never leads to perfection.

Furthermore, Darwin established the basis for entirely new approaches in philosophy. At a time when the philosophy of science was dominated by a methodology based on mathematical principles, physical laws, and determinism, Darwin introduced the concepts of probability, chance, and uniqueness into scientific discourse. His work embodied the principle that observation and the making of hypotheses are as important to the advancement of knowledge as experimentation.

Darwin would be remembered as an outstanding scientist even if he had never written a word about evolution. Indeed, the evolutionist J. B. S. Haldane went so far as to say that Darwin's most original contribution to biology was not the theory of evolution but his series of books on experimental botany published nearer the end of his life. This achievement is little known among nonbiologists, and the same is true for his equally outstanding work on the adaptation of flowers and on animal psy-

† From *One Long Argument* (Cambridge, Mass.: 1991). Reprinted by permission of the publisher: Harvard University Press, Copyright © 1991 by Ernst Mayr. Ernst Mayr (b. 1904) is Alexander Agassiz Professor of Zoology, Emeritus, Harvard University. Two excellent biographies of Darwin are Adrian Desmond and James A. Moore, *Darwin* (New York, 1991) and Janet Browne, *Charles Darwin, I: Voyaging* (London, 1995).

chology, as well as his competent work on the barnacles and his imaginative work on earthworms. In all these areas Darwin was a pioneer, and
although in some areas more than a half a century passed before others
built on the foundations he laid, it is now clear that Darwin attacked
important problems with extraordinary originality, thereby becoming the
founder of several now well-recognized separate disciplines. Darwin was
the first person to work out a sound theory of classification, one which is
still adopted by the majority of taxonomists. His approach to biogeography,
in which so much emphasis was placed on the behavior and the ecology
of organisms as factors of distribution, is much closer to modern biogeography than the purely descriptive-geographical approach that dominated
biogeography for more than a half-century after Darwin's death.

Who was this extraordinary man, and how did he come to his ideas?
Was it his training, his personality, his industry, or his genius that accounts
for his success? Indeed, as we shall see, all were involved.

The Man and His Work

Charles Darwin was born on February 12, 1809, at Shrewsbury, England, the fifth of six children and the second son of Dr. Robert Darwin,
an eminently successful physician. His grandfather was Erasmus Darwin,
the author of *Zoonomia*, a work which anticipated his grandson's evolutionary interests by attempting to explain organic life according to evolutionary principles. His mother, the daughter of Josiah Wedgwood, the
celebrated potter, died when Charles was only eight years old, and his
elder sisters tried to fill her place.

From his earliest youth, Darwin was a passionate lover of the outdoors.
As he himself said, "I was born a naturalist." Every aspect of nature intrigued him. He loved to collect, to fish and hunt, and to read nature
books. Shrewsbury was a country town of about 20,000 inhabitants—a
perfect place for the development of a naturalist, much better than either
a big city or a strictly rural area would be. *Why?*

School, consisting largely of the study of the classics, bored the young
naturalist intolerably. Before he turned seventeen years old, Darwin's father
sent him to the University of Edinburgh to study medicine like his older
brother. But medicine appalled Charles, and he continued to devote much
of his time to the study of nature. When it became clear that he did not
want to become a physician, his father sent him early in 1828 to Cambridge to study theology. This seemed a reasonable choice, since virtually
all the naturalists in England at that time were ordained ministers, as were
the professors at Cambridge who taught botany (J. S. Henslow) and geology (Adam Sedgwick). Darwin's letters and biographical notes give the
impression that in Cambridge he devoted more time to collecting beetles,
discussing botany and geology with his professors, and hunting and riding
with similarly inclined friends than to his prescribed studies. Yet he did
well in his examinations, and when he took his B.A. in 1831 he stood
tenth on the list of nonhonors students. More importantly, when Darwin
had completed his Cambridge years he was an accomplished young
naturalist.

Immediately upon finishing his studies Darwin received an invitation to join *H. M. S. Beagle* as naturalist and gentleman companion of Captain Robert FitzRoy. FitzRoy had been commissioned to survey the coasts of Patagonia, Tierra del Fuego, Chile, and Peru to provide information for making better charts. The voyage was to be completed within two or three years but actually lasted five. The *Beagle* left Plymouth on December 27, 1831, when Darwin was twenty-two years old, and returned to England on October 2, 1836. Darwin used these five years to their fullest extent. In an eminently readable travelogue (*Journal of Researches*) he tells about all the places he visited—volcanic and coral islands, tropical forests in Brazil, the vast pampas of Patagonia, a crossing of the Andes from Chile to Tucuman in Argentina, and much, much more. Every day brought unforgettable new experiences, an invaluable background for his life's work. He collected specimens from widely different groups of organisms, he dug out important fossils in Patagonia, he devoted much of his time to geology, but most of all he observed aspects of nature and asked himself innumerable questions as to the how and why of natural processes. He asked "why" questions not only about geological features and animal life, but also about political and social situations. And it was his ability to ask profound questions and his perseverance in trying to answer them that would eventually make Darwin a great scientist.

In spite of being desperately seasick every time the ship encountered rough weather, Darwin managed to read a great deal of important scientific literature that he brought along on the voyage. No scientific work was more critical to his further thinking than the first two volumes of Charles Lyell's *Principles of Geology* (1832), which not only gave Darwin an advanced course in uniformitarian geology—a theory that changes in the earth's surface have occurred gradually over long periods of time—but also introduced him to Jean Baptiste Lamarck's arguments for, and Lyell's arguments against, evolutionary thinking.

When Darwin boarded the *Beagle* he still believed in the fixity of species, as did Lyell and all of his teachers at Cambridge. Yet during the South American phase of the *Beagle* voyage Darwin made many observations that greatly puzzled him and that shook his belief in the fixity of species. But it was really his visit to the Galapagos in September and October 1835 that provided him with the crucial evidence, even though —being preoccupied during his stay with geological researches—he did not at first realize it. However, nine months later, in July 1836, he penned these words in his diary: "When I see these islands in sight of each other and possessed of but a scanty stock of animals, tenanted by these birds but slightly differing in structure and filling the same place in nature, I must suspect they are varieties . . . if there is the slightest foundation for these remarks, the zoology of the archipelagoes will be well worth examining: for such facts would undermine the stability of species."

After his arrival in England in October 1836 Darwin sorted his collections and sent them to various specialists to be described in the official account of the *Beagle* expedition. In March 1837, when the celebrated ornithologist John Gould insisted that the mockingbirds (*Mimus*) collected by Darwin on three different islands in the Galapagos were three distinct species rather than varieties, as Darwin had thought, Darwin first understood the process of geographic speciation: that a new species can develop when a population becomes geographically isolated from its parental species. Furthermore, if colonists derived from a single South American ancestor could become three species in the Galapagos, then all the species of mockingbirds on the mainland could have been derived from an ancestral species, and so could have, at an earlier time, the species of related genera, and so forth. Numerous statements in Darwin's writings confirm that from the spring of 1837 on he firmly believed in the gradual origin of new species through geographic speciation, and in the theory of evolution by common descent. But another year and a half would pass before Darwin figured out the mechanism of evolution, the principle of natural selection. This happened on September 28, 1838, as he was reading Malthus's *Essay on the Principle of Population*.

In January 1839 Darwin married his cousin Emma Wedgwood, and in September 1842 the young couple moved from London to a country house in the small village of Downe (Kent), sixteen miles south of London, where Darwin lived until he died on April 19, 1882. Darwin's health required the move to a quiet place in the country. After he had passed his thirtieth year there were often long periods when he was unable to work more than two or three hours a day—indeed, when he was completely incapacitated for months on end. The exact nature of his illness is still controversial, but all the symptoms indicate a malfunctioning of the autonomous nervous system.

On the Origin of Species

Darwin did not publish his theories about evolution for another twenty years, even though he wrote some preliminary manuscript essays in 1842 and 1844. He devoted these years to his geological books and papers and to his monumental two-volume monograph on the barnacles (*Cirripedia*). Why did Darwin spend eight years on this piece of taxonomy instead of rushing into print with his important discovery of evolution by common descent through natural selection? Modern historical researches by M. T. Ghiselin and others have clearly shown that the barnacle studies were, for Darwin, an advanced graduate course in taxonomy, morphology, and ontogenetic research and not at all a waste of time. The experience he gained in these researches was an invaluable preparation for writing the *Origin*.

Finally, in April 1856, Darwin began to compose what he considered to be his "big species book." About two years later, after he had finished the first nine or ten chapters of this book, he received a letter from the naturalist Alfred Russel Wallace, who at that time was collecting specimens in the Moluccas. This letter, which Darwin received in June 1858, was accompanied by a manuscript that Wallace asked Darwin to read and submit to some journal if he found it acceptable. When Darwin read the manuscript, he was thunderstruck. Wallace had arrived at essentially the same theory of evolution by common descent through natural selection as he. On July 1, 1858, Darwin's friends Charles Lyell and the botanist Joseph Hooker presented Wallace's manuscript, together with excerpts from

Darwin's manuscripts and letters, at a meeting of the Linnean Society of London. This presentation amounted to a simultaneous publication of the findings of Darwin and Wallace. Darwin quickly abandoned his idea of finishing his monumental work on the species and wrote instead what he called an "abstract," which became his famous *On the Origin of the Species*, published November 24, 1859.

The impact of the *Origin* was enormous. Quite rightly it has been referred to as "the book that shook the world." In its first year the work sold 3,800 copies, and in Darwin's lifetime the British printings alone sold more than 27,000 copies. Several American printings, as well as innumerable translations, also appeared. Nevertheless, only in our lifetime have historians understood how fundamental the influence of this work has been. Every modern discussion of man's future, the population explosion, the struggle for existence, the purpose of man and the universe, and man's place in nature rests on Darwin.

In the ensuing twenty-three years of his life Darwin worked steadily on certain aspects of evolution he had not been able to cover adequately in the *Origin*. In a two-volume work, *The Variation of Animals and Plants under Domestication* (1868), he struggled valiantly with the problem of how genetic variation originates. In *The Descent of Man and Selection in Relation to Sex* (1871) he dealt with the evolution of the human species and expanded on his theory of sexual selection. *The Expression of the Emotions in Man and Animals* (1872) laid a foundation for the study of animal behavior. *Insectivorous Plants* (1875) described the remarkable adaptation of the sun-dew and other plants for catching and digesting insects. In *The Effects of Cross- and Self-Fertilization in the Vegetable Kingdom* (1876), in *The Different Forms of Flowers on Plants of the Same Species* (1877), and in *The Power of Movement in Plants* (1880), Darwin discussed aspects of plant growth and physiology, as indicated in the titles. And finally in *The Formation of Vegetable Mold, through the Action of Worms, with Observations on Their Habits* (1881), he described the important role played by earthworms in the formation of the topsoil.

How could one man achieve so much in a lifetime, particularly considering the constraints imposed by his illness? Only by retreating into the quiet of the countryside, refusing to accept most offered offices or memberships on committees, and, through the generosity of his father, living on his inherited income was Darwin able to complete his task. Yet Darwin was not a recluse. He kept in touch with the scientific world through an extensive correspondence and occasional visits to London, and he was a devoted husband and dedicated father to his ten children.

Darwin was described by his contemporaries as an extraordinarily modest, gentle person who went out of his way to avoid hurting anyone's feelings. He worked so hard because he had an unquenchable thirst for learning, not in order to get advancement or honors. In his publications he was a scientist's scientist. He did not write for the general public; when some of his works had great popular success, he was always astonished.

Nevertheless, Darwin fought for the recognition of his findings among scientists, and he was supported by a small band of loyal friends—among them Lyell, Hooker, and the morphologist T. H. Huxley, often referred to as Darwin's bulldog because it was he who in public debates most often defended Darwin's theories. The most fervent of Darwin's admirers were the naturalists. These included the codiscoverer of evolution by natural selection, A. R. Wallace, the entomologist Henry Walter Bates, and the naturalist Fritz Müller.

To have a loyal group of defenders was very important because Darwin was attacked with unusual ferocity. In 1860 the Harvard University zoologist Louis Agassiz wrote that Darwin's theory was a "scientific mistake, untrue in its facts, unscientific in its methods, and mischievous in its tendency." The *Origin* was extensively reviewed in journals by the leading philosophers, theologians, literary men, and scientists of the day. By far the majority of the reviews were negative, if not extremely hostile. Curiously, this negative reception continued after Darwin's death in 1882 and has lasted in certain circles to the present day.

Darwin's Scientific Method

The years during which Darwin worked on the manuscript for his big species book happened to be the same years in which the field of study known as the philosophy of science originated in England. While still a student, Darwin had read with enthusiasm John Herschel's *Preliminary Discourse on the Study of Natural Philosophy* (1830), and this work continued to be one of his favorite readings. He also read William Whewell's and John Stuart Mill's books and tried conscientiously to follow their prescriptions for the study of natural history. This was rather difficult, since the recommendations of the various authors were often contradictory; as a result, so were Darwin's own statements on the subject. To satisfy some of his readers Darwin asserted that he followed "the true Baconian method," that is, straight induction. In reality, he "speculated" on any subject he encountered. He realized that one cannot make observations unless one has some hypothesis on the basis of which to make the appropriate observations. Therefore, "I can have no doubt that speculative men, with a curb on, make far the best observers." He stated his views most clearly in a letter to Henry Fawcett. "About 30 years ago there was much talk that geologists ought to observe and not to theorize; and I well remember someone saying that at this rate a man might as well go into a gravel pit and count the pebbles and describe the colors. How odd it is that anyone should not see that all observation must be for or against some view if it is to be of any service!"

Darwin's method was actually the time-honored method of the best naturalists. They observe numerous phenomena and always try to understand the how and why of their observations. When something does not at once fall into place, they make a conjecture and test it by additional observations, leading either to a refutation or strengthening of the original assumption. This procedure does not fit well into the classical prescriptions of the philosophy of science, because it consists of continually going back and forth between making observations, posing questions, establishing hypotheses or models, testing them by making further observations, and so forth. Darwin's speculation was a well-disciplined process, used by him, as by every modern scientist, to give direction to the planning of experiments and to the collecting of further observations. I know of no forerunner of Darwin who used this method as consistently and with as much success.

That Darwin was a genius is hardly any longer questioned, some of his earlier detractors notwithstanding. But there must have been a score of other biologists of equal intelligence who failed to match Darwin's achievement. What is it that distinguishes Darwin from all the others? Perhaps we can answer this question by investigating what kind of scientist Darwin was. As he has said, he was first and foremost a naturalist. He was a splendid observer, and like all other naturalists he was interested in organic diversity and in adaptation. Naturalists are, on the whole, describers and particularizers, but Darwin was also a great theoretician, something only very few naturalists have ever been. In that respect Darwin resembles much more some of the leading physical scientists of his day. But Darwin differed from the run-of-the-mill naturalists also in another way. He was not only an observer but also a gifted and indefatigable experimenter whenever he dealt with a problem whose solution could be advanced by an experiment.

I think this suggests some of the sources of Darwin's greatness. The universality of his talents and interests had preadapted him to become a bridge-builder between fields. It enabled him to use his background as a naturalist to theorize about some of the most challenging problems that pique our curiosity. And, in the face of widespread beliefs to the contrary, Darwin was utterly bold in his theorizing. A brilliant mind, great intellectual boldness, and an ability to combine the best qualities of a naturalist-observer, philosophical theoretician, and experimentalist —the world has so far seen such a combination only once, and it was in the man Charles Darwin.

PART III
SCIENTIFIC THOUGHT:
JUST BEFORE DARWIN

As a record of a former state of things, I have retained in the foregoing paragraphs, and elsewhere, several sentences which imply that naturalists believe in the separate creation of each species; and I have been much censured for having thus expressed myself. But undoubtedly this was the general belief when the first edition of the present work appeared. I formerly spoke to very many naturalists on the subject of evolution, and never once met with any sympathetic agreement. It is probable that some did then believe in evolution, but they were either silent, or expressed themselves so ambiguously that it was not easy to understand their meaning. Now things are wholly changed, and almost every naturalist admits the great principle of evolution.

—Charles Darwin, 1872

He succeeded in putting the *whole* of past life into *every* aspect of *every* form of present life. In this respect Darwin has no precursor.

—Bert James Loewenberg, 1965

GAVIN DE BEER

Biology before the *Beagle* (1964)†

*   *   *

The subject of mutability of species had been taken up in speculative manner by a group of French philosophers including Montesquieu, Maupertuis, and Diderot. Basing themselves on certain facts such as the gradations that can be imagined between different species arranged in series, the appearance of new varieties of cultivated plants and domestic animals and of hereditary sports such as six-fingered men, the significance of monstrous births and imperfections of development, and the changes undergone by animals during their own life-histories, these thinkers concluded by deduction that species must have been mutable. Diderot even suggested that there was a prototype from which all living beings were descended and that the agent responsible for change was the age-old folk-belief that characters impressed on an organism during its life were transmitted by inheritance to the offspring. This, in his view, would account for the supposed perpetuation of the effects of use and disuse of organs, while the principle that if an animal experienced a need this need would provoke the formation of an organ that satisfied the need, accounted for the origin of such an organ.

In substantial agreement with these speculations was Erasmus Darwin, physician-philosopher-poet, whose work *Zoönomia or the Laws of Organic Life* was published in 1794. Like his French predecessors, Erasmus Darwin believed in the mutability of species because of the changes undergone by animals during embryonic development, particularly the metamorphoses of the caterpillar into the moth and the tadpole into the frog, because of the changes brought about by domestication and resulting from hybridization, because of the significance of monstrous births, and the similarity in plan of structure of vertebrate animals. He believed that the modification of species was brought about by the satisfaction of wants due to "lust, hunger, and danger," and as a result of "their own exertions in consequence of their desires and aversions, of their pleasures and pains, or of irritations, or of associations; and many of these acquired forms or propensities are transmitted to their posterity." He recognized the importance of adaptation of organisms to their environments in the struggle for existence, of protective coloration; of artificial selection and sexual selection in bringing about change; of cross-fertilization in maintaining vigor; of the significance of vestigial organs that were without function in their possessors but presupposed a former function; of monstrous births as disproof of the notion that the embryo is preformed in the germ; and of sports or mutations such as six-toed cats and rumpless fowls. But when it came to

† From Chapter 1 of *Charles Darwin: A Scientific Biography* (New York, 1964). Used by permission of International Thomson Publishing Company. Gavin de Beer (1899–1972) was director of the Natural History Department of the British Museum and professor of embryology at the University of London.

explaining how adaptations were produced in an organism, Erasmus Darwin had nothing to offer but "the power of acquiring new parts, attended with new propensities, directed by irritations, sensations, volitions, and associations; and thus possessing the faculties of continuing to improve by its own inherent activity, and of delivering down those improvements to its posterity, world without end."

Independently, although heir to the same speculative background, Jean-Baptiste de Lamarck came to conclusions very similar to those of Erasmus Darwin. A soldier of outstanding gallantry in the Seven Years War who had subsequently become fascinated by the luxuriance of plants in his garrison stations in the south of France, Lamarck abandoned the army as a profession and took up the study of natural history. In his book *Hydro-géologie* published in 1802 he opposed the "catastrophic" theories of geological causes then in vogue which required fantastic catastrophes to explain the state of the earth and, like James Hutton, advocated the uninterrupted continuity of past and present causes and effects. Lamarck recognized the unlimited amount of time required to account for the history of the earth, deduced the organic origin of sedimentary rocks, and pointed out the importance of fossils for the estimation of past changes of climate, valuable services to science, largely ignored even today.

It is for his *Philosophie zoologique* published in 1809 that Lamarck is remembered in the history of science. Confronted with the task of classifying the collections in the Paris Museum of Natural History, he experienced such difficulty in distinguishing between species and varieties of species that he concluded that there was no basic difference between them. He argued that if enough closely related species were studied together, differences between them could no longer be made out and they merged into one another. In fact this is not the case, because the barrier between species is always discernible even if very difficult to detect, but the appearance that species graded into one another led Lamarck to put forward a full theory of "transformism" or evolution, which he was the first to do, invoking descent of species during long periods of time from other species, so that the Animal Kingdom could be represented by a genealogy of branching lines, the last branch being that of man. Fossil organisms he thought had not become extinct but had been transmuted into their living descendants.

Lamarck accounted for evolution by means of the action of two factors. The first was a supposed tendency to perfection and to increased complexity, which he held responsible for the existence of the scale of beings from the simplest organisms at the bottom to man at the top. He regarded this concept as so self-evident as not to require proof, of which in fact it is incapable, being inaccessible to scientific investigation. It led him to suppose that as simple lowly organisms exist today without having been perfected or made complex, they must have arisen recently by spontaneous generation. Lamarck's second factor was introduced because the scale of beings is not a perfect series graded from the lowest to the highest but shows anomalies, deviations, and branchings from what it might and in his view would have been if the environment had not interfered. Like Diderot and Erasmus Darwin, Lamarck supposed that as a result of new needs experienced by the animal in its environment, its "inner feeling," comparable to Erasmus Darwin's "internal impulse" or "living force," set in motion bodily movements and instituted habits that produced new organs satisfying those needs, in other words, adapting the animal to its environment. These organs, and the effects of their use and disuse, he thought were then transmitted by heredity. As this explanation could not be applied to plants or to the lowest animals, Lamarck concluded that their evolution was conditioned by the direct effects of the environment. He was therefore unable to provide a unitary theory of evolution.

These views led contemporary scientists to reject them, and with them the theory of transmutation. Even Étienne Geoffroy-Saint-Hilaire, who accepted the transmutation of species, regretted that by his speculations Lamarck had compromised it. Scientists like Baron Georges Cuvier who rejected transmutation were even more opposed to Lamarck. It is, however, only fair to say that Lamarck has been treated with less than justice by history, for his name is associated with a hypothetic cause of evolution that he did not invent and that is unacceptable, whereas it was his genius in proposing a scheme of evolution that deserves commemoration in the term Lamarckism.

As a result of his extensive researches in comparative anatomy and paleontology published in 1812, Cuvier was struck by the fact that in the rocks of the Paris basin some strata contained fossils of marine animals, others fossils of fresh-water animals, and others again no fossils at all. From the apparently sudden appearance and equally sudden disappearance of these remains of bygone life, Cuvier concluded that catastrophes similar to the Biblical Flood had repeatedly destroyed life, and that after each catastrophe it had blossomed out afresh through successive creations and immigrations of such organisms as had escaped destruction because they had previously lived elsewhere on earth, out of reach of that particular catastrophe. There had therefore been extensive extinction of species, which was a new concept involving the abandonment of some objects of creation to their melancholy fate by the Supreme Being. It was not many years since John Wesley, in 1770, had written, "Death . . . is never permitted to destroy the most inconsiderable species," and Thomas Jefferson, referring to fossil bones of the American mastodon, which he refused to regard as extinct, wrote, "Such is the economy of nature, that no instance can be produced, of her having permitted any one race of her animals to become extinct; of her having formed any link in her great work, so weak as to be broken."

It was also obvious to Cuvier that after each "catastrophe" there was an advance in the complexity of life, so that each new wave of living beings showed a superiority of organization over their extinct predecessors. The younger the strata, the more fossils they contained belonging to animals similar to those living. A transcendental principle of progressionism had therefore to be invoked to account for this, since two reasons prevented him from accepting transmutation: the absence of any known intermediate forms, and the fact that organisms found in the oldest tombs of Egypt were identical with those still living and had therefore undergone no transmutation during the intervening period of time. Finally, Cuvier showed that the anatomical diversity exhibited by different groups of animals could not be accommodated on any single plan of structure undergoing progression from the simplest to the most complex. He therefore introduced the concept of four major groups or *embranchements* into which the Animal Kingdom was divided: Radiata (jellyfish, starfish), Articulata (worms, insects), Mollusca (snails, octopus), and Vertebrata. In other words, for the single scale of beings Cuvier substituted four plans of structure, which introduced the concept of divergence.

Another concept introduced by Cuvier was that of correlation of parts. His mastery of comparative anatomy enabled him to claim that "the smallest fragment of bone, even the most apparently insignificant apophysis, possesses a fixed and determinate character, relative to the class, order, genus and species of the animal to which it belonged; insomuch, that when we find merely the extremity of a well-preserved bone, we are able by careful examination, assisted by analogy and exact comparison, to determine the species to which it once belonged, as certainly as if we had the entire animal before us." * * *

Cuvier's principle of correlation was, in fact, based on his recognition of the fact and importance of adaptation; organs serve functions that adapt the organisms to their environments or conditions of existence, and in his view, as in that of many of his contemporaries, this fact of adaptation was evidence of purpose or of final causes: organisms had been created with their organs as they are in order that they might exploit their several ways of life and enjoy their environments. Teleology had been introduced into the details of anatomy and physiology.

To the geologist Charles Lyell, Cuvier's theories of catastrophism and progressionism were unacceptable, first because Lyell's observations and researches had convinced him that the geological agents that were to be seen operating in the present could, given sufficient time, have caused everything that had happened in the past history of the earth. This was the principle of uniformitarianism, first introduced by James Hutton in 1785 and developed independently by Lyell in his *Principles of Geology* (1830) to a point where it could not fail to prevail over the speculations of catastrophism. Lyell's objection to progressionism was due partly to its association with catastrophism and partly to his opinion that the paleontological evidence obtainable from the fossil record as known in his day was insufficient to support progressionism. Dicotyledonous plants, the highest types of the vegetable kingdom, had been found in coal measures of the Carboniferous period, and mammals in Secondary strata. Lyell therefore rejected progressionism and, with it, Lamarck's theory of transmutation, all the more because "if we look for some of those essential changes which would be required to lend even the semblance of a foundation for the theory of Lamarck, respecting the growth of new organs and the gradual obliteration of others, we find nothing of the kind." In his view, the theory lacked evidence, no intermediate forms were known, he thought it extravagant to claim that organisms could vary sufficiently to account for the differences between species, and the notion that when organs were needed they arose, removed the problem out of the realm of science into that of fanciful speculation. It must be added that Lamarck's inclusion of man in his scheme of evolution could not fail to disturb Lyell, for he was not yet prepared to contemplate unorthodox opinion where man was concerned, notwithstanding his scientific approach and rejection of scriptural interpretation in problems of geology. The result was that Lyell accepted the fact that species could become extinct, as a result of failure in the struggle for existence, and he knew that extinct species had been replaced by other species, but as to how this occurred and by what process fresh species originated, he had nothing to offer.

The problem of the origination of fresh species had, however, to be answered somehow, and the inability of the uniformitarian view to provide an answer drove its critics to adopt the only alternative known to them, namely miraculous interposition by the Creator. * * * The theory of evolution was tinged with political overtones that still persist. Then, they resulted in the writing of two books that had profound though unexpected effects on the future of natural history. On the sociological plane, a valiant attempt to stem the tide of the French ungodly was made by Thomas Robert Malthus with his *Essay on Population*, while on the theological side William Paley set out in his *Natural Theology* to prove that the study of natural history inevitably led to belief in a divine Creator.

* * * [Malthus] generalized the principle that "Population, when unchecked, increases in a geometrical ratio. Subsistence increases only in an arithmetical ratio. . . . I can see no way by which man can escape from the weight of this law which pervades all animate nature." Unwittingly, no doubt, Malthus here placed man on the same plane as the rest of the animal kingdom. Among plants and animals the growth of population was kept down by mortality due to "want of room and nourishment" and falling a prey to predators. In man, if in spite of famines and epidemics and the preventive checks imposed by reason, population nevertheless increased too fast, those of its members who could least afford the necessities of life were doomed to misery and death. On the other hand, if the checks to the increase in numbers of a population through delayed marriage and abstinence were artificial and too effective, there would be no competition or compulsion to work exerted on those whose livelihood depended on it, and the results would equally be misery from the effects of immorality, idleness, and sloth.

It followed, as H. N. Brailsford has pointed out, that all attempts to preserve life were contrary to the correct application of principle, charity was an economic sin, altruism "unscientific," and presumably the medical profession pursued an anti-social aim. Since the possibilities of variation, shown by cultivated plants and domestic animals, were in Malthus' view strictly limited, progress was impossible; attempts to achieve it as in the French Revolution were doomed to failure; and mankind could neither improve nor be perfected. Malthus' book was reprinted several times and the main lines of evidence on which his argument rested were on his own admission more and more undermined, but he nevertheless stuck to the sloganlike antithesis between geometrical and arithmetical rates of increase for growth of population and of subsistence. In this, Malthus performed a service to science, because most of those of his contemporaries who were aware of the struggle for existence in nature ran away from the horrors of tooth and claw and tried to veil it, minimize it, or moralize on the greater resulting happiness for the survivors. As will be seen, this aspect of Malthus' work had far-reaching effects.

Among Malthus' adherents was William Paley, who based his *Natural Theology* (1802) on the argument that a contrivance implies a contriver, just as a design implies a designer, and illustrated this analogy by means of a watch. Passing from horology to natural history he pointed out that the lens of the eye in fishes is more spherical than that of the eye of land vertebrates, which showed that each eye is *adapted* to the refractive index of the medium, water or air, in which the animal lives. "What plainer manifestation of design can there be than this instance?" he asked. The function of the iris diaphragm, accommodation for distance, the fact that the blind spots of the two eyes of an individual are not at conjugate points on the retina, that the eyebrow and eyelid protect the eye, all pointed to intelligent construction: "it is only by the display of contrivance, that the existence, the agency, the wisdom, of the Deity *could* be testified to his rational creatures." The same argument applied to the ear and to the function of all organs and tissues: down-feathers for warmth, flight-feathers for flight, webbed feet for progression in water, poison-fangs for defense in snakes, pouches for containing the young in marsupials, the long tongue of the woodpecker for catching grubs, the complicated life history of mistletoe. Some adaptations are even anticipatory, such as migration in birds, a contrivance to avoid and survive a cold season that has not yet arrived, or the foramen ovale and ductus arteriosus of the mammalian embryo, which enable it to switch instantly at birth from the intra-uterine to the aerial type of respiration and blood-circulation. All these were adaptations and Paley summed them up with the words: "The marks of *design* are too strong to be gotten over. Design must have had a designer. That designer must have been a person. That person is God." * * *

It is in the treatment of the problem of suffering that Paley had the greatest difficulty in making his case. "Pain, no doubt, and privations exist . . . Evil, no doubt, exists; but it is never, that we can perceive, the *object* of contrivance. Teeth are contrived to eat, not to ache." The "aches" caused in what teeth kill and eat are ignored, although the undeniable carnage of nature forces Paley to admit that "We cannot avoid the difficulty by saying that the effect was not intended. The only question open to us is whether it be ultimately evil. From the confessed and felt imperfection of our knowledge, we ought to presume that there may be consequences of this economy which are hidden from us," a form of argument that will be met again in very different circumstances. In an attempt to minimize the horror of the war of nature, he continues, "I believe the cases of bites which produce death in large animals (of stings I think there are none) to be very few."

Again, "Pain also itself is not without its *alleviations*. It may be violent and frequent; but it is seldom violent and long-continued; and its pauses and intermissions become positive pleasures. Of *mortal* diseases the great use is to reconcile us to death." In any case, by Malthus' principle, death is necessary to prevent over-population, and therefore beneficial. In compensation, "The Deity has super-added *pleasure* to animal sensations, beyond what was necessary for any purpose . . . it is a happy world after all." Then, as a parting shot, "The appearance of chance will always bear a proportion to the ignorance of the observer," with which Paley was confident that he had defended his religion and confounded the infidel. * * *

What Paley had, in fact, done was to provide a catalogue of adaptations that was shortly to come in very useful, and this is why it has been necessary to allot to Paley, as to Malthus, more space than would be justified by the intrinsic merits of their special pleading, masquerading as science. Furthermore, Paley's works, which were prescribed reading in British universities for many years, represent the prevailing points of view and attitudes of mind that had to be overcome by hard scientific evidence before the theory of evolution could be established, and, by an astonishing irony of history, his and Malthus' works unwittingly contributed more than any other publications to the establishment of that theory.

Such were the tides, currents, and backwaters of thought when on December 27, 1831 H.M.S. *Beagle* set sail from Plymouth.

THOMAS ROBERT MALTHUS

An Essay on the Principle of Population (1798)†

*   *   *

I think I may fairly make two postulata.

⎧ First, That food is necessary to the existence of man.

⎩ Secondly, That the passion between the sexes is necessary and will remain nearly in its present state.

These two laws, ever since we have had any knowledge of mankind, appear to have been fixed laws of our nature, and, as we have not hitherto seen any alteration in them, we have no right to conclude that they will ever cease to be what they now are.

*   *   *

Assuming then, my postulata as granted, I say that the power of population is indefinitely greater than the power in the earth to produce subsistence for man.

Population, when unchecked, increases in a geometrical ratio. Subsistence increases only in an arithmetical ratio. A slight acquaintance with numbers will shew the immensity of the first power in comparison of the second.

By that law of our nature which makes food necessary to the life of man, the effects of these two unequal powers must be kept equal.

† From *An Essay on the Principle of Population* (London, 1798; rev. ed., 1803). Thomas Robert Malthus (1766–1834) was professor of political economy at the East India College, Hertfordshire. His essay was widely read and often reprinted. Darwin credited the central idea of that book, reprinted here, as giving him the clue to natural selection.

{   This implies a strong and constantly operating check on population from the difficulty of subsistence. This difficulty must fall some where and must necessarily be severely felt by a large portion of mankind.

Through the animal and vegetable kingdoms, nature has scattered the seeds of life abroad with the most profuse and liberal hand. She has been comparatively sparing in the room and the nourishment necessary to rear them. The germs of existence contained in this spot of earth, with ample food and ample room to expand in, would fill millions of worlds in the course of a few thousand years. Necessity, that imperious all pervading law of nature, restrains them within the prescribed bounds. The race of plants and the race of animals shrink under this great restrictive law. And the race of man cannot, by any efforts of reason, escape from it. Among plants and animals its effects are waste of seed, sickness, and premature death. Among mankind, misery and vice.

*   *   *

Taking the population of the world at any number, a thousand millions, for instance, the human species would increase in the ratio of—1, 2, 4, 8, 16, 32, 64, 128, 256, 512, &c. and subsistence as—1, 2, 3, 4, 5, 6, 7, 8, 9, 10, &c. In two centuries and a quarter, the population would be to the means of subsistence as 512 to 10, in three centuries as 4096 to 13, and in two thousand years the difference would be almost incalculable, though the produce in that time would have increased to an immense extent.

No limits whatever are placed to the productions of the earth; they may increase for ever and be greater than any assignable quantity; yet still the power of population being a power of a superior order, the increase of the human species can only be kept commensurate to the increase of the means of subsistence by the constant operation of the strong law of necessity acting as a check upon the greater power.

The effects of this check remain now to be considered.

Among plants and animals the view of the subject is simple. They are all impelled by a powerful instinct to the increase of their species, and this instinct is interrupted by no reasoning or doubts about providing for their offspring. Wherever therefore there is liberty, the power of increase is exerted, and the super-abundant effects are repressed afterwards by want of room and nourishment, which is common to animals and plants, and among animals, by becoming the prey of others. *   *   *

WILLIAM PALEY

Natural Theology (1802)†

State of the Argument

In crossing a heath, suppose I pitched my foot against a *stone*, and were asked how the stone came to be there, I might possibly answer, that for any thing I knew to the contrary it had lain there for ever; nor would it, perhaps, be very easy to show the absurdity of this answer. But suppose I had found a *watch* upon the ground, and it should be inquired how the watch happened to be in that place, I should hardly think of the answer which I had before given, that for any thing I knew the watch might have always been there. Yet why should not this answer serve for the watch as well as for the stone; why is it not as admissible in the second case as in the first? For this reason, and for no other, namely, that when we come to inspect the watch, we perceive—what we could not discover in the stone—that its several parts are framed and put together for a purpose, *e.g.* that they are so formed and adjusted as to produce motion, and that motion so regulated as to point out the hour of· the day; that if the different parts had been differently shaped from what they are, or placed after any other manner or in any other order than that in which they are placed, either no motion at all would have been carried on in the machine, or none which would have answered the use that is now served by it. To reckon up a few of the plainest of these parts and of their offices, all tending to one result: We see a cylindrical box containing a coiled elastic spring, which, by its endeavor to relax itself, turns round the box. We next observe a flexible chain—artificially wrought for the sake of flexure—communicating the action of the spring from the box to the fusee. We then find a series of wheels, the teeth of which catch in and apply to each other, conducting the motion from the fusee to the balance and from the balance to the pointer, and at the same time, by the size and shape of those wheels, so regulating that motion as to terminate in causing an index, by an equable and measured progression, to pass over a given space in a given time. We take notice that the wheels are made of brass, in order to keep them from rust; the springs of steel, no other metal being so elastic; that over the face of the watch there is placed a glass, a material employed in no other part of the work, but in the room of which, if there had been any other than a transparent substance, the hour could not be seen without opening the case. This mechanism being observed—it requires indeed an examination of the instrument, and perhaps some previous knowledge of the subject, to perceive and understand it; but being once, as we have said, observed and understood, the inference we think is inevitable, that the watch must have had a maker—that there must have existed, at some

† From *Natural Theology: or Evidences of the Existence and Attributes of the Deity Collected from the Appearances of Nature* (London, 1802). William Paley (1743–1805), English ecclesiastic and moralist, was author of several influential works on natural theology, including this text, which Darwin studied carefully at Cambridge.

time and at some place or other, an artificer or artificers who formed it for the purpose which we find it actually to answer, who comprehended its construction and designed its use.

Suppose, in the next place, that the person who found the watch should after some time discover, that in addition to all the properties which he had hitherto observed in it, it possessed the unexpected property of producing in the course of its movement another watch like itself—the thing is conceivable; that it contained within it a mechanism, a system of parts —a mould, for instance, or a complex adjustment of lathes, files, and other tools—evidently and separately calculated for this purpose; let us inquire what effect ought such a discovery to have upon his former conclusion.

I. The first effect would be to increase his admiration of the contrivance, and his conviction of the consummate skill of the contriver. Whether he regarded the object of the contrivance, the distinct apparatus, the intricate, yet in many parts intelligible mechanism by which it was carried on, he would perceive in this new observation nothing but an additional reason for doing what he had already done—for referring the construction of the watch to design and to supreme art. If that construction *without* this property, or which is the same thing, before this property had been noticed, proved intention and art to have been employed about it, still more strong would the proof appear when he came to the knowledge of this further property, the crown and perfection of all the rest.

II. He would reflect, that though the watch before him were *in some sense* the maker of the watch which was fabricated in the course of its movements, yet it was in a very different sense from that in which a carpenter, for instance, is the maker of a chair—the author of its contrivance, the cause of the relation of its parts to their use. With respect to these, the first watch was no cause at all to the second; in no such sense as this was it the author of the constitution and order, either of the parts which the new watch contained, or of the parts by the aid and instrumentality of which it was produced. We might possibly say, but with great latitude of expression, that a stream of water ground corn; but no latitude of expression would allow us to say, no stretch of conjecture could lead us to think, that the stream of water built the mill, though it were too ancient for us to know who the builder was. What the stream of water does in the affair is neither more nor less than this: by the application of an unintelligent impulse to a mechanism previously arranged, arranged independently of it and arranged by intelligence, an effect is produced, namely, the corn is ground. But the effect results from the arrangement. The force of the stream cannot be said to be the cause or the author of the effect, still less of the arrangement. Understanding and plan in the formation of the mill were not the less necessary for any share which the water has in grinding the corn; yet is this share the same as that which the watch would have contributed to the production of the new watch, upon the supposition assumed in the last section. Therefore,

III. Though it be now no longer probable that the individual watch which our observer had found was made immediately by the hand of an artificer, yet doth not this alteration in anywise affect the inference, that an artificer had been originally employed and concerned in the production. The argument from design remains as it was. Marks of design and contrivance are no more accounted for now than they were before. In the same thing, we may ask for the cause of different properties. We may ask for the cause of the color of a body, of its hardness, of its heat; and these causes may be all different. We are now asking for the cause of that subserviency to a use, that relation to an end, which we have remarked in the watch before us. No answer is given to this question, by telling us that a preceding watch produced it. There cannot be design without a designer; contrivance, without a contriver; order, without choice; arrangement, without any thing capable of arranging; subserviency and relation to a purpose, without that which could intend a purpose; means suitable to an end, and executing their office in accomplishing that end, without the end ever having been contemplated, or the means accommodated to it. Arrangement, disposition of parts, subserviency of means to an end, relation of instruments to a use, imply the presence of intelligence and mind. No one, therefore, can rationally believe that the insensible, inanimate watch, from which the watch before us issued, was the proper cause of the mechanism we so much admire in it—could be truly said to have constructed the instrument, disposed its parts, assigned their office, determined their order, action, and mutual dependency, combined their several motions into one result, and that also a result connected with the utilities of other beings. All these properties, therefore, are as much unaccounted for as they were before.

The conclusion which the *first* examination of the watch, of its works, construction, and movement, suggested, was, that it must have had, for cause and author of that construction, an artificer who understood its mechanism and designed its use. This conclusion is invincible. A *second* examination presents us with a new discovery. The watch is found, in the course of its movement, to produce another watch similar to itself; and not only so, but we perceive in it a system or organization separately calculated for that purpose. What effect would this discovery have, or ought it to have, upon our former inference? What, as hath already been said, but to increase beyond measure our admiration of the skill which had been employed in the formation of such a machine? Or shall it, instead of this, all at once turn us round to an opposite conclusion, namely, that no art or skill whatever has been concerned in the business, although all other evidences of art and skill remain as they were, and this last and supreme piece of art be now added to the rest? Can this be maintained without absurdity? Yet this is atheism.

Application of the Argument

This is atheism; for every indication of contrivance, every manifestation of design which existed in the watch, exists in the works of nature, with the difference on the side of nature of being greater and more, and that in a degree which exceeds all computation. I mean, that the contrivances of nature surpass the contrivances of art, in the complexity, subtilty, and curiosity of the mechanism; and still more, if possible, do they go beyond them in number and variety; yet, in a multitude of cases, are not less evidently mechanical, not less evidently contrivances, not less evidently accommodated to their end or suited to their office, than are the most perfect productions of human ingenuity.

I know no better method of introducing so large a subject, than that of comparing a single thing with a single thing: an eye, for example, with a telescope. As far as the examination of the instrument goes, there is precisely the same proof that the eye was made for vision, as there is that the telescope was made for assisting it. They are made upon the same principles; both being adjusted to the laws by which the transmission and refraction of rays of light are regulated. I speak not of the origin of the laws themselves; but such laws being fixed, the construction in both cases is adapted to them. For instance, these laws require, in order to produce the same effect, that the rays of light, in passing from water into the eye, should be refracted by a more convex surface than when it passes out of air into the eye. Accordingly we find that the eye of a fish, in that part of it called the crystalline lens, is much rounder than the eye of terrestrial animals. What plainer manifestation of design can there be than this difference? What could a mathematical instrument maker have done more to show his knowledge of his principle, his application of that knowledge, his suiting of his means to his end—I will not say to display the compass or excellence of his skill and art, for in these all comparison is indecorous, but to testify counsel, choice, consideration, purpose?

JEAN BAPTISTE PIERRE ANTOINE DE MONET LAMARCK

Zoological Philosophy (1809)†

* * *

The conditions necessary to the existence of life are all present in the lowest organisations, and they are here also reduced to their simplest expression. It became therefore of importance to know how this organisation, by some sort of change, had succeeded in giving rise to others less simple, and indeed to the gradually increasing complexity observed throughout the animal scale. By means of the two following principles, to which observation had led me, I believed I perceived the solution of the problem at issue.

Firstly, a number of known facts proves that the continued use of any organ leads to its development, strengthens it and even enlarges it, while permanent disuse of any organ is injurious to its development, causes it to deteriorate and ultimately disappear if the disuse continues for a long period through successive generations. Hence we may infer that when some change in the environment leads to a change of habit in some race

---

† From *Zoological Philosophy* (Paris, 1809). Jean Baptiste Lamarck (1744–1829), French naturalist and professor of zoology, brought attention to the idea of evolution; but without a persuasive causal mechanism, his work was dismissed by contemporary scientists.

of animals, the organs that are less used die away little by little, while those which are more used develop better, and acquire a vigour and size proportional to their use.

Secondly, when reflecting upon the power of the movement of the fluids in the very supple parts which contain them, I soon became convinced that, according as this movement is accelerated, the fluids modify the cellular tissue in which they move, open passages in them, form various canals, and finally create different organs, according to the state of the organisation in which they are placed.

*   *   *

The belief has long been held that there exists a sort of scale or graduated chain among living bodies. Bonnet has developed this view; but he did not prove it by facts derived from their organisation; yet this was necessary especially with regard to animals. He was unable to prove it, since at the time when he lived the means did not exist.

In the study of all classes of animals there are many other things to be seen besides the animal complexity. Among the subjects of greatest importance in framing a rational philosophy are the effect of the environment in the creation of new needs; the effect of the needs in giving rise to actions, and of repeated actions in creating habits and inclinations; the results of increased or diminished use of any organ, and the means adopted by nature to maintain and to perfect all that has been acquired in organisation.

*   *   *

It is not a futile purpose to decide definitely what we mean by the so-called *species* among living bodies, and to enquire if it is true that species are of absolute constancy, as old as nature, and have all existed from the beginning just as we see them to-day; or if, as a result of changes in their environment, albeit extremely slow, they have not in course of time changed their characters and shape.

The solution of this question is of importance not only for our knowledge of zoology and botany, but also for the history of the world.

I shall show in one of the following chapters that every species has derived from the action of the environment in which it has long been placed the *habits* which we find in it. These habits have themselves influenced the parts of every individual in the species, to the extent of modifying those parts and bringing them into relation with the acquired habits. Let us first see what is meant by the name of species.

Any collection of like individuals which were produced by others similar to themselves is called a species.

This definition is exact; for every individual possessing life always resembles very closely those from which it sprang; but to this definition is added the allegation that the individuals composing a species never vary in their specific characters, and consequently that species have an absolute constancy in nature.

It is just this allegation that I propose to attack, since clear proofs drawn from observation show that it is ill-founded.

* * *

The idea formed of species among living bodies was quite simple, easy to understand, and seemed confirmed by the constancy in the shapes of individuals, perpetuated by reproduction or generation. Such are a great number of these alleged species that we see every day.

Meanwhile, the farther we advance in our knowledge of the various organised bodies which cover almost every part of the earth's surface, the greater becomes our difficulty in determining what should be regarded as a species, and still more in finding the boundaries and distinctions of genera.

According as the productions of nature are collected and our museums grow richer, we see nearly all the gaps filled up and the lines of demarcation effaced. We find ourselves reduced to an arbitrary decision which sometimes leads us to take the smallest differences of varieties and erect them into what we call species, and sometimes leads us to describe as a variety of some species slightly differing individuals which others regard as constituting a separate species.

* * *

If the factor which is incessantly working towards complicating organisation were the only one which had any influence on the shape and organs of animals, the growing complexity of organisation would everywhere be very regular. But it is not; nature is forced to submit her works to the influence of their environment, and this environment everywhere produces variations in them. This is the special factor which occasionally produces in the course of the degradation that we are about to exemplify, the often curious deviations that may be observed in the progression.

We shall attempt to set forth in full both the progressive degradation of animal organisation and the cause of the anomalies in the progress of that degradation, in the course of the animal series.

It is obvious that, if nature had given existence to none but aquatic animals and if all these animals had always lived in the same climate, the same kind of water, the same depth, etc., etc., we should then no doubt have found a regular and even continuous gradation in the organisation of these animals.

But the power of nature is not confined within such limits.

It first has to be observed that even in the waters she has established considerable diversity of conditions: fresh-water, sea water, still or stagnant water, running water, the water of hot climates, of cold climates, and lastly shallow water and very deep water; these provide as many special conditions which each act differently on the animals living in them. Now the races of animals exposed to any of these conditions have undergone special influences from them and have been varied by them all the while that their complexity of organisation has been advancing.

After having produced aquatic animals of all ranks and having caused extensive variations in them by the different environments provided by the waters, nature led them little by little to the habit of living in the air, first by the water's edge and afterwards on all the dry parts of the globe. These animals have in course of time been profoundly altered by such novel conditions; which so greatly influenced their habits and organs that the regular gradation which they should have exhibited in complexity of organisation is often scarcely recognisable.

These results which I have long studied, and shall definitely prove, lead me to state the following zoological principle, the truth of which appears to me beyond question.

Progress in complexity of organisation exhibits anomalies here and there in the general series of animals, due to the influence of environment and of acquired habits.

* * *

I must now explain what I mean by this statement: *the environment affects the shape and organisation of animals,* that is to say that when the environment becomes very different, it produces in course of time corresponding modifications in the shape and organisation of animals.

It is true if this statement were to be taken literally, I should be convicted of an error; for, whatever the environment may do, it does not work any direct modification whatever in the shape and organisation of animals.

But great alterations in the environment of animals lead to great alterations in their needs, and these alterations in their needs necessarily lead to others in their activities. Now if the new needs become permanent, the animals then adopt new habits which last as long as the needs that evoked them. This is easy to demonstrate, and indeed requires no amplification.

It is then obvious that a great and permanent alteration in the environment of any race of animals induces new habits in these animals.

Now, if a new environment, which has become permanent for some race of animals, induces new habits in these animals, that is to say, leads them to new activities which become habitual, the result will be the use of some one part in preference to some other part, and in some cases the total disuse of some part no longer necessary.

Nothing of all this can be considered as hypothesis or private opinion; on the contrary, they are truths which, in order to be made clear, only require attention and the observation of facts.

We shall shortly see by the citation of known facts in evidence, in the first place, that new needs which establish a necessity for some part really bring about the existence of that part, as a result of efforts; and that subsequently its continued use gradually strengthens, develops and finally greatly enlarges it; in the second place, we shall see that in some cases, when the new environment and the new needs have altogether destroyed the utility of some part, the total disuse of that part has resulted in its gradually ceasing to share in the development of the other parts of the animal; it shrinks and wastes little by little, and ultimately, when there has been total disuse for a long period, the part in question ends by disappearing. All this is positive; I propose to furnish the most convincing proofs of it.

*   *   *

In the various habitable parts of the earth's surface, the character and situation of places and climates constitute both for animals and plants environmental influences of extreme variability. The animals living in these various localities must therefore differ among themselves, not only by reason of the state of complexity of organisation attained in each race, but also by reason of the habits which each race is forced to acquire; thus when the observing naturalist travels over large portions of the earth's surface and sees conspicuous changes occurring in the environment, he invariably finds that the characters of species undergo a corresponding change.

Now the true principle to be noted in all this is as follows:

1. Every fairly considerable and permanent alteration in the environment of any race of animals works a real alteration in the needs of that race.

2. Every change in the needs of animals necessitates new activities on their part for the satisfaction of those needs, and hence new habits.

3. Every new need, necessitating new activities for its satisfaction, requires the animal, either to make more frequent use of some of its parts which it previously used less, and thus greatly to develop and enlarge them; or else to make use of entirely new parts, to which the needs have imperceptibly given birth by efforts of its inner feeling; this I shall shortly prove by means of known facts.

Thus to obtain a knowledge of the true causes of that great diversity of shapes and habits found in the various known animals, we must reflect that the infinitely diversified but slowly changing environment in which the animals of each race have successively been placed, has involved each of them in new needs and corresponding alterations in their habits. This is a truth which, once recognised, cannot be disputed. Now we shall easily discern how the new needs may have been satisfied, and the new habits acquired, if we pay attention to the two following laws of nature, which are always verified by observation.

FIRST LAW.

In every animal which has not passed the limit of its development, a more frequent and continuous use of any organ gradually strengthens, develops and enlarges that organ, and gives it a power proportional to the length of time it has been so used; while the permanent disuse of any organ imperceptibly weakens and deteriorates it, and progressively diminishes its functional capacity, until it finally disappears.

SECOND LAW.

All the acquisitions or losses wrought by nature on individuals, through the influence of the environment in which their race has long been placed, and hence through the influence of the predominant use or permanent disuse of any organ; all these are preserved by reproduction to the new individuals which arise, provided that the acquired modifications are common to both sexes, or at least to the individuals which produce the young.

Here we have two permanent truths, which can only be doubted by those who have never observed or followed the operations of nature.

*   *   *

CHARLES LYELL

Principles of Geology (1830–33)†

Modern Progress of Geology

No period could have been more fortunate for the discovery, in the immediate neighbourhood of Paris, of a rich store of well-preserved fossils, than the commencement of the present century; for at no former era had Natural History been cultivated with such enthusiasm in the French metropolis. The labours of Cuvier in comparative osteology, and of Lamarck in recent and fossil shells, had raised these departments of study to a rank of which they had never previously been deemed susceptible. Their investigations had eventually a powerful effect in dispelling the illusion which had long prevailed concerning the absence of analogy between the ancient and modern state of our planet. A close comparison of the recent and fossil species, and the inferences drawn in regard to their habits, accustomed the geologist to contemplate the earth as having been at successive periods the dwelling-place of animals and plants of different races, some terrestrial, and others aquatic—some fitted to live in seas, others in the waters of lakes and rivers. By the consideration of these topics, the mind was slowly and insensibly withdrawn from imaginary pictures of catastrophes and chaotic confusion, such as haunted the imagination of the early cosmogonists. Numerous proofs were discovered of the tranquil deposition of sedimentary matter, and the slow development of organic life. If many writers, and Cuvier himself in the number, still continued to maintain, that 'the thread of induction was broken,' yet, in reasoning by the strict rules of induction from recent to fossil species, they in a great measure disclaimed the dogma which in theory they professed. The adop-

---

† From *Principles of Geology* (London, 1830–33). Charles Lyell (1797–1875) was a fellow of the Royal Society and president of the British Association. His three-volume *Principles of Geology*, which went through eleven editions in his lifetime, was highly influential. Darwin read the first two volumes during the *Beagle* voyage, and they helped shape his thinking about evolution.

tion of the same generic, and, in some cases, even of the same specific, names for the exuviae of fossil animals and their living analogues, was an important step towards familiarising the mind with the idea of the identity and unity of the system in distant eras. It was an acknowledgment, as it were, that part at least of the ancient memorials of nature were written in a living language. The growing importance, then, of the natural history of organic remains may be pointed out as the characteristic feature of the progress of the science during the present century. This branch of knowledge has already become an instrument of great utility in geological classification, and is continuing daily to unfold new data for grand and enlarged views respecting the former changes of the earth.

*   *   *

When difficulties arise in interpreting the monuments of the past, I deem it more consistent with philosophical caution to refer them to our present ignorance of all the existing agents, or all their possible effects in an indefinite lapse of time, than to causes formerly in operation, but which have ceased to act; and if in any part of the globe the energy of a cause appears to have decreased, I consider it more probable that the diminution of intensity in its action is merely local, than that its force is impaired throughout the whole globe. But should there appear reason to believe that certain agents have, at particular periods of past time, been more potent instruments of change over the entire surface of the earth than they now are, it is still more consistent with analogy to presume, that after an interval of quiescence they will recover their pristine vigour, than to imagine that they are worn out.

The geologist who assents to the truth of these principles will deem it incumbent on him to examine with minute attention all the changes now in progress on the earth, and will regard every fact collected respecting the causes in diurnal action, as affording him a key to the interpretation of some mystery in the archives of remote ages. His estimate of the value of geological evidence, and his interest in the investigation of the earth's history, will depend entirely on the degree of confidence which he feels in regard to the permanency of the great causes of change. Their constancy alone will enable him to reason from analogy, and to arrive, by a comparison of the state of things at distinct epochs, at the knowledge of the general laws which govern the economy of our system.

The uniformity of the plan being once assumed, events which have occurred at the most distant periods in the animate and inanimate world will be acknowledged to throw light on each other, and the deficiency of our information respecting some of the most obscure parts of the present creation will be removed. For as, by studying the external configuration of the existing land and its inhabitants, we may restore in imagination the appearance of the ancient continents which have passed away, so may we obtain from the deposits of ancient seas and lakes an insight into the nature of the subaqueous processes now in operation, and of many forms of organic life, which, though now existing, are veiled from sight. Rocks, also, produced by subterranean fire in former ages at great depths in the bowels of the earth, present us, when upraised by gradual movements, and exposed to the light of heaven, with an image of those changes which the deep-seated volcano may now occasion in the nether regions. Thus, although we are mere sojourners on the surface of the planet, chained to a mere point in space, enduring but for a moment of time, the human mind is not only enabled to number worlds beyond the unassisted ken of mortal eye, but to trace the events of indefinite ages before the creation of our race, and is not even withheld from penetrating into the dark secrets of the ocean, or the interior of the solid globe.

*   *   *

Position of Former Continents

The existence of land as well as sea, at every geological period, is attested by the remains of terrestrial plants imbedded in the deposits of all ages, even the most remote. We find fluviatile shells not unfrequently in the secondary strata, and here and there some freshwater formations; but the latter are less common than in the tertiary series. For this fact the reader's mind has been prepared, by the views advanced in the third chapter respecting the different circumstances under which the secondary and tertiary strata appear to have originated. The secondary, it was suggested, may have been accumulated in an ocean like the Pacific, where coralline and shelly limestones are forming; or in a basin like the bed of the western Atlantic, which may have received, for ages, the turbid waters of great rivers, such as the Amazon and Orinoco, each draining a considerable extent of continent. The *tertiary* deposits, on the other hand, very probably accumulated during the growth of a continent, by successive emergence of new lands, and the uniting together of islands. During such changes, inland seas and lakes would be caused, and their basins afterwards filled up with sediment, and then raised above the level of the waters.

That the greater part of the space now occupied by the European continent was sea when some of the secondary rocks were produced, must be inferred from the wide areas over which several of the marine groups are diffused; but we need not suppose that the quantity of land was less in those remote ages, but merely that its position was very different.

*   *   *

Concluding Remarks

In the history of the progress of geology, it has been stated that the opinion originally promulgated by Hutton, 'that the strata called *primitive* were mere altered sedimentary rocks,' was vehemently opposed for a time, on the ground of its supposed tendency to promote a belief in the past eternity of our planet. Before that period the absence of animal and vegetable remains in the so-called primitive strata had been appealed to, as proving that there had been an era when the planet was uninhabited by living beings, and when, as was also inferred, it was uninhabitable, and, therefore, probably in a nascent state.

The opposite doctrine, that the oldest visible strata might be the monuments of an antecedent period, when the animate world was already in existence, was declared to be equivalent to the assumption that there never was a beginning to the present order of things. The unfairness of this charge was clearly pointed out by Playfair, who observed, 'that it was one thing to declare that we had not yet discovered the traces of a beginning, and another to deny that the earth ever had a beginning.'

*   *   *

As geologists, we learn that it is not only the present condition of the globe which has been suited to the accommodation of myriads of living creatures, but that many former states also have been adapted to the organisation and habits of prior races of beings. The disposition of the seas, continents, and islands, and the climates, have varied; the species likewise have been changed; and yet they have all been so modelled, on types analogous to those of existing plants and animals, as to indicate throughout a perfect harmony of design and unity of purpose. To assume that the evidence of the beginning or end of so vast a scheme lies within the reach of our philosophical inquiries, or even of our speculations, appears to be inconsistent with a just estimate of the relations which subsist between the finite powers of man and the attributes of an Infinite and Eternal Being.

JOHN HERSCHEL

The Study of Natural Philosophy (1830)†

*   *   *

(137.) The first thing that a philosophic mind considers, when any new phenomenon presents itself, is its *explanation*, or reference to an immediate producing cause. If that cannot be ascertained, the next is to *generalize* the phenomenon, and include it, with others analogous to it, in the expression of some law, in the hope that its consideration, in a more advanced state of knowledge, may lead to the discovery of an adequate proximate cause.

(138.) Experience having shown us the manner in which one phenomenon depends on another in a great variety of cases, we find ourselves provided, as science extends, with a continually increasing stock of such antecedent phenomena, or causes (meaning at present merely proximate causes), competent, under different modifications, to the production of a

---

† From *Preliminary Discourse on the Study of Natural Philosophy* (London, 1830). John Frederick William Herschel (1792–1871) was a highly influential British astronomer and physicist, for whose principles of induction Darwin had great respect. Darwin sent Herschel a copy of the *Origin of Species* in 1859, telling Herschel that "scarcely anything in my life made so deep an impression on me" as Herschel's *Discourse*.

great multitude of effects, besides those which originally led to a knowledge of them. To such causes Newton has applied the term *veræ causæ*;
that is, causes recognized as having a real existence in nature, and not
being mere hypotheses or figments of the mind.

* * *

(139.) The fact of a great change in the general climate of large tracts
of the globe, if not of the whole earth, and of a diminution of general
temperature, having been recognised by geologists, from their examination
of the remains of animals and vegetables of former ages enclosed in the
strata, various causes for such diminution of temperature have been assigned. Some consider the whole globe as having gradually cooled from
absolute fusion; some regard the immensely superior activity of former
volcanoes, and consequent more copious communication of internal heat
to the surface, in former ages, as the cause. Neither of these can be regarded as real causes in the sense here intended; for we do not *know* that
the globe has so cooled from fusion, nor are we sure that such supposed
greater activity of former than of present volcanoes really did exist. A cause,
possessing the essential requisites of a *vera causa*, has, however, been
brought forward in the varying influence of the distribution of land and
sea over the surface of the globe: a change of such distribution, in the
lapse of ages, by the degradation of the old continents, and the elevation
of new, being a demonstrated fact; and the influence of such a change on
the climates of particular regions, if not of the whole globe, being a perfectly fair conclusion, from what we know of continental, insular, and
oceanic climates by actual observation. Here, then, we have, at least, a
cause on which a philosopher may consent to reason.

* * *

(145.) When we would lay down general rules for guiding and facili-
tating our search, among a great mass of assembled facts, for their common
cause, we must have regard to the characters of that relation which we
intend by cause and effect. Now, these are,—

> 1st, Invariable connection, and, in particular, invariable antecedence
> of the cause and consequence of the effect, unless prevented by
> some counteracting cause. But it must be observed, that, in a
> great number of natural phenomena, the effect is produced grad-
> ually, while the cause often goes on increasing in intensity; so
> that the antecedence of the one and consequence of the other
> becomes difficult to trace, though it really exists. On the other
> hand, the effect often follows the cause so instantaneously, that
> the interval cannot be perceived. In consequence of this, it is
> sometimes difficult to decide, of two phenomena constantly ac-
> companying one another, which is cause or which effect.
> 2d, Invariable negation of the effect with absence of the cause, unless
> some other cause be capable of producing the same effect.
> 3d, Increase or diminution of the effect, with the increased or dimin-

ished intensity of the cause, in cases which admit of increase and diminution.

4th, Proportionality of the effect to its cause in all cases of *direct unimpeded* action.

5th, Reversal of the effect with that of the cause.

(146.) From these characters we are led to the following observations, which may be considered as so many propositions readily applicable to particular cases, or rules of philosophizing: we conclude, 1st, That if in our group of facts there be one in which any assigned peculiarity, or attendant circumstance, is wanting or opposite, such peculiarity cannot be the cause we seek.

(147.) 2d, That any circumstance in which all the facts without exception agree, *may* be the cause in question, or, if not, at least a collateral effect of the same cause: if there be but one such point of agreement, this possibility becomes a certainty; and, on the other hand, if there be more than one, they may be concurrent causes.

(148.) 3d, That we are not to deny the existence of a cause in favour of which we have a unanimous agreement of strong analogies, though it may not be apparent how such a cause can produce the effect, or even though it may be difficult to conceive its existence under the circumstances of the case; in such cases we should rather appeal to experience when possible, than decide *à priori* against the cause, and try whether it cannot be made apparent. * * *

(150.) 4th, That contrary or opposing facts are equally instructive for the discovery of causes with favourable ones.

*   *   *

(152.) 5th, That causes will very frequently become obvious, by a mere arrangement of our facts in the order of intensity in which some peculiar quality subsists; though not of necessity, because counteracting or modifying causes may be at the same time in action.

*   *   *

(154.) 6th, That such counteracting or modifying causes may subsist unperceived, and annul the effects of the cause we seek, in instances which, but for their action, would have come into our class of favourable facts; and that, therefore, exceptions may often be made to disappear by removing or allowing for such counteracting causes. This remark becomes of the greatest importance, when (as is often the case) a single striking exception stands out, as it were, against an otherwise unanimous array of facts in favour of a certain cause.

*   *   *

(156.) 7th, If we can either find produced by nature, or produce designedly for ourselves, two instances which agree *exactly* in all but one

particular, and differ in that one, its influence in producing the phenomenon, if it have any, *must* thereby be rendered sensible.

*　*　*

(157.) 8th, If we cannot obtain a complete negative or opposition of the
circumstance whose influence we would ascertain, we must endeavour to
find cases where it varies considerably in degree. If *this* cannot be done,
we may perhaps be able to weaken or exalt its influence by the introduction of some fresh circumstance, which, abstractedly considered, seems
likely to produce this effect, and thus obtain indirect evidence of its
influence. *　*　*

(158.) 9th, Complicated phenomena, in which several causes concur-
ring, opposing, or quite independent of each other, operate at once, so as
to produce a compound effect, may be simplified by subducting the effect
of all the known causes, as well as the nature of the case permits, either
by deductive reasoning or by appeal to experience, and thus leaving, as it
were, a *residual phenomenon* to be explained. It is by this process, in fact,
that science, in its present advanced state, is chiefly promoted. Most of
the phenomena which nature presents are very complicated; and when
the effects of all known causes are estimated with exactness, and sub-
ducted, the residual facts are constantly appearing in the form of phenomena altogether new, and leading to the most important conclusions.

*　*　*

(180.) The surest and best characteristic of a well-founded and extensive
induction, however, is when verifications of it spring up, as it were, spontaneously, into notice, from quarters where they might be least expected,
or even among instances of that very kind which were at first considered
hostile to them. Evidence of this kind is irresistible, and compels assent
with a weight which scarcely any other possesses.

*　*　*

(201.) As particular inductions and laws of the first degree of generality
are obtained from the consideration of individual facts, so Theories result
from a consideration of these laws, and of the proximate causes brought
into view in the previous process, regarded all together as constituting a
new set of phenomena, the creatures of reason rather than of sense, and
each representing under general language innumerable particular facts. In
raising these higher inductions, therefore, more scope is given to the exercise of pure reason than in slowly groping out our first results. The mind
is more disencumbered of matter, and moves as it were in its own element.
What is now before it, it perceives more intimately, and less through the
medium of sense, or at least not in the same manner as when actually at
work on the immediate objects of sense. But it must not be therefore
supposed that, in the formation of theories, we are abandoned to the un-
restrained exercise of imagination, or at liberty to lay down arbitrary prin-

ciples, or assume the existence of mere fanciful causes. The liberty of speculation which we possess in the domains of theory is not like the wild licence of the slave broke loose from his fetters, but rather like that of the freeman who has learned the lessons of self-restraint in the school of just subordination. The ultimate objects we pursue in the highest theories are the same as those of the lowest inductions; and the means by which we can most securely attain them bear a close analogy to those which we have found successful in such inferior cases.

* * *

(208.) Now, are we to be deterred from framing hypotheses and constructing theories, because we meet with such dilemmas, and find ourselves frequently beyond our depth? Undoubtedly not. * * * Hypotheses, with respect to theories, are what presumed proximate causes are with respect to particular inductions: they afford us motives for searching into analogies; grounds of citation to bring before us all the cases which seem to bear upon them, for examination. A well imagined hypothesis, if it have been suggested by a fair inductive consideration of general laws, can hardly fail at least of enabling us to generalize a step farther, and group together several such laws under a more universal expression. But this is taking a very limited view of the value and importance of hypotheses: it may happen (and it has happened in the case of the undulatory doctrine of light) that such a weight of analogy and probability may become accumulated on the side of an hypothesis, that we are compelled to admit one of two things; either that it is an actual statement of what really passes in nature, or that the reality, whatever it be, must run so close a parallel with it, as to admit of some mode of expression common to both, at least in so far as the phenomena actually known are concerned. Now, this is a very great step, not only for its own sake, as leading us to a high point in philosophical speculation, but for its applications; because whatever conclusions we deduce from an hypothesis so supported must have at least a strong presumption in their favour: and we may be thus led to the trial of many curious experiments, and to the imagining of many useful and important contrivances, which we should never otherwise have thought of, and which, at all events, *if* verified in practice, are real additions to our stock of knowledge and to the arts of life.

(209.) In framing a theory which shall render a rational account of any natural phenomenon, we have *first* to consider the agents on which it depends, or the causes to which we regard it as ultimately referable. These agents are not to be arbitrarily assumed; they must be such as we have good inductive grounds to believe do exist in nature, and do perform a part in phenomena analogous to those we would render an account of; or such, whose presence in the actual case can be demonstrated by unequivocal signs. They must be *veræ causæ*, in short, which we can not only show to exist and to act, but the laws of whose action we can derive independently, by direct induction, from experiments purposely instituted; or at least make such suppositions respecting them as shall not be contrary to our experience, and which will remain to be verified by the coincidence of the conclusions we shall deduce from them, with facts.

*   *   *

(391.) Finally, when we look back on what has been accomplished in science, and compare it with what remains to be done, it is hardly possible to avoid being strongly impressed with the idea that we have been and are still executing the labour by which succeeding generations are to profit. In a few instances only have we arrived at those general axiomatic laws which admit of direct deductive inference, and place the solutions of physical phenomena before us as so many problems, whose principles of solution we fully possess, and which require nothing but acuteness of reasoning to pursue even into their farthest recesses. In fewer still have we reached that command of abstract reasoning itself which is necessary for the accomplishment of so arduous a task. Science, therefore, in relation to our faculties, still remains boundless and unexplored, and, after the lapse of a century and a half from the æra of Newton's discoveries, during which every department of it has been cultivated with a zeal and energy which have assuredly met their full return, we remain in the situation in which he figured himself,—standing on the shore of a wide ocean, from whose beach we may have culled some of those innumerable beautiful productions it casts up with lavish prodigality, but whose acquisition can be regarded as no diminution of the treasures that remain.

*   *   *

WILLIAM WHEWELL

Astronomy and General Physics Considered with Reference to Natural Theology (1833)†

*   *   *

It may be interesting to show how the views of the creation, preservation, and government of the universe, which natural science opens to us, harmonize with our belief in a Creator, Governor, and Preserver of the world. To do this with respect to certain departments of Natural Philosophy is the object of the following pages.

*   *   *

† From *Astronomy and General Physics Considered with Reference to Natural Theology* (London, 1833). William Whewell (1794–1866) was professor of Moral Philosophy at Trinity College, Cambridge, and a member of the Royal Society. His works on induction were widely read, as was this text, one of the Bridgewater Treatises, which were intended to illustrate "the power, wisdom, and goodness of God as manifested in the Creation."

Nature acts by general laws; that is, the occurrences of the world in which we find ourselves, result from causes which operate according to fixed and constant rules. The succession of days, and seasons, and years, is produced by the motions of the earth; and these again are governed by the attraction of the sun, a force which acts with undeviating steadiness and regularity. The changes of winds and skies, seemingly so capricious and casual, are produced by the operation of the sun's heat upon air and moisture, land and sea; and though in this case we cannot trace the particular events to their general causes, as we can trace the motions of the sun and moon, no philosophical mind will doubt the generality and fixity of the rules by which these causes act. * * *

The world then is governed by general laws; and in order to collect from the world itself a judgment concerning the nature and character of its government, we must consider the import and tendency of such laws, so far as they come under our knowledge. If there be, in the administration of the universe, intelligence and benevolence, superintendence and foresight, grounds for love and hope, such qualities may be expected to appear in the constitution and combination of those fundamental regulations by which the course of nature is brought about, and made to be what it is.

* * *

However strong and solemn be the conviction which may be derived from a contemplation of nature, concerning the existence, the power, the wisdom, the goodness of our Divine Governor, we cannot expect that this conviction, as resulting from the extremely complex spectacle of the material world, should be capable of being irresistibly conveyed by a few steps of reasoning, like the conclusion of a geometrical proposition, or the result of an arithmetical calculation.

We shall, therefore, endeavour to point out cases and circumstances in which the different parts of the universe exhibit this mutual adaptation, and thus to bring before the mind of the reader the evidence of wisdom and providence, which the external world affords. * * *

We proceed in this Book to point out relations which subsist between the laws of the inorganic world, that is, the general facts of astronomy and meteorology; and the laws which prevail in the organic world, the properties of plants and animals.

* * *

Now a general fact, which we shall endeavour to exemplify in the following chapters, is this:—That those properties of plants and animals which have reference to agencies of a periodical character, have also by their nature a periodical mode of working; while those properties which refer to agencies of constant intensity, are adjusted to this constant intensity: and again, there are peculiarities in the nature of organized beings which have reference to a variety in the conditions of the external world, as, for instance, the difference of the organized population of different regions: and there are other peculiarities which have a reference to the constancy of the average of such conditions, and the limited range of the deviations from that average; as for example, that constitution by which each plant and animal is fitted to exist and prosper in its usual place in the world.

And not only is there this general agreement between the nature of the laws which govern the organic and inorganic world, but also there is a coincidence between the *arbitrary magnitudes* which such laws involve on the one hand and on the other. Plants and animals have, in their construction, certain periodical functions, which have a reference to alternations of heat and cold; the length of the period which belongs to these functions by their construction, appears to be that of the period which belongs to the actual alternations of heat and cold, namely, a year. Plants and animals have again in their construction certain other periodical functions, which have a reference to alternations of light and darkness; the length of the period of such functions appears to coincide with the natural day. In like manner the other arbitrary magnitudes which enter into the laws of gravity, of the effects of air and moisture, and of other causes of permanence, and of change, by which the influences of the elements operate, are the same arbitrary magnitudes to which the members of the organic world are adapted by the various peculiarities of their construction.

The illustration of this view will be pursued in the succeeding chapters; and when the coincidence here spoken of is distinctly brought before the reader, it will, we trust, be found to convey the conviction of a wise and benevolent design, which has been exercised in producing such an agreement between the internal constitution and the external circumstances of organized beings. * * *

Chapter I. The Length of the Year.

A year is the most important and obvious of the periods which occur in the organic, and especially in the vegetable world. In this interval of time the cycle of most of the external influences which operate upon plants is completed. There is also in plants a cycle of internal functions, corresponding to this succession of external causes. The length of either of these periods might have been different from what it is, according to any grounds of necessity which we can perceive. But a certain length is selected in both instances, and in both instances the same. The length of the year is so determined as to be adapted to the constitution of most vegetables; or the construction of vegetables is so adjusted as to be suited to the length which the year really has, and unsuited to a duration longer or shorter by any considerable portion. The vegetable clock-work is so set as to go for a year.

The length of the year or interval of recurrence of the seasons is determined by the time which the earth employs in performing its revolution round the sun: and we can very easily conceive the solar system so adjusted that the year should be longer or shorter than it actually is. We can imagine the earth to revolve round the sun at a distance greater or less than that which it at present has, all the forces of the system remaining unaltered. If the earth were removed towards the centre by about one-eighth of its distance, the year would be diminished by about a month; and in the same manner it would be increased by a month on increasing the distance by one-eighth. * * *

Now, if any change of this kind were to take place, the working of the botanical world would be thrown into utter disorder, the functions of plants would be entirely deranged, and the whole vegetable kingdom involved in instant decay and rapid extinction.

That this would be the case, may be collected from innumerable indications. Most of our fruit trees, for example, require the year to be of its present length. If the summer and the autumn were much shorter, the fruit could not ripen; if these seasons were much longer, the tree would put forth a fresh suit of blossoms; to be cut down by the winter. Or if the year were twice its present length, a second crop of fruit would probably not be matured, for want, among other things, of an intermediate season of rest and consolidation, such as the winter is.

* * *

But in the existing state of things, the duration of the earth's revolution round the sun, and the duration of the revolution of the vegetable functions of most plants are equal. These two periods are *adjusted* to each other. The stimulants which the elements apply come at such intervals and continue for such times, that the plant is supported in health and vigour, and enabled to reproduce its kind. Just such a portion of time is measured out for the vegetable powers to execute their task, as enables them to do so in the best manner.

Now such an adjustment must surely be accepted as a proof of design, exercised in the formation of the world. Why should the solar year be so long and no longer? or, this being of such a length, why should the vegetable cycle be exactly of the same length? Can this be chance? And this occurs, it is to be observed, not in one, or in a few species of plants, but in thousands. Take a small portion only of known species, as the most obviously endowed with this adjustment, and say ten thousand. How should all these organized bodies be constructed for the same period of a year. How should all these machines be wound up so as to go for the same time? Even allowing that they could bear a year of a month longer or shorter, how do they all come within such limits? No chance could produce such a result.

* * *

The same kind of argument might be applied to the animal creation. The pairing, nesting, hatching, fledging, and flight of birds, for instance, occupy each its peculiar time of the year; and, together with a proper period of rest, fill up the twelve months. The transformations of most insects have a similar reference to the seasons, their progress and duration. "In every species" (except man), says a writer on animals, "there is a particular period of the year in which the reproductive system exercises its energies. And the season of love and the period of gestation are so arranged that the young ones are produced at the time wherein the conditions of temperature are most suited to the commencement of life." It is not our business here to consider the details of such provisions, beautiful and striking as they are. But the prevalence of the great law of periodicity in the vital functions of organized beings will be allowed to have a claim to be considered in its reference to astronomy, when it is seen that their periodical constitution derives its use from the periodical nature of the motions of the planets round the sun; and that the duration of such cycles in the existence of plants and animals has a reference to the arbitrary elements of the solar system: a reference which, we maintain, is inexplicable and unintelligible, except by admitting into our conceptions an intelligent Author, alike of the organic and inorganic universe.

*   *   *

ALFRED RUSSEL WALLACE

On the Tendency of Varieties to Depart Indefinitely from the Original Type (1858)†

*   *   *

One of the strongest arguments which have been adduced to prove the original and permanent distinctness of species is, that *varieties* produced in a state of domesticity are more or less unstable, and often have a tendency, if left to themselves, to return to the normal form of the parent species; and this instability is considered to be a distinctive peculiarity of all varieties, even of those occurring among wild animals in a state of nature, and to constitute a provision for preserving unchanged the originally created distinct species.

In the absence or scarcity of facts and observations as to *varieties* occurring among wild animals, this argument has had great weight with naturalists, and has led to a very general and somewhat prejudiced belief in the stability of species. Equally general, however, is the belief in what are called "permanent or true varieties,"—races of animals which continually propagate their like, but which differ so slightly (although constantly) from some other race, that the one is considered to be a *variety* of the other. Which is the *variety* and which the original *species*, there is generally no means of determining, except in those rare cases in which the one race has been known to produce an offspring unlike itself and resembling the other. This, however, would seem quite incompatible with the "permanent invariability of species," but the difficulty is overcome by assuming that

† From the *Journal of the Proceedings of the Linnean Society, Zoology* 3 (Aug. 20, 1858). Alfred Russel Wallace (1823–1913) was a young British naturalist working in Malaya when he, prompted like Darwin by Malthus's ideas, arrived at the idea of natural selection. Having written this account, he sent it to Darwin, and their ideas were presented jointly to the Linnean Society in London. Darwin then went on to finish his *Origin of Species* the next year.

such varieties have strict limits, and can never again vary further from the original type, although they may return to it, which, from the analogy of the domesticated animals, is considered to be highly probable, if not certainly proved.

It will be observed that this argument rests entirely on the assumption, that *varieties* occurring in a state of nature are in all respects analogous to or even identical with those of domestic animals, and are governed by the same laws as regards their permanence or further variation. But it is the object of the present paper to show that this assumption is altogether false, that there is a general principle in nature which will cause many varieties to survive the parent species, and to give rise to successive variations departing further and further from the original type, and which also produces, in domesticated animals, the tendency of varieties to return to the parent form.

The life of wild animals is a struggle for existence. The full exertion of all their faculties and all their energies is required to preserve their own existence and provide for that of their infant offspring. The possibility of procuring food during the least favourable seasons, and of escaping the attacks of their most dangerous enemies, are the primary conditions which determine the existence both of individuals and of entire species. These conditions will also determine the population of a species; and by a careful consideration of all the circumstances we may be enabled to comprehend, and in some degree to explain, what at first sight appears so inexplicable —the excessive abundance of some species, while others closely allied to them are very rare. * * *

Now it is clear that what takes place among the individuals of a species must also occur among the several allied species of a group,—viz. that those which are best adapted to obtain a regular supply of food, and to defend themselves against the attacks of their enemies and the vicissitudes of the seasons, must necessarily obtain and preserve a superiority in population; while those species which from some defect of power or organization are the least capable of counteracting the vicissitudes of food, supply, &c., must diminish in numbers, and, in extreme cases, become altogether extinct. Between these extremes the species will present various degrees of capacity for ensuring the means of preserving life; and it is thus we account for the abundance or rarity of species. Our ignorance will generally prevent us from accurately tracing the effects to their causes; but could we become perfectly acquainted with the organization and habits of the various species of animals, and could we measure the capacity of each for performing the different acts necessary to its safety and existence under all the varying circumstances by which it is surrounded, we might be able even to calculate the proportionate abundance of individuals which is the necessary result.

If now we have succeeded in establishing these two points—1st, *that the animal population of a country is generally stationary, being kept down by a periodical deficiency of food, and other checks*; and, 2nd, *that the comparative abundance or scarcity of the individuals of the several species is entirely due to their organization and resulting habits, which, rendering it more difficult to procure a regular supply of food and to provide for their personal safety in some cases than in others, can only be balanced by a difference in the population which have to exist in a given area*—we shall be in a condition to proceed to the consideration of *varieties*, to which the preceding remarks have a direct and very important application.

Most or perhaps all the variations from the typical form of a species must have some definite effect, however slight, on the habits or capacities of the individuals. Even a change of colour might, by rendering them more or less distinguishable, affect their safety; a greater or less development of hair might modify their habits. More important changes, such as an increase in the power or dimensions of the limbs or any of the external organs, would more or less affect their mode of procuring food or the range of country which they inhabit. It is also evident that most changes would affect, either favourably or adversely, the powers of prolonging existence. An antelope with shorter or weaker legs must necessarily suffer more from the attacks of the feline carnivora; the passenger pigeon with less powerful wings would sooner or later be affected in its powers of procuring a regular supply of food; and in both cases the result must necessarily be a diminution of the population of the modified species. If, on the other hand, any species should produce a variety having slightly increased powers of preserving existence, that variety must inevitably in time acquire a superiority in numbers. These results must follow as surely as old age, intemperance, or scarcity of food produce an increased mortality. In both cases there may be many individual exceptions; but on the average the rule will invariably be found to hold good. All varieties will therefore fall into two classes—those which under the same conditions would never reach the population of the parent species, and those which would in time obtain and keep a numerical superiority. Now, let some alteration of physical conditions occur in the district—a long period of drought, a destruction of vegetation by locusts, the irruption of some new carnivorous animal seeking "pastures new"—any change in fact tending to render existence more difficult to the species in question, and tasking its utmost powers to avoid complete extermination; it is evident that, of all the individuals composing the species, those forming the least numerous and most feebly organized variety would suffer first, and, were the pressure severe, must soon become extinct. The same causes continuing in action, the parent species would next suffer, would gradually diminish in numbers, and with a recurrence of similar unfavourable conditions might also become extinct. The superior variety would then alone remain, and on a return to favourable circumstances would rapidly increase in numbers and occupy the place of the extinct species and variety.

The *variety* would now have replaced the *species*, of which it would be a more perfectly developed and more highly organized form. It would be in all respects better adapted to secure its safety, and to prolong its individual existence and that of the race. Such a variety *could not* return to the original form; for that form is an inferior one, and could never compete with it for existence. Granted, therefore, a "tendency" to reproduce the original type of the species, still the variety must ever remain preponderant in numbers, and under adverse physical conditions *again alone survive*. But this new, improved, and populous race might itself, in course of time, give rise to new varieties, exhibiting several diverging modifications of form, any of which, tending to increase the facilities for preserving existence, must, by the same general law, in their turn become predominant. Here, then, we have *progression and continued divergence* deduced from the general laws which regulate the existence of animals in a state of nature, and from the undisputed fact that varieties do frequently occur.

* * *

We believe we have now shown that there is a tendency in nature to the continued progression of certain classes of *varieties* further and further from the original type—a progression to which there appears no reason to assign any definite limits—and that the same principle which produces this result in a state of nature will also explain why domestic varieties have a tendency to revert to the original type. This progression, by minute steps, in various directions, but always checked and balanced by the necessary conditions, subject to which alone existence can be preserved, may, it is believed, be followed out so as to agree with all the phenomena presented by organized beings, their extinction and succession in past ages, and all the extraordinary modifications of form, instinct, and habits which they exhibit.

Ternate, February, 1858.

PART IV
SELECTIONS FROM
DARWIN'S WORK

We are not here concerned with hopes or fears, only with the truth as far as our reason permits us to discover it; and I have given the evidence to the best of my ability. We must, however, acknowledge, as it seems to me, that man with all his noble qualities . . . still bears in his bodily frame the indelible stamp of his lowly origin.

—Charles Darwin, 1871

Darwin's *essential* achievement was the demonstration that the almost incredible variety of life, with all its complex and puzzling relations to its environment, was explicable in scientific terms.

—Julian Huxley, 1958

The Voyage of the *Beagle*:
Galapagos Archipelago (1845)†

Chapter I. St. Jago—Cape de Verd Islands

After having been twice driven back by heavy south-western gales, Her Majesty's ship *Beagle*, a ten-gun brig, under the command of Captain Fitz Roy, R.N., sailed from Devonport on the 27th of December, 1831. The object of the expedition was to complete the survey of Patagonia and Tierra del Fuego, commenced under Captain King in 1826 to 1830—to survey the shores of Chile, Peru, and of some islands in the Pacific—and to carry a chain of chronometrical measurements round the World. On the 6th of January we reached Teneriffe, but were prevented landing, by fears of our bringing the cholera: the next morning we saw the sun rise behind the rugged outline of the Grand Canary island, and suddenly illumine the Peak of Teneriffe, whilst the lower parts were veiled in fleecy clouds. This was the first of many delightful days never to be forgotten.

* * *

Chapter XVII. Galapagos Archipelago

September 15th.—This archipelago consists of ten principal islands, of which five exceed the others in size. They are situated under the Equator, and between five and six hundred miles westward of the coast of America. They are all formed of volcanic rocks; a few fragments of granite curiously glazed and altered by the heat, can hardly be considered as an exception. Some of the craters, surmounting the larger islands, are of immense size, and they rise to a height of between three and four thousand feet. Their flanks are studded by innumerable smaller orifices. I scarcely hesitate to affirm, that there must be in the whole archipelago at least two thousand craters. These consist either of lava and scoriæ, or of finely-stratified, sand-stone-like tuff. Most of the latter are beautifully symmetrical; they owe their origin to eruptions of volcanic mud without any lava: it is a remark-able circumstance that every one of the twenty-eight tuff-craters which were examined, had their southern sides either much lower than the other sides, or quite broken down and removed. As all these craters have appar-ently been formed when standing in the sea, and as the waves from the trade-wind and the swell from the open Pacific here unite their forces on the southern coasts of all the islands, this singular uniformity in the broken

† The text is from the second edition of *The Voyage of the Beagle* (London, 1845), originally published in 1839 as *Journal of Researches during the Voyage of H.M.S. Beagle*, but here revised and expanded. By good fortune, and because his science instructor at Cambridge considered him to be "the best qualified person I know of who is likely to undertake such a situation," Darwin was invited to join the *Beagle* voyage of exploration when he was only twenty-two years old, fresh out of college. His discoveries on this five-year expedition were instrumental in develop-ing his theory of natural selection. (See Ernst Mayr, "Who Is Darwin?" [p. 23] and the map on p. xvii.)

state of the craters, composed of the soft and yielding tuff, is easily explained.

Considering that these islands are placed directly under the equator, the climate is far from being excessively hot; this seems chiefly caused by the singularly low temperature of the surrounding water, brought here by the great southern Polar current. Excepting during one short season, very little rain falls, and even then it is irregular; but the clouds generally hang low. Hence, whilst the lower parts of the island are very sterile, the upper parts, at a height of a thousand feet and upwards, possess a damp climate and a tolerably luxuriant vegetation. This is especially the case on the windward sides of the islands, which first receive and condense the moisture from the atmosphere.

In the morning (17th) we landed on Chatham Island, which, like the others, rises with a tame and rounded outline, broken here and there by scattered hillocks, the remains of former craters. Nothing could be less inviting than the first appearance. A broken field of black basaltic lava, thrown into the most rugged waves, and crossed by great fissures, is every where covered by stunted, sunburnt brushwood, which shows little signs of life. The dry and parched surface, being heated by the noonday sun, gave to the air a close and sultry feeling, like that from a stove: we fancied even that the bushes smelt unpleasantly. Although I diligently tried to collect as many plants as possible, I succeeded in getting very few; and such wretched-looking little weeds would have better become an arctic than an equatorial Flora. The brushwood appears, from a short distance, as leafless as our trees during winter; and it was some time before I discovered that not only almost every plant was now in full leaf, but that the greater number were in flower. The commonest bush is one of the Euphorbiaceæ: an acacia and a great odd-looking cactus are the only trees which afford any shade. After the season of heavy rains, the islands are said to appear for a short time partially green. The volcanic island of Fernando Noronha, placed in many respects under nearly similar conditions, is the only other country where I have seen a vegetation at all like this of the Galapagos islands.

The *Beagle* sailed round Chatham Island, and anchored in several bays. One night I slept on shore on a part of the island, where black truncated cones were extraordinarily numerous: from one small eminence I counted sixty of them, all surmounted by craters more or less perfect. The greater number consisted merely of a ring of red scoriæ or slags, cemented together: and their height above the plain of lava was not more than from fifty to a hundred feet: none had been very lately active. The entire surface of this part of the island seems to have been permeated, like a sieve, by the subterranean vapours: here and there the lava, whilst soft, has been blown into great bubbles; and in other parts, the tops of caverns similarly formed have fallen in, leaving circular pits with steep sides. From the regular form of the many craters, they gave to the country an artificial appearance, which vividly reminded me of those parts of Staffordshire, where the great iron-foundries are most numerous. The day was glowing hot, and the scrambling over the rough surface and through the intricate thickets, was very fatiguing; but I was well repaid by the strange Cyclopean scene. As I was walking along I met two large tortoises, each of which must have weighed at least two hundred pounds: one was eating a piece of cactus, and as I approached, it stared at me and slowly stalked away; the other gave a deep hiss, and drew in its head. These huge reptiles, surrounded by the black lava, the leafless shrubs, and large cacti, seemed to my fancy like some antediluvian animals. The few dull-coloured birds cared no more for me, than they did for the great tortoises.

23rd.—The *Beagle* proceeded to Charles Island. This archipelago has long been frequented, first by the Bucaniers, and latterly by whalers, but it is only within the last six years, that a small colony has been established here. The inhabitants are between two and three hundred in number: they are nearly all people of colour, who have been banished for political crimes from the Republic of the Equator, of which Quito is the capital. The settlement is placed about four and a half miles inland, and at a height probably of a thousand feet. In the first part of the road we passed through leafless thickets, as in Chatham Island. Higher up, the woods gradually became greener: and as soon as we crossed the ridge of the island, we were cooled by a fine southerly breeze, and our sight refreshed by a green and thriving vegetation. In this upper region coarse grasses and ferns abound; but there are no tree-ferns: I saw nowhere any member of the Palm family, which is the more singular, as 360 miles northward, Cocos Island takes its name from the number of cocoa-nuts. The houses are irregularly scattered over a flat space of ground, which is cultivated with sweet potatoes and bananas. It will not easily be imagined how pleasant the sight of black mud was to us, after having been so long accustomed to the parched soil of Peru and northern Chile. The inhabitants, although complaining of poverty, obtain, without much trouble, the means of sub-sistence. In the woods there are many wild pigs and goats; but the staple article of animal food is supplied by the tortoises. Their numbers have of course been greatly reduced in this island, but the people yet count on two days' hunting giving them food for the rest of the week. It is said that formerly single vessels have taken away as many as seven hundred, and that the ship's company of a frigate some years since brought down in one day two hundred tortoises to the beach.

*   *   *

The natural history of these islands is eminently curious, and well de-serves attention. Most of the organic productions are aboriginal creations, found nowhere else; there is even a difference between the inhabitants of the different islands; yet all show a marked relationship with those of Amer-ica, though separated from that continent by an open space of ocean, between 500 and 600 miles in width. The archipelago is a little world within itself, or rather a satellite attached to America, whence it has derived a few stray colonists, and has received the general character of its indige-nous productions. Considering the small size of these islands, we feel the more astonished at the number of their aboriginal beings, and at their confined range. Seeing every height crowned with its crater, and the boundaries of most of the lava-streams still distinct, we are led to believe that within a period, geologically recent, the unbroken ocean was here spread out. Hence, both in space and time, we seem to be brought somewhat near to that great fact—that mystery of mysteries—the first appearance of new beings on this earth.

Of terrestrial mammals, there is only one which must be considered as indigenous, namely, a mouse (Mus Galapagoensis), and this is confined, as far as I could ascertain, to Chatham Island, the most easterly island of the group. It belongs, as I am informed by Mr. Waterhouse, to a division of the family of mice characteristic of America. At James Island, there is a rat sufficiently distinct from the common kind to have been named and described by Mr. Waterhouse; but as it belongs to the old-world division of the family, and as this island has been frequented by ships for the last hundred and fifty years, I can hardly doubt that this rat is merely a variety, produced by the new and peculiar climate, food, and soil, to which it has been subjected. Although no one has a right to speculate without distinct facts, yet even with respect to the Chatham Island mouse, it should be borne in mind, that it may possibly be an American species imported here; for I have seen, in a most unfrequented part of the Pampas, a native mouse living in the roof of a newly-built hovel, and therefore its transportation in a vessel is not improbable: analogous facts have been observed by Dr. Richardson in North America.

Of land-birds I obtained twenty-six kinds, all peculiar to the group and found nowhere else, with the exception of one lark-like finch from North America (Dolichonyx oryzivorus), which ranges on that continent as far north as 54°, and generally frequents marshes. The other twenty-five birds consist, firstly, of a hawk, curiously intermediate in structure between a Buzzard and the American group of carrion-feeding Polybori; and with these latter birds it agrees most closely in every habit and even tone of voice. Secondly, there are two owls, representing the short-eared and white barn-owls of Europe. Thirdly, a wren, three tyrant fly-catchers (two of them species of Pyrocephalus, one or both of which would be ranked by some ornithologists as only varieties), and a dove—all analogous to, but distinct from, American species. Fourthly, a swallow, which though differing from the Progne purpurea of both Americas, only in being rather duller coloured, smaller, and slenderer, is considered by Mr. Gould as specifically distinct. Fifthly, there are three species of mocking-thrush—a form highly characteristic of America. The remaining land-birds form a most singular group of finches, related to each other in the structure of their beaks, short tails, form of body, and plumage: there are thirteen species, which Mr. Gould has divided into four sub-groups. All these species are peculiar to this archipelago; and so is the whole group, with the exception of one species of the sub-group Cactornis, lately brought from Bow Island, in the Low Archipelago. Of Cactornis, the two species may be often seen climbing about the flowers of the great cactus-trees; but all the other species of this group of finches, mingled together in flocks, feed on the dry and sterile ground of the lower districts. The males of all, or certainly of the greater number, are jet black; and the females (with perhaps one or two exceptions) are brown. The most curious fact is the perfect gradation in the size of the beaks in the different species of Geospiza, from one as large as that of a hawfinch to that of a chaffinch, and (if Mr. Gould is right in including his sub-group, Certhidea, in the main group), even to that of a warbler. The largest beak in the genus Geospiza is shown in Fig. 1, and the smallest in Fig. 3; but instead of their being only one intermediate species, with a beak of the size shown in Fig. 2, there are no less than six species with insensibly graduated beaks. The beak of the sub-group Certhidea, is shown in Fig. 4. The beak of Cactornis is somewhat like that of a starling; and that of the fourth sub-group, Camarhynchus, is slightly parrot-shaped. Seeing this gradation and diversity of structure in one small, intimately related group of birds, one might really fancy that from an original paucity of birds in this archipelago, one species had been taken and modified for different ends. In a like manner it might be fancied that a bird originally a buzzard, had been induced here to undertake the office of the carrion-feeding Polybori of the American continent.

*   *   *

We will now turn to the order of reptiles, which gives the most striking character to the zoology of these islands. The species are not numerous, but the numbers of individuals of each species are extraordinarily great. There is one small lizard belonging to a South American genus, and two species (and probably more) of the Amblyrhynchus—a genus confined to the Galapagos Islands. There is one snake which is numerous; it is identical, as I am informed by M. Bibron, with the Psammophis Temminckii from Chile. Of sea-turtle I believe there is more than one species; and of tortoises there are, as we shall presently show, two or three species or races. Of toads and frogs there are none: I was surprised at this, considering how well suited for them the temperate and damp upper woods appeared to be. It recalled to my mind the remark made by Bory St. Vincent,[1] namely,

1. Voyage aux Quatre Iles d'Afrique. With respect to the Sandwich Islands, see Tyerman and Bennett's Journal, vol. i. p. 434. For Mauritius, see Voyage par un Officier, &c., Part i. p. 170. There are no frogs in the Canary Islands (Webb et Berthelot, Hist. Nat. des Iles Canaries). I saw none at St. Jago in the Cape de Verds. There are none at St. Helena.

that none of this family are found on any of the volcanic islands in the great oceans. As far as I can ascertain from various works, this seems to hold good throughout the Pacific, and even in the large islands of the Sandwich archipelago. Mauritius offers an apparent exception, where I saw the Rana Mascariensis in abundance: this frog is said now to inhabit the Seychelles, Madagascar, and Bourbon; but on the other hand, Du Bois, in his voyage of 1669, states that there were no reptiles in Bourbon except tortoises; and the Officier du Roi asserts that before 1768 it had been attempted, without success, to introduce frogs into Mauritius—I presume, for the purpose of eating: hence it may be well doubted whether this frog is an aboriginal of these islands. The absence of the frog family in the oceanic islands is the more remarkable, when contrasted with the case of lizards, which swarm on most of the smallest islands. May this difference not be caused, by the greater facility with which the eggs of lizards, protected by calcareous shells, might be transported through salt-water, than could the slimy spawn of frogs?

I will first describe the habits of the tortoise (Testudo nigra, formerly called Indica), which has been so frequently alluded to. These animals are found, I believe, on all the islands of the Archipelago; certainly on the greater number. They frequent in preference the high damp parts, but they likewise live in the lower and arid districts. I have already shown, from the numbers which have been caught in a single day, how very numerous they must be. Some grow to an immense size: Mr. Lawson, an Englishman, and vice-governor of the colony, told us that he had seen several so large, that it required six or eight men to lift them from the ground; and that some had afforded as much as two hundred pounds of meat. The old males are the largest, the females rarely growing to so great a size: the male can readily be distinguished from the female by the greater length of its tail. The tortoises which live on those islands where there is no water, or in the lower and arid parts of the others, feed chiefly on the succulent cactus. Those which frequent the higher and damp regions, eat the leaves of various trees, a kind of berry (called guayavita) which is acid and austere, and likewise a pale green filamentous lichen (Usnera plicata), that hangs in tresses from the boughs of the trees.

The tortoise is very fond of water, drinking large quantities, and wallowing in the mud. The larger islands alone possess springs, and these are always situated towards the central parts, and at a considerable height. The tortoises, therefore, which frequent the lower districts, when thirsty, are obliged to travel from a long distance. Hence broad and well-beaten paths branch off in every direction from the wells down to the sea-coast; and the Spaniards by following them up, first discovered the watering-places. When I landed at Chatham Island, I could not imagine what animal travelled so methodically along well-chosen tracks. Near the springs it was a curious spectacle to behold many of these huge creatures, one set eagerly travelling onwards with outstretched necks, and another set returning, after having drunk their fill. When the tortoise arrives at the spring, quite regardless of any spectator, he buries his head in the water above his eyes, and greedily swallows great mouthfuls, at the rate of about ten in a minute. The inhabitants say each animal stays three or four days in the neighbourhood of the water, and then returns to the lower country; but they differed respecting the frequency of these visits. The animal probably regulates them according to the nature of the food on which it has lived. It is, however, certain, that tortoises can subsist even on those islands, where there is no other water than what falls during a few rainy days in the year.

I believe it is well ascertained, that the bladder of the frog acts as a reservoir for the moisture necessary to its existence: such seems to be the case with the tortoise. For some time after a visit to the springs, their urinary bladders are distended with fluid, which is said gradually to decrease in volume, and to become less pure. The inhabitants, when walking in the lower district, and overcome with thirst, often take advantage of this circumstance, and drink the contents of the bladder if full: in one I saw killed, the fluid was quite limpid, and had only a very slightly bitter taste. The inhabitants, however, always first drink the water in the pericardium, which is described as being best.

The tortoises, when purposely moving towards any point, travel by night and day, and arrive at their journey's end much sooner than would be expected. The inhabitants, from observing marked individuals, consider that they travel a distance of about eight miles in two or three days. One large tortoise, which I watched, walked at the rate of sixty yards in ten minutes, that is 360 yards in the hour, or four miles a day,—allowing a little time for it to eat on the road. During the breeding season, when the male and female are together, the male utters a hoarse roar or bellowing, which, it is said, can be heard at the distance of more than a hundred yards. The female never uses her voice, and the male only at these times; so that when the people hear this noise, they know that the two are together. They were at this time (October) laying their eggs. The female, where the soil is sandy, deposits them together, and covers them up with sand; but where the ground is rocky she drops them indiscriminately in any hole: Mr. Bynoe found seven placed in a fissure. The egg is white and spherical; one which I measured was seven inches and three-eighths in circumference, and therefore larger than a hen's egg. The young tortoises, as soon as they are hatched, fall a prey in great numbers to the carrion-feeding buzzard. The old ones seem generally to die from accidents, as from falling down precipices: at least, several of the inhabitants told me, that they had never found one dead without some evident cause.

The inhabitants believe that these animals are absolutely deaf; certainly they do not overhear a person walking close behind them. I was always amused when overtaking one of these great monsters, as it was quietly pacing along, to see how suddenly, the instant I passed, it would draw in its head and legs, and uttering a deep hiss fall to the ground with a heavy sound, as if struck dead. I frequently got on their backs, and then giving a few raps on the hinder part of their shells, they would rise up and walk away;—but I found it very difficult to keep my balance. The flesh of this animal is largely employed, both fresh and salted; and a beautifully clear oil is prepared from the fat. When a tortoise is caught, the man makes a slit in the skin near its tail, so as to see inside its body, whether the fat under the dorsal plate is thick. If it is not, the animal is liberated; and it is said to recover soon from this strange operation. In order to secure the tortoises, it is not sufficient to turn them like turtle, for they are often able to get on their legs again.

There can be little doubt that this tortoise is an aboriginal inhabitant of the Galapagos; for it is found on all, or nearly all, the islands, even on some of the smaller ones where there is no water; had it been an imported species, this would hardly have been the case in a group which has been so little frequented. Moreover, the old Bucaniers found this tortoise in greater numbers even than at present: Wood and Rogers also, in 1708, say that it is the opinion of the Spaniards, that it is found nowhere else in this quarter of the world. It is now widely distributed; but it may be questioned whether it is in any other place an aboriginal. The bones of a tortoise at Mauritius, associated with those of the extinct Dodo, have generally been considered as belonging to this tortoise: if this had been so, undoubtedly it must have been there indigenous; but M. Bibron informs me that he believes that it was distinct, as the species now living there certainly is.

The Amblyrhynchus, a remarkable genus of lizards, is confined to this archipelago: there are two species, resembling each other in general form, one being terrestrial and the other aquatic. This latter species (A. cristatus) was first characterized by Mr. Bell, who well foresaw, from its short, broad head, and strong claws of equal length, that its habits of life would turn out very peculiar, and different from those of its nearest ally, the Iguana. It is extremely common on all the islands throughout the group, and lives exclusively on the rocky sea-beaches, being never found, at least I never saw one, even ten yards in-shore. It is a hideous-looking creature, of a dirty black colour, stupid, and sluggish in its movements. The usual length of a full-grown one is about a yard, but there are some even four feet long; a large one weighed twenty pounds: on the island of Albemarle they seem to grow to a greater size than elsewhere. Their tails are flattened sideways, and all four feet partially webbed. They are occasionally seen some hundred yards from the shore, swimming about; and Captain Collnett, in his Voyage, says, "They go to sea in herds a-fishing, and sun themselves on the rocks; and may be called alligators in miniature." It must not, however, be supposed that they live on fish. When in the water this lizard swims with perfect ease and quickness, by a serpentine movement of its body and flattened tail—the legs being motionless and closely collapsed on its sides. A seaman on board sank one, with a heavy weight attached to it, thinking thus to kill it directly; but when, an hour afterwards, he drew up the line, it was quite active. Their limbs and strong claws are admirably adapted for crawling over the rugged and fissured masses of lava, which everywhere form the coast. In such situations, a group of six or seven of these hideous reptiles may oftentimes be seen on the black rocks, a few feet above the surf, basking in the sun with outstretched legs.

I opened the stomachs of several, and found them largely distended with minced sea-weed (Ulvæ), which grows in thin foliaceous expansions of a bright green or a dull red colour. I do not recollect having observed this sea-weed in any quantity on the tidal rocks; and I have reason to believe it grows at the bottom of the sea, at some little distance from the

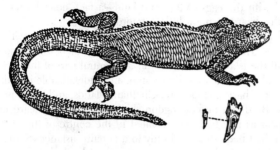

Amblyrhynchus cristatus. *Insert*: Tooth of natural size, and likewise magnified.

coast. If such be the case, the object of these animals occasionally going out to sea is explained. The stomach contained nothing but the sea-weed. Mr. Bynoe, however, found a piece of a crab in one; but this might have got in accidentally, in the same manner as I have seen a caterpillar, in the midst of some lichen, in the paunch of a tortoise. The intestines were large, as in other herbivorous animals. The nature of this lizard's food, as well as the structure of its tail and feet, and the fact of its having been seen voluntarily swimming out at sea, absolutely prove its aquatic habits; yet there is in this respect one strange anomaly, namely, that when frightened it will not enter the water. Hence it is easy to drive these lizards down to any little point overhanging the sea, where they will sooner allow a person to catch hold of their tails than jump into the water. They do not seem to have any notion of biting; but when much frightened they squirt a drop of fluid from each nostril. I threw one several times as far as I could, into a deep pool left by the retiring tide; but it invariably returned in a direct line to the spot where I stood. It swam near the bottom, with a very graceful and rapid movement, and occasionally aided itself over the uneven ground with its feet. As soon as it arrived near the edge, but still being under water, it tried to conceal itself in the tufts of sea-weed, or it entered some crevice. As soon as it thought the danger was past, it crawled out on the dry rocks, and shuffled away as quickly as it could. I several times caught this same lizard, by driving it down to a point, and though possessed of such perfect powers of diving and swimming, nothing would induce it to enter the water; and as often as I threw it in, it returned in the manner above described. Perhaps this singular piece of apparent stupidity may be accounted for by the circumstance, that this reptile has no enemy whatever on shore, whereas at sea it must often fall a prey to the numerous sharks. Hence, probably, urged by a fixed and hereditary instinct that the shore is its place of safety, whatever the emergency may be, it there takes refuge.

During our visit (in October), I saw extremely few small individuals of this species, and none I should think under a year old. From this circumstance it seems probable that the breeding season had not then commenced. I asked several of the inhabitants if they knew where it laid its eggs: they said that they knew nothing of its propagation, although well acquainted with the eggs of the land kind—a fact, considering how very common this lizard is, not a little extraordinary.

We will now turn to the terrestial species (A. Demarlii), with a round tail, and toes without webs. This lizard, instead of being found like the other on all the islands, is confined to the central part of the archipelago, namely to Albemarle, James, Barrington, and Indefatigable islands. To the southward, in Charles, Hood, and Chatham islands, and to the northward, in Towers, Bindloes, and Abingdon, I neither saw nor heard of any. It would appear as if it had been created in the centre of the archipelago, and thence had been dispersed only to a certain distance. Some of these lizards inhabit the high and damp parts of the islands, but they are much more numerous in the lower and sterile districts near the coast. I cannot give a more forcible proof of their numbers, than by stating that when we were left at James Island, we could not for some time find a spot free from their burrows on which to pitch our single tent. Like their brothers the sea-kind, they are ugly animals, of a yellowish orange beneath, and of a brownish red colour above: from their low facial angle they have a singularly stupid appearance. They are, perhaps, of a rather less size than the marine species; but several of them weighed between ten and fifteen pounds. In their movements they are lazy and half torpid. When not frightened, they slowly crawl along with their tails and bellies dragging on the ground. They often stop, and doze for a minute or two, with closed eyes and hind legs spread out on the parched soil.

They inhabit burrows, which they sometimes make between fragments of lava, but more generally on level patches of the soft sandstone-like tuff. The holes do not appear to be very deep, and they enter the ground at a small angle; so that when walking over these lizard-warrens, the soil is constantly giving way, much to the annoyance of the tired walker. This animal, when making its burrow, works alternately the opposite sides of its body. One front leg for a short time scratches up the soil, and throws it towards the hind foot, which is well placed so as to heave it beyond the mouth of the hole. That side of the body being tired, the other takes up the task, and so on alternately. I watched one for a long time, till half its body was buried; I then walked up and pulled it by the tail; at this it was greatly astonished, and soon shuffled up to see what was the matter; and then stared me in the face, as much as to say, "What made you pull my tail?"

They feed by day, and do not wander far from their burrows; if frightened, they rush to them with a most awkward gait. Except when running down hill, they cannot move very fast, apparently from the lateral position of their legs. They are not at all timorous: when attentively watching any one, they curl their tails, and, raising themselves on their front legs, nod their heads vertically, with a quick movement, and try to look very fierce: but in reality they are not at all so; if one just stamps on the ground, down go their tails, and off they shuffle as quickly as they can. I have frequently observed small fly-eating lizards, when watching anything, nod their heads in precisely the same manner; but I do not at all know for what purpose. If this Amblyrhynchus is held and plagued with a stick, it will bite it very severely; but I caught many by the tail, and they never tried to bite me. If two are placed on the ground and held together, they will fight, and bite each other till blood is drawn.

The individuals, and they are the greater number, which inhabit the lower country, can scarcely taste a drop of water throughout the year; but they consume much of the succulent cactus, the branches of which are occasionally broken off by the wind. I several times threw a piece to two or three of them when together; and it was amusing enough to see them trying to seize and carry it away in their mouths, like so many hungry dogs with a bone. They eat very deliberately, but do not chew their food. The little birds are aware how harmless these creatures are: I have seen one of the thick-billed finches picking at one end of a piece of cactus (which is much relished by all the animals of the lower region), whilst a lizard was eating at the other end; and afterwards the little bird with the utmost indifference hopped on the back of the reptile.

I opened the stomachs of several, and found them full of vegetable fibres and leaves of different trees, especially of an acacia. In the upper region they live chiefly on the acid and astringent berries of the guayavita, under which trees I have seen these lizards and huge tortoises feeding together. To obtain the acacia-leaves they crawl up the low stunted trees; and it is not uncommon to see a pair quietly browsing, whilst seated on a branch several feet above the ground. These lizards, when cooked, yield a white meat, which is liked by those whose stomachs soar above all prejudices. Humboldt has remarked that in intertropical South America, all lizards which inhabit dry regions are esteemed delicacies for the table. The inhabitants state that those which inhabit the upper damp parts drink water, but that the others do not, like the tortoises, travel up for it from the lower sterile country. At the time of our visit, the females had within their bodies numerous large, elongated eggs, which they lay in their burrows: the inhabitants seek them for food.

These two species of Amblyrhynchus agree, as I have already stated, in their general structure, and in many of their habits. Neither have that rapid movement, so characteristic of the genera Lacerta and Iguana. They are both herbivorous, although the kind of vegetation on which they feed is so very different. Mr. Bell has given the name to the genus from the shortness of the snout; indeed, the form of the mouth may almost be compared to that of the tortoise: one is led to suppose that this is an adaptation to their herbivorous appetites. It is very interesting thus to find a well-characterized genus, having its marine and terrestrial species, belonging to so confined a portion of the world. The aquatic species is by far the most remarkable, because it is the only existing lizard which lives on marine vegetable productions. As I at first observed, these islands are not so remarkable for the number of the species of reptiles, as for that of the individuals; when we remember the well-beaten paths made by the thousands of huge tortoises—the many turtles—the great warrens of the terrestrial Amblyrhynchus—and the groups of the marine species basking on the coast-rocks of every island—we must admit that there is no other quarter of the world where this Order replaces the herbivorous mammalia in so extraordinary a manner. The geologist on hearing this will probably refer back in his mind to the Secondary epochs, when lizards, some herbivorous, some carnivorous, and of dimensions comparable only with our existing whales, swarmed on the land and in the sea. It is, therefore, worthy of his observation, that this archipelago, instead of possessing a humid climate and rank vegetation, cannot be considered otherwise than extremely arid, and, for an equatorial region, remarkably temperate.

* * *

If this character were owing merely to immigrants from America, there would be little remarkable in it; but we see that a vast majority of all the land animals, and that more than half of the flowering plants, are aboriginal productions. It was most striking to be surrounded by new birds, new reptiles, new shells, new insects, new plants, and yet by innumerable trifling details of structure, and even by the tones of voice and plumage of the birds, to have the temperate plains of Patagonia, or the hot dry deserts of Northern Chile, vividly brought before my eyes. Why, on these small points of land, which within a late geological period must have been covered by the ocean, which are formed of basaltic lava, and therefore differ in geological character from the American continent, and which are placed under a peculiar climate,—why were their aboriginal inhabitants, associated, I may add, in different proportions both in kind and number from those on the continent, and therefore acting on each other in a different manner—why were they created on American types of organization? It is probable that the islands of the Cape de Verd group resemble, in all their physical conditions, far more closely the Galapagos Islands than these latter physically resemble the coast of America; yet the aboriginal inhabitants of the two groups are totally unlike; those of the Cape de Verd Islands bearing the impress of Africa, as the inhabitants of the Galapagos Archipelago are stamped with that of America.

I have not as yet noticed by far the most remarkable feature in the natural history of this archipelago; it is, that the different islands to a considerable extent are inhabited by a different set of beings. My attention was first called to this fact by the Vice-Governor, Mr. Lawson, declaring that the tortoises differed from the different islands, and that he could with certainty tell from which island any one was brought. I did not for some time pay sufficient attention to this statement, and I had already partially mingled together the collections from two of the islands. I never dreamed that islands, about fifty or sixty miles apart, and most of them in sight of each other, formed of precisely the same rocks, placed under a quite similar climate, rising to a nearly equal height, would have been differently tenanted; but we shall soon see that this is the case. It is the fate of most voyagers, no sooner to discover what is most interesting in any locality, than they are hurried from it; but I ought, perhaps, to be thankful that I obtained sufficient material to establish this most remarkable fact in the distribution of organic beings.

The inhabitants, as I have said, state that they can distinguish the tortoises from the different islands; and that they differ not only in size, but in other characters. Captain Porter has described[2] those from Charles and from the nearest island to it, namely, Hood Island, as having their shells in front thick and turned up like a Spanish saddle, whilst the tortoises from James Island are rounder, blacker, and have a better taste when cooked. M. Bibron, moreover, informs me that he has seen what he considers two distinct species of tortoise from the Galapagos, but he does not know from which islands. The specimens that I brought from three islands were young ones; and probably owing to this cause, neither Mr. Gray nor myself could find in them any specific differences. I have remarked that the marine Amblyrhynchus was larger at Albemarle Island than elsewhere; and M. Bibron informs me that he has seen two distinct aquatic species of this genus; so that the different islands probably have their representative species or races of the Amblyrhynchus, as well as of the tortoise. My attention was first thoroughly aroused, by comparing together the numerous specimens, shot by myself and several other parties on board, of the mocking-thrushes, when, to my astonishment, I discovered that all those from Charles Island belonged to one species (Mimus trifasciatus); all from Albemarle Island to M. parvulus; and all from James and Chatham Islands (between which two other islands are situated, as connecting links) belonged to M. melanotis. These two latter species are closely allied, and would by some ornithologists be considered as only well-marked races or varieties; but the Mimus trifasciatus is very distinct. Unfortunately most of the specimens of the finch tribe were mingled together; but I have strong reasons to suspect that some of the species of the sub-group Geospiza are confined to separate islands. If the different islands have their representatives of Geospiza, it may help to explain the singularly large number of the species of this sub-group in this one small archipelago, and as a probable consequence of their numbers, the perfectly graduated series in the size of their beaks. Two species of the sub-group Cactornis, and two of Camarhynchus, were procured in the archipelago; and of the numerous specimens of these two sub-groups shot by four collectors at James Island, all were found to belong to one species of each; whereas the numerous specimens shot either on Chatham or Charles Island (for the two sets were mingled together) all belonged to the two other species: hence we may feel almost sure that these islands possess their representative species of these two sub-groups. In land-shells this law of distribution does not appear to hold good. In my very small collection of insects, Mr. Waterhouse remarks, that of those which were ticketed with their locality, not one was common to any two of the islands.

*   *   *

The only light which I can throw on this remarkable difference in the inhabitants of the different islands, is, that very strong currents of the sea running in a westerly and W.N.W. direction must separate, as far as transportal by the sea is concerned, the southern islands from the northern ones; and between these northern islands a strong N.W. current was ob-

2. Voyage in the U. S. ship *Essex*, vol. i. p. 215.

served, which must effectually separate James and Albemarle Islands. As
the archipelago is free to a most remarkable degree from gales of wind,
neither the birds, insects, nor lighter seeds, would be blown from island
to island. And lastly, the profound depth of the ocean between the islands,
and their apparently recent (in a geological sense) volcanic origin, render
it highly unlikely that they were ever united; and this, probably, is a far
more important consideration than any other, with respect to the geographical distribution of their inhabitants. Reviewing the facts here given, one
is astonished at the amount of creative force, if such an expression may
be used, displayed on these small, barren, and rocky islands; and still more
so, at its diverse yet analogous action on points so near each other. I have
said that the Galapagos Archipelago might be called a satellite attached to
America, but it should rather be called a group of satellites, physically
similar, organically distinct, yet intimately related to each other, and all
related in a marked, though much lesser degree, to the great American
continent.

I will conclude my description of the natural history of these islands, by
giving an account of the extreme tameness of the birds.

This disposition is common to all the terrestrial species; namely, to the
mocking-thrushes, the finches, wrens, tyrant-flycatchers, the dove, and
carrion-buzzard. All of them often approached sufficiently near to be killed
with a switch, and sometimes, as I myself tried, with a cap or hat. A gun
is here almost superfluous; for with the muzzle I pushed a hawk off the
branch of a tree. One day, whilst lying down, a mocking-thrush alighted
on the edge of a pitcher, made of the shell of a tortoise, which I held in
my hand, and began very quietly to sip the water; it allowed me to lift it
from the ground whilst seated on the vessel: I often tried, and very nearly
succeeded, in catching these birds by their legs. Formerly the birds appear
to have been even tamer than at present. Cowley (in the year 1684) says
that the "Turtle-doves were so tame, that they would often alight upon our
hats and arms, so as that we could take them alive: they not fearing man,
until such time as some of our company did fire at them, whereby they
were rendered more shy." Dampier also, in the same year, says that a man
in a morning's walk might kill six or seven dozen of these doves. At present,
although certainly very tame, they do not alight on people's arms, nor do
they suffer themselves to be killed in such large numbers. It is surprising
that they have not become wilder; for these islands during the last hundred
and fifty years have been frequently visited by bucaniers and whalers; and
the sailors, wandering through the woods in search of tortoises, always take
cruel delight in knocking down the little birds.

These birds, although now still more persecuted, do not readily become
wild: in Charles Island, which had then been colonized about six years, I
saw a boy sitting by a well with a switch in his hand, with which he killed
the doves and finches as they came to drink. He had already procured a
little heap of them for his dinner; and he said that he had constantly been
in the habit of waiting by this well for the same purpose. It would appear
that the birds of this archipelago, not having as yet learnt that man is a
more dangerous animal than the tortoise or the Amblyrhynchus, disregard

him, in the same manner as in England shy birds, such as magpies, disregard the cows and horses grazing in our fields.

The Falkland Islands offer a second instance of birds with a similar disposition. The extraordinary tameness of the little Opetiorhynchus has been remarked by Pernety, Lesson, and other voyagers. It is not, however, peculiar to that bird: the Polyborus, snipe, upland and lowland goose, thrush, bunting, and even some true hawks, are all more or less tame. As the birds are so tame there, where foxes, hawks, and owls occur, we may infer that the absence of all rapacious animals at the Galapagos, is not the cause of their tameness here. The upland geese at the Falklands show, by the precaution they take in building on the islets, that they are aware of their danger from the foxes; but they are not by this rendered wild towards man. This tameness of the birds, especially of the waterfowl, is strongly contrasted with the habits of the same species in Tierra del Fuego, where for ages past they have been persecuted by the wild inhabitants. In the Falklands, the sportsman may sometimes kill more of the upland geese in one day than he can carry home; whereas in Tierra del Fuego, it is nearly as difficult to kill one, as it is in England to shoot the common wild goose.

*   *   *

From these several facts we may, I think, conclude, first, that the wildness of birds with regard to man, is a particular instinct directed against *him*, and not dependent on any general degree of caution arising from other sources of danger; secondly, that it is not acquired by individual birds in a short time, even when much persecuted; but that in the course of successive generations it becomes hereditary. With domesticated animals we are accustomed to see new mental habits or instincts acquired and rendered hereditary; but with animals in a state of nature, it must always be most difficult to discover instances of acquired hereditary knowledge. In regard to the wildness of birds towards man, there is no way of accounting for it, except as an inherited habit: comparatively few young birds, in any one year, have been injured by man in England, yet almost all, even nestlings, are afraid of him; many individuals, on the other hand, both at the Galapagos and at the Falklands, have been pursued and injured by man, but yet have not learned a salutary dread of him. We may infer from these facts, what havoc the introduction of any new beast of prey must cause in a country, before the instincts of the indigenous inhabitants have become adapted to the stranger's craft or power.

On the Tendency of Species to Form Varieties; and On the Perpetuation of Varieties and Species by Natural Means of Selection (1858)†

I—Extract from an unpublished Work on Species,
by C. DARWIN, Esq.

De Candolle, in an eloquent passage, has declared that all nature is at war, one organism with another, or with external nature. Seeing the contented face of nature, this may at first well be doubted; but reflection will inevitably prove it to be true. The war, however, is not constant, but recurrent in a slight degree at short periods, and more severely at occasional more distant periods; and hence its effects are easily overlooked. It is the doctrine of Malthus applied in most cases with tenfold force. As in every climate there are seasons, for each of its inhabitants, of greater and less abundance, so all annually breed; and the moral restraint which in some small degree checks the increase of mankind is entirely lost. Even slow-breeding mankind has doubled in twenty-five years; and if he could increase his food with greater ease, he would double in less time. But for animals without artificial means, the amount of food for each species must, *on an average*, be constant, whereas the increase of all organisms tends to be geometrical, and in a vast majority of cases at an enormous ratio. Suppose in a certain spot there are eight pairs of birds, and that *only* four pairs of them annually (including double hatches) rear only four young, and that these go on rearing their young at the same rate, then at the end of seven years (a short life, excluding violent deaths, for any bird) there will be 2048 birds, instead of the original sixteen. As this increase is quite impossible, we must conclude either that birds do not rear nearly half their young, or that the average life of a bird is, from accident, not nearly seven years. Both checks probably concur. The same kind of calculation applied to all plants and animals affords results more or less striking, but in very few instances more striking than in man.

Many practical illustrations of this rapid tendency to increase are on record, among which, during peculiar seasons, are the extraordinary numbers of certain animals; for instance, during the years 1826 to 1828, in La Plata, when from drought some millions of cattle perished, the whole country *swarmed* with mice. Now I think it cannot be doubted that during the breeding-season all the mice (with the exception of a few males or females in excess) ordinarily pair, and therefore that this astounding increase during three years must be attributed to a greater number than usual surviving the first year, and then breeding, and so on till the third year, when their numbers were brought down to their usual limits on the return of wet weather. Where man has introduced plants and animals into a new

† From the *Journal of the Proceedings of the Linnean Society, Zoology* 3 (Aug. 20, 1858). Darwin sketched out these ideas in 1839 and sent a revised copy of them to Joseph Hooker in 1844; but he didn't publish any such thoughts until prompted by A. R. Wallace's own remarkably similar sketch (see p. 61).

and favourable country, there are many accounts in how surprisingly few years the whole country has become stocked with them. This increase would necessarily stop as soon as the country was fully stocked; and yet we have every reason to believe, from what is known of wild animals, that *all* would pair in the spring. In the majority of cases it is most difficult to imagine where the checks fall—though generally, no doubt, on the seeds, eggs, and young; but when we remember how impossible, even in mankind (so much better known than any other animal), it is to infer from repeated casual observations what the average duration of life is, or to discover the different percentage of deaths to births in different countries, we ought to feel no surprise at our being unable to discover where the check falls in any animal or plant. It should always be remembered, that in most cases the checks are recurrent yearly in a small, regular degree, and in an extreme degree during unusually cold, hot, dry, or wet years, according to the constitution of the being in question. Lighten any check in the least degree, and the geometrical powers of increase in every organism will almost instantly increase the average number of the favoured species. Nature may be compared to a surface on which rest ten thousand sharp wedges touching each other and driven inwards by incessant blows. Fully to realize these views much reflection is requisite. Malthus on man should be studied; and all such cases as those of the mice in La Plata, of the cattle and horses when first turned out in South America, of the birds by our calculation, &c., should be well considered. Reflect on the enormous multiplying power *inherent and annually in action* in all animals; reflect on the countless seeds scattered by a hundred ingenious contrivances, year after year, over the whole face of the land; and yet we have every reason to suppose that the average percentage of each of the inhabitants of a country usually remains constant. Finally, let it be borne in mind that this average number of individuals (the external conditions remaining the same) in each country is kept up by recurrent struggles against other species or against external nature (as on the borders of the Arctic regions, where the cold checks life), and that ordinarily each individual of every species holds its place, either by its own struggle and capacity of acquiring nourishment in some period of its life, from the egg upwards; or by the struggle of its parents (in short-lived organisms, when the main check occurs at longer intervals) with other individuals of the *same* or *different* species.

But let the external conditions of a country alter. If in a small degree, the relative proportions of the inhabitants will in most cases simply be slightly changed; but let the number of inhabitants be small, as on an island, and free access to it from other countries be circumscribed, and let the change of conditions continue progressing (forming new stations), in such a case the original inhabitants must cease to be as perfectly adapted to the changed conditions as they were originally. It has been shown in a former part of this work, that such changes of external conditions would, from their acting on the reproductive system, probably cause the organization of those beings which were most affected to become, as under domestication, plastic. Now, can it be doubted, from the struggle each individual has to obtain subsistence, that any minute variation in structure, habits, or instincts, adapting that individual better to the new conditions, would tell upon its vigour and health? In the struggle it would have a better *chance* of surviving; and those of its offspring which inherited the variation, be it ever so slight, would also have a better *chance*. Yearly more are bred than can survive; the smallest grain in the balance, in the long run, must tell on which death shall fall, and which shall survive. Let this work of selection on the one hand, and death on the other, go on for a thousand generations, who will pretend to affirm that it would produce no effect, when we remember what, in a few years, Bakewell effected in cattle, and Western in sheep, by this identical principle of selection?

To give an imaginary example from changes in progress on an island: —let the organization of a canine animal which preyed chiefly on rabbits, but sometimes on hares, become slightly plastic; let these same changes cause the number of rabbits very slowly to decrease, and the number of hares to increase; the effect of this would be that the fox or dog would be driven to try to catch more hares: his organization, however, being slightly plastic, those individuals with the lightest forms, longest limbs, and best eyesight, let the difference be ever so small, would be slightly favoured, and would tend to live longer, and to survive during that time of the year when food was scarcest; they would also rear more young, which would tend to inherit these slight peculiarities. The less fleet ones would be rigidly destroyed. I can see no more reason to doubt that these causes in a thousand generations would produce a marked effect, and adapt the form of the fox or dog to the catching of hares instead of rabbits, than that greyhounds can be improved by selection and careful breeding. So would it be with plants under similar circumstances. If the number of individuals of a species with plumed seeds could be increased by greater powers of dissemination within its own area (that is, if the check to increase fell chiefly on the seeds), those seeds which were provided with ever so little more down, would in the long run be most disseminated; hence a greater number of seeds thus formed would germinate; and would tend to produce plants inheriting the slightly better-adapted down.

Besides this natural means of selection, by which those individuals are preserved, whether in their egg, or larval, or mature state, which are best adapted to the place they fill in nature, there is a second agency at work in most unisexual animals, tending to produce the same effect, namely, the struggle of the males for the females. These struggles are generally decided by the law of battle, but in the case of birds, apparently, by the charms of their song, by their beauty or their power of courtship, as in the dancing rock-thrush of Guiana. The most vigorous and healthy males, implying perfect adaptation, must generally gain the victory in their con-tests. This kind of selection, however, is less rigorous than the other; it does not require the death of the less successful, but gives to them fewer descendants. The struggle falls, moreover, at a time of year when food is generally abundant, and perhaps the effect chiefly produced would be the modification of the secondary sexual characters, which are not related to the power of obtaining food, or to defence from animals, but to fighting with or rivalling other males. The result of this struggle amongst the males

may be compared in some respects to that produced by those agricultur-
alists who pay less attention to the careful selection of all their young
animals, and more to the occasional use of a choice mate.

II—Abstract of a Letter from C. Darwin, *Esq., to* Prof. Asa Gray,
Boston, U.S., dated Down, September 5th, 1857.

1. It is wonderful what the principle of selection by man, that is the
picking out of individuals with any desired quality, and breeding from
them, and again picking out, can do. Even breeders have been astounded
at their own results. They can act on differences inappreciable to an uneducated eye. Selection has been *methodically* followed in *Europe* for only
the last half century; but it was occasionally, and even in some degree
methodically, followed in the most ancient times. There must have been
also a kind of unconscious selection from a remote period, namely in the
preservation of the individual animals (without any thought of their offspring) most useful to each race of man in his particular circumstances.
The "roguing," as nurserymen call the destroying of varieties which depart
from their type, is a kind of selection. I am convinced that intentional and
occasional selection has been the main agent in the production of our
domestic races; but however this may be, its great power of modification
has been indisputably shown in later times. Selection acts only by the
accumulation of slight or greater variations, caused by external conditions,
or by the mere fact that in generation the child is not absolutely similar
to its parent. Man, by this power of accumulating variations, adapts living
beings to his wants—may be said to make the wool of one sheep good for
carpets, of another for cloth, &c.

2. Now suppose there were a being who did not judge by mere external
appearances, but who could study the whole internal organization, who
was never capricious, and should go on selecting for one object during
millions of generations; who will say what he might not effect? In nature
we have some *slight* variation occasionally in all parts; and I think it can
be shown that changed conditions of existence is the main cause of the
child not exactly resembling its parents; and in nature geology shows us
what changes have taken place, and are taking place. We have almost
unlimited time; no one but a practical geologist can fully appreciate this.
Think of the Glacial period, during the whole of which the same species
at least of shells have existed; there must have been during this period
millions on millions of generations.

3. I think it can be shown that there is such an unerring power at work
in *Natural Selection* (the title of my book), which selects exclusively for
the good of each organic being. The elder De Candolle, W. Herbert, and
Lyell have written excellently on the struggle for life; but even they have
not written strongly enough. Reflect that every being (even the elephant)
breeds at such a rate, that in a few years, or at most a few centuries, the
surface of the earth would not hold the progeny of one pair. I have found
it hard constantly to bear in mind that the increase of every single species
is checked during some part of its life, or during some shortly recurrent

generation. Only a few of those annually born can live to propagate their kind. What a trifling difference must often determine which shall survive, and which perish!

4. Now take the case of a country undergoing some change. This will tend to cause some of its inhabitants to vary slightly—not but that I believe most beings vary at all times enough for selection to act on them. Some of its inhabitants will be exterminated; and the remainder will be exposed to the mutual action of a different set of inhabitants, which I believe to be far more important to the life of each being than mere climate. Considering the infinitely various methods which living beings follow to obtain food by struggling with other organisms, to escape danger at various times of life, to have their eggs or seeds disseminated, &c. &c., I cannot doubt that during millions of generations individuals of a species will be occasionally born with some slight variation, profitable to some part of their economy. Such individuals will have a better chance of surviving, and of propagating their new and slightly different structure; and the modification may be slowly increased by the accumulative action of natural selection to any profitable extent. The variety thus formed will either coexist with, or, more commonly, will exterminate its parent form. An organic being, like the woodpecker or misseltoe, may thus come to be adapted to a score of contingences—natural selection accumulating those slight variations in all parts of its structure, which are in any way useful to it during any part of its life.

5. Multiform difficulties will occur to every one, with respect to this theory. Many can, I think, be satisfactorily answered. *Natura non facit saltum* answers some of the most obvious. The slowness of the change, and only a very few individuals undergoing change at any one time, answers others. The extreme imperfection of our geological records answers others.

6. Another principle, which may be called the principle of divergence, plays, I believe, an important part in the origin of species. The same spot will support more life if occupied by very diverse forms. We see this in the many generic forms in a square yard of turf, and in the plants or insects on any little uniform islet, belonging almost invariably to as many genera and families as species. We can understand the meaning of this fact amongst the higher animals, whose habits we understand. We know that it has been experimentally shown that a plot of land will yield a greater weight if sown with several species and genera of grasses, than if sown with only two or three species. Now, every organic being, by propagating so rapidly, may be said to be striving its utmost to increase in numbers. So it will be with the offspring of any species after it has become diversified into varieties, or subspecies, or true species. And it follows, I think, from the foregoing facts, that the varying offspring of each species will try (only few will succeed) to seize on as many and as diverse places in the economy of nature as possible. Each new variety or species, when formed, will generally take the place of, and thus exterminate its less well-fitted parent. This I believe to be the origin of the classification and affinities of organic beings at all times; for organic beings always *seem* to branch and sub-branch like the limbs of a tree from a common trunk, the flourishing and

diverging twigs destroying the less vigorous—the dead and lost branches rudely representing extinct genera and families.

This sketch is *most* imperfect; but in so short a space I cannot make it better. Your imagination must fill up very wide blanks.

An Historical Sketch of the Progress of Opinion on the Origin of Species, previously to the Publication of This Work (1861)†

I will here give a brief sketch of the progress of opinion on the Origin of Species. Until recently the great majority of naturalists believed that species were immutable productions, and had been separately created. This view has been ably maintained by many authors. Some few naturalists, on the other hand, have believed that species undergo modification and that the existing forms of life are the descendants by true generation of pre-existing forms. Passing over allusions to the subject in the classical writers,[1] the first author who in modern times has treated it in a scientific spirit was Buffon. But as his opinions fluctuated greatly at different periods, and as he does not enter on the causes or means of the transformation of species, I need not here enter on details.

Lamarck was the first man whose conclusions on the subject excited much attention. This justly celebrated naturalist first published his views in 1801; he much enlarged them in 1809 in his 'Philosophie Zoologique,' and subsequently, in 1815, in the Introduction to his 'Hist. Nat. des Animaux sans Vertèbres.' In these works he upholds the doctrine that all species, including man, are descended from other species. He first did the eminent service of arousing attention to the probability of all changes in the organic, as well as in the inorganic world, being the result of law, and not of miraculous interposition. Lamarck seems to have been chiefly led to his conclusion on the gradual change of species, by the difficulty of distinguishing species and varieties, by the almost perfect gradation of forms in certain groups, and by the analogy of domestic productions. With respect to the means of modification, he attributed something to the direct action of the physical conditions of life, something to the crossing of already existing forms, and much to use and disuse, that is, to the effects of

---

† This sketch was first added to *The Origin of Species* in the third edition (1861) and was supplemented in later editions. Darwin had been criticized from various quarters for giving insufficient credit to his "predecessors." The text is from the sixth edition of the *Origin*, the last in Darwin's lifetime.

1. Aristotle, in his 'Physicae Auscultationes' (lib. 2, cap. 8, s. 2), after remarking that rain does not fall in order to make the corn grow, any more than it falls to spoil the farmer's corn when threshed out of doors, applies the same argument to organisation; and adds (as translated by Mr. Clair Grece, who first pointed out the passage to me), "So what hinders the different parts [of the body] from having this merely accidental relation in nature? as the teeth, for example, grow by necessity, the front ones sharp, adapted for dividing, and the grinders flat, and serviceable for masticating the food; since they were not made for the sake of this, but it was the result of accident. And in like manner as to the other parts in which there appears to exist an adaptation to an end. Wheresoever, therefore, all things together (that is all the parts of one whole) happened like as if they were made for the sake of something, these were preserved, having been appropriately constituted by an internal spontaneity; and whatsoever things were not thus constituted, perished, and still perish." We here see the principle of natural selection shadowed forth, but how little Aristotle fully comprehended the principle, is shown by his remarks on the formation of the teeth.

habit. To this latter agency he seems to attribute all the beautiful adaptations in nature;—such as the long neck of the giraffe for browsing on the
branches of trees. But he likewise believed in a law of progressive development; and as all the forms of life thus tend to progress, in order to
account for the existence at the present day of simple productions, he
maintains that such forms are now spontaneously generated.[2]

Geoffroy Saint-Hilaire, as is stated in his 'Life,' written by his son, suspected, as early as 1795, that what we call species are various degenerations
of the same type. It was not until 1828 that he published his conviction
that the same forms have not been perpetuated since the origin of all
things. Geoffroy seems to have relied chiefly on the conditions of life, or
the 'monde ambiant' as the cause of change. He was cautious in drawing
conclusions, and did not believe that existing species are now undergoing
modification; and, as his son adds, "C'est donc un problème à réserver
entièrement à l'avenir, supposé même que l'avenir doive avoir prise sur
lui."[3]

In 1813, Dr. W. C. Wells read before the Royal Society 'An Account
of a White female, part of whose skin resembles that of a Negro'; but his
paper was not published until his famous 'Two Essays upon Dew and
Single Vision' appeared in 1818. In this paper he distinctly recognises the
principle of natural selection, and this is the first recognition which has
been indicated; but he applies it only to the races of man, and to certain
characters alone. After remarking that Negroes and mulattoes enjoy an
immunity from certain tropical diseases, he observes, firstly, that all animals tend to vary in some degree, and, secondly, that agriculturists improve
their domesticated animals by selection; and then, he adds, but what is
done in this latter case "by art, seems to be done with equal efficacy,
though more slowly, by nature, in the formation of varieties of mankind,
fitted for the country which they inhabit. Of the accidental varieties of
man, which would occur among the first few and scattered inhabitants of
the middle regions of Africa, some one would be better fitted than the
others to bear the diseases of the country. This race would consequently
multiply, while the others would decrease; not only from their inability to
sustain the attacks of disease, but from their incapacity of contending with
their more vigorous neighbours. The colour of this vigorous race I take
for granted, from what has been already said, would be dark. But the same
disposition to form varieties still existing, a darker and a darker race would

2. I have taken the date of the first publication of Lamarck from Isid. Geoffroy Saint-Hilaire's ('Hist.
Nat. Générale,' tom. ii. p. 405, 1859) excellent history of opinion on this subject. In this work a
full account is given of Buffon's conclusions on the same subject. It is curious how largely my
grandfather, Dr. Erasmus Darwin, anticipated the views and erroneous grounds of opinion of
Lamarck in his 'Zoonomia' (vol. i. pp. 500–510), published in 1794. According to Isid. Geoffroy
there is no doubt that Goethe was an extreme partisan of similar views, as shown in the Introduction to a work written in 1794 and 1795, but not published till long afterwards: he has pointedly
remarked ('Goethe als Naturforscher,' von Dr. Karl Meding, s. 34) that the future question for
naturalists will be how, for instance, cattle got their horns, and not for what they are used. It is
rather a singular instance of the manner in which similar views arise at about the same time, that
Goethe in Germany, Dr. Darwin in England, and Geoffroy Saint-Hilaire (as we shall immediately
see) in France, came to the same conclusion on the origin of species, in the years 1794–5.
3. "It is therefore a problem to hold over for the future, supposing that the future might take it upon
itself." I am grateful to Quentin Hope for all translations from the French in Darwin's works.
[Editor]

in the course of time occur: and as the darkest would be the best fitted for the climate, this would at length become the most prevalent, if not the only race, in the particular country in which it had originated." He then extends these same views to the white inhabitants of colder climates. I am indebted to Mr. Rowley, of the United States, for having called my attention, through Mr. Brace, to the above passage in Dr. Wells' work.

The Hon. and Rev. W. Herbert, afterwards Dean of Manchester, in the fourth volume of the 'Horticultural Transactions,' 1822, and in his work on the 'Amaryllidaceæ' (1837, pp. 19, 339), declares that "horticultural experiments have established, beyond the possibility of refutation, that botanical species are only a higher and more permanent class of varieties." He extends the same view to animals. The Dean believes that single species of each genus were created in an originally highly plastic condition, and that these have produced, chiefly by intercrossing, but likewise by variation, all our existing species.

In 1826 Professor Grant, in the concluding paragraph in his well-known paper ('Edinburgh Philosophical Journal,' vol. xiv. p. 283) on the Spongilla, clearly declares his belief that species are descended from other species, and that they become improved in the course of modification. This same view was given in his 55th Lecture, published in the 'Lancet' in 1834.

In 1831 Mr. Patrick Matthew published his work on 'Naval Timber and Arboriculture,' in which he gives precisely the same view on the origin of species as that (presently to be alluded to) propounded by Mr. Wallace and myself in the 'Linnean Journal,' and as that enlarged in the present volume. Unfortunately the view was given by Mr. Matthew very briefly in scattered passages in an Appendix to a work on a different subject, so that it remained unnoticed until Mr. Matthew himself drew attention to it in the 'Gardener's Chronicle,' on April 7th, 1860. The differences of Mr. Matthew's view from mine are not of much importance: he seems to consider that the world was nearly depopulated at successive periods, and then re-stocked; and he gives as an alternative, that new forms may be generated "without the presence of any mould or germ of former aggregates." I am not sure that I understand some passages; but it seems that he attributes much influence to the direct action of the conditions of life. He clearly saw, however, the full force of the principle of natural selection.

The celebrated geologist and naturalist, Von Buch, in his excellent 'Description Physique des Isles Canaries' (1836, p. 147), clearly expresses his belief that varieties slowly become changed into permanent species, which are no longer capable of intercrossing.

Rafinesque, in his 'New Flora of North America,' published in 1836, wrote (p. 6) as follows:—"All species might have been varieties once, and many varieties are gradually becoming species by assuming constant and peculiar characters"; but farther on (p. 18) he adds, "except the original types or ancestors of the genus."

In 1843–44 Professor Haldeman ('Boston Journal of Nat. Hist. U. States,' vol. iv. p. 468) has ably given the arguments for and against the hypothesis of the development and modification of species: he seems to lean towards the side of change.

The 'Vestiges of Creation' appeared in 1844. In the tenth and much improved edition (1853) the anonymous author says (p. 155):—"The proposition determined on after much consideration is, that the several series of animated beings, from the simplest and oldest up to the highest and most recent, are, under the providence of God, the results, *first*, of an impulse which has been imparted to the forms of life, advancing them, in definite times, by generation, through grades of organisation terminating in the highest dicotyledons and vertebrata, these grades being few in number, and generally marked by intervals of organic character, which we find to be a practical difficulty in ascertaining affinities; *second*, of another impulse connected with the vital forces, tending, in the course of generations, to modify organic structures in accordance with external circumstances, as food, the nature of the habitat, and the meteoric agencies, these being the 'adaptations' of the natural theologian." The author apparently believes that organisation progresses by sudden leaps, but that the effects produced by the conditions of life are gradual. He argues with much force on general grounds that species are not immutable productions. But I cannot see how the two supposed "impulses" account in a scientific sense for the numerous and beautiful coadaptations which we see throughout nature; I cannot see that we thus gain any insight how, for instance, a woodpecker has become adapted to its peculiar habits of life. The work, from its powerful and brilliant style, though displaying in the earlier editions little accurate knowledge and a great want of scientific caution, immediately had a very wide circulation. In my opinion it has done excellent service in this country in calling attention to the subject, in removing prejudice, and in thus preparing the ground for the reception of analogous views.

In 1846 the veteran geologist M. J. d'Omalius d'Halloy published in an excellent though short paper ('Bulletins de l'Acad. Roy. Bruxelles,' tom. xiii. p. 581) his opinion that it is more probable that new species have been produced by descent with modification than that they have been separately created: the author first promulgated this opinion in 1831.

Professor Owen, in 1849 ('Nature of Limbs,' p. 86), wrote as follows:— "The archetypal idea was manifested in the flesh under diverse such modifications, upon this planet, long prior to the existence of those animal species that actually exemplify it. To what natural laws or secondary causes the orderly succession and progression of such organic phenomena may have been committed, we, as yet, are ignorant." In his Address to the British Association, in 1858, he speaks (p. li.) of "the axiom of the continuous operation of creative power, or of the ordained becoming of living things." Farther on (p. xc.), after referring to geographical distribution, he adds, "These phenomena shake our confidence in the conclusion that the Apteryx of New Zealand and the Red Grouse of England were distinct creations in and for those islands respectively. Always, also, it may be well to bear in mind that by the word 'creation' the zoologist means 'a process he knows not what.' " He amplifies this idea by adding that when such cases as that of the Red Grouse are "enumerated by the zoologist as evidence of distinct creation of the bird in and for such islands, he chiefly expresses that he knows not how the Red Grouse came to be there, and there exclusively; signifying also, by this mode of expressing such ignorance, his belief that both the bird and the islands owed their origin to a great first Creative Cause." If we interpret these sentences given in the same Address, one by the other, it appears that this eminent philosopher felt in 1858 his confidence shaken that the Apteryx and the Red Grouse first appeared in their respective homes, "he knew not how," or by some process "he knew not what."

This Address was delivered after the papers by Mr. Wallace and myself on the Origin of Species, presently to be referred to, had been read before the Linnean Society. When the first edition of this work was published, I was so completely deceived, as were many others, by such expressions as "the continuous operation of creative power," that I included Professor Owen with other palæontologists as being firmly convinced of the immutability of species; but it appears ('Anat. of Vertebrates,' vol. iii. p. 796) that this was on my part a preposterous error. In the last edition of this work I inferred, and the inference still seems to me perfectly just, from a passage beginning with the words "no doubt the type-form," &c. (Ibid. vol. i. p. xxxv.), that Professor Owen admitted that natural selection may have done something in the formation of a new species; but this it appears (Ibid. vol. iii. p. 798) is inaccurate and without evidence. I also gave some extracts from a correspondence between Professor Owen and the Editor of the 'London Review,' from which it appeared manifest to the Editor as well as myself, that Professor Owen claimed to have promulgated the theory of natural selection before I had done so; and I expressed my surprise and satisfaction at this announcement; but as far as it is possible to understand certain recently published passages (Ibid vol. iii. p. 798) I have either partially or wholly again fallen into error. It is consolatory to me that others find Professor Owen's controversial writings as difficult to understand and to reconcile with each other, as I do. As far as the mere enunciation of the principle of natural selection is concerned, it is quite immaterial whether or not Professor Owen preceded me, for both of us, as shown in this historical sketch, were long ago preceded by Dr. Wells and Mr. Matthew.

M. Isidore Geoffroy Saint-Hilaire, in his lectures delivered in 1850 (of which a Résumé appeared in the 'Revue et Mag. de Zoolog.,' Jan. 1851), briefly gives his reason for believing that specific characters "sont fixés, pour chaque espèce, tant qu'elle se perpétue au milieu des mêmes circonstances: ils se modifient, si les circonstances ambiantes viennent à changer." "En-résumé, *l'observation* des animaux sauvages démontre déjà la variabilité *limitée* des espèces. Les *expériences* sur les animaux sauvages, devenus domestiques, et sur les animaux domestiques redevenus sauvages, la démontrent plus clairement encore. Ces mêmes expériences prouvent, de plus, que les différences produites peuvent être de *valeur générique*."[4]

---

4. "are fixed, for each species, as long as it remains in the same environment: they will change if the environment changes" "To sum up, *observation* of wild animals demonstrates a *limited* variability in species. *Experiments* on wild animals that have been domesticated, and of domestic animals returned to the wild state, demonstrate it even more clearly. These experiences prove further that the differences produced can be of *general value*." [Editor].

In his 'Hist. Nat. Générale' (tom. ii. p. 430, 1859) he amplifies analogous conclusions.

From a circular lately issued it appears that Dr. Freke, in 1851 ('Dublin Medical Press,' p. 322), propounded the doctrine that all organic beings have descended from one primordial form. His grounds of belief and treatment of the subject are wholly different from mine; but as Dr. Freke has now (1861) published his Essay on the 'Origin of Species by means of Organic Affinity,' the difficult attempt to give any idea of his views would be superfluous on my part.

Mr. Herbert Spencer, in an Essay (originally published in the 'Leader,' March, 1852, and republished in his 'Essays,' in 1858), has contrasted the theories of the Creation and the Development of organic beings with remarkable skill and force. He argues from the analogy of domestic productions, from the changes which the embryos of many species undergo, from the difficulty of distinguishing species and varieties, and from the principle of general gradation, that species have been modified; and he attributes the modification to the change of circumstances. The author (1855) has also treated Psychology on the principle of the necessary acquirement of each mental power and capacity by gradation.

In 1852 M. Naudin, a distinguished botanist, expressly stated, in an admirable paper on the Origin of Species ('Revue Horticole,' p. 102; since partly republished in the 'Nouvelles Archives du Muséum,' tom. i. p. 171), his belief that species are formed in an analogous manner as varieties are under cultivation; and the latter process he attributes to man's power of selection. But he does not show how selection acts under nature. He believes, like Dean Herbert, that species, when nascent, were more plastic than at present. He lays weight on what he calls the principle of finality, "puissance mystérieuse, indéterminée; fatalité pour les uns; pour les autres, volonté providentielle, dont l'action incessante sur les êtres vivants détermine, à toutes les époques de l'existence du monde, la forme, le volume, et la durée de chacun d'eux, en raison de sa destinée dans l'ordre de choses dont il fait partie. C'est cette puissance qui harmonise chaque membre à l'ensemble, en l'appropriant à la fonction qu'il doit remplir dans l'organisme général de la nature, fonction qui est pour lui sa raison d'être."[5]

In 1853 a celebrated geologist, Count Keyserling ('Bulletin de la Soc. Géolog.,' 2nd Ser., tom x. p. 357), suggested that as new diseases, supposed

---

5. From references in Bronn's 'Untersuchungen über die Entwickelungs-Gesetze,' it appears that the celebrated botanist and palaeontologist Unger published, in 1852, his belief that species undergo development and modification. Dalton, likewise, in Pander and Dalton's work on Fossil Sloths, expressed, in 1821, a similar belief. Similar views have, as is well known, been maintained by Oken in his mystical 'Natur-Philosophie.' From other references in Godron's work 'Sur l'Espèce,' it seems that Bory St. Vincent, Burdach, Poiret, and Fries, have all admitted that new species are continually being produced.

I may add, that of the thirty-four authors named in this Historical Sketch, who believe in the modification of species, or at least disbelieve in separate acts of creation, twenty-seven have written on special branches of natural history or geology.

"A force that is mysterious and indeterminate: fate for one, providential will for another; its unceasing action on living beings determines, at all periods of the world's existence, the form, the number, and the duration of each of them, by reason of its destiny in the order of things of which it is a part. It is this power that integrates each part to the whole, assigning it the function that it must perform in the natural order of things, a function that is its *raison d'être*." [Editor] to have been caused by some miasma, have arisen and spread over the world, so at certain periods the germs of existing species may have been chemically affected by circumambient molecules of a particular nature, and thus have given rise to new forms.

In this same year, 1853, Dr. Schaaffhausen published an excellent pamphlet ('Verhand. des Naturhist. Vereins der Preuss. Rheinlands,' &c.), in which he maintains the development of organic forms on the earth. He infers that many species have kept true for long periods, whereas a few have become modified. The distinction of species he explains by the destruction of intermediate graduated forms. "Thus living plants and animals are not separated from the extinct by new creations, but are to be regarded as their descendants through continued reproduction."

A well-known French botanist, M. Lecoq, writes in 1854 (Etudes sur Géograph. Bot.,' tom. i. p. 250), "On voit que nos recherches sur la fixité ou la variation de l'espèce, nous conduisent directement aux idées émises, par deux hommes justement célèbres, Geoffroy Saint-Hilaire et Goethe."[6] Some other passages scattered through M. Lecoq's large work, make it a little doubtful how far he extends his views on the modification of species.

The 'Philosophy of Creation' has been treated in a masterly manner by the Rev. Baden Powell, in his 'Essays on the Unity of Worlds,' 1855. Nothing can be more striking than the manner in which he shows that the introduction of new species is "a regular, not a casual phenomenon," or, as Sir John Herschel expresses it, "a natural in contradistinction to a miraculous process."

The third volume of the 'Journal of the Linnean Society' contains papers, read July 1st, 1858, by Mr. Wallace and myself, in which, as stated in the introductory remarks to this volume, the theory of Natural Selection is promulgated by Mr. Wallace with admirable force and clearness.

Von Baer, towards whom all zoologists feel so profound a respect, expressed about the year 1859 (see Prof. Rudolph Wagner, "Zoologisch-Anthropologische Untersuchungen,' 1861, s. 51) his conviction, chiefly grounded on the laws of geographical distribution, that forms now perfectly distinct have descended from a single parent-form.

In June, 1859, Professor Huxley gave a lecture before the Royal Institution on the 'Persistent Types of Animal Life.' Referring to such cases, he remarks, "It is difficult to comprehend the meaning of such facts as these, if we suppose that each species of animal and plant, or each great type of organisation, was formed and placed upon the surface of the globe at long intervals by a distinct act of creative power; and it is well to recollect that such an assumption is as unsupported by tradition or revelation as it is opposed to the general analogy of nature. If, on the other hand, we view 'Persistent Types' in relation to that hypothesis which supposes the species living at any time to be the result of the gradual modification of preexisting species, a hypothesis which, though unproven, and sadly damaged by some of its supporters, is yet the only one to which physiology lends any countenance; their existence would seem to show that the amount of modifi-

6. "Thus our research on the fixity or the variation of species leads us directly to ideas put forth by two justly celebrated men, Geoffroy Saint-Hilaire and Goethe." [Editor]

cation which living beings have undergone during geological time is but very small in relation to the whole series of changes which they have suffered."

In December, 1859, Dr. Hooker published his 'Introduction to the Australian Flora.' In the first part of this great work he admits the truth of the descent and modification of species, and supports this doctrine by many original observations.

The first edition of this work was published on November 24th, 1859, and the second edition on January 7th, 1860.

The Origin of Species (1859)†

Introduction

When on board H.M.S. 'Beagle,' as naturalist, I was much struck with certain facts in the distribution of the inhabitants of South America, and in the geological relations of the present to the past inhabitants of that continent. These facts seemed to me to throw some light on the origin of species—that mystery of mysteries, as it has been called by one of our greatest philosophers. On my return home, it occurred to me, in 1837, that something might perhaps be made out on this question by patiently accumulating and reflecting on all sorts of facts which could possibly have any bearing on it. After five years' work I allowed myself to speculate on the subject, and drew up some short notes; these I enlarged in 1844 into a sketch of the conclusions, which then seemed to me probable: from that period to the present day I have steadily pursued the same object. I hope that I may be excused for entering on these personal details, as I give them to show that I have not been hasty in coming to a decision.

My work is now nearly finished; but as it will take me two or three more years to complete it, and as my health is far from strong, I have been urged to publish this Abstract. I have more especially been induced to do this, as Mr. Wallace, who is now studying the natural history of the Malay archipelago, has arrived at almost exactly the same general conclusions that I have on the origin of species. Last year he sent to me a memoir on this subject, with a request that I would forward it to Sir Charles Lyell, who sent it to the Linnean Society, and it is published in the third volume of the Journal of that Society. Sir C. Lyell and Dr. Hooker, who both knew of my work—the latter having read my sketch of 1844—honoured me by thinking it advisable to publish, with Mr. Wallace's excellent memoir, some brief extracts from my manuscripts.

This Abstract, which I now publish, must necessarily be imperfect. I cannot here give references and authorities for my several statements; and I must trust to the reader reposing some confidence in my accuracy. No doubt errors will have crept in, though I hope I have always been cautious in trusting to good authorities alone. I can here give only the general conclusions at which I have arrived, with a few facts in illustration, but which, I hope, in most cases will suffice. No one can feel more sensible than I do of the necessity of hereafter publishing in detail all the facts, with references, on which my conclusions have been grounded; and I hope in a future work to do this. For I am well aware that scarcely a single point is discussed in this volume on which facts cannot be adduced, often apparently leading to conclusions directly opposite to those at which I have arrived. A fair result can be obtained only by fully stating and balancing the facts and arguments on both sides of each question; and this cannot possibly be here done.

† The text is excerpted from the first edition of *The Origin of Species* (London, 1859). Darwin's title for the first edition of the book was *On the Origin of Species*, but he dropped the *On* in the sixth (and last) edition of his lifetime, and the shorter title has been commonly used ever since.

I much regret that want of space prevents my having the satisfaction of acknowledging the generous assistance which I have received from very many naturalists, some of them personally unknown to me. I cannot, however, let this opportunity pass without expressing my deep obligations to Dr. Hooker, who for the last fifteen years has aided me in every possible way by his large stores of knowledge and his excellent judgment.

In considering the Origin of Species, it is quite conceivable that a naturalist, reflecting on the mutual affinities of organic beings, on their embryological relations, their geographical distribution, geological succession, and other such facts, might come to the conclusion that each species had not been independently created, but had descended, like varieties, from other species. Nevertheless, such a conclusion, even if well founded, would be unsatisfactory, until it could be shown how the innumerable species inhabiting this world have been modified, so as to acquire that perfection of structure and coadaptation which most justly excites our admiration. Naturalists continually refer to external conditions, such as climate, food, &c., as the only possible cause of variation. In one very limited sense, as we shall hereafter see, this may be true; but it is preposterous to attribute to mere external conditions, the structure, for instance, of the woodpecker, with its feet, tail, beak, and tongue, so admirably adapted to catch insects under the bark of trees. In the case of the misseltoe, which draws its nourishment from certain trees, which has seeds that must be transported by certain birds, and which has flowers with separate sexes absolutely requiring the agency of certain insects to bring pollen from one flower to the other, it is equally preposterous to account for the structure of this parasite, with its relations to several distinct organic beings, by the effects of external conditions, or of habit, or of the volition of the plant itself.

The author of the 'Vestiges of Creation' would, I presume, say that, after a certain unknown number of generations, some bird had given birth to a woodpecker, and some plant to the misseltoe, and that these had been produced perfect as we now see them; but this assumption seems to me to be no explanation, for it leaves the case of the coadaptations of organic beings to each other and to their physical conditions of life, untouched and unexplained.

It is, therefore, of the highest importance to gain a clear insight into the means of modification and coadaptation. At the commencement of my observations it seemed to me probable that a careful study of domesticated animals and of cultivated plants would offer the best chance of making out this obscure problem. Nor have I been disappointed; in this and in all other perplexing cases I have invariably found that our knowledge, imperfect though it be, of variation under domestication, afforded the best and safest clue. I may venture to express my conviction of the high value of such studies, although they have been very commonly neglected by naturalists.

From these considerations, I shall devote the first chapter of this Abstract to Variation under Domestication. We shall thus see that a large amount of hereditary modification is at least possible; and, what is equally or more important, we shall see how great is the power of man in accumulating by his Selection successive slight variations. I will then pass on to the variability of species in a state of nature; but I shall, unfortunately, be compelled to treat this subject far too briefly, as it can be treated properly only by giving long catalogues of facts. We shall, however, be enabled to discuss what circumstances are most favourable to variation. In the next chapter the Struggle for Existence amongst all organic beings throughout the world, which inevitably follows from their high geometrical powers of increase, will be treated of. This is the doctrine of Malthus, applied to the whole animal and vegetable kingdoms. As many more individuals of each species are born than can possibly survive; and as, consequently, there is a frequently recurring struggle for existence, it follows that any being, if it vary however slightly in any manner profitable to itself, under the complex and sometimes varying conditions of life, will have a better chance of surviving, and thus be *naturally selected*. From the strong principle of inheritance, any selected variety will tend to propagate its new and modified form.

This fundamental subject of Natural Selection will be treated at some length in the fourth chapter; and we shall then see how Natural Selection almost inevitably causes much Extinction of the less improved forms of life, and induces what I have called Divergence of Character. In the next chapter I shall discuss the complex and little known laws of variation and of correlation of growth. In the four succeeding chapters, the most apparent and gravest difficulties on the theory will be given: namely, first, the difficulties of transitions, or in understanding how a simple being or a simple organ can be changed and perfected into a highly developed being or elaborately constructed organ; secondly, the subject of Instinct, or the mental powers of animals; thirdly, Hybridism, or the infertility of species and the fertility of varieties when intercrossed; and fourthly, the imperfection of the Geological Record. In the next chapter I shall consider the geological succession of organic beings throughout time; in the eleventh and twelfth, their geographical distribution throughout space; in the thirteenth, their classification or mutual affinities, both when mature and in an embryonic condition. In the last chapter I shall give a brief recapitulation of the whole work, and a few concluding remarks.

No one ought to feel surprise at much remaining as yet unexplained in regard to the origin of species and varieties, if he makes due allowance for our profound ignorance in regard to the mutual relations of all the beings which live around us. Who can explain why one species ranges widely and is very numerous, and why another allied species has a narrow range and is rare? Yet these relations are of the highest importance, for they determine the present welfare, and, as I believe, the future success and modification of every inhabitant of this world. Still less do we know of the mutual relations of the innumerable inhabitants of the world during the many past geological epochs in its history. Although much remains obscure, and will long remain obscure, I can entertain no doubt, after the most deliberate study and dispassionate judgment of which I am capable, that the view which most naturalists entertain, and which I formerly entertained—namely, that each species has been independently created— is erroneous. I am fully convinced that species are not immutable; but that those belonging to what are called the same genera are lineal descendants of some other and generally extinct species, in the same manner as the acknowledged varieties of any one species are the descendants of that species. Furthermore, I am convinced that Natural Selection has been the main but not exclusive means of modification.

Chapter I. *Variation under Domestication*

Causes of Variability—Effects of Habit—Correlation of Growth—Inheritance—Character of Domestic Varieties—Difficulty of distinguishing between Varieties and Species—Origin of Domestic Varieties from one or more Species—Domestic Pigeons, their Differences and Origin—Principle of Selection anciently followed, its Effects—Methodical and Unconscious Selection—Unknown Origin of our Domestic Productions—Circumstances favourable to Man's power of Selection.

When we look to the individuals of the same variety or sub-variety of our older cultivated plants and animals, one of the first points which strikes us, is, that they generally differ much more from each other, than do the individuals of any one species or variety in a state of nature. When we reflect on the vast diversity of the plants and animals which have been cultivated, and which have varied during all ages under the most different climates and treatment, I think we are driven to conclude that this greater variability is simply due to our domestic productions having been raised under conditions of life not so uniform as, and somewhat different from, those to which the parent-species have been exposed under nature. There is, also, I think, some probability in the view propounded by Andrew Knight, that this variability may be partly connected with excess of food. It seems pretty clear that organic beings must be exposed during several generations to the new conditions of life to cause any appreciable amount of variation; and that when the organisation has once begun to vary, it generally continues to vary for many generations. No case is on record of a variable being ceasing to be variable under cultivation. Our oldest cultivated plants, such as wheat, still often yield new varieties: our oldest domesticated animals are still capable of rapid improvement or modification.

* * *

The result of the various, quite unknown, or dimly seen laws of variation is infinitely complex and diversified. It is well worth while carefully to study the several treatises published on some of our old cultivated plants, as on the hyacinth, potato, even the dahlia, &c.; and it is really surprising to note the endless points in structure and constitution in which the varieties and subvarieties differ slightly from each other. The whole organisation seems to have become plastic, and tends to depart in some small degree from that of the parental type.

Any variation which is not inherited is unimportant for us. But the number and diversity of inheritable deviations of structure, both those of slight and those of considerable physiological importance, is endless. Dr. Prosper Lucas's treatise, in two large volumes, is the fullest and the best on this subject. No breeder doubts how strong is the tendency to inheritance: like produces like is his fundamental belief: doubts have been thrown on this principle by theoretical writers alone. When a deviation appears not unfrequently, and we see it in the father and child, we cannot tell whether it may not be due to the same original cause acting on both; but when amongst individuals, apparently exposed to the same conditions, any very rare deviation, due to some extraordinary combination of circumstances, appears in the parent—say, once amongst several million individuals—and it reappears in the child, the mere doctrine of chances almost compels us to attribute its reappearance to inheritance. Every one must have heard of cases of albinism, prickly skin, hairy bodies, &c., appearing in several members of the same family. If strange and rare deviations of structure are truly inherited, less strange and commoner deviations may be freely admitted to be inheritable. Perhaps the correct way of viewing the whole subject, would be, to look at the inheritance of every character whatever as the rule, and non-inheritance as the anomaly.

The laws governing inheritance are quite unknown; no one can say why the same peculiarity in different individuals of the same species, and in individuals of different species, is sometimes inherited and sometimes not so; why the child often reverts in certain characters to its grandfather or grandmother or other much more remote ancestor; why a peculiarity is often transmitted from one sex to both sexes, or to one sex alone, more commonly but not exclusively to the like sex. It is a fact of some little importance to us, that peculiarities appearing in the males of our domestic breeds are often transmitted either exclusively, or in a much greater degree, to males alone. A much more important rule, which I think may be trusted, is that, at whatever period of life a peculiarity first appears, it tends to appear in the offspring at a corresponding age, though sometimes earlier. In many cases this could not be otherwise: thus the inherited peculiarities in the horns of cattle could appear only in the offspring when nearly mature; peculiarities in the silkworm are known to appear at the corresponding caterpillar or cocoon stage. But hereditary diseases and some other facts make me believe that the rule has a wider extension, and that when there is no apparent reason why a peculiarity should appear at any particular age, yet that it does tend to appear in the offspring at the same period at which it first appeared in the parent. I believe this rule to be of the highest importance in explaining the laws of embryology. These remarks are of course confined to the first *appearance* of the peculiarity, and not to its primary cause, which may have acted on the ovules or male element; in nearly the same manner as in the crossed offspring from a short-horned cow by a long-horned bull, the greater length of horn, though appearing late in life, is clearly due to the male element.

*   *   *

When we look to the hereditary varieties or races of our domestic animals and plants, and compare them with species closely allied together, we generally perceive in each domestic race, as already remarked, less uniformity of character than in true species. Domestic races of the same species, also, often have a somewhat monstrous character; by which I mean, that, although differing from each other, and from the other species of the same genus, in several trifling respects, they often differ in an extreme degree in some one part, both when compared one with another, and more especially when compared with all the species in nature to which they are nearest allied. With these exceptions (and with that of the perfect fertility of varieties when crossed,—a subject hereafter to be discussed), domestic races of the same species differ from each other in the same manner as, only in most cases in a lesser degree than, do closely-allied species of the same genus in a state of nature. I think this must be admitted, when we find that there are hardly any domestic races, either amongst animals or plants, which have not been ranked by some competent judges as mere varieties, and by other competent judges as the descendants of aboriginally distinct species. If any marked distinction existed between domestic races and species, this source of doubt could not so perpetually recur. It has often been stated that domestic races do not differ from each other in characters of generic value. I think it could be shown that this statement is hardly correct; but naturalists differ most widely in determining what characters are of generic value; all such valuations being at present empirical. Moreover, on the view of the origin of genera which I shall presently give, we have no right to expect often to meet with generic differences in our domesticated productions.

When we attempt to estimate the amount of structural difference between the domestic races of the same species, we are soon involved in doubt, from not knowing whether they have descended from one or several parent-species. This point, if it could be cleared up, would be interesting; if, for instance, it could be shown that the greyhound, bloodhound, terrier, spaniel, and bull-dog, which we all know propagate their kind so truly, were the offspring of any single species, then such facts would have great weight in making us doubt about the immutability of the many very closely allied and natural species—for instance, of the many foxes—inhabiting different quarters of the world. I do not believe, as we shall presently see, that all our dogs have descended from any one wild species; but, in the case of some other domestic races, there is presumptive, or even strong, evidence in favour of this view.

*   *   *

ON THE BREEDS OF THE DOMESTIC PIGEON

Believing that it is always best to study some special group, I have, after deliberation, taken up domestic pigeons. I have kept every breed which I could purchase or obtain, and have been most kindly favoured with skins from several quarters of the world, more especially by the Hon. W. Elliot from India, and by the Hon. C. Murray from Persia. Many treatises in different languages have been published on pigeons, and some of them are very important, as being of considerable antiquity. I have associated with several eminent fanciers, and have been permitted to join two of the

London Pigeon Clubs. The diversity of the breeds is something astonishing. Compare the English carrier and the short-faced tumbler, and see the wonderful difference in their beaks, entailing corresponding differences in their skulls. The carrier, more especially the male bird, is also remarkable from the wonderful development of the carunculated skin about the head, and this is accompanied by greatly elongated eyelids, very large external orifices to the nostrils, and a wide gape of mouth. The short-faced tumbler has a beak in outline almost like that of a finch; and the common tumbler has the singular and strictly inherited habit of flying at a great height in a compact flock, and tumbling in the air head over heels. The runt is a bird of great size, with long, massive beak and large feet; some of the sub-breeds of runts have very long necks, others very long wings and tails, others singularly short tails. The barb is allied to the carrier, but, instead of a very long beak, has a very short and very broad one. The pouter has a much elongated body, wings, and legs; and its enormously developed crop, which it glories in inflating, may well excite astonishment and even laughter. The turbit has a very short and conical beak, with a line of reversed feathers down the breast; and it has the habit of continually expanding slightly the upper part of the œsophagus. The Jacobin has the feathers so much reversed along the back of the neck that they form a hood, and it has, proportionally to its size, much elongated wing and tail feathers. The trumpeter and laugher, as their names express, utter a very different coo from the other breeds. The fantail has thirty or even forty tail-feathers, instead of twelve or fourteen, the normal number in all members of the great pigeon family; and these feathers are kept expanded, and are carried so erect that in good birds the head and tail touch; the oil-gland is quite aborted. Several other less distinct breeds might have been specified.

In the skeletons of the several breeds, the development of the bones of the face in length and breadth and curvature differs enormously. The shape, as well as the breadth and length of the ramus of the lower jaw, varies in a highly remarkable manner. The number of the caudal and sacral vertebræ vary; as does the number of the ribs, together with their relative breadth and the presence of processes. The size and shape of the apertures in the sternum are highly variable; so is the degree of divergence and relative size of the two arms of the furcula. The proportional width of the gape of mouth, the proportional length of the eyelids, of the orifice of the nostrils, of the tongue (not always in strict correlation with the length of beak), the size of the crop and of the upper part of the œsophagus; the development and abortion of the oil-gland; the number of the primary wing and caudal feathers; the relative length of wing and tail to each other and to the body; the relative length of leg and of the feet; the number of scutellæ on the toes, the development of skin between the toes, are all points of structure which are variable. The period at which the perfect plumage is acquired varies, as does the state of the down with which the nestling birds are clothed when hatched. The shape and size of the eggs vary. The manner of flight differs remarkably; as does in some breeds the voice and disposition. Lastly, in certain breeds, the males and females have come to differ to a slight degree from each other.

Altogether at least a score of pigeons might be chosen, which if shown to an ornithologist, and he were told that they were wild birds, would certainly, I think, be ranked by him as well-defined species. Moreover, I do not believe that any ornithologist would place the English carrier, the short-faced tumbler, the runt, the barb, pouter, and fantail in the same genus; more especially as in each of these breeds several truly-inherited sub-breeds, or species as he might have called them, could be shown him.

Great as the differences are between the breeds of pigeons, I am fully convinced that the common opinion of naturalists is correct, namely, that all have descended from the rock-pigeon (Columba livia), including under this term several geographical races or sub-species, which differ from each other in the most trifling respects.

*   *   *

From these several reasons, namely, the improbability of man having formerly got seven or eight supposed species of pigeons to breed freely under domestication; these supposed species being quite unknown in a wild state, and their becoming nowhere feral; these species having very abnormal characters in certain respects, as compared with all other Columbidæ, though so like in most other respects to the rock-pigeon; the blue colour and various marks occasionally appearing in all the breeds, both when kept pure and when crossed; the mongrel offspring being perfectly fertile;—from these several reasons, taken together, I can feel no doubt that all our domestic breeds have descended from the Columba livia with its geographical sub-species.

In favour of this view, I may add, firstly, that C. livia, or the rock-pigeon, has been found capable of domestication in Europe and in India; and that it agrees in habits and in a great number of points of structure with all the domestic breeds. Secondly, although an English carrier or short-faced tumbler differs immensely in certain characters from the rock-pigeon, yet by comparing the several sub-breeds of these breeds, more especially those brought from distant countries, we can make an almost perfect series between the extremes of structure. Thirdly, those characters which are mainly distinctive of each breed, for instance the wattle and length of beak of the carrier, the shortness of that of the tumbler, and the number of tail-feathers in the fantail, are in each breed eminently variable; and the explanation of this fact will be obvious when we come to treat of selection. Fourthly, pigeons have been watched, and tended with the utmost care, and loved by many people. They have been domesticated for thousands of years in several quarters of the world; the earliest known record of pigeons is in the fifth Ægyptian dynasty, about 3000 B.C., as was pointed out to me by Professor Lepsius; but Mr. Birch informs me that pigeons are given in a bill of fare in the previous dynasty. In the time of the Romans, as we hear from Pliny, immense prices were given for pigeons; "nay, they are come to this pass, that they can reckon up their pedigree and race." Pigeons were much valued by Akber Khan in India, about the year 1600; never less than 20,000 pigeons were taken with the court. "The monarchs of Iran and Turan sent him some very rare birds;" and, continues the courtly historian, "His Majesty by crossing the breeds, which method was never practised before, has improved them astonishingly." About this same period the Dutch were as eager about pigeons as were the old Romans. The paramount importance of these considerations in explaining the immense amount of variation which pigeons have undergone, will be obvious when we treat of Selection. We shall then, also, see how it is that the breeds so often have a somewhat monstrous character. It is also a most favourable circumstance for the production of distinct breeds, that male and female pigeons can be easily mated for life; and thus different breeds can be kept together in the same aviary.

I have discussed the probable origin of domestic pigeons at some, yet quite insufficient, length; because when I first kept pigeons and watched the several kinds, knowing well how true they bred, I felt fully as much difficulty in believing that they could ever have descended from a common parent, as any naturalist could in coming to a similar conclusion in regard to the many species of finches, or other large groups of birds, in nature. One circumstance has struck me much; namely, that all the breeders of the various domestic animals and the cultivators of plants, with whom I have ever conversed, or whose treatises I have read, are firmly convinced that the several breeds to which each has attended, are descended from so many aboriginally distinct species. Ask, as I have asked, a celebrated raiser of Hereford cattle, whether his cattle might not have descended from long-horns, and he will laugh you to scorn. I have never met a pigeon, or poultry, or duck, or rabbit fancier, who was not fully convinced that each main breed was descended from a distinct species. Van Mons, in his treatise on pears and apples, shows how utterly he disbelieves that the several sorts, for instance a Ribston-pippin or Codlin-apple, could ever have proceeded from the seeds of the same tree. Innumerable other examples could be given. The explanation, I think, is simple: from long-continued study they are strongly impressed with the differences between the several races; and though they well know that each race varies slightly, for they win their prizes by selecting such slight differences, yet they ignore all general arguments, and refuse to sum up in their minds slight differences accumulated during many successive generations. May not those naturalists who, knowing far less of the laws of inheritance than does the breeder, and knowing no more than he does of the intermediate links in the long lines of descent, yet admit that many of our domestic races have descended from the same parents—may they not learn a lesson of caution, when they deride the idea of species in a state of nature being lineal descendants of other species?

SELECTION

Let us now briefly consider the steps by which domestic races have been produced, either from one or from several allied species. Some little effect may, perhaps, be attributed to the direct action of the external conditions of life, and some little to habit; but he would be a bold man who would account by such agencies for the differences of a dray and race horse, a greyhound and bloodhound, a carrier and tumbler pigeon. One of the most remarkable features in our domesticated races is that we see in them adaptation, not indeed to the animal's or plant's own good, but to man's use or fancy. Some variations useful to him have probably arisen suddenly, or by one step; many botanists, for instance, believe that the fuller's teazle, with its hooks, which cannot be rivalled by any mechanical contrivance, is only a variety of the wild Dipsacus; and this amount of change may have suddenly arisen in a seedling. So it has probably been with the turn-spit dog; and this is known to have been the case with the ancon sheep. But when we compare the dray-horse and race-horse, the dromedary and camel, the various breeds of sheep fitted either for cultivated land or moun-tain pasture, with the wool of one breed good for one purpose, and that of another breed for another purpose; when we compare the many breeds of dogs, each good for man in very different ways; when we compare the game-cock, so pertinacious in battle, with other breeds so little quarrel-some, with "everlasting layers" which never desire to sit, and with the bantam so small and elegant; when we compare the host of agricultural, culinary, orchard, and flower-garden races of plants, most useful to man at different seasons and for different purposes, or so beautiful in his eyes, we must, I think, look further than to mere variability. We cannot suppose that all the breeds were suddenly produced as perfect and as useful as we now see them; indeed, in several cases, we know that this has not been their history. The key is man's power of accumulative selection: nature gives successive variations; man adds them up in certain directions useful to him. In this sense he may be said to make for himself useful breeds.

* * *

At the present time, eminent breeders try by methodical selection, with a distinct object in view, to make a new strain or sub-breed, superior to anything existing in the country. But, for our purpose, a kind of Selection, which may be called Unconscious, and which results from every one trying to possess and breed from the best individual animals, is more important. Thus, a man who intends keeping pointers naturally tries to get as good dogs as he can, and afterwards breeds from his own best dogs, but he has no wish or expectation of permanently altering the breed. Nevertheless I cannot doubt that this process, continued during centuries, would improve and modify any breed, in the same way as Bakewell, Collins, &c., by this very same process, only carried on more methodically, did greatly modify, even during their own lifetimes, the forms and qualities of their cattle. Slow and insensible changes of this kind could never be recognised unless actual measurements or careful drawings of the breeds in question had been made long ago, which might serve for comparison. In some cases, however, unchanged or but little changed individuals of the same breed may be found in less civilised districts, where the breed has been less improved. There is reason to believe that King Charles's spaniel has been unconsciously modified to a large extent since the time of that monarch. Some highly competent authorities are convinced that the setter is directly derived from the spaniel, and has probably been slowly altered from it. It is known that the English pointer has been greatly changed within the last century, and in this case the change has, it is believed, been chiefly effected by crosses with the fox-hound; but what concerns us is, that the change has been effected unconsciously and gradually, and yet so effectually, that, though the old Spanish pointer certainly came from Spain, Mr. Borrow has not seen, as I am informed by him, any native dog in Spain like our pointer.

By a similar process of selection, and by careful training, the whole body of English racehorses have come to surpass in fleetness and size the parent Arab stock, so that the latter, by the regulations for the Goodwood Races, are favoured in the weights they carry. Lord Spencer and others have shown how the cattle of England have increased in weight and in early maturity, compared with the stock formerly kept in this country. By comparing the accounts given in old pigeon treatises of carriers and tumblers with these breeds as now existing in Britain, India, and Persia, we can, I think, clearly trace the stages through which they have insensibly passed, and come to differ so greatly from the rock-pigeon.

*　*　*

To sum up on the origin of our Domestic Races of animals and plants. I believe that the conditions of life, from their action on the reproductive system, are so far of the highest importance as causing variability. I do not believe that variability is an inherent and necessary contingency, under all circumstances, with all organic beings, as some authors have thought. The effects of variability are modified by various degrees of inheritance and of reversion. Variability is governed by many unknown laws, more especially by that of correlation of growth. Something may be attributed to the direct action of the conditions of life. Something must be attributed to use and disuse. The final result is thus rendered infinitely complex. In some cases, I do not doubt that the intercrossing of species, aboriginally distinct, has played an important part in the origin of our domestic productions. When in any country several domestic breeds have once been established, their occasional intercrossing, with the aid of selection, has, no doubt, largely aided in the formation of new sub-breeds; but the importance of the crossing of varieties has, I believe, been greatly exaggerated, both in regard to animals and to those plants which are propagated by seed. In plants which are temporarily propagated by cuttings, buds, &c., the importance of the crossing both of distinct species and of varieties is immense; for the cultivator here quite disregards the extreme variability both of hybrids and mongrels, and the frequent sterility of hybrids; but the cases of plants not propagated by seed are of little importance to us, for their endurance is only temporary. Over all these causes of Change I am convinced that the accumulative action of Selection, whether applied methodically and more quickly, or unconsciously and more slowly, but more efficiently, is by far the predominant Power.

Chapter II. Variation under Nature

Variability—Individual differences—Doubtful species—Wide ranging, much diffused, and common species vary most—Species of the larger genera in any country vary more than the species of the smaller genera—Many of the species of the larger genera resemble varieties in being very closely, but unequally, related to each other, and in having restricted ranges.

Before applying the principles arrived at in the last chapter to organic beings in a state of nature, we must briefly discuss whether these latter are subject to any variation. To treat this subject at all properly, a long catalogue of dry facts should be given; but these I shall reserve for my future work. Nor shall I here discuss the various definitions which have been given of the term species. No one definition has as yet satisfied all naturalists; yet every naturalist knows vaguely what he means when he speaks of a species. Generally the term includes the unknown element of a distinct act of creation. The term "variety" is almost equally difficult to define; but here community of descent is almost universally implied, though it can rarely be proved.

*　*　*

Alph. De Candolle and others have shown that plants which have very wide ranges generally present varieties; and this might have been expected, as they become exposed to diverse physical conditions, and as they come into competition (which, as we shall hereafter see, is a far more important circumstance) with different sets of organic beings. But my tables further show that, in any limited country, the species which are most common, that is abound most in individuals, and the species which are most widely diffused within their own country (and this is a different consideration from wide range, and to a certain extent from commonness), often give rise to varieties sufficiently well-marked to have been recorded in botanical works. Hence it is the most flourishing, or, as they may be called, the dominant species,—those which range widely over the world, are the most diffused in their own country, and are the most numerous in individuals,—which oftenest produce well-marked varieties, or, as I consider them, incipient species. And this, perhaps, might have been anticipated; for, as varieties, in order to become in any degree permanent, necessarily have to struggle with the other inhabitants of the country, the species which are already dominant will be the most likely to yield offspring which, though in some slight degree modified, will still inherit those advantages that enabled their parents to become dominant over their compatriots.

*　*　*

Finally, then, varieties have the same general characters as species, for they cannot be distinguished from species,—except, firstly, by the discovery of intermediate linking forms, and the occurrence of such links cannot affect the actual characters of the forms which they connect; and except, secondly, by a certain amount of difference, for two forms, if differing very little, are generally ranked as varieties, notwithstanding that intermediate linking forms have not been discovered; but the amount of difference considered necessary to give to two forms the rank of species is quite indefinite. In genera having more than the average number of species in any country, the species of these genera have more than the average number of varieties. In large genera the species are apt to be closely, but unequally, allied together, forming little clusters round certain species. Species very closely allied to other species apparently have restricted ranges. In all these several respects the species of large genera present a strong analogy with varieties. And we can clearly understand these analogies, if species have once existed as varieties, and have thus originated: whereas, these analogies are utterly inexplicable if each species has been independently created.

We have, also, seen that it is the most flourishing and dominant species of the larger genera which on an average vary most; and varieties, as we shall hereafter see, tend to become converted into new and distinct species. The larger genera thus tend to become larger; and throughout nature the forms of life which are now dominant tend to become still more dominant by leaving many modified and dominant descendants. But by steps hereafter to be explained, the larger genera also tend to break up into smaller genera. And thus, the forms of life throughout the universe become divided into groups subordinate to groups.

⤳ Chapter III. Struggle for Existence

Bears on natural selection—The term used in a wide sense—Geometrical powers of increase—Rapid increase of naturalised animals and plants—Nature of the checks to increase—Competition universal—Effects of climate—Protection from the number of individuals—Complex relations of all animals and plants throughout nature—Struggle for life most severe between individuals and varieties of the same species; often severe between species of the same genus—The relation of organism to organism the most important of all relations.

Before entering on the subject of this chapter, I must make a few preliminary remarks, to show how the struggle for existence bears on Natural Selection. It has been seen in the last chapter that amongst organic beings in a state of nature there is some individual variability; indeed I am not aware that this has ever been disputed. It is immaterial for us whether a multitude of doubtful forms be called species or sub-species or varieties; what rank, for instance, the two or three hundred doubtful forms of British plants are entitled to hold, if the existence of any well-marked varieties be admitted. But the mere existence of individual variability and of some few well-marked varieties, though necessary as the foundation for the work, helps us but little in understanding how species arise in nature. How have all those exquisite adaptations of one part of the organisation to another part, and to the conditions of life, and of one distinct organic being to another being, been perfected? We see these beautiful co-adaptations most plainly in the woodpecker and missletoe; and only a little less plainly in the humblest parasite which clings to the hairs of a quadruped or feathers of a bird; in the structure of the beetle which dives through the water; in the plumed seed which is wafted by the gentlest breeze; in short, we see beautiful adaptations everywhere and in every part of the organic world.

Again, it may be asked, how is it that varieties, which I have called incipient species, become ultimately converted into good and distinct species, which in most cases obviously differ from each other far more than do the varieties of the same species? How do those groups of species, which constitute what are called distinct genera, and which differ from each other more than do the species of the same genus, arise? All these results, as we shall more fully see in the next chapter, follow inevitably from the struggle for life. Owing to this struggle for life, any variation, however slight and from whatever cause proceeding, if it be in any degree profitable to an individual of any species, in its infinitely complex relations to other organic beings and to external nature, will tend to the preservation of that individual, and will generally be inherited by its offspring. The offspring, also, will thus have a better chance of surviving, for, of the many individuals of any species which are periodically born, but a small number can survive. I have called this principle, by which each slight variation, if useful, is preserved, by the term of Natural Selection, in order to mark its relation to man's power of selection. We have seen that man by selection can certainly produce great results, and can adapt organic beings to his own uses, through the accumulation of slight but useful variations, given to him by the hand of Nature. But Natural Selection, as we shall hereafter see, is a power incessantly ready for action, and is as immeasurably superior to man's feeble efforts, as the works of Nature are to those of Art.

We will now discuss in a little more detail the struggle for existence. In my future work this subject shall be treated, as it well deserves, at much greater length. The elder De Candolle and Lyell have largely and philosophically shown that all organic beings are exposed to severe competition. In regard to plants, no one has treated this subject with more spirit and ability than W. Herbert, Dean of Manchester, evidently the result of his great horticultural knowledge. Nothing is easier than to admit in words the truth of the universal struggle for life, or more difficult—at least I have found it so—than constantly to bear this conclusion in mind. Yet unless it be thoroughly engrained in the mind, I am convinced that the whole economy of nature, with every fact on distribution, rarity, abundance, extinction, and variation, will be dimly seen or quite misunderstood. We behold the face of nature bright with gladness, we often see superabundance of food; we do not see, or we forget, that the birds which are idly singing round us mostly live on insects or seeds, and are thus constantly destroying life; or we forget how largely these songsters, or their eggs, or their nestlings, are destroyed by birds and beasts of prey; we do not always bear in mind, that though food may be now superabundant, it is not so at all seasons of each recurring year.

I should premise that I use the term Struggle for Existence in a large and metaphorical sense, including dependence of one being on another, and including (which is more important) not only the life of the individual, but success in leaving progeny. Two canine animals in a time of dearth, may be truly said to struggle with each other which shall get food and live. But a plant on the edge of a desert is said to struggle for life against the drought, though more properly it should be said to be dependent on the moisture. A plant which annually produces a thousand seeds, of which on an average only one comes to maturity, may be more truly said to struggle with the plants of the same and other kinds which already clothe the ground. The missletoe is dependent on the apple and a few other trees, but can only in a far-fetched sense be said to struggle with these trees, for if too many of these parasites grow on the same tree, it will languish and die. But several seedling missletoes, growing close together on the same branch, may more truly be said to struggle with each other. As the missle- toe is disseminated by birds, its existence depends on birds; and it may metaphorically be said to struggle with other fruit-bearing plants, in order to tempt birds to devour and thus disseminate its seeds rather than those of other plants. In these several senses, which pass into each other, I use for convenience sake the general term of struggle for existence.

A struggle for existence inevitably follows from the high rate at which all organic beings tend to increase. Every being, which during its natural lifetime produces several eggs or seeds, must suffer destruction during some period of its life, and during some season or occasional year, oth- erwise, on the principle of geometrical increase, its numbers would quickly become so inordinately great that no country could support the product. Hence, as more individuals are produced than can possibly survive, there must in every case be a struggle for existence, either one individual with another of the same species, or with the individuals of distinct species, or with the physical conditions of life. It is the doctrine of Malthus applied with manifold force to the whole animal and vegetable kingdoms; for in this case there can be no artificial increase of food, and no prudential restraint from marriage. Although some species may be now increasing, more or less rapidly, in numbers, all cannot do so, for the world would not hold them.

There is no exception to the rule that every organic being naturally increases at so high a rate, that if not destroyed, the earth would soon be covered by the progeny of a single pair. Even slow-breeding man has dou- bled in twenty-five years, and at this rate, in a few thousand years, there would literally not be standing room for his progeny. Linnæus has calcu- lated that if an annual plant produced only two seeds—and there is no plant so unproductive as this—and their seedlings next year produced two, and so on, then in twenty years there would be a million plants. The elephant is reckoned to be the slowest breeder of all known animals, and I have taken some pains to estimate its probable minimum rate of natural increase: it will be under the mark to assume that it breeds when thirty years old, and goes on breeding till ninety years old, bringing forth three pair of young in this interval; if this be so, at the end of the fifth century there would be alive fifteen million elephants, descended from the first pair.

But we have better evidence on this subject than mere theoretical cal- culations, namely, the numerous recorded cases of the astonishingly rapid increase of various animals in a state of nature, when circumstances have been favourable to them during two or three following seasons. Still more striking is the evidence from our domestic animals of many kinds which have run wild in several parts of the world: if the statements of the rate of increase of slow-breeding cattle and horses in South-America, and latterly in Australia, had not been well authenticated, they would have been quite incredible. So it is with plants: cases could be given of introduced plants which have become common throughout whole islands in a period of less than ten years. Several of the plants now most numerous over the wide plains of La Plata, clothing square leagues of surface almost to the exclusion of all other plants, have been introduced from Europe; and there are plants which now range in India, as I hear from Dr. Falconer, from Cape Comorin to the Himalaya, which have been imported from America since its discovery. In such cases, and endless instances could be given, no one supposes that the fertility of these animals or plants has been suddenly and temporarily increased in any sensible degree. The obvious explanation is that the conditions of life have been very favourable, and that there has consequently been less destruction of the old and young, and that nearly all the young have been enabled to breed. In such cases the geometrical ratio of increase, the result of which never fails to be surprising, simply explains the extraordinarily rapid increase and wide diffusion of naturalised productions in their new homes.

In a state of nature almost every plant produces seed, and amongst animals there are very few which do not annually pair. Hence we may confidently assert, that all plants and animals are tending to increase at a geometrical ratio, that all would most rapidly stock every station in which they could any how exist, and that the geometrical tendency to increase must be checked by destruction at some period of life. Our familiarity with the larger domestic animals tends, I think, to mislead us: we see no great destruction falling on them, and we forget that thousands are annually slaughtered for food, and that in a state of nature an equal number would have somehow to be disposed of.

The only difference between organisms which annually produce eggs or seeds by the thousand, and those which produce extremely few, is, that the slow-breeders would require a few more years to people, under favourable conditions, a whole district, let it be ever so large. The condor lays a couple of eggs and the ostrich a score, and yet in the same country the condor may be the more numerous of the two: the Fulmar petrel lays but one egg, yet it is believed to be the most numerous bird in the world. One fly deposits hundreds of eggs, and another, like the hippobosca, a single one; but this difference does not determine how many individuals of the two species can be supported in a district. A large number of eggs is of some importance to those species, which depend on a rapidly fluctuating amount of food, for it allows them rapidly to increase in number. But the real importance of a large number of eggs or seeds is to make up for much destruction at some period of life; and this period in the great majority of cases is an early one. If an animal can in any way protect its own eggs or young, a small number may be produced, and yet the average stock be fully kept up; but if many eggs or young are destroyed, many must be produced, or the species will become extinct. It would suffice to keep up the full number of a tree, which lived on an average for a thousand years, if a single seed were produced once in a thousand years, supposing that this seed were never destroyed, and could be ensured to germinate in a fitting place. So that in all cases, the average number of any animal or plant depends only indirectly on the number of its eggs or seeds.

In looking at Nature, it is most necessary to keep the foregoing considerations always in mind—never to forget that every single organic being around us may be said to be striving to the utmost to increase in numbers; that each lives by a struggle at some period of its life; that heavy destruction inevitably falls either on the young or old, during each generation or at recurrent intervals. Lighten any check, mitigate the destruction ever so little, and the number of the species will almost instantaneously increase to any amount. The face of Nature may be compared to a yielding surface, with ten thousand sharp wedges packed close together and driven inwards by incessant blows, sometimes one wedge being struck, and then another with greater force.

*   *   *

Chapter IV. Natural Selection

Natural Selection—its power compared with man's selection—its power on characters of trifling importance—its power at all ages and on both sexes—Sexual Selection— On the generality of intercrosses between individuals of the same species—Circumstances favourable and unfavourable to Natural Selection, namely, intercrossing, isolation, number of individuals—Slow action—Extinction caused by Natural Selection —Divergence of Character, related to the diversity of inhabitants of any small area, and to naturalisation—Action of Natural Selection, through Divergence of Character and Extinction, on the descendants from a common parent—Explains the Grouping of all organic beings.

How will the struggle for existence, discussed too briefly in the last chapter, act in regard to variation? Can the principle of selection, which we have seen is so potent in the hands of man, apply in nature? I think we shall see that it can act most effectually. Let it be borne in mind in what an endless number of strange peculiarities our domestic productions, and, in a lesser degree, those under nature, vary; and how strong the hereditary tendency is. Under domestication, it may be truly said that the whole organisation becomes in some degree plastic. Let it be borne in mind how infinitely complex and close-fitting are the mutual relations of all organic beings to each other and to their physical conditions of life. Can it, then, be thought improbable, seeing that variations useful to man have undoubtedly occurred, that other variations useful in some way to each being in the great and complex battle of life, should sometimes occur in the course of thousands of generations? If such do occur, can we doubt (remembering that many more individuals are born than can possibly survive) that individuals having any advantage, however slight, over others, would have the best chance of surviving and of procreating their kind? On the other hand, we may feel sure that any variation in the least degree injurious would be rigidly destroyed. This preservation of favourable variations and the rejection of injurious variations, I call Natural Selection. Variations neither useful nor injurious would not be affected by natural selection, and would be left a fluctuating element, as perhaps we see in the species called polymorphic.

We shall best understand the probable course of natural selection by taking the case of a country undergoing some physical change, for instance, of climate. The proportional numbers of its inhabitants would almost immediately undergo a change, and some species might become extinct. We may conclude, from what we have seen of the intimate and complex manner in which the inhabitants of each country are bound together, that any change in the numerical proportions of some of the inhabitants, independently of the change of climate itself, would most seriously affect many of the others. If the country were open on its borders, new forms would certainly immigrate, and this also would seriously disturb the relations of some of the former inhabitants. Let it be remembered how powerful the influence of a single introduced tree or mammal has been shown to be. But in the case of an island, or of a country partly surrounded by barriers, into which new and better adapted forms could not freely enter, we should then have places in the economy of nature which would assuredly be better filled up, if some of the original inhabitants were in some manner modified; for, had the area been open to immigration, these same places would have been seized on by intruders. In such case, every slight modification, which in the course of ages chanced to arise, and which in any way favoured the individuals of any of the species, by better adapting them to their altered conditions, would tend to be preserved; and natural selection would thus have free scope for the work of improvement.

We have reason to believe, as stated in the first chapter, that a change in the conditions of life, by specially acting on the reproductive system, causes or increases variability; and in the foregoing case the conditions of life are supposed to have undergone a change, and this would manifestly be favourable to natural selection, by giving a better chance of profitable variations occurring; and unless profitable variations do occur, natural selection can do nothing. Not that, as I believe, any extreme amount of variability is necessary; as man can certainly produce great results by adding up in any given direction mere individual differences, so could Nature, but far more easily, from having incomparably longer time at her disposal. Nor do I believe that any great physical change, as of climate, or any unusual degree of isolation to check immigration, is actually necessary to produce new and unoccupied places for natural selection to fill up by modifying and improving some of the varying inhabitants. For as all the inhabitants of each country are struggling together with nicely balanced forces, extremely slight modifications in the structure or habits of one inhabitant would often give it an advantage over others; and still further modifications of the same kind would often still further increase the advantage. No country can be named in which all the native inhabitants are now so perfectly adapted to each other and to the physical conditions under which they live, that none of them could anyhow be improved; for in all countries, the natives have been so far conquered by naturalised productions, that they have allowed foreigners to take firm possession of the land. And as foreigners have thus everywhere beaten some of the natives, we may safely conclude that the natives might have been modified with advantage, so as to have better resisted such intruders.

As man can produce and certainly has produced a great result by his methodical and unconscious means of selection, what may not nature effect? Man can act only on external and visible characters: nature cares nothing for appearances, except in so far as they may be useful to any being. She can act on every internal organ, on every shade of constitutional difference, on the whole machinery of life. Man selects only for his own good; Nature only for that of the being which she tends. Every selected character is fully exercised by her; and the being is placed under well-suited conditions of life. Man keeps the natives of many climates in the same country; he seldom exercises each selected character in some peculiar and fitting manner; he feeds a long and a short beaked pigeon on the same food; he does not exercise a long-backed or long-legged quadruped in any peculiar manner; he exposes sheep with long and short wool to the same climate. He does not allow the most vigorous males to struggle for the females. He does not rigidly destroy all inferior animals, but protects during each varying season, as far as lies in his power, all his productions. He often begins his selection by some half-monstrous form; or at least by some modification prominent enough to catch his eye, or to be plainly useful to him. Under nature, the slightest difference of structure or constitution may well turn the nicely-balanced scale in the struggle for life, and so be preserved. How fleeting are the wishes and efforts of man! how short his time! and consequently how poor will his products be, compared with those accumulated by nature during whole geological periods. Can we wonder, then, that nature's productions should be far "truer" in character than man's productions; that they should be infinitely better adapted to the most complex conditions of life, and should plainly bear the stamp of far higher workmanship?

It may be said that natural selection is daily and hourly scrutinising, throughout the world, every variation, even the slightest; rejecting that which is bad, preserving and adding up all that is good; silently and insensibly working, whenever and wherever opportunity offers, at the improvement of each organic being in relation to its organic and inorganic conditions of life. We see nothing of these slow changes in progress, until the hand of time has marked the long lapse of ages, and then so imperfect is our view into long past geological ages, that we only see that the forms of life are now different from what they formerly were.

Although natural selection can act only through and for the good of each being, yet characters and structures, which we are apt to consider as of very trifling importance, may thus be acted on. When we see leaf-eating insects green, and bark-feeders mottled-grey; the alpine ptarmigan white in winter, the red-grouse the colour of heather, and the black-grouse that of peaty earth, we must believe that these tints are of service to these birds and insects in preserving them from danger. Grouse, if not destroyed at some period of their lives, would increase in countless numbers; they are known to suffer largely from birds of prey; and hawks are guided by eyesight to their prey,—so much so, that on parts of the Continent persons are warned not to keep white pigeons, as being the most liable to destruction. Hence I can see no reason to doubt that natural selection might be most effective in giving the proper colour to each kind of grouse, and in keeping that colour, when once acquired, true and constant. Nor ought we to think that the occasional destruction of an animal of any particular colour would produce little effect: we should remember how essential it is in a flock of white sheep to destroy every lamb with the faintest trace of black. In plants the down on the fruit and the colour of the flesh are considered by botanists as characters of the most trifling importance: yet we hear from an excellent horticulturist, Downing, that in the United States smooth-skinned fruits suffer far more from a beetle, a curculio, than those with down; that purple plums suffer far more from a certain disease than yellow plums; whereas another disease attacks yellow-fleshed peaches far more than those with other coloured flesh. If, with all the aids of art, these slight differences make a great difference in cultivating the several varieties, assuredly, in a state of nature, where the trees would have to struggle with other trees and with a host of enemies, such differences would effectually settle which variety, whether a smooth or downy, a yellow or purple fleshed fruit, should succeed.

In looking at many small points of difference between species, which, as far as our ignorance permits us to judge, seem to be quite unimportant, we must not forget that climate, food, &c., probably produce some slight and direct effect. It is, however, far more necessary to bear in mind that there are many unknown laws of correlation of growth, which, when one part of the organisation is modified through variation, and the modifications are accumulated by natural selection for the good of the being, will cause other modifications, often of the most unexpected nature.

As we see that those variations which under domestication appear at any particular period of life, tend to reappear in the offspring at the same period;—for instance, in the seeds of the many varieties of our culinary and agricultural plants; in the caterpillar and cocoon stages of the varieties of the silkworm; in the eggs of poultry, and in the colour of the down of their chickens; in the horns of our sheep and cattle when nearly adult;— so in a state of nature, natural selection will be enabled to act on and modify organic beings at any age, by the accumulation of profitable variations at that age, and by their inheritance at a corresponding age. If it profit a plant to have its seeds more and more widely disseminated by the wind, I can see no greater difficulty in this being effected through natural selection, than in the cotton-planter increasing and improving by selection the down in the pods on his cotton-trees. Natural selection may modify and adapt the larva of an insect to a score of contingencies, wholly different from those which concern the mature insect. These modifications will no doubt affect, through the laws of correlation, the structure of the adult; and probably in the case of those insects which live only for a few hours, and which never feed, a large part of their structure is merely the correlated result of successive changes in the structure of their larvæ. So, conversely, modifications in the adult will probably often affect the structure of the larva; but in all cases natural selection will ensure that modifications consequent on other modifications at a different period of life, shall not be in the least degree injurious: for if they became so, they would cause the extinction of the species.

Natural selection will modify the structure of the young in relation to the parent, and of the parent in relation to the young. In social animals it will adapt the structure of each individual for the benefit of the community; if each in consequence profits by the selected change. What natural selection cannot do, is to modify the structure of one species, without giving it any advantage, for the good of another species; and though statements to this effect may be found in works of natural history, I cannot find one case which will bear investigation. A structure used only once in an animal's whole life, if of high importance to it, might be modified to any extent by natural selection; for instance, the great jaws possessed by certain insects, and used exclusively for opening the cocoon—or the hard tip to the beak of nestling birds, used for breaking the egg. It has been asserted, that of the best short-beaked tumbler-pigeons more perish in the egg than are able to get out of it; so that fanciers assist in the act of hatching. Now, if nature had to make the beak of a full-grown pigeon very short for the bird's own advantage, the process of modification would be very slow, and there would be simultaneously the most rigorous selection of the young birds within the egg, which had the most powerful and hardest beaks, for all with weak beaks would inevitably perish: or, more delicate and more easily broken shells might be selected, the thickness of the shell being known to vary like every other structure.

SEXUAL SELECTION

Inasmuch as peculiarities often appear under domestication in one sex and become hereditarily attached to that sex, the same fact probably occurs under nature, and if so, natural selection will be able to modify one sex in its functional relations to the other sex, or in relation to wholly different habits of life in the two sexes, as is sometimes the case with insects. And this leads me to say a few words on what I call Sexual Selection. This depends, not on a struggle for existence, but on a struggle between the males for possession of the females; the result is not death to the unsuccessful competitor, but few or no offspring. Sexual selection is, therefore, less rigorous than natural selection. Generally, the most vigorous males, those which are best fitted for their places in nature, will leave most progeny. But in many cases, victory will depend not on general vigour, but on having special weapons, confined to the male sex. A hornless stag or spurless cock would have a poor chance of leaving offspring. Sexual selection by always allowing the victor to breed might surely give indomitable courage, length to the spur, and strength to the wing to strike in the spurred leg, as well as the brutal cockfighter, who knows well that he can improve his breed by careful selection of the best cocks. How low in the scale of nature this law of battle descends, I know not; male alligators have been described as fighting, bellowing, and whirling round, like Indians in a wardance, for the possession of the females; male salmons have been seen fighting all day long; male stag-beetles often bear wounds from the huge mandibles of other males. The war is, perhaps, severest between the males of polygamous animals, and these seem oftenest provided with special weapons. The males of carnivorous animals are already well armed; though to them and to others, special means of defence may be given through means of sexual selection, as the mane to the lion, the shoulder-pad to the boar, and the hooked jaw to the male salmon; for the shield may be as important for victory, as the sword or spear.

Amongst birds, the contest is often of a more peaceful character. All those who have attended to the subject, believe that there is the severest rivalry between the males of many species to attract by singing the females. The rock-thrush of Guiana, birds of Paradise, and some others, congregate; and successive males display their gorgeous plumage and perform strange antics before the females, which standing by as spectators, at last choose the most attractive partner. Those who have closely attended to birds in confinement well know that they often take individual preferences and dislikes: thus Sir R. Heron has described how one pied peacock was eminently attractive to all his hen birds. It may appear childish to attribute any effect to such apparently weak means: I cannot here enter on the details necessary to support this view; but if man can in a short time give elegant carriage and beauty to his bantams, according to his standard of beauty, I can see no good reason to doubt that female birds, by selecting, during thousands of generations, the most melodious or beautiful males, according to their standard of beauty, might produce a marked effect. I strongly suspect that some well-known laws with respect to the plumage of male and female birds, in comparison with the plumage of the young, can be explained on the view of plumage having been chiefly modified by sexual selection, acting when the birds have come to the breeding age or during the breeding season; the modifications thus produced being inherited at corresponding ages or seasons, either by the males alone, or by the males and females; but I have not space here to enter on this subject.

Thus it is, as I believe, that when the males and females of any animal have the same general habits of life, but differ in structure, colour, or ornament, such differences have been mainly caused by sexual selection; that is, individual males have had, in successive generations, some slight advantage over other males, in their weapons, means of defence, or charms; and have transmitted these advantages to their male offspring. Yet, I would not wish to attribute all such sexual differences to this agency: for we see peculiarities arising and becoming attached to the male sex in our domestic animals (as the wattle in male carriers, horn-like protuberances in the cocks of certain fowls, &c.), which we cannot believe to be either useful to the males in battle, or attractive to the females. We see analogous cases under nature, for instance, the tuft of hair on the breast of the turkey-cock, which can hardly be either useful or ornamental to this bird;—indeed, had the tuft appeared under domestication, it would have been called a monstrosity.

ILLUSTRATIONS OF THE ACTION OF NATURAL SELECTION

In order to make it clear how, as I believe, natural selection acts, I must beg permission to give one or two imaginary illustrations. Let us take the case of a wolf, which preys on various animals, securing some by craft, some by strength, and some by fleetness; and let us suppose that the fleetest prey, a deer for instance, had from any change in the country increased in numbers, or that other prey had decreased in numbers, during that season of the year when the wolf is hardest pressed for food. I can under such circumstances see no reason to doubt that the swiftest and slimmest wolves would have the best chance of surviving, and so be preserved or selected,—provided always that they retained strength to master their prey at this or at some other period of the year, when they might be compelled to prey on other animals. I can see no more reason to doubt this, than that man can improve the fleetness of his grey-hounds by careful and methodical selection, or by that unconscious selection which results from each man trying to keep the best dogs without any thought of modifying the breed.

Even without any change in the proportional numbers of the animals on which our wolf preyed, a cub might be born with an innate tendency to pursue certain kinds of prey. Nor can this be thought very improbable; for we often observe great differences in the natural tendencies of our domestic animals; one cat, for instance, taking to catch rats, another mice; one cat, according to Mr. St. John, bringing home winged game, another hares or rabbits, and another hunting on marshy ground and almost nightly catching woodcocks or snipes. The tendency to catch rats rather than mice is known to be inherited. Now, if any slight innate change of habit or of structure benefited an individual wolf, it would have the best chance of surviving and of leaving offspring. Some of its young would probably inherit the same habits or structure, and by the repetition of this process, a new variety might be formed which would either supplant or coexist with the parent-form of wolf. Or, again, the wolves inhabiting a mountainous district, and those frequenting the lowlands, would naturally be forced to hunt different prey; and from the continued preservation of the individuals best fitted for the two sites, two varieties might slowly be formed. These varieties would cross and blend where they met; but to this subject of intercrossing we shall soon have to return. I may add, that, according to Mr. Pierce, there are two varieties of the wolf inhabiting the Catskill Mountains in the United States, one with a light greyhound-like form, which pursues deer, and the other more bulky, with shorter legs, which more frequently attacks the shepherd's flocks.

Let us now take a more complex case. Certain plants excrete a sweet juice, apparently for the sake of eliminating something injurious from their sap: this is effected by glands at the base of the stipules in some Leguminosæ, and at the back of the leaf of the common laurel. This juice, though small in quantity, is greedily sought by insects. Let us now suppose a little sweet juice or nectar to be excreted by the inner bases of the petals of a flower. In this case insects in seeking the nectar would get dusted with pollen, and would certainly often transport the pollen from one flower to the stigma of another flower. The flowers of two distinct individuals of the same species would thus get crossed; and the act of crossing, we have good reason to believe (as will hereafter be more fully alluded to), would produce very vigorous seedlings, which consequently would have the best chance of flourishing and surviving. Some of these seedlings would probably inherit the nectar-excreting power. Those individual flowers which had the largest glands or nectaries, and which excreted most nectar, would be oftenest visited by insects, and would be oftenest crossed; and so in the long-run would gain the upper hand. Those flowers, also, which had their stamens and pistils placed, in relation to the size and habits of the particular insects which visited them, so as to favour in any degree the transportal of their pollen from flower to flower, would likewise be favoured or selected. We might have taken the case of insects visiting flowers for the sake of collecting pollen instead of nectar; and as pollen is formed for the sole object of fertilisation, its destruction appears a simple loss to the plant; yet if a little pollen were carried, at first occasionally and then habitually, by the pollen-devouring insects from flower to flower, and a cross thus effected, although nine-tenths of the pollen were destroyed, it might still be a great gain to the plant; and those individuals which produced more and more pollen, and had larger and larger anthers, would be selected.

When our plant, by this process of the continued preservation or natural selection of more and more attractive flowers, had been rendered highly attractive to insects, they would, unintentionally on their part, regularly carry pollen from flower to flower; and that they can most effectually do this, I could easily show by many striking instances. I will give only one —not as a very striking case, but as likewise illustrating one step in the separation of the sexes of plants, presently to be alluded to. Some holly-trees bear only male flowers, which have four stamens producing rather a small quantity of pollen, and a rudimentary pistil; other holly-trees bear only female flowers; these have a full-sized pistil, and four stamens with shrivelled anthers, in which not a grain of pollen can be detected. Having found a female tree exactly sixty yards from a male tree, I put the stigmas of twenty flowers, taken from different branches, under the microscope, and on all, without exception, there were pollen-grains, and on some a profusion of pollen. As the wind had set for several days from the female to the male tree, the pollen could not thus have been carried. The weather had been cold and boisterous, and therefore not favourable to bees, nevertheless every female flower which I examined had been effectually fertilised by the bees, accidentally dusted with pollen, having flown from tree to tree in search of nectar. But to return to our imaginary case: as soon as the plant had been rendered so highly attractive to insects that pollen was regularly carried from flower to flower, another process might commence. No naturalist doubts the advantage of what has been called the "physiological division of labour;" hence we may believe that it would be advantageous to a plant to produce stamens alone in one flower or on one whole plant, and pistils alone in another flower or on another plant. In plants under culture and placed under new conditions of life, sometimes the male organs and sometimes the female organs become more or less impotent; now if we suppose this to occur in ever so slight a degree under nature, then as pollen is already carried regularly from flower to flower, and as a more complete separation of the sexes of our plant would be advantageous on the principle of the division of labour, individuals with this tendency more and more increased, would be continually favoured or selected, until at last a complete separation of the sexes would be effected.

Let us now turn to the nectar-feeding insects in our imaginary case: we may suppose the plant of which we have been slowly increasing the nectar by continued selection, to be a common plant; and that certain insects depended in main part on its nectar for food. I could give many facts, showing how anxious bees are to save time; for instance, their habit of cutting holes and sucking the nectar at the bases of certain flowers, which they can, with a very little more trouble, enter by the mouth. Bearing such facts in mind, I can see no reason to doubt that an accidental deviation in the size and form of the body, or in the curvature and length of the proboscis, &c., far too slight to be appreciated by us, might profit a bee or other insect, so that an individual so characterised would be able to obtain its food more quickly, and so have a better chance of living and leaving descendants. Its descendants would probably inherit a tendency to a similar slight deviation of structure. The tubes of the corollas of the common red and incarnate clovers (Trifolium pratense and incarnatum) do not on a hasty glance appear to differ in length; yet the hive-bee can easily suck the nectar out of the incarnate clover, but not out of the common red clover, which is visited by humble-bees alone; so that whole fields of the red clover offer in vain an abundant supply of precious nectar to the hive-bee. Thus it might be a great advantage to the hive-bee to have a slightly longer or differently constructed proboscis. On the other hand, I have found by experiment that the fertility of clover greatly depends on bees visiting and moving parts of the corolla, so as to push the pollen on to the stigmatic surface. Hence, again, if humble-bees were to become rare in any country, it might be a great advantage to the red clover to have a shorter or more deeply divided tube to its corolla, so that the hive-bee could visit its flowers. Thus I can understand how a flower and a bee might slowly become, either simultaneously or one after the other, modified and adapted in the most perfect manner to each other, by the continued preservation of individuals presenting mutual and slightly favourable deviations of structure.

I am well aware that this doctrine of natural selection, exemplified in the above imaginary instances, is open to the same objections which were at first urged against Sir Charles Lyell's noble views on "the modern changes of the earth, as illustrative of geology;" but we now very seldom hear the action, for instance, of the coastwaves, called a trifling and insignificant cause, when applied to the excavation of gigantic valleys or to the formation of the longest lines of inland cliffs. Natural selection can act only by the preservation and accumulation of infinitesimally small inherited modifications, each profitable to the preserved being; and as modern geology has almost banished such views as the excavation of a great valley by a single diluvial wave, so will natural selection, if it be a true principle, banish the belief of the continued creation of new organic beings, or of any great and sudden modification in their structure.

* * *

CIRCUMSTANCES FAVOURABLE TO NATURAL SELECTION

This is an extremely intricate subject. A large amount of inheritable and diversified variability is favourable, but I believe mere individual differences suffice for the work. A large number of individuals, by giving a better chance for the appearance within any given period of profitable variations, will compensate for a lesser amount of variability in each individual, and is, I believe, an extremely important element of success. Though nature grants vast periods of time for the work of natural selection, she does not grant an indefinite period; for as all organic beings are striving, it may be said, to seize on each place in the economy of nature, if any one species does not become modified and improved in a corresponding degree with its competitors, it will soon be exterminated.

In man's methodical selection, a breeder selects for some definite object, and free intercrossing will wholly stop his work. But when many men, without intending to alter the breed, have a nearly common standard of perfection, and all try to get and breed from the best animals, much improvement and modification surely but slowly follow from this unconscious process of selection, notwithstanding a large amount of crossing with inferior animals. Thus it will be in nature; for within a confined area, with some place in its polity not so perfectly occupied as might be, natural selection will always tend to preserve all the individuals varying in the right direction, though in different degrees, so as better to fill up the unoccupied place. But if the area be large, its several districts will almost certainly present different conditions of life; and then if natural selection be modifying and improving a species in the several districts, there will be intercrossing with the other individuals of the same species on the confines of each. And in this case the effects of intercrossing can hardly be counterbalanced by natural selection always tending to modify all the individuals in each district in exactly the same manner to the conditions of each; for in a continuous area, the conditions will generally graduate away insensibly from one district to another. The intercrossing will most affect those animals which unite for each birth, which wander much, and which do not breed at a very quick rate. Hence in animals of this nature, for instance in birds, varieties will generally be confined to separated countries; and this I believe to be the case. In hermaphrodite organisms which cross only occasionally, and likewise in animals which unite for each birth, but which wander little and which can increase at a very rapid rate, a new and improved variety might be quickly formed on any one spot, and might there maintain itself in a body, so that whatever intercrossing took place would be chiefly between the individuals of the same new variety. A local variety when once thus formed might subsequently slowly spread to other districts. On the above principle, nurserymen always prefer getting seed from a large body of plants of the same variety, as the chance of inter-crossing with other varieties is thus lessened.

Even in the case of slow-breeding animals, which unite for each birth, we must not overrate the effects of intercrosses in retarding natural selection; for I can bring a considerable catalogue of facts, showing that within the same area, varieties of the same animal can long remain distinct, from haunting different stations, from breeding at slightly different seasons, or from varieties of the same kind preferring to pair together.

Intercrossing plays a very important part in nature in keeping the individuals of the same species, or of the same variety, true and uniform in character. It will obviously thus act far more efficiently with those animals which unite for each birth; but I have already attempted to show that we have reason to believe that occasional intercrosses take place with all animals and with all plants. Even if these take place only at long intervals, I am convinced that the young thus produced will gain so much in vigour and fertility over the offspring from long-continued self-fertilisation, that they will have a better chance of surviving and propagating their kind; and thus, in the long run, the influence of intercrosses, even at rare intervals, will be great. If there exist organic beings which never intercross, uniformity of character can be retained amongst them, as long as their conditions of life remain the same, only through the principle of inheritance, and through natural selection destroying any which depart from the proper type; but if their conditions of life change and they undergo modification, uniformity of character can be given to their modified offspring, solely by natural selection preserving the same favourable variations.

Isolation, also, is an important element in the process of natural selection. In a confined or isolated area, if not very large, the organic and inorganic conditions of life will generally be in a great degree uniform; so that natural selection will tend to modify all the individuals of a varying species throughout the area in the same manner in relation to the same conditions. Intercrosses, also, with the individuals of the same species, which otherwise would have inhabited the surrounding and differently circumstanced districts, will be prevented. But isolation probably acts more efficiently in checking the immigration of better adapted organisms, after any physical change, such as of climate or elevation of the land, &c.; and thus new places in the natural economy of the country are left open for the old inhabitants to struggle for, and become adapted to, through modifications in their structure and constitution. Lastly, isolation, by checking immigration and consequently competition, will give time for any new variety to be slowly improved; and this may sometimes be of importance in the production of new species. If, however, an isolated area be very small, either from being surrounded by barriers, or from having very peculiar physical conditions, the total number of the individuals supported on it will necessarily be very small; and fewness of individuals will greatly retard the production of new species through natural selection, by decreasing the chance of the appearance of favourable variations.

If we turn to nature to test the truth of these remarks, and look at any small isolated area, such as an oceanic island, although the total number

of the species inhabiting it, will be found to be small, as we shall see in
our chapter on geographical distribution; yet of these species a very large
proportion are endemic,—that is, have been produced there, and nowhere
else. Hence an oceanic island at first sight seems to have been highly
favourable for the production of new species. But we may thus greatly
deceive ourselves, for to ascertain whether a small isolated area, or a large
open area like a continent, has been most favourable for the production
of new organic forms, we ought to make the comparison within equal
times; and this we are incapable of doing.

Although I do not doubt that isolation is of considerable importance in
the production of new species, on the whole I am inclined to believe that
largeness of area is of more importance, more especially in the production
of species, which will prove capable of enduring for a long period, and of
spreading widely. Throughout a great and open area, not only will there
be a better chance of favourable variations arising from the large number
of individuals of the same species there supported, but the conditions of
life are infinitely complex from the large number of already existing species; and if some of these many species become modified and improved,
others will have to be improved in a corresponding degree or they will be
exterminated. Each new form, also, as soon as it has been much improved,
will be able to spread over the open and continuous area, and will thus
come into competition with many others. Hence more new places will be
formed, and the competition to fill them will be more severe, on a large
than on a small and isolated area. Moreover, great areas, though now
continuous, owing to oscillations of level, will often have recently existed
in a broken condition, so that the good effects of isolation will generally,
to a certain extent, have concurred. Finally, I conclude that, although
small isolated areas probably have been in some respects highly favourable
for the production of new species, yet that the course of modification will
generally have been more rapid on large areas; and what is more important, that the new forms produced on large areas, which already have been
victorious over many competitors, will be those that will spread most
widely, will give rise to most new varieties and species, and will thus play
an important part in the changing history of the organic world.

We can, perhaps, on these views, understand some facts which will be
again alluded to in our chapter on geographical distribution; for instance,
that the productions of the smaller continent of Australia have formerly
yielded, and apparently are now yielding, before those of the larger
Europæo-Asiatic area. Thus, also, it is that continental productions have
everywhere become so largely naturalised on islands. On a small island,
the race for life will have been less severe, and there will have been less
modification and less extermination. Hence, perhaps, it comes that the
flora of Madeira, according to Oswald Heer, resembles the extinct tertiary
flora of Europe. All fresh-water basins, taken together, make a small area
compared with that of the sea or of the land; and, consequently, the competition between fresh-water productions will have been less severe than
elsewhere; new forms will have been more slowly formed, and old forms
more slowly exterminated. And it is in fresh water that we find seven genera
of Ganoid fishes, remnants of a once preponderant order: and in fresh

water we find some of the most anomalous forms now known in the world, as the Ornithorhynchus and Lepidosiren, which, like fossils, connect to a certain extent orders now widely separated in the natural scale. These anomalous forms may almost be called living fossils; they have endured to the present day, from having inhabited a confined area, and from having thus been exposed to less severe competition.

To sum up the circumstances favourable and unfavourable to natural selection, as far as the extreme intricacy of the subject permits. I conclude, looking to the future, that for terrestrial productions a large continental area, which will probably undergo many oscillations of level, and which consequently will exist for long periods in a broken condition, will be the most favourable for the production of many new forms of life, likely to endure long and to spread widely. For the area will first have existed as a continent, and the inhabitants, at this period numerous in individuals and kinds, will have been subjected to very severe competition. When converted by subsidence into large separate islands, there will still exist many individuals of the same species on each island: intercrossing on the confines of the range of each species will thus be checked: after physical changes of any kind, immigration will be prevented, so that new places in the polity of each island will have to be filled up by modifications of the old inhabitants; and time will be allowed for the varieties in each to become well modified and perfected. When, by renewed elevation, the islands shall be re-converted into a continental area, there will again be severe competition: the most favoured or improved varieties will be enabled to spread: there will be much extinction of the less improved forms, and the relative proportional numbers of the various inhabitants of the renewed continent will again be changed; and again there will be a fair field for natural selection to improve still further the inhabitants, and thus produce new species.

That natural selection will always act with extreme slowness, I fully admit. Its action depends on there being places in the polity of nature, which can be better occupied by some of the inhabitants of the country undergoing modification of some kind. The existence of such places will often depend on physical changes, which are generally very slow, and on the immigration of better adapted forms having been checked. But the action of natural selection will probably still oftener depend on some of the inhabitants becoming slowly modified; the mutual relations of many of the other inhabitants being thus disturbed. Nothing can be effected, unless favourable variations occur, and variation itself is apparently always a very slow process. The process will often be greatly retarded by free intercrossing. Many will exclaim that these several causes are amply sufficient wholly to stop the action of natural selection. I do not believe so. On the other hand, I do believe that natural selection will always act very slowly, often only at long intervals of time, and generally on only a very few of the inhabitants of the same region at the same time. I further believe, that this very slow, intermittent action of natural selection accords perfectly well with what geology tells us of the rate and manner at which the inhabitants of this world have changed.

Slow though the process of selection may be, if feeble man can do much by his powers of artificial selection, I can see no limit to the amount of change, to the beauty and infinite complexity of the coadaptations between all organic beings, one with another and with their physical conditions of life, which may be effected in the long course of time by nature's power of selection.

*   *   *

DIVERGENCE OF CHARACTER

The principle, which I have designated by this term, is of high importance on my theory, and explains, as I believe, several important facts. In the first place, varieties, even strongly-marked ones, though having somewhat of the character of species—as is shown by the hopeless doubts in many cases how to rank them—yet certainly differ from each other far less than do good and distinct species. Nevertheless, according to my view, varieties are species in the process of formation, or are, as I have called them, incipient species. How, then, does the lesser difference between varieties become augmented into the greater difference between species? That this does habitually happen, we must infer from most of the innumerable species throughout nature presenting well-marked differences; whereas varieties, the supposed prototypes and parents of future well-marked species, present slight and ill-defined differences. Mere chance, as we may call it, might cause one variety to differ in some character from its parents, and the offspring of this variety again to differ from its parent in the very same character and in a greater degree; but this alone would never account for so habitual and large an amount of difference as that between varieties of the same species and species of the same genus.

As has always been my practice, let us seek light on this head from our domestic productions. We shall here find something analogous. A fancier is struck by a pigeon having a slightly shorter beak; another fancier is struck by a pigeon having a rather longer beak; and on the acknowledged principle that "fanciers do not and will not admire a medium standard, but like extremes," they both go on (as has actually occurred with tumbler-pigeons) choosing and breeding from birds with longer and longer beaks, or with shorter and shorter beaks. Again, we may suppose that at an early period one man preferred swifter horses; another stronger and more bulky horses. The early differences would be very slight; in the course of time, from the continued selection of swifter horses by some breeders, and of stronger ones by others, the differences would become greater, and would be noted as forming two sub-breeds; finally, after the lapse of centuries, the sub-breeds would become converted into two well-established and distinct breeds. As the differences slowly become greater, the inferior animals with intermediate characters, being neither very swift nor very strong, will have been neglected, and will have tended to disappear. Here, then, we see in man's productions the action of what may be called the principle of divergence, causing differences, at first barely appreciable, steadily to increase, and the breeds to diverge in character both from each other and from their common parent.

But how, it may be asked, can any analogous principle apply in nature? I believe it can and does apply most efficiently, from the simple circumstance that the more diversified the descendants from any one species become in structure, constitution, and habits, by so much will they be better enabled to seize on many and widely diversified places in the polity of nature, and so be enabled to increase in numbers.

We can clearly see this in the case of animals with simple habits. Take the case of a carnivorous quadruped, of which the number that can be supported in any country has long ago arrived at its full average. If its natural powers of increase be allowed to act, it can succeed in increasing (the country not undergoing any change in its conditions) only by its varying descendants seizing on places at present occupied by other animals: some of them, for instance, being enabled to feed on new kinds of prey, either dead or alive; some inhabiting new stations, climbing trees, frequenting water, and some perhaps becoming less carnivorous. The more diversified in habits and structure the descendants of our carnivorous animal became, the more places they would be enabled to occupy. What applies to one animal will apply throughout all time to all animals—that is, if they vary—for otherwise natural selection can do nothing. So it will be with plants. It has been experimentally proved, that if a plot of ground be sown with one species of grass, and a similar plot be sown with several distinct genera of grasses, a greater number of plants and a greater weight of dry herbage can thus be raised. The same has been found to hold good when first one variety and then several mixed varieties of wheat have been sown on equal spaces of ground. Hence, if any one species of grass were to go on varying, and those varieties were continually selected which differed from each other in at all the same manner as distinct species and genera of grasses differ from each other, a greater number of individual plants of this species of grass, including its modified descendants, would succeed in living on the same piece of ground. And we well know that each species and each variety of grass is annually sowing almost countless seeds; and thus, as it may be said, is striving its utmost to increase its numbers. Consequently, I cannot doubt that in the course of many thousands of generations, the most distinct varieties of any one species of grass would always have the best chance of succeeding and of increasing in numbers, and thus of supplanting the less distinct varieties; and varieties, when rendered very distinct from each other, take the rank of species.

The truth of the principle, that the greatest amount of life can be supported by great diversification of structure, is seen under many natural circumstances. In an extremely small area, especially if freely open to immigration, and where the contest between individual and individual must be severe, we always find great diversity in its inhabitants. For instance, I found that a piece of turf, three feet by four in size, which had been exposed for many years to exactly the same conditions, supported twenty species of plants, and these belonged to eighteen genera and to eight orders, which shows how much these plants differed from each other.

So it is with the plants and insects on small and uniform islets; and so in small ponds of fresh water. Farmers find that they can raise most food by a rotation of plants belonging to the most different orders: nature follows what may be called a simultaneous rotation. Most of the animals and plants which live close round any small piece of ground, could live on it (supposing it not to be in any way peculiar in its nature), and may be said to be striving to the utmost to live there; but, it is seen, that where they come into the closest competition with each other, the advantages of diversification of structure, with the accompanying differences of habit and constitution, determine that the inhabitants, which thus jostle each other most closely, shall, as a general rule, belong to what we call different genera and orders.

The same principle is seen in the naturalisation of plants through man's agency in foreign lands. It might have been expected that the plants which have succeeded in becoming naturalised in any land would generally have been closely allied to the indigenes; for these are commonly looked at as specially created and adapted for their own country. It might, also, perhaps have been expected that naturalised plants would have belonged to a few groups more especially adapted to certain stations in their new homes. But the case is very different; and Alph. De Candolle has well remarked in his great and admirable work, that floras gain by naturalisation, proportionally with the number of the native genera and species, far more in new genera than in new species. To give a single instance: in the last edition of Dr. Asa Gray's 'Manual of the Flora of the Northern United States,' 260 naturalised plants are enumerated, and these belong to 162 genera. We thus see that these naturalised plants are of a highly diversified nature. They differ, moreover, to a large extent from the indigenes, for out of the 162 genera, no less than 100 genera are not there indigenous, and thus a large proportional addition is made to the genera of these States.

By considering the nature of the plants or animals which have struggled successfully with the indigenes of any country, and have there become naturalised, we can gain some crude idea in what manner some of the natives would have had to be modified, in order to have gained an advantage over the other natives; and we may, I think, at least safely infer that diversification of structure, amounting to new generic differences, would have been profitable to them.

The advantage of diversification in the inhabitants of the same region is, in fact, the same as that of the physiological division of labour in the organs of the same individual body—a subject so well elucidated by Milne Edwards. No physiologist doubts that a stomach by being adapted to digest vegetable matter alone, or flesh alone, draws most nutriment from these substances. So in the general economy of any land, the more widely and perfectly the animals and plants are diversified for different habits of life, so will a greater number of individuals be capable of there supporting themselves. A set of animals, with their organisation but little diversified, could hardly compete with a set more perfectly diversified in structure. It may be doubted, for instance, whether the Australian marsupials, which are divided into groups differing but little from each other, and feebly representing, as Mr. Waterhouse and others have remarked, our carnivorous, ruminant, and rodent mammals, could successfully compete with these well-pronounced orders. In the Australian mammals, we see the process of diversification in an early and incomplete stage of development.

After the foregoing discussion, which ought to have been much amplified, we may, I think, assume that the modified descendants of any one species will succeed by so much the better as they become more diversified in structure, and are thus enabled to encroach on places occupied by other beings. Now let us see how this principle of great benefit being derived from divergence of character, combined with the principles of natural selection and of extinction, will tend to act.

The accompanying diagram will aid us in understanding this rather perplexing subject. Let A to L represent the species of a genus large in its own country; these species are supposed to resemble each other in unequal degrees, as is so generally the case in nature, and as is represented in the diagram by the letters standing at unequal distances. I have said a large genus, because we have seen in the second chapter, that on an average more of the species of large genera vary than of small genera; and the varying species of the large genera present a greater number of varieties. We have, also, seen that the species, which are the commonest and the most widely-diffused, vary more than rare species with restricted ranges. Let (A) be a common, widely-diffused, and varying species, belonging to a genus large in its own country. The little fan of diverging dotted lines of unequal lengths proceeding from (A), may represent its varying offspring. The variations are supposed to be extremely slight, but of the most diversified nature; they are not supposed all to appear simultaneously, but often after long intervals of time; nor are they all supposed to endure for equal periods. Only those variations which are in some way profitable will be preserved or naturally selected. And here the importance of the principle of benefit being derived from divergence of character comes in; for this will generally lead to the most different or divergent variations (represented by the outer dotted lines) being preserved and accumulated by natural selection. When a dotted line reaches one of the horizontal lines, and is there marked by a small numbered letter, a sufficient amount of variation is supposed to have been accumulated to have formed a fairly well-marked variety, such as would be thought worthy of record in a systematic work.

The intervals between the horizontal lines in the diagram, may represent each a thousand generations; but it would have been better if each had represented ten thousand generations. After a thousand generations, species (A) is supposed to have produced two fairly well-marked varieties, namely a^1 and m^1. These two varieties will generally continue to be exposed to the same conditions which made their parents variable, and the tendency to variability is in itself hereditary, consequently they will tend to vary, and generally to vary in nearly the same manner as their parents varied. Moreover, these two varieties, being only slightly modified forms, will tend to inherit those advantages which made their common parent (A) more numerous than most of the other inhabitants of the same country; they will likewise partake of those more general advantages which made the genus to which the parent-species belonged, a large genus in its

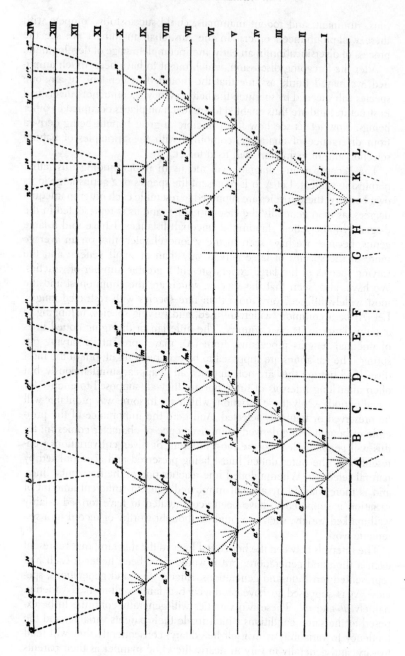

own country. And these circumstances we know to be favourable to the production of new varieties.

If, then, these two varieties be variable, the most divergent of their variations will generally be preserved during the next thousand generations. And after this interval, variety a^1 is supposed in the diagram to have produced variety a^2, which will, owing to the principle of divergence, differ more from (A) than did variety a^1. Variety m^1 is supposed to have produced two varieties, namely m^2 and s^3, differing from each other, and more considerably from their common parent (A). We may continue the process by similar steps for any length of time; some of the varities, after each thousand generations, producing only a single variety, but in a more and more modified condition, some producing two or three varieties, and some failing to produce any. Thus the varieties or modified descendants, proceeding from the common parent (A), will generally go on increasing in number and diverging in character. In the diagram the process is represented up to the ten-thousandth generation, and under a condensed and simplified form up to the fourteen-thousandth generation.

But I must here remark that I do not suppose that the process ever goes on so regularly as is represented in the diagram, though in itself made somewhat irregular. I am far from thinking that the most divergent varieties will invariably prevail and multiply: a medium form may often long endure, and may or may not produce more than one modified descendant; for natural selection will always act according to the nature of the places which are either unoccupied or not perfectly occupied by other beings; and this will depend on infinitely complex relations. But as a general rule, the more diversified in structure the descendants from any one species can be rendered, the more places they will be enabled to seize on, and the more their modified progeny will be increased. In our diagram the line of succession is broken at regular intervals by small numbered letters marking the successive forms which have become sufficiently distinct to be recorded as varieties. But these breaks are imaginary, and might have been inserted anywhere, after intervals long enough to have allowed the accumulation of a considerable amount of divergent variation.

As all the modified descendants from a common and widely-diffused species, belonging to a large genus, will tend to partake of the same advantages which made their parent successful in life, they will generally go on multiplying in number as well as diverging in character: this is represented in the diagram by the several divergent branches proceeding from (A). The modified offspring from the later and more highly improved branches in the lines of descent, will, it is probable, often take the place of, and so destroy, the earlier and less improved branches: this is represented in the diagram by some of the lower branches not reaching to the upper horizontal lines. In some cases I do not doubt that the process of modification will be confined to a single line of descent, and the number of the descendants will not be increased; although the amount of divergent modification may have been increased in the successive generations. This case would be represented in the diagram, if all the lines proceeding from (A) were removed, excepting that from a^1 to a^{10}. In the same way, for instance, the English race-horse and English pointer have apparently both gone on slowly diverging in character from their original stocks, without either having given off any fresh branches or races.

After ten thousand generations, species (A) is supposed to have produced three forms, a^{10}, f^{10}, and m^{10}, which, from having diverged in character during the successive generations, will have come to differ largely, but perhaps unequally, from each other and from their common parent. If we suppose the amount of change between each horizontal line in our diagram to be excessively small, these three forms may still be only well-marked varieties; or they may have arrived at the doubtful category of sub-species; but we have only to suppose the steps in the process of modification to be more numerous or greater in amount, to convert these three forms into well-defined species: thus the diagram illustrates the steps by which the small differences distinguishing varieties are increased into the larger differences distinguishing species. By continuing the same process for a greater number of generations (as shown in the diagram in a condensed and simplified manner), we get eight species, marked by the letters between a^{14} and m^{14}, all descended from (A). Thus, as I believe, species are multiplied and genera are formed.

In a large genus it is probable that more than one species would vary. In the diagram I have assumed that a second species (I) has produced, by analogous steps, after ten thousand generations, either two well-marked varieties (w^{10} and z^{10}) or two species, according to the amount of change supposed to be represented between the horizontal lines. After fourteen thousand generations, six new species, marked by the letters n^{14} to z^{14}, are supposed to have been produced. In each genus, the species, which are already extremely different in character, will generally tend to produce the greatest number of modified descendants; for these will have the best chance of filling new and widely different places in the polity of nature: hence in the diagram I have chosen the extreme species (A), and the nearly extreme species (I), as those which have largely varied, and have given rise to new varieties and species. The other nine species (marked by capital letters) of our original genus, may for a long period continue transmitting unaltered descendants; and this is shown in the diagram by the dotted lines not prolonged far upwards from want of space.

But during the process of modification, represented in the diagram, another of our principles, namely that of extinction, will have played an important part. As in each fully stocked country natural selection necessarily acts by the selected form having some advantage in the struggle for life over other forms, there will be a constant tendency in the improved descendants of any one species to supplant and exterminate in each stage of descent their predecessors and their original parent. For it should be remembered that the competition will generally be most severe between those forms which are most nearly related to each other in habits, constitution, and structure. Hence all the intermediate forms between the earlier and later states, that is between the less and more improved state of a species, as well as the original parent-species itself, will generally tend to become extinct. So it probably will be with many whole collateral lines of descent, which will be conquered by later and improved lines of descent.

If, however, the modified offspring of a species get into some distinct country, or become quickly adapted to some quite new station, in which child and parent do not come into competition, both may continue to exist.

If then our diagram be assumed to represent a considerable amount of modification, species (A) and all the earlier varieties will have become extinct, having been replaced by eight new species (a^{14} to m^{14}); and (I) will have been replaced by six (n^{14} to z^{14}) new species.

But we may go further than this. The original species of our genus were supposed to resemble each other in unequal degrees, as is so generally the case in nature; species (A) being more nearly related to B, C, and D, than to the other species; and species (I) more to G, H, K, L, than to the others. These two species (A) and (I), were also supposed to be very common and widely diffused species, so that they must originally have had some advantage over most of the other species of the genus. Their modified descendants, fourteen in number at the fourteen-thousandth generation, will probably have inherited some of the same advantages: they have also been modified and improved in a diversified manner at each stage of descent, so as to have become adapted to many related places in the natural economy of their country. It seems, therefore, to me extremely probable that they will have taken the places of, and thus exterminated, not only their parents (A) and (I), but likewise some of the original species which were most nearly related to their parents. Hence very few of the original species will have transmitted offspring to the fourteen-thousandth generation. We may suppose that only one (F), of the two species which were least closely related to the other nine original species, has transmitted descendants to this late stage of descent.

The new species in our diagram descended from the original eleven species, will now be fifteen in number. Owing to the divergent tendency of natural selection, the extreme amount of difference in character between species a^{14} and z^{14} will be much greater than that between the most different of the original eleven species. The new species, moreover, will be allied to each other in a widely different manner. Of the eight descendants from (A) the three marked a^{14}, q^{14}, p^{14}, will be nearly related from having recently branched off from a^{10}; b^{14} and f^{14}, from having diverged at an earlier period from a^5, will be in some degree distinct from the three first-named species; and lastly, o^{14}, e^{14}, and m^{14}, will be nearly related one to the other, but from having diverged at the first commencement of the process of modification, will be widely different from the other five species, and may constitute a sub-genus or even a distinct genus.

The six descendants from (I) will form two sub-genera or even genera. But as the original species (I) differed largely from (A), standing nearly at the extreme points of the original genus, the six descendants from (I) will, owing to inheritance, differ considerably from the eight descendants from (A); the two groups, moreover, are supposed to have gone on diverging in different directions. The intermediate species, also (and this is a very important consideration), which connected the original species (A) and (I), have all become, excepting (F), extinct, and have left no descendants.

Hence the six new species descended from (I), and the eight descended from (A), will have to be ranked as very distinct genera, or even as distinct sub-families.

Thus it is, as I believe, that two or more genera are produced by descent, with modification, from two or more species of the same genus. And the two or more parent-species are supposed to have descended from some one species of an earlier genus. In our diagram, this is indicated by the broken lines, beneath the capital letters, converging in sub-branches downwards towards a single point; this point representing a single species, the supposed single parent of our several new sub-genera and genera.

It is worth while to reflect for a moment on the character of the new species F^{14}, which is supposed not to have diverged much in character, but to have retained the form of (F), either unaltered or altered only in a slight degree. In this case, its affinities to the other fourteen new species will be of a curious and circuitous nature. Having descended from a form which stood between the two parent-species (A) and (I), now supposed to be extinct and unknown, it will be in some degree intermediate in character between the two groups descended from these species. But as these two groups have gone on diverging in character from the type of their parents, the new species (F^{14}) will not be directly intermediate between them, but rather between types of the two groups; and every naturalist will be able to bring some such case before his mind.

In the diagram, each horizontal line has hitherto been supposed to represent a thousand generations, but each may represent a million or hundred million generations, and likewise a section of the successive strata of the earth's crust including extinct remains. We shall, when we come to our chapter on Geology, have to refer again to this subject, and I think we shall then see that the diagram throws light on the affinities of extinct beings, which, though generally belonging to the same orders, or families, or genera, with those now living, yet are often, in some degree, intermediate in character between existing groups; and we can understand this fact, for the extinct species lived at very ancient epochs when the branching lines of descent had diverged less.

I see no reason to limit the process of modification, as now explained, to the formation of genera alone. If, in our diagram, we suppose the amount of change represented by each successive group of diverging dotted lines to be very great, the forms marked a^{14} to p^{14}, those marked b^{14} and f^{14}, and those marked o^{14} to m^{14}, will form three very distinct genera. We shall also have two very distinct genera descended from (I); and as these latter two genera, both from continued divergence of character and from inheritance from a different parent, will differ widely from the three genera descended from (A), the two little groups of genera will form two distinct families, or even orders, according to the amount of divergent modification supposed to be represented in the diagram. And the two new families, or orders, will have descended from two species of the original genus; and these two species are supposed to have descended from one species of a still more ancient and unknown genus.

We have seen that in each country it is the species of the larger genera which oftenest present varieties or incipient species. This, indeed, might have been expected; for as natural selection acts through one form having some advantage over other forms in the struggle for existence, it will chiefly act on those which already have some advantage; and the largeness of any group shows that its species have inherited from a common ancestor some advantage in common. Hence, the struggle for the production of new and modified descendants, will mainly lie between the larger groups, which are all trying to increase in number. One large group will slowly conquer another large group, reduce its numbers, and thus lessen its chance of further variation and improvement. Within the same large group, the later and more highly perfected sub-groups, from branching out and seizing on many new places in the polity of Nature, will constantly tend to supplant and destroy the earlier and less improved sub-groups. Small and broken groups and sub-groups will finally tend to disappear. Looking to the future, we can predict that the groups of organic beings which are now large and triumphant, and which are least broken up, that is, which as yet have suffered least extinction, will for a long period continue to increase. But which groups will ultimately prevail, no man can predict; for we well know that many groups, formerly most extensively developed, have now become extinct. Looking still more remotely to the future, we may predict that, owing to the continued and steady increase of the larger groups, a multitude of smaller groups will become utterly extinct, and leave no modified descendants; and consequently that of the species living at any one period, extremely few will transmit descendants to a remote futurity. I shall have to return to this subject in the chapter on Classification, but I may add that on this view of extremely few of the more ancient species having transmitted descendants, and on the view of all the descendants of the same species making a class, we can understand how it is that there exist but very few classes in each main division of the animal and vegetable kingdoms. Although extremely few of the most ancient species may now have living and modified descendants, yet at the most remote geological period, the earth may have been as well peopled with many species of many genera, families, orders, and classes, as at the present day.

SUMMARY OF CHAPTER

If during the long course of ages and under varying conditions of life, organic beings vary at all in the several parts of their organisation, and I think this cannot be disputed; if there be, owing to the high geometrical powers of increase of each species, at some age, season, or year, a severe struggle for life, and this certainly cannot be disputed; then, considering the infinite complexity of the relations of all organic beings to each other and to their conditions of existence, causing an infinite diversity in structure, constitution, and habits, to be advantageous to them, I think it would be a most extraordinary fact if no variation ever had occurred useful to each being's own welfare, in the same way as so many variations have occurred useful to man. But if variations useful to any organic being do occur, assuredly individuals thus characterised will have the best chance of being preserved in the struggle for life; and from the strong principle of inheritance they will tend to produce offspring similarly characterised.

This principle of preservation, I have called, for the sake of brevity, Natural Selection. Natural selection, on the principle of qualities being inherited at corresponding ages, can modify the egg, seed, or young, as easily as the adult. Amongst many animals, sexual selection will give its aid to ordinary selection, by assuring to the most vigorous and best adapted males the greatest number of offspring. Sexual selection will also give characters useful to the males alone, in their struggles with other males.

Whether natural selection has really thus acted in nature, in modifying and adapting the various forms of life to their several conditions and stations, must be judged of by the general tenour and balance of evidence given in the following chapters. But we already see how it entails extinction; and how largely extinction has acted in the world's history, geology plainly declares. Natural selection, also, leads to divergence of character; for more living beings can be supported on the same area the more they diverge in structure, habits, and constitution, of which we see proof by looking at the inhabitants of any small spot or at naturalised productions. Therefore during the modification of the descendants of any one species, and during the incessant struggle of all species to increase in numbers, the more diversified these descendants become, the better will be their chance of succeeding in the battle of life. Thus the small differences distinguishing varieties of the same species, will steadily tend to increase till they come to equal the greater differences between species of the same genus, or even of distinct genera.

We have seen that it is the common, the widely-diffused, and widely-ranging species, belonging to the larger genera, which vary most; and these will tend to transmit to their modified offspring that superiority which now makes them dominant in their own countries. Natural selection, as has just been remarked, leads to divergence of character and to much extinction of the less improved and intermediate forms of life. On these principles, I believe, the nature of the affinities of all organic beings may be explained. It is a truly wonderful fact—the wonder of which we are apt to overlook from familiarity—that all animals and all plants throughout all time and space should be related to each other in group subordinate to group, in the manner which we everywhere behold—namely, varieties of the same species most closely related together, species of the same genus less closely and unequally related together, forming sections and sub-genera, species of distinct genera much less closely related, and genera related in different degrees, forming sub-families, families, orders, sub-classes, and classes. The several subordinate groups in any class cannot be ranked in a single file, but seem rather to be clustered round points, and these round other points, and so on in almost endless cycles. On the view that each species has been independently created, I can see no explanation of this great fact in the classification of all organic beings; but, to the best of my judgment, it is explained through inheritance and the complex action of natural selection, entailing extinction and divergence of character, as we have seen illustrated in the diagram.

The affinities of all the beings of the same class have sometimes been represented by a great tree. I believe this simile largely speaks the truth. The green and budding twigs may represent existing species; and those produced during each former year may represent the long succession of extinct species. At each period of growth all the growing twigs have tried to branch out on all sides, and to overtop and kill the surrounding twigs and branches, in the same manner as species and groups of species have tried to overmaster other species in the great battle for life. The limbs divided into great branches, and these into lesser and lesser branches, were themselves once, when the tree was small, budding twigs; and this connexion of the former and present buds by ramifying branches may well represent the classification of all extinct and living species in groups subordinate to groups. Of the many twigs which flourished when the tree was a mere bush, only two or three, now grown into great branches, yet survive and bear all the other branches; so with the species which lived during long-past geological periods, very few now have living and modified descendants. From the first growth of the tree, many a limb and branch has decayed and dropped off; and these lost branches of various sizes may represent those whole orders, families, and genera which have now no living representatives, and which are known to us only from having been found in a fossil state. As we here and there see a thin straggling branch springing from a fork low down in a tree, and which by some chance has been favoured and is still alive on its summit, so we occasionally see an animal like the Ornithorhynchus or Lepidosiren, which in some small degree connects by its affinities two large branches of life, and which has apparently been saved from fatal competition by having inhabited a protected station. As buds give rise by growth to fresh buds, and these, if vigorous, branch out and overtop on all sides many a feebler branch, so by generation I believe it has been with the great Tree of Life, which fills with its dead and broken branches the crust of the earth, and covers the surface with its ever branching and beautiful ramifications.

Chapter VI. Difficulties on Theory

Difficulties on the theory of descent with modification—Transitions—Absence or rarity of transitional varieties—Transitions in habits of life—Diversified habits in the same species—Species with habits widely different from those of their allies—Organs of extreme perfection—Means of transition—Cases of difficulty—Natura non facit saltum—Organs of small importance—Organs not in all cases absolutely perfect—The law of Unity of Type and of the Conditions of Existence embraced by the theory of Natural Selection.

Long before having arrived at this part of my work, a crowd of difficulties will have occurred to the reader. Some of them are so grave that to this day I can never reflect on them without being staggered; but, to the best of my judgment, the greater number are only apparent, and those that are real are not, I think, fatal to my theory.

These difficulties and objections may be classed under the following heads:—Firstly, why, if species have descended from other species by insensibly fine gradations, do we not everywhere see innumerable transitional forms? Why is not all nature in confusion instead of the species being, as we see them, well defined?

Secondly, is it possible that an animal having, for instance, the structure and habits of a bat, could have been formed by the modification of some animal with wholly different habits? Can we believe that natural selection could produce, on the one hand, organs of trifling importance, such as the tail of a giraffe, which serves as a fly-flapper, and, on the other hand, organs of such wonderful structure, as the eye, of which we hardly as yet fully understand the inimitable perfection?

Thirdly, can instincts be acquired and modified through natural selection? What shall we say to so marvellous an instinct as that which leads the bee to make cells, which have practically anticipated the discoveries of profound mathematicians?

Fourthly, how can we account for species, when crossed, being sterile and producing sterile offspring, whereas, when varieties are crossed, their fertility is unimpaired?

The two first heads shall be here discussed—Instinct and Hybridism in separate chapters.

ON THE ABSENCE OR RARITY OF TRANSITIONAL VARIETIES

As natural selection acts solely by the preservation of profitable modifications, each new form will tend in a fully-stocked country to take the place of, and finally to exterminate, its own less improved parent or other less-favoured forms with which it comes into competition. Thus extinction and natural selection will, as we have seen, go hand in hand. Hence, if we look at each species as descended from some other unknown form, both the parent and all the transitional varieties will generally have been exterminated by the very process of formation and perfection of the new form.

But, as by this theory innumerable transitional forms must have existed, why do we not find them embedded in countless numbers in the crust of the earth? It will be much more convenient to discuss this question in the chapter on the Imperfection of the geological record; and I will here only state that I believe the answer mainly lies in the record being incomparably less perfect than is generally supposed; the imperfection of the record being chiefly due to organic beings not inhabiting profound depths of the sea, and to their remains being embedded and preserved to a future age only in masses of sediment sufficiently thick and extensive to withstand an enormous amount of future degradation; and such fossiliferous masses can be accumulated only where much sediment is deposited on the shallow bed of the sea, whilst it slowly subsides. These contingencies will concur only rarely, and after enormously long intervals. Whilst the bed of the sea is stationary or is rising, or when very little sediment is being deposited, there will be blanks in our geological history. The crust of the earth is a vast museum; but the natural collections have been made only at intervals of time immensely remote.

But it may be urged that when several closely-allied species inhabit the same territory we surely ought to find at the present time many transitional forms. Let us take a simple case: in travelling from north to south over a continent, we generally meet at successive intervals with closely allied or representative species, evidently filling nearly the same place in the natural economy of the land. These representative species often meet and interlock; and as the one becomes rarer and rarer, the other becomes more and more frequent, till the one replaces the other. But if we compare these species where they intermingle, they are generally as absolutely distinct from each other in every detail of structure as are specimens taken from the metropolis inhabited by each. By my theory these allied species have descended from a common parent; and during the process of modification, each has become adapted to the conditions of life of its own region, and has supplanted and exterminated its original parent and all the transitional varieties between its past and present states. Hence we ought not to expect at the present time to meet with numerous transitional varieties in each region, though they must have existed there, and may be embedded there in a fossil condition. But in the intermediate region, having intermediate conditions of life, why do we not now find closely-linking intermediate varieties? This difficulty for a long time quite confounded me. But I think it can be in large part explained.

In the first place we should be extremely cautious in inferring, because an area is now continuous, that it has been continuous during a long period. Geology would lead us to believe that almost every continent has been broken up into islands even during the later tertiary periods; and in such islands distinct species might have been separately formed without the possibility of intermediate varieties existing in the intermediate zones. By changes in the form of the land and of climate, marine areas now continuous must often have existed within recent times in a far less continuous and uniform condition than at present. But I will pass over this way of escaping from the difficulty; for I believe that many perfectly defined species have been formed on strictly continuous areas; though I do not doubt that the formerly broken condition of areas now continuous has played an important part in the formation of new species, more especially with freely-crossing and wandering animals.

In looking at species as they are now distributed over a wide area, we generally find them tolerably numerous over a large territory, then becoming somewhat abruptly rarer and rarer on the confines, and finally disappearing. Hence the neutral territory between two representative species is generally narrow in comparison with the territory proper to each. We see the same fact in ascending mountains, and sometimes it is quite remarkable how abruptly, as Alph. De Candolle has observed, a common alpine species disappears. The same fact has been noticed by Forbes in sounding the depths of the sea with the dredge. To those who look at climate and the physical conditions of life as the all-important elements of distribution, these facts ought to cause surprise, as climate and height or depth graduate away insensibly. But when we bear in mind that almost every species, even in its metropolis, would increase immensely in numbers, were it not for other competing species; that nearly all either prey on or serve as prey for others; in short, that each organic being is either directly or indirectly related in the most important manner to other organic beings, we must see that the range of the inhabitants of any country by no means exclusively depends on insensibly changing physical conditions, but in large part on the presence of other species, on which it depends, or by which it is destroyed, or with which it comes into competition; and as these species are already defined objects (however they may have become so), not blending one into another by insensible gradations, the range of any one species, depending as it does on the range of others, will tend to be sharply defined. Moreover, each species on the confines of its range, where it exists in lessened numbers, will, during fluctuations in the number of its enemies or of its prey, or in the seasons, be extremely liable to utter extermination; and thus its geographical range will come to be still more sharply defined.

If I am right in believing that allied or representative species, when inhabiting a continuous area, are generally so distributed that each has a wide range, with a comparatively narrow neutral territory between them, in which they become rather suddenly rarer and rarer; then, as varieties do not essentially differ from species, the same rule will probably apply to both; and if we in imagination adapt a varying species to a very large area, we shall have to adapt two varieties to two large areas, and a third variety to a narrow intermediate zone. The intermediate variety, consequently, will exist in lesser numbers from inhabiting a narrow and lesser area; and practically, as far as I can make out, this rule holds good with varieties in a state of nature. I have met with striking instances of the rule in the case of varieties intermediate between well-marked varieties in the genus Balanus. And it would appear from information given me by Mr. Watson, Dr. Asa Gray, and Mr. Wollaston, that generally when varieties intermediate between two other forms occur, they are much rarer numerically than the forms which they connect. Now, if we may trust these facts and inferences, and therefore conclude that varieties linking two other varieties together have generally existed in lesser numbers than the forms which they connect, then, I think, we can understand why intermediate varieties should not endure for very long periods;—why as a general rule they should be exterminated and disappear, sooner than the forms which they originally linked together.

For any form existing in lesser numbers would, as already remarked, run a greater chance of being exterminated than one existing in large numbers; and in this particular case the intermediate form would be eminently liable to the inroads of closely allied forms existing on both sides of it. But a far more important consideration, as I believe, is that, during the process of further modification, by which two varieties are supposed on my theory to be converted and perfected into two distinct species, the two which exist in larger numbers from inhabiting larger areas, will have a great advantage over the intermediate variety, which exists in smaller numbers in a narrow and intermediate zone. For forms existing in larger numbers will always have a better chance, within any given period, of presenting further favourable variations for natural selection to seize on, than will the rarer forms which exist in lesser numbers. Hence, the more common forms, in the race for life, will tend to beat and supplant the less common forms, for these will be more slowly modified and improved. It is the same principle which, as I believe, accounts for the common species in each country, as shown in the second chapter, presenting on an average a greater number of well-marked varieties than do the rarer species. I may illustrate what I mean by supposing three varieties of sheep to be kept, one adapted to an extensive mountainous region; a second to a comparatively narrow, hilly tract; and a third to wide plains at the base; and that the inhabitants are all trying with equal steadiness and skill to improve their stocks by selection; the chances in this case will be strongly in favour of the great holders on the mountains or on the plains improving their breeds more quickly than the small holders on the intermediate narrow, hilly tract; and consequently the improved mountain or plain breed will soon take the place of the less improved hill breed; and thus the two breeds, which originally existed in greater numbers, will come into close contact with each other, without the interposition of the supplanted, intermediate hill-variety.

To sum up, I believe that species come to be tolerably well-defined objects, and do not at any one period present an inextricable chaos of varying and intermediate links: firstly, because new varieties are very slowly formed, for variation is a very slow process, and natural selection can do nothing until favourable variations chance to occur, and until a place in the natural polity of the country can be better filled by some modification of some one or more of its inhabitants. And such new places will depend on slow changes of climate, or on the occasional immigration of new inhabitants, and, probably, in a still more important degree, on some of the old inhabitants becoming slowly modified, with the new forms thus produced and the old ones acting and reacting on each other. So that, in any one region and at any one time, we ought only to see a few species presenting slight modifications of structure in some degree permanent; and this assuredly we do see.

Secondly, areas now continuous must often have existed within the recent period in isolated portions, in which many forms, more especially amongst the classes which unite for each birth and wander much, may have separately been rendered sufficiently distinct to rank as representative species. In this case, intermediate varieties between the several representative species and their common parent, must formerly have existed in each broken portion of the land, but these links will have been supplanted and exterminated during the process of natural selection, so that they will no longer exist in a living state.

Thirdly, when two or more varieties have been formed in different portions of a strictly continuous area, intermediate varieties will, it is probable, at first have been formed in the intermediate zones, but they will generally have had a short duration. For these intermediate varieties will, from reasons already assigned (namely from what we know of the actual distribution of closely allied or representative species, and likewise of acknowledged varieties), exist in the intermediate zones in lesser numbers than the varieties which they tend to connect. From this cause alone the intermediate varieties will be liable to accidental extermination; and during the process of further modification through natural selection, they will almost certainly be beaten and supplanted by the forms which they connect; for these from existing in greater numbers will, in the aggregate, present more variation, and thus be further improved through natural selection and gain further advantages.

Lastly, looking not to any one time, but to all time, if my theory be true, numberless intermediate varieties, linking most closely all the species of the same group together, must assuredly have existed; but the very process of natural selection constantly tends, as has been so often remarked, to exterminate the parent-forms and the intermediate links. Consequently evidence of their former existence could be found only amongst fossil remains, which are preserved, as we shall in a future chapter attempt to show, in an extremely imperfect and intermittent record.

ON THE ORIGIN AND TRANSITIONS OF ORGANIC BEINGS WITH PECULIAR HABITS AND STRUCTURE

It has been asked by the opponents of such views as I hold, how, for instance, a land carnivorous animal could have been converted into one with aquatic habits; for how could the animal in its transitional state have subsisted? It would be easy to show that within the same group carnivorous animals exist having every intermediate grade between truly aquatic and strictly terrestrial habits; and as each exists by a struggle for life, it is clear that each is well adapted in its habits to its place in nature. Look at the Mustela vison of North America, which has webbed feet and which resembles an otter in its fur, short legs, and form of tail; during summer this animal dives for and preys on fish, but during the long winter it leaves the frozen waters, and preys like other pole-cats on mice and land animals. If a different case had been taken, and it had been asked how an insectivorous quadruped could possibly have been converted into a flying bat, the question would have been far more difficult, and I could have given no answer. Yet I think such difficulties have very little weight.

Here, as on other occasions, I lie under a heavy disadvantage, for out of the many striking cases which I have collected, I can give only one or two instances of transitional habits and structures in closely allied species of the same genus; and of diversified habits, either constant or occasional, in the same species. And it seems to me that nothing less than a long list of such cases is sufficient to lessen the difficulty in any particular case like that of the bat.

Look at the family of squirrels; here we have the finest gradation from animals with their tails only slightly flattened, and from others, as Sir J. Richardson has remarked, with the posterior part of their bodies rather wide and with the skin on their flanks rather full, to the so-called flying squirrels; and flying squirrels have their limbs and even the base of the tail united by a broad expanse of skin, which serves as a parachute and allows them to glide through the air to an astonishing distance from tree to tree. We cannot doubt that each structure is of use to each kind of squirrel in its own country, by enabling it to escape birds or beasts of prey, or to collect food more quickly, or, as there is reason to believe, by lessening the danger from occasional falls. But it does not follow from this fact that the structure of each squirrel is the best that it is possible to conceive under all natural conditions. Let the climate and vegetation change, let other competing rodents or new beasts of prey immigrate, or old ones become modified, and all analogy would lead us to believe that

some at least of the squirrels would decrease in numbers or become exterminated, unless they also became modified and improved in structure
in a corresponding manner. Therefore, I can see no difficulty, more especially under changing conditions of life, in the continued preservation
of individuals with fuller and fuller flank-membranes, each modification
being useful, each being propagated, until by the accumulated effects of
this process of natural selection, a perfect so-called flying squirrel was
produced.

Now look at the Galeopithecus or flying lemur, which formerly was
falsely ranked amongst bats. It has an extremely wide flank-membrane,
stretching from the corners of the jaw to the tail, and including the limbs
and the elongated fingers: the flank-membrane is, also, furnished with an
extensor muscle. Although no graduated links of structure, fitted for gliding
through the air, now connect the Galeopithecus with the other Lemuridæ,
yet I can see no difficulty in supposing that such links formerly existed,
and that each had been formed by the same steps as in the case of the
less perfectly gliding squirrels; and that each grade of structure had been
useful to its possessor. Nor can I see any insuperable difficulty in further
believing it possible that the membrane-connected fingers and fore-arm of
the Galeopithecus might be greatly lengthened by natural selection; and
this, as far as the organs of flight are concerned, would convert it into a
bat. In bats which have the wing-membrane extended from the top of the
shoulder to the tail, including the hind-legs, we perhaps see traces of an
apparatus originally constructed for gliding through the air rather than for
flight.

If about a dozen genera of birds had become extinct or were unknown,
who would have ventured to have surmised that birds might have existed
which used their wings solely as flappers, like the logger-headed duck
(Micropterus of Eyton); as fins in the water and front legs on the land,
like the penguin; as sails, like the ostrich; and functionally for no purpose,
like the Apteryx. Yet the structure of each of these birds is good for it,
under the conditions of life to which it is exposed, for each has to live by
a struggle; but it is not necessarily the best possible under all possible
conditions. It must not be inferred from these remarks that any of the
grades of wing-structure here alluded to, which perhaps may all have resulted from disuse, indicate the natural steps by which birds have acquired
their perfect power of flight; but they serve, at least, to show what diversified means of transition are possible.

Seeing that a few members of such water-breathing classes as the Crustacea and Mollusca are adapted to live on the land, and seeing that we
have flying birds and mammals, flying insects of the most diversified types,
and formerly had flying reptiles, it is conceivable that flying-fish, which
now glide far through the air, slightly rising and turning by the aid of their
fluttering fins, might have been modified into perfectly winged animals.
If this had been effected, who would have ever imagined that in an early
transitional state they had been inhabitants of the open ocean, and had
used their incipient organs of flight exclusively, as far as we know, to escape
being devoured by other fish?

When we see any structure highly perfected for any particular habit, as the wings of a bird for flight, we should bear in mind that animals displaying early transitional grades of the structure will seldom continue to exist to the present day, for they will have been supplanted by the very process of perfection through natural selection. Furthermore, we may conclude that transitional grades between structures fitted for very different habits of life will rarely have been developed at an early period in great numbers and under many subordinate forms. Thus, to return to our imaginary illustration of the flying-fish, it does not seem probable that fishes capable of true flight would have been developed under many subordinate forms, for taking prey of many kinds in many ways, on the land and in the water, until their organs of flight had come to a high stage of perfection, so as to have given them a decided advantage over other animals in the battle for life. Hence the chance of discovering species with transitional grades of structure in a fossil condition will always be less, from their having existed in lesser numbers, than in the case of species with fully developed structures.

I will now give two or three instances of diversified and of changed habits in the individuals of the same species. When either case occurs, it would be easy for natural selection to fit the animal, by some modification of its structure, for its changed habits, or exclusively for one of its several different habits. But it is difficult to tell, and immaterial for us, whether habits generally change first and structure afterwards; or whether slight modifications of structure lead to changed habits; both probably often change almost simultaneously. Of cases of changed habits it will suffice merely to allude to that of the many British insects which now feed on exotic plants, or exclusively on artificial substances. Of diversified habits innumerable instances could be given: I have often watched a tyrant flycatcher (Saurophagus sulphuratus) in South America, hovering over one spot and then proceeding to another, like a kestrel, and at other times standing stationary on the margin of water, and then dashing like a kingfisher at a fish. In our own country the larger titmouse (Parus major) may be seen climbing branches, almost like a creeper; it often, like a shrike, kills small birds by blows on the head; and I have many times seen and heard it hammering the seeds of the yew on a branch, and thus breaking them like a nuthatch. In North America the black bear was seen by Hearne swimming for hours with widely open mouth, thus catching, like a whale, insects in the water. Even in so extreme a case as this, if the supply of insects were constant, and if better adapted competitors did not already exist in the country, I can see no difficulty in a race of bears being rendered, by natural selection, more and more aquatic in their structure and habits, with larger and larger mouths, till a creature was produced as monstrous as a whale.

As we sometimes see individuals of a species following habits widely different from those both of their own species and of the other species of the same genus, we might expect, on my theory, that such individuals would occasionally have given rise to new species, having anomalous habits, and with their structure either slightly or considerably modified from that of their proper type. And such instances do occur in nature. Can a more striking instance of adaptation be given than that of a woodpecker for climbing trees and for seizing insects in the chinks of the bark? Yet in North America there are woodpeckers which feed largely on fruit, and others with elongated wings which chase insects on the wing; and on the plains of La Plata, where not a tree grows, there is a woodpecker, which in every essential part of its organisation, even in its colouring, in the harsh tone of its voice, and undulatory flight, told me plainly of its close blood-relationship to our common species; yet it is a woodpecker which never climbs a tree!

Petrels are the most aërial and oceanic of birds, yet in the quiet Sounds of Tierra del Fuego, the Puffinuria berardi, in its general habits, in its astonishing power of diving, its manner of swimming, and of flying when unwillingly it takes flight, would be mistaken by any one for an auk or grebe; nevertheless, it is essentially a petrel, but with many parts of its organisation profoundly modified. On the other hand, the acutest observer by examining the dead body of the water-ouzel would never have suspected its sub-aquatic habits; yet this anomalous member of the strictly terrestrial thrush family wholly subsists by diving,—grasping the stones with its feet and using its wings under water.

He who believes that each being has been created as we now see it, must occasionally have felt surprise when he has met with an animal having habits and structure not at all in agreement. What can be plainer than that the webbed feet of ducks and geese are formed for swimming? yet there are upland geese with webbed feet which rarely or never go near the water; and no one except Audubon has seen the frigate-bird, which has all its four toes webbed, alight on the surface of the sea. On the other hand, grebes and coots are eminently aquatic, although their toes are only bordered by membrane. What seems plainer than that the long toes of grallatores are formed for walking over swamps and floating plants, yet the water-hen is nearly as aquatic as the coot; and the landrail nearly as terrestrial as the quail or partridge. In such cases, and many others could be given, habits have changed without a corresponding change of structure. The webbed feet of the upland goose may be said to have become rudimentary in function, though not in structure. In the frigate-bird, the deeply-scooped membrane between the toes shows that structure has begun to change.

He who believes in separate and innumerable acts of creation will say, that in these cases it has pleased the Creator to cause a being of one type to take the place of one of another type; but this seems to me only restating the fact in dignified language. He who believes in the struggle for existence and in the principle of natural selection, will acknowledge that every organic being is constantly endeavouring to increase in numbers; and that if any one being vary ever so little, either in habits or structure, and thus gain an advantage over some other inhabitant of the country, it will seize on the place of that inhabitant, however different it may be from its own place. Hence it will cause him no surprise that there should be geese and frigate-birds with webbed feet, either living on the dry land or most rarely alighting on the water; that there should be long-toed corncrakes living in meadows instead of in swamps; that there should be woodpeckers where not a tree grows; that there should be diving thrushes, and petrels with the habits of auks.

ORGANS OF EXTREME PERFECTION AND COMPLICATION

To suppose that the eye, with all its inimitable contrivances for adjusting the focus to different distances, for admitting different amounts of light, and for the correction of spherical and chromatic aberration, could have been formed by natural selection, seems, I freely confess, absurd in the highest possible degree. Yet reason tells me, that if numerous gradations from a perfect and complex eye to one very imperfect and simple, each grade being useful to its possessor, can be shown to exist; if further, the eye does vary ever so slightly, and the variations be inherited, which is certainly the case; and if any variation or modification in the organ be ever useful to an animal under changing conditions of life, then the difficulty of believing that a perfect and complex eye could be formed by natural selection, though insuperable by our imagination, can hardly be considered real. How a nerve comes to be sensitive to light, hardly concerns us more than how life itself first originated; but I may remark that several facts make me suspect that any sensitive nerve may be rendered sensitive to light, and likewise to those coarser vibrations of the air which produce sound.

In looking for the gradations by which an organ in any species has been perfected, we ought to look exclusively to its lineal ancestors; but this is scarcely ever possible, and we are forced in each case to look to species of the same group, that is to the collateral descendants from the same original parent-form, in order to see what gradations are possible, and for the chance of some gradations having been transmitted from the earlier stages of descent, in an unaltered or little altered condition. Amongst existing Vertebrata, we find but a small amount of gradation in the structure of the eye, and from fossil species we can learn nothing on this head. In this great class we should probably have to descend far beneath the lowest known fossiliferous stratum to discover the earlier stages, by which the eye has been perfected.

In the Articulata we can commence a series with an optic nerve merely coated with pigment, and without any other mechanism; and from this low stage, numerous gradations of structure, branching off in two fundamentally different lines, can be shown to exist, until we reach a moderately high stage of perfection. In certain crustaceans, for instance, there is a double cornea, the inner one divided into facets, within each of which there is a lens shaped swelling. In other crustaceans the transparent cones which are coated by pigment, and which properly act only by excluding lateral pencils of light, are convex at their upper ends and must act by convergence; and at their lower ends there seems to be an imperfect vitreous substance. With these facts, here far too briefly and imperfectly given, which show that there is much graduated diversity in the eyes of living crustaceans, and bearing in mind how small the number of living animals is in proportion to those which have become extinct, I can see no very great difficulty (not more than in the case of many other structures) in believing that natural selection has converted the simple apparatus of an optic nerve merely coated with pigment and invested by transparent membrane, into an optical instrument as perfect as is possessed by any member of the great Articulate class.

He who will go thus far, if he find on finishing this treatise that large bodies of facts, otherwise inexplicable, can be explained by the theory of descent, ought not to hesitate to go further, and to admit that a structure even as perfect as the eye of an eagle might be formed by natural selection, although in this case he does not know any of the transitional grades. His reason ought to conquer his imagination; though I have felt the difficulty far too keenly to be surprised at any degree of hesitation in extending the principle of natural selection to such startling lengths.

It is scarcely possible to avoid comparing the eye to a telescope. We know that this instrument has been perfected by the long-continued efforts of the highest human intellects; and we naturally infer that the eye has been formed by a somewhat analogous process. But may not this inference be presumptuous? Have we any right to assume that the Creator works by intellectual powers like those of man? If we must compare the eye to an optical instrument, we ought in imagination to take a thick layer of transparent tissue, with a nerve sensitive to light beneath, and then suppose every part of this layer to be continually changing slowly in density, so as to separate into layers of different densities and thicknesses, placed at different distances from each other, and with the surfaces of each layer slowly changing in form. Further we must suppose that there is a power always intently watching each slight accidental alteration in the transparent layers; and carefully selecting each alteration which, under varied circumstances, may in any way, or in any degree, tend to produce a distincter image. We must suppose each new state of the instrument to be multiplied by the million; and each to be preserved till a better be produced, and then the old ones to be destroyed. In living bodies, variation will cause the slight alterations, generation will multiply them almost infinitely, and natural selection will pick out with unerring skill each improvement. Let this process go on for millions on millions of years; and during each year on millions of individuals of many kinds; and may we not believe that a living optical instrument might thus be formed as superior to one of glass, as the works of the Creator are to those of man?

*   *   *

SUMMARY OF CHAPTER

We have in this chapter discussed some of the difficulties and objections which may be urged against my theory. Many of them are very grave; but I think that in the discussion light has been thrown on several facts, which on the theory of independent acts of creation are utterly obscure. We have seen that species at any one period are not indefinitely variable, and are not linked together by a multitude of intermediate gradations, partly because the process of natural selection will always be very slow, and will act, at any one time, only on a very few forms; and partly because the very process of natural selection almost implies the continual supplanting and extinction of preceding and intermediate gradations. Closely allied species, now living on a continuous area, must often have been formed when the area was not continuous, and when the conditions of life did not insensibly graduate away from one part to another. When two varieties are formed in two districts of a continuous area, an intermediate variety will often be formed, fitted for an intermediate zone; but from reasons assigned, the intermediate variety will usually exist in lesser numbers than the two forms which it connects; consequently the two latter, during the course of further modification, from existing in greater numbers, will have a great advantage over the less numerous intermediate variety, and will thus generally succeed in supplanting and exterminating it.

We have seen in this chapter how cautious we should be in concluding that the most different habits of life could not graduate into each other; that a bat, for instance, could not have been formed by natural selection from an animal which at first could only glide through the air.

We have seen that a species may under new conditions of life change its habits, or have diversified habits, with some habits very unlike those of its nearest congeners. Hence we can understand, bearing in mind that each organic being is trying to live wherever it can live, how it has arisen that there are upland geese with webbed feet, ground woodpeckers, diving thrushes, and petrels with the habits of auks.

Although the belief that an organ so perfect as the eye could have been formed by natural selection, is more than enough to stagger any one; yet in the case of any organ, if we know of a long series of gradations in complexity, each good for its possessor, then, under changing conditions of life, there is no logical impossibility in the acquirement of any conceivable degree of perfection through natural selection. In the cases in which we know of no intermediate or transitional states, we should be very cautious in concluding that none could have existed, for the homologies of many organs and their intermediate states show that wonderful metamorphoses in function are at least possible. For instance, a swim-bladder has apparently been converted into an air-breathing lung. The same organ having performed simultaneously very different functions, and then having been specialised for one function; and two very distinct organs having performed at the same time the same function, the one having been perfected whilst aided by the other, must often have largely facilitated transitions.

We are far too ignorant, in almost every case, to be enabled to assert that any part or organ is so unimportant for the welfare of a species, that modifications in its structure could not have been slowly accumulated by means of natural selection. But we may confidently believe that many modifications, wholly due to the laws of growth, and at first in no way advantageous to a species, have been subsequently taken advantage of by the still further modified descendants of this species. We may, also, believe that a part formerly of high importance has often been retained (as the tail of an aquatic animal by its terrestrial descendants), though it has become of such small importance that it could not, in its present state, have been acquired by natural selection,—a power which acts solely by the preservation of profitable variations in the struggle for life.

Natural selection will produce nothing in one species for the exclusive good or injury of another; though it may well produce parts, organs, and excretions highly useful or even indispensable, or highly injurious to another species, but in all cases at the same time useful to the owner. Natural selection in each well-stocked country, must act chiefly through the competition of the inhabitants one with another, and consequently will produce perfection, or strength in the battle for life, only according to the standard of that country. Hence the inhabitants of one country, generally the smaller one, will often yield, as we see they do yield, to the inhabitants of another and generally larger country. For in the larger country there will have existed more individuals, and more diversified forms, and the competition will have been severer, and thus the standard of perfection will have been rendered higher. Natural selection will not necessarily produce absolute perfection; nor, as far as we can judge by our limited faculties, can absolute perfection be everywhere found.

On the theory of natural selection we can clearly understand the full meaning of that old canon in natural history, "Natura non facit saltum." This canon, if we look only to the present inhabitants of the world, is not strictly correct, but if we include all those of past times, it must by my theory be strictly true.

It is generally acknowledged that all organic beings have been formed on two great laws—Unity of Type, and the Conditions of Existence. By unity of type is meant that fundamental agreement in structure, which we see in organic beings of the same class, and which is quite independent of their habits of life. On my theory, unity of type is explained by unity of descent. The expression of conditions of existence, so often insisted on by the illustrious Cuvier, is fully embraced by the principle of natural selection. For natural selection acts by either now adapting the varying parts of each being to its organic and inorganic conditions of life; or by having adapted them during long-past periods of time: the adaptations being aided in some cases by use and disuse, being slightly affected by the direct action of the external conditions of life, and being in all cases subjected to the several laws of growth. Hence, in fact, the law of the Conditions of Existence is the higher law; as it includes, through the inheritance of former adaptations, that of Unity of Type.

Chapter IX. On the Imperfection of the Geological Record

On the absence of intermediate varieties at the present day—On the nature of extinct intermediate varieties; on their number—On the vast lapse of time, as inferred from the rate of deposition and of denudation—On the poorness of our palæontological collections—On the intermittence of geological formations—On the absence of intermediate varieties in any one formation—On the sudden appearance of groups of species—On their sudden appearance in the lowest known fossiliferous strata.

In the sixth chapter I enumerated the chief objections which might be justly urged against the views maintained in this volume. Most of them have now been discussed. One, namely the distinctness of specific forms, and their not being blended together by innumerable transitional links, is a very obvious difficulty. I assigned reasons why such links do not commonly occur at the present day, under the circumstances apparently most favourable for their presence, namely on an extensive and continuous area with graduated physical conditions. I endeavoured to show, that the life of each species depends in a more important manner on the presence of other already defined organic forms, than on climate; and, therefore, that the really governing conditions of life do not graduate away quite insensibly like heat or moisture. I endeavoured, also, to show that intermediate varieties, from existing in lesser numbers than the forms which they connect, will generally be beaten out and exterminated during the course of further modification and improvement. The main cause, however, of innumerable intermediate links not now occurring everywhere throughout nature depends on the very process of natural selection, through which new varieties continually take the places of and exterminate their parent-forms. But just in proportion as this process of extermination has acted on an enormous scale, so must the number of intermediate varieties, which have formerly existed on the earth, be truly enormous. Why then is not every geological formation and every stratum full of such intermediate links? Geology assuredly does not reveal any such finely graduated organic chain; and this, perhaps, is the most obvious and gravest objection which can be urged against my theory. The explanation lies, as I believe, in the extreme imperfection of the geological record.

In the first place it should always be borne in mind what sort of intermediate forms must, on my theory, have formerly existed. I have found it difficult, when looking at any two species, to avoid picturing to myself, forms *directly* intermediate between them. But this is a wholly false view; we should always look for forms intermediate between each species and a common but unknown progenitor; and the progenitor will generally have differed in some respects from all its modified descendants. To give a simple illustration: the fantail and pouter pigeons have both descended from the rock-pigeon; if we possessed all the intermediate varieties which have ever existed, we should have an extremely close series between both and the rock-pigeon; but we should have no varieties directly intermediate between the fantail and pouter; none, for instance, combining a tail somewhat expanded with a crop somewhat enlarged, the characteristic features of these two breeds. These two breeds, moreover, have become so much modified, that if we had no historical or indirect evidence regarding their origin, it would not have been possible to have determined from a mere comparison of their structure with that of the rock-pigeon, whether they had descended from this species or from some other allied species, such as C. oenas.

So with natural species, if we look to forms very distinct, for instance to the horse and tapir, we have no reason to suppose that links ever existed directly intermediate between them, but between each and an unknown common parent. The common parent will have had in its whole organisation much general resemblance to the tapir and to the horse; but in some points of structure may have differed considerably from both, even perhaps more than they differ from each other. Hence in all such cases, we should be unable to recognise the parent-form of any two or more species, even if we closely compared the structure of the parent with that of its modified descendants, unless at the same time we had a nearly perfect chain of the intermediate links.

It is just possible by my theory, that one of two living forms might have descended from the other; for instance, a horse from a tapir; and in this case *direct* intermediate links will have existed between them. But such a case would imply that one form had remained for a very long period unaltered, whilst its descendants had undergone a vast amount of change; and the principle of competition between organism and organism, between child and parent, will render this a very rare event; for in all cases the new and improved forms of life will tend to supplant the old and unimproved forms.

By the theory of natural selection all living species have been connected with the parent-species of each genus, by differences not greater than we see between the varieties of the same species at the present day; and these parent-species, now generally extinct, have in their turn been similarly connected with more ancient species; and so on backwards, always converging to the common ancestor of each great class. So that the number of intermediate and transitional links, between all living and extinct species, must have been inconceivably great. But assuredly, if this theory be true, such have lived upon this earth.

ON THE LAPSE OF TIME

Independently of our not finding fossil remains of such infinitely numerous connecting links, it may be objected, that time will not have sufficed for so great an amount of organic change, all changes having been effected very slowly through natural selection. It is hardly possible for me even to recall to the reader, who may not be a practical geologist, the facts leading the mind feebly to comprehend the lapse of time. He who can read Sir Charles Lyell's grand work on the Principles of Geology, which the future historian will recognise as having produced a revolution in natural science, yet does not admit how incomprehensibly vast have been the past periods of time, may at once close this volume. Not that it suffices to study the Principles of Geology, or to read special treatises by different observers on separate formations, and to mark how each author attempts to give an inadequate idea of the duration of each formation or even each stratum. A man must for years examine for himself great piles of superimposed strata, and watch the sea at work grinding down old rocks and making fresh sediment, before he can hope to comprehend anything of the lapse of time, the monuments of which we see around us.

*   *   *

ON THE POORNESS OF OUR PALÆONTOLOGICAL COLLECTIONS

That our palæontological collections are very imperfect, is admitted by every one. The remark of that admirable palæontologist, the late Edward Forbes, should not be forgotten, namely, that numbers of our fossil species are known and named from single and often broken specimens, or from a few specimens collected on some one spot. Only a small portion of the surface of the earth has been geologically explored, and no part with sufficient care, as the important discoveries made every year in Europe prove. No organism wholly soft can be preserved. Shells and bones will decay and disappear when left on the bottom of the sea, where sediment is not accumulating. I believe we are continually taking a most erroneous view, when we tacitly admit to ourselves that sediment is being deposited over nearly the whole bed of the sea, at a rate sufficiently quick to embed and preserve fossil remains. Throughout an enormously large proportion of the ocean, the bright blue tint of the water bespeaks its purity. The many cases on record of a formation conformably covered, after an enormous interval of time, by another and later formation, without the underlying bed having suffered in the interval any wear and tear, seem explicable only on the view of the bottom of the sea not rarely lying for ages in an unaltered condition. The remains which do become embedded, if in sand or gravel, will when the beds are upraised generally be dissolved by the percolation of rain-water. I suspect that but few of the very many animals which live on the beach between high and low watermark are preserved. For instance, the several species of the Chthamalinæ (a sub-family of sessile cirripedes) coat the rocks all over the world in infinite numbers: they are all strictly littoral, with the exception of a single Mediterranean species, which inhabits deep water and has been found fossil in Sicily, whereas not one other species has hitherto been found in any tertiary formation: yet it is now known that the genus Chthamalus existed during the chalk period. The molluscan genus Chiton offers a partially analogous case.

With respect to the terrestrial productions which lived during the Secondary and Palæozoic periods, it is superfluous to state that our evidence from fossil remains is fragmentary in an extreme degree. For instance, not a land shell is known belonging to either of these vast periods, with one exception discovered by Sir C. Lyell in the carboniferous strata of North America. In regard to mammiferous remains, a single glance at the historical table published in the Supplement to Lyell's Manual, will bring home the truth, how accidental and rare is their preservation, far better than pages of detail. Nor is their rarity surprising, when we remember how large a proportion of the bones of tertiary mammals have been discovered either in caves or in lacustrine deposits; and that not a cave or true lacustrine bed is known belonging to the age of our secondary or palæozoic formations.

But the imperfection in the geological record mainly results from another and more important cause than any of the foregoing; namely, from the several formations being separated from each other by wide intervals of time. When we see the formations tabulated in written works, or when we follow them in nature, it is difficult to avoid believing that they are closely consecutive. But we know, for instance, from Sir R. Murchison's great work on Russia, what wide gaps there are in that country between the superimposed formations; so it is in North America, and in many other parts of the world. The most skilful geologist, if his attention had been exclusively confined to these large territories, would never have suspected that during the periods which were blank and barren in his own country, great piles of sediment, charged with new and peculiar forms of life, had elsewhere been accumulated. And if in each separate territory, hardly any idea can be formed of the length of time which has elapsed between the consecutive formations, we may infer that this could nowhere be ascertained. The frequent and great changes in the mineralogical composition of consecutive formations, generally implying great changes in the geography of the surrounding lands, whence the sediment has been derived, accords with the belief of vast intervals of time having elapsed between each formation.

* * *

Those who think the natural geological record in any degree perfect, and who do not attach much weight to the facts and arguments of other kinds given in this volume, will undoubtedly at once reject my theory. For my part, following out Lyell's metaphor, I look at the natural geological record, as a history of the world imperfectly kept, and written in a changing dialect; of this history we possess the last volume alone, relating only to two or three countries. Of this volume, only here and there a short chapter has been preserved; and of each page, only here and there a few lines. Each word of the slowly-changing language, in which the history is supposed to be written, being more or less different in the interrupted succession of chapters, may represent the apparently abruptly changed forms of life, entombed in our consecutive, but widely separated, formations. On this view, the difficulties above discussed are greatly diminished, or even disappear.

Chapter XIII. Mutual Affinities of Organic Beings: Morphology: Embryology: Rudimentary Organs

CLASSIFICATION, groups subordinate to groups—Natural system—Rules and difficulties in classification, explained on the theory of descent with modification—Classification of varieties—Descent always used in classification—Analogical or adaptive characters —Affinities, general, complex and radiating—Extinction separates and defines groups—MORPHOLOGY, between members of the same class, between parts of the same individual—EMBRYOLOGY, laws of, explained by variations not supervening at an early age, and being inherited at a corresponding age—RUDIMENTARY ORGANS; their origin explained—Summary.

From the first dawn of life, all organic beings are found to resemble each other in descending degrees, so that they can be classed in groups under groups. This classification is evidently not arbitrary like the grouping of the stars in constellations. The existence of groups would have been of simple signification, if one group had been exclusively fitted to inhabit the land, and another the water; one to feed on flesh, another on vegetable matter, and so on; but the case is widely different in nature; for it is notorious how commonly members of even the same sub-group have different habits. In our second and fourth chapters, on Variation and on Natural Selection, I have attempted to show that it is the widely ranging, the much diffused and common, that is the dominant species belonging to the larger genera, which vary most. The varieties, or incipient species, thus produced ultimately become converted, as I believe, into new and distinct species; and these, on the principle of inheritance, tend to produce other new and dominant species. Consequently the groups which are now large, and which generally include many dominant species, tend to go on increasing indefinitely in size. I further attempted to show that from the varying descendants of each species trying to occupy as many and as different places as possible in the economy of nature, there is a constant tendency in their characters to diverge. This conclusion was supported by looking at the great diversity of the forms of life which, in any small area, come into the closest competition, and by looking to certain facts in naturalisation.

I attempted also to show that there is a constant tendency in the forms which are increasing in number and diverging in character, to supplant and exterminate the less divergent, the less improved, and preceding forms. I request the reader to turn to the diagram illustrating the action, as formerly explained, of these several principles; and he will see that the inevitable result is that the modified descendants proceeding from one progenitor become broken up into groups subordinate to groups. In the diagram each letter on the uppermost line may represent a genus including several species; and all the genera on this line form together one class, for all have descended from one ancient but unseen parent, and, consequently, have inherited something in common. But the three genera on the left hand have, on this same principle, much in common, and form a sub-family, distinct from that including the next two genera on the right hand, which diverged from a common parent at the fifth stage of descent. These five genera have also much, though less, in common; and they form a family distinct from that including the three genera still further to the right hand, which diverged at a still earlier period. And all these genera, descended from (A), form an order distinct from the genera descended from (I). So that we here have many species descended from a single progenitor grouped into genera; and the genera are included in, or subordinate to, sub-families, families, and orders, all united into one class. Thus, the grand fact in natural history of the subordination of group under group, which, from its familiarity, does not always sufficiently strike us, is in my judgment fully explained.

Naturalists try to arrange the species, genera, and families in each class, on what is called the Natural System. But what is meant by this system? Some authors look at it merely as a scheme for arranging together those living objects which are most alike, and for separating those which are most unlike; or as an artificial means for enunciating, as briefly as possible, general propositions,—that is, by one sentence to give the characters common, for instance, to all mammals, by another those common to all carnivora, by another those common to the dog-genus, and then by adding a single sentence, a full description is given of each kind of dog. The ingenuity and utility of this system are indisputable. But many naturalists think that something more is meant by the Natural System; they believe that it reveals the plan of the Creator; but unless it be specified whether order in time or space, or what else is meant by the plan of the Creator, it seems to me that nothing is thus added to our knowledge. Such expressions as that famous one of Linnæus, and which we often meet with in a more or less concealed form, that the characters do not make the genus, but that the genus gives the characters, seem to imply that something more is included in our classification, than mere resemblance. I believe that something more is included; and that propinquity of descent,—the only known cause of the similarity of organic beings,—is the bond, hidden as it is by various degrees of modification, which is partially revealed to us by our classifications.

＊　＊　＊

But I must explain my meaning more fully. I believe that the *arrangement* of the groups within each class, in due subordination and relation to the other groups, must be strictly genealogical in order to be natural; but that the *amount* of difference in the several branches or groups, though allied in the same degree in blood to their common progenitor, may differ greatly, being due to the different degrees of modification which they have undergone; and this is expressed by the forms being ranked under different genera, families, sections, or orders. The reader will best understand what is meant, if he will take the trouble of referring to the diagram in the fourth chapter. We will suppose the letters A to L to represent allied genera, which lived during the Silurian epoch, and these have descended from a species which existed at an unknown anterior period. Species of three of these genera (A, F, and I) have transmitted modified descendants to the present day, represented by the fifteen genera (a^{14} to z^{14}) on the uppermost horizontal line. Now all these modified descendants from a single species, are represented as related in blood or descent to the same degree; they may metaphorically be called cousins to the same millionth degree; yet they differ widely and in different degrees from each other. The forms descended from A, now broken up into two or three families, constitute a distinct order from those descended from I, also broken up into two families. Nor can the existing species, descended from A, be ranked in the same genus with the parent A; or those from I, with the parent I. But the existing genus F^{14} may be supposed to have been but slightly modified; and it will then rank with the parent-genus F; just as some few still living organic beings belong to Silurian genera. So that the amount or value of the differences between organic beings all related to each other in the same degree in blood, has come to be widely different. Nevertheless their genealogical *arrangement* remains strictly true, not only at the present time, but at each successive period of descent. All the modified descendants from A will have inherited something in common from their common parent, as will all the descendants from I; so will it be with each subordinate branch of descendants, at each successive period. If, however, we choose to suppose that any of the descendants of A or of I have been so much modified as to have more or less completely lost traces of their parentage, in this case, their places in a natural classification will have been more or less completely lost,—as sometimes seems to have occurred with existing organisms. All the descendants of the genus F, along its whole line of descent, are supposed to have been but little modified, and they yet form a single genus. But this genus, though much isolated, will still occupy its proper intermediate position; for F originally was intermediate in character between A and I, and the several genera descended from these two genera will have inherited to a certain extent their characters. This natural arrangement is shown, as far as is possible on paper, in the diagram, but in much too simple a manner. If a branching diagram had not been used, and only the names of the groups had been written in a linear series, it would have been still less possible to have given a natural arrangement; and it is notoriously not possible to represent in a series, on a flat surface, the affinities which we discover in nature amongst the beings of the same group. Thus, on the view which I hold, the natural system is genealogical in its arrangement, like a pedigree; but the degrees of modification which the different groups have undergone, have to be expressed by ranking them under different so-called genera, sub-families, families, sections, orders, and classes.

* * *

On the principle of the multiplication and gradual divergence in character of the species descended from a common parent, together with their retention by inheritance of some characters in common, we can understand the excessively complex and radiating affinities by which all the members of the same family or higher group are connected together. For the common parent of a whole family of species, now broken up by extinction into distinct groups and sub-groups, will have transmitted some of its characters, modified in various ways and degrees, to all; and the several species will consequently be related to each other by circuitous lines of affinity of various lengths (as may be seen in the diagram so often referred to), mounting up through many predecessors. As it is difficult to show the blood-relationship between the numerous kindred of any ancient and noble family, even by the aid of a genealogical tree, and almost impossible to do this without this aid, we can understand the extraordinary difficulty which naturalists have experienced in describing, without the aid of a diagram, the various affinities which they perceive between the many living and extinct members of the same great natural class.

Extinction, as we have seen in the fourth chapter, has played an important part in defining and widening the intervals between the several groups in each class. We may thus account even for the distinctness of whole classes from each other—for instance, of birds from all other vertebrate animals—by the belief that many ancient forms of life have been utterly lost, through which the early progenitors of birds were formerly connected with the early progenitors of the other vertebrate classes. There has been less entire extinction of the forms of life which once connected fishes with batrachians. There has been still less in some other classes, as in that of the Crustacea, for here the most wonderfully diverse forms are still tied together by a long, but broken, chain of affinities. Extinction has only separated groups: it has by no means made them; for if every form which has ever lived on this earth were suddenly to reappear, though it would be quite impossible to give definitions by which each group could be distinguished from other groups, as all would blend together by steps as fine as those between the finest existing varieties, nevertheless a natural classification, or at least a natural arrangement, would be possible. * * *

Finally, we have seen that natural selection, which results from the struggle for existence, and which almost inevitably induces extinction and divergence of character in the many descendants from one dominant parent-species, explains that great and universal feature in the affinities of all organic beings, namely, their subordination in group under group. We use the element of descent in classing the individuals of both sexes and of all ages, although having few characters in common, under one species; we use descent in classing acknowledged varieties, however different they may be from their parent; and I believe this element of descent is the hidden bond of connexion which naturalists have sought under the term of the Natural System. On this idea of the natural system being, in so far as it has been perfected, genealogical in its arrangement, with the grades of difference between the descendants from a common parent, expressed by the terms genera, families, orders, &c., we can understand the rules which we are compelled to follow in our classification. We can understand why we value certain resemblances far more than others; why we are permitted to use rudimentary and useless organs, or others of trifling physiological importance; why, in comparing one group with a distinct group, we summarily reject analogical or adaptive characters, and yet use these same characters within the limits of the same group. We can clearly see how it is that all living and extinct forms can be grouped together in one great system; and how the several members of each class are connected together by the most complex and radiating lines of affinities. We shall never, probably, disentangle the inextricable web of affinities between the members of any one class; but when we have a distinct object in view, and do not look to some unknown plan of creation, we may hope to make sure but slow progress.

Morphology.—We have seen that the members of the same class, independently of their habits of life, resemble each other in the general plan of their organisation. This resemblance is often expressed by the term "unity of type;" or by saying that the several parts and organs in the different species of the class are homologous. The whole subject is included under the general name of Morphology. This is the most interesting department of natural history, and may be said to be its very soul. What can be more curious than that the hand of a man, formed for grasping, that of a mole for digging, the leg of the horse, the paddle of the porpoise, and the wing of the bat, should all be constructed on the same pattern, and should include the same bones, in the same relative positions? Geoffroy St. Hilaire has insisted strongly on the high importance of relative connexion in homologous organs: the parts may change to almost any extent in form and size, and yet they always remain connected together in the same order. We never find, for instance, the bones of the arm and forearm, or of the thigh and leg, transposed. Hence the same names can be given to the homologous bones in widely different animals. We see the same great law in the construction of the mouths of insects: what can be more different than the immensely long spiral proboscis of a sphinx-moth, the curious folded one of a bee or bug, and the great jaws of a beetle?—yet all these organs, serving for such different purposes, are formed by infinitely numerous modifications of an upper lip, mandibles, and two pairs of maxillæ. Analogous laws govern the construction of the mouths and limbs of crustaceans. So it is with the flowers of plants.

Nothing can be more hopeless than to attempt to explain this similarity of pattern in members of the same class, by utility or by the doctrine of final causes. The hopelessness of the attempt has been expressly admitted by Owen in his most interesting work on the 'Nature of Limbs.' On the ordinary view of the independent creation of each being, we can only say that so it is;—that it has so pleased the Creator to construct each animal and plant.

The explanation is manifest on the theory of the natural selection of successive slight modifications,—each modification being profitable in some way to the modified form, but often affecting by correlation of growth other parts of the organisation. In changes of this nature, there will be little or no tendency to modify the original pattern, or to transpose parts. The bones of a limb might be shortened and widened to any extent, and become gradually enveloped in thick membrane, so as to serve as a fin; or a webbed foot might have all its bones, or certain bones, lengthened to any extent, and the membrane connecting them increased to any extent, so as to serve as a wing: yet in all this great amount of modification there will be no tendency to alter the framework of bones or the relative connexion of the several parts. If we suppose that the ancient progenitor, the archetype as it may be called, of all mammals, had its limbs constructed on the existing general pattern, for whatever purpose they served, we can at once perceive the plain signification of the homologous construction of the limbs throughout the whole class. So with the mouths of insects, we have only to suppose that their common progenitor had an upper lip, mandibles, and two pair of maxillæ, these parts being perhaps very simple in form; and then natural selection will account for the infinite diversity in structure and function of the mouths of insects. Nevertheless, it is conceivable that the general pattern of an organ might become so much obscured as to be finally lost, by the atrophy and ultimately by the complete abortion of certain parts, by the soldering together of other parts, and by the doubling or multiplication of others,—variations which we know to be within the limits of possibility. In the paddles of the extinct gigantic sea-lizards, and in the mouths of certain suctorial crustaceans, the general pattern seems to have been thus to a certain extent obscured.

* * *

SUMMARY

In this chapter I have attempted to show, that the subordination of group to group in all organisms throughout all time; that the nature of the relationship, by which all living and extinct beings are united by complex, radiating, and circuitous lines of affinities into one grand system; the rules followed and the difficulties encountered by naturalists in their classifications; the value set upon characters, if constant and prevalent, whether of high vital importance, or of the most trifling importance, or, as in rudimentary organs, of no importance; the wide opposition in value between analogical or adaptive characters, and characters of true affinity; and other such rules;—all naturally follow on the view of the common parentage of those forms which are considered by naturalists as allied, together with their modification through natural selection, with its contingencies of extinction and divergence of character. In considering this view of classification, it should be borne in mind that the element of descent has been universally used in ranking together the sexes, ages, and acknowledged varieties of the same species, however different they may be in structure. If we extend the use of this element of descent,—the only certainly known cause of similarity in organic beings,—we shall understand what is meant by the natural system: it is genealogical in its attempted arrangement, with the grades of acquired difference marked by the terms varieties, species, genera, families, orders, and classes.

On this same view of descent with modification, all the great facts in Morphology become intelligible,—whether we look to the same pattern displayed in the homologous organs, to whatever purpose applied, of the different species of a class; or to the homologous parts constructed on the same pattern in each individual animal and plant.

On the principle of successive slight variations, not necessarily or generally supervening at a very early period of life, and being inherited at a corresponding period, we can understand the great leading facts in Embryology; namely, the resemblance in an individual embryo of the homologous parts, which when matured will become widely different from each other in structure and function; and the resemblance in different species of a class of the homologous parts or organs, though fitted in the adult members for purposes as different as possible. Larvae are active embryos, which have become specially modified in relation to their habits of life, through the principle of modifications being inherited at corresponding ages. On this same principle—and bearing in mind, that when organs are reduced in size, either from disuse or selection, it will generally be at that period of life when the being has to provide for its own wants, and bearing in mind how strong is the principle of inheritance—the occurrence of rudimentary organs and their final abortion, present to us no inexplicable difficulties; on the contrary, their presence might have been

even anticipated. The importance of embryological characters and of rudimentary organs in classification is intelligible, on the view that an arrangement is only so far natural as it is genealogical.

Finally, the several classes of facts which have been considered in this
chapter, seem to me to proclaim so plainly, that the inumerable species,
genera, and families of organic beings, with which this world is peopled,
have all descended, each within its own class or group, from common
parents, and have all been modified in the course of descent, that I should
without hesitation adopt this view, even if it were unsupported by other
facts or arguments.

Chapter XIV. Recapitulation and Conclusion

Recapitulation of the difficulties on the theory of Natural Selection—Recapitulation of
the general and special circumstances in its favour—Causes of the general belief in
the immutability of species—How far the theory of natural selection may be
extended—Effects of its adoption on the study of Natural history—Concluding
remarks.

As this whole volume is one long argument, it may be convenient to
the reader to have the leading facts and inferences briefly recapitulated.

That many and grave objections may be advanced against the theory of
descent with modification through natural selection, I do not deny. I have
endeavoured to give to them their full force. Nothing at first can appear
more difficult to believe than that the more complex organs and instincts
should have been perfected, not by means superior to, though analogous
with, human reason, but by the accumulation of innumerable slight variations, each good for the individual possessor. Nevertheless, this difficulty,
though appearing to our imagination insuperably great, cannot be considered real if we admit the following propositions, namely,—that gradations
in the perfection of any organ or instinct, which we may consider, either
do now exist or could have existed, each good of its kind,—that all organs
and instincts are, in ever so slight a degree, variable,—and, lastly, that there
is a struggle for existence leading to the preservation of each profitable
deviation of structure or instinct. The truth of these propositions cannot,
I think, be disputed.

It is, no doubt, extremely difficult even to conjecture by what gradations
many structures have been perfected, more especially amongst broken and
failing groups of organic beings; but we see so many strange gradations in
nature, as is proclaimed by the canon, "Natura non facit saltum," that we
ought to be extremely cautious in saying that any organ or instinct, or any
whole being, could not have arrived at its present state by many graduated
steps. There are, it must be admitted, cases of special difficulty on the
theory of natural selection; and one of the most curious of these is the existence of two or three defined castes of workers or sterile females in the
same community of ants; but I have attempted to show how this difficulty
can be mastered.

With respect to the almost universal sterility of species when first
crossed, which forms so remarkable a contrast with the almost universal

fertility of varieties when crossed, I must refer the reader to the recapitulation of the facts given at the end of the eighth chapter, which seem to me conclusively to show that this sterility is no more a special endowment than is the incapacity of two trees to be grafted together; but that it is incidental on constitutional differences in the reproductive systems of the intercrossed species. We see the truth of this conclusion in the vast difference in the result, when the same two species are crossed reciprocally; that is, when one species is first used as the father and then as the mother.

The fertility of varieties when intercrossed and of their mongrel offspring cannot be considered as universal; nor is their very general fertility surprising when we remember that it is not likely that either their constitutions or their reproductive systems should have been profoundly modified. Moreover, most of the varieties which have been experimentised on have been produced under domestication; and as domestication apparently tends to eliminate sterility, we ought not to expect it also to produce sterility.

The sterility of hybrids is a very different case from that of first crosses, for their reproductive organs are more or less functionally impotent; whereas in first crosses the organs on both sides are in a perfect condition. As we continually see that organisms of all kinds are rendered in some degree sterile from their constitutions having been disturbed by slightly different and new conditions of life, we need not feel surprise at hybrids being in some degree sterile, for their constitutions can hardly fail to have been disturbed from being compounded of two distinct organisations. This parallelism is supported by another parallel, but directly opposite, class of facts; namely, that the vigour and fertility of all organic beings are increased by slight changes in their conditions of life, and that the offspring of slightly modified forms or varieties acquire from being crossed increased vigour and fertility. So that, on the one hand, considerable changes in the conditions of life and crosses between greatly modified forms, lessen fertility; and on the other hand, lesser changes in the conditions of life and crosses between less modified forms, increase fertility.

Turning to geographical distribution, the difficulties encountered on the theory of descent with modification are grave enough. All the individuals of the same species, and all the species of the same genus, or even higher group, must have descended from common parents; and therefore, in however distant and isolated parts of the world they are now found, they must in the course of successive generations have passed from some one part to the others. We are often wholly unable even to conjecture how this could have been effected. Yet, as we have reason to believe that some species have retained the same specific form for very long periods, enormously long as measured by years, too much stress ought not to be laid on the occasional wide diffusion of the same species; for during very long periods of time there will always be a good chance for wide migration by many means. A broken or interrupted range may often be accounted for by the extinction of the species in the intermediate regions. It cannot be denied that we are as yet very ignorant of the full extent of the various climatal and geographical changes which have affected the earth during modern periods; and such changes will obviously have greatly facilitated migration. As an example, I have attempted to show how potent has been the influence of the Glacial period on the distribution both of the same and of representative species throughout the world. We are as yet profoundly ignorant of the many occasional means of transport. With respect to distinct species of the same genus inhabiting very distant and isolated regions, as the process of modification has necessarily been slow, all the means of migration will have been possible during a very long period; and consequently the difficulty of the wide diffusion of species of the same genus is in some degree lessened.

As on the theory of natural selection an interminable number of intermediate forms must have existed, linking together all the species in each group by gradations as fine as our present varieties, it may be asked, Why do we not see these linking forms all around us? Why are not all organic beings blended together in an inextricable chaos? With respect to existing forms, we should remember that we have no right to expect (excepting in rare cases) to discover *directly* connecting links between them, but only between each and some extinct and supplanted form. Even on a wide area, which has during a long period remained continuous, and of which the climate and other conditions of life change insensibly in going from a district occupied by one species into another district occupied by a closely allied species, we have no just right to expect often to find intermediate varieties in the intermediate zone. For we have reason to believe that only a few species are undergoing change at any one period; and all changes are slowly effected. I have also shown that the intermediate varieties which will at first probably exist in the intermediate zones, will be liable to be supplanted by the allied forms on either hand; and the latter, from existing in greater numbers, will generally be modified and improved at a quicker rate than the intermediate varieties, which exist in lesser numbers; so that the intermediate varieties will, in the long run, be supplanted and exterminated.

On this doctrine of the extermination of an infinitude of connecting links, between the living and extinct inhabitants of the world, and at each successive period between the extinct and still older species, why is not every geological formation charged with such links? Why does not every collection of fossil remains afford plain evidence of the gradation and mutation of the forms of life? We meet with no such evidence, and this is the most obvious and forcible of the many objections which may be urged against my theory. Why, again, do whole groups of allied species appear, though certainly they often falsely appear, to have come in suddenly on the several geological stages? Why do we not find great piles of strata beneath the Silurian system, stored with the remains of the progenitors of the Silurian groups of fossils? For certainly on my theory such strata must somewhere have been deposited at these ancient and utterly unknown epochs in the world's history.

I can answer these questions and grave objections only on the supposition that the geological record is far more imperfect than most geologists believe. It cannot be objected that there has not been time sufficient for any amount of organic change; for the lapse of time has been so great as to be utterly inappreciable by the human intellect. The number of specimens in all our museums is absolutely as nothing compared with the countless generations of countless species which certainly have existed. We should not be able to recognise a species as the parent of any one or more species if we were to examine them ever so closely, unless we likewise possessed many of the intermediate links between their past or parent and present states; and these many links we could hardly ever expect to discover, owing to the imperfection of the geological record. Numerous existing doubtful forms could be named which are probably varieties; but who will pretend that in future ages so many fossil links will be discovered, that naturalists will be able to decide, on the common view, whether or not these doubtful forms are varieties? As long as most of the links between any two species are unknown, if any one link or intermediate variety be discovered, it will simply be classed as another and distinct species. Only a small portion of the world has been geologically explored. Only organic beings of certain classes can be preserved in a fossil condition, at least in any great number. Widely ranging species vary most, and varieties are often at first local,—both causes rendering the discovery of intermediate links less likely. Local varieties will not spread into other and distant regions until they are considerably modified and improved; and when they do spread, if discovered in a geological formation, they will appear as if suddenly created there, and will be simply classed as new species. Most formations have been intermittent in their accumulation; and their duration, I am inclined to believe, has been shorter than the average duration of specific forms. Successive formations are separated from each other by enormous blank intervals of time; for fossiliferous formations, thick enough to resist future degradation, can be accumulated only where much sediment is deposited on the subsiding bed of the sea. During the alternate periods of elevation and of stationary level the record will be blank. During these latter periods there will probably be more variability in the forms of life; during periods of subsidence, more extinction.

With respect to the absence of fossiliferous formations beneath the lowest Silurian strata, I can only recur to the hypothesis given in the ninth chapter. That the geological record is imperfect all will admit; but that it is imperfect to the degree which I require, few will be inclined to admit. If we look to long enough intervals of time, geology plainly declares that all species have changed; and they have changed in the manner which my theory requires, for they have changed slowly and in a graduated manner. We clearly see this in the fossil remains from consecutive formations invariably being much more closely related to each other, than are the fossils from formations distant from each other in time.

Such is the sum of the several chief objections and difficulties which may justly be urged against my theory; and I have now briefly recapitulated the answers and explanations which can be given to them. I have felt these difficulties far too heavily during many years to doubt their weight. But it deserves especial notice that the more important objections relate to questions on which we are confessedly ignorant; nor do we know how ignorant we are. We do not know all the possible transitional gradations between the simplest and the most perfect organs; it cannot be pretended that we know all the varied means of Distribution during the long lapse of years, or that we know how imperfect the Geological Record is. Grave as these several difficulties are, in my judgment they do not overthrow the theory of descent with modification.

Now let us turn to the other side of the argument. Under domestication we see much variability. This seems to be mainly due to the reproductive system being eminently susceptible to changes in the conditions of life; so that this system, when not rendered impotent, fails to reproduce offspring exactly like the parent-form. Variability is governed by many complex laws,—by correlation of growth, by use and disuse, and by the direct action of the physical conditions of life. There is much difficulty in ascertaining how much modification our domestic productions have undergone; but we may safely infer that the amount has been large, and that modifications can be inherited for long periods. As long as the conditions of life remain the same, we have reason to believe that a modification, which has already been inherited for many generations, may continue to be inherited for an almost infinite number of generations. On the other hand we have evidence that variability, when it has once come into play, does not wholly cease; for new varieties are still occasionally produced by our most anciently domesticated productions.

Man does not actually produce variability; he only unintentionally exposes organic beings to new conditions of life, and then nature acts on the organisation, and causes variability. But man can and does select the variations given to him by nature, and thus accumulate them in any desired manner. He thus adapts animals and plants for his own benefit or pleasure. He may do this methodically, or he may do it unconsciously by preserving the individuals most useful to him at the time, without any thought of altering the breed. It is certain that he can largely influence the character of a breed by selecting, in each successive generation, individual differences so slight as to be quite inappreciable by an uneducated eye. This process of selection has been the great agency in the production of the most distinct and useful domestic breeds. That many of the breeds produced by man have to a large extent the character of natural species, is shown by the inextricable doubts whether very many of them are varieties or aboriginal species.

There is no obvious reason why the principles which have acted so efficiently under domestication should not have acted under nature. In the preservation of favoured individuals and races, during the constantly-recurrent Struggle for Existence, we see the most powerful and ever-acting means of selection. The struggle for existence inevitably follows from the high geometrical ratio of increase which is common to all organic beings. This high rate of increase is proved by calculation, by the effects of a succession of peculiar seasons, and by the results of naturalisation, as explained in the third chapter. More individuals are born than can possibly survive. A grain in the balance will determine which individual shall live and which shall die,—which variety or species shall increase in number, and which shall decrease, or finally become extinct. As the individuals of the same species come in all respects into the closest competition with each other, the struggle will generally be most severe between them; it will be almost equally severe between the varieties of the same species, and next in severity between the species of the same genus. But the struggle will often be very severe between beings most remote in the scale of nature. The slightest advantage in one being, at any age or during any season, over those with which it comes into competition, or better adaptation in however slight a degree to the surrounding physical conditions, will turn the balance.

With animals having separated sexes there will in most cases be a struggle between the males for possession of the females. The most vigorous individuals, or those which have most successfully struggled with their conditions of life, will generally leave most progeny. But success will often depend on having special weapons or means of defence, or on the charms of the males; and the slightest advantage will lead to victory.

As geology plainly proclaims that each land has undergone great physical changes, we might have expected that organic beings would have varied under nature, in the same way as they generally have varied under the changed conditions of domestication. And if there be any variability under nature, it would be an unaccountable fact if natural selection had not come into play. It has often been asserted, but the assertion is quite incapable of proof, that the amount of variation under nature is a strictly limited quantity. Man, though acting on external characters alone and often capriciously, can produce within a short period a great result by adding up mere individual differences in his domestic productions; and every one admits that there are at least individual differences in species under nature. But, besides such differences, all naturalists have admitted the existence of varieties, which they think sufficiently distinct to be worthy of record in systematic works. No one can draw any clear distinction between individual differences and slight varieties; or between more plainly marked varieties and sub-species, and species. Let it be observed how naturalists differ in the rank which they assign to the many representative forms in Europe and North America.

If then we have under nature variability and a powerful agent always ready to act and select, why should we doubt that variations in any way useful to beings, under their excessively complex relations of life, would be preserved, accumulated, and inherited? Why, if man can by patience select variations most useful to himself, should nature fail in selecting variations useful, under changing conditions of life, to her living products? What limit can be put to this power, acting during long ages and rigidly scrutinising the whole constitution, structure, and habits of each creature,—favouring the good and rejecting the bad? I can see no limit to this power, in slowly and beautifully adapting each form to the most complex relations of life. The theory of natural selection, even if we looked no further than this, seems to me to be in itself probable. I have already recapitulated, as fairly as I could, the opposed difficulties and objections: now let us turn to the special facts and arguments in favour of the theory.

On the view that species are only strongly marked and permanent varieties, and that each species first existed as a variety, we can see why it is that no line of demarcation can be drawn between species, commonly supposed to have been produced by special acts of creation, and varieties which are acknowledged to have been produced by secondary laws. On this same view we can understand how it is that in each region where many species of a genus have been produced, and where they now flourish, these same species should present many varieties; for where the manufactory of species has been active, we might expect, as a general rule, to find it still in action; and this is the case if varieties be incipient species. Moreover, the species of the larger genera, which afford the greater number of varieties or incipient species, retain to a certain degree the character of varieties; for they differ from each other by a less amount of difference than do the species of smaller genera. The closely allied species also of the larger genera apparently have restricted ranges, and they are clustered in little groups round other species—in which respects they resemble varieties. These are strange relations on the view of each species having been independently created, but are intelligible if all species first existed as varieties.

As each species tends by its geometrical ratio of reproduction to increase inordinately in number; and as the modified descendants of each species will be enabled to increase by so much the more as they become more diversified in habits and structure, so as to be enabled to seize on many and widely different places in the economy of nature, there will be a constant tendency in natural selection to preserve the most divergent offspring of any one species. Hence during a long-continued course of modification, the slight differences, characteristic of varieties of the same species, tend to be augmented into the greater differences characteristic of species of the same genus. New and improved varieties will inevitably supplant and exterminate the older, less improved and intermediate varieties; and thus species are rendered to a large extent defined and distinct objects. Dominant species belonging to the larger groups tend to give birth to new and dominant forms; so that each large group tends to become still larger, and at the same time more divergent in character. But as all groups cannot thus succeed in increasing in size, for the world would not hold them, the more dominant groups beat the less dominant. This tendency in the large groups to go on increasing in size and diverging in character, together with the almost inevitable contingency of much extinction, explains the arrangement of all the forms of life, in groups subordinate to groups, all within a few great classes, which we now see everywhere around us, and which has prevailed throughout all time. This grand fact of the grouping of all organic beings seems to me utterly inexplicable on the theory of creation.

As natural selection acts solely by accumulating slight, successive, favourable variations, it can produce no great or sudden modification; it can act only by very short and slow steps. Hence the canon of "Natura non facit saltum," which every fresh addition to our knowledge tends to make more strictly correct, is on this theory simply intelligible. We can plainly see why nature is prodigal in variety, though niggard in innovation. But why this should be a law of nature if each species has been independently created, no man can explain.

Many other facts are, as it seems to me, explicable on this theory. How strange it is that a bird, under the form of woodpecker, should have been created to prey on insects on the ground; that upland geese, which never or rarely swim, should have been created with webbed feet; that a thrush should have been created to dive and feed on sub-aquatic insects; and that a petrel should have been created with habits and structure fitting it for the life of an auk or grebe! and so on in endless other cases. But on the view of each species constantly trying to increase in number, with natural selection always ready to adapt the slowly varying descendants of each to any unoccupied or ill-occupied place in nature, these facts cease to be strange, or perhaps might even have been anticipated.

As natural selection acts by competition, it adapts the inhabitants of each country only in relation to the degree of perfection of their associates; so that we need feel no surprise at the inhabitants of any one country, although on the ordinary view supposed to have been specially created and adapted for that country, being beaten and supplanted by the naturalised productions from another land. Nor ought we to marvel if all the contrivances in nature be not, as far as we can judge, absolutely perfect; and if some of them be abhorrent to our ideas of fitness. We need not marvel at the sting of the bee causing the bee's own death; at drones being produced in such vast numbers for one single act, and being then slaughtered by their sterile sisters; at the astonishing waste of pollen by our fir-trees; at the instinctive hatred of the queen bee for her own fertile daughters; at ichneumonidæ feeding within the live bodies of caterpillars; and at other such cases. The wonder indeed is, on the theory of natural selection, that more cases of the want of absolute perfection have not been observed.

The complex and little known laws governing variation are the same, as far as we can see, with the laws which have governed the production of so-called specific forms. In both cases physical conditions seem to have produced but little direct effect; yet when varieties enter any zone, they occasionally assume some of the characters of the species proper to that zone. In both varieties and species, use and disuse seem to have produced some effect; for it is difficult to resist this conclusion when we look, for instance, at the logger-headed duck, which has wings incapable of flight, in nearly the same condition as in the domestic duck; or when we look at the burrowing tucutucu, which is occasionally blind, and then at certain moles, which are habitually blind and have their eyes covered with skin; or when we look at the blind animals inhabiting the dark caves of America and Europe. In both varieties and species correlation of growth seems to have played a most important part, so that when one part has been modified other parts are necessarily modified. In both varieties and species reversions to long-lost characters occur. How inexplicable on the theory of creation is the occasional appearance of stripes on the shoulder and legs of the several species of the horse-genus and in their hybrids! How simply is this fact explained if we believe that these species have descended from a striped progenitor, in the same manner as the several domestic breeds of pigeon have descended from the blue and barred rock-pigeon!

On the ordinary view of each species having been independently created, why should the specific characters, or those by which the species of the same genus differ from each other, be more variable than the generic characters in which they all agree? Why, for instance, should the colour of a flower be more likely to vary in any one species of a genus, if the other species, supposed to have been created independently, have differently coloured flowers, than if all the species of the genus have the same coloured flowers? If species are only well-marked varieties, of which the characters have become in a high degree permanent, we can understand this fact; for they have already varied since they branched off from a common progenitor in certain characters, by which they have come to be specifically distinct from each other; and therefore these same characters would be more likely still to be variable than the generic characters which have been inherited without change for an enormous period. It is inexplicable on the theory of creation why a part developed in a very unusual manner in any one species of a genus, and therefore, as we may naturally infer, of great importance to the species, should be eminently liable to variation; but, on my view, this part has undergone, since the several species branched off from a common progenitor, an unusual amount of variability and modification, and therefore we might expect this part generally to be still variable. But a part may be developed in the most unusual manner, like the wing of a bat, and yet not be more variable than any other structure, if the part be common to many subordinate forms, that is, if it has been inherited for a very long period; for in this case it will have been rendered constant by long-continued natural selection.

Glancing at instincts, marvellous as some are, they offer no greater difficulty than does corporeal structure on the theory of the natural selection of successive, slight, but profitable modifications. We can thus understand why nature moves by graduated steps in endowing different animals of the same class with their several instincts. I have attempted to show how much light the principle of gradation throws on the admirable architectural powers of the hive-bee. Habit no doubt sometimes comes into play in modifying instincts; but it certainly is not indispensable, as we see, in the case of neuter insects, which leave no progeny to inherit the effects of long-continued habit. On the view of all the species of the same genus having descended from a common parent, and having inherited much in common, we can understand how it is that allied species, when placed under considerably different conditions of life, yet should follow nearly the same instincts; why the thrush of South America, for instance, lines her nest with mud like our British species. On the view of instincts having been slowly acquired through natural selection we need not marvel at some instincts being apparently not perfect and liable to mistakes, and at many instincts causing other animals to suffer.

If species be only well-marked and permanent varieties, we can at once see why their crossed offspring should follow the same complex laws in their degrees and kinds of resemblance to their parents,—in being absorbed into each other by successive crosses, and in other such points,—as do the crossed offspring of acknowledged varieties. On the other hand, these would be strange facts if species have been independently created, and varieties have been produced by secondary laws.

If we admit that the geological record is imperfect in an extreme degree, then such facts as the record gives, support the theory of descent with modification. New species have come on the stage slowly and at successive intervals; and the amount of change, after equal intervals of time, is widely different in different groups. The extinction of species and of whole groups of species, which has played so conspicuous a part in the history of the organic world, almost inevitably follows on the principle of natural selection; for old forms will be supplanted by new and improved forms. Neither single species nor groups of species reappear when the chain of ordinary generation has once been broken. The gradual diffusion of dominant forms, with the slow modification of their descendants, causes the forms of life, after long intervals of time, to appear as if they had changed simultaneously throughout the world. The fact of the fossil remains of each formation being in some degree intermediate in character between the fossils in the formations above and below, is simply explained by their intermediate position in the chain of descent. The grand fact that all extinct organic beings belong to the same system with recent beings, falling either into the same or into intermediate groups, follows from the living and the extinct being the offspring of common parents. As the groups which have descended from an ancient progenitor have generally diverged in character, the progenitor with its early descendants will often be intermediate in character in comparison with its later descendants; and thus we can see why the more ancient a fossil is, the oftener it stands in some degree intermediate between existing and allied groups. Recent forms are generally looked at as being, in some vague sense, higher than ancient and extinct forms; and they are in so far higher as the later and more improved forms have conquered the older and less improved organic beings in the struggle for life. Lastly, the law of the long endurance of allied forms on the same continent,—of marsupials in Australia, of edentata in America, and other such cases,—is intelligible, for within a confined country, the recent and the extinct will naturally be allied by descent.

Looking to geographical distribution, if we admit that there has been during the long course of ages much migration from one part of the world to another, owing to former climatal and geographical changes and to the many occasional and unknown means of dispersal, then we can understand, on the theory of descent with modification, most of the great leading facts in Distribution. We can see why there should be so striking a parallelism in the distribution of organic beings throughout space, and in their geological succession throughout time; for in both cases the beings have been connected by the bond of ordinary generation, and the means of modification have been the same. We see the full meaning of the wonderful fact, which must have struck every traveller, namely, that on the same continent, under the most diverse conditions, under heat and cold, on mountain and lowland, on deserts and marshes, most of the inhabitants within each great class are plainly related; for they will generally be descendants of the same progenitors and early colonists. On this same principle of former migration, combined in most cases with modification, we can understand, by the aid of the Glacial period, the identity of some few plants, and the close alliance of many others, on the most distant mountains, under the most different climates; and likewise the close alliance of some of the inhabitants of the sea in the northern and southern temperate zones, though separated by the whole intertropical ocean. Although two areas may present the same physical conditions of life, we need feel no surprise at their inhabitants being widely different, if they have been for a long period completely separated from each other; for as the relation of organism to organism is the most important of all relations, and as the two areas will have received colonists from some third source or from each other, at various periods and in different proportions, the course of modification in the two areas will inevitably be different.

On this view of migration, with subsequent modification, we can see why oceanic islands should be inhabited by few species, but of these, that many should be peculiar. We can clearly see why those animals which cannot cross wide spaces of ocean, as frogs and terrestrial mammals, should not inhabit oceanic islands; and why, on the other hand, new and peculiar species of bats, which can traverse the ocean, should so often be found on islands far distant from any continent. Such facts as the presence of peculiar species of bats, and the absence of all other mammals, on oceanic islands, are utterly inexplicable on the theory of independent acts of creation.

The existence of closely allied or representative species in any two areas, implies, on the theory of descent with modification, that the same parents formerly inhabited both areas; and we almost invariably find that wherever many closely allied species inhabit two areas, some identical species common to both still exist. Wherever many closely allied yet distinct species occur, many doubtful forms and varieties of the same species likewise occur. It is a rule of high generality that the inhabitants of each area are related to the inhabitants of the nearest source whence immigrants might have been derived. We see this in nearly all the plants and animals of the Galapagos archipelago, of Juan Fernandez, and of the other American islands being related in the most striking manner to the plants and animals of the neighbouring American mainland; and those of the Cape de Verde archipelago and other African islands to the African mainland. It must be admitted that these facts receive no explanation on the theory of creation.

The fact, as we have seen, that all past and present organic beings constitute one grand natural system, with group subordinate to group, and with extinct groups often falling in between recent groups, is intelligible on the theory of natural selection with its contingencies of extinction and divergence of character. On these same principles we see how it is, that the mutual affinities of the species and genera within each class are so complex and circuitous. We see why certain characters are far more serviceable than others for classification;—why adaptive characters, though of paramount importance to the being, are of hardly any importance in classification; why characters derived from rudimentary parts, though of no service to the being, are often of high classificatory value; and why embryological characters are the most valuable of all. The real affinities of all organic beings are due to inheritance or community of descent. The natural system is a genealogical arrangement, in which we have to discover the lines of descent by the most permanent characters, however slight their vital importance may be.

The framework of bones being the same in the hand of a man, wing of a bat, fin of the porpoise, and leg of the horse,—the same number of vertebræ forming the neck of the giraffe and of the elephant,—and innumerable other such facts, at once explain themselves on the theory of descent with slow and slight successive modifications. The similarity of pattern in the wing and leg of a bat, though used for such different purpose,—in the jaws and legs of a crab,—in the petals, stamens, and pistils of a flower, is likewise intelligible on the view of the gradual modification of parts or organs, which were alike in the early progenitor of each class. On the principle of successive variations not always supervening at an early age, and being inherited at a corresponding not early period of life, we can clearly see why the embryos of mammals, birds, reptiles, and fishes should be so closely alike, and should be so unlike the adult forms. We may cease marvelling at the embryo of an air-breathing mammal or bird having branchial slits and arteries running in loops, like those in a fish which has to breathe the air dissolved in water, by the aid of well-developed branchiæ.

Disuse, aided sometimes by natural selection, will often tend to reduce an organ, when it has become useless by changed habits or under changed conditions of life; and we can clearly understand on this view the meaning of rudimentary organs. But disuse and selection will generally act on each creature, when it has come to maturity and has to play its full part in the struggle for existence, and will thus have little power of acting on an organ during early life; hence the organ will not be much reduced or rendered rudimentary at this early age. The calf, for instance, has inherited teeth, which never cut through the gums of the upper jaw, from an early progenitor having well-developed teeth; and we may believe, that the teeth in the mature animal were reduced, during successive generations, by disuse or by the tongue and palate having been fitted by natural selection to browse without their aid; whereas in the calf, the teeth have been left untouched by selection or disuse, and on the principle of inheritance at corresponding ages have been inherited from a remote period to the present day. On the view of each organic being and each separate organ having been specially created, how utterly inexplicable it is that parts, like the teeth in the embryonic calf or like the shrivelled wings under the soldered wing-covers of some beetles, should thus so frequently bear the plain stamp of inutility! Nature may be said to have taken pains to reveal, by rudimentary organs and by homologous structures, her scheme of modification, which it seems that we wilfully will not understand.

I have now recapitulated the chief facts and considerations which have thoroughly convinced me that species have changed, and are still slowly changing by the preservation and accumulation of successive slight favourable variations. Why, it may be asked, have all the most eminent living naturalists and geologists rejected this view of the mutability of species? It cannot be asserted that organic beings in a state of nature are subject to no variation; it cannot be proved that the amount of variation in the course of long ages is a limited quantity; no clear distinction has been, or can be, drawn between species and well-marked varieties. It cannot be maintained that species when intercrossed are invariably sterile, and varieties invariably fertile; or that sterility is a special endowment and sign of creation. The belief that species were immutable productions was almost unavoidable as long as the history of the world was thought to be of short duration; and now that we have acquired some idea of the lapse of time, we are too apt to assume, without proof, that the geological record is so perfect that it would have afforded us plain evidence of the mutation of species, if they had undergone mutation.

But the chief cause of our natural unwillingness to admit that one species has given birth to other and distinct species, is that we are always slow in admitting any great change of which we do not see the intermediate steps. The difficulty is the same as that felt by so many geologists, when Lyell first insisted that long lines of inland cliffs had been formed, and great valleys excavated, by the slow action of the coast-waves. The mind cannot possibly grasp the full meaning of the term of a hundred million years; it cannot add up and perceive the full effects of many slight variations, accumulated during an almost infinite number of generations.

Although I am fully convinced of the truth of the views given in this volume under the form of an abstract, I by no means expect to convince experienced naturalists whose minds are stocked with a multitude of facts all viewed, during a long course of years, from a point of view directly opposite to mine. It is so easy to hide our ignorance under such expressions as the "plan of creation," "unity of design," &c., and to think that we give an explanation when we only restate a fact. Any one whose disposition leads him to attach more weight to unexplained difficulties than to the explanation of a certain number of facts will certainly reject my theory. A few naturalists, endowed with much flexibility of mind, and who have already begun to doubt on the immutability of species, may be influenced by this volume; but I look with confidence to the future, to young and rising naturalists, who will be able to view both sides of the question with impartiality. Whoever is led to believe that species are mutable will do good service by conscientiously expressing his conviction; for only thus can the load of prejudice by which this subject is overwhelmed be removed.

Several eminent naturalists have of late published their belief that a multitude of reputed species in each genus are not real species; but that other species are real, that is, have been independently created. This seems to me a strange conclusion to arrive at. They admit that a multitude of forms, which till lately they themselves thought were special creations, and which are still thus looked at by the majority of naturalists, and which consequently have every external characteristic feature of true species,— they admit that these have been produced by variation, but they refuse to extend the same view to other and very slightly different forms. Nevertheless they do not pretend that they can define, or even conjecture, which are the created forms of life, and which are those produced by secondary laws. They admit variation as a *vera causa* in one case, they arbitrarily reject it in another, without assigning any distinction in the two cases. The day will come when this will be given as a curious illustration of the blindness of preconceived opinion. These authors seem no more startled at a miraculous act of creation than at an ordinary birth. But do they really believe that at innumerable periods in the earth's history certain elemental atoms have been commanded suddenly to flash into living tissues? Do they believe that at each supposed act of creation one individual or many were produced? Were all the infinitely numerous kinds of animals and plants created as eggs or seed, or as full grown? and in the case of mammals, were they created bearing the false marks of nourishment from the mother's womb? Although naturalists very properly demand a full explanation of every difficulty from those who believe in the mutability of species, on their own side they ignore the whole subject of the first appearance of species in what they consider reverent silence.

It may be asked how far I extend the doctrine of the modification of species. The question is difficult to answer, because the more distinct the forms are which we may consider, by so much the arguments fall away in force. But some arguments of the greatest weight extend very far. All the members of whole classes can be connected together by chains of affinities, and all can be classified on the same principle, in groups subordinate to groups. Fossil remains sometimes tend to fill up very wide intervals between existing orders. Organs in a rudimentary condition plainly show that an early progenitor had the organ in a fully developed state; and this in some instances necessarily implies an enormous amount of modification in the descendants. Throughout whole classes various structures are formed on the same pattern, and at an embryonic age the species closely resemble each other. Therefore I cannot doubt that the theory of descent with modification embraces all the members of the same class. I believe that animals have descended from at most only four or five progenitors, and plants from an equal or lesser number.

Analogy would lead me one step further, namely, to the belief that all animals and plants have descended from some one prototype. But analogy may be a deceitful guide. Nevertheless all living things have much in common, in their chemical composition, their germinal vesicles, their cellular structure, and their laws of growth and reproduction. We see this even in so trifling a circumstance as that the same poison often similarly affects plants and animals; or that the poison secreted by the gall-fly produces monstrous growths on the wild rose or oak-tree. Therefore I should infer from analogy that probably all the organic beings which have ever lived on this earth have descended from some one primordial form, into which life was first breathed.

When the views entertained in this volume on the origin of species, or when analogous views are generally admitted, we can dimly foresee that there will be a considerable revolution in natural history. Systematists will be able to pursue their labours as at present; but they will not be incessantly haunted by the shadowy doubt whether this or that form be in essence a species. This I feel sure, and I speak after experience, will be no slight relief. The endless disputes whether or not some fifty species of British brambles are true species will cease. Systematists will have only to decide (not that this will be easy) whether any form be sufficiently constant and distinct from other forms, to be capable of definition; and if definable, whether the differences be sufficiently important to deserve a specific name. This latter point will become a far more essential consideration than it is at present; for differences, however slight, between any two forms, if not blended by intermediate gradations, are looked at by most naturalists as sufficient to raise both forms to the rank of species. Hereafter we shall be compelled to acknowledge that the only distinction between species and well-marked varieties is, that the latter are known, or believed, to be connected at the present day by intermediate gradations, whereas species were formerly thus connected. Hence, without quite rejecting the consideration of the present existence of intermediate gradations between any two forms, we shall be led to weigh more carefully and to value higher the actual amount of difference between them. It is quite possible that forms now generally acknowledged to be merely varieties may hereafter be thought worthy of specific names, as with the primrose and cowslip; and in this case scientific and common language will come into accordance. In short, we shall have to treat species in the same manner as those naturalists treat genera, who admit that genera are merely artificial combinations made for convenience. This may not be a cheering prospect; but we shall at least be freed from the vain search for the undiscovered and undiscoverable essence of the term species.

The other and more general departments of natural history will rise greatly in interest. The terms used by naturalists of affinity, relationship, community of type, paternity, morphology, adaptive characters, rudimentary and aborted organs, &c., will cease to be metaphorical, and will have a plain signification. When we no longer look at an organic being as a savage looks at a ship, as at something wholly beyond his comprehension; when we regard every production of nature as one which has had a history; when we contemplate every complex structure and instinct as the summing up of many contrivances, each useful to the possessor, nearly in the same way as when we look at any great mechanical invention as the summing up of the labour, the experience, the reason, and even the blunders of numerous workmen; when we thus view each organic being, how far more interesting, I speak from experience, will the study of natural history become!

A grand and almost untrodden field of inquiry will be opened, on the causes and laws of variation, on correlation of growth, on the effects of use and disuse, on the direct action of external conditions, and so forth. The study of domestic productions will rise immensely in value. A new variety raised by man will be a far more important and interesting subject for study than one more species added to the infinitude of already recorded species. Our classifications will come to be, as far as they can be so made, genealogies; and will then truly give what may be called the plan of creation. The rules for classifying will no doubt become simpler when we have a definite object in view. We possess no pedigrees or armorial bearings; and we have to discover and trace the many diverging lines of descent in our natural genealogies, by characters of any kind which have long been inherited. Rudimentary organs will speak infallibly with respect to the nature of long-lost structures. Species and groups of species, which are called aberrant, and which may fancifully be called living fossils, will aid us in forming a picture of the ancient forms of life. Embryology will reveal to us the structure, in some degree obscured, of the prototypes of each great class.

When we can feel assured that all the individuals of the same species, and all the closely allied species of most genera, have within a not very remote period descended from one parent, and have migrated from some one birthplace; and when we better know the many means of migration, then, by the light which geology now throws, and will continue to throw, on former changes of climate and of the level of the land, we shall surely be enabled to trace in an admirable manner the former migrations of the inhabitants of the whole world. Even at present, by comparing the differences of the inhabitants of the sea on the opposite sides of a continent, and the nature of the various inhabitants of that continent in relation to their apparent means of immigration, some light can be thrown on ancient geography.

The noble science of Geology loses glory from the extreme imperfection of the record. The crust of the earth with its embedded remains must not be looked at as a well-filled museum, but as a poor collection made at hazard and at rare intervals. The accumulation of each great fossiliferous formation will be recognised as having depended on an unusual concurrence of circumstances, and the blank intervals between the successive stages as having been of vast duration. But we shall be able to gauge with some security the duration of these intervals by a comparison of the preceding and succeeding organic forms. We must be cautious in attempting to correlate as strictly contemporaneous two formations, which include few identical species, by the general succession of their forms of life. As species are produced and exterminated by slowly acting and still existing causes, and not by miraculous acts of creation and by catastrophes; and as the most important of all causes of organic change is one which is almost independent of altered and perhaps suddenly altered physical conditions, namely, the mutual relation of organism to organism,—the improvement of one being entailing the improvement or the extermination of others; it follows, that the amount of organic change in the fossils of consecutive formations probably serves as a fair measure of the lapse of actual time. A number of species, however, keeping in a body might remain for a long period unchanged, whilst within this same period, several of these species, by migrating into new countries and coming into competition with foreign associates, might become modified; so that we must not overrate the accuracy of organic change as a measure of time. During early periods of the earth's history, when the forms of life were probably fewer and simpler, the rate of change was probably slower; and at the first dawn of life, when very few forms of the simplest structure existed, the rate of change may have been slow in an extreme degree. The whole history of the world, as at present known, although of a length quite incomprehensible by us, will hereafter be recognised as a mere fragment of time, compared with the ages which have elapsed since the first creature, the progenitor of innumerable extinct and living descendants, was created.

In the distant future I see open fields for far more important researches. Psychology will be based on a new foundation, that of the necessary acquirement of each mental power and capacity by gradation. Light will be thrown on the origin of man and his history.

Authors of the highest eminence seem to be fully satisfied with the view that each species has been independently created. To my mind it accords better with what we know of the laws impressed on matter by the Creator, that the production and extinction of the past and present inhabitants of the world should have been due to secondary causes, like those determining the birth and death of the individual. When I view all beings not as special creations, but as the lineal descendants of some few beings which lived long before the first bed of the Silurian system was deposited, they seem to me to become ennobled. Judging from the past, we may safely infer that not one living species will transmit its unaltered likeness to a distant futurity. And of the species now living very few will transmit progeny of any kind to a far distant futurity; for the manner in which all organic beings are grouped, shows that the greater number of species of each genus, and all the species of many genera, have left no descendants, but have become utterly extinct. We can so far take a prophetic glance into futurity as to foretel that it will be the common and widely-spread species, belonging to the larger and dominant groups, which will ultimately prevail and procreate new and dominant species. As all the living forms of life are the lineal descendants of those which lived long before the Silurian epoch, we may feel certain that the ordinary succession by generation has never once been broken, and that no cataclysm has desolated the whole world. Hence we may look with some confidence to a secure future of equally inappreciable length. And as natural selection works solely by and for the good of each being, all corporeal and mental endowments will tend to progress towards perfection.

It is interesting to contemplate an entangled bank, clothed with many plants of many kinds, with birds singing on the bushes, with various insects flitting about, and with worms crawling through the damp earth, and to reflect that these elaborately constructed forms, so different from each other, and dependent on each other in so complex a manner, have all been produced by laws acting around us. These laws, taken in the largest sense, being Growth with Reproduction; Inheritance which is almost implied by reproduction; Variability from the indirect and direct action of the external conditions of life, and from use and disuse; a Ratio of Increase so high as to lead to a Struggle for Life, and as a consequence to Natural Selection, entailing Divergence of Character and the Extinction of lessimproved forms. Thus, from the war of nature, from famine and death, the most exalted object which we are capable of conceiving, namely, the production of the higher animals, directly follows. There is grandeur in this view of life, with its several powers, having been originally breathed into a few forms or into one; and that, whilst this planet has gone cycling on according to the fixed law of gravity, from so simple a beginning endless forms most beautiful and most wonderful have been, and are being, evolved.

The Descent of Man (1871)†

Introduction

The nature of the following work will be best understood by a brief account of how it came to be written. During many years I collected notes on the origin or descent of man, without any intention of publishing on the subject, but rather with the determination not to publish, as I thought that I should thus only add to the prejudices against my views. It seemed to me sufficient to indicate, in the first edition of my 'Origin of Species,' that by this work "light would be thrown on the origin of man and his history;" and this implies that man must be included with other organic beings in any general conclusion respecting his manner of appearance on this earth. Now the case wears a wholly different aspect. When a naturalist like Carl Vogt ventures to say in his address as President of the National Institution of Geneva (1869), "personne, en Europe au moins, n'ose plus soutenir la création indépendante et de toutes pièces, des espèces,"[1] it is manifest that at least a large number of naturalists must admit that species are the modified descendants of other species; and this especially holds good with the younger and rising naturalists. The greater number accept the agency of natural selection; though some urge, whether with justice the future must decide, that I have greatly overrated its importance. Of the older and honoured chiefs in natural science, many unfortunately are still opposed to evolution in every form.

In consequence of the views now adopted by most naturalists, and which will ultimately, as in every other case, be followed by others who are not scientific, I have been led to put together my notes, so as to see how far the general conclusions arrived at in my former works were applicable to man. This seemed all the more desirable, as I had never deliberately applied these views to a species taken singly. When we confine our attention to any one form, we are deprived of the weighty arguments derived from the nature of the affinities which connect together whole groups of organisms—their geographical distribution in past and present times, and their geological succession. The homological structure, embryological development, and rudimentary organs of a species remain to be considered, whether it be man or any other animal, to which our attention may be directed; but these great classes of facts afford, as it appears to me, ample and conclusive evidence in favour of the principle of gradual evolution. The strong support derived from the other arguments should, however, always be kept before the mind.

The sole object of this work is to consider, firstly, whether man, like every other species, is descended from some pre-existing form; secondly, the manner of his development; and thirdly, the value of the differences

---

† The text is excerpted from the second edition (1874), an extensive revision that contains a note by T. H. Huxley on the brains of humans and apes.
1. "No one, in Europe at least, dares any longer to assert the wholly independent creation of species." I am grateful to Quentin Hope for all translations from the French in Darwin's works. [Editor]

between the so-called races of man. As I shall confine myself to these points, it will not be necessary to describe in detail the differences between the several races—an enormous subject which has been fully discussed in many valuable works. The high antiquity of man has recently been demonstrated by the labours of a host of eminent men, beginning with M. Boucher de Perthes; and this is the indispensable basis for understanding his origin. I shall, therefore, take this conclusion for granted, and may refer my readers to the admirable treatises of Sir Charles Lyell, Sir John Lubbock, and others. Nor shall I have occasion to do more than to allude to the amount of difference between man and the anthropomorphous apes; for Prof. Huxley, in the opinion of most competent judges, has conclusively shewn that in every visible character man differs less from the higher apes, than these do from the lower members of the same order of Primates.

This work contains hardly any original facts in regard to man; but as the conclusions at which I arrived, after drawing up a rough draft, appeared to me interesting, I thought that they might interest others. It has often and confidently been asserted, that man's origin can never be known: but ignorance more frequently begets confidence than does knowledge: it is those who know little, and not those who know much, who so positively assert that this or that problem will never be solved by science. The conclusion that man is the co-descendant with other species of some ancient, lower, and extinct form, is not in any degree new. Lamarck long ago came to this conclusion, which has lately been maintained by several eminent naturalists and philosophers; for instance, by Wallace, Huxley, Lyell, Vogt, Lubbock, Büchner, Rolle, &c.,[2] and especially by Häckel. This last naturalist, besides his great work, 'Generelle Morphologie' (1866), has recently (1868, with a second edit. in 1870), published his 'Natürliche Schöpfungsgeschichte,' in which he fully discusses the genealogy of man. If this work had appeared before my essay had been written, I should probably never have completed it. Almost all the conclusions at which I have arrived I find confirmed by this naturalist, whose knowledge on many points is much fuller than mine. Wherever I have added any fact or view from Prof. Häckel's writings, I give his authority in the text; other statements I leave as they originally stood in my manuscript, occasionally giving in the footnotes references to his works, as a confirmation of the more doubtful or interesting points.

During many years it has seemed to me highly probable that sexual selection has played an important part in differentiating the races of man; but in my 'Origin of Species' (first edition, p. 199) I contented myself by

---

2. As the works of the first-named authors are so well known, I need not give the titles; but as those of the latter are less well known in England, I will give them:—'Sechs Vorlesungen über die Darwin'sche Theorie:' zweite Auflage, 1868, von Dr. L. Büchner; translated into French under the title 'Conférences sur la Théorie Darwinienne,' 1869. 'Der Mensch, im Lichte der Darwin'sche Lehre,' 1865, von Dr. F. Rolle. I will not attempt to give references to all the authors who have taken the same side of the question. Thus G. Canestrini has published ('Annuario della Soc. d. Nat.,' Modena, 1867, p. 81) a very curious paper on rudimentary characters, as bearing on the origin of man. Another work has (1869) been published by Dr. Francesco Barrago, bearing in Italian the title of "Man, made in the image of God, was also made in the image of the ape."

merely alluding to this belief. When I came to apply this view to man, I found it indispensable to treat the whole subject in full detail.[3] Consequently the second part of the present work, treating of sexual selection, has extended to an inordinate length, compared with the first part; but this could not be avoided.

I had intended adding to the present volumes an essay on the expression of the various emotions by man and the lower animals. My attention was called to this subject many years ago by Sir Charles Bell's admirable work. This illustrious anatomist maintains that man is endowed with certain muscles solely for the sake of expressing his emotions. As this view is obviously opposed to the belief that man is descended from some other and lower form, it was necessary for me to consider it. I likewise wished to ascertain how far the emotions are expressed in the same manner by the different races of man. But owing to the length of the present work, I have thought it better to reserve my essay for separate publication.

Chapter I. The Evidence of the Descent of Man from Some Lower Form

Nature of the evidence bearing on the origin of man—Homologous structures in man and the lower animals—Miscellaneous points of correspondence—Development—Rudimentary structures, muscles, sense-organs, hair, bones, reproductive organs, &c.—The bearing of these three great classes of facts on the origin of man.

He who wishes to decide whether man is the modified descendant of some pre-existing form, would probably first enquire whether man varies, however slightly, in bodily structure and in mental faculties; and if so, whether the variations are transmitted to his offspring in accordance with the laws which prevail with the lower animals. Again, are the variations the result, as far as our ignorance permits us to judge, of the same general causes, and are they governed by the same general laws, as in the case of other organisms; for instance, by correlation, the inherited effects of use and disuse, &c.? Is man subject to similar malconformations, the result of arrested development, of reduplication of parts, &c., and does he display in any of his anomalies reversion to some former and ancient type of structure? It might also naturally be enquired whether man, like so many other animals, has given rise to varieties and sub-races, differing but slightly from each other, or to races differing so much that they must be classed as doubtful species? How are such races distributed over the world; and how, when crossed, do they react on each other in the first and succeeding generations? And so with many other points.

The enquirer would next come to the important point, whether man tends to increase at so rapid a rate, as to lead to occasional severe struggles for existence; and consequently to beneficial variations, whether in body or mind, being preserved, and injurious ones eliminated. Do the races or species of men, whichever term may be applied, encroach on and replace

3. Prof. Häckel was the only author who, at the time when this work first appeared, had discussed the subject of sexual selection, and had seen its full importance, since the publication of the 'Origin'; and this he did in a very able manner in his various works.

one another, so that some finally become extinct? We shall see that all these questions, as indeed is obvious in respect to most of them, must be answered in the affirmative, in the same manner as with the lower animals. But the several considerations just referred to may be conveniently deferred for a time: and we will first see how far the bodily structure of man shows traces, more or less plain, of his descent from some lower form. In succeeding chapters the mental powers of man, in comparison with those of the lower animals, will be considered.

THE BODILY STRUCTURE OF MAN

It is notorious that man is constructed on the same general type or model as other mammals. All the bones in his skeleton can be compared with corresponding bones in a monkey, bat, or seal. So it is with his muscles, nerves, blood-vessels and internal viscera. The brain, the most important of all the organs, follows the same law, as shewn by Huxley and other anatomists. Bischoff,[4] who is a hostile witness, admits that every chief fissure and fold in the brain of man has its analogy in that of the orang; but he adds that at no period of development do their brains perfectly agree; nor could perfect agreement by expected, for otherwise their mental powers would have been the same. Vulpian[5] remarks: "Les différences réelles qui existent entre l'encéphale de l'homme et celui des singes supérieurs, sont bien minimes. Il ne faut pas se faire d'illusions à cet égard. L'homme est bien plus près des singes anthropomorphes par les caractères anatomiques de son cerveau que ceux-ci ne le sont non seulement des autres mammifères, mais même de certains quadrumanes, des guenons et des macaques."[6] But it would be superfluous here to give further details on the correspondence between man and the higher mammals in the structure of the brain and all other parts of the body.

It may, however, be worth while to specify a few points, not directly or obviously connected with structure, by which this correspondence or relationship is well shewn.

Man is liable to receive from the lower animals, and to communicate to them, certain diseases, as hydrophobia, variola, the glanders, syphilis, cholera, herpes, &c.;[7] and this fact proves the close similarity[8] of their

---

4. 'Grosshirnwindungen des Menschen,' 1868, s. 96. The conclusions of this author, as well as those of Gratiolet and Aeby, concerning the brain, will be discussed by Prof. Huxley in the Appendix alluded to in the Preface to this edition.
5. 'Leç. sur la Phys.' 1866, p. 890, as quoted by M. Dally, 'L'Ordre des Primates et le Transformisme,' 1868, p. 29.
6. "The real differences that exist between the brain of man and that of the higher apes are very small. We shouldn't have any illusions about that. Man is much closer to the anthropomorphic apes, in the anatomical structure of the brain, than the apes are, not only to other mammals, but even to certain of the quadrumana, the guenons and the macaques." [Editor]
7. Dr. W. Lauder Lindsay has treated this subject at some length in the 'Journal of Mental Science,' July 1871; and in the 'Edinburgh Veterinary Review,' July 1858.
8. A Reviewer has criticised ('British Quarterly Review,' Oct. 1st, 1871, p. 472) what I have here said with much severity and contempt; but as I do not use the term identity, I cannot see that I am greatly in error. There appears to me a strong analogy between the same infection or contagion producing the same result, or one closely similar, in two distinct animals, and the testing of two distinct fluids by the same chemical reagent.

tissues and blood, both in minute structure and composition, far more plainly than does their comparison under the best microscope, or by the aid of the best chemical analysis. Monkeys are liable to many of the same non-contagious diseases as we are; thus Rengger,[9] who carefully observed for a long time the *Cebus Azarae* in its native land, found it liable to catarrh, with the usual symptoms, and which, when often recurrent, led to consumption. These monkeys suffered also from apoplexy, inflammation of the bowels, and cataract in the eye. The younger ones when shedding their milk-teeth often died from fever. Medicines produced the same effect on them as on us. Many kinds of monkeys have a strong taste for tea, coffee, and spirituous liquors: they will also, as I have myself seen, smoke tobacco with pleasure.[1] Brehm asserts that the natives of north-eastern Africa catch the wild baboons by exposing vessels with strong beer, by which they are made drunk. He has seen some of these animals, which he kept in confinement, in this state; and he gives a laughable account of their behaviour and strange grimaces. On the following morning they were very cross and dismal; they held their aching heads with both hands, and wore a most pitiable expression: when beer or wine was offered them, they turned away with disgust, but relished the juices of lemons.[2] An American monkey, an Ateles, after getting drunk on brandy, would never touch it again, and thus was wiser than many men. These trifling facts prove how similar the nerves of taste must be in monkeys and man, and how similarly their whole nervous system is affected.

Man is infested with internal parasites, sometimes causing fatal effects; and is plagued by external parasites, all of which belong to the same genera or families as those infesting other mammals, and in the case of scabies to the same species.[3] Man is subject, like other mammals, birds, and even insects,[4] to that mysterious law, which causes certain normal processes, such as gestation, as well as the maturation and duration of various diseases, to follow lunar periods. His wounds are repaired by the same process of healing; and the stumps left after the amputation of his limbs, especially during an embryonic period, occasionally possess some power of regeneration, as in the lowest animals.[5]

The whole process of that most important function, the reproduction of the species, is strikingly the same in all mammals, from the first act of

9. 'Naturgeschichte der Säugethiere von Paraguay,' 1830, s. 50.
1. The same tastes are common to some animals much lower in the scale. Mr. A. Nicols informs me that he kept in Queensland, in Australia, three individuals of the *Phaseolarctus cinereus*; and that, without having been taught in any way, they acquired a strong taste for rum, and for smoking tobacco.
2. Brehm, 'Thierleben,' B. i. 1864, s. 75, 86. On the Ateles, s. 105. For other analogous statements, see s. 25, 107.
3. Dr. W. Lauder Lindsay, 'Edinburgh Vet. Review,' July 1858, p. 13.
4. With respect to insects see Dr. Laycock, "On a General Law of Vital Periodicity," 'British Association,' 1842. Dr. Macculloch, 'Silliman's North American Journal of Science,' vol. xvii. p. 305, has seen a dog suffering from tertian ague. Hereafter I shall return to this subject.
5. I have given the evidence on this head in my 'Variation of Animals and Plants under Domestication,' vol. ii. p. 15, and more could be added.

courtship by the male,[6] to the birth and nurturing of the young. Monkeys are born in almost as helpless a condition as our own infants; and in certain genera the young differ fully as much in appearance from the adults, as do our children from their full-grown parents.[7] It has been urged by some writers, as an important distinction, that with man the young arrive at maturity at a much later age than with any other animal: but if we look to the races of mankind which inhabit tropical countries the difference is not great, for the orang is believed not to be adult till the age of from ten to fifteen years.[8] Man differs from woman in size, bodily strength, hairiness, &c., as well as in mind, in the same manner as do the two sexes of many mammals. So that the correspondence in general structure, in the minute structure of the tissues, in chemical composition and in constitution, between man and the higher animals, especially the anthropomorphous apes, is extremely close.

EMBRYONIC DEVELOPMENT

Man is developed from an ovule, about the 125th of an inch in diameter, which differs in no respect from the ovules of other animals. The embryo itself at a very early period can hardly be distinguished from that of other members of the vertebrate kingdom. At this period the arteries run in arch-like branches, as if to carry the blood to branchiæ which are not present in the higher vertebrate, though the slits on the sides of the neck still remain (f, g, fig. 1), marking their former position. At a somewhat later period, when the extremities are developed, "the feet of lizards and mammals," as the illustrious Von Baer remarks, "the wings and feet of birds, no less than the hands and feet of man, all arise from the same fundamental form." It is, says Prof. Huxley,[9] quite in the later stages of development that the young human being presents marked differences from the young ape, while the latter departs as much from the dog in its developments, as the man does. Startling as this last assertion may appear to be, it is demonstrably true.

6. Mares e diversis generibus Quadrumanorum sine dubio dignoscunt feminas humanas a maribus. Primum, credo, odoratu, postea aspectu. Mr. Youatt, qui diu in Hortis Zoologicis (Bestiariis) medicus animalium erat, vir in rebus observandis cautus et sagax, hoc mihi certissime probavit, et curatores ejusdem loci et alii e ministris confirmaverunt. Sir Andrew Smith et Brehm notabant idem in Cynocephalo. Illustrissimus Cuvier etiam narrat multa de hâc re, quâ ut opinor, nihil turpius potest indicari inter omnia hominibus et Quadrumanis communia. Narrat enim Cynocephalum quendam in furorem incidere aspectu feminarum aliquarem, sed nequaquam accendi tanto furore ab omnibus. Semper eligebat juniores, et dignoscebat in turbâ, et advocabat voce gestûque. "Males from diverse genuses of four-handed creatures undoubtedly distinguish human females from males. First, I believe, by scent, than by sight. Mr. Youatt, who for a long time was the animal doctor in the Zoological Garden (for animals), a most cautious and sagacious observer, assured me that this was true; and the curators of the same place and other caretakers confirmed it. Sir Andrew Smith and Brehm remarked the same in the dog-headed ape (mandrills, etc.). The famous Cuvier also tells much about this—a matter, to my way of thinking, than which nothing baser can be witnessed among all those things that are common to humankind and four-handed creatures. For he tells us that a certain dog-headed ape fell into heat at the sight of females, but was by no means aroused with so great heat by all. Always he chose the younger and picked them out in the crowd and summoned them by voice and gesture." I am grateful to John Van Sickle for all translations from the Latin in Darwin's works. [Editor]
7. This remark is made with respect to Cynocephalus and the anthropomorphous apes by Geoffroy Saint-Hilaire and F. Cuvier, 'Hist. Nat. des Mammifères.' tom. i. 1824.
8. Huxley, 'Man's Place in Nature,' 1863, p. 34.
9. 'Man's Place in Nature,' 1863, p. 67.

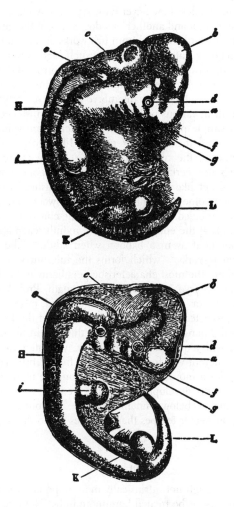

FIG. I. — Upper figure human embryo, from Ecker. Lower figure that of a dog, from Bischoff.

    a. Fore-brain, cerebral hemispheres, &c.

    b. Mid-brain, corpora, quadrigemina.

    c. Hind-brain, cerebellum, medulla oblongata.

    d. Eye.   e. Ear.   f. First visceral arch.   g. Second visceral arch.

    H. Vertebral columns and muscles in process of development.

    i. Anterior
             } extremities.
    K. Posterior

    L. Tail or os coccyx.

As some of my readers may never have seen a drawing of an embryo, I have given one of man and another of a dog, at about the same early stage of development, carefully copied from two works of undoubted accuracy.[1]

After the foregoing statements made by such high authorities, it would be superfluous on my part to give a number of borrowed details, shewing that the embryo of man closely resembles that of other mammals. It may, however, be added, that the human embryo likewise resembles certain low forms when adult in various points of structure. For instance, the heart at first exists as a simple pulsating vessel; the excreta are voided through a cloacal passage; and the os coccyx projects like a true tail, "extending considerably beyond the rudimentary legs."[2] In the embryos of all air-breathing vertebrates, certain glands, called the corpora Wolffiana, correspond with, and act like the kidneys of mature fishes.[3] Even at a later embryonic period, some striking resemblances between man and the lower animals may be observed. Bischoff says "that the convolutions of the brain in a human fœtus at the end of the seventh month reach about the same stage of development as in a baboon when adult."[4] The great toe, as Professor Owen remarks,[5] "which forms the fulcrum when standing or walking, is perhaps the most characteristic peculiarity in the human structure;" but in an embryo, about an inch in length, Prof. Wyman[6] found "that the great toe was shorter than the others; and, instead of being parallel to them, projected at an angle from the side of the foot, thus corresponding with the permanent condition of this part in the quadrumana." I will conclude with a quotation from Huxley,[7] who after asking, does man originate in a different way from a dog, bird, frog or fish? says, "the reply is not doubtful for a moment; without question, the mode of origin, and the early stages of the development of man, are identical with those of the animals immediately below him in the scale: without a doubt in these respects, he is far nearer to apes than the apes are to the dog."

RUDIMENTS

This subject, though not intrinsically more important than the two last, will for several reasons be treated here more fully.[8] Not one of the higher animals can be named which does not bear some part in a rudimentary

1. The human embryo (upper fig.) is from Ecker, 'Icones Phys.,' 1851–1859, tab. xxx. fig. 2. This embryo was ten lines in length, so that the drawing is much magnified. The embryo of the dog is from Bischoff, 'Entwicklungsgeschichte des Hunde-Eies,' 1845, tab. xi. fig. 42 B. This drawing is five times magnified, the embryo being twenty-five days old. The internal viscera have been omitted, and the uterine appendages in both drawings removed. I was directed to these figures by Prof. Huxley, from whose work, 'Man's Place in Nature,' the idea of giving them was taken. Häckel has also given analogous drawings in his 'Schöpfungsgeschichte.'
2. Prof. Wyman in 'Proc. of American Acad. of Sciences,' vol. iv. 1860, p. 17.
3. Owen, 'Anatomy of Vertebrates,' vol. i. p. 533.
4. 'Die Grosshirnwindungen des Menschen,' 1868, s. 95.
5. 'Anatomy of Vertebrates,' vol. ii. p. 553.
6. 'Proc. Soc. Nat. Hist.' Boston; 1863, vol. ix. p. 185.
7. 'Man's Place in Nature,' p. 65.
8. I had written a rough copy of this chapter before reading a valuable paper, "Caratteri rudimentali in ordine all' origine dell' uomo" ('Annuario della Soc. d. Nat.,' Modena, 1867, p. 81), by G. Canestrini, to which paper I am considerably indebted. Häckel has given admirable discussions on this whole subject, under the title of Dysteleology, in his 'Generelle Morphologie' and 'Schöpfungsgeschichte.'

condition; and man forms no exception to the rule. Rudimentary organs must be distinguished from those that are nascent; though in some cases the distinction is not easy. The former are either absolutely useless, such as the mammæ of male quadrupeds, or the incisor teeth of ruminants which never cut through the gums; or they are of such slight service to their present possessors, that we can hardly suppose that they were developed under the conditions which now exist. Organs in this latter state are not strictly rudimentary, but they are tending in this direction. Nascent organs, on the other hand, though not fully developed, are of high service to their possessors, and are capable of further development. Rudimentary organs are eminently variable; and this is partly intelligible, as they are useless, or nearly useless, and consequently are no longer subjected to natural selection. They often become wholly suppressed. When this occurs, they are nevertheless liable to occasional reappearance through reversion—a circumstance well worthy of attention.

The chief agents in causing organs to become rudimentary seem to have been disuse at that period of life when the organ is chiefly used (and this is generally during maturity), and also inheritance at a corresponding period of life. The term "disuse" does not relate merely to the lessened action of muscles, but includes a diminished flow of blood to a part or organ, from being subjected to fewer alterations of pressure, or from becoming in any way less habitually active. Rudiments, however, may occur in one sex of those parts which are normally present in the other sex; and such rudiments, as we shall hereafter see, have often originated in a way distinct from those here referred to. In some cases, organs have been reduced by means of natural selection, from having become injurious to the species under changed habits of life. The process of reduction is probably often aided through the two principles of compensation and economy of growth; but the later stages of reduction, after disuse has done all that can fairly be attributed to it, and when the saving to be effected by the economy of growth would be very small,[9] are difficult to understand. The final and complete suppression of a part, already useless and much reduced in size, in which case neither compensation nor economy can come into play, is perhaps intelligible by the aid of the hypothesis of pangenesis. But as the whole subject of rudimentary organs has been discussed and illustrated in my former works,[1] I need here say no more on this head.

Rudiments of various muscles have been observed in many parts of the human body;[2] and not a few muscles, which are regularly present in some of the lower animals can occasionally be detected in man in a greatly reduced condition. Every one must have noticed the power which many animals, especially horses, possess of moving or twitching their skin; and this is effected by the *panniculus carnosus*. Remnants of this muscle in an

---

9. Some good criticisms on this subject have been given by Messrs. Murie and Mivart, in 'Transact. Zoolog. Soc.' 1869, vol, vii p. 92.

1. 'Variation of Animals and Plants under Domestication,' vol. ii. pp. 317 and 397. See also 'Origin of Species,' fifth edition, p. 535.

2. For instance, M. Richard ('Annales des Sciences Nat.,' 3d series, Zoolog. 1852, tom. xviii, p. 13) describes and figures rudiments of what he calls the "muscle pédieux de la main," which he says is sometimes "infiniment petit." Another muscle, called "le tibial postérieur," is generally quite absent in the hand, but appears from time to time in a more or less rudimentary condition.

efficient state are found in various parts of our bodies; for instance, the muscle on the forehead, by which the eyebrows are raised. The *platysma myoides*, which is well developed on the neck, belongs to this system. Prof. Turner, of Edinburgh, has occasionally detected, as he informs me, muscular fasciculi in five different situations, namely in the axillæ, near the scapulæ, &c., all of which must be referred to the system of the *panniculus*. He has also shewn[3] that the *musculus sternalis* or *sternalis brutorum*, which is not an extension of the *rectus abdominalis*, but is closely allied to the *panniculus*, occurred in the proportion of about three percent. in upward of 600 bodies: he adds, that this muscle affords "an excellent illustration of the statement that occasional and rudimentary structures are especially liable to variation in arrangement."

Some few persons have the power of contracting the superficial muscles on their scalps; and these muscles are in a variable and partially rudimentary condition. M. A. de Candolle has communicated to me a curious instance of the long-continued persistence or inheritance of this power, as well as of its unusual development. He knows a family, in which one member, the present head of the family, could, when a youth, pitch several heavy books from his head by the movement of the scalp alone; and he won wagers by performing this feat. His father, uncle, grandfather, and his three children possess the same power to the same unusual degree. This family became divided eight generations ago into two branches; so that the head of the above-mentioned branch is cousin in the seventh degree to the head of the other branch. This distant cousin resides in another part of France; and on being asked whether he possessed the same faculty, immediately exhibited his power. This case offers a good illustration how persistent may be the transmission of an absolutely useless faculty, probably derived from our remote semi-human progenitors; since many monkeys have, and frequently use the power, of largely moving their scalps up and down.[4]

The extrinsic muscles which serve to move the external ear, and the intrinsic muscles which move the different parts, are in a rudimentary condition in man, and they all belong to the system of the *panniculus*; they are also variable in development, or at least in function. I have seen one man who could draw the whole ear forwards; other men can draw it upwards; another who could draw it backwards;[5] and from what one of these persons told me, it is probable that most of us, by often touching our ears, and thus directing our attention towards them, could recover some power of movement by repeated trials. The power of erecting and directing the shell of the ears to the various points of the compass, is no doubt of the highest service to many animals, as they thus perceive the direction of danger; but I have never heard, on sufficient evidence, of a man who possessed this power, the one which might be of use to him. The whole external shell may be considered a rudiment, together with the various folds and prominences (helix and anti-helix, tragus and anti-tragus,

3. Prof. W. Turner, 'Proc. Royal Soc. Edinburgh,' 1866–67, p. 65.
4. See my 'Expression of the Emotions in Man and Animals,' 1872, p. 144.
5. Canestrini quotes Hyrtl. ('Annuario della Soc. dei Naturalisti,' Modena, 1897, p. 97) to the same effect.

&c.) which in the lower animals strengthen and support the ear when erect, without adding much to its weight. Some authors, however, suppose that the cartilage of the shell serves to transmit vibrations to the acoustic nerve; but Mr. Toynbee,[6] after collecting all the known evidence on this head, concludes that the external shell is of no distinct use. The ears of the chimpanzee and orang are curiously like those of man, and the proper muscles are likewise but very slightly developed.[7] I am also assured by the keepers in the Zoological Gardens that these animals never move or erect their ears; so that they are in an equally rudimentary condition with those of man, as far as function is concerned. Why these animals, as well as the progenitors of man, should have lost the power of erecting their ears, we can not say. It may be, though I am not satisfied with this view, that owing to their arboreal habits and great strength they were but little exposed to danger, and so during a lengthened period moved their ears but little, and thus gradually lost the power of moving them. This would be a parallel case with that of those large and heavy birds, which, from inhabiting oceanic islands, have not exposed to the attacks of beasts of prey, and have consequently lost the power of using their wings for flight. The inability to move the ears in man and several apes is, however, partly compensated by the freedom with which they can move the head in a horizontal plane, so as to catch sounds from all directions. It has been asserted that the ear of man alone possesses a lobule; but "a rudiment of it is found in the gorilla;"[8] and, as I hear from Prof. Preyer, it is not rarely absent in the negro.

The celebrated sculptor, Mr. Woolner, informs me of one little peculiarity in the external ear, which he has often observed both in men and women, and of which he perceived the full significance. His attention was first called to the subject whilst at work on his figure of Puck, to which he had given pointed ears. He was thus led to examine the ears of various monkeys, and subsequently more carefully those of man. The peculiarity consists in a little blunt point, projecting from the inwardly folded margin, or helix. When present, it is developed at birth, and according to Prof. Ludwig Meyer, more frequently in man than in woman. Mr. Woolner made an exact model of one such case, and sent me the accompanying drawing. (Fig. 2.) These points not only project inwards towards the centre of the ear, but often a little outwards from its plane, so as to be visible when the head is viewed from directly in front or behind. They are variable in size, and somewhat in position, standing either a little higher or lower; and they sometimes occur on one ear and not on the other. They are not confined to mankind, for I observed a case in one of the spider-monkeys (*Ateles beelzebuth*) in our Zoological Gardens; and Mr. E. Ray Lankester informs me of another case in a chimpanzee in the gardens at Hamburg. The helix obviously consists of the extreme margin of the ear folded inwards; and this folding appears to be in some manner connected with the

6. 'The Diseases of the Ear,' by J. Toynbee, F. R. S., 1860, p. 12. A distinguished physiologist, Prof. Preyer, informs me that he had lately been experimenting on the function of the shell of the ear, and has come to nearly the same conclusion as that given here.
7. Prof. A. Macalister, 'Annals and Mag. of Nat. History,' vol. vii., 1871, p. 342.
8. Mr. St. George Mivart, 'Elementary Anatomy,' 1873, p. 396.

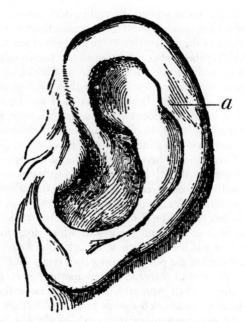

FIG. 2.—Human Ear, modelled and drawn by Mr. Woolner.
  a. *The projecting point.*

whole external ear being permanently pressed backwards. In many monkeys, which do not stand high in the order, as baboons and some species of macacus,[9] the upper portion of the ear is slightly pointed, and the margin is not at all folded inwards; but if the margin were to be thus folded, a slight point would necessarily project inwards towards the centre, and probably a little outwards from the plane of the ear; and this I believe to be their origin in many cases. On the other hand, Prof. L. Meyer, in an able paper recently published,[1] maintains that the whole case is one of mere variability; and that the projections are not real ones, but are due to the internal cartilage on each side of the points not having been fully developed. I am quite ready to admit that this is the correct explanation in many instances, as in those figured by Prof. Meyer, in which there are several minute points, or the whole margin is sinuous. I have myself seen, through the kindness of Dr. L. Down, the ear of a microcephalous idiot, on which there is a projection on the outside of the helix, and not on the inward folded edge, so that this point can have no relation to a former apex of the ear. Nevertheless in some cases, my original view, that the points are vestiges of the tips of formerly erect and pointed ears, still seems to me probable. I think so from the frequency of their occurrence, and from the general correspondence in position with that of the tip of a pointed ear. In one case, of which a photograph has been sent me, the

9. See also some remarks, and the drawings of the ears of the Lemuroidea, in Messrs. Murie and Mivart's excellent paper in 'Transact. Zoolog. Soc.' vol. vii. 1869, pp. 6 and 90.
1. Ueber das Darwin'sche Spitzohr, Archiv für Path. Anat. und Phys. 1871, p. 485.

projection is so large, that supposing, in accordance with Prof. Meyer's view, the ear to be made perfect by the equal development of the cartilage throughout the whole extent of the margin, it would have covered fully one-third of the whole ear. Two cases have been communicated to me, one in North America, and the other in England, in which the upper margin is not at all folded inwards, but is pointed, so that it closely resembles the pointed ear of an ordinary quadruped in outline. In one of these cases, which was that of a young child, the father compared the ear with the drawing which I have given[2] of the ear of a monkey, the *Cynopithecus niger*, and says that their outlines are closely similar. If, in these two cases, the margin had been folded inwards in the normal manner, an inward projection must have been formed. I may add that in two other cases the outline still remains somewhat pointed, although the margin of the upper part of the ear is normally folded inwards—in one of them, however, very narrowly. The following woodcut (No. 3) is an accurate copy of a photograph of the fœtus of an orang (kindly sent me by Dr. Nitsche), in which it may be seen how different the pointed outline of the ear is at this period from its adult condition, when it bears a close general resemblance to that of man. It is evident that the folding over of the tip of such an ear, unless it changed greatly during its further development, would give rise to a point projecting inwards. On the whole, it still seems to me probable that the points in question are in some cases, both in man and apes, vestiges of a former condition.

The nictitating membrane, or third eyelid, with its accessory muscles and other structures, is especially well developed in birds, and is of much functional importance to them, as it can be rapidly drawn across the whole eye-ball. It is found in some reptiles and amphibians, and in certain fishes, as in sharks. It is fairly well developed in the two lower divisions of the mammalian series, namely, in the monotremata and marsupials, and in some few of the higher mammals, as in the walrus. But in man, the quadrumana, and most other mammals, it exists, as is admitted by all anatomists, as a mere rudiment, called the semilunar fold.[3]

The sense of smell is of the highest importance to the greater number of mammals—to some, as the ruminants, in warning them of danger; to others, as the carnivora, in finding their prey; to others, again, as the wild boar, for both purposes combined. But the sense of smell is of extremely slight service, if any, even to the dark coloured races of men, in whom it is much more highly developed than in the white and civilised races.[4]

---

2. 'The Expression of the Emotions,' p. 136.
3. Müller's 'Elements of Physiology.' Eng. translat., 1842, vol. ii. p. 1117. Owen, 'Anatomy of Vertebrates,' vol. iii. p. 260; ibid. on the Walrus, 'Proc. Zoolog. Soc.' November 8th, 1854. See also R. Knox, 'Great Artists and Anatomists,' p. 106. This rudiment apparently is somewhat larger in Negroes and Australians than in Europeans, see Carl Vogt, 'Lectures on Man,' Eng. translat. p. 129.
4. The account given by Humboldt of the power of smell possessed by the natives of South America is well known, and has been confirmed by others. M. Houzeau ('Études sur les Facultés Mentales,' &c., tom. i. 1872, p. 91) asserts that he repeatedly made experiments, and proved that Negroes and Indians could recognise persons in the dark by their odour. Dr. W. Ogle has made some curious observations on the connection between the power of smell and the colouring matter of the membrane of the olfactory region as well as of the skin of the body. I have, therefore, spoken in the text of the dark-coloured races having a finer sense of smell than the white races. See his paper, 'Medico-Chirurgical Transactions,' London, vol. liii., 1870, p. 276.

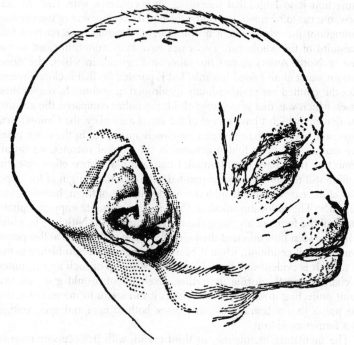

FIG. 3.—Fœtus of an Orang. Exact copy of a photograph, showing the form of the ear at this early age.

Nevertheless it does not warn them of danger, nor guide them to their food; nor does it prevent the Esquimaux from sleeping in the most fetid atmosphere, nor many savages from eating half-putrid meat. In Europeans the power differs greatly in different individuals, as I am assured by an eminent naturalist who possesses this sense highly developed, and who has attended to the subject. Those who believe in the principle of gradual evolution, will not readily admit that the sense of smell in its present state was originally acquired by man, as he now exists. He inherits the power in an enfeebled and so far rudimentary condition, from some early progenitor, to whom it was highly serviceable, and by whom it was continually used. In those animals which have this sense highly developed, such as dogs and horses, the recollection of persons and of places is strongly associated with their odour; and we can thus perhaps understand how it is, as Dr. Maudsley has truly remarked,[5] that the sense of smell in man "is singularly effective in recalling vividly the ideas and images of forgotten scenes and places."

Man differs conspicuously from all the other Primates in being almost naked. But a few short straggling hairs are found over the greater part of the body in the man, and fine down on that of a woman. The different

5. 'The Physiology and Pathology of Mind,' 2nd edit, 1868, p. 134.

races differ much in hairiness; and in the individuals of the same race the
hairs are highly variable, not only in abundance, but likewise in position:
thus in some Europeans the shoulders are quite naked, whilst in others
they bear thick tufts of hair.[6] There can be little doubt that the hairs thus
scattered over the body are the rudiments of the uniform hairy coat of the
lower animals. This view is rendered all the more probable, as it is known
that fine, short, and pale-coloured hairs on the limbs and other parts of
the body, occasionally become developed into "thickset, long, and rather
coarse dark hairs," when abnormally nourished near old-standing inflamed
surfaces.[7]

I am informed by Sir James Paget that often several members of a family
have a few hairs in their eyebrows much longer than the others; so that
even this slight peculiarity seems to be inherited. These hairs, too, seem
to have their representatives; for in the chimpanzee, and in certain species
of Macacus, there are scattered hairs of considerable length rising from
the naked skin above the eyes, and corresponding to our eyebrows; similar
long hairs project from the hairy covering of the superciliary ridges in some
baboons.

The fine wool-like hair, or so-called lanugo, with which the human
fœtus during the sixth month is thickly covered, offers a more curious
case. It is first developed, during the fifth month, on the eyebrows and
face, and especially round the mouth, where it is much longer than that
on the head. A moustache of this kind was observed by Eschricht[8] on a
female fœtus; but this is not so surprising a circumstance as it may at first
appear, for the two sexes generally resemble each other in all external
characters during an early period of growth. The direction and arrangement of the hairs on all parts of the fœtal body are the same as in the
adult, but are subject to much variability. The whole surface, including
even the forehead and ears, is thus thickly clothed; but it is a significant
fact that the palms of the hands and the soles of the feet are quite naked,
like the inferior surfaces of all four extremities in most of the lower animals. As this can hardly be an accidental coincidence, the woolly covering
of the fœtus probably represents the first permanent coat of hair in those
mammals which are born hairy. Three or four cases have been recorded
of persons born with their whole bodies and faces thickly covered with
fine long hairs; and this strange condition is strongly inherited, and is
correlated with an abnormal condition of the teeth.[9] Prof. Alex. Brandt
informs me that he has compared the hair from the face of a man thus
characterised, aged thirty-five, with the lanugo of a fœtus, and finds it quite
similar in texture; therefore, as he remarks, the case may be attributed to
an arrest of development in the hair, together with its continued growth.
Many delicate children, as I have been assured by a surgeon to a hospital

---

6. Eschricht, Ueber die Richtung der Haare am menschlichen Körper, 'Müller's Archiv für Anat.
und Phys. 1837, s. 47. I shall often have to refer to this very curious paper.
7. Paget, 'Lectures on Surgical Pathology,' 1853, vol. i. p. 71.
8. Eschricht, ibid. s. 40, 47.
9. See my 'Variation of Animals and Plants under Domestication,' vol. ii. p. 327. Prof. Alex Brandt
has recently sent me an additional case of a father and son, born in Russia, with these peculiarities.
I have received drawings of both from Paris.

for children, have their backs covered by rather long silky hairs; and such cases probably come under the same head.

It appears as if the posterior molar or wisdom-teeth were tending to become rudimentary in the more civilised races of man. These teeth are rather smaller than the other molars, as is likewise the case with the corresponding teeth in the chimpanzee and orang; and they have only two separate fangs. They do not cut through the gums till about the seventeenth year, and I have been assured that they are much more liable to decay, and are earlier lost than the other teeth; but this is denied by some eminent dentists. They are also much more liable to vary, both in structure and in the period of their development, than the other teeth.[1] In the Melanian races, on the other hand, the wisdom-teeth are usually furnished with three separate fangs, and are generally sound; they also differ from the other molars in size, less than in the Caucasian races.[2] Prof. Schaaffhausen accounts for this difference between the races by "the posterior dental portion of the jaw being always shortened" in those that are civilised,[3] and this shortening may, I presume, be attributed to civilised men habitually feeding on soft, cooked food, and thus using their jaws less: I am informed by Mr. Brace that it is becoming quite a common practice in the United States to remove some of the molar teeth of children, as the jaw does not grow large enough for the perfect development of the normal number.[4]

With respect to the alimentary canal, I have met with an account of only a single rudiment, namely the vermiform appendage of the cæcum. The cæcum is a branch or diverticulum of the intestine, ending in a cul-de-sac, and is extremely long in many of the lower vegetable-feeding mammals. In the marsupial koala it is actually more than thrice as long as the whole body.[5] It is sometimes produced into a long gradually-tapering point, and is sometimes constricted in parts. It appears as if, in consequence of changed diet or habits, the cæcum had become much shortened in various animals, the vermiform appendage being left as a rudiment of the shortened part. That this appendage is a rudiment, we may infer from its small size, and from the evidence which Prof. Canestrini[6] has collected of its variability in man. It is occasionally quite absent, or again is largely developed. The passage is sometimes completely closed for half or two-thirds of its length, with the terminal part consisting of a flattened solid expansion. In the orang this appendage is long and convoluted: in man it arises from the end of the short cæcum, and is commonly from four to five inches in length, being only about the third of an inch in diameter. Not only is it useless, but it is sometimes the cause of death, of which fact I

1. Dr. Webb, 'Teeth in Man and the Anthropoid Apes,' as quoted by Dr. C. Carter Blake in 'Anthropological Review,' July 1867, p. 299.
2. Owen, 'Anatomy of Vertebrates,' vol. iii. pp. 320, 321, and 325.
3. 'On the Primitive Form of the Skull,' Eng. translat. in 'Anthropological Review,' Oct. 1868, p. 426.
4. Prof. Montegazza writes to me from Florence, that he has lately been studying the last molar teeth in the different races of man, and has come to the same conclusion as that given in my text, viz., that in the higher or civilized races they are on the road towards atrophy or elimination.
5. Owen, 'Anatomy of Vertebrates,' vol. iii. pp. 416, 434, 441.
6. 'Annuario della Soc. d. Nat.' Modena, 1867, p. 94.

have lately heard two instances: this is due to small hard bodies, such as seeds, entering the passage, and causing inflammation.[7]

In some of the lower Quadrumana, in the Lemuridæ and Carnivora, as well as in many marsupials, there is a passage near the lower end of the humerus, called the supra-condyloid foramen, through which the great nerve of the fore limb and often the great artery pass. Now in the humerus of man, there is generally a trace of this passage, which is sometimes fairly well developed, being formed by a depending hook-like process of bone, completed by a band of ligament. Dr. Struthers,[8] who has closely attended to the subject, has now shewn that this peculiarity is sometimes inherited, as it has occurred in a father, and in no less than four out of his seven children. When present, the great nerve invariably passes through it; and this clearly indicates that it is the homologue and rudiment of the supra-condyloid foramen of the lower animals. Prof. Turner estimates, as he informs me, that it occurs in about one per cent. of recent skeletons. But if the occasional development of this structure in man is, as seems probable, due to reversion, it is a return to a very ancient state of things, because in the higher Quadrumana it is absent.

There is another foramen or perforation in the humerus, occasionally present in man, which may be called the inter-condyloid. This occurs, but not constantly, in various anthropoid and other apes,[9] and likewise in many of the lower animals. It is remarkable that this perforation seems to have been present in man much more frequently during ancient times than recently. Mr. Busk[1] has collected the following evidence on this head: Prof. Broca "noticed the perforation in four and a half per cent. of the arm-bones collected in the 'Cimetière du Sud,' at Paris; and in the Grotto of Orrony, the contents of which are referred to the Bronze period, as many as eight humeri out of thirty-two were perforated; but this extraordinary proportion, he thinks, might be due to the cavern having been a sort of 'family vault.' Again, M. Dupont found thirty per cent. of perforated bones in the caves of the Valley of the Lesse, belonging to the Reindeer period; whilst M. Leguay, in a sort of *dolmen* at Argenteuil, observed twenty-five per cent. to be perforated; and M. Pruner-Bey found twenty-six per cent. in the same condition in bones from Vauréal. Nor should it be left unnoticed that M. Pruner-Bey states that this condition is common in Guanche skeletons." It is an interesting fact that ancient races, in this and several other cases, more frequently present structures which resemble those of the lower animals than do the modern. One chief cause seems

---

7. M. C. Martins ("De l'Unité Organique," in 'Revue des Deux Mondes,' June 15, 1862, p. 16), and Häckel ("Génerelle Morphologie,' B. ii. s. 278), have both remarked on the singular fact of this rudiment sometimes causing death.
8. With respect to inheritance, see Dr. Struthers in the 'Lancet,' Feb. 15, 1873, and another important paper, ibid., Jan. 24, 1863, p. 83. Dr. Knox, as I am informed, was the first anatomist who drew attention to this peculiar structure in man; see his 'Great Artists and Anatomists,' p. 63. See also an important memoir on this process by Dr. Gruber, in the 'Bulletin de l'Acad. Imp. de St. Pétersbourg,' tom xii. 1867, p. 448.
9. Mr. St. George Mivart, 'Transact. Phil. Soc.' 1867, p. 310.
1. "On the Caves of Gibraltar," "Transact. Internat. Congress of Prehist. Arch.' Third Session, 1869, p. 159. Prof. Wyman has lately shown (Fourth Annual Report, Peabody Museum, 1871, p. 20), that this perforation is present in thirty-one per cent. of some human remains from ancient mounds in the Western United States, and in Florida. It frequently occurs in the negro.

to be that the ancient races stand somewhat nearer in the long line of descent to their remote animal-like progenitors.

In man, the os coccyx, together with certain other vertebræ hereafter to be described, though functionless as a tail, plainly represent this part in other vertebrate animals. At an early embryonic period it is free, and projects beyond the lower extremities; as may be seen in the drawing (Fig. 1.) of a human embryo. Even after birth it has been known, in certain rare and anomalous cases,[2] to form a small external rudiment of a tail. The os coccyx is short, usually including only four vertebræ, all anchylosed together: and these are in a rudimentary condition, for they consist, with the exception of the basal one, of the centrum alone.[3] They are furnished with some small muscles; one of which, as I am informed by Prof. Turner, has been expressly described by Theile as a rudimentary repetition of the extensor of the tail, a muscle which is so largely developed in many mammals.

The spinal cord in man extends only as far downwards as the last dorsal or first lumbar vertebra; but a thread-like structure (the *filum terminale*) runs down the axis of the sacral part of the spinal canal, and even along the back of the coccygeal bones. The upper part of this filament, as Prof. Turner informs me, is undoubtedly homologous with the spinal cord; but the lower part apparently consists merely of the *pia mater*, or vascular investing membrane. Even in this case the os coccyx may be said to possess a vestige of so important a structure as the spinal cord, though no longer enclosed within a bony canal. The following fact, for which I am also indebted to Prof. Turner, shews how closely the os coccyx corresponds with the true tail in the lower animals: Luschka has recently discovered at the extremity of the coccygeal bones a very peculiar convoluted body, which is continuous with the middle sacral artery; and this discovery led Krause and Meyer to examine the tail of a monkey (Macacus), and of a cat, in both of which they found a similarly convoluted body, though not at the extremity.

The reproductive system offers various rudimentary structures; but these differ in one important respect from the foregoing cases. Here we are not concerned with the vestige of a part which does not belong to the species in an efficient state, but with a part efficient in the one sex, and represented in the other by a mere rudiment. Nevertheless, the occurrence of such rudiments is as difficult to explain, on the belief of the separate creation of each species, as in the foregoing cases. Hereafter I shall have to recur to these rudiments, and shall shew that their presence generally depends merely on inheritance, that is, on parts acquired by one sex having been partially transmitted to the other. I will in this place only give some instances of such rudiments. It is well known that in the males of all mammals, including man, rudimentary mammæ exist. These in several

2. Quatrefages has lately collected the evidence on this subject. 'Revue des Cours Scientifiques,' 1867–1868, p. 625. In 1840 Fleischmann exhibited a human fœtus bearing a free tail, which, as is not always the case, included vertebral bodies; and this tail was critically examined by the many anatomists present at the meeting of naturalists at Erlangen (see Marshall in Niederländischen Archiv Für Zoologie, December 1871).

3. Owen, 'On the Nature of Limbs,' 1849, p. 114.

instances have become well developed, and have yielded a copious supply of milk. Their essential identity in the two sexes is likewise shewn by their occasional sympathetic enlargement in both during an attack of the measles. The *vesicula prostatica*, which has been observed in many male mammals, is now universally acknowledged to be the homologue of the female uterus, together with the connected passage. It is impossible to read Leuckart's able description of this organ, and his reasoning, without admitting the justness of his conclusion. This is especially clear in the case of those mammals in which the true female uterus bifurcates, for in the males of these the vesicula likewise bifurcates.[4] Some other rudimentary structures belonging to the reproductive system might have been here adduced.[5]

The bearing of the three great classes of facts now given is unmistakable. But it would be superfluous fully to recapitulate the line of argument given in detail in my 'Origin of Species.' The homological construction of the whole frame in the members of the same class is intelligible, if we admit their descent from a common progenitor, together with their subsequent adaptation to diversified conditions. On any other view, the similarity of pattern between the hand of a man or monkey, the foot of a horse, the flipper of a seal, the wing of a bat, &c., is utterly inexplicable.[6] It is no scientific explanation to assert that they have all been formed on the same ideal plan. With respect to development, we can clearly understand, on the principle of variation supervening at a rather late embryonic period, and being inherited at a corresponding period, how it is that the embryos of wonderfully different forms should still retain, more or less perfectly, the structure of their common progenitor. No other explanation has ever been given of the marvellous fact that the embryos of a man, dog, seal, bat, reptile, &c., can at first hardly be distinguished from each other. In order to understand the existence of rudimentary organs, we have only to suppose that a former progenitor possessed the parts in question in a perfect state, and that under changed habits of life they became greatly reduced, either from simple disuse, or through the natural selection of those individuals which were least encumbered with a superfluous part, aided by the other means previously indicated.

Thus we can understand how it has come to pass that man and all other

4. Leuckart, in Todd's 'Cyclop. of Anat.' 1849–52, vol. iv. p. 1415. In man this organ is only from three to six lines in length, but, like so many other rudimentary parts, it is variable in development as well as in other characters.
5. See, on this subject, Owen, 'Anatomy of Vertebrates,' vol. iii. pp. 675, 676, 706.
6. Prof. Bianconi, in a recently published work, illustrated by admirable engravings ('La Théorie Darwinienne et la création dite indépendante,' 1874), endeavours to show that homological structures, in the above and other cases, can be fully explained on mechanical principles, in accordance with their uses. No one has shewn so well, how admirably such structures are adapted for their final purpose; and this adaptation can, as I believe, be explained through natural selection. In considering the wing of a bat, he brings forward (p. 218) what appears to me (to use Auguste Comte's words) a mere metaphysical principle, namely, the preservation "in its integrity of the mammalian nature of the animal." In only a few cases does he discuss rudiments, and then only those parts which are partially rudimentary, such as the little hoofs of the pig and ox, which do not touch the ground; these he shows clearly to be of service to the animal. It is unfortunate that he did not consider such cases as the minute teeth, which never cut through the jaw in the ox, or the mammæ of male quadrupeds, or the wings of certain beetles, existing under the soldered wing-covers, or the vestiges of the pistil and stamens in various flowers, and many other such cases. Although I greatly admire Prof. Bianconi's work, yet the belief now held by most naturalists seems to me left unshaken, that homological structures are inexplicable on the principle of mere adaptation.

vertebrate animals have been constructed on the same general model, why they pass through the same early stages of development, and why they retain certain rudiments in common. Consequently we ought frankly to admit their community of descent; to take any other view, is to admit that our own structure, and that of all the animals around us, is a mere snare laid to entrap our judgment. This conclusion is greatly strengthened, if we look to the members of the whole animal series, and consider the evidence derived from their affinities or classification, their geographical distribution and geological succession. It is only our natural prejudice, and that arrogance which made our forefathers declare that they were descended from demi-gods, which leads us to demur to this conclusion. But the time will before long come, when it will be thought wonderful that naturalists, who were well acquainted with the comparative structure and development of man, and other mammals, should have believed that each was the work of a separate act of creation.

Chapter II. On the Manner of Development of Man from Some Lower Form

Variability of body and mind in man—Inheritance—Causes of variability—Laws of variation the same in man as in the lower animals—Direct action of the conditions of life—Effects of the increased use and disuse of parts—Arrested development—Reversion—Correlated variation—Rate of increase—Checks to increase—Natural selection—Man the most dominant animal in the world—Importance of his corporeal structure—The causes which have led to his becoming erect—Consequent changes of structure—Decrease in size of the canine teeth—Increased size and altered shape of the skull—Nakedness—Absence of a tail—Defenceless condition of man.

It is manifest that man is now subject to much variability. No two individuals of the same race are quite alike. We may compare millions of faces, and each will be distinct. There is an equally great amount of diversity in the proportions and dimensions of the various parts of the body; the length of the legs being one of the most variable points.[7] Although in some quarters of the world an elongated skull, and in other quarters a short skull prevails, yet there is great diversity of shape even within the limits of the same race, as with the aborigines of America and South Australia—the latter a race "probably as pure and homogeneous in blood, customs, and language as any in existence"—and even with the inhabitants of so confined an area as the Sandwich Islands.[8] An eminent dentist assures me that there is nearly as much diversity in the teeth as in the features. The chief arteries so frequently run in abnormal courses, that it has been useful for surgical purposes to calculate from 1040 corpses how often each course prevails.[9] The muscles are eminently variable: thus those of the foot

7. Investigations in Military and Anthropolog. Statistics of American Soldiers,' by B. A. Gould, 1869, p. 256.
8. With respect to the "Cranial forms of the American aborigines," see Dr. Aitken Meigs in 'Proc. Acad. Nat. Sci.' Philadelphia, May, 1868. On the Australians, see Huxley, in Lyell's 'Antiquity of Man,' 1863, p. 87. On the Sandwich Islanders, Prof. J. Wyman, 'Observations on Crania,' Boston, 1868, p. 18.
9. 'Anatomy of the Arteries,' by R. Quain. Preface, vol. i. 1844.

were found by Prof. Turner[1] not to be strictly alike in any two out of fifty bodies; and in some the deviations were considerable. He adds, that the power of performing the appropriate movements must have been modified in accordance with the several deviations. Mr. J. Wood has recorded[2] the occurrence of 295 muscular variations in thirty-six subjects, and in another set of the same number no less than 558 variations, those occurring on both sides of the body being only reckoned as one. In the last set, not one body out of the thirty-six was "found totally wanting in departures from the standard descriptions of the muscular system given in anatomical text books." A single body presented the extraordinary number of twenty-five distinct abnormalities. The same muscle sometimes varies in many ways: thus Prof. Macalister describes[3] no less than twenty distinct variations in the *palmaris accessorius.*

The famous old anatomist, Wolff,[4] insists that the internal viscera are more variable than the external parts: *Nulla particula est quæ non aliter et aliter in aliis se habeat hominibus.*[5] He has even written a treatise on the choice of typical examples of the viscera for representation. A discussion on the beau-ideal of the liver, lungs, kidneys, &c., as of the human face divine, sounds strange in our ears.

The variability or diversity of the mental faculties in men of the same race, not to mention the greater differences between the men of distinct races, is so notorious that not a word need here be said. So it is with the lower animals. All who have had charge of menageries admit this fact, and we see it plainly in our dogs and other domestic animals. Brehm especially insists that each individual monkey of those which he kept tame in Africa had its own peculiar disposition and temper: he mentions one baboon remarkable for its high intelligence; and the keepers in the Zoological Gardens pointed out to me a monkey, belonging to the New World division, equally remarkable for intelligence. Rengger, also, insists on the diversity in the various mental characters of the monkeys of the same species which he kept in Paraguay; and this diversity, as he adds, is partly innate, and partly the result of the manner in which they have been treated or educated.[6]

I have elsewhere[7] so fully discussed the subject of Inheritance, that I need here add hardly anything. A greater number of facts have been collected with respect to the transmission of the most trifling, as well as of the most important characters in man, than in any of the lower animals: though the facts are copious enough with respect to the latter. So in regard to mental qualities, their transmission is manifest in our dogs, horses, and other domestic animals. Besides special tastes and habits, general intelligence, courage, bad and good temper, &c., are certainly transmitted. With man we see similar facts in almost every family; and we now know, through

---

1. 'Transact. Royal Soc. Edinburgh,' vol. xxiv. pp. 175, 189.
2. 'Proc. Royal Soc.' 1867, p. 544; also 1868, pp. 483, 524. There is a previous paper, 1866, p. 229.
3. 'Proc. R. Irish Academy,' vol. x. 1868, p. 141.
4. "There is no part that does not dispose itself now one way and now another in one man and in another." [Editor]
5. 'Act. Acad. St. Petersburg,' 1778, part ii. p. 217.
6. Brehm, 'Thierleben,' B. i. s. 58, 87; Rengger, 'Säugethiere von Paraguay, s. 57.
7. Variation of Animals and Plants under Domestication,' vol. ii. chap. xii.

the admirable labours of Mr. Galton,[8] that genius which implies a won-derfully complex combination of high faculties, tends to be inherited; and, on the other hand, it is too certain that insanity and deteriorated mental powers likewise run in families.

With respect to the causes of variability, we are in all cases very ignorant; but we can see that in man as in the lower animals, they stand in some relation to the conditions to which each species has been exposed, during several generations. Domesticated animals vary more than those in a state of nature; and this is apparently due to the diversified and changing nature of the conditions to which they have been subjected. In this respect the different races of man resemble domesticated animals, and so do the in-dividuals of the same race, when inhabiting a very wide area, like that of America. We see the influence of diversified conditions in the more civ-ilised nations; for the members belonging to different grades of rank, and following different occupations, present a greater range of character than do the members of barbarous nations. But the uniformity of savages has often been exaggerated, and in some cases can hardly be said to exist.[9] It is, nevertheless, an error to speak of man, even if we look only to the conditions to which he has been exposed, as "far more domesticated"[1] than any other animal. Some savage races, such as the Australians, are not exposed to more diversified conditions than are many species which have a wide range. In another and much more important respect, man differs widely from any strictly domesticated animal; for his breeding has never long been controlled, either by methodical or unconscious selection. No race or body of men has been so completely subjugated by other men, as that certain individuals should be preserved, and thus unconsciously se-lected, from somehow excelling in utility to their masters. Nor have certain male and female individuals been intentionally picked out and matched, except in the well-known case of the Prussian grenadiers; and in this case man obeyed, as might have been expected, the law of methodical selec-tion; for it is asserted that many tall men were reared in the villages in-habited by the grenadiers and their tall wives. In Sparta, also, a form of selection was followed, for it was enacted that all children should be ex-amined shortly after birth; the well-formed and vigorous being preserved, the others left to perish.[2]

If we consider all the races of man as forming a single species, his range

8. 'Hereditary Genius: an Inquiry into its Laws and Consequences, 1869.
9. Mr. Bates remarks ('The Naturalist on the Amazons,' 1863, vol. ii. p. 159), with respect to the Indians of the same South American tribe, "no two of them were at all similar in the shape of the head; one man had an oval visage with fine features, and another was quite Mongolian in breadth and prominence of cheek, spread of nostrils, and obliquity of eyes."
1. Blumenbach, 'Treatises on Anthropolog.' Eng. translat., 1865, p. 205.
2. Mitlord's 'History of Greece,' vol. i. p. 282. It appears also from a passage in Xenophon's 'Mem-orabilia,' B. ii. 4 (to which my attention has been called by the Rev. J. N. Hoare), that it was a well recognised principle with the Greeks, that men ought to select their wives with a view to the health and vigour of their children. The Grecian poet, Theognis, who lived 550 B. C., clearly saw how important selection, if carefully applied, would be for the improvement of mankind. He saw, likewise, that wealth often checks the proper action of sexual selection. He thus writes:

> "With kine and horses, Kurnus! we proceed
> By reasonable rules, and choose a breed
> For profit and increase, at any price:
> Of a sound stock, without defect or vice.

is enormous; but some separate races, as the Americans and Polynesians, have very wide ranges. It is a well-known law that widely-ranging species are much more variable than species with restricted ranges; and the variability of man may with more truth be compared with that of widely-ranging species, than with that of domesticated animals.

Not only does variability appear to be induced in man and the lower animals by the same general causes, but in both the same parts of the body are effected in a closely analogous manner. This has been proved in such full detail by Godron and Quatrefages, that I need here only refer to their works.[3] Monstrosities, which graduate into slight variations, are likewise so similar in man and the lower animals, that the same classification and the same terms can be used for both, as has been shewn by Isidore Geoffroy St. Hilaire.[4] In my work on the variation of domestic animals, I have attempted to arrange in a rude fashion the laws of variation under the following heads:—The direct and definite action of changed conditions, as exhibited by all or nearly all the individuals of the same species, varying in the same manner under the same circumstances. The effects of the long-continued use or disuse of parts. The cohesion of homologous parts. The variability of multiple parts. Compensation of growth; but of this law I have found no good instance in the case of man. The effects of the mechanical pressure of one part on another; as of the pelvis on the cranium of the infant in the womb. Arrests of development, leading to the diminution or suppression of parts. The reappearance of long-lost characters through reversion. And lastly, correlated variation. All these so-called laws apply equally to man and the lower animals; and most of them even to plants. It would be superfluous here to discuss all of them;[5] but several are so important, that they must be treated at considerable length. * * *

RATE OF INCREASE

Civilised populations have been known under favourable conditions, as in the United States, to double their numbers in twenty-five years; and, according to a calculation, by Euler, this might occur in a little over twelve years.[6] At the former rate, the present population of the United States (thirty millions), would in 657 years cover the whole terraqueous globe so thickly, that four men would have to stand on each square yard of surface. The primary or fundamental check to the continued increase of man is the difficulty of gaining subsistence, and of living in comfort. We may infer that this is the case from what we see, for instance, in the United States, where subsistence is easy, and there is plenty of room. If such means were suddenly doubled in Great Britain, our number would be quickly doubled. With civilised nations, this primary check acts chiefly by restrain-

3. Godron, 'De l'Espèce,' 1859, tom. ii. livre 3. Quatrefages, 'Unité de l'Espèce Humaine,' 1861. Also Lectures on Anthropology, given in the 'Revue des Cours Scientifiques,' 1866–1868.
4. 'Hist. Gén. et Part. des Anomalies de l'Organisation,' in three volumes, tom. i. 1832.
5. I have fully discussed these laws in my 'Variation of Animals and Plants under Domestication,' vol. ii. chap. xxii, and xxiii. M. J. P. Durand has lately (1868) published a valuable essay 'De l'Influence des Milieux,' &c. He lays much stress, in the case of plants, on the nature of the soil.
6. See the ever memorable 'Essay on the Principle of Population,' by the Rev. T. Malthus, vol. i. 1826, pp. 6, 517.

ing marriages. The greater death-rate of infants in the poorest classes is also very important; as well as the greater mortality, from various diseases, of the inhabitants of crowded and miserable houses, at all ages. The effects of severe epidemics and wars are soon counterbalanced, and more than counterbalanced, in nations placed under favourable conditions. Emigration also comes in aid as a temporary check, but, with the extremely poor classes, not to any great extent.

There is great reason to suspect, as Malthus has remarked, that the reproductive power is actually less in barbarous, than in civilised races. We know nothing positively on this head, for with savages no census has been taken; but from the concurrent testimony of missionaries, and of others who have long resided with such people, it appears that their families are usually small, and large ones rare. This may be partly accounted for, as it is believed, by the women suckling their infants during a long time; but it is highly probable that savages, who often suffer much hardships, and who do not obtain so much nutritious food as civilised men, would be actually less prolific. I have shewn in a former work,[7] that all our domesticated quadrupeds and birds, and all our cultivated plants, are more fertile than the corresponding species in a state of nature. It is no valid objection to this conclusion that animals suddenly supplied with an excess of food, or when grown very fat; and that most plants on sudden removal from very poor to very rich soil, are rendered more or less sterile. We might, therefore, expect that civilised men, who in one sense are highly domesticated, would be more prolific than wild men. It is also probable that the increased fertility of civilised nations would become, as with our domestic animals, an inherited character: it is at least known that with mankind a tendency to produce twins runs in families.[8]

Notwithstanding that savages appear to be less prolific than civilised people, they would no doubt rapidly increase if their numbers were not by some means rigidly kept down. The Santali, or hill-tribes of India, have recently afforded a good illustration of this fact; for, as shewn by Mr. Hunter,[9] they have increased at an extraordinary rate since vaccination has been introduced, other pestilences mitigated, and war sternly repressed. This increase, however, would not have been possible had not these rude people spread into the adjoining districts, and worked for hire. Savages almost always marry; yet there is some prudential restraint, for they do not commonly marry at the earliest possible age. The young men are often required to shew that they can support a wife; and they generally have first to earn the price with which to purchase her from her parents. With savages the difficulty of obtaining subsistence occasionally limits their number in a much more direct manner than with civilised people, for all tribes periodically suffer from severe famines. At such times savages are forced to devour much bad food, and their health can hardly fail to be injured. Many accounts have been published of their protruding stomachs and emaciated limbs after and during famines. They are then, also, com-

7. 'Variation of Animals and Plants under Domestication,' vol. ii, pp. 111–113, 163.
8. Mr. Sedgwick, 'British and Foreign Medico-Chirurg. Review,' July, 1863, p. 170.
9. 'The Animals of Rural Bengal,' by W. W. Hunter, 1868, p. 259.

pelled to wander much, and, as I was assured in Australia, their infants perish in large numbers. As famines are periodical, depending chiefly on extreme seasons, all tribes must fluctuate in number. They cannot steadily and regularly increase, as there is no artificial increase in the supply of food. Savages, when hard pressed, encroach on each other's territories, and war is the result; but they are indeed almost always at war with their neighbours. They are liable to many accidents on land and water in their search for food; and in some countries they suffer much from the larger beasts of prey. Even in India, districts have been depopulated by the ravages of tigers.

Malthus has discussed these several checks, but he does not lay stress enough on what is probably the most important of all, namely infanticide, especially of female infants and the habit of procuring abortion. These practices now prevail in many quarters of the world; and infanticide seems formerly to have prevailed, as Mr. M'Lennan[1] has shewn on a still more extensive scale. These practices appear to have originated in savages recognising the difficulty, or rather the impossibility of supporting all the infants that are born. Licentiousness may also be added to the foregoing checks; but this does not follow from failing means of subsistence; though there is reason to believe that in some cases (as in Japan) it has been intentionally encouraged as a means of keeping down the population.

If we look back to an extremely remote epoch, before man had arrived at the dignity of manhood, he would have been guided more by instinct and less by reason than are the lowest savages at the present time. Our early semi-human progenitors would not have practised infanticide or polyandry; for the instincts of the lower animals are never so perverted[2] as to lead them regularly to destroy their own offspring, or to be quite devoid of jealousy. There would have been no prudential restraint from marriage, and the sexes would have freely united at an early age. Hence the progenitors of man would have tended to increase rapidly; but checks of some kind, either periodical or constant, must have kept down their numbers, even more severely than with existing savages. What the precise nature of these checks were, we cannot say, any more than with most other animals. We know that horses and cattle, which are not extremely prolific animals, when first turned loose in South America, increased at an enormous rate. The elephant, the slowest breeder of all known animals, would in a few thousand years stock the whole world. The increase of every species of monkey must be checked by some means; but not, as Brehm remarks, by the attacks of beasts of prey. No one will assume that the actual power of reproduction in the wild horses and cattle of America, was at first in any sensible degree increased; or that, as each district became fully stocked,

---

1. 'Primitive Marriage,' 1865.
2. A writer in the 'Spectator' (March 12th, 1871, p. 320) comments as follows on this passage:—
"Mr. Darwin finds himself compelled to reintroduce a new doctrine of the fall of man. He shews that the instincts of the higher animals are far nobler than the habits of savage races of men, and he finds himself, therefore, compelled to re-introduce,—in a form of the substantial orthodoxy of which he appears to be quite unconscious,—and to introduce as a scientific hypothesis the doctrine that man's gain of *knowledge* was the cause of a temporary but long-enduring moral deterioration as indicated by the many foul customs, especially as to marriage, of savage tribes. What does the Jewish tradition of the moral degeneration of man through his snatching at a knowledge forbidden him by his highest instinct assert beyond this?"

this same power was diminished. No doubt in this case, and in all others, many checks concur, and different checks under different circumstances; periodical dearths, depending on unfavourable seasons, being probably the most important of all. So it will have been with the early progenitors of man.

NATURAL SELECTION

We have now seen that man is variable in body and mind; and that the variations are induced, either directly or indirectly, by the same general causes, and obey the same general laws, as with the lower animals. Man has spread widely over the face of the earth, and must have been exposed, during his incessant migration,[3] to the most diversified conditions. The inhabitants of Tierra del Fuego, the Cape of Good Hope, and Tasmania in the one hemisphere, and of the Arctic regions in the other, must have passed through many climates, and changed their habits many times, before they reached their present homes.[4] The early progenitors of man must also have tended, like all other animals, to have increased beyond their means of subsistence; they must, therefore, occasionally have been exposed to a struggle for existence, and consequently to the rigid law of natural selection. Beneficial variations of all kinds will thus, either occasionally or habitually, have been preserved and injurious ones eliminated. I do not refer to strongly-marked deviations of structure, which occur only at long intervals of time, but to mere individual differences. We know, for instance, that the muscles of our hands and feet, which determine our powers of movement, are liable, like those of the lower animals,[5] to incessant variability. If then the progenitors of man inhabiting any district, especially one undergoing some change in its conditions, were divided into two equal bodies, the one half which included all the individuals best adapted by their powers of movement for gaining subsistence, or for defending themselves, would on an average survive in greater numbers, and procreate more offspring than the other and less well endowed half.

 Man in the rudest state in which he now exists is the most dominant animal that has ever appeared on this earth. He has spread more widely than any other highly organised form: and all others have yielded before him. He manifestly owes this immense superiority to his intellectual faculties, to his social habits, which lead him to aid and defend his fellows, and to his corporeal structure. The supreme importance of these characters has been proved by the final arbitrament of the battle for life. Through his powers of intellect, articulate language has been evolved; and on this his wonderful advancement has mainly depended. As Mr. Chauncey Wright remarks:[6] "a psychological analysis of the faculty of language shews,

---

3. See some good remarks to this effect by W. Stanley Jevons, "A Deduction from Darwin's Theory,' 'Nature,' 1869, p. 231.
4. Latham, 'Man and his Migrations,' 1851, p. 135.
5. Messrs. Murie and Mivart in their 'Anatomy of the Lemuroidea' ('Transact. Zoolog. Soc.' vol. vii. 1869, pp. 96–98) say, "some muscles are so irregular in their distribution that they cannot be well classed in any of the above groups." These muscles differ even on the opposite sides of the same individual.
6. Limits of Natural Selection, 'North American Review,' Oct. 1870, p. 295.

that even the smallest proficiency in it might require more brain power than the greatest proficiency in any other direction." He has invented and is able to use various weapons, tools, traps, &c. with which he defends himself, kills or catches prey, and otherwise obtains food. He has made rafts or canoes for fishing or crossing over to neighbouring fertile islands. He has discovered the art of making fire, by which hard and stringy roots can be rendered digestible, and poisonous roots or herbs innocuous. This discovery of fire, probably the greatest ever made by man, excepting language, dates from before the dawn of history. These several inventions, by which man in the rudest state has become so pre-eminent, are the direct results of the development of his powers of observation, memory, curiosity, imagination, and reason. I cannot, therefore, understand how it is that Mr. Wallace[7] maintains, that "natural selection could only have endowed the savage with a brain a little superior to that of an ape."

Although the intellectual powers and social habits of man are of paramount importance to him, we must not underrate the importance of his bodily structure, to which subject the remainder of this chapter will be devoted; the development of the intellectual and social or moral faculties being discussed in a later chapter.

Even to hammer with precision is no easy matter, as every one who has tried to learn carpentry will admit. To throw a stone with as true an aim as a Fuegian in defending himself, or in killing birds, requires the most consummate perfection in the correlated action of the muscles of the hand, arm, and shoulder, and, further, a fine sense of touch. In throwing a stone or spear, and in many other actions, a man must stand firmly on his feet; and this again demands the perfect co-adaptation of numerous muscles. To chip a flint into the rudest tool, or to form a barbed spear or hook from a bone, demands the use of a perfect hand; for, as a most capable judge, Mr. Schoolcraft,[8] remarks, the shaping fragments of stone into knives, lances, or arrow-heads, shews "extraordinary ability and long practice." This is to a great extent proved by the fact that primeval men practised a division of labour; each man did not manufacture his own flint tools or rude pottery, but certain individuals appear to have devoted themselves to such work, no doubt receiving in exchange the produce of the chase. Archæologists are convinced that an enormous interval of time elapsed before our ancestors thought of grinding chipped flints into smooth tools. One can hardly doubt, that a man-like animal who possessed a hand and arm sufficiently perfect to throw a stone with precision, or to form a

7. 'Quarterly Review,' April 1869, p. 392. This subject is more fully discussed in Mr. Wallace's 'Contributions to the Theory of Natural Selection,' 1870, in which all the essays referred to in this work are republished. The 'Essay on Man,' has been ably criticised by Prof. Claparède, one of the most distinguished zoologists in Europe, in an article published in the 'Bibliothèque Universelle,' June 1870. The remark quoted in my text will surprise every one who has read Mr. Wallace's celebrated paper on 'The origin of Human Races deduced from the Theory of Natural Selection,' originally published in the 'Anthropological Review,' May 1864, p. clviii. I cannot here resist quoting a most just remark by Sir J. Lubbock ('Prehistoric Times,' 1865, p. 479) in reference to this paper, namely, that Mr. Wallace, "with characteristic unselfishness, ascribes it (i. e. the idea of natural selection) unreservedly to Mr. Darwin, although, as is well known, he struck out the idea independently, and published it, though not with the same elaboration, at the same time."

8. Quoted by Mr. Lawson Tait in his 'Law of Natural Selection,'—'Dublin Quarterly Journal of Medical Science,' Feb. 1869. Dr. Keller is likewise quoted to the same effect.

flint into a rude tool, could, with sufficient practice, as far as mechanical skill alone is concerned, make almost anything which a civilised man can make. The structure of the hand in this respect may be compared with that of the vocal organs, which in the apes are used for uttering various signal-cries, as in one genus, musical cadences; but in man the closely similar vocal organs have become adapted through the inherited effects of use for the utterance of articulate language.

Turning now to the nearest allies of man, and therefore to the best representatives of our early progenitors, we find that the hands of the Quadrumana are constructed on the same general pattern as our own, but are far less perfectly adapted for diversified uses. Their hands do not serve for locomotion so well as the feet of a dog; as may be seen in such monkeys as the chimpanzee and orang, which walk on the outer margins of the palms, or on the knuckles.[9] Their hands, however, are admirably adapted for climbing trees. Monkeys seize thin branches or ropes, with the thumb on one side and the fingers and palm on the other, in the same manner as we do. They can thus also lift rather large objects, such as the neck of a bottle, to their mouths. Baboons turn over stones, and scratch up roots with their hands. They seize nuts, insects, or other small objects with the thumb in opposition to the fingers, and no doubt they thus extract eggs and young from the nests of birds. American monkeys beat the wild oranges on the branches until the rind is cracked, and then tear it off with the fingers of the two hands. In a wild state they break open hard fruits with stones. Other monkeys open mussel-shells with the two thumbs. With their fingers they pull out thorns and burs, and hunt for each other's parasites. They roll down stones, or throw them at their enemies: nevertheless, they are clumsy in these various actions, and, as I have myself seen, are quite unable to throw a stone with precision.

It seems to me far from true that because "objects are grasped clumsily" by monkeys, "a much less specialised organ of prehension" would have served them[1] equally well with their present hands. On the contrary, I see no reason to doubt that more perfectly constructed hands would have been an advantage to them, provided that they were not thus rendered less fitted for climbing trees. We may suspect that a hand as perfect as that of man would have been disadvantageous for climbing; for the most arboreal monkeys in the world, namely, Ateles in America, Colobus in Africa, and Hylobates in Asia, are either thumbless, or their toes partially cohere, so that their limbs are converted into mere grasping hooks.[2]

As soon as some ancient member in the great series of the Primates came to be less aboreal, owing to a change in its manner of procuring subsistence, or to some change in the surrounding conditions, its habitual manner of progression would have been modified: and thus it would have been rendered more strictly quadrupedal or bipedal. Baboons frequent

---

9. Owen, 'Anatomy of Vertebrates,' vol. iii. p. 71.
1. 'Quarterly Review,' April 1869, p. 392.
2. In *Hylobates syndactylus*, as the name expresses, two of the toes regularly cohere; and this, as Mr. Blyth informs me, is occasionally the case with the toes of *H. agilis, lar,* and *leuciscus*. Colobus is strictly arboreal and extraordinarily active (Brehm, 'Thierleben,' B. i. s. 50), but whether a better climber than the species of the allied genera, I do not know. It deserves notice that the feet of the sloths, the most arboreal animals in the world, are wonderfully hook-like.

hilly and rocky districts, and only from necessity climb high trees;[3] and they have acquired almost the gait of a dog. Man alone has become a biped; and we can, I think, partly see how he has come to assume his erect attitude, which forms one of his most conspicuous characters. Man could not have attained his present dominant position in the world without the use of his hands, which are so admirably adapted to act in obedience to his will. Sir C. Bell[4] insists that "the hand supplies all instruments, and by its correspondence with the intellect gives him universal dominion." But the hands and arms could hardly have become perfect enough to have manufactured weapons, or to have hurled stones and spears with a true aim, as long as they were habitually used for locomotion and for supporting the whole weight of the body, or, as before remarked, so long as they were especially fitted for climbing trees. Such rough treatment would also have blunted the sense of touch, on which their delicate use largely depends. From these causes alone it would have been an advantage to man to become a biped; but for many actions it is indispensable that the arms and whole upper part of the body should be free; and he must for this end stand firmly on his feet. To gain this great advantage, the feet have been rendered flat; and the great toe has been peculiarly modified, though this has entailed the almost complete loss of its power of prehension. It accords with the principle of the division of physiological labour, prevailing throughout the animal kingdom, that as the hands became perfected for prehension, the feet should have become perfected for support and locomotion. With some savages, however, the foot has not altogether lost its prehensile power, as shewn by their manner of climbing trees, and of using them in other ways.[5]

If it be an advantage to man to stand firmly on his feet and to have his hands and arms free, of which, from his pre-eminent success in the battle of life, there can be no doubt, then I can see no reason why it should not have been advantageous to the progenitors of man to have become more and more erect or bipedal. They would thus have been better able to defend themselves with stones or clubs, to attack their prey, or otherwise to obtain food. The best built individuals would in the long run have succeeded best, and have survived in large numbers. If the gorilla and a few allied forms had become extinct, it might have been argued, with great force and apparent truth, that an animal could not have been gradually converted from a quadruped into a biped, as all the individuals in an intermediate condition would have been miserably ill-fitted for progression. But we know (and this is well worthy of reflection) that the anthropomorphous apes are now actually in an intermediate condition; and no one doubts that they are on the whole well adapted for their conditions of life. Thus the gorilla runs with a sidelong shambling gait, but more commonly progresses by resting on its bent hands. The long-armed apes

3. Brehm, 'Thierleben,' B. i. s. 80.
4. "The Hand," &c. 'Bridgewater Treatise,' 1833, p. 38.
5. Häckel has an excellent discussion on the steps by which man became a biped: 'Natürliche Schöpfungsgeschichte,' 1868, s. 507. Dr. Büchner ('Conférences sur la Théorie Darwinienne,' 1869, p. 135) has given good cases of the use of the foot as a prehensile organ by man; and has also written on the manner of progression of the higher apes, to which I allude in the following paragraph: see also Owen ('Anatomy of Vertebrates,' vol. iii. p. 71) on this latter subject.

occasionally use their arms like crutches, swinging their bodies forward between them, and some kinds of Hylobates, without having been taught, can walk or run upright with tolerable quickness; yet they move awkwardly, and much less securely than man. We see, in short, in existing monkeys a manner of progression intermediate between that of a quadruped and a biped; but, as an unprejudiced judge[6] insists, the anthropomorphous apes approach in structure more nearly to the bipedal than to the quadrupedal type.

As the progenitors of man became more and more erect, with their hands and arms more and more modified for prehension and other purposes, with their feet and legs at the same time transformed for firm support and progression, endless other changes of structure would have become necessary. The pelvis would have to be broadened, the spine peculiarly curved, and the head fixed in an altered position, all which changes have been attained by man. Prof. Schaaffhausen[7] maintains that "the powerful mastoid processes of the human skull are the result of his erect position;" and these processes are absent in the orang, chimpanzee, &c., and are smaller in the gorilla than in man. Various other structures, which appear connected with man's erect position, might here have been added. It is very difficult to decide how far these correlated modifications are the result of natural selection, and how far of the inherited effects of the increased use of certain parts, or of the action of one part on another. No doubt these means of change often co-operate: thus when certain muscles, and the crests of bone to which they are attached, become enlarged by habitual use, this shews that certain actions are habitually performed and must be serviceable. Hence the individuals which performed them best, would tend to survive in greater numbers.

The free use of the arms and hands, partly the cause and partly the result of man's erect position, appears to have led to an indirect manner to other modifications of structure. The early male forefathers of man were, as previously stated, probably furnished with great canine teeth; but as they gradually acquired the habit of using stones, clubs, or other weapons, for fighting with their enemies or rivals, they would use their jaws and teeth less and less. In this case, the jaws, together with the teeth, would become reduced in size, as we may feel almost sure from innumerable analogous cases. In a future chapter we shall meet with a closely parallel case, in the reduction or complete disappearance of the canine teeth in male ruminants, apparently in relation with the development of their horns; and in horses, in relation to their habit of fighting with their incisor teeth and hoofs.

In the adult male anthropomorphous apes, as Rütimeyer,[8] and others, have insisted, it is the effect on the skull of the great development of the jaw-muscles that causes it to differ so greatly in many respects from that of man, and has given to these animals "a truly frightful physiognomy."

6. Prof. Broca, La Constitution des Vertèbres caudales; 'La Revue d'Anthropologie,' 1872, p. 26, (separate copy).
7. 'On the Primitive Form of the Skull,' translated in 'Anthropological Review,' Oct. 1868, p. 428. Owen ('Anatomy of Vertebrates,' vol. ii. 1866, p. 551) on the mastoid processes in the higher apes.
8. 'Die Grenzen der Thierwelt, eine Betrachtung zu Darwin's Lehre,' 1868, s. 51.

Therefore, as the jaws and teeth in man's progenitors gradually become reduced in size, the adult skull would have come to resemble more and more that of existing man. As we shall hereafter see, a great reduction of the canine teeth in the males would almost certainly affect the teeth of the females through inheritance.

As the various mental faculties gradually developed themselves the brain would almost certainly become larger. No one, I presume, doubts that the large proportion which the size of man's brain bears to his body, compared to the same proportion in the gorilla or orang, is closely connected with his higher mental powers. We meet with closely analogous facts with insects, for in ants the cerebral ganglia are of extraordinary dimensions, and in all the Hymenoptera these ganglia are many times larger than in the less intelligent orders, such as beetles.[9] On the other hand, no one supposes that the intellect of any two animals or of any two men can be accurately gauged by the cubic contents of their skulls. It is certain that there may be extraordinary mental activity with an extremely small absolute mass of nervous matter: thus the wonderfully diversified instincts, mental powers, and affections of ants are notorious, yet their cerebral ganglia are not so large as the quarter of a small pin's head. Under this point of view, the brain of an ant is one of the most marvellous atoms of matter in the world, perhaps more so than the brain of a man.

The belief that there exists in man some close relation between the size of the brain and the development of the intellectual faculties is supported by the comparison of the skulls of savage and civilised races, of ancient and modern people, and by the analogy of the whole vertebrate series. Dr. J. Bernard Davis has proved,[1] by many careful measurements, that the mean internal capacity of the skull in Europeans is 92.3 cubic inches; in Americans 87.5; in Asiatics 87.1; and in Australians only 81.9 cubic inches. Professor Broca[2] found that the nineteenth century skulls from graves in Paris were larger than those from vaults of the twelfth century, in the proportion of 1484 to 1426; and that the increased size, as ascertained by measurements, was exclusively in the frontal part of the skull—the seat of the intellectual faculties. Prichard is persuaded that the present inhabitants of Britain have "much more capacious braincases" than the ancient inhabitants. Nevertheless, it must be admitted that some skulls of very high antiquity, such as the famous one of Neanderthal, are well developed and capacious.[3] With respect to the lower animals, M. E. Lartet,[4] by comparing

---

9. Dujardin, 'Annales des Sc. Nat.' 3rd series Zoolog. tom. xiv. 1850. p. 203. See also Mr. Lowne, 'Anatomy and Phys. of the *Musca vomitoria*,' 1870, p. 14. My son, Mr. F. Darwin, dissected for me the cerebral ganglia of the *Formica rufa*.
1. 'Philosophical Transactions,' 1869, p. 513.
2. 'Les Sélections,' M. P. Broca, 'Revue d'Anthroplogies,' 1873; see also, as quoted in C. Vogt's 'Lectures on Man,' Eng. Translat. 1864, pp. 88, 90. Prichard, 'Phys. Hist. of Mankind,' vol. i. 1838, p. 305.
3. In the interesting article just referred to, Prof. Broca has well remarked, that in civilised nations, the average capacity of the skull must be lowered by the preservation of a considerable number of individuals, weak in mind and body, who would have been promptly eliminated in the savage state. On the other hand, with savages, the average includes only the more capable individuals, who have been able to survive under extremely hard conditions of life. Broca thus explains the otherwise inexplicable fact, that the mean capacity of the skull of the ancient Troglodytes of Lozère is greater than that of modern Frenchmen.
4. 'Comptes-rendus des Sciences,' &c., June 1, 1868.

the crania of tertiary and recent mammals belonging to the same groups, has come to the remarkable conclusion that the brain is generally larger and the convolutions are more complex in the more recent forms. On the other hand, I have shewn[5] that the brains of domestic rabbits are considerably reduced in bulk, in comparison with those of the wild rabbit or hare; and this may be attributed to their having been closely confined during many generations, so that they have exerted their intellect, instincts, senses, and voluntary movements but little.

The gradually increasing weight of the brain and skull in man must have influenced the development of the supporting spinal column, more especially whilst he was becoming erect. As this change of position was being brought about, the internal pressure of the brain will also have influenced the form of the skull; for many facts shew how easily the skull is thus affected. Ethnologists believe that it is modified by the kind of cradle in which infants sleep. Habitual spasms of the muscles, and a cicatrix from a severe burn, have permanently modified the facial bones. In young persons whose heads have become fixed either sideways or backwards, owing to disease, one of the two eyes has changed its position, and the shape of the skull has been altered apparently by the pressure of the brain in a new direction.[6] I have shewn that with long-eared rabbits even so trifling a cause as the lopping forward of one ear drags forward almost every bone of the skull on that side; so that the bones on the opposite side no longer strictly correspond. Lastly, if any animal were to increase or diminish much in general size, without any change in its mental powers, or if the mental powers were to be much increased or diminished, without any great change in the size of the body, the shape of the skull would almost certainly be altered. I infer this from my observations on domestic rabbits, some kinds of which have become very much larger than the wild animal, whilst others have retained nearly the same size, but in both cases the brain has been much reduced relatively to the size of the body. Now I was at first much surprised on finding that in all these rabbits the skull had become elongated or dolichocephalic; for instance, of two skulls of nearly equal breadth, the one from a wild rabbit and the other from a large domestic kind, the former was 3.15 and the latter 4.3 inches in length.[7] One of the most marked distinctions in different races of men is that the skull in some is elongated, and in others rounded; and here the explanation suggested by the case of the rabbits may hold good; for Welcker finds that short "men incline more to brachycephaly, and tall men to dolichocephaly;"[8] and tall men may be compared with the larger and longer-bodied rabbits, all of which have elongated skulls, or are dolichocephalic.

5. 'The Variation of Animals and Plants under Domestication,' vol. i. pp. 124–129.
6. Schaaffhausen gives from Blumenbach and Busch, the cases of the spasms and cicatrix, in 'Anthropolog. Review,' Oct. 1868, p. 420. Dr. Jarrold ('Anthropologia,' 1808, pp. 115, 116) adduces from Camper and from his own observations, cases of the modification of the skull from the head being fixed in an unnatural position. He believes that in certain trades, such as that of a shoemaker, where the head is habitually held forward, the forehead becomes more rounded and prominent.
7. 'Variation of Animals', &c., vol. i. p. 117, on the elongation of the skull; p. 119, on the effect of the lopping of one ear.
8. Quoted by Schaaffhausen, in 'Anthropolog. Review,' Oct. 1868, p. 419.

From these several facts we can understand, to a certain extent, the means by which the great size and more or less rounded form of the skull have been acquired by man; and these are characters eminently distinctive of him in comparison with the lower animals.

Another most conspicuous difference between man and the lower animals is the nakedness of his skin. Whales and porpoises (Cetacea), dugongs (Sirenia) and the hippopotamus are naked; and this may be advantageous to them for gliding through the water; nor would it be injurious to them from the loss of warmth, as the species, which inhabit the colder regions, are protected by a thick layer of blubber, serving the same purpose as the fur of seals and others. Elephants and rhinoceroses are almost hairless; and as certain extinct species, which formerly lived under an Arctic climate, were covered with long wool or hair, it would almost appear as if the existing species of both genera had lost their hairy covering from exposure to heat. This appears the most probable, as the elephants in India which live on elevated and cool districts are more hairy[9] than those on the lowlands. May we then infer that man became divested of hair from having aboriginally inhabited some tropical land? That the hair is chiefly retained in the male sex on the chest and face, and in both sexes at the junction of all four limbs with the trunk, favours this inference—on the assumption that the hair was lost before man became erect; for the parts which now retain most hair would then have been most protected from the heat of the sun. The crown of the head, however, offers a curious exception, for at all times it must have been one of the most exposed parts, yet it is thickly clothed with hair. The fact, however, that the other members of the order of Primates, to which man belongs, although inhabiting various hot regions, are well clothed with hair, generally thickest on the upper surface,[1] is opposed to the supposition that man became naked through the action of the sun. Mr. Belt believes[2] that within the tropics it is an advantage to man to be destitute of hair, as he is thus enabled to free himself of the multitude of ticks (acari) and other parasites, with which he is often infested, and which sometimes cause ulceration. But whether this evil is of sufficient magnitude to have led to the denudation of his body through natural selection, may be doubted, since none of the many quadrupeds inhabiting the tropics have, as far as I know, acquired any specialised means of relief. The view which seems to me the most probable is that man, or rather primarily woman, became divested of hair for ornamental purposes, as we shall see under Sexual Selection; and, according to this belief, it is not surprising that man should differ so greatly in hair-

---

9. Owen, 'Anatomy of Vertebrates,' vol. iii, p. 619.
1. Isidore Geoffroy St.-Hilaire remarks ('Hist. Nat. Générale,' tom. ii. 1859, pp. 215–217) on the head of man being covered with long hair; also on the upper surfaces of monkeys and of other mammals being more thickly clothed than the lower surfaces. This has likewise been observed by various authors. Prof. P. Gervais ('Hist. Nat. des Mammifères,' tom. i. 1854, p. 28), however, states that in the Gorilla the hair is thinner on the back, where it is partly rubbed off, than on the lower surface.
2. The 'Naturalist in Nicaragua,' 1874, p. 209. As some confirmation of Mr. Belt's view, I may quote the following passage from Sir W. Denison ('Varieties of Vice-Regal Life,' vol. i. 1870, p. 440): "It is said to be a practice with the Australians, when the vermin get troublesome, to singe themselves."

iness from all other Primates, for characters, gained through sexual selection, often differ to an extraordinary degree in closely related forms.

According to a popular impression, the absence of a tail is eminently
distinctive of man; but as those apes which come nearest to him are destitute of this organ, its disappearance does not relate exclusively to man.
The tail often differs remarkably in length within the same genus: thus in
some species of Macacus it is·longer than the whole body, and is formed
of twenty-four vertebræ; in others it consists of a scarcely visible stump,
containing only three or four vertebræ. In some kinds of baboons there
are twenty-five, whilst in the mandrill there are ten very small stunted
caudal vertebræ, or, according to Cuvier,[3] sometimes only five. The tail,
whether it be long or short, almost always tapers toward the end; and this,
I presume, results from the atrophy of the terminal muscles, together with
their arteries and nerves, through disuse, leading to the atrophy of the
terminal bones. But no explanation can at present be given of the great
diversity which often occurs in its length. Here, however, we are more
specially concerned with the complete external disappearance of the tail.
Professor Broca has recently shewn[4] that the tail in all quadrupeds consists
of two portions, generally separated abruptly from each other; the basal
portion consists of vertebræ, more or less perfectly channelled and furnished with apophyses like ordinary vertebræ; whereas those of the terminal portion are not channelled, are almost smooth, and scarcely
resemble true vertebræ. A tail, though not externally visible, is really present in man and the anthropomorphous apes, and is constructed on exactly
the same pattern in both. In the terminal portion the vertebræ, constituting
the os coccyx, are quite rudimentary, being much reduced in size and
number. In the basal portion, the vertebræ are likewise few, are united
firmly together, and are arrested in development; but they have been rendered much broader and flatter than the corresponding vertebræ in the
tails of other animals: they constitute what Broca calls the accessory sacral
vertebræ. These are of functional importance by supporting certain internal parts and in other ways; and their modification is directly connected
with the erect or semi-erect attitude of man and the anthropomorphous
apes. This conclusion is the more trustworthy, as Broca formerly held a
different view, which he has now abandoned. The modification, therefore,
of the basal caudal vertebræ in man and the higher apes may have been
effected, directly or indirectly, through natural selection.

But what are we to say about the rudimentary and variable vertebræ of
the terminal portion of the tail, forming the os coccyx? A notion which has
often been, and will no doubt again be ridiculed, namely, that friction has
had something to do with the disappearance of the external portion of the
tail, is not so ridiculous as it at first appears. Dr. Anderson[5] states that the
extremely short tail of Macacus brunneus is formed of eleven vertebræ,
including the imbedded basal ones. The extremity is tendonous and con-

3. Mr. St. George Mivart, 'Proc. Zoolog. Soc.' 1865, pp. 562, 583. Dr. J. E. Gray, 'Cat. Brit. Mus.:
    Skeletons.' Owen. 'Anatomy of Vertebrates,' vol. ii. p. 517. Isidore Geoffroy, 'Hist. Nat. Gén.' tom.
    ii. p. 244.
4. 'Revue d'Anthropologie,' 1872; 'La Constitution des Vertèbres caudales.'
5. 'Proc. Zoolog. Soc.,' 1872, p. 210.

tains no vertebræ; this is succeeded by five rudimentary ones, so minute
that together they are only one line and a half in length, and these are
permanently bent to one side in the shape of a hook. The free part of the
tail, only a little above an inch in length, includes only four more small
vertebræ. This short tail is carried erect; but about a quarter of its total
length is doubled on to itself to the left; and this terminal part, which
includes the hook-like portion, serves "to fill up the interspace between
the upper divergent portion of the callosities;" so that the animal sits on
it, and thus renders it rough and callous. Dr. Anderson thus sums up his
observations: "These facts seem to me to have only one explanation; this
tail, from its short size, is in the monkey's way when it sits down, and
frequently becomes placed under the animal while it is in this attitude;
and from the circumstance that it does not extend beyond the extremity
of the ischial tuberosities, it seems as if the tail originally had been bent
round by the will of the animal, into the interspace between the callosities,
to escape being pressed between them and the ground, and that in time
the curvature became permanent, fitting in of itself when the organ happens to be sat upon." Under these circumstances it is not surprising that
the surface of the tail should have been roughened and rendered callous,
and Dr. Murie,[6] who carefully observed this species in the Zoological
Gardens, as well as three other closely allied forms with slightly longer
tails, says that when the animal sits down, the tail "is necessarily thrust to
one side of the buttocks; and whether long or short its root is consequently
liable to be rubbed or chafed." As we now have evidence that mutilations
occasionally produce an inherited effect,[7] it is not very improbable that in
short-tailed monkeys, the projecting part of the tail, being functionally
useless, should after many generations have become rudimentary and distorted, from being continually rubbed and chafed. We see the projecting
part in this condition in the *Macacus brunneus*, and absolutely aborted in
the *M. ecaudatus* and in several of the higher apes. Finally, then, as far
as we can judge, the tail has disappeared in man and the anthropomorphous apes, owing to the terminal portion having been injured by friction
during a long lapse of time; the basal and embedded portion having been
reduced and modified, so as to become suitable to the erect or semi-erect
position.

I have now endeavoured to shew that some of the most distinctive characters of man have in all probability been acquired, either directly, or more
commonly indirectly, through natural selection. We should bear in mind
that modifications in structure or constitution which do not serve to adapt
an organism to its habits of life, to the food which it consumes, or passively
to the surrounding conditions, cannot have been thus acquired. We must
not, however, be too confident in deciding what modifications are of serv-

6. 'Proc. Zoolog. Soc.,' 1872, p. 786.
7. I allude to Dr. Brown-Séquard's observations on the transmitted effect of an operation causing
epilepsy in guinea-pigs, and likewise more recently on the analogous effects of cutting the sympathetic nerve in the neck. I shall hereafter have occasion to refer to Mr. Salvin's interesting case
of the apparently inherited effects of motmots biting off the barbs of their own tail-feathers. See
also on the general subject 'Variation of Animals and Plants under Domestication.' vol. ii. pp.
22–24.

ice to each being: we should remember how little we know about the use of many parts, or what changes in the blood tissues may serve to fit an organism for a new climate or new kinds of food. Nor must we forget the principle of correlation, by which, as Isidore Geoffroy has shewn in the case of man, many strange deviations of structure are tied together. Independently of correlation, a change in one part often leads, through the increased or decreased use of other parts, to other changes of a quite unexpected nature. It is also well to reflect on such facts, as the wonderful growth of galls on plants caused by the poison of an insect, and on the remarkable changes of colour in the plumage of parrots when fed on certain fishes, or inoculated with the poison of toads;[8] for we can thus see that the fluids of the system, if altered for some special purpose, might induce other changes. We should especially bear in mind that modifications acquired and continually used during past ages for some useful purpose, would probably become firmly fixed, and might be long inherited.

Thus a large yet undefined extension may safely be given to the direct and indirect results of natural selection; but I now admit, after reading the essay by Nägeli on plants, and the remarks by various authors with respect to animals, more especially those recently made by Professor Broca, that in the earlier editions of my 'Origin of Species' I perhaps attributed too much to the action of natural selection or the survival of the fittest. I have altered the fifth edition of the 'Origin' so as to confine my remarks to adaptive changes of structure; but I am convinced, from the light gained during even the last few years, that very many structures which now appear to us useless, will hereafter be proved to be useful, and will therefore come within the range of natural selection. Nevertheless, I did not formerly consider sufficiently the existence of structures, which, as far as we can at present judge, are neither beneficial nor injurious; and this I believe to be one of the greatest oversights as yet detected in my work. I may be permitted to say, as some excuse, that I had two distinct objects in view; firstly, to shew that species had not been separately created, and secondly, that natural selection had been the chief agent of change, though largely aided by the inherited effects of habit, and slightly by the direct action of the surrounding conditions. I was not, however, able to annul the influence of my former belief, then almost universal, that each species had been purposely created; and this led to my tacit assumption that every detail of structure, excepting rudiments, was of some special, though unrecognised, service. Any one with this assumption in his mind would naturally extend too far the action of natural selection, either during past or present times. Some of those who admit the principle of evolution, but reject natural selection, seem to forget, when criticising my book, that I had the above two objects in view; hence if I have erred in giving to natural selection great power, which I am very far from admitting, or in having exaggerated its power, which is in itself probable, I have at least, as I hope, done good service in aiding to overthrow the dogma of separate creations.

It is, as I can now see, probable that all organic beings, including man, possess peculiarities of structure, which neither are now, nor were formerly

8. "The Variation of Animals and Plants under Domestication,' vol. ii. pp. 280, 282.

of any service to them, and which, therefore, are of no physiological importance. We know not what produces the numberless slight differences between the individuals of each species, for reversion only carries the problem a few steps backwards, but each peculiarity must have had its efficient cause. If these causes, whatever they may be, were to act more uniformly and energetically during a lengthened period (and against this no reason can be assigned), the result would probably be not a mere slight individual difference, but a well-marked and constant modification, though one of no physiological importance. Changed structures, which are in no way beneficial, cannot be kept uniform through natural selection, though the injurious will be thus eliminated. Uniformity of character would, however, naturally follow from the assumed uniformity of the exciting causes, and likewise from the free intercrossing of many individuals. During successive periods, the same organism might in this manner acquire successive modifications, which would be transmitted in a nearly uniform state as long as the exciting causes remained the same and there was free intercrossing. With respect to the exciting causes we can only say, as when speaking of so-called spontaneous variations, that they relate much more closely to the constitution of the varying organism, than to the nature of the conditions to which it has been subjected.

CONCLUSION

In this chapter we have seen that as man at the present day is liable, like every other animal, to multiform individual differences or slight variations, so no doubt were the early progenitors of man; the variations being formerly induced by the same general causes, and governed by the same general and complex laws as at present. As all animals tend to multiply beyond their means of subsistence, so it must have been with the progenitors of man; and this would inevitably lead to a struggle for existence and to natural selection. The latter process would be greatly aided by the inherited effects of the increased use of parts, and these two processes would incessantly react on each other. It appears, also, as we shall hereafter see, that various unimportant characters have been acquired by man through sexual selection. An unexplained residuum of change must be left to the assumed uniform action of those unknown agencies, which occasionally induce strongly marked and abrupt deviations of structure in our domestic productions.

Judging from the habits of savages and of the greater number of the Quadrumana, primeval men, and even their ape-like progenitors, probably lived in society. With strictly social animals, natural selection sometimes acts on the individual, through the preservation of variations which are beneficial to the community. A community which includes a large number of well-endowed individuals increases in number, and is victorious over other less favoured ones; even although each separate member gains no advantage over the others of the same community. Associated insects have thus acquired many remarkable structures, which are of little or no service to the individual, such as the pollen-collecting apparatus, or the sting of the worker-bee, or the great jaws of soldier-ants. With the higher social animals, I am not aware that any structure has been modified solely for the good of the community, though some are of secondary service to it. For instance, the horns of ruminants and the great canine teeth of baboons appear to have been acquired by the males as weapons for sexual strife, but they are used in defence of the herd or troop. In regard to certain mental powers the case, as we shall see in the fifth chapter, is wholly different; for these faculties have been chiefly, or even exclusively, gained for the benefit of the community, and the individuals thereof have at the same time gained an advantage indirectly.

It has often been objected to such views as the foregoing, that man is one of the most helpless and defenceless creatures in the world; and that during his early and less well-developed condition, he would have been still more helpless. The Duke of Argyll, for instance, insists[9] that "the human frame has diverged from the structure of brutes, in the direction of greater physical helplessness and weakness. That is to say, it is a divergence which of all others it is most impossible to ascribe to mere natural selection." He adduces the naked and unprotected state of the body, the absence of great teeth or claws for defence, the small strength and speed of man, and his slight power of discovering food or of avoiding danger by smell. To these deficiencies there might be added one still more serious, namely, that he cannot climb quickly, and so escape from enemies. The loss of hair would not have been a great injury to the inhabitants of a warm country. For we know that the unclothed Fuegians can exist under a wretched climate. When we compare the defenceless state of man with that of apes, we must remember that the great canine teeth with which the latter are provided, are possessed in their full development by the males alone, and are chiefly used by them for fighting with their rivals; yet the females, which are not thus provided, manage to survive.

In regard to bodily size or strength, we do not know whether man is descended from some small species, like the chimpanzee, or from one as powerful as the gorilla; and, therefore, we cannot say whether man has become larger and stronger, or smaller and weaker, than his ancestors. We should, however, bear in mind that an animal possessing great size, strength, and ferocity, and which, like the gorilla, could defend itself from all enemies, would not perhaps have become social: and this would most effectually have checked the acquirement of the higher mental qualities, such as sympathy and the love of his fellows. Hence it might have been an immense advantage to man to have sprung from some comparatively weak creature.

The small strength and speed of man, his want of natural weapons, &c., are more than counterbalanced, firstly, by his intellectual powers, through which he has formed for himself weapons, tools, &c., though still remaining in a barbarous state, and secondly, by his social qualities which lead him to give and receive aid from his fellow-men. No country in the world abounds in a greater degree with dangerous beasts than Southern Africa; no country presents more fearful physical hardships than the Arctic

9. 'Primeval Man,' 1869, p. 66.

regions; yet one of the puniest of races, that of the Bushmen, maintains itself in Southern Africa, as do the dwarfed Esquimaux in the Arctic regions. The ancestors of man were, no doubt, inferior in intellect, and probably in social disposition, to the lowest existing savages; but it is quite conceivable that they might have existed, or even flourished, if they had advanced in intellect, whilst gradually losing their brute-like powers, such as that of climbing trees, &c. But these ancestors would not have been exposed to any special danger, even if far more helpless and defenceless than any existing savages, had they inhabited some warm continent or large island, such as Australia, New Guinea, or Borneo, which is now the home of the orang. And natural selection arising from the competition of tribe with tribe, in some large area as one of these, together with the inherited effects of habit, would, under favourable conditions, have sufficed to raise man to his present high position in the organic scale.

Chapter III. Comparison of the Mental Powers of Man and the Lower Animals

The difference in mental power between the highest ape and the lowest savage, immense—Certain instincts in common—The emotions—Curiosity—Imitation—Attention—Memory—Imagination—Reason—Progressive improvement—Tools and weapons used by animals—Abstraction, self-consciousness—Language—Sense of Beauty—Belief in God, spiritual agencies, superstitions.

We have seen in the last two chapters that man bears in his bodily structure clear traces of his descent from some lower form; but it may be urged that, as man differs so greatly in his mental power from all other animals, there must be some error in this conclusion. No doubt the difference in this respect is enormous, even if we compare the mind of one of the lowest savages, who has no words to express any number higher than four, and who uses hardly any abstract terms for common objects or for the affections,[1] with that of the most highly organised ape. The difference would, no doubt, still remain immense, even if one of the higher apes had been improved or civilised as much as a dog has been in comparison with its parent-form, the wolf or jackal. The Fuegians rank amongst the lowest barbarians; but I was continually struck with surprise how closely the three natives on board H. M. S. "Beagle," who had lived some years in England, and could talk a little English, resembled us in disposition and in most of our mental faculties. If no organic being excepting man had possessed any mental power, or if his powers had been of a wholly different nature from those of the lower animals, then we should never have been able to convince ourselves that our high faculties had been gradually developed. But it can be shewn that there is no fundamental difference of this kind. We must also admit that there is a much wider interval in mental power between one of the lowest fishes, as a lamprey or lancelet, and one of the higher apes, than between an ape and man; yet this interval is filled up by numberless gradations.

1. See the evidence on those points, as given by Lubbock, 'Prehistoric Times,' p. 354, &c.

Nor is the difference slight in moral disposition between a barbarian, such as the man described by the old navigator Byron, who dashed his child on the rocks for dropping a basket of sea-urchins, and a Howard or Clarkson; and in intellect, between a savage who uses hardly any abstract terms, and a Newton or Shakespeare. Differences of this kind between the highest men of the highest races and the lowest savages, are connected by the finest gradations. Therefore it is possible that they might pass and be developed into each other.

My object in this chapter is to shew that there is no fundamental difference between man and the higher mammals in their mental faculties. Each division of the subject might have been extended into a separate essay, but must here be treated briefly. As no classification of the mental powers has been universally accepted, I shall arrange my remarks in the order most convenient for my purpose; and will select those facts which have struck me most, with the hope that they may produce some effect on the reader.

* * * The lower animals, like man, manifestly feel pleasure and pain, happiness and misery. Happiness is never better exhibited than by young animals, such as puppies, kittens, lambs, &c., when playing together, like our own children. Even insects play together, as has been described by that excellent observer, P. Huber,[2] who saw ants chasing and pretending to bite each other, like so many puppies.

The fact that the lower animals are excited by the same emotions as ourselves is so well established, that it will not be necessary to weary the reader by many details. Terror acts in the same manner on them as on us, causing the muscles to tremble, the heart to palpitate, the sphincters to be relaxed, and the hair to stand on end. Suspicion, the offspring of fear, is eminently characteristic of most wild animals. It is, I think, impossible to read the account given by Sir E. Tennent, of the behaviour of the female elephants, used as decoys, without admitting that they intentionally practise deceit, and well know what they are about. Courage and timidity are extremely variable qualities in the individuals of the same species, as is plainly seen in our dogs. Some dogs and horses are ill-tempered, and easily turn sulky; others are good-tempered; and these qualities are certainly inherited. Every one knows how liable animals are to furious rage, and how plainly they shew it. Many, and probably true, anecdotes have been published on the long-delayed and artful revenge of various animals. The accurate Rengger, and Brehm[3] state that the American and African monkeys which they kept tame, certainly revenged themselves. Sir Andrew Smith, a zoologist whose scrupulous accuracy was known to many persons, told me the following story of which he was himself an eye-witness; at the Cape of Good Hope an officer had often plagued a certain baboon, and the animal, seeing him approaching one Sunday for parade, poured water into a hole and hastily made some thick mud, which he skilfully dashed over the officer as he passed by, to the

---

2. 'Recherches sur les Mœurs des Fourmis,' 1810, p. 173.
3. All the following statements, given on the authority of these two naturalists, are taken from Rengger's 'Naturgesch. der Säugethiere von Paraguay,' 1830, s. 41–57, and from Brehm's 'Thierleben,' B. i. s. 10–87.

amusement of many bystanders. For long afterwards the baboon rejoiced and triumphed whenever he saw his victim.

The love of a dog for his master is notorious; as an old writer quaintly says,[4] "A dog is the only thing on this earth that luvs you more than he luvs himself."

In the agony of death a dog has been known to caress his master, and every one has heard of the dog suffering under vivisection, who licked the hand of the operator; this man, unless the operation was fully justified by an increase of our knowledge, or unless he had a heart of stone, must have felt remorse to the last hour of his life.

As Whewell[5] has well asked, "who that reads the touching instances of maternal affection, related so often of the women of all nations, and of the females of all animals, can doubt that the principle of action is the same in the two cases?" We see maternal affection exhibited in the most trifling details; thus Rengger observed an American monkey (a Cebus) carefully driving away the flies which plagued her infant; and Duvaucel saw a Hylobates washing the faces of her young ones in a stream. So intense is the grief of female monkeys for the loss of their young, that it invariably caused the death of certain kinds kept under confinement by Brehm in N. Africa. Orphan monkeys were always adopted and carefully guarded by the other monkeys, both males and females. One female baboon had so capacious a heart that she not only adopted young monkeys of other species, but stole young dogs and cats, which she continually carried about. Her kindness, however, did not go so far as to share her food with her adopted offspring, at which Brehm was surprised, as his monkeys always divided everything quite fairly with their own young ones. An adopted kitten scratched this affectionate baboon, who certainly had a fine intellect, for she was much astonished at being scratched, and immediately examined the kitten's feet, and without more ado bit off the claws.[6] In the Zoological Gardens, I heard from the keeper that an old baboon (C. chacma) had adopted a Rhesus monkey; but when a young drill and mandrill were placed in the cage, she seemed to perceive that these monkeys, though distinct species, were her nearer relatives, for she at once rejected the Rhesus and adopted both of them. The young Rhesus, as I saw, was greatly discontented at being thus rejected, and it would, like a naughty child, annoy and attack the young drill and mandrill whenever it could do so with safety; this conduct exciting great indignation in the old baboon. Monkeys will also, according to Brehm, defend their master when attacked by any one, as well as dogs to whom they are attached, from the attacks of other dogs. But we here trench on the subjects of sympathy and fidelity, to which I shall recur. Some of Brehm's monkeys took much delight in teasing a certain old dog whom they disliked, as well as other animals, in various ingenious ways.

4. Quoted by Dr. Lauder Lindsay, in his 'Physiology of Mind in the Lower Animals,' 'Journal of Mental Science,' April 1871, p. 38.
5. 'Bridgewater Treatise,' p. 263.
6. A critic, without any grounds ('Quarterly Review,' July, 1871, p. 72), disputes the possibility of this act as described by Brehm, for the sake of discrediting my work. Therefore I tried, and found that I could readily seize with my own teeth the sharp little claws of a kitten nearly five weeks old.

Most of the more complex emotions are common to the higher animals and ourselves. Every one has seen how jealous a dog is of his master's affection, if lavished on any other creature; and I have observed the same fact with monkeys. This shews that animals not only love, but have desire to be loved. Animals manifestly feel emulation. They love approbation or praise; and a dog carrying a basket for his master exhibits in a high degree self-complacency or pride. There can, I think, be no doubt that a dog feels shame, as distinct from fear, and something very like modesty when begging too often for food. A great dog scorns the snarling of a little dog, and this may be called magnanimity. Several observers have stated that monkeys certainly dislike being laughed at; and they sometimes invent imaginary offences. In the Zoological Gardens I saw a baboon who always got into a furious rage when his keeper took out a letter or book and read it aloud to him; and his rage was so violent that, as I witnessed on one occasion, he bit his own leg till the blood flowed. Dogs shew what may be fairly called a sense of humour, as distinct from mere play; if a bit of stick or other such object be thrown to one, he will often carry it away for a short distance; and then squatting down with it on the ground close before him, will wait until his master comes quite close to take it away. The dog will then seize it and rush away in triumph, repeating the same manœuvre, and evidently enjoying the practical joke.

We will now turn to the more intellectual emotions and faculties, which are very important, as forming the basis for the development of the higher mental powers. Animals manifestly enjoy excitement, and suffer from ennui, as may be seen with dogs, and, according to Rengger, with monkeys. All animals feel Wonder, and many exhibit Curiosity. They sometimes suffer from this latter quality, as when the hunter plays antics and thus attracts them; I have witnessed this with deer, and so it is with the wary chamois, and with some kinds of wild-ducks. Brehm gives a curious account of the instinctive dread, which his monkeys exhibited, for snakes; but their curiosity was so great that they could not desist from occasionally satiating their horror in a most human fashion, by lifting up the lid of the box in which the snakes were kept. I was so much surprised at this account, that I took a stuffed and coiled-up snake into the monkey-house at the Zoological Gardens, and the excitement thus caused was one of the most curious spectacles which I ever beheld. Three species of Cercopithecus were the most alarmed; they dashed about their cages, and uttered sharp signal cries of danger, which were understood by the other monkeys. A few young monkeys and one old Anubis baboon alone took no notice of the snake. I then placed the stuffed specimen on the ground in one of the larger compartments. After a time all the monkeys collected round it in a large circle, and staring intently, presented a most ludicrous appearance. They became extremely nervous; so that when a wooden ball, with which they were familiar as a plaything, was accidentally moved in the straw, under which it was partly hidden, they all instantly started away. These monkeys behaved very differently when a dead fish, a mouse,[7] a living

---

7. I have given a short account of their behaviour on this occasion in my "Expression of the Emotions," p. 43.

turtle, and other new objects were placed in their cages; for though at first frightened, they soon approached, handled and examined them. I then placed a live snake in a paper bag, with the mouth loosely closed, in one of the larger compartments. One of the monkeys immediately approached, cautiously opened the bag a little, peeped in, and instantly dashed away. Then I witnessed what Brehm has described, for monkey after monkey, with head raised high and turned on one side, could not resist taking a momentary peep into the upright bag, at the dreadful object lying quietly at the bottom. It would almost appear as if monkeys had some notion of zoological affinities, for those kept by Brehm exhibited a strange, though mistaken, instinctive dread of innocent lizards and frogs. An orang, also, has been known to be much alarmed at the first sight of a turtle.[8]

The principle of Imitation is strong in man, and especially, as I have myself observed, with savages. In certain morbid states of the brain this tendency is exaggerated to an extraordinary degree: some hemiplegic patients and others, at the commencement of inflammatory softening of the brain, unconsciously imitate every word which is uttered, whether in their own or in a foreign language, and every gesture or action which is performed near them.[9] Desor[1] has remarked that no animal voluntarily imitates an action performed by man, until in the ascending scale we come to monkeys, which are well known to be ridiculous mockers. Animals, however, sometimes imitate each other's actions: thus two species of wolves, which had been reared by dogs, learned to bark, as does sometimes the jackal,[2] but whether this can be called voluntary imitation is another question. Birds imitate the songs of their parents, and sometimes of other birds; and parrots are notorious imitators of any sound which they often hear. Dureau de la Malle gives an account[3] of a dog reared by a cat, who learnt to imitate the well-known action of a cat licking her paws, and thus washing her ears and face; this was also witnessed by the celebrated naturalist Audouïn. I have received several confirmatory accounts; in one of these, a dog had not been suckled by a cat, but had been brought up with one, together with kittens, and had thus acquired the above habit, which he ever afterwards practised during his life of thirteen years. Dureau de la Malle's dog likewise learnt from the kittens to play with a ball by rolling it about with his fore paws, and springing on it. A correspondent assures me that a cat in his house used to put her paws into jugs of milk having too narrow a mouth for her head. A kitten of this cat soon learned the same trick, and practised it ever afterwards, whenever there was an opportunity.

The parents of many animals, trusting to the principle of imitation in their young, and more especially to their instinctive or inherited tendencies, may be said to educate them. We see this when a cat brings a live mouse to her kittens; and Dureau de la Malle has given a curious account (in the paper above quoted) of his observations on hawks which taught

8. W. C. L. Martin, 'Nat. Hist. of Mammalia,' 1841, p. 405.
9. Dr. Bateman 'On Aphasia,' 1870, p. 110.
1. Quoted by Vogt, 'Mémoire sur les Microcéphales,' 1867, p. 168.
2. 'The Variation of Animals and Plants under Domestication,' vol. i. p. 27.
3. 'Annales des Sc. Nat.' (1st Series), tom, xxii, p. 397.

their young dexterity, as well as judgment of distances, by first dropping through the air dead mice and sparrows, which the young generally failed to catch, and then bringing them live birds and letting them loose.

Hardly any faculty is more important for the intellectual progress of man than Attention. Animals clearly manifest this power, as when a cat watches by a hole and prepares to spring on its prey. Wild animals sometimes become so absorbed when thus engaged, that they may be easily approached. Mr. Bartlett has given me a curious proof how variable this faculty is in monkeys. A man who trains monkeys to act in plays, used to purchase common kinds from the Zoological Society at the price of five pounds for each; but he offered to give double the price, if he might keep three or four of them for a few days, in order to select one. When asked how he could possibly learn so soon, whether a particular monkey would turn out a good actor, he answered that it all depended on their power of attention. If when he was talking and explaining anything to a monkey, its attention was easily distracted, as by a fly on the wall or other trifling object, the case was hopeless. If he tried by punishment to make an inattentive monkey act, it turned sulky. On the other hand, a monkey which carefully attended to him could always be trained.

It is almost superfluous to state that animals have excellent Memories for persons and places. A baboon at the Cape of Good Hope, as I have been informed by Sir Andrew Smith, recognised him with joy after an absence of nine months. I had a dog who was savage and averse to all strangers, and I purposely tried his memory after an absence of five years and two days. I went near the stable where he lived, and shouted to him in my old manner; he shewed no joy, but instantly followed me out walking, and obeyed me, exactly as if I had parted with him only half an hour before. A train of old associations, dormant during five years, had thus been instantaneously awakened in his mind. Even ants, as P. Huber[4] has clearly shewn, recognised their fellow-ants belonging to the same community after a separation of four months. Animals can certainly by some means judge of the intervals of time between recurrent events.

The Imagination is one of the highest prerogatives of man. By this faculty he unites former images and ideas, independently of the will, and thus creates brilliant and novel results. A poet, as Jean Paul Richter remarks,[5] "who must reflect whether he shall make a character say yes or no—to the devil with him; he is only a stupid corpse." Dreaming gives us the best notion of this power; as Jean Paul again says, "The dream is an involuntary art of poetry." The value of the products of our imagination depends of course on the number, accuracy, and clearness of our impressions, on our judgment and taste in selecting or rejecting the involuntary combinations, and to a certain extent on our power of voluntarily combining them. As dogs, cats, horses, and probably all the higher animals, even birds[6] have vivid dreams, and this is shewn by their movements and the sounds uttered, we must admit that they possess some power of imag-

---

4. 'Les Mœurs des Fourmis,' 1810, p. 150.
5. Quoted in Dr. Maudsley's 'Physiology and Pathology of Mind,' 1868, pp. 19, 220.
6. Dr. Jerdon, 'Birds of India,' vol. i. 1862, p. xxi. Houzeau says that his parokeets and canary-birds dreamt: 'Facultés Mentales,' tom. ii. p. 136.

ination. There must be something special, which causes dogs to howl in the night, and especially during moonlight, in that remarkable and melancholy manner called baying. All dogs do not do so; and, according to Houzeau,[7] they do not then look at the moon, but at some fixed point near the horizon. Houzeau thinks that their imaginations are disturbed by the vague outlines of the surrounding objects, and conjure up before them fantastic images: if this be so, their feelings may almost be called superstitious.

   Of all the faculties of the human mind, it will, I presume, be admitted that Reason stands at the summit. Only a few persons now dispute that animals possess some power of reasoning. Animals may constantly be seen to pause, deliberate, and resolve. It is a significant fact, that the more the habits of any particular animal are studied by a naturalist, the more he attributes to reason and the less to unlearnt instincts.[8] In future chapters we shall see that some animals extremely low in the scale apparently display a certain amount of reason. No doubt it is often difficult to distinguish between the power of reason and that of instinct. For instance, Dr. Hayes, in his work on 'The Open Polar Sea,' repeatedly remarks that his dogs, instead of continuing to draw the sledges in a compact body, diverged and separated when they came to thin ice, so that their weight might be more evenly distributed. This was often the first warning which the travellers received that the ice was becoming thin and dangerous. Now, did the dogs act thus from the experience of each individual, or from the example of the older and wiser dogs, or from an inherited habit, that is from instinct? This instinct, may possibly have arisen since the time, long ago, when dogs were first employed by the natives in drawing their sledges; or the Arctic wolves, the parent-stock of the Esquimaux dog, may have acquired an instinct impelling them not to attack their prey in a close pack, when on thin ice.

   We can only judge by the circumstances under which actions are performed, whether they are due to instinct, or to reason, or to the mere association of ideas: this latter principle, however, is intimately connected with reason. A curious case has been given by Prof. Möbius,[9] of a pike, separated by a plate of glass from an adjoining aquarium stocked with fish, and who often dashed himself with such violence against the glass in trying to catch the other fishes, that he was sometimes completely stunned. The pike went on thus for three months, but at last learnt caution, and ceased to do so. The plate of glass was then removed, but the pike would not attack these particular fishes, though he would devour others which were afterwards introduced; so strongly was the idea of a violent shock associated in his feeble mind with the attempt on his former neighbours. If a savage, who had never seen a large plate-glass window, were to dash himself even once against it, he would for a long time afterwards associate a shock with a window-frame; but very differently from the pike, he would probably reflect on the nature of the impediment, and be cautious under analogous

7. 'Facultés Mentales des Animaux,' 1872, tom. ii. p. 181.
8. Mr. L. H. Morgan's work on 'The American Beaver,' 1868, offers a good illustration of this remark. I cannot help thinking, however, that he goes too far in underrating the power of instinct.
9. 'Die Bewegungen der Thiere,' &c., 1873, p. 11.

circumstances. Now with monkeys, as we shall presently see, a painful or merely a disagreeable impression, from an action once performed, is sometimes sufficient to prevent the animal from repeating it. If we attribute this difference between the monkey and the pike solely to the association of ideas being so much stronger and more persistent in the one than the other, though the pike often received much the more severe injury, can we maintain in the case of man that a similar difference implies the possession of a fundamentally different mind?

Houzeau relates[1] that, whilst crossing a wide and arid plain in Texas, his two dogs suffered greatly from thirst, and that between thirty and forty times they rushed down the hollows to search for water. These hollows were not valleys, and there were no trees in them, or any other difference in the vegetation, and as they were absolutely dry there could have been no smell of damp earth. The dogs behaved as if they knew that a dip in the ground offered them the best chance of finding water, and Houzeau has often witnessed the same behaviour in other animals.

I have seen, as I daresay have others, that when a small object is thrown on the ground beyond the reach of one of the elephants in the Zoological Gardens, he blows through his trunk on the ground beyond the object, so that the current reflected on all sides may drive the object within his reach. Again a well-known ethnologist, Mr. Westropp, informs me that he observed in Vienna a bear deliberately making with his paw a current in some water, which was close to the bars of his cage, so as to draw a piece of floating bread within his reach. These actions of the elephant and bear can hardly be attributed to instinct or inherited habit, as they would be of little use to an animal in a state of nature. Now, what is the difference between such actions, when performed by an uncultivated man, and by one of the higher animals?

The savage and the dog have often found water at a low level, and the coincidence under such circumstances has become associated in their minds. A cultivated man would perhaps make some general proposition on the subject; but from all that we know of savages it is extremely doubtful whether they would do so, and a dog certainly would not. But a savage, as well as a dog, would search in the same way, though frequently disappointed; and in both it seems to be equally an act of reason, whether or not any general proposition on the subject is consciously placed before the mind.[2] The same would apply to the elephant and the bear making currents in the air or water. The savage would certainly neither know nor care by what law the desired movements were effected; yet his act would be guided by a rude process of reasoning, as surely as would a philosopher in his longest chain of deductions. There would no doubt be this difference between him and one of the higher animals, that he would take notice of much slighter circumstances and conditions, and would observe any connection between them after much less experience and this would

1. 'Facultés Mentales des Animaux,' 1872, tom. ii. p. 265.
2. Prof. Huxley has analysed with admirable clearness the mental steps by which a man, as well as a dog, arrives at a conclusion in a case analogous to that given in my text. See his article, 'Mr. Darwin's Critics,' in the 'Contemporary Review,' Nov. 1871, p. 462, and in his 'Critiques and Essays,' 1873, p. 279.

be of paramount importance. I kept a daily record of the actions of one of my infants, and when he was about eleven months old, and before he could speak a single word, I was continually struck with the greater quickness, with which all sorts of objects and sounds were associated together in his mind, compared with that of the most intelligent dogs I ever knew. But the higher animals differ in exactly the same way in this power of association from those low in the scale, such as the pike, as well as in that of drawing inferences and of observation.

The prompting of reason, after very short experience, are well shewn by the following actions of American monkeys, which stand low in their order. Rengger, a most careful observer, states that when he first gave eggs to his monkeys in Paraguay, they smashed them, and thus lost much of their contents; afterwards they gently hit one end against some hard body, and picked off the bits of shell with their fingers. After cutting themselves only *once* with any sharp tool, they would not touch it again, or would handle it with the greatest caution. Lumps of sugar were often given them wrapped up in paper; and Rengger sometimes put a live wasp in the paper, so that in hastily unfolding it they got stung; after this had *once* happened, they always first held the packet to their ears to detect any movement within.[3]

The following cases relate to dogs. Mr. Colquhoun[4] winged two wild-ducks, which fell on the further side of a stream; his retriever tried to bring over both at once, but could not succeed; she then, though never before known to ruffle a feather, deliberately killed one, brought over the other, and returned for the dead bird. Col. Hutchinson relates that two partridges were shot at once, one being killed, the other wounded; the latter ran away, and was caught by the retriever, who on her return came across the dead bird; "she stopped, evidently greatly puzzled, and after one or two trials, finding she could not take it up without permitting the escape of the winged bird, she considered a moment, then deliberately murdered it by giving it a severe crunch, and afterwards brought away both together. This was the only known instance of her ever having wilfully injured any game." Here we have reason though not quite perfect, for the retriever might have brought the wounded bird first and then returned for the dead one, as in the case of the two wild-ducks. I give the above cases, as resting on the evidence of two independent witnesses, and because in both instances the retrievers, after deliberation, broke through a habit which is inherited by them (that of not killing the game retrieved), and because they shew how strong their reasoning faculty must have been to overcome a fixed habit.

I will conclude by quoting a remark by the illustrious Humboldt.[5] "The muleteers in S. America say, 'I will not give you the mule whose step is easiest, but *la mas racional*,—the one that reasons best;' " and as he adds, "this popular expression, dictated by long experience, combats the system of animated machines, better perhaps than all the arguments of speculative

3. Mr. Belt, in his most interesting work, 'The Naturalist in Nicaragua,' 1874 (p. 119), likewise describes various actions of a tamed Cebus, which, I think, clearly shew that this animal possessed some reasoning power.
4. 'The Moor and the Loch,' p. 45. Col. Hutchinson on 'Dog Breaking,' 1850, p. 46.
5. 'Personal Narrative,' Eng. translat., vol. iii. p. 106.

philosophy." Nevertheless some writers even yet deny that the higher animals possess a trace of reason; and they endeavor to explain away, by what
appears to be mere verbiage,[6] all such facts as those above given.

It has, I think, now been shewn that man and the higher animals, especially the Primates, have some few instincts in common.

*   *   *

Chapter VI. On the Affinities and Genealogy of Man

Position of man in the animal series—The natural system genealogical—Adaptive characters of slight value—Various small points of resemblance between man and the
Quadrumana—Rank of man in the natural system—Birthplace and antiquity of man
—Absence of fossil connecting links—Lower stages in the genealogy of man, as inferred, firstly from his affinities and secondly from his structure—Early androgynous
condition of the Vertebrata—Conclusion.

Even if it be granted that the difference between man and his nearest
allies is as great in corporeal structure as some naturalists maintain, and
although we must grant that the difference between them is immense in
mental power, yet the facts given in the earlier chapters appear to declare,
in the plainest manner, that man is descended from some lower form,
notwithstanding that connecting-links have not hitherto been discovered.

Man is liable to numerous, slight, and diversified variations, which are
induced by the same general causes, are governed and transmitted in accordance with the same general laws, as in the lower animals. Man has
multiplied so rapidly, that he has necessarily been exposed to struggle for
existence, and consequently to natural selection. He has given rise to many
races, some of which differ so much from each other, that they have often
been ranked by naturalists as distinct species. His body is constructed on
the same homological plan as that of other mammals. He passes through
the same phases of embryological development. He retains many rudimentary and useless structures, which no doubt were once serviceable.
Characters occasionally make their re-appearance in him, which we have
reason to believe were possessed by his early progenitors. If the origin of
man had been wholly different from that of all other animals, these various
appearances would be mere empty deceptions; but such an admission is
incredible. These appearances, on the other hand, are intelligible, at least
to a large extent, if man is the co-descendant with other mammals of some
unknown and lower form.

Some naturalists, from being deeply impressed with the mental and
spiritual powers of man, have divided the whole organic world into three
kingdoms, the Human, the Animal, and the Vegetable, thus giving to man

---

6. I am glad to find that so acute a reasoner as Mr. Leslie Stephen ('Darwinism and Divinity, Essays
on Free-thinking,' 1873, p. 80), in speaking of the supposed impassable barrier between the minds
of man and the lower animals, says, "The distinctions, indeed, which have been drawn, seem to
us to rest upon no better foundation than a great many other metaphysical distinctions; that is,
the assumption that because you can give two things different names, they must therefore have
different natures. It is difficult to understand how anybody who has ever kept a dog, or seen an
elephant, can have any doubt as to an animal's power of performing the essential processes of
reasoning."

a separate kingdom.[7] Spiritual powers cannot be compared or classed by the naturalist: but he may endeavour to shew, as I have done, that the mental faculties of man and the lower animals do not differ in kind, although immensely in degree. A difference in degree, however great, does not justify us in placing man in a distinct kingdom, as will perhaps be best illustrated by comparing the mental powers of two insects, namely, a coccus or scale-insect and an ant, which undoubtedly belong to the same class. The difference is here greater than, though of a somewhat different kind from, that between man and the highest mammal. The female coccus, whilst young, attaches itself by its proboscis to a plant; sucks the sap, but never moves again; is fertilised and lays eggs; and this is its whole history. On the other hand, to describe the habits and mental powers of worker-ants, would require, as Pierre Huber has shewn, a large volume; I may, however, briefly specify a few points. Ants certainly communicate information to each other, and several unite for the same work, or for games of play. They recognise their fellow-ants after months of absence, and feel sympathy for each other. They build great edifices, keep them clean, close the doors in the evening, and post sentries. They make roads as well as tunnels under rivers, and temporary bridges over them, by clinging together. They collect food for the community, and when an object, too large for entrance, is brought to the nest, they enlarge the door, and afterwards build it up again. They store up seeds, of which they prevent the germination, and which, if damp, are brought up to the surface to dry. They keep aphides and other insects as milch-cows. They go out to battle in regular bands, and freely sacrifice their lives for the common weal. They emigrate according to a preconcerted plan. They capture slaves. They move the eggs of their aphides, as well as their own eggs and cocoons, into warm parts of the nest, in order that they may be quickly hatched; and endless similar facts could be given.[8] On the whole, the difference in mental power between an ant and a coccus is immense; yet no one has ever dreamed of placing these insects in distinct classes, much less in distinct kingdoms. No doubt the difference is bridged over by other insects; and this is not the case with man and the higher apes. But we have every reason to believe that the breaks in the series are simply the results of many forms having become extinct.

Professor Owen, relying chiefly on the structure of the brain, has divided the mammalian series into four sub-classes. One of these he devotes to man; in another he places both the Marsupials and the Monotremata; so that he makes man as distinct from all other mammals as are these two latter groups conjoined. This view has not been accepted, as far as I am aware, by any naturalist capable of forming an independent judgment and therefore need not here be further considered.

We can understand why a classification founded on any single character

7. Isidore Geoffroy St.-Hilaire gives a detailed account of the position assigned to man by various naturalists in their classifications: 'Hist. Nat. Gén.', tom. ii. 1859, pp. 170–189.
8. Some of the most interesting facts ever published on the habits of ants are given by Mr. Belt, in his 'Naturalist in Nicaragua,' 1874. See also Mr. Moggridge's admirable work, 'Harvesting Ants,' &c., 1873, also L'Instinct chez les Insectes,' by M. George Pouchet, 'Revue des Deux Mondes,' Feb. 1870, p. 682.

or organ—even an organ so wonderfully complex and important as the brain—or on the high development of the mental faculties, is almost sure to prove unsatisfactory. This principle has indeed been tried with hymenopterous insects; but when thus classed by their habits or instincts, the arrangement proved thoroughly artificial.[9] Classifications may, of course, be based on any character whatever, as on size, colour, or the element inhabited; but naturalists have long felt a profound conviction that there is a natural system. This system, it is now generally admitted, must be, as far as possible, genealogical in arrangement,—that is the co-descendants of the same form must be kept together in one group, apart from the co-descendants of any other form; but if the parent-forms are related, so will be their descendants, and the two groups together will form a larger group. The amount of difference between the several groups—that is the amount of modification which each has undergone—is expressed by such terms as genera, families, orders, and classes. As we have no record of the lines of descent, the pedigree can be discovered only by observing the degrees of resemblance between the beings which are to be classed. For this object numerous points of resemblance are of much more importance than the amount of similarity or dissimilarity in a few points. If two languages were found to resemble each other in a multitude of words and points of construction, they would be universally recognised as having sprung from a common source, notwithstanding that they differed greatly in some few words or points of construction. But with organic beings the points of resemblance must not consist of adaptations to similar habits of life: two animals may, for instance, have had their whole frames modified for living in the water, and yet they will not be brought any nearer to each other in the natural system. Hence we can see how it is that resemblances in several unimportant structures, in useless and rudimentary organs, or not now functionally active, or in an embryological condition, are by far the most serviceable for classification; for they can hardly be due to adaptations within a late period; and thus they reveal the old lines of descent or of true affinity.

We can further see why a great amount of modification in some one character ought not to lead us to separate widely any two organisms. A part which already differs much from the same part in other allied forms has already, according to the theory of evolution, varied much; consequently it would (as long as the organism remained exposed to the same exciting conditions) be liable to further variations of the same kind; and these, if beneficial, would be preserved, and thus be continually augmented. In many cases the continued development of a part, for instance, of the beak of a bird, or of the teeth of a mammal, would not aid the species in gaining its food, or for any other object; but with man we can see no definite limit to the continued development of the brain and mental faculties, as far as advantage is concerned. Therefore in determining the position of man in the natural or genealogical system, the extreme development of his brain ought not to outweigh a multitude of resemblances in other less important or quite unimportant points.

The greater number of naturalists who have taken into consideration

9. Westwood, 'Modern Class of Insects,' vol. ii. 1840, p. 87.

the whole structure of man, including his mental faculties, have followed Blumenbach and Cuvier, and have placed man in a separate Order, under the title of the Bimana, and therefore on an equality with the orders of the Quadrumana, Carnivora, &c. Recently many of our best naturalists have recurred to the view first propounded by Linnæus, so remarkable for his sagacity, and have placed man in the same Order with the Quadrumana, under the title of the Primates. The justice of this conclusion will be admitted: for in the first place, we must bear in mind the comparative insignificance for classification of the great development of the brain in man, and that the strongly-marked differences between the skulls of man and the Quadrumana (lately insisted upon by Bischoff, Aeby, and others) apparently follow from their differently developed brains. In the second place, we must remember that nearly all the other and more important differences between man and the quadrumana are manifestly adaptive in their nature, and relate chiefly to the erect position of man; such as the structure of his hand, foot, and pelvis, the curvature of his spine, and the position of his head. The family of Seals offers a good illustration of the small importance of adaptive characters for classification. These animals differ from all other Carnivora in the form of their bodies and in the structure of their limbs, far more than does man from the higher apes; yet in most systems, from that of Cuvier to the most recent one by Mr. Flower,[1] seals are ranked as a mere family in the Order of the Carnivora. If man had not been his own classifier, he would never have thought of founding a separate order for his own reception.

It would be beyond my limits, and quite beyond my knowledge, even to name the innumerable points of structure in which man agrees with the other Primates. Our great anatomist and philosopher, Prof. Huxley, has fully discussed this subject,[2] and concludes that man in all parts of his organization differs less from the higher apes, than these do from the lower members of the same group. Consequently there "is no justification for placing man in a distinct order." * * *

LOWER STAGES IN THE GENEALOGY OF MAN

* * * We have thus far endeavoured rudely to trace the genealogy of the Vertebrata by the aid of their mutual affinities. We will now look to man as he exists; and we shall, I think, be able partially to restore the structure of our early progenitors, during successive periods, but not in due order of time. This can be effected by means of the rudiments which man still retains, by the characters which occasionally make their appearance in him through reversion, and by the aid of the principles of morphology and embryology. The various facts, to which I shall here allude, have been given in the previous chapters.

The early progenitors of man must have been once covered with hair, both sexes having beards; their ears were probably pointed, and capable of movement; and their bodies were provided with a tail, having the proper

1. 'Proc. Zoolog. Soc.' 1863, p. 4.
2. 'Evidence as to Man's Place in Nature,' 1863, p. 70, *et passim*.

muscles. Their limbs and bodies were also acted on by many muscles which now only occasionally reappear, but are normally present in the Quadrumana. At this or some earlier period, the great artery and nerve of the humerus ran through a supra-condyloid foramen. The intestine gave forth a much larger diverticulum or cæcum than that now existing. The foot was then prehensile, judging from the condition of the great toe in the fœtus; and our progenitors, no doubt, were arboreal in their habits, and frequented some warm, forest-clad land. The males had great canine teeth, which served them as formidable weapons. At a much earlier period the uterus was double; the excreta were voided through a cloaca; and the eye was protected by a third eyelid or nictitating membrane. At a still earlier period the progenitors of man must have been aquatic in their habits; for morphology plainly tells us that our lungs consist of a modified swim-bladder, which once served as a float. The clefts on the neck in the embryo of man show where the branchiæ once existed. In the lunar or weekly recurrent periods of some of our functions we apparently still retain traces of our primordial birthplace, a shore washed by the tides. At about this same early period the true kidneys were replaced by the corpora wolf-fiana. The heart existed as a simple pulsating vessel; and the chorda dor-salis took the place of a vertebral column. These early ancestors of man, thus seen in the dim recesses of time, must have been as simply, or even still more simply organised than the lancelet or amphioxus.

There is one other point deserving a fuller notice. It has long been known that in the vertebrate kingdom one sex bears rudiments of various accessory parts, appertaining to the reproductive system, which properly belongs to the opposite sex; and it has now been ascertained that at a very early embryonic period both sexes possess true male and female glands. Hence some remote progenitor of the whole vertebrate kingdom appears to have been hermaphrodite or androgynous.[3] But here we encounter a singular difficulty. In the mammalian class the males possess rudiments of a uterus with the adjacent passage, in their vesiculæ prostaticæ; they bear also rudiments of mammæ, and some male Marsupials have traces of a marsupial sack.[4] Other analogous facts could be added. Are we, then, to suppose that some extremely ancient mammal continued androgynous, after it had acquired the chief distinctions of its class, and therefore after it had diverged from the lower classes of the vertebrate kingdom? This seems very improbable, for we have to look to fishes, the lowest of all the classes, to find any still existent androgynous forms.[5] That various accessory

3. This is the conclusion of Prof. Gegenbaur, one of the highest authorities in comparative anatomy: see 'Grundzüge der vergleich. Anat.' 1870, s. 876. The result has been arrived at chiefly from the study of the Amphibia; but it appears from the researches of Waldeyer (as quoted in 'Journal of Anat. and Phys.' 1869, p. 161), that the sexual organs of even "the higher vertebrata are, in their early condition, hermaphrodite." Similar views have long been held by some authors, though until recently without a firm basis.
4. The male Thylacinus offers the best instance. Owen, 'Anatomy of Vertebrates,' vol. iii. p. 771.
5. Hermaphroditism has been observed in several species of Serranus, as well as in some other fishes, where it is either normal and symmetrical, or abnormal and unilateral. Dr. Zouteveen has given me references on this subject, more especially to a paper by Prof. Halbertsma, in the 'Transact. of the Dutch Acad. of Sciences,' vol. xvi. Dr. Günther doubts the fact, but it has now been recorded by too many good observers to be any longer disputed. Dr. M. Lessona writes to me, that he has verified the observations made by Cavolini on Serranus. Prof. Ercolani has recently shewn ('Acad. delle Scienze,' Bologna, Dec. 28, 1871) that eels are androgynous.

parts, proper to each sex, are found in a rudimentary condition in the opposite sex, may be explained by such organs having been gradually acquired by the one sex, and then transmitted in a more or less imperfect state to the other. When we treat of sexual selection, we shall meet with innumerable instances of this form of transmission,—as in the case of the spurs, plumes, and brilliant colours, acquired for battle or ornament by male birds, and inherited by the females in an imperfect or rudimentary condition.

The possession by male mammals of functionally imperfect mammary organs is, in some respects, especially curious. The Monotremata have the proper milk-secreting glands with orifices, but no nipples; and as these animals stand at the very base of the mammalian series, it is probable that the progenitors of the class also had milk-secreting glands, but no nipples. This conclusion is supported by what is known of their manner of development; for Professor Turner informs me, on the authority of Kölliker and Langer, that in the embryo the mammary glands can be distinctly traced before the nipples are in the least visible; and the development of successive parts in the individual generally represents and accords with the development of successive beings in the same line of descent. The Marsupials differ from the Monotremata by possessing nipples; so that probably these organs were first acquired by the Marsupials, after they had diverged from, and risen above, the Monotremata, and were then transmitted to the placental mammals.[6] No one will suppose that the Marsupials still remained androgynous, after they had approximately acquired their present structure. How then are we to account for male mammals possessing mammæ? It is possible that they were first developed in the females and then transferred to the males, but from what follows this is hardly probable.

It may be suggested, as another view, that long after the progenitors of the whole mammalian class had ceased to be androgynous, both sexes yielded milk, and thus nourished their young; and in the case of the Marsupials, that both sexes carried their young in marsupial sacks. This will not appear altogether improbable, if we reflect that the males of existing syngnathous fishes receive the eggs of the females in their abdominal pouches, hatch them, and afterwards, as some believe, nourish the young;[7]—that certain other male fishes hatch the eggs within their mouths or branchial cavities;—that certain male toads take the chaplets of eggs from the females, and wind them round their own thighs, keeping them there until the tadpoles are born;—that certain male birds undertake the whole duty of incubation, and that male pigeons, as well as the females, feed their nestlings with a secretion from their crops. But the above suggestion first occurred to me from mammary glands of male mammals

6. Prof. Gegenbaur has shewn ('Jenaische Zeitschrift,' Bd. vii. p. 212) that two distinct types of nipples prevail throughout the several mammalian orders, but that it is quite intelligible how both could have been derived from the nipples of the Marsupials, and the latter from those of the Monotremata. See, also, a memoir by Dr. Max Huss, on the mammary glands, ibid. B. viii. p. 176.
7. Mr. Lockwood believes (as quoted in 'Quart. Journal of Science,' April, 1868, p. 269), from what he has observed of the development of Hippocampus, that the walls of the abdominal pouch of the male in some way afford nourishment. On male fishes hatching the ova in their mouths, see a very interesting paper by Prof. Wyman, in 'Proc. Boston Soc. of Nat. Hist.' Sept. 15, 1857; also Prof. Turner, in 'Journal of Anat. and Phys.' Nov. 1, 1866, p. 78. Dr. Günther has likewise described similar cases.

being so much more perfectly developed than the rudiments of the other accessory reproductive parts, which are found in the one sex though proper to the other. The mammary glands and nipples, as they exist in male mammals, can indeed hardly be called rudimentary; they are merely not fully developed, and not functionally active. They are sympathetically affected under the influence of certain diseases, like the same organs in the female. They often secrete a few drops of milk at birth and at puberty: this latter fact occurred in the curious case before referred to, where a young man possessed two pairs of mammæ. In man and some other male mammals these organs have been known occasionally to become so well developed during maturity as to yield a fair supply of milk. Now if we suppose that during a former prolonged period male mammals aided the females in nursing their offspring,[8] and that afterwards from some cause (as from the production of a smaller number of young) the males ceased to give this aid, disuse of the organs during maturity would lead to their becoming inactive; and from two well-known principles of inheritance, this state of inactivity would probably be transmitted to the males at the corresponding age of maturity. But at an earlier age these organs would be left unaffected, so that they would be almost equally well developed in the young of both sexes.

CONCLUSION

Von Baer has defined advancement or progress in the organic scale better than any one else, as resting on the amount of differentiation and specialisation of the several parts of a being,—when arrived at maturity, as I should be inclined to add. Now as organisms have become slowly adapted to diversified lines of life by means of natural selection, their parts will have become more and more differentiated and specialised for various functions from the advantage gained by the division of physiological labour. The same part appears often to have been modified first for one purpose, and then long afterwards for some other and quite distinct purpose; and thus all the parts are rendered more and more complex. But each organism still retains the general type of structure of the progenitor from which it was aboriginally derived. In accordance with this view it seems, if we turn to geological evidence, that organisation on the whole has advanced throughout the world by slow and interrupted steps. In the great kingdom of the Vertebrata it has culminated in man. It must not, however, be supposed that groups of organic beings are always supplanted, and disappear as soon as they have given birth to other and more perfect groups. The latter, though victorious over their predecessors, may not have become better adapted for all places in the economy of nature. Some old forms appear to have survived from inhabiting protected sites, where they have not been exposed to very severe competition; and these often aid us in constructing our genealogies, by giving us a fair idea of former and lost populations. But we must not fall into the error of looking at the existing

---

8. Maddle. C. Royer has suggested a similar view in her 'Origine de l'Homme,' &c., 1870.

members of any lowly-organised group as perfect representatives of their ancient predecessors.

The most ancient progenitors in the kingdom of the Vertebrata, at which we are able to obtain an obscure glance, apparently consisted of a group of marine animals,[9] resembling the larvæ of existing Ascidians. These animals probably gave rise to a group of fishes, as lowly organised as the lancelet; and from these the Ganoids, and other fishes like the Lepidosiren, must have been developed. From such fish a very small advance would carry us on to the Amphibians. We have seen that birds and reptiles were once intimately connected together; and the Monotremata now connect mammals with reptiles in a slight degree. But no one can at present say by what line of descent the three higher and related classes, namely, mammals, birds, and reptiles, were derived from the two lower vertebrate classes, namely, amphibians and fishes. In the class of mammals the steps are not difficult to conceive which led from the ancient Monotremata to the ancient Marsupials; and from these to the early progenitors of the placental mammals. We may thus ascend to the Lemuridæ; and the interval is not very wide from these to the Simiadæ. The Simiadæ then branched off into two great stems, the New World and Old World monkeys; and from the latter, at a remote period, Man, the wonder and glory of the Universe, proceeded.

Thus we have given to man a pedigree of prodigious length, but not, it may be said, of noble quality. The world, it has often been remarked, appears as if it had long been preparing for the advent of man: and this, in one sense is strictly true, for he owes his birth to a long line of progenitors. If any single link in this chain had never existed, man would not have been exactly what he now is. Unless we wilfully close our eyes, we may, with our present knowledge, approximately recognise our parentage; nor need we feel ashamed of it. The most humble organism is something much higher than the inorganic dust under our feet; and no one with an unbiased mind can study any living creature, however humble, without being struck with enthusiasm at its marvellous structure and properties.

*   *   *

9. The inhabitants of the seashore must be greatly affected by the tides; animals living either about the *mean* high-water mark, or about the *mean* low-water mark, pass through a complete cycle of tidal changes in a fortnight. Consequently, their food supply will undergo marked changes week by week. The vital functions of such animals, living under these conditions for many generations, can hardly fail to run their course in regular weekly periods. Now it is a mysterious fact that in the highest and now terrestrial Vertebrata, as well as in other classes, many normal and abnormal processes have one or more whole weeks as their periods; this would be rendered intelligible if the Vertebrata are descended from an animal allied to the existing tidal Ascidians. Many instances of such periodic processes might be given, as the gestation of mammals, the duration of fevers, &c. The hatching of eggs affords also a good example, for, according to Mr. Bartlett ('Land and Water,' Jan. 7, 1871), the eggs of the pigeon are hatched in two weeks; those of the fowl in three; those of the duck in four; those of the goose in five; and those of the ostrich in seven weeks. As far as we can judge, a recurrent period, if approximately of the right duration for any process or function, would not, when once gained, be liable to change; consequently it might be thus transmitted through almost any number of generations. But if the function changed, the period would have to change, and would be apt to change almost abruptly by a whole week. This conclusion, if sound, is highly remarkable; for the period of gestation in each mammal, and the hatching of each bird's eggs, and many other vital processes, thus betray to us the primordial birthplace of these animals.

Chapter VIII. Principles of Sexual Selection

Secondary sexual characters—Sexual selection—Manner of action—Excess of males—
  Polygamy—The male alone generally modified through sexual selection—Eagerness
  of the male—Variability of the male—Choice exerted by the female—Sexual compared with natural selection—Inheritance, at corresponding periods of life, at corresponding seasons of the year, and as limited by sex—Relations between the several
  forms of inheritance—Causes why one sex and the young are not modified through
  sexual selection—Supplement on the proportional numbers of the two sexes throughout the animal kingdom—The proportion of the sexes in relation to natural selection.

With animals which have their sexes separated, the males necessarily differ
from the females in their organs of reproduction; and these are the primary
sexual characters. But the sexes often differ in what Hunter has called
secondary sexual characters, which are not directly connected with the act
of reproduction; for instance, the male possesses certain organs of sense
or locomotion, of which the female is quite destitute, or has them more
highly-developed, in order that he may readily find or reach her; or again
the male has special organs of prehension for holding her securely. These
latter organs, of infinitely diversified kinds, graduate into those which are
commonly ranked as primary, and in some cases can hardly be distinguished from them; we see instances of this in the complex appendages
at the apex of the abdomen in male insects. Unless indeed we confine the
term "primary" to the reproductive glands, it is scarcely possible to decide
which ought to be called primary and which secondary.

* * *

  We are, however, here concerned only with sexual selection. This depends on the advantage which certain individuals have over others of the
same sex and species solely in respect of reproduction. When, as in the
cases above mentioned, the two sexes differ in structure in relation to
different habits of life, they have no doubt been modified through natural
selection, and by inheritance, limited to one and the same sex. So again
the primary sexual organs, and those for nourishing or protecting the
young, come under the same influence; for those individuals which generated or nourished their offspring best, would leave, *cœteris paribus*, the
greatest number to inherit their superiority; whilst those which generated
or nourished their offspring badly, would leave but few to inherit their
weaker powers. As the male has to find the female, he requires organs of
sense and locomotion, but if these organs are necessary for the other purposes of life, as is generally the case, they will have been developed through
natural selection. * * *
  When the two sexes follow exactly the same habits of life, and the male
has the sensory or locomotive organs more highly developed than those of
the female, it may be that the perfection of these is indispensable to the
male for finding the female; but in the vast majority of cases, they serve
only to give one male an advantage over another, for with sufficient time,
the less well-endowed males would succeed in pairing with the females;

and judging from the structure of the female, they would be in all other respects equally well adapted for their ordinary habits of life. Since in such cases the males have acquired their present structure, not from being better fitted to survive in the struggle for existence, but from having gained an advantage over other males, and from having transmitted this advantage to their male offspring alone, sexual selection must here have come into action. It was the importance of this distinction which led me to designate this form of selection as Sexual Selection. So again, if the chief service rendered to the male by his prehensile organs is to prevent the escape of the female before the arrival of other males, or when assaulted by them, these organs will have been perfected through sexual selection, that is by the advantage acquired by certain individuals over their rivals. But in most cases of this kind it is impossible to distinguish between the effects of natural and sexual selection.

* * *

Let us take any species, a bird for instance, and divide the females inhabiting a district into two equal bodies, the one consisting of the more vigorous and better-nourished individuals, and the other of the less vigorous and healthy. The former, there can be little doubt, would be ready to breed in the spring before the others; and this is the opinion of Mr. Jenner Weir, who has carefully attended to the habits of birds during many years. There can also be no doubt that the most vigorous, best-nourished and earliest breeders would on an average succeed in rearing the largest number of fine offspring.[1] The males, as we have seen, are generally ready to breed before the females; the strongest, and with some species the best armed of the males, drive away the weaker; and the former would then unite with the more vigorous and better-nourished females, because they are the first to breed.[2] Such vigorous pairs would surely rear a larger number of offspring than the retarded females, which would be compelled to unite with the conquered and less powerful males, supposing the sexes to be numerically equal; and this is all that is wanted to add, in the course of successive generations, to the size, strength and courage of the males, or to improve their weapons.

But in very many cases the males which conquer their rivals, do not obtain possession of the females, independently of the choice of the latter. The courtship of animals is by no means so simple and short an affair as might be thought. The females are most excited by, or prefer pairing with, the more ornamented males, or those which are the best songsters, or play the best antics; but it is obviously probable that they would at the same

1. Here is excellent evidence on the character of the offspring from an experienced ornithologist. Mr. J. A. Allen, in speaking ('Mammals and Winter Birds of E. Florida,' p. 229) of the later broods, after the accidental destruction of the first, says, that these "are found" to be smaller and paler-coloured than those hatched earlier in the season. In cases where several broods are reared each year, as a general rule the birds of the earlier broods seem in all respects the most perfect and vigorous."
2. Hermann Müller has come to this same conclusion with respect to those female bees which are the first to emerge from the pupa each year. See his remarkable essay, 'Anwendung den Darwin'schen Lehre auf Bienen,' 'Verh. d. V. Jahrg,' xxix. p. 45.

time prefer the more vigorous and lively males, and this has in some cases been confirmed by actual observation.[3] Thus the more vigorous females, which are the first to breed, will have the choice of many males; and though they may not always select the strongest or best armed, they will select those which are vigorous and well armed, and in other respects the most attractive. Both sexes, therefore, of such early pairs would as above explained, have an advantage over others in rearing offspring; and this apparently has sufficed during a long course of generations to add not only to the strength and fighting powers of the males, but likewise to their various ornaments or other attractions.

In the converse and much rarer case of the males selecting particular females, it is plain that those which were the most vigorous and had conquered others, would have the freest choice; and it is almost certain that they would select vigorous as well as attractive females. Such pairs would have an advantage in rearing offspring, more especially if the male had the power to defend the female during the pairing-season as occurs with some of the higher animals, or aided her in providing for the young. The same principles would apply if each sex preferred and selected certain individuals of the opposite sex; supposing that they selected not only the more attractive, but likewise the more vigorous individuals. * * *

Chapter XIX. Secondary Sexual Characters of Man

Differences between man and woman—Causes of such differences and of certain characters common to both sexes—Law of Battle—Difference in mental powers, and voice—On the influence of beauty in determining the marriages of mankind—Attention paid by savages to ornaments—Their ideas of beauty in woman—The tendency to exaggerate each natural peculiarity.

With mankind the differences between the sexes are greater than in most of the Quadrumana, but not so great as in some, for instance, the mandrill. Man on an average is considerably taller, heavier, and stronger than woman, with squarer shoulders and more plainly-pronounced muscles. Owing to the relation which exists between muscular development and the projection of the brows,[4] the superciliary ridge is generally more marked in man than in woman. His body, and especially his face, is more hairy, and his voice has a different and more powerful tone. In certain races the women are said to differ slightly in tint from the men. For instance, Schweinfurth, in speaking of a negress belonging to the Monbuttoos, who inhabit the interior of Africa a few degrees north of the Equator, says, "Like all her race, she had a skin several shades lighter than her husband's, being something of the colour of half-roasted coffee."[5] As the women labour in the fields and are quite unclothed, it is not likely that they differ in colour from the men owing to less exposure to the weather.

3. With respect to poultry, I have received information, hereafter to be given, to this effect. Even with birds, such as pigeons, which pair for life, the female, as I hear from Mr. Jenner Weir, will desert her mate if he is injured or grows weak.
4. Schaaffhausen, translation in 'Anthropological Review,' Oct. 1868, pp. 419, 420, 427.
5. 'The Heart of Africa,' English transl. 1873, vol. i. p. 544.

European women are perhaps the brighter coloured of the two sexes, as may be seen when both have been equally exposed.

Man is more courageous, pugnacious and energetic than woman, and has a more inventive genius. His brain is absolutely larger, but whether or not proportionately to his larger body, has not, I believe, been fully ascertained. In woman the face is rounder; the jaws and the base of the skull smaller; the outlines of the body rounder, in parts more prominent; and her pelvis is broader than in man;[6] but this latter character may perhaps be considered rather as a primary than a secondary sexual character. She comes to maturity at an earlier age than man.

As with animals of all classes, so with man, the distinctive characters of the male sex are not fully developed until he is nearly mature; and if emasculated they never appear. The beard, for instance is a secondary sexual character, and male children are beardless, though at an early age they have abundant hair on the head. It is probably due to the rather late appearance in life of the successive variations whereby man has acquired his masculine characters, that they are transmitted to the male sex alone. Male and female children resemble each other closely, like the young of so many other animals in which the adult sexes differ widely; they likewise resemble the mature female much more closely than the mature male. The female, however, ultimately assumes certain distinctive characters, and in the formation of her skull, is said to be intermediate between the child and the man.[7] Again, as the young of closely allied though distinct species do not differ nearly so much from each other as do the adults, so it is with the children of the different races of man. Some have even maintained that race-differences cannot be detected in the infantile skull.[8] In regard to colour, the new-born negro child is reddish nut-brown, which soon becomes slaty-grey; the black colour being fully developed within a year in the Soudan, but not until three years in Egypt. The eyes of the negro are at first blue, and the hair chestnut-brown rather than black, being curled only at the ends. The children of the Australians immediately after birth are yellowish-brown, and become dark at a later age. Those of the Guaranys of Paraguay are whitish-yellow, but they acquire in the course of a few weeks the yellowish-brown tint of their parents. Similar observations have been made in other parts of America.[9]

I have specified the foregoing differences between the male and female sex in mankind, because they are curiously like those of the Quadrumana.

*   *   *

6. Ecker, translation in 'Anthropological Review,' Oct. 1868, pp. 351–356. The comparison of the form of the skull in men and women has been followed out with much care by Welcker.
7. Ecker and Welcker, ibid. pp. 352, 355; Vogt, 'Lectures on Man,' Eng. translat. p. 81.
8. Schaaffhausen, 'Anthropolog. Review,' ibid. p. 429.
9. Pruner-Bey, on negro infants as quoted by Vogt, 'Lectures on Man,' Eng. translat. 1864, p. 189: for further facts on negro infants, as quoted from Winterbottom and Camper, see Lawrence, 'Lectures on Physiology,' &c. 1822, p. 451. For the infants of the Guaranys, see Rengger, 'Säugethiere,' &c. s. 3. See also Godron, 'De l'Espèce,' tom. ii. 1859, p. 253. For the Australians, Waitz, 'Introduct. to Anthropology,' Eng. translat. 1863, p. 99.

There can be little doubt that the greater size and strength of man, in comparison with woman, together with his broader shoulders, more developed muscles, rugged outline of body, his greater courage and pugnacity, are all due in chief part to inheritance from his half-human male ancestors. These characters would, however, have been preserved or even augmented during the long ages of man's savagery, by the success of the strongest and boldest men, both in the general struggle for life and in their contests for wives; a success which would have ensured their leaving a more numerous progeny than their less favoured brethren. It is not probable that the greater strength of man was primarily acquired through the inherited effects of his having worked harder than woman for his own subsistence and that of his family; for the women in all barbarous nations are compelled to work at least as hard as the men. With civilised people the arbitrament of battle for the possession of the women has long ceased; on the other hand, the men, as a general rule, have to work harder than the women for their joint subsistence, and thus their greater strength will have been kept up.

DIFFERENCE IN THE MENTAL POWERS OF THE TWO SEXES

With respect to differences of this nature between man and woman, it is probable that sexual selection has played a highly important part. I am aware that some writers doubt whether there is any such inherent difference; but this is at least probable from the analogy of the lower animals which present other secondary sexual characters. No one disputes that the bull differs in disposition from the cow, the wild-boar from the sow, the stallion from the mare, and, as is well known to the keepers of menageries, the males of the larger apes from the females. Woman seems to differ from man in mental disposition, chiefly in her greater tenderness and less selfishness; and this holds good even with savages, as shewn by a well-known passage in Mungo Park's Travels, and by statements made by many other travellers. Woman, owing to her maternal instincts, displays these qualities towards her infants in an eminent degree; therefore it is likely that she would often extend them towards her fellow-creatures. Man is the rival of other men; he delights in competition, and this leads to ambition which passes too easily into selfishness. These latter qualities seem to be his natural and unfortunate birthright. It is generally admitted that with woman the powers of intuition, of rapid perception, and perhaps of imitation, are more strongly marked than in man; but some, at least, of these faculties are characteristic of the lower races, and therefore of a past and lower state of civilisation.

The chief distinction in the intellectual powers of the two sexes is shewn by man's attaining to a higher eminence, in whatever he takes up, than can woman—whether requiring deep thought, reason, or imagination, or merely the use of the senses and hands. If two lists were made of the most eminent men and women in poetry, painting, sculpture, music (inclusive both of composition and performance), history, science, and philosophy, with half-a-dozen names under each subject, the two lists would not bear comparison. We may also infer, from the law of the deviation from averages, so well illustrated by Mr. Galton, in his work on 'Hereditary Genius,' that if men are capable of a decided pre-eminence over women in many subjects, the average of mental power in man must be above that of woman.

Amongst the half-human progenitors of man, and amongst savages, there have been struggles between the males during many generations for the possession of the females. But mere bodily strength and size would do little for victory, unless associated with courage, perseverance, and determined energy. With social animals, the young males have to pass through many a contest before they win a female, and the older males have to retain their females by renewed battles. They have, also, in the case of mankind, to defend their females, as well as their young, from enemies of all kinds, and to hunt for their joint subsistence. But to avoid enemies or to attack them with success, to capture wild animals, and to fashion weapons, requires the aid of the higher mental faculties, namely, observation, reason, invention, or imagination. These various faculties will thus have been continually put to the test and selected during manhood; they will, moreover, have been strengthened by use during this same period of life. Consequently in accordance with the principle often alluded to, we might expect that they would at least tend to be transmitted chiefly to the male offspring at the corresponding period of manhood.

Now, when two men are put into competition, or a man with a woman, both possessed of every mental quality in equal perfection, save that one has higher energy, perseverance, and courage, the latter will generally become more eminent in every pursuit, and will gain the ascendancy.[1] He may be said to possess genius—for genius has been declared by a great authority to be patience; and patience, in this sense, means unflinching, undaunted perseverance. But this view of genius is perhaps deficient; for without the higher powers of the imagination and reason, no eminent success can be gained in many subjects. These latter faculties, as well as the former, will have been developed in man, partly through sexual selection,—that is, through the contest of rival males, and partly through natural selection,—that is, from success in the general struggle for life; and as in both cases the struggle will have been during maturity, the characters gained will have been transmitted more fully to the male than to the female offspring. It accords in a striking manner with this view of the modification and re-inforcement of many of our mental faculties by sexual selection, that, firstly, they notoriously undergo a considerable change at puberty,[2] and, secondly, that eunuchs remain throughout life inferior in these same qualities. Thus man has ultimately become superior to woman. It is, indeed, fortunate that the law of the equal transmission of characters to both sexes prevails with mammals; otherwise it is probable that man

---

1. J. Stuart Mill remarks ('The Subjection of Women,' 1869, p. 122), "The things in which man most excels woman are those which require most plodding, and long hammering at single thoughts." What is this but energy and perseverance?
2. Maudsley, 'Mind and Body,' p. 31.

would have become as superior in mental endowment to woman, as the peacock is in ornamental plumage to the peahen.

*   *   *

A critic has asked how the ears of man, and he ought to have added of other animals, could have been adapted by selection so as to distinguish musical notes. But this question shows some confusion on the subject; a noise is the sensation resulting from the co-existence of several aërial "simple vibrations" of various periods, each of which intermits so frequently that its separate existence cannot be perceived. It is only in the want of continuity of such vibrations, and in their want of harmony *inter se*, that a noise differs from a musical note. Thus an ear to be capable of discriminating noises—and the high importance of this power to all animals is admitted by every one—must be sensitive to musical notes. We have evidence of this capacity even low down in the animal scale: thus Crustaceans are provided with auditory hairs of different lengths, which have been seen to vibrate when the proper musical notes are struck.[3] As stated in a previous chapter, similar observations have been made on the hairs of the antennæ of gnats. It has been positively asserted by good observers that spiders are attracted by music. It is also well known that some dogs howl when hearing particular tones.[4] Seals apparently appreciate music, and their fondness for it "was well known to the ancients, and is often taken advantage of by the hunters at the present day."[5]

Therefore, as far as the mere perception of musical notes is concerned, there seems no special difficulty in the case of man or of any other animal. Helmholtz has explained on physiological principles why concords are agreeable, and discords disagreeable to the human ear; but we are little concerned with these, as music in harmony is a late invention. We are more concerned with melody, and here again, according to Helmholtz, it is intelligible why the notes of our musical scale are used. The ear analyses all sounds into their component "simple vibrations," although we are not conscious of this analysis. In a musical note the lowest in pitch of these is generally predominant; and the others which are less marked are the octave, the twelfth, the second octave, &c., all harmonies of the fundamental predominant note; any two notes of our scale have many of these harmonic over-tones in common. It seems pretty clear then, that if an animal always wished to sing precisely the same song, he would guide himself by sounding those notes in succession, which possess many overtones in common—that is, he would choose for his song, notes which belong to our musical scale.

But if it be further asked why musical tones in a certain order and rhythm give man and other animals pleasure, we can no more give the reason than for the pleasantness of certain tastes and smells. That they do

---

3. Helmholtz, 'Théorie Phys. de la Musique,' 1868, p. 187.
4. Several accounts have been published to this effect. Mr. Peach writes to me that an old dog of his howls when B flat is sounded on the flute, and to no other note. I may add another instance of a dog always whining, when one note on a concertina, which was out of tune, was played.
5. Mr. R. Brown, in 'Proc. Zool. Soc.' 1868, p. 410.

give pleasure of some kind to animals, we may infer from their being produced during the season of courtship by many insects, spiders, fishes, amphibians, and birds; for unless the females were able to appreciate such sounds and were excited or charmed by them, the persevering efforts of the males, and the complex structures often possessed by them alone, would be useless; and this it is impossible to believe.

Human song is generally admitted to be the basis or origin of instrumental music. As neither the enjoyment nor the capacity of producing musical notes are faculties of the least use to man in reference to his daily habits of life, they must be ranked amongst the most mysterious with which he is endowed. They are present, though in a very rude condition, in men of all races, even the most savage; but so different is the taste of the several races, that our music gives no pleasure to savages, and their music is to us in most cases hideous and unmeaning. Dr. Seemann, in some interesting remarks on this subject,[6] "doubt whether even amongst the nations of Western Europe, intimately connected as they are by close and frequent intercourse, the music of the one is interpreted in the same sense by the others. By travelling eastwards we find that there is certainly a different language of music. Songs of joy and dance-accompaniments are no longer, as with us, in the major keys, but always in the minor." Whether or not the half-human progenitors of man possessed, like the singing gibbons, the capacity of producing, and therefore no doubt of appreciating, musical notes, we know that man possessed these faculties at a very remote period. M. Lartet has described two flutes made out of the bones and horns of the reindeer, found in caves together with flint tools and the remains of extinct animals. The arts of singing and of dancing are also very ancient, and are now practised by all or nearly all the lowest races of man. Poetry, which may be considered as the offspring of song, is likewise so ancient, that many persons have felt astonished that it should have arisen during the earliest ages of which we have any record.

We see that the musical faculties, which are not wholly deficient in any race, are capable of prompt and high development, for Hottentots and Negroes have become excellent musicians, although in their native countries they rarely practise anything that we should consider music. Schweinfurth, however, was pleased with some of the simple melodies which he heard in the interior of Africa. But there is nothing anomalous in the musical faculties lying dormant in man: some species of birds which never naturally sing, can without much difficulty be taught to do so; thus a house-sparrow has learnt the song of a linnet. As these two species are closely allied, and belong to the order of Insessores, which includes nearly all the singing-birds in the world, it is possible that a progenitor of the sparrow may have been a songster. It is more remarkable that parrots, belonging to a group distinct from the Insessores, and having differently constructed vocal organs, can be taught not only to speak, but to pipe or whistle tunes invented by man, so that they must have some musical

6. 'Journal of Anthropolog. Soc.' Oct. 1870, p. clv. See also the several later chapters in Sir John Lubbock's 'Prehistoric Times,' second edition, 1869, which contain an admirable account of the habits of savages.

capacity. Nevertheless it would be very rash to assume that parrots are descended from some ancient form which was a songster. Many cases could be advanced of organs and instincts originally adapted for one purpose, having been utilised for some distinct purpose.[7] Hence the capacity for high musical development which the savage races of man possess, may be due either to the practice by our semi-human progenitors of some rude form of music, or simply to their having acquired the proper vocal organs for a different purpose. But in this latter case we must assume, as in the above instance of parrots, and as seems to occur with many animals, that they already possessed some sense of melody.

Music arouses in us various emotions, but not the more terrible ones of horror, fear, rage, &c. It awakens the gentler feelings of tenderness and love, which readily pass into devotion. In the Chinese annals it is said, "Music hath the power of making heaven descend upon earth." It likewise stirs up in us the sense of triumph and the glorious ardour for war. These powerful and mingled feelings may well give rise to the sense of sublimity. We can concentrate, as Dr. Seemann observes, greater intensity of feeling in a single musical note than in pages of writing. It is probable that nearly the same emotions, but much weaker and far less complex, are felt by birds when the male pours forth his full volume of song, in rivalry with other males, to captivate the female. Love is still the commonest theme of our songs. As Herbert Spencer remarks, "music arouses dormant sentiments of which we had not conceived the possibility, and do not know the meaning; or, as Richter says, tells us of things we have not seen and shall not see." Conversely, when vivid emotions are felt and expressed by the orator, or even in common speech, musical cadences and rhythm are instinctively used. The negro in Africa when excited often bursts forth in song; "another will reply in song, whilst the company, as if touched by a musical wave, murmur a chorus in perfect unison."[8] Even monkeys express strong feelings in different tones—anger and impatience by low,—fear and pain by high notes.[9] The sensations and ideas thus excited in us by music, or expressed by the cadences of oratory, appear from their vagueness, yet depth, like mental reversions to the emotions and thoughts of a long-past age.

All these facts with respect to music and impassioned speech become intelligible to a certain extent, if we may assume that musical tones and rhythm were used by our half-human ancestors, during the season of courtship, when animals of all kinds are excited not only by love, but by the strong passions of jealousy, rivalry, and triumph. From the deeply-laid principle of inherited associations, musical tones in this case would be likely to call up vaguely and indefinitely the strong emotions of a long-past age.

7. Since this chapter was printed, I have seen a valuable article by Mr. Chauncey Wright ('North American Review,' Oct. 1870, page 293), who, in discussing the above subject, remarks, "There are many consequences of the ultimate laws or uniformities of nature, through which the acquisition of one useful power will bring with it many resulting advantages as well as limiting disadvantages, actual or possible, which the principle of utility may not have comprehended in its action." As I have attempted to shew in an early chapter of this work, this principle has an important bearing on the acquisition by man of some of his mental characteristics.
8. Winwood Reade, 'The Martyrdom of Man,' 1872, p. 441, and 'African Sketch Book,' 1873, vol. ii. p. 313.
9. Rengger, 'Säugethiere von Paraguay,' s. 49.

As we have every reason to suppose that articulate speech is one of the latest, as it certainly is the highest, of the arts acquired by man, and as the instinctive power of producing musical notes and rhythms is developed low down in the animal series, it would be altogether opposed to the principle of evolution, if we were to admit that man's musical capacity has been developed from the tones used in impassioned speech. We must suppose that the rhythms and cadences of oratory are derived from previously developed musical powers.[1] We can thus understand how it is that music, dancing, song, and poetry are such very ancient arts. We may go even further than this, and, as remarked in a former chapter, believe that musical sounds afforded one of the bases for the development of language.[2]

*   *   *

Chapter XX. Secondary Sexual Characters of Man—continued

On the effects of the continued selection of women according to a different standard of beauty in each race—On the causes which interfere with sexual selection in civilised and savage nations—Conditions favourable to sexual selection during primeval times—On the manner of action of sexual selection with mankind—On the women in savage tribes having some power to choose their husbands—Absence of hair on the body, and development of the beard—Colour of the skin—Summary.

We have seen in the last chapter that with all barbarous races ornaments, dress, and external appearance are highly valued; and that the men judge of the beauty of their women by widely different standards. We must next inquire whether this preference and the consequent selection during many generations of those women, which appear to the men of each race the most attractive, has altered the character either of the females alone, or of both sexes. With mammals the general rule appears to be that characters of all kinds are inherited equally by the males and females; we might therefore expect that with mankind any characters gained by the females or by the males through sexual selection would commonly be transferred to the offspring of both sexes. If any change has thus been effected, it is almost certain that the different races would be differently modified, as each has its own standard of beauty.

With mankind, especially with savages, many causes interfere with the

1. See the very interesting discussion on the 'Origin and Function of Music,' by Mr. Herbert Spencer, in his collected 'Essays,' 1858, p. 359. Mr. Spencer comes to an exactly opposite conclusion to that at which I have arrived. He concludes, as did Diderot formerly, that the cadences used in emotional speech afford the foundation from which music has been developed; whilst I conclude that musical notes and rhythm were first acquired by the male or female progenitors of mankind for the sake of charming the opposite sex. Thus musical tones became firmly associated with some of the strongest passions an animal is capable of feeling, and are consequently used instinctively, or through association when strong emotions are expressed in speech. Mr. Spencer does not offer any satisfactory explanation, nor can I, why high or deep notes should be expressive, both with man and the lower animals, of certain emotions. Mr. Spencer gives also an interesting discussion on the relations between poetry, recitative and song.
2. I find in Lord Monboddo's 'Origin of Language,' vol. i. (1774), p. 469, that Dr. Blacklock likewise thought "that the first language among men was music, and that before our ideas were expressed by articulate sounds, they were communicated by tones varied according to different degrees of gravity and acuteness."

action of sexual selection as far as the bodily frame is concerned. Civilised men are largely attracted by the mental charms of women, by their wealth, and especially by their social position; for men rarely marry into a much lower rank. The men who succeed in obtaining the more beautiful women will not have a better chance of leaving a long line of descendants than other men with plainer wives, save the few who bequeath their fortunes according to primogeniture. With respect to the opposite form of selection, namely, of the more attractive men by the women, although in civilised nations women have free or almost free choice, which is not the case with barbarous races, yet their choice is largely influenced by the social position and wealth of the men; and the success of the latter in life depends much on their intellectual powers and energy, or on the fruits of these same powers in their forefathers. No excuse is needed for treating this subject in some detail; for, as the German philosopher Schopenhauer remarks, "the final aim of all love intrigues, be they comic or tragic, is really of more importance than all other ends in human life. What it all turns upon is nothing less than the composition of the next generation. . . . It is not the weal or woe of any one individual, but that of the human race to come, which is here at stake."[3]

There is, however, reason to believe that in certain civilised and semi-civilised nations sexual selection has effected something in modifying the bodily frame of some of the members. Many persons are convinced, as it appears to me with justice, that our aristocracy, including under this term all wealthy families in which primogeniture has long prevailed, from having chosen during many generations from all classes the more beautiful women as their wives, have become handsomer, according to the European standard, than the middle classes; yet the middle classes are placed under equally favourable conditions of life for the perfect development of the body.

*   *   *

Although the manner of development of the marriage-tie is an obscure subject, as we may infer from the divergent opinions on several points between the three authors who have studied it most closely, namely, Mr. Morgan, Mr. M'Lennan, and Sir J. Lubbock, yet from the foregoing and several other lines of evidence it seems probable[4] that the habit of marriage, in any strict sense of the word, has been gradually developed; and that almost promiscuous or very loose intercourse was once extremely common throughout the world. Nevertheless, from the strength of the feeling of jealousy all through the animal kingdom, as well as from the analogy of the lower animals, more particularly of those which come nearest to man, I cannot believe that absolutely promiscuous intercourse prevailed in times past, shortly before man attained to his present rank in the zoological scale. Man, as I have attempted to shew, is certainly descended

---

3. 'Schopenhauer and Darwinism,' in 'Journal of Anthropology,' Jan. 1871, p. 323.
4. Mr. C. Staniland Wake argues strongly ('Anthropologia,' March, 1874, p. 197) against the views held by these three writers on the former prevalence of almost promiscuous intercourse; and he thinks that the classificatory system of relationship can be otherwise explained.

from some ape-like creature. With the existing Quadrumana, as far as their habits are known, the males of some species are monogamous, but live during only a part of the year with the females: of this the orang seems to afford an instance. Several kinds, for example some of the Indian and American monkeys, are strictly monogamous, and associate all the year round with their wives. Others are polygamous, for example the gorilla and several American species, and each family lives separate. Even when this occurs, the families inhabiting the same district are probably somewhat social; the chimpanzee, for instance, is occasionally met with in large bands. Again, other species are polygamous, but several males, each with his own females, live associated in a body, as with several species of baboons.[5] We may indeed conclude from what we know of the jealousy of all male quadrupeds, armed, as many of them are, with special weapons for battling with their rivals, that promiscuous intercourse in a state of nature is extremely improbable. The pairing may not last for life, but only for each birth; yet if the males which are the strongest and best able to defend or otherwise assist their females and young, were to select the more attractive females, this would suffice for sexual selection.

Therefore, looking far enough back in the stream of time, and judging from the social habits of man as he now exists, the most probable view is that he aboriginally lived in small communities, each with a single wife, or if powerful with several, whom he jealously guarded against all other men. Or he may not have been a social animal, and yet have lived with several wives, like the gorilla; for all the natives "agree that but one adult male is seen in a band; when the young male grows up, a contest takes place for mastery, and the strongest, by killing and driving out the others, establishes himself as the head of the community."[6] The younger males, being thus expelled and wandering about, would, when at last successful in finding a partner, prevent too close interbreeding within the limits of the same family.

*   *   *

With animals in a state of nature, many characters proper to the males, such as size, strength, special weapons, courage and pugnacity, have been acquired through the law of battle. The semi-human progenitors of man, like their allies the Quadrumana, will almost certainly have been thus modified; and, as savages still fight for the possession of their women, a similar process of selection has probably gone on in a greater or less degree to the present day. Other characters proper to the males of the lower animals, such as bright colours and various ornaments, have been acquired by the more attractive males having been preferred by the females. There are, however, exceptional cases in which the males are the selectors, instead of having been the selected. We recognise such cases by the females

5. Brehm ('Illust. Thierleben,' B. i. p. 77) says *Cynocephalus hamadryas* lives in great troops containing twice as many adult females as adult males. See Rengger on American polygamous species, and Owen ('Anat. of Vertebrates,' vol. iii. p. 746) on American monogamous species. Other references might be added.
6. Dr. Savage, in 'Boston Journal of Nat. Hist.' vol. v. 1845–47, p. 423.

being more highly ornamented than the males,—their ornamental characters having been transmitted exclusively or chiefly to their female offspring. One such case has been described in the order to which man belongs, that of the Rhesus monkey.

Man is more powerful in body and mind than woman, and in the savage state he keeps her in a far more abject state of bondage than does the male of any other animal; therefore it is not surprising that he should have gained the power of selection. Women are everywhere conscious of the value of their own beauty; and when they have the means, they take more delight in decorating themselves with all sorts of ornaments than do men. They borrow the plumes of male birds, with which nature has decked this sex, in order to charm the females. As women have long been selected for beauty, it is not surprising that some of their successive variations should have been transmitted exclusively to the same sex; consequently that they should have transmitted beauty in a somewhat higher degree to their female than to their male offspring, and thus have become more beautiful, according to general opinion, than men. Women, however, certainly transmit most of their characters, including some beauty, to their offspring of both sexes; so that the continued preference by the men of each race for the more attractive women, according to their standard of taste, will have tended to modify in the same manner all the individuals of both sexes belonging to the race.

With respect to the other form of sexual selection (which with the lower animals is much the more common), namely, when the females are the selectors, and accept only those males which excite or charm them most, we have reason to believe that it formerly acted on our progenitors. Man in all probability owes his beard, and perhaps some other characters, to inheritance from an ancient progenitor who thus gained his ornaments. But this form of selection may have occasionally acted during later times; for in utterly barbarous tribes the women have more power in choosing, rejecting, and tempting their lovers, or of afterwards changing their husbands, than might have been expected.

*　*　*

SUMMARY

We may conclude that the greater size, strength, courage, pugnacity, and energy of man, in comparison with woman, were acquired during primeval times, and have subsequently been augmented, chiefly through the contests of rival males for the possession of the females. The greater intellectual vigour and power of invention in man is probably due to natural selection, combined with the inherited effects of habit, for the most able men will have succeeded best in defending and providing for themselves and for their wives and offspring. As far as the extreme intricacy of the subject permits us to judge, it appears that our male ape-like progenitors acquired their beards as an ornament to charm or excite the opposite sex, and transmitted them only to their male offspring. The females apparently first had their bodies denuded of hair, also as a sexual ornament;

but they transmitted this character almost equally to both sexes. It is not improbable that the females were modified in other respects for the same purpose and by the same means; so that women have acquired sweeter voices and become more beautiful than men.

It deserves attention that with mankind the conditions were in many respects much more favourable for sexual selection during a very early period, when man had only just attained to the rank of manhood, than during later times. For he would then, as we may safely conclude, have been guided more by his instinctive passions, and less by foresight or reason. He would have jealously guarded his wife or wives. He would not have practised infanticide; nor valued his wives merely as useful slaves; nor have been betrothed to them during infancy. Hence we may infer that the races of men were differentiated, as far as sexual selection is concerned, in chief part at a very remote epoch; and this conclusion throws light on the remarkable fact that at the most ancient period, of which we have as yet any record, the races of man had already come to differ nearly or quite as much as they do at the present day.

The views here advanced, on the part which sexual selection has played in the history of man, want scientific precision. He who does not admit this agency in the case of the lower animals, will disregard all that I have written in the later chapters on man. We cannot positively say that this character, but not that, has been thus modified; it has however, been shewn that the races of man differ from each other and from their nearest allies, in certain characters which are of no service to them in their daily habits of life, and which it is extremely probable would have been modified through sexual selection. We have seen that with the lowest savages the people of each tribe admire their own characteristic qualities,—the shape of the head and face, the squareness of the cheek-bones, the prominence or depression of the nose, the colour of the skin, the length of the hair on the head, the absence of hair on the face and body, or the presence of a great beard, and so forth. Hence these and other such points could hardly fail to be slowly and gradually exaggerated, from the more powerful and able men in each tribe, who would succeed in rearing the largest number of off-spring, having selected during many generations for their wives the most strongly characterised and therefore most attractive women. For my own part I conclude that of all the causes which have led to the differences in external appearance between the races of man, and to a certain extent between man and the lower animals, sexual selection has been the most efficient.

Chapter XXI. General Summary and Conclusion

Main conclusion that man is descended from some lower form—Manner of development—Genealogy of man—Intellectual and moral faculties—Sexual Selection—Concluding remarks.

A brief summary will be sufficient to recall to the reader's mind the more salient points in this work. Many of the views which have been advanced are highly speculative, and some no doubt will prove erroneous;

but I have in every case given the reasons which have led me to one view rather than to another. It seemed worth while to try how far the principle of evolution would throw light on some of the more complex problems in the natural history of man. False facts are highly injurious to the progress of science, for they often endure long; but false views, if supported by some evidence, do little harm, for every one takes a salutary pleasure in proving their falseness and when this is done, one path towards error is closed and the road to truth is often at the same time opened.

The main conclusion here arrived at, and now held by many naturalists who are well competent to form a sound judgment, is that man is descended from some less highly organised form. The grounds upon which this conclusion rests will never be shaken, for the close similarity between man and the lower animals in embryonic development, as well as in innumerable points of structure and constitution, both of high and of the most trifling importance,—the rudiments which he retains, and the abnormal reversions to which he is occasionally liable,—are facts which cannot be disputed. They have long been known, but until recently they told us nothing with respect to the origin of man. Now when viewed by the light of our knowledge of the whole organic world, their meaning is unmistakable. The great principle of evolution stands up clear and firm, when these groups or facts are considered in connection with others, such as the mutual affinities of the members of the same group, their geographical distribution in past and present times, and their geological succession. It is incredible that all these facts should speak falsely. He who is not content to look, like a savage, at the phenomena of nature as disconnected, cannot any longer believe that man is the work of a separate act of creation. He will be forced to admit that the close resemblance of the embryo of man to that, for instance, of a dog—the construction of his skull, limbs and whole frame on the same plan with that of other mammals, independently of the uses to which the parts may be put—the occasional re-appearance of various structures, for instance of several muscles, which man does not normally possess, but which are common to the Quadrumana—and a crowd of analogous facts—all point in the plainest manner to the conclusion that man is the co-descendant with other mammals of a common progenitor.

We have seen that man incessantly presents individual differences in all parts of his body and in his mental faculties. These differences or variations seem to be induced by the same general causes, and to obey the same laws as with the lower animals. In both cases similar laws of inheritance prevail. Man tends to increase at a greater rate than his means of subsistence; consequently he is occasionally subjected to a severe struggle for existence, and natural selection will have effected whatever lies within its scope. A succession of strongly-marked variations of a similar nature is by no means requisite; slight fluctuating differences in the individual suffice for the work of natural selection; not that we have any reason to suppose that in the same species, all parts of the organisation tend to vary to the same degree. We may feel assured that the inherited effects of the long-continued use or disuse of parts will have done much in the same direction with natural selection. Modifications formerly of importance, though no longer of any special use, are long-inherited. When one part is modified, other parts change through the principle of correlation, of which we have instances in many curious cases of correlated monstrosities. Something may be attributed to the direct and definite action of the surrounding conditions of life, such as abundant food, heat or moisture; and lastly, many characters of slight physiological importance, some indeed of considerable importance, have been gained through sexual selection.

No doubt man, as well as every other animal, presents structures, which seem to our limited knowledge, not to be now of any service to him, nor to have been so formerly, either for the general conditions of life, or in the relations of one sex to the other. Such structures cannot be accounted for by any form of selection, or by the inherited effects of the use and disuse of parts. We know, however, that many strange and strongly-marked peculiarities of structure occasionally appear in our domesticated productions, and if their unknown causes were to act more uniformly, they would probably become common to all the individuals of the species. We may hope hereafter to understand something about the causes of such occasional modifications, especially through the study of monstrosities: hence the labours of experimentalists such as those of M. Camille Dareste, are full of promise for the future. In general we can only say that the cause of each slight variation and of each monstrosity lies much more in the constitution of the organism, than in the nature of the surrounding conditions; though new and changed conditions certainly play an important part in exciting organic changes of many kinds.

Through the means just specified, aided perhaps by others as yet undiscovered, man has been raised to his present state. But since he attained to the rank of manhood, he has diverged into distinct races, or as they may be more fitly called, sub-species. Some of these, such as the Negro and European, are so distinct that, if specimens had been brought to a naturalist without any further information, they would undoubtedly have been considered by him as good and true species. Nevertheless all the races agree in so many unimportant details of structure and in so many mental peculiarities that these can be accounted for only by inheritance from a common progenitor; and a progenitor thus characterised would probably deserve to rank as man.

It must not be supposed that the divergence of each race from the other races, and of all from a common stock, can be traced back to any one pair of progenitors. On the contrary, at every stage in the process of modification, all the individuals which were in any way better fitted for their conditions of life, though in different degrees, would have survived in greater numbers than the less well-fitted. The process would have been like that followed by man, when he does not intentionally select particular individuals, but breeds from all the superior individuals, and neglects the inferior. He thus slowly but surely modifies his stock, and unconciously forms a new strain. So with respect to modifications acquired independently of selection, and due to variations arising from the nature of the organism and the action of the surrounding conditions, or from changed habits of life, no single pair will have been modified much more than the other pairs inhabiting the same country, for all will have been continually blended through free intercrossing.

By considering the embryological structure of man,—the homologies which he presents with the lower animals,—the rudiments which he retains,—and the reversions to which he is liable, we can partly recall in imagination the former condition of our early progenitors; and can approximately place them in their proper place in the zoological series. We thus learn that man is descended from a hairy, tailed quadruped, probably arboreal in its habits, and an inhabitant of the Old World. This creature, if its whole structure had been examined by a naturalist, would have been classed amongst the Quadrumana, as surely as the still more ancient progenitor of the Old and New World monkeys. The Quadrumana and all the higher mammals are probably derived from an ancient marsupial animal, and this through a long series of diversified forms, from some amphibian-like creature, and this again from some fish-like animal. In the dim obscurity of the past we can see that the early progenitor of all the Vertebrata must have been an aquatic animal provided with branchiæ, with the two sexes united in the same individual, and with the most important organs of the body (such as the brain and heart) imperfectly or not at all developed. This animal seems to have been more like the larvæ of the existing marine Ascidians than any other known form.

The high standard of our intellectual powers and moral disposition is the greatest difficulty which presents itself, after we have been driven to this conclusion on the origin of man. But every one who admits the principle of evolution, must see that the mental powers of the higher animals, which are the same in kind with those of man, though so different in degree, are capable of advancement. Thus the interval between the mental powers of one of the higher apes and of a fish, or between those of an ant and scale-insect, is immense; yet their development does not offer any special difficulty; for with our domesticated animals, the mental faculties are certainly variable, and the variations are inherited. No one doubts that they are of the utmost importance to animals in a state of nature. Therefore the conditions are favourable for their development through natural selection. The same conclusion may be extended to man; the intellect must have been all-important to him, even at a very remote period, as enabling him to invent and use language, to make weapons, tools, traps, &c., whereby with the aid of his social habits, he long ago became the most dominant of all living creatures.

A great stride in the development of the intellect will have followed, as soon as the half-art and half-instinct of language came into use; for the continued use of language will have reacted on the brain and produced an inherited effect; and this again will have reacted on the improvement of language. As Mr. Chauncey Wright[7] has well remarked, the largeness of the brain in man relatively to his body, compared with the lower animals, may be attributed in chief part to the early use of some simple form

---

7. 'On the Limits of Natural Selection,' in the 'North American Review,' Oct. 1870, p. 295.

of language,—that wonderful engine which affixes signs to all sorts of objects and qualities, and excites trains of thought which would never arise from the mere impression of the senses, or if they did arise could not be followed out. The higher intellectual powers of man, such as those of ratiocination, abstraction, self-consciousness, &c., probably follow from the continued improvement and exercise of the other mental faculties.

The development of the moral qualities is a more interesting problem. The foundation lies in the social instincts, including under this term the family ties. These instincts are highly complex, and in the case of the lower animals give special tendencies towards certain definite actions; but the more important elements are love, and the distinct emotion of sympathy. Animals endowed with the social instincts take pleasure in one another's company, warn one another of danger, defend and aid one another in many ways. These instincts do not extend to all the individuals of the species, but only to those of the same community. As they are highly beneficial to the species, they have in all probability been acquired through natural selection.

A moral being is one who is capable of reflecting on his past actions and their motives—of approving of some and disapproving of others; and the fact that man is the one being who certainly deserves this designation, is the greatest of all distinctions between him and the lower animals. But in the fourth chapter I have endeavoured to shew that the moral sense follows, firstly, from the enduring and ever-present nature of the social instincts; secondly, from man's appreciation of the approbation and disapprobation of his fellows; and thirdly, from the high activity of his mental faculties, with past impressions extremely vivid; and in these latter respects he differs from the lower animals. Owing to this condition of mind, man cannot avoid looking both backwards and forwards, and comparing past impressions. Hence after some temporary desire or passion has mastered his social instincts, he reflects and compares the now weakened impression of such past impulses with the ever-present social instincts; and he then feels that sense of dissatisfaction which all unsatisfied instincts leave behind them, he therefore resolves to act differently for the future,—and this is conscience. Any instinct, permanently stronger or more enduring than another, gives rise to a feeling which we express by saying that it ought to be obeyed. A pointer dog, if able to reflect on his past conduct, would say to himself, I ought (as indeed we say of him) to have pointed at that hare and not have yielded to the passing temptation of hunting it.

Social animals are impelled partly by a wish to aid the members of their community in a general manner, but more commonly to perform certain definite actions. Man is impelled by the same general wish to aid his fellows; but has few or no special instincts. He differs also from the lower animals in the power of expressing his desires by words, which thus become a guide to the aid required and bestowed. The motive to give aid is likewise much modified in man: it no longer consists solely of a blind instinctive impulse, but is much influenced by the praise or blame of his fellows. The appreciation and the bestowal of praise and blame both rest on sympathy; and this emotion, as we have seen, is one of the most important elements of the social instincts. Sympathy, though gained as an instinct, is also much strengthened by exercise or habit. As all men desire their own happiness, praise or blame is bestowed on actions and motives, according as they lead to this end; and as happiness is an essential part of the general good, the greatest-happiness principle indirectly serves as a nearly safe standard of right and wrong. As the reasoning powers advance and experience is gained, the remoter effects of certain lines of conduct on the character of the individual, and on the general good, are perceived; and then the self-regarding virtues come within the scope of public opinion, and receive praise, and their opposites blame. But with the less civilised nations reason often errs, and many bad customs and base superstitions come within the same scope, and are then esteemed as high virtues, and their breach as heavy crimes.

The moral faculties are generally and justly esteemed as of higher value than the intellectual powers. But we should bear in mind that the activity of the mind in vividly recalling past impressions is one of the fundamental though secondary bases of conscience. This affords the strongest argument for educating and stimulating in all possible ways the intellectual faculties of every human being. No doubt a man with a torpid mind, if his social affections and sympathies are well developed, will be led to good actions, and may have a fairly sensitive conscience. But whatever renders the imagination more vivid and strengthens the habit of recalling and comparing past impressions, will make the conscience more sensitive, and may even somewhat compensate for weak social affections and sympathies.

The moral nature of man has reached its present standard, partly through the advancement of his reasoning powers and consequently of a just public opinion, but especially from his sympathies having been rendered more tender and widely diffused through the effects of habit, example, instruction, and reflection. It is not improbable that after long practice virtuous tendencies may be inherited. With the more civilised races, the conviction of the existence of an all-seeing Deity has had a potent influence on the advance of morality. Ultimately man does not accept the praise or blame of his fellows as his sole guide, though few escape this influence, but his habitual convictions, controlled by reason, afford him the safest rule. His conscience then becomes the supreme judge and monitor. Nevertheless the first foundation or origin of the moral sense lies in the social instincts, including sympathy; and these instincts no doubt were primarily gained, as in the case of the lower animals, through natural selection.

The belief in God has often been advanced as not only the greatest, but the most complete of all the distinctions between man and the lower animals. It is however impossible, as we have seen, to maintain that this belief is innate or instinctive in man. On the other hand a belief in all-pervading spiritual agencies seems to be universal; and apparently follows from a considerable advance in man's reason, and from a still greater advance in his faculties of imagination, curiosity and wonder. I am aware that the assumed instinctive belief in God has been used by many persons as an argument for His existence. But this is a rash argument, as we should thus be compelled to believe in the existence of many cruel and malignant spirits, only a little more powerful than man; for the belief in them is far more general than in a beneficent Deity. The idea of a universal and beneficent Creator does not seem to arise in the mind of man, until he has been elevated by long-continued culture.

He who believes in the advancement of man from some low organised form, will naturally ask how does this bear on the belief in the immortality of the soul. The barbarous races of man, as Sir J. Lubbock has shewn, possess no clear belief of this kind; but arguments derived from the primeval beliefs of savages are, as we have just seen, of little or no avail. Few persons feel any anxiety from the impossibility of determining at what precise period in the development of the individual, from the first trace of a minute germinal vesicle, man becomes an immortal being; and there is no greater cause for anxiety because the period cannot possibly be determined in the gradually ascending organic scale.[8]

I am aware that the conclusions arrived at in this work will be denounced by some as highly irreligious; but he who denounces them is bound to shew why it is more irreligious to explain the origin of man as a distinct species by descent from some lower form, through the laws of variation and natural selection, than to explain the birth of the individual through the laws of ordinary reproduction. The birth both of the species and of the individual are equally parts of that grand sequence of events, which our minds refuse to accept as the result of blind chance. The understanding revolts at such a conclusion, whether or not we are able to believe that every slight variation of structure,—the union of each pair in marriage,—the dissemination of each seed,—and other such events, have all been ordained for some special purpose.

Sexual selection has been treated at great length in this work; for, as I have attempted to shew, it has played an important part in the history of the organic world. I am aware that much remains doubtful, but I have endeavoured to give a fair view of the whole case. In the lower divisions of the animal kingdom, sexual selection seems to have done nothing: such animals are often affixed for life to the same spot, or have the sexes combined in the same individual, or what is still more important, their perceptive and intellectual faculties are not sufficiently advanced to allow of the feelings of love and jealousy, or of the exertion of choice. When, however, we come to the Arthropoda and Vertebrata, even to the lowest classes in these two great Sub-Kingdoms, sexual selection has effected much.

In the several great classes of the animal kingdom,—in mammals, birds, reptiles, fishes, insects, and even crustaceans,—the differences between the sexes follow nearly the same rules. The males are almost always the wooers; and they alone are armed with special weapons for fighting with their rivals. They are generally stronger and larger than the females, and are endowed with the requisite qualities of courage and pugnacity. They are provided, either exclusively or in a much higher degree than the females, with organs for vocal or instrumental music, and with odoriferous glands.

8. The Rev. J. A. Picton gives a discussion to this effect in his 'New Theories and the Old Faith,' 1870.

They are ornamental with infinitely diversified appendages, and with the most brilliant or conspicuous colours, often arranged in elegant patterns, whilst the females are unadorned. When the sexes differ in more important structures, it is the male which is provided with special sense-organs for discovering the female, with locomotive organs for reaching her, and often with prehensile organs for holding her. These various structures for charming or securing the female are often developed in the male during only part of the year, namely the breeding-season. They have in many cases been more or less transferred to the females; and in the latter case they often appear in her as mere rudiments. They are lost or never gained by the males after emasculation. Generally they are not developed in the male during early youth, but appear a short time before the age for reproduction. Hence in most cases the young of both sexes resemble each other; and the female somewhat resembles her young offspring throughout life. In almost every great class a few anomalous cases occur, where there has been an almost complete transposition of the characters proper to the two sexes; the females assuming characters which properly belong to the males. This surprising uniformity in the laws regulating the differences between the sexes in so many and such widely separated classes, is intelligible if we admit the action of one common cause, namely sexual selection.

Sexual selection depends on the success of certain individuals over others of the same sex, in relation to the propagation of the species; whilst natural selection depends on the success of both sexes, at all ages, in relation to the general conditions of life. The sexual struggle is of two kinds; in the one it is between individuals of the same sex, generally the males, in order to drive away or kill their rivals, the females remaining passive; whilst in the other, the struggle is likewise between the individuals of the same sex, in order to excite or charm those of the opposite sex, generally the females, which no longer remain passive, but select the more agreeable partners. This latter kind of selection is closely analogous to that which man unintentionally, yet effectually, brings to bear on his domesticated productions, when he preserves during a long period the most pleasing or useful individuals, without any wish to modify the breed.

The laws of inheritance determine whether characters gained through sexual selection by either sex shall be transmitted to the same sex, or to both; as well as the age at which they shall be developed. It appears that variations arising late in life are commonly transmitted to one and the same sex. Variability is the necessary basis for the action of selection, and is wholly independent of it. It follows from this, that variations of the same general nature have often been taken advantage of and accumulated through sexual selection in relation to the propagation of the species, as well as through natural selection in relation to the general purposes of life. Hence secondary sexual characters, when equally transmitted to both sexes can be distinguished from ordinary specific characters only by the light of analogy. The modifications acquired through sexual selection are often so strongly pronounced that the two sexes have frequently been ranked as distinct species, or even as distinct genera. Such strongly-marked differences must be in some manner highly important; and we know that they have been acquired in some instances at the cost not only of inconvenience, but of exposure to actual danger.

The belief in the power of sexual selection rests chiefly on the following considerations. Certain characters are confined to one sex; and this alone renders it probable that in most cases they are connected with the act of reproduction. In innumerable instances these characters are fully developed only at maturity, and often during only a part of the year, which is always the breeding-season. The males (passing over a few exceptional cases) are the more active in courtship; they are the better armed, and are rendered the more attractive in various ways. It is to be especially observed that the males display their attractions with elaborate care in the presence of the females; and that they rarely or never display them excepting during the season of love. It is incredible that all this should be purposeless. Lastly we have distinct evidence with some quadrupeds and birds, that the individuals of one sex are capable of feeling a strong antipathy or preference for certain individuals of the other sex.

Bearing in mind these facts, and the marked results of man's unconscious selection, when applied to domesticated animals and cultivated plants, it seems to me almost certain that if the individuals of one sex were during a long series of generations to prefer pairing with certain individuals of the other sex, characterised in some peculiar manner, the offspring would slowly but surely become modified in this same manner. I have not attempted to conceal that, excepting when the males are more numerous than the females, or when polygamy prevails, it is doubtful how the more attractive males succeed in leaving a large number of offspring to inherit their superiority in ornaments or other charms than the less attractive males; but I have shewn that this would probably follow from the females,—especially the more vigorous ones, which would be the first to breed,—preferring not only the more attractive but at the same time the more vigorous and victorious males.

Although we have some positive evidence that birds appreciate bright and beautiful objects, as with the bower-birds of Australia, and although they certainly appreciate the power of song, yet I fully admit that it is astonishing that the females of many birds and some mammals should be endowed with sufficient taste to appreciate ornaments, which we have reason to attribute to sexual selection; and this is even more astonishing in the case of reptiles, fish, and insects. But we really know little about the minds of the lower animals. It cannot be supposed, for instance, that male birds of paradise or peacocks should take such pains in erecting, spreading, and vibrating their beautiful plumes before the females for no purpose. We should remember the fact given on excellent authority in a former chapter, that several peahens, when debarred from an admired male, remained widows during a whole season rather than pair with another bird.

Nevertheless I know of no fact in natural history more wonderful than that of the female Argus pheasant should appreciate the exquisite shading of the ball-and-socket ornaments and the elegant patterns on the wing-feathers of the male. He who thinks that the male was created as he now exists must admit that the great plumes, which prevent the wings from being used for flight, and which are displayed during courtship and at no other time in a manner quite peculiar to this one species, were given to him as an ornament. If so, he must likewise admit that the female was created and endowed with the capacity of appreciating such ornaments. I differ only in the conviction that the male Argus pheasant acquired his beauty gradually, through the preference of the females during many generations for the more highly ornamented males; the æsthetic capacity of the females having been advanced through exercise or habit, just as our own taste is gradually improved. In the male through the fortunate chance of a few feathers being left unchanged, we can distinctly trace how simple spots with a little fulvous shading on one side may have been developed by small steps into the wonderful ball-and-socket ornaments; and it is probable that they were actually thus developed.

Everyone who admits the principle of evolution, and yet feels great difficulty in admitting that female mammals, birds, reptiles, and fish, could have acquired the high taste implied by the beauty of the males, and which generally coincides with our own standard, should reflect that the nerve-cells of the brain in the highest as well as in the lowest members of the Vertebrate series, are derived from those of the common progenitor of this great Kingdom. For we can thus see how it has come to pass that certain mental faculties, in various and widely distinct groups of animals, have been developed in nearly the same manner and to nearly the same degree.

The reader who has taken the trouble to go through the several chapters devoted to sexual selection, will be able to judge how far the conclusions at which I have arrived are supported by sufficient evidence. If he accepts these conclusions he may, I think, safely extend them to mankind; but it would be superfluous here to repeat what I have so lately said on the manner in which sexual selection apparently has acted on man, both on the male and female side, causing the two sexes to differ in body and mind, and the several races to differ from each other in various characters, as well as from their ancient and lowly-organised progenitors.

He who admits the principle of sexual selection will be led to the remarkable conclusion that the nervous system not only regulates most of the existing functions of the body, but has indirectly influenced the progressive development of various bodily structures and of certain mental qualities. Courage, pugnacity, perseverance, strength and size of body, weapons of all kinds, musical organs, both vocal and instrumental, bright colours and ornamental appendages, have all been indirectly gained by the one sex or the other, through the exertion of choice, the influence of love and jealousy, and the appreciation of the beautiful in sound, colour or form; and these powers of the mind manifestly depend on the development of the brain.

Man scans with scrupulous care the character and pedigree of his horses, cattle, and dogs before he matches them; but when he comes to his own marriage he rarely, or never, takes any such care. He is impelled by nearly the same motives as the lower animals, when they are left to their own free choice, though he is in so far superior to them that he highly values mental charms and virtues. On the other hand he is strongly attracted by mere wealth or rank. Yet he might by selection do something not only for the bodily constitution and frame of his offspring, but for their intellectual and moral qualities. Both sexes ought to refrain from marriage if they are in any marked degree inferior in body or mind; but such hopes are Utopian and will never be even partially realised until the laws of inheritance are thoroughly known. Everyone does good service, who aids toward this end. When the principles of breeding and inheritance are better understood, we shall not hear ignorant members of our legislature rejecting with scorn a plan for ascertaining whether or not consanguineous marriages are injurious to man.

The advancement of the welfare of mankind is a most intricate problem: all ought to refrain from marriage who cannot avoid abject poverty for their children; for poverty is not only a great evil, but tends to its own increase by leading to recklessness in marriage. On the other hand, as Mr. Galton has remarked, if the prudent avoid marriage, whilst the reckless marry, the inferior members tend to supplant the better members of society. Man, like every other animal, has no doubt advanced to his present high condition through a struggle for existence consequent on his rapid multiplication; and if he is to advance still higher, it is to be feared that he must remain subject to a severe struggle. Otherwise he would sink into indolence, and the more gifted men would not be more successful in the battle of life than the less gifted. Hence our natural rate of increase, though leading to many and obvious evils, must not be greatly diminished by any means. There should be open competition for all men; and the most able should not be prevented by laws or customs from succeeding best and rearing the largest number of offspring. Important as the struggle for existence has been and even still is, yet as far as the highest part of man's nature is concerned there are other agencies more important. For the moral qualities are advanced, either directly or indirectly, much more through the effects of habit, the reasoning powers, instruction, religion, &c., than through natural selection; though to this latter agency may be safely attributed the social instincts, which afforded the basis for the development of the moral sense.

The main conclusion arrived at in this work, namely, that man is descended from some lowly organised form, will, I regret to think, be highly distasteful to many. But there can hardly be a doubt that we are descended from barbarians. The astonishment which I felt on first seeing a party of Fuegians on a wild and broken shore will never be forgotten by me, for the reflection at once rushed into my mind—such were our ancestors. These men were absolutely naked and bedaubed with paint, their long hair was tangled, their mouths, frothed with excitement, and their expression was wild, startled, and distrustful. They possessed hardly any arts, and like wild animals lived on what they could catch; they had no government, and were merciless to every one not of their own small tribe. He who has seen a savage in his native land will not feel much shame, if forced to acknowledge that the blood of some more humble creature flows in his veins. For my own part I would as soon be descended from that heroic little monkey, who braved his dreaded enemy in order to save the life of his keeper, or from that old baboon, who descending from the mountains, carried away in triumph his young comrade from a crowd of astonished dogs—as from a savage who delights to torture his enemies, offers up bloody sacrifices, practises infanticide without remorse, treats his wives like slaves, knows no decency, and is haunted by the grossest superstitions.

Man may be excused for feeling some pride at having risen, though not through his own exertions, to the very summit of the organic scale; and the fact of his having thus risen, instead of having been aboriginally placed there, may give him hope for a still higher destiny in the distant future. But we are not here concerned with hopes or fears, only with the truth as far as our reason permits us to discover it; and I have given the evidence to the best of my ability. We must, however, acknowledge, as it seems to me, that man with all his noble qualities, with sympathy which feels for the most debased, with benevolence which extends not only to other men but to the humblest living creature, with his god-like intellect which has penetrated into the movements and constitution of the solar system—with all these exalted powers—Man still bears in his bodily frame the indelible stamp of his lowly origin.

PART V
DARWIN'S INFLUENCE
ON SCIENCE

Nothing in biology makes sense, except in the light of evolution.
—Theodosius Dobzhansky, 1973

I see a continued mapping of the links between genes and behavior, a much more precise knowledge of how the brain works, and a gradual adoption of the evolutionary paradigm in the social sciences. Charles Darwin's portrait will finally decorate the walls of departments of psychology and sociology!
—Frans De Waal, 1999

The concept of biological evolution is one of the most important ideas ever generated by the application of scientific methods to the natural world. The evolution of all the organisms that live on Earth today from ancestors that lived in the past is at the core of genetics, biochemistry, neurobiology, physiology, ecology, and other biological disciplines. It helps to explain the emergence of new infectious diseases, the development of antiobiotic resistance in bacteria, the agricultural relationships among wild and domestic plants and animals, the composition of Earth's atmosphere, the molecular machinery of the cell, the similarities between human beings and other primates, and countless other features of the biological and physical world.
—Bruce Alberts, 1999

Looking at the genome, and taking it as a kind of image of who we are, places us squarely with the rest of nature. You can see the same genes in flies, worms, monkeys, mice, and people. It's evolution laid out for all to see.
—Jon Seger, on the deciphering of the human genome, June 2000

PART V

DARWIN'S INFLUENCE ON SCIENCE

Nothing in biology makes sense except in the light of evolution.

—Theodosius Dobzhansky, 1973

—Frans De Waal, 1999

—Bruce Alberts, 1998

The Victorian Opposition to Darwin

DAVID L. HULL

Darwin and His Critics (1983)†

Darwin expected theologians, people untrained in scientific investigation, and even those scientists who were strongly religious to object violently to his theory of evolution. He had also anticipated the skepticism of even the most dispassionate scientists. He had not labored over twenty years for nothing gathering facts to support his theory and attempting to discount those that apparently conflicted with it. But he had not anticipated the vehemence with which even the most respected scientists and philosophers in his day would denounce his efforts as not being properly "scientific." To the extent that these latter reactions were genuine and not the result of religious bigotry, they can be explained by reference to the philosophies of science popular in Darwin's day. * * *

Darwin had both the good fortune and the misfortune to begin his scientific career at precisely that moment in history when philosophy of science came into its own in England. Of course, philosophers from Plato and Aristotle had always written on epistemology and, after the scientific revolution, they were presented with the added advantage and obligation of reconciling their philosophies with the current state of science. Some of these philosophers were also themselves scientists. But the works of Descartes, Locke, Hume, Berkeley, Leibnitz, and Kant do not exhibit the same concern with the accomplishments of science and the nature of the "scientific method" which has come to characterize philosophy of science.

Commencing with John Herschel's *Preliminary Discourse on the Study of Natural Philosophy* (1830), English-speaking scientists became self-conscious about the proper method of doing science. During the years 1837–1842, when Darwin was residing in London and working on the species problem, the great debate on the philosophy of science erupted between William Whewell (1794–1866) and John Stuart Mill (1806–1873). In 1833 Whewell contributed his *Astronomy and General Physics Considered with reference to Natural Theology* to the Bridgewater Treatises. In 1837 he published his *History of the Inductive Sciences* and in 1840

† From *Darwin and His Critics: The Reception of Darwin's Theory of Evolution by the Scientific Community* (Chicago, 1983). Reprinted by permission of The University of Chicago Press. Copyright © 1983. David L. Hull (b. 1935) is professor of philosophy at Northwestern University.

The Philosophy of Inductive Sciences, Founded upon their History. Darwin was impressed by the breadth of knowledge exhibited in these five volumes and remembered Whewell as one of the best conversers on grave subjects to whom he had ever listened.

In 1843 Mill brought out his influential *System of Logic, Ratiocinative and Inductive, Being a Connected View of the Principles of Evidence, and the Methods of Scientific Investigation.* Although Mill had gathered most of what he knew of science from reading Whewell's volumes, his *System of Logic* was largely an empiricist attack on Whewell's reworking of Kant's rationalist philosophy. The key word in this dispute and in the methodological objections raised to Darwin's theory was "induction." It would be nice to be able to set out at this point the meaning which the disputants attached to this word, but I cannot. Everyone meant something different by it, and in the works of a single man, one is likely to find many different uses of the word. Initially it was used by Francis Bacon (1561–1626) to contrast his abortive "inductive method" with the Aristotelian "deductive method." As popularly misconceived, the deductive method consisted in an irresponsible leap to a conclusion of high generality and the subsequent deduction of consequences of these generalizations regardless of observed facts. Perhaps the scholastics at their worst were guilty of such maneuvers, but the above characterization was not only a parody of Aristotle but also fails to identify the actual weaknesses in Aristotle's system. The inductive method, also as popularly misconceived, began with observation and proceeded by the cautious construction of generalizations of greater and greater generality. The deductive method proceeded from the peak of the pyramid of knowledge down to its base, whereas the inductive method started at the base and worked up. The superiority of a pyramid resting on its base rather than its peak was obvious.

Although Bacon came close to advocating the inductive method as set out above, Herschel, Whewell, and Mill were all aware of its shortcomings. Science had not and could not proceed by the method set out by Bacon. Yet Bacon was the patron saint of the scientific revolution, and "inductive" was an honorific title not to be discarded lightly. All three men wanted to reserve the term "induction" for the process by which scientific knowledge is attained. Simultaneously they also wanted to use it to refer to the means by which such knowledge was proved factual. For Herschel and Mill induction was the discovery of empirical laws in the facts, reasoning from the known to the unknown. Concurrently, this inductive method insured the truth of these laws. For Whewell, induction was the superinducing of concepts on the facts by the mind. Experience might stimulate the mind to form a concept, but once the appropriate concept had been conceived, truth was guaranteed. For Herschel and Mill, both Kepler's laws and the parallel line postulate of Euclidean geometry were inductions from experience; for Whewell they were self-evident truths whose truth could be known *a priori.*

Whewell did not reply to Mill for six years, then published his *Of Induction, with Especial Reference to Mr. J. Stuart Mill's System of Logic* (1849), just in time for the third edition of Mill's *System of Logic.* The controversy which ensued was gradually decided in Mill's favor, not because Mill's position was especially superior to that of Whewell, but because Whewell's version of Kantian philosophy ran contrary to the rising empiricism of the time. It was in the midst of this controversy over scientific method that Darwin published his *On the Origin of Species by Means of Natural Selection, or the Preservation of Favoured Races in the Struggle for Life* (1859). For Darwin, this coincidence was, to say the least, a mixed blessing.

In his last year at Cambridge, Darwin read Herschel's *Discourse* which, along with Humboldt's *Personal Narrative* (1818), stirred in him "a burning zeal to add even the most humble contribution to the noble structure of Natural Science." Herschel had written his book to elicit precisely this reaction in his readers. Newton had brought about *the* scientific revolution. Henceforth, all scientists had to do was to fill in the details of Newton's great structure, perhaps expanding upon it, but always within the Newtonian framework. Nor was there any conflict between science and religion. Geology had challenged the literal interpretation of the Bible, but scientists and theologians had made their peace. Scientists could concern themselves with the workings of the material world, once created, but the first creation, life, mind and soul were the province of the theologian. "To ascend to the origin of things, and to speculate on the creation, is not the business of the natural philosopher." Not only were scientists making great contributions to the noble edifice of science and to mankind by applications of science in medicine and industry, but their discoveries also lent support to religion through natural theology. As they discovered more clearly how nature worked, they showed how great the creator's wisdom had been. In his youth Darwin had hoped to join in this great parade of scientists and men of God marching arm in arm to produce a better world. Instead he stopped it dead in its tracks.

In his early publications, Darwin gave every appearance of contributing his share to received science. His journals concerning the voyage of the *Beagle* were in the best tradition of such narratives. His monographs on living and fossil barnacles certainly were in no way controversial. Even the publication of his papers on the formation of the Parallel Roads of Glen Roy (1839) and of coral reefs (1842), though theoretical in nature, did not detract from his growing reputation as a true inductive scientist. In the first, he explained the appearance of a series of parallel shelves on the sides of a glen in Scotland in terms of the gradual elevation of the land. The parallel roads were actually the remnants of former beaches. In the second, he explained the formation of coral reefs in terms of the gradual subsidence of the ocean floor. New coral grew on the old as it fell beneath the surface of the water. But with the publication of the *Origin of Species*, large segments of the scientific and intellectual community, turned on him. Both Adam Sedgwick, the eminent geologist, and Richard Owen, the leading comparative anatomist of the day, had encouraged Darwin in his early work. After the *Origin*, their praise turned to ridicule. Sedgwick (1860) complained that Darwin had "departed from the true inductive track." Owen, while admitting that he himself had casually entertained the notion of natural selection, had judiciously refrained from enunciating it. It was "just one of those obvious possibilities that might float through the imagination of any speculative naturalist; only the sober searcher after truth would prefer a blameless silence to sending the proposition forth as explanatory of the origin of species, without its inductive foundations."

Darwin was prepared for the abuse which the *content* of his theory, especially its implications for man, was to receive from certain quarters, but he was not prepared for the criticism which his *methodology* was to receive from the most respected philosophers and scientists of his day. Most contemporary commentators tend to dismiss these criticisms as facile, disingenuous and superficial, suspecting that they stemmed more from a distaste of the content of Darwin's theory than from his methodology, but this dismissal is itself too facile. Certainly the repeated invocation of the Baconian method by many of Darwin's critics and even by Darwin himself indicated no great understanding of the actual nature of this method or the philosophy from which it stemmed, but the leading philosophers contemporary with Darwin, John Herschel, William Whewell, and John Stuart Mill, were equally adamant in their conviction that the *Origin of Species* was just one mass of conjecture. Darwin had proved nothing! From a philosophical point of view, evolutionary theory was sorely deficient. Even today, both Darwin's original efforts and more recent reformulations are repeatedly found philosophically objectionable. Evolutionary theory seems capable of offending almost everyone.

In the nineteenth century, "to be scientific" meant to be like John Herschel's extension of physical astronomy to the sidereal regions. Thus, Darwin was especially anxious to hear the opinion of Herschel, the "great philosopher" referred to in the opening paragraph of the *Origin*. He sent Herschel a copy of his book and wrote to Lyell to pass on any comments which the great physicist might make since "I should excessively like to hear whether I produce any effect on such a mind."[1] Herschel's opinion was rapidly forthcoming. Darwin wrote to Lyell, "I have heard, by a roundabout channel, that Herschel says my book 'is the law of higgeldy-piggeldy.' What this exactly means I do not know, but it is evidently very contemptuous. If true this is a great blow and discouragement."[2] In the face of such a rejection by the most eminent philosopher-scientist of the century, it is easy to understand Darwin's pleasure when he discovered in an equally roundabout way that another great philosopher, John Stuart Mill, thought that his reasoning in the *Origin* was "in the most exact accordance with the strict principles of logic."[3] On closer examination, however, Mill's endorsement can be seen to be not nearly reassuring. Darwin had properly used the Method of Hypothesis, but this method belonged to the logic of discovery, not proof. In spite of twenty years' labor, Darwin had failed to provide proof for his theory of evolution by natural selection.

Darwin's own views on the nature of science exhibited the conflicts and inconsistencies typical of his day. He evidenced the usual distrust of "hypotheses" while grudgingly admitting their necessity. For example, in a

1. Letter of Nov. 23, 1859 in Francis Darwin, *The Life and Letters of Charles Darwin*, Vol. 2. (London, 1887): 26.
2. Letter of Dec. 12, 1859 in *Life and Letters*, Vol. 2, 37.
3. See Francis Darwin, *More Letters of Charles Darwin*, Vol. 1 (London, 1903): 189.

letter to Hooker, Darwin claimed that he looked upon "a strong tendency to generalize as an entire evil"[4] and yet admitted in his *Autobiography*: "I cannot resist forming one in every subject."[5] In the opening paragraph of the *Origin of Species* Darwin sketched the following history of the development of his theory:

> When on board H.M.S. "Beagle," as naturalist, I was much struck with certain facts in the distribution of the inhabitants of South America, and in the geological relations of the present to the past inhabitants of that continent. These facts seemed to me to throw some light on the origin of species—that mystery of mysteries, as it has been called by one of our greatest philosophers. On my return home, it occurred to me, in 1837, that something might perhaps be made out on this question by patiently accumulating and reflecting on all sorts of facts which could possibly have any bearing on it. After five years' work I allowed myself to speculate on the subject, and drew up some short notes; these I enlarged in 1844 into a sketch of the conclusions, which then seemed to me probable: from that period to the present day I have steadily pursued the same object (p. 1).

In his *Autobiography* Darwin recalls roughly this same sequence of events but adds that he "worked on true Baconian principles and without any theory collected facts on a wholesale scale."[6] But Darwin was well aware that the possibility of species evolving had occurred to him soon after his return from his voyage on the *Beagle* (if not before) and his principle of natural selection not much later, in October 1838. Five years may have elapsed before he permitted himself to write an essay on the subject, but he had speculated and collected facts in the light of these speculations from the very first.

The source of this fabrication is easy to uncover. One of the most prevalent confusions in the work of even the best scientists and philosophers was between the temporal order of an actual scientific investigation and the logical order of a reconstruction of scientific method. According to empiricist epistemology, all knowledge has its foundation in experience. This tenet was mistakenly taken to imply that all scientific investigation has to *begin* with observation. The true inductive scientist began collecting data indiscriminately, with no preconceived ideas, and gradually evolved broader and broader generalizations. The process of scientific investigation assured both the truth and the empirical meaningfulness of the resultant propositions. Deductivists approached nature with a hypothesis already in mind, and speculators flew too quickly to generalizations of too great a scope. Thus, Darwin can be found saying of his coral reef paper, "No other work of mine was begun in so deductive a spirit as this; for the whole theory was thought out on the west coast of S. America before I had seen a true coral reef."[7] Similarly with respect to his theory of evolution, he conceded to Asa Gray, "What you hint at generally is very, very true: that

---

4. Letter of Jan. 11, 1844 in *More Letters*, Vol. 1, 39.
5. Nora Barlow, ed., *The Autobiography of Charles Darwin, 1809–1882* (London, 1958): 141.
6. *Autobiography*, 119.
7. *Autobiography*, 98.

my work will be grievously hypothetical, and large parts by no means worthy of being called induction, my commonest error being probably induction from too few facts."[8]

In a letter to Henry Fawcett, however, Darwin indicated that he realized that data cannot be gathered efficiently without some hypothesis in mind:

> About thirty years ago there was much talk that geologists ought only to observe and not to theorize; and I well remember someone saying that at this rate a man might as well go into a gravel-pit and count the pebbles and describe the colours. How odd it is that anyone should not see that all observation must be for or against some view if it is to be of any service![9]

What mattered was that the hypothesis be an empirical hypothesis, one that could be verified or refuted by observation, and that serious attempts be made to gather the relevant data. Immediately after saying that his coral reef paper was begun in a deductive manner, Darwin adds, "I had therefore only to verify and extend my views by a careful examination of coral reefs."[1] Darwin's own experience as a scientist forced him to recognize that the order in which hypotheses were formed and the relevant data gathered was not rigidly set. It helped to have a hypothesis in mind, but hypotheses had to be changed as the investigation proceeded.

* * *

Darwin's conservative views on publication were rewarded to some degree. His *Origin of Species* did not suffer the same fate as those works on evolution that had preceded it. It was treated as a serious work of science even by those who denounced it. But a similar reticence on the part of Gregor Mendel resulted in his laws of heredity being overlooked for almost forty years. Mendel published his laws in 1865, soon after the appearance of the *Origin*. He too wanted to avoid being branded a speculator. In his original paper he barely alludes to his unobservable "factors," though the cogency of his entire argument rested upon their existence. In a letter to Carl Nägeli, he claimed that, "as an empirical worker" he had to "define constancy of type as the retention of a character during the period of observation." Perhaps Darwin's advice might protect scientists from being engulfed in half-baked scientific publications, but it also contributed to the obscurity of Mendel's potentially great contribution to science. Because Lamarck neglected the niceties of the sociology of science, his work was ignored with disdainful embarrassment. Because Mendel was too scrupulous in observing them, his work was overlooked. Darwin struck an appropriate compromise.

Darwin's beliefs on the ethics of publication go a great way toward explaining his reticence in publishing his own views on the origin of spe-

8. Letter of Nov. 29, 1859 in *More Letters*, Vol. 1, 126.
9. Letter of Sept. 18, 1861 in *More Letters*, Vol. 1, 195.
1. *Autobiography*, 98.

cies until his big book was complete. Darwin emphasized the importance of providing empirical evidence for scientific hypotheses for still another reason. The science of Darwin's day was filled with metaphysical principles enunciated as if they were scientific laws. Darwin found Herbert Spencer to be one of the chief offenders in this regard. Because of the jargon of the period, Darwin's discussions of the differences between scientific laws, the axioms of mathematics, and metaphysical principles are none too clear, but in these matters he was no worse than the leading empiricist philosophers of the day. He tended to distinguish the formal from the empirical sciences by the prevalence of deductive reasoning in the former. Of Spencer, Darwin complained:

> His deductive manner of treating any subject is wholly opposed to my frame of mind. His conclusions never convince me; and over and over again I have said to myself, after reading one of his discussions, — "Here would be a fine subject for half-a-dozen years' work." His fundamental generalizations (which have been compared in importance by some persons with Newton's Laws!) which I daresay may be very valuable under a philosophical point of view, are of such a nature that they do not seem to me to be of any strictly scientific use. They partake more of the nature of definitions than of laws of nature. They do not aid me in predicting what will happen in any particular case. Anyhow they have not been of any use to me.[2]

The distinction which Darwin discerned in the works of Spencer was between a scientific hypothesis which has not yet been verified and a purely metaphysical principle which, by the methods of science, cannot be confronted by empirical data at all. He felt "inclined to cavil at speculation when the direct and immediate effect of a cause in question cannot be shown."[3] Darwin doubted the merits of Spencer's scientific work, not merely because the evidential basis was frequently lacking but because Darwin doubted that there was any.

*   *   *

One reason which Darwin frequently gave for the *Origin's* being so maligned and misunderstood was that Wallace's joint discovery had forced him into premature publication. No similar pressure forced Darwin to publish his theory of pangenesis, and it met with even more resistance than the *Origin* had. In reality, all of Darwin's theoretical work had much the same structure. As Darwin put it: "The line of argument often pursued throughout my theory is to establish a point as a probability by induction and to apply it as hypotheses to other parts and see whether it will solve them."[4] If it did solve them, then Darwin thought that there was good

---

2. *Autobiography*, 109. See also Letter of Dec. 8, 1874 in *Life and Letters*, Vol. 2, 371.
3. Letter of Mar. 4, 1850 in *More Letters*, vol. 2, 133.
4. Gavin DeBeer, "Darwin's Notebooks on 'Transmutation of Species,' " *Bulletin of the British Museum* 2 (1960): 1–83.

reason to accept the hypotheses tentatively. As Darwin wrote of F. W. Hutton's review of the *Origin*:

> He is one of the very few who see that the change of species cannot be directly proved, and that the doctrine must sink or swim according as it groups and explains phenomena. It is really curious how few judge it in this way, which is clearly the right way.[5]

And in his autobiography he says of his theory of pangenesis:

> Towards the end of the work I give my well-abused hypothesis of pangenesis. An unverified hypothesis is of little or no value. But if anyone should hereafter be led to make observations by which some such hypothesis could be established, I shall have done good service, as an astonishing number of isolated facts can thus be connected together and rendered intelligible.[6]

Darwin produced several theoretical works in his career: two were in error (pangenesis and his explanation of the Parallel Roads of Glen Roy) and two correct (evolutionary theory and his explanation of the formation of coral reefs). His procedures in formulating, articulating, and verifying these theories and explanations were roughly the same, yet no one complained of the methodology of his Glen Roy or coral reefs papers. If Darwin's methodology was faulty in the *Origin*, then it should have been equally faulty in all of his scientific works.

What was wrong with Darwin's theories? Was his methodology faulty? What is the nature of inductive formulation and proof which eluded Darwin? These are the questions which occur to the modern reader when first confronted by the reviews of the *Origin of Species* and Darwin's later work, especially the *Descent of Man*. Some of the reviewers were obviously biased. Some were merely mouthing undigested platitudes. But many of the reviewers were competent scientists honestly trying to evaluate a novel theory against the commonly accepted standards of scientific excellence, and evolutionary theory consistently came up wanting. The solution to these puzzles can be found in the philosophies of science promulgated by such philosophers as Herschel, Whewell, and Mill and their most important predecessors, Aristotle, Bacon, and Newton. Darwin was caught in the middle of a great debate over some of the most fundamental issues in the philosophy of science—the difference between deduction and induction and the role of each in science, the difference between concept formation and the discovery of scientific laws, the relation between the logic of discovery and the logic of justification, the nature of mathematical axioms and their relation to experience, the distinction between occult qualities and theoretical entities, and the role of God's direct intervention in nature. Before philosophers of science had thoroughly sorted out these issues, they were presented with an original and highly problematic scientific theory to evaluate. That they rejected evolutionary theory, a theory which has outlasted many of the theories judged to be exemplars of scientific method,

5. *Life and Letters*, vol. 2, 155.
6. *Autobiography*, 120.

says something about the views of science held by these philosophers and scientists.

⁕   ⁕   ⁕

ADAM SEDGWICK

Objections to Mr. Darwin's Theory of the Origin of Species (1860)†

[The Archbishop of Dublin has received the following remarks, in answer to an inquiry he had made of a friend (eminent in the world of science) on the subject of Darwin's theory of the origin of species.]

⁕ ⁕ ⁕ I must in the first place observe that Darwin's theory is not *inductive*,—not based on a series of acknowledged facts pointing to a *general* conclusion,—not a proposition evolved out of the facts, logically, and of course including them. To use an old figure, I look on the theory as a vast pyramid resting on its apex, and that apex a mathematical point. The only facts he pretends to adduce, as true elements of proof, are the *varieties* produced by domestication, or the *human artifice* of cross-breeding. We all admit the varieties, and the very wide limits of variation, among domestic animals. How very unlike are poodles and greyhounds. Yet they are of one species. And how nearly alike are many animals,—allowed to be of distinct species, on any acknowledged views of species. Hence there may have been very many blunders among naturalists, in the discrimination and enumeration of species. But this does not undermine the grand truth of nature, and the continuity of species. Again, the varieties, built upon by Mr. Darwin, are varieties of domestication and human *design*. Such varieties could have no existence in the old world. Something may be done by cross-breeding; but mules are generally sterile, or the progeny (in some rare instances) passes into one of the original crossed forms. The Author of Nature will not permit His work to be spoiled by the wanton curiosity of Man. And in a state of nature (such as that of the old world before Man came upon it) wild animals of different species do not desire to cross and unite.

Species have been constant for thousands of years; and time (so far as I see my way) though multiplied by millions and billions would never change them, so long as the conditions remained constant. Change the conditions, and old species would disappear; and new species *might* have room to come in and flourish. But how, and by what causation? I say by *creation*. But, what do I mean by creation? I reply, the operation of a power quite beyond the powers of a pigeon-fancier, a cross-breeder, or hybridizer; a power I cannot imitate or comprehend; but in which I can

† This review appeared anonymously in *The Spectator* 33 (Mar. 24, 1860): 285–86. Adam Sedgwick (1785–1873) was Woodwardian Professor of geology at Cambridge and president of the Geological Society and of the British Association.

believe, by a legitimate conclusion of sound reason drawn from the laws and harmonies of Nature,—proving in all around me, a design and purpose, and a mutual adaptation of parts, which I *can* comprehend,—and which prove that there is exterior to, and above, the mere phenomena of Nature a great prescient and designing cause. Believing this, I have no difficulty in the repetition of new species.

But Darwin would say that I am introducing a *miracle* by the supposition. In one sense I am; in another I am not. The hypothesis does not suspend or interrupt an established law of Nature. It does suppose the introduction of a new phenomenon unaccounted for by the operation of any *known* law of Nature; and it appeals to a power above established laws, and yet acting in conformity with them. * * *

I place the theory against facts viewed collectively. 1st. I see no proofs of enormous *gaps* of geological time, (I say nothing of years or centuries,) in those cases where there is a sudden change in the ancient fauna and flora. I am willing, out of the stock of past time, to lavish millions or billions upon each epoch, if thereby we can gain rational results from the operation of *true causes*. But time and "natural selection" can do nothing if there be not a vera causa working in them. I must confine myself to a few of the collective instances.

2d. Towards the end of the carboniferous period, there was a vast extinction of animal and vegetable life. We can, I think, account for this extinction mechanically. The old crust was broken up. The sea bottom underwent a great change. The old flora and fauna went out; a new flora and fauna appeared, in the ground now called Permian, at the base of the new red sandstone, which overlie the carboniferous. I take the fact as it *is*, and I have no difficulty. The time in which all this was brought *may* have been very long, even upon a geological scale of time. But where do the *intervening* and connecting types exist, which are to mark the *work of natural selection*? We do not find them. Therefore the step onwards gives no true resting-place to a baseless theory; and is, in fact, a stumbling-block in its way.

3d. Before we rise through the new red sandstone, we find the muschel-kalk (wanting in England, though its place on the scale is well-known) with *an entirely new* fauna: where have we a proof of any enormous lapse of geological time to account for the change? We have no proof in the deposits themselves: the presumption they offer to our senses is of a contrary kind.

4th. If we rise from the muschel-kalk to the Lias, we find again a new fauna. All the anterior species are gone. Yet the passage through the upper members of the new red sandstone to the Lias is by insensible gradation, and it is no easy matter to fix the physical line of their demarcation. I think it would be a very rash assertion to affirm that a great interval took place between the formation of the upper part of the new red sandstone and the Lias. Physical evidence is against it. To support a baseless theory, Darwin would require a countless lapse of ages of which we have *no* commensurate physical monuments; and he is unable to supply any of the connecting organic links that ought to bind together the older fauna with that of the Lias.

I need hardly go on any further with these objections. But I cannot conclude without expressing my detestation of the theory, because of its unflinching materialism;—because it has deserted the inductive track, the only track that leads to physical truth;—because it utterly repudiates final causes, and thereby indicates a demoralized understanding on the part of its advocates. In some rare instances it shows a wonderful credulity. Darwin seems to believe that a white bear, by being confined to the slops floating in the Polar basin, might be turned into a whale; that a Lemur might easily be turned into a bat; that a three-toed Tapir might be the great grandfather of a horse! or the progeny of a horse may (in America) have gone back to the tapir.

But any startling and (supposed) novel paradox, maintained very boldly and with something of imposing plausibility, produces, in some minds, a kind of pleasing excitement, which predisposes them in its favour; and if they are unused to careful reflection, and averse to the labour of accurate investigation, they will be likely to conclude that what is (apparently) *original*, must be a production of original *genius*, and that anything very much opposed to prevailing notions must be a grand *discovery*,—in short, that whatever comes from "the bottom of a well" must be the "truth" supposed to be hidden there.

RICHARD OWEN

Darwin on the Origin of Species (1860)†

* * * Mr. Darwin refers to the multitude of the individuals of every species, which, from one cause or another, perish either before, or soon after attaining maturity.

> 'Owing to this struggle for life, any variation, however slight and from whatever cause proceeding, if it be in any degree profitable to an individual of any species, in its infinitely complex relations to other organic beings and to external nature, will tend to the preservation of that individual, and will generally be inherited by its offspring. The offspring, also, will thus have a better chance of surviving, for, of the many individuals of any species which are periodically born, but a small number can survive. I have called this principle, by which each slight variation, if useful, is preserved, by the term of Natural Selection, in order to mark its relation to man's power of selection. We have seen that man by selection can certainly produce great results, and can adapt organic beings to his own uses, through the accumulation of slight but useful variations, given to him by the hand of Nature. But Natural Selection, as we shall hereafter see, is a power incessantly ready for action, and is as immeasurably superior to man's feeble efforts, as the works of Nature are to those of Art.' (P. 61.)

† This review appeared anonymously in the *Edinburgh Review* 111 (1860): 487–532. Richard Owen (1804–1892), superintendent of the natural history department of the British Museum, was a distinguished comparative anatomist and a pioneer in vertebrate paleontology.

The scientific world has looked forward with great interest to the facts which Mr. Darwin might finally deem adequate to the support of his theory on this supreme question in biology, and to the course of inductive original research which might issue in throwing light on 'that mystery of mysteries.' But having now cited the chief, if not the whole, of the original observations adduced by its author in the volume now before us, our disappointment may be conceived. Failing the adequacy of such observations, not merely to carry conviction, but to give a colour to the hypothesis, we were then left to confide in the superior grasp of mind, strength of intellect, clearness and precision of thought and expression, which might raise one man so far above his contemporaries, as to enable him to discern in the common stock of facts, of coincidences, correlations and analogies in Natural History, deeper and truer conclusions than his fellow-labourers had been able to reach.

These expectations, we must confess, received a check on perusing the first sentence in the book.

> 'When on board H.M.S "Beagle," as naturalist, I was much struck with certain facts in the distribution of the inhabitants of South America, and in the geological relations of the present to the past inhabitants of that continent. These facts seemed to me to throw some light on the origin of species—that mystery of mysteries, as it has been called by some of our greatest philosophers.' (P. 1.)

What is there, we asked ourselves, as we closed the volume to ponder on this paragraph,—what can there possibly be in the inhabitants, we suppose he means aboriginal inhabitants, of South America, or in their distribution on that continent, to have suggested to any mind that man might be a transmuted ape, or to throw any light on the origin of the human or other species? Mr. Darwin must be aware of what is commonly understood by an 'un-inhabited island;' he may, however, mean by the inhabitants of South America, not the human kind only, whether aboriginal or otherwise, but all the lower animals. Yet again, why are the fresh-water polypes or sponges to be called 'inhabitants' more than the plants? Perhaps what was meant might be, that the distribution and geological relations of the organised beings generally in South America, had suggested transmutational views. They have commonly suggested ideas as to the independent origin of such localized kinds of plants and animals. But what the 'certain facts' were, and what may be the nature of the light which they threw upon the mysterious beginning of species, is not mentioned or further alluded to in the present work. * * *

'Isolation also,' says Mr. Darwin, 'is an important element in the process of natural selection.' But how can one select if a thing be 'isolated'? Even using the word in the sense of a confined area, Mr. Darwin admits that the conditions of life 'throughout such area, will tend to modify all the individuals of a species in the same manner, in relation to the same conditions.' (P. 104.) No evidence, however, is given of a species having ever been created in that way; but granting the hypothetical influence and transmutation, there is no selection here. The author adds, 'Although I do not doubt that isolation is of considerable importance in the production of new species, on the whole, I am inclined to believe, that largeness of area is of more importance in the production of species capable of spreading widely.' (P. 105.)

Now, on such a question as the origin of species, and in an express, formal, scientific treatise on the subject, the expression of a belief, where one looks for a demonstration, is simply provoking. We are not concerned in the author's beliefs or inclinations to believe. Belief is a state of mind short of actual knowledge. It is a state which may govern action, when based upon a tacit admission of the mind's incompetency to prove a proposition, coupled with submissive acceptance of an authoritative dogma, or worship of a favourite idol of the mind. We readily concede, and it needs, indeed, no ghost to reveal the fact, that the wider the area in which a species may be produced, the more widely it will spread. But we fail to discern its import in respect of the great question at issue.

We have read and studied with care most of the monographs conveying the results of close investigations of particular groups of animals, but have not found, what Darwin asserts to be the fact, at least as regards all those investigators of particular groups of animals and plants whose treatises he has read, viz., that their authors 'are one and all firmly convinced that each of the well-marked forms or species was at the first independently created.' Our experience has been that the monographers referred to have rarely committed themselves to any conjectural hypothesis whatever, upon the origin of the species which they have closely studied.

Darwin appeals from the 'experienced naturalists whose minds are stocked with a multitude of facts' which he assumes to have been 'viewed from a point of view opposite to his own,' to the 'few naturalists endowed with much flexibility of mind,' for a favourable reception of his hypothesis. We must confess that the minds to whose conclusions we incline to bow belong to that truth-loving, truth-seeking, truth-imparting class, which Robert Brown,[1] Bojanus,[2] Rudolphi, Cuvier,[3] Ehrenberg,[4] Herold, Kölliker,[5] and Siebold,[6] worthily exemplify. The rightly and sagaciously generalising intellect is associated with the power of endurance of continuous and laborious research, exemplarily manifested in such monographs as we have quoted below. Their authors are the men who trouble the intellectual world little with their beliefs, but enrich it greatly with their proofs. If close and long-continued research, sustained by the determination to get accurate results, blunted, as Mr. Darwin seems to imply, the far-seeing discovering faculty, then are we driven to this paradox, viz., that the elucidation of the higher problems, nay the highest, in Biology, is to be sought for or expected in the lucubrations of those naturalists whose minds are not weighed or troubled with more than a discursive and superficial knowledge of nature.

Lasting and fruitful conclusions have, indeed, hitherto been based only

1. Prodromus Floræ Novæ Hollandiæ.
2. Anatome Testudinis Europæ.
3. Mémoires pour servir à l'Anatomie des Mollusques.
4. Die Infusionsthierchen, als vollkommene Organismen.
5. Disquisitiones de Animalium vertebris carentium, &c.
6. Entwickelungsgeschichte des Cephalopoden.

on the possession of knowledge; now we are called upon to accept an hypothesis on the plea of want of knowledge. The geological record, it is averred, is so imperfect! But what human record is not? Especially must the record of past organisms be must less perfect than of present ones. We freely admit it. But when Mr. Darwin, in reference to the absence of the intermediate fossil forms required by his hypothesis—and only the zootomical zoologist can approximately appreciate their immense numbers—the countless hosts of transitional links which, on 'natural selection,' must certainly have existed at one period or another of the world's history—when Mr. Darwin exclaims what may be, or what may not be, the forms yet forthcoming out of the graveyards of strata, we would reply, that our only ground for prophesying of what may come, is by the analogy of what has come to light. We may expect, e.g., a chambered-shell from a secondary rock; but not the evidence of a creature linking on the cuttle-fish to the lump-fish.

Mr. Darwin asks, 'How is it that varieties, which I have called incipient species, become ultimately good and distinct species?' To which we rejoin with the question:—Do they become good and distinct species? Is there any one instance proved by observed facts of such transmutation? We have searched the volume in vain for such. When we see the intervals that divide most species from their nearest congeners, in the recent and especially the fossil series, we either doubt the fact of progressive conversion, or, as Mr. Darwin remarks in his letter to Dr. Asa Gray,[7] one's 'imagination must fill up very wide blanks.' * * *

The essential element in the complex idea of species, as it has been variously framed and defined by naturalists, viz., the blood-relationship between all the individuals of such species, is annihilated on the hypothesis of 'natural selection.' According to this view a genus, a family, an order, a class, a sub-kingdom,—the individuals severally representing these grades of difference or relationship,—now differ from individuals of the same species only in degree: the species, like every other group, is a mere creature of the brain; it is no longer from nature. With the present evidence from form, structure, and procreative phenomena, of the truth of the opposite proposition, that 'classification is the task of science, but species the work of nature,' we believe that this aphorism will endure; we are certain that it has not yet been refuted; and we repeat in the words of Linnæus, '*Classis et Ordo* est sapientiæ, *Species* naturæ opus.'[8]

---

7. Proceedings of the Linnæan Society, 1858, p. 61.
8. For Darwin's response to Owen, see *Historical Sketch*, p. 91. [Editor]

FLEEMING JENKIN

Review of the Origin of Species (1867)†

The theory proposed by Mr. Darwin as sufficient to account for the origin of species has been received as probable, and even as certainly true, by many who from their knowledge of physiology, natural history, and geology, are competent to form an intelligent opinion. The facts, they think, are consistent with the theory. Small differences are observed between animals and their offspring. Greater differences are observed between varieties known to be sprung from a common stock. The differences between what have been termed species are sometimes hardly greater in appearance than those between varieties owning a common origin. Even when species differ more widely, the difference they say, is one of degree only, not of kind. They can see no clear, definite distinction by which to decide in all cases, whether two animals have sprung from a common ancestor or not. They feel warranted in concluding, that for aught the structure of animals shows to the contrary, they may be descended from a few ancestors only,—nay, even from a single pair.

* * *

Some persons seem to have thought his theory dangerous to religion, morality, and what not. Others have tried to laugh it out of court. We can share neither the fears of the former nor the merriment of the latter; and, on the contrary, own to feeling the greatest admiration both for the ingenuity of the doctrine and for the temper in which it was broached, although, from a consideration of the following arguments, our opinion is adverse to its truth.

Variability

Darwin's theory requires that there shall be no limit to the possible differences between descendants and their progenitors, or, at least, that if there be limits, they shall be at so great a distance as to comprehend the utmost differences between any known forms of life. The variability required, if not infinite, is indefinite. Experience with domestic animals and cultivated plants shows that great variability exists. Darwin calls special attention to the differences between the various fancy pigeons, which, he says, are descended from one stock; between various breeds of cattle and horses, and some other domestic animals. He states that these differences are greater than those which induce some naturalists to class many specimens as distinct species. These differences are infinitely small as compared with the range required by his theory, but he assumes that by

† From *The North British Review*, 46 (1867). Fleeming Jenkin (1833–1885) was a professor of engineering at University College, London, and a Fellow of the Royal Society.

accumulation of successive difference any degree of variation may be produced.

*   *   *

We are thus led to believe that whatever new point in the variable beast, bird, or flower, be chosen as desirable by a fancier, this point can be rapidly approached at first, but that the rate of approach quickly diminishes, tending to a limit never to be attained. Darwin says that our oldest cultivated plants still yield new varieties. Granted; but the new variations are not successive variations in one direction. Horses could be produced with very long or with very short ears, very long or short hair, with large or small hooves, with peculiar colour, eyes, teeth, perhaps. In short whatever variation we perceive of ordinary occurrence might by selection be carried to an extravagant excess. If a large annual prize were offered for any of these novel peculiarities, probably the variation in the first few years would be remarkable, but in twenty years' time the judges would be much puzzled to which breeder the prize should fall, and the maximum excellence would be known and expressed in figures, so that an eighth of an inch more or less would determine success or failure.

A given animal or plant appears to be contained, as it were, within a sphere of variation; one individual lies near one portion of the surface, another individual, of the same species, near another part of the surface; the average animal at the centre.

*   *   *

We hope this argument is now plain. However slow the rate of variation might be, even though it were only one part in a thousand per twenty or two thousand generations, yet if it were constant or erratic we might believe that, in untold time, it would lead to untold distance; but if in every case we find that deviation from an average individual can be rapidly effected at first, and that the rate of deviation steadily diminishes till it reaches an almost imperceptible amount, then we are as much entitled to assume a limit to the possible deviation as we are to the progress of a cannon-ball from a knowledge of the law of diminution in its speed. This limit to the variation of species seems to be established for all cases of man's selection. What argument does Darwin offer showing that the law of variation will be different when the variation occurs slowly, not rapidly? The law may be different, but is there any experimental ground for believing that it *is* different? Darwin says (p. 153), 'The struggle between natural selection, on the one hand, and the tendency to reversion and variability on the other hand, will in the course of time cease, and that the most abnormally developed organs may be made constant, I can see no reason to doubt.' But what reason have we to believe this? Darwin says the variability will disappear by the continued rejection of the individuals tending to revert to a former condition; but is there any experimental ground for believing that the variability *will* disappear; and, secondly, if the variety can become fixed, that it will in time become ready to vary still more in the original direction, passing that limit which we think has just been shown to exist in the case of man's selection? It is peculiarly difficult to see how natural selection could reject individuals having a tendency to produce offspring reverting to an original stock. The tendency to produce offspring more like their superior parents than their inferior grandfathers can surely be of no advantage to any individual in the struggle for life.

＊   ＊   ＊

Although many domestic animals and plants are highly variable, there appears to be a limit to their variation in any one direction. This limit is shown by the fact that new points are at first rapidly gained, but afterwards more slowly, while finally no further perceptible change can be effected. Great, therefore, as the variability is, we are not free to assume that successive variations of the same kind can be accumulated. There is no experimental reason for believing that the limit would be removed to a greater distance, or passed, simply because it was approached by very slow degrees, instead of by more rapid steps. There is no reason to believe that a fresh variability is acquired by long selection of one form; on the contrary, we know that with the oldest breeds it is easier to bring about a diminution than an increase in the points of excellence. The sphere of variation is a simile embodying this view;—each point of the sphere corresponding to a different individual of the same race, the centre to the average animal, the surface to the limit in various directions. The individual near the centre may have offspring varying in all directions with nearly equal rapidity. A variety near the surface may be made to approach it still nearer, but has a greater tendency to vary in every other direction. The sphere may be conceived as large for some species and small for others.

Efficiency of Natural Selection

Those individuals of any species which are most adapted to the life they lead, live on an average longer than those which are less adapted to the circumstances in which the species is placed. The individuals which live the longest will have the most numerous offspring, and as the offspring on the whole resemble their parents, the descendants from any given generation will on the whole resemble the more favoured rather than the less favoured individuals of the species. So much of the theory of natural selection will hardly be denied; but it will be worth while to consider how far this process can tend to cause a variation in some one direction. It is clear that it will frequently, and indeed generally, tend to prevent any deviation from the common type. The mere existence of a species is a proof that it is tolerably well adapted to the life it must lead; many of the variations which may occur will be variations for the worse, and natural selection will assuredly stamp these out. A white grouse in the heather, or a white hare on a fallow would be sooner detected by its enemies than one of the usual plumage or colour. Even so, any favourable deviation must, according to the very terms of the statement, give its fortunate possesor a better chance of life; but this conclusion differs widely from the supposed consequence that a whole species may or will gradually acquire some one new quality, or wholly change in one direction and in the same manner.

* * *

The vague use of an imperfectly understood doctrine of chance has led Darwinian supporters * * * to imagine that a very slight balance in favour of some individual sport must lead to its perpetuation. All that can be said, is that in the above example the favoured sport would be preserved once in fifty times. Let us consider what will be its influence on the main stock when preserved. It will breed and have a progeny of say 100; now this progeny will, on the whole, be intermediate between the average individual and the sport. The odds in favour of one of this generation of the new breed will be, say 1½ to 1, as compared with the average individual; the odds in their favour will therefore be less than that of their parent; but owing to their greater number, the chances are that about 1½ of them would survive. Unless these breed together, a most improbable event, their progeny would again approach the average individual; there would be 150 of them, and their superiority would be say in the ratio of 1¼ to 1; the probability would now be that nearly two of them would survive, and have 200 children, with an eighth superiority. Rather more than two of these would survive; but the superiority would again dwindle, until after a few generations it would no longer be observed and would count for no more in the struggle for life, than any of the hundred trifling advantages which occur in the ordinary organs. * * *

Darwin says that in the struggle for life a grain may turn the balance in favour of a given structure, which will then be preserved. But one of the weights in the scale of nature is due to the number of a given tribe. Let there be 7000 A's and 7000 B's, representing two varieties of a given animal, and let all the B's, in virtue of a slight difference of structure, have the better chance of life by 1/7000th part. We must allow that there is a slight probability that the descendants of B will supplant the descendants of A; but let there be only 7001 A's against 7000 B's at first, and the chances are once more equal, while if there be 7002 A's to start, the odds would be laid on the A's. True, they stand a greater chance of being killed; but then they can better afford to be killed. The grain will only turn the scales when these are very nicely balanced, and an advantage in numbers counts for weight, even as an advantage in structure. As the numbers of the favoured variety diminish, so must its relative advantage increase, if the chance of its existence is to surpass the chance of its extinction, until hardly any conceivable advantage would enable the descendants of a single pair to exterminate the descendants of many thousands if they and their descendants are supposed to breed freely with the inferior variety, and so gradually lose their ascendency. If it is impossible that any sport or accidental variation in a single individual, however favourable to life, should be preserved and transmitted by natural selection, still less can slight and imperceptible variations, occurring in single individuals be garnered up and transmitted to continually increasing numbers; for if a very highly-favoured white cannot blanch a nation of negroes, it will hardly be contended that a comparatively very dull mulatto has a good chance of producing a tawny tribe; the idea, which seems almost absurd when presented in connexion with a practical case, rests on a fallacy of exceedingly common occurrence in mechanics and physics generally. When a man shows that a tendency to produce a given effect exists he often thinks he has proved that the effect must follow. He does not take into account the opposing tendencies, much less does he measure the various forces, with a view to calculate the result.

* * *

Victorian Supporters of Darwin

JOSEPH DALTON HOOKER

Flora Tasmaniae (1859)†

* * * In the Introductory Essay to the New Zealand Flora, I advanced certain general propositions as to the origin of species, which I refrained from endorsing as articles of my own creed: amongst others was the still prevalent doctrine that these are, in the ordinary acceptation of the term, created as such, and are immutable. In the present Essay I shall advance the opposite hypothesis, that species are derivative and mutable; and this chiefly because, whatever opinions a naturalist may have adopted with regard to the origin and variation of species, every candid mind must admit that the facts and arguments upon which he has grounded his convictions require revision since the recent publication by the Linnean Society of the ingenious and original reasonings and theories of Mr. Darwin and Mr. Wallace. * * *

With regard to my own views on the subjects of the variability of existing species and the fallacy of supposing we can ascertain anything through these alone of their ancestry or of originally created types, they are, in so far as they are liable to influence my estimate of the value of the facts collected for the analysis of the Australian Flora, unaltered from those which I maintained in the 'Flora of New Zealand:' on such theoretical questions, however, as the origin and ultimate permanence of species, they have been greatly influenced by the views and arguments of Mr. Darwin and Mr. Wallace above alluded to, which incline me to regard more favourably the hypothesis that it is to variation that we must look as the means which Nature has adopted for peopling the globe with those diverse existing forms which, when they tend to transmit their characters unchanged through many generations, are called species. * * *

In conformity with my plan of starting from the variable and not the

---

† From Chapter 2 of "Introductory Essay," *The Botany of the Antarctic Voyage of H.M. Discovery and Terror, in the years 1839–1843*, Vol. 2 (London, 1859). Joseph Dalton Hooker (1817–1911), Fellow (and for five years president) of the Royal Society, shared with Darwin and Thomas Henry Huxley the valuable experience of a long voyage of exploration. The fruits of his travels were published in the three volumes of *Botany of the Antarctic*. Hooker and Huxley were two of the earliest of Victorian scientists to rally to Darwin's support. This essay appeared in December 1859, thus putting Hooker in public support of Darwin almost at the moment *The Origin of Species* was published.

fixed aspect of Nature, I have now set down the prominent features of the Vegetable Kingdom, as surveyed from this point of view. From the preceding paragraphs the evidence appears to be certainly in favour of proneness to change in individuals, and of the power to change ceasing only with the life of the individual; and we have still to account for the fact that there are limits to these mutations, and laws that control the changes both as to degree and kind; that species are neither visionary nor even arbitrary creations of the naturalist; that they are, in short, realities, whether only temporarily so or not.

13. Granting then that the tendency of Nature is first to multiply forms of existing plants by graduated changes, and next by destroying some to isolate the rest in area and in character, we are now in a condition to seek some theory of the *modus operandi* of Nature that will give temporary permanence of character to these changelings. And here we must appeal to theory or speculation; for our knowledge of the history of species in relation to one another, and to the incessant mutations of their environing physical conditions, is far too limited and incomplete to afford data for demonstrating the effects of these in the production of any one species in a native state.

Of these speculations by far the most important and philosophical is that of the delimitation of species by natural selection, for which we are indebted to two wholly independent and original thinkers, Mr. Darwin and Mr. Wallace. These authors assume that all animal and vegetable forms are variable, that the average amount of space and annual supply of food for each species (or other group of individuals) is limited and constant, but that the increase of all organisms tends to proceed annually in a geometrical ratio; and that, as the sum of organic life on the surface of the globe does not increase, the individuals annually destroyed must be incalculably great; also that each species is ever warring against many enemies, and only holding its own by a slender tenure. In the ordinary course of nature this annual destruction falls upon the eggs or seeds and young of the organisms, and as it is effected by a multitude of antagonistic, ever-changing natural causes, each more destructive of one organism than of any other, it operates with different effect on each group of individuals, in every locality, and at every returning season. Here then we have an infinite number of varying conditions, and a superabundant supply of variable organisms, to accommodate themselves to these conditions. Now the organisms can have no power of surviving any change in these conditions, except they are endowed with the means of accommodating themselves to it. The exercise of this power may be accompanied by a visible (morphological) change in the form or structure of the individual, or it may not, in which case there is still a change, but a physiological one, not outwardly manifested; but there is always a morphological change if the change of conditions be sudden, or when, through lapse of time, it becomes extreme. The new form is necessarily that best suited to the changed condition, and as its progeny are henceforth additional enemies to the old, they will eventually tend to replace their parent form in the same locality. Further, a greater proportion of the seeds and young of the old will annually be destroyed than of the new, and the survivors of the old, being less well adapted to the locality, will yield less seed, and hence have fewer descendants. * * *

35. From the sum then of our theories, as arranged in accordance with ascertained facts, we may make the following assumptions:—That the principal recognized families of plants which inhabited the globe at and since the Palæozoic period still exist, and therefore have as families survived all intervening geological changes. That of these types some have been transferred, or have migrated, from one hemisphere to another. That it is not unreasonable to suppose that further evidence may be forthcoming which will show that all existing species may have descended genealogically from fewer preexisting ones; that we owe their different forms to the variation of individuals, and the power of limiting them into genera and species to the destruction of some of these varieties, etc., and the increase in individuals of others. Lastly, that the fact of species being with so much uniformity the ultimate and most definable group (the leaves as it were of the family tree), may possibly be owing to the tendency to vary being checked, partly by the ample opportunities each brood of a variety possesses of being fertilized by the pollen of its nearest counterpart, partly by the temporary stability of its surrounding physical conditions, and partly by the superabundance of seeds shed by each individual, those only vegetating which are well suited to existing conditions: an appearance of stability is also, in the case of many perennials, due to the fact that the individuals normally attain a great age,[1] and thus survive many generations of other species, of which generations some present characters foreign to their parents. * * *

37. Again, it is argued by both Mr. Darwin and Mr. Wallace that the general effects of variation by selection must be to establish a general progressive development of the whole animal kingdom. But here again in botany we are checked by the question, What is the standard of progression? Is it physiological or morphological? Is it evidenced by the power of overcoming physical obstacles to dispersion or propagation, or by a nice adaptation of structure or constitution to very restricted or complex conditions? Are cosmopolites to be regarded as superior to plants of restricted range, hermaphrodite plants to unisexual, parasites to self-sustainers, albuminous-seeded to exalbuminous, gymnosperms to angiosperms, water plants to land, trees to herbs, perennials to annuals, insular plants to continental? and, in fine, what is the significance of the multitudinous differences in point of structure and complexity, and powers of endurance, presented by the members of the Vegetable Kingdom, and which have no

---

1. In considering the relative amount and rate at which different plants vary, it should be remembered that we habitually estimate them not only loosely but falsely. We assume annuals to be more variable than perennials, but we probably greatly overrate the amount to which they really are so, because a brief personal experience enables us to study many generations of an annual under many combinations of physical conditions; whereas the same experience embraces but a fractional period of the duration of (comparatively) very few perennials. It has also been well shown by Bentham (in his paper on the British Flora, read (1858) before the Linnæan Society) that an appearance of stability is given to many varieties of perennials, through their habitual increase by buds, offsets, etc., which propagate the individual; and in the case of *Rubi*, which comparatively seldom propagate by seed, a large tract of ground may be peopled by parts of a single individual.

recognized physiological end and interpretation, nor importance in a classificatory point of view? It is extremely easy to answer any of these questions, and to support the opinion by a host of arguments, morphological, physiological, and teleological; but any one gifted with a quick perception of relations, and whose mind is stored with a sufficiency of facts, will turn every argument to equal advantage for both sides of the question.

To my mind, however, the doctrine of progression, if considered in connection with the hypothesis of the origin of species being by variation, is by far the most profound of all that have ever agitated the schools of Natural History, and I do not think that it has yet been treated in the unprejudiced spirit it demands. The elements for its study are the vastest and most complicated which the naturalist can contemplate, and reside in the comprehension of the reciprocal action of the so-called inorganic on the organic world. Granting that multiplication and specialization of organs is the evidence and measure of progression, that variation explains the *rationale* of the operation which results in this progression, the question arises, What are the limits to the combinations of physical causes which determine this progression, and how can the specializing power of Nature stop short of causing every race or family ultimately to represent a species? While the psychological philosophers persuade us that we see the tendency to specialize pervading every attribute of organic life, mental and physical; and the physicists teach that there are limits to the amount and duration of heat, light, and every other manifestation of physical force which our senses present or our intellects perceive, and which are all in process of consumption; the reflecting botanist, knowing that his ultimate results must accord with these facts, is perplexed at feeling that he has failed to establish on independent evidence the doctrines of variation and progressive specialization, or to co-ordinate his attempts to do so with the successive discoveries in physical science. * * *

The arguments deduced from genetic resemblance being (in the present state of science), as far as I can discover, exhausted, I have felt it my duty to re-examine the phenomena of variation in reference to the origin of existing species; these phenomena I have long studied independently of this question, and when treating either of whole Floras or of species. I have made it my constant aim to demonstrate how much more important and prevalent this element of variability is than is usually admitted, as also how deep it lies beneath the foundations of all our facts and reasonings concerning classification and distribution. I have hitherto endeavoured to keep my ideas upon variation in subjection to the hypothesis of species being immutable, both because a due regard to that theory checks any tendency to careless observation of minute facts, and because the opposite one is apt to lead to a precipitate conclusion that slight differences have no significance; whereas, though not of specific importance, they may be of high structural and physiological value, and hence reveal affinities that might otherwise escape us. I have already stated how greatly I am indebted to Mr. Darwin's[2] *rationale* of the phenomena of variation and natural

---

2. In this Essay I refer to the brief abstract only (Linn. Journ.) of my friend's views, not to his work now in the press, a deliberate study of which may modify my opinion on some points whereon we differ. Matured conclusions on these subjects are very slowly developed.

selection in the production of species; and though it does not positively establish the doctrine of creation by variation, I expect that every additional fact and observation relating to species will gain great additional value from being viewed in reference to it, and that it will materially assist in developing the principles of classification and distribution.

THOMAS HENRY HUXLEY

On the Relations of Man to the Lower Animals (1863)†

* * * The question of questions for mankind—the problem which underlies all others, and is more deeply interesting than any other—is the ascertainment of the place which Man occupies in nature and of his relations to the universe of things. Whence our race has come; what are the limits of our power over nature, and of nature's power over us; to what goal we are tending; are the problems which present themselves anew and with undiminished interest to every man born into the world. * * *

As if to demonstrate, by a striking example, the impossibility of erecting any cerebral barrier between man and the apes, Nature has provided us, in the latter animals, with an almost complete series of gradations from brains little higher than that of a Rodent, to brains little lower than that of Man. And it is a remarkable circumstance that though, so far as our present knowledge extends, there *is* one true structural break in the series of forms of Simian brains, this hiatus does not lie between Man and the man-like apes, but between the lower and the lowest Simians; or, in other words, between the old and new world apes and monkeys, and the Lemurs. Every Lemur which has yet been examined, in fact, has its cerebellum partially visible from above, and its posterior lobe, with the contained posterior cornu and hippocampus minor, more or less rudimentary. Every Marmoset, American monkey, old world monkey, Baboon, or Man-like ape, on the contrary, has its cerebellum entirely hidden, posteriorly, by the cerebral lobes, and possesses a large posterior cornu, with a well-developed hippocampus minor. * * *

As to the convolutions, the brains of the apes exhibit every stage of progress, from the almost smooth brain of the Marmoset, to the Orang and the Chimpanzee, which fall but little below Man. And it is most remarkable that, as soon as all the principal sulci appear, the pattern according to which they are arranged is identical with that of the corresponding sulci of man. The surface of the brain of a monkey exhibits a sort of skeleton map of man's, and in the man-like apes the details become more and more filled in, until it is only in minor characters, such as the greater excavation of the anterior lobes, the constant presence of fissures usually absent in man, and the different disposition and proportions of some con-

† From Chapter 2, *Man's Place in Nature* (London, 1863). Thomas Henry Huxley (1825–1895) studied medicine as a young man and matured as a naturalist during a voyage of discovery aboard H. M. S. *Rattlesnake,* at the end of which he was elected a Fellow of the Royal Society. His review of the *Origin* in the London *Times* was an important contribution to public understanding of the book, and for years Huxley was Darwin's ablest advocate, "Darwin's bulldog."

volutions, that the Chimpanzee's or the Orang's brain can be structurally distinguished from Man's.

So far as cerebral structure goes, therefore, it is clear that Man differs less from the Chimpanzee or the Orang, than these do even from the Monkeys, and that the difference between the brains of the Chimpanzee and of Man is almost insignificant, when compared with that between the Chimpanzee brain and that of a Lemur.

It must not be overlooked, however, that there is a very striking difference in the absolute mass and weight between the lowest human brain and that of the highest ape—a difference which is all the more remarkable when we recollect that a full grown Gorilla is probably pretty nearly twice as heavy as a Bosjes man, or as many an European woman. It may be doubted whether a healthy human adult brain ever weighed less than thirty-one or two ounces, or that the heaviest Gorilla brain has exceeded twenty ounces.

This is a very noteworthy circumstance, and doubtless will one day help to furnish an explanation of the great gulf which intervenes between the lowest man and the highest ape in intellectual power,[1] but it has little systematic value, for the simple reason that, as may be concluded from what has been already said respecting cranial capacity, the difference in weight of brain between the highest and the lowest men is far greater, both relatively and absolutely, than that between the lowest man and the highest ape. The latter, as has been seen, is represented by, say twelve, ounces of cerebral substance absolutely, or by 32:20 relatively; but as the largest

---

1. I say *help* to furnish: for I by no means believe that it was any original difference of cerebral quality, or quantity, which caused that divergence between the human and the pithecoid stirpes, which has ended in the present enormous gulf between them. It is no doubt perfectly true, in a certain sense, that all difference of function is a result of difference of structure; or, in other words, of difference in the combination of the primary molecular forces of living substance; and, starting from this undeniable axiom, objectors occasionally, and with much seeming plausibility, argue that the vast intellectual chasm between the Ape and Man implies a corresponding structural chasm in the organs of the intellectual functions; so that, it is said, the non-discovery of such vast differences proves, not that they are absent, but that Science is incompetent to detect them. A very little consideration, however, will, I think, show the fallacy of this reasoning. Its validity hangs upon the assumption, that intellectual power depends altogether on the brain—whereas the brain is only one condition out of many on which intellectual manifestations depend; the others being, chiefly, the organs of the senses and the motor apparatuses, especially those which are concerned in prehension and in the production of articulate speech.

A man born dumb, notwithstanding his great cerebral mass and his inheritance of strong intellectual instincts, would be capable of few higher intellectual manifestations than an Orang or a Chimpanzee, if he were confined to the society of dumb associates. And yet there might not be the slightest discernible difference between his brain and that of a highly intelligent and cultivated person. The dumbness might be the result of a defective structure of the mouth, or of the tongue, or a mere defective innervation of these parts; or it might result from congenital deafness, caused by some minute defect of the internal ear, which only a careful anatomist could discover.

The argument, that because there is an immense difference between a Man's intelligence and an Ape's, therefore, there must be an equally immense difference between their brains, appears to me to be about as well based as the reasoning by which one should endeavour to prove that, because there is a "great gulf" between a watch that keeps accurate time and another that will not go at all, there is therefore a great structural hiatus between the two watches. A hair in the balance-wheel, a little rust on a pinion, a bend in a tooth of the escapement, a something so slight that only the practised eye of the watchmaker can discover it, may be the source of all the difference.

And believing, as I do, with Cuvier, that the possession of articulate speech is the grand distinctive character of man (whether it be absolutely peculiar to him or not), I find it very easy to comprehend, that some equally inconspicuous structural difference may have been the primary cause of the immeasurable and practically infinite divergence of the Human from the Simian Stirps.

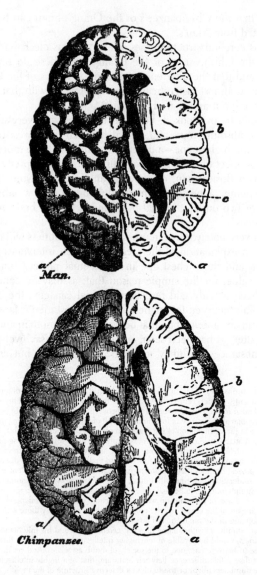

Drawings of the cerebral hemispheres of a Man and of a Chimpanzee of
the same length, in order to show the relative proportions of the parts: the
former taken from a specimen, which Mr. Flower, Conservator of the
Museum of the Royal College of Surgeons, was good enough to dissect
for me; the latter, from the photograph of a similarly dissected Chimpanzee's brain, given in Mr. Marshall's paper above referred to. *a*, posterior
lobe; *b*, lateral ventricle; *c*, posterior cornu; *x*, the hippocampus minor.

recorded human brain weighed between 65 and 66 ounces, the former difference is represented by more than 33 ounces absolutely, or by 65:32 relatively. Regarded systematically the cerebral differences, of man and apes, are not of more than genetic value—his Family distinction resting chiefly on his dentition, his pelvis, and his lower limbs.

Thus, whatever system of organs be studied, the comparison of their modifications in the ape series leads to one and the same result—that the structural differences which separate Man from the Gorilla and the Chimpanzee are not so great as those which separate the Gorilla from the lower apes.

But in enunciating this important truth I must guard myself against a form of misunderstanding, which is very prevalent. I find, in fact, that those who endeavour to teach what nature so clearly shows us in this matter, are liable to have their opinions misrepresented and their phraseology garbled, until they seem to say that the structural differences between man and even the highest apes are small and insignificant. Let me take this opportunity then of distinctly asserting, on the contrary, that they are great and significant; that every bone of a Gorilla bears marks by which it might be distinguished from the corresponding bone of a Man; and that, in the present creation, at any rate, no intermediate link bridges over the gap between *Homo* and *Troglodytes*.

It would be no less wrong than absurd to deny the existence of this chasm; but it is at least equally wrong and absurd to exaggerate its magnitude, and, resting on the admitted fact of its existence, to refuse to inquire whether it is wide or narrow. Remember, if you will, that there is no existing link between Man and the Gorilla, but do not forget that there is no less sharp line of demarcation, a no less complete absence of any transitional form, between the Gorilla and the Orang, or the Orang and the Gibbon. I say, not less sharp, though it is somewhat narrower. The structural differences between Man and the Man-like apes certainly justify our regarding him as constituting a family apart from them; though, inasmuch as he differs less from them than they do from other families of the same order, there can be no justification for placing him in a distinct order.

And thus the sagacious foresight of the great lawgiver of systematic zoology, Linnæus, becomes justified, and a century of anatomical research brings us back to his conclusion, that man is a member of the same order (for which the Linnæan term PRIMATES ought to be retained) as the Apes and Lemurs. This order is now divisible into seven families, of about equal systematic value: the first, the ANTHROPINI, contains Man alone; the second, the CATARHINI, embraces the old world apes; the third, the PLATYRHINI, all new world apes, except the Marmosets; the fourth, the ARCTOPITHECINI, contains the Marmosets; the fifth, the LEMURINI, the Lemurs—from which *Cheiromys* should probably be excluded to form a sixth distinct family, the CHEIROMYINI; while the seventh, the GALEOPITHECINI, contains only the flying Lemur *Galeopithecus*,—a strange form which almost touches on the Bats, as the *Cheiromys* puts on a rodent clothing, and the Lemurs simulate Insectivora.

Perhaps no order of mammals presents us with so extraordinary a series of gradations as this—leading us insensibly from the crown and summit of the animal creation down to creatures, from which there is but a step, as it seems, to the lowest, smallest, and least intelligent of the placental Mammalia. It is as if nature herself had foreseen the arrogance of man, and with Roman severity had provided that his intellect, by its very triumphs, should call into prominence the slaves, admonishing the conqueror that he is but dust.

These are the chief facts, this the immediate conclusion from them to which I adverted the commencement of this Essay. The facts, I believe, cannot be disputed; and if so, the conclusion appears to me to be inevitable.

But if Man be separated by no greater structural barrier, from the brutes than they are from one another—then it seems to follow that if any process of physical causation can be discovered by which the genera and families of ordinary animals have been produced, that process of causation is amply sufficient to account for the origin of Man. In other words, if it could be shown that the Marmosets, for example, have arisen by gradual modification of the ordinary Platyrhini, or that both Marmosets and Platyrhini are modified ramifications of a primitive stock—then, there would be no rational ground for doubting that man might have originated, in the one case, by the gradual modification of a man-like ape; or, in the other case, as a ramification of the same primitive stock as those apes.

At the present moment, but one such process of physical causation has any evidence in its favour; or, in other words, there is but one hypothesis regarding the origin of species of animals in general which has any scientific existence—that propounded by Mr. Darwin. For Lamarck, sagacious as many of his views were, mingled them with so much that was crude and even absurd, as to neutralize the benefit which his originality might have effected, had he been a more sober and cautious thinker; and though I have heard of the announcement of a formula touching "the ordained continuous becoming of organic forms," it is obvious that it is the first duty of a hypothesis to be intelligible, and that a qua-quâ-versal proposition of this kind, which may be read backwards, or forwards, or sideways, with exactly the same amount of signification, does not really exist, though it may seem to do so.

At the present moment, therefore, the question of the relation of man to the lower animals resolves itself, in the end, into the larger question of the tenability or untenability of Mr. Darwin's views. But here we enter upon difficult ground, and it behoves us to define our exact position with the greatest care.

It cannot be doubted, I think, that Mr. Darwin has satisfactorily proved that what he terms selection, or selective modification, must occur, and does occur, in nature; and he has also proved to superfluity that such selection is competent to produce forms as distinct structurally, as some genera even are. If the animated world presented us with none but structural differences, I should have no hesitation in saying that Mr. Darwin had demonstrated the existence of a true physical cause, amply competent to account for the origin of living species, and of man among the rest.

But, in addition to their structural distinctions, the species of animals and plants, or at least a great number of them, exhibit physiological characters—what are known as distinct species, structurally, being for the most part either altogether incompetent to breed one with another; or if they breed, the resulting mule, or hybrid, is unable to perpetuate its race with another hybrid of the same kind.

A true physical cause is, however, admitted to be such only on one condition—that it shall account for all the phenomena which come within the range of its operation. If it is inconsistent with any one phenomenon, it must be rejected; if it fails to explain any one phenomenon, it is so far weak, so far to be suspected; though it may have a perfect right to claim provisional acceptance.

Now, Mr. Darwin's hypothesis is not, so far as I am aware, inconsistent with any known biological fact; on the contrary, if admitted, the facts of Development, of Comparative Anatomy, of Geographical Distribution, and of Palæontology, become connected together, and exhibit a meaning such as they never possessed before; and I, for one, am fully convinced, that if not precisely true, that hypothesis is as near an approximation to the truth as, for example, the Copernican hypothesis was to the true theory of the planetary motions. * * *

CHARLES LYELL

Principles of Geology (1867)†

* * * In former editions of this work from 1832 to 1853, I did not venture to differ from the opinion of Linnæus, that each species had remained from its origin such as we now see it, being variable, but only within certain fixed limits. The mystery in which the origin of each species was involved seemed to me no greater than that in which the beginning of all vital phenomena on the earth is shrouded. * * *

* * * Mr. Charles Darwin* * * had been for many years busily engaged in collecting materials for a great work on the origin of species; having made for that purpose a vast series of original observations and experiments on domesticated animals and cultivated plants, and having reflected profoundly on those problems in geology and biology which were calculated to throw most light on that question. For eighteen years these researches had all been pointing to the same conclusion, namely, that the species now living had been derived by variation and generation from those which had pre-existed, and these again from others of still older date.

† From Chapter 35, *Principles of Geology*, 11th ed. (New York, 1883). Charles Lyell (1797–1875) was a Fellow of the Royal Society and president of the British Association. His three-volume *Principles of Geology*, which went through eleven editions in his lifetime, illustrates by its continual accretions the progress of geology over half a century. Lyell was the most reluctant of Darwin's several confidants to come out publicly in support of evolution. His remarks on the subject in *The Antiquity of Man* (1863) were deeply disappointing to Darwin, and there was no new edition of the *Principles* until 1867, in which the passage printed here appeared.

Several of his MS. volumes on this subject had been read by Dr. Hooker as long ago as 1844, and how long the ever-accumulating store of facts and reasonings might have remained unknown to the general public, had no one else attempted to work out the same problem, it is impossible to say. But at length Mr. Darwin received a communication, dated February 1858, from Mr. Wallace, then residing at Ternate in the Malay Archipelago, entitled 'On the Tendency of Varieties to depart indefinitely from the Original Type.'

The Author requested Mr. Darwin to show this essay to me should he think it sufficiently novel and interesting. It was brought to me by Dr. Hooker, who remarked how complete was the coincidence of Mr. Wallace's new views and those contained in one of the chapters of Mr. Darwin's unpublished work. Accordingly, he suggested that it would be unfair to let Mr. Wallace's essay go to press unaccompanied by the older memoir on the same subject. Although, therefore, Mr. Darwin was willing to waive his claim to priority, the two papers were read on the same evening to the Linnæn Society and published in their Proceedings for 1858. The title of the chapter extracted from Mr. Darwin's MS. ran as follows: 'On the Tendency of Species to form Varieties, and on the Perpetuation of Species and Varieties by Natural Means of Selection.'

Already in the previous year, September 1857, Mr. Darwin had sent to Professor Asa Gray, the celebrated American botanist, a brief sketch of his forthcoming treatise on what he then termed 'Natural Selection.' This letter, also printed by the Linnæn Society together with the papers above alluded to, contained an outline of the leading features of his theory of selection as since explained, showing how new races were formed by the breeder, and how analogous results might or must occur in nature under changed conditions in the animate and inanimate world. Reference was made in the same letter to the law of human population first enunciated by Malthus, or the tendency in man to increase in a geometrical ratio, while the means of subsistence cannot be made to augment in the same ratio. We were reminded that in some countries the human population has doubled in twenty-five years, and would have multiplied faster if food could have been supplied. In like manner every animal and plant is capable of increasing so rapidly, that if it were unchecked by other species, it would soon occupy the greater part of the habitable globe; but in the general struggle for life few only of those which are born into the world can obtain subsistence and arrive at maturity. In any given species those alone survive which have some advantage over others, and this is often determined by a slight peculiarity capable in a severe competition of turning the scale in their favour. Notwithstanding the resemblance to each other and to their parents of all the individuals of the same family, no two of them are exactly alike. The breeder chooses out from among the varieties presented to him those best suited to his purpose, and the divergence from the original stock is more and more increased by breeding in each successive generation from individuals which possess the desired characters in the most marked degree. In this manner Mr. Darwin suggests that as the surrounding conditions in the organic and inorganic world slowly alter in the course of geological periods, new races which are more in harmony with the altered state of things must be formed in a state of nature, and must often supplant the parent type.

Although this law of natural selection constituted one only of the grounds on which Mr. Darwin relied for establishing his views as to the origin of species by variation, yet it formed so original and prominent a part of his theory that the fact of Mr. Wallace having independently thought out the same principle and illustrated it by singularly analogous examples, is remarkable. It raises at the same time a strong presumption in favour of the truth of the doctrine. * * *

After the publication of the detached chapter of his book in the Linnæan Proceedings, Mr. Darwin was persuaded by his friends that he ought no longer to withhold from the world the result of his investigations on the nature and origin of species, and his theory of Natural Selection. Great was the sensation produced in the scientific world by the appearance of the abridged and condensed statement of his views comprised in his work entitled 'On the Origin of Species by means of Natural Selection, or the Preservation of Favoured Races in the Struggle for Life.' From the hour of its appearance it gave, as Professor Huxley truly said, 'a new direction to biological speculation,' for even where it failed to make proselytes, it gave a shock to old and time-honoured opinions from which they have never since recovered. It effected this not merely by the manner in which it explained how new races and species might be formed by Natural Selection, but also by showing that, if we assume this principle, much light is thrown on many very distinct and otherwise unconnected classes of phenomena, both in the present condition and past history of the organic world. * * *

ALFRED RUSSEL WALLACE

The Debt of Science to Darwin (1883)†

These works [Darwin's early works], * * * great as is each of them separately, and, taken altogether, amazing as the production of one man, sink into insignificance as compared with the vast body of research and of thought of which the *Origin of Species* is the brief epitome, and with which alone the name of Darwin is associated by the mass of educated men. I have here endeavoured, however imperfectly, to enable non-specialists to judge of the character and extent of this work, and of the vast revolution it has effected in our conception of nature,—a revolution altogether independent of the question whether the theory of "natural selection" is or is not as important a factor in bringing about changes of animal and vegetable forms as its author maintained. Let us consider for a moment the state of mind induced by the new theory and that which preceded it. So long as men believed that every species was the immediate handiwork of

† From *Natural Selection and Tropical Nature* (London, 1883). Alfred Russel Wallace (1823–1913), co-discoverer of natural selection, became a friend of Darwin's and a lifelong supporter. This tribute was published a year after Darwin's death.

the Creator, and was therefore absolutely perfect, they remained altogether
blind to the meaning of the countless variations and adaptations of the
parts and organs of plants and animals. They who were always repeating,
parrot-like, that every organism was exactly adapted to its conditions and
surroundings by an all-wise being, were apparently dulled or incapacitated
by this belief from any inquiry into the inner meaning of what they saw
around them, and were content to pass over whole classes of facts as inexplicable, and to ignore countless details of structure under vague notions
of a "general plan," or of variety and beauty being "ends in themselves";
while he whose teachings were at first stigmatised as degrading or even
atheistical, by devoting to the varied phenomena of living things the loving,
patient, and reverent study of one who really had *faith* in the beauty and
harmony and perfection of creation, was enabled to bring to light innumerable hidden adaptations, and to prove that the most insignificant parts
of the meanest living things had a use and a purpose, were worthy of our
earnest study, and fitted to excite our highest and most intelligent admiration.

   That he has done this is the sufficient answer to his critics and to his
few detractors. However much our knowledge of nature may advance in
the future, it will certainly be by following in the pathways he has made
clear for us; and for long years to come the name of Darwin will stand
for the typical example of what the student of nature ought to be. And if
we glance back over the whole domain of science, we shall find none to
stand beside him as equals; for in him we find a patient observation and
collection of facts, as in Tycho Brahe; the power of using those facts in
the determination of laws, as in Kepler, combined with the inspirational
genius of a Newton, through which he was enabled to grasp fundamental
principles, and so apply them as to bring order out of chaos, and illuminate
the world of life as Newton illuminated the material universe. * * *

Darwin and the Shaping of Modern Science

Scientific Method in Evolution

NATIONAL ACADEMY OF SCIENCES

Evolution and the Nature of Science (1999)†

Science is a particular way of knowing about the world. In science, explanations are limited to those based on observations and experiments that can be substantiated by other scientists. Explanations that cannot be based on empirical evidence are not a part of science.

In the quest for understanding, science involves a great deal of careful observation that eventually produces an elaborate written description of the natural world. Scientists communicate their findings and conclusions to other scientists through publications, talks at conferences, hallway conversations, and many other means. Other scientists then test those ideas and build on preexisting work. In this way, the accuracy and sophistication of descriptions of the natural world tend to increase with time, as subsequent generations of scientists correct and extend the work done by their predecessors.

Progress in science consists of the development of better explanations for the causes of natural phenomena. Scientists never can be sure that a given explanation is complete and final. Some of the hypotheses advanced by scientists turn out to be incorrect when tested by further observations or experiments. Yet many scientific explanations have been so thoroughly tested and confirmed that they are held with great confidence.

The theory of evolution is one of these well-established explanations. An enormous amount of scientific investigation since the mid-19th century has converted early ideas about evolution proposed by Darwin and others into a strong and well-supported theory. Today, evolution is an extremely active field of research, with an abundance of new discoveries that are continually increasing our understanding of how evolution occurs.

* * *

† From *Science and Creationism: A View from the National Academy of Sciences* (Washington, D.C., 1999). Copyright © 1999 by the National Academy of Sciences.

The theory of evolution has become the central unifying concept of biology and is a critical component of many related scientific disciplines. In contrast, the claims of creation science lack empirical support and cannot be meaningfully tested. These observations lead to two fundamental conclusions: the teaching of evolution should be an integral part of science instruction, and creation science is in fact not science and should not be presented as such in science classes.

Terms Used in Describing the Nature of Science[1]

Fact: In science, an observation that has been repeatedly confirmed and for all practical purposes is accepted as "true." Truth in science, however, is never final, and what is accepted as a fact today may be modified or even discarded tomorrow.

Hypothesis: A tentative statement about the natural world leading to deductions that can be tested. If the deductions are verified, it becomes more probable that the hypothesis is correct. If the deductions are incorrect, the original hypothesis can be abandoned or modified. Hypotheses can be used to build more complex inferences and explanations.

Law: A descriptive generalization about how some aspect of the natural world behaves under stated circumstances.

Theory: In science, a well-substantiated explanation of some aspect of the natural world that can incorporate facts, laws, inferences, and tested hypotheses.

The contention that evolution should be taught as a "theory, not as a fact" confuses the common use of these words with the scientific use. In science, theories do not turn into facts through the accumulation of evidence. Rather, theories are the end points of science. They are understandings that develop from extensive observation, experimentation, and creative reflection. They incorporate a large body of scientific facts, laws, tested hypotheses, and logical inferences. In this sense, evolution is one of the strongest and most useful scientific theories we have.

1. Adapted from *Teaching About Evolution and the Nature of Science* by the National Academy of Sciences (Washington, D.C.: National Academy Press, 1998).

Evidence Supporting Biological Evolution

A long path leads from the origins of primitive "life," which existed at least 3.5 billion years ago, to the profusion and diversity of life that exists today. This path is best understood as a product of evolution.

Contrary to popular opinion, neither the term nor the idea of biological evolution began with Charles Darwin and his foremost work, *On the Origin of Species by Means of Natural Selection* (1859). Many scholars from the ancient Greek philosophers on had inferred that similar species were descended from a common ancestor. The word "evolution" first appeared in the English language in 1647 in a nonbiological connection, and it became widely used in English for all sorts of progressions from simpler beginnings. The term Darwin most often used to refer to biological evolution was "descent with modification," which remains a good brief definition of the process today.

Darwin proposed that evolution could be explained by the differential survival of organisms following their naturally occurring variation—a process he termed "natural selection." According to this view, the offspring of organisms differ from one another and from their parents in ways that are heritable—that is, they can pass on the differences genetically to their own offspring. Furthermore, organisms in nature typically produce more offspring than can survive and reproduce given the constraints of food, space, and other environmental resources. If a particular offspring has traits that give it an advantage in a particular environment, that organism will be more likely to survive and pass on those traits. As differences accumulate over generations, populations of organisms diverge from their ancestors.

Darwin's original hypothesis has undergone extensive modification and expansion, but the central concepts stand firm. Studies in genetics and molecular biology—fields unknown in Darwin's time—have explained the occurrence of the hereditary variations that are essential to natural selection. Genetic variations result from changes, or mutations, in the nucleotide sequence of DNA, the molecule that genes are made from. Such changes in DNA now can be detected and described with great precision.

Genetic mutations arise by chance. They may or may not equip the organism with better means for surviving in its environment. But if a gene variant improves adaptation to the environment (for example, by allowing an organism to make better use of an available nutrient, or to escape predators more effectively—such as through stronger legs or disguising coloration), the organisms carrying that gene are more likely to survive and reproduce than those without it. Over time, their descendants will tend to increase, changing the average characteristics of the population. Although the genetic variation on which natural selection works is based on random or chance elements, natural selection itself produces "adaptive" change—the very opposite of chance.

Scientists also have gained an understanding of the processes by which new species originate. A new species is one in which the individuals cannot mate and produce viable descendants with individuals of a preexisting species. The split of one species into two often starts because a group of individuals becomes geographically separated from the rest. This is particularly apparent in distant remote islands, such as the Galápagos and the Hawaiian archipelago, whose great distance from the Americas and Asia means that arriving colonizers will have little or no opportunity to mate with individuals remaining on those continents. Mountains, rivers, lakes, and other natural barriers also account for geographic separation between populations that once belonged to the same species.

Once isolated, geographically separated groups of individuals become genetically differentiated as a consequence of mutation and other processes, including natural selection. The origin of a species is often a gradual process, so that at first the reproductive isolation between separated groups of organisms is only partial, but it eventually becomes complete. Scientists pay special attention to these intermediate situations, because they help to reconstruct the details of the process and to identify particular genes or sets of genes that account for the reproductive isolation between species.

A particularly compelling example of speciation involves the 13 species of finches studied by Darwin on the Galápagos Islands, now known as Darwin's finches. The ancestors of these finches appear to have immigrated from the South American mainland to the Galápagos. Today the different species of finches on the island have distinct habitats, diets, and behaviors, but the mechanisms involved in speciation continue to operate. A research group led by Peter and Rosemary Grant of Princeton University has shown that a single year of drought on the islands can drive evolutionary changes in the finches. Drought diminishes supplies of easily cracked nuts but permits the survival of plants that produce larger, tougher nuts. Droughts thus favor birds with strong, wide beaks that can break these tougher seeds, producing populations of birds with these traits. The Grants have estimated that if droughts occur about once every 10 years on the islands, a new species of finch might arise in only about 200 years.

The following sections consider several aspects of biological evolution in greater detail, looking at paleontology, comparative anatomy, biogeography, embryology, and molecular biology for further evidence supporting evolution.

THE FOSSIL RECORD

Although it was Darwin, above all others, who first marshaled convincing evidence for biological evolution, earlier scholars had recognized that organisms on Earth had changed systematically over long periods of time. For example, in 1799 an engineer named William Smith reported that, in undisrupted layers of rock, fossils occurred in a definite sequential order, with more modern-appearing ones closer to the top. Because bottom layers of rock logically were laid down earlier and thus are older than top layers, the sequence of fossils also could be given a chronology from oldest to youngest. His findings were confirmed and extended in the 1830s by the paleontologist William Lonsdale, who recognized that fossil remains of organisms from lower strata were more primitive than the ones above. Today, many thousands of ancient rock deposits have been identified that show corresponding successions of fossil organisms.

Thus, the general sequence of fossils had already been recognized before Darwin conceived of descent with modification. But the paleontologists and geologists before Darwin used the sequence of fossils in rocks not as proof of biological evolution, but as a basis for working out the original sequence of rock strata that had been structurally disturbed by earthquakes and other forces.

In Darwin's time, paleontology was still a rudimentary science. Large parts of the geological succession of stratified rocks were unknown or inadequately studied. Darwin, therefore, worried about the rarity of intermediate forms between some major groups of organisms.

Today, many of the gaps in the paleontological record have been filled by the research of paleontologists. Hundreds of thousands of fossil organisms, found in well-dated rock sequences, represent successions of forms through time and manifest many evolutionary transitions. As mentioned earlier, microbial life of the simplest type was already in existence 3.5 billion years ago. The oldest evidence of more complex organisms (that is, eucaryotic cells, which are more complex than bacteria) has been discovered in fossils sealed in rocks approximately 2 billion years old. Multicellular organisms, which are the familiar fungi, plants, and animals, have been found only in younger geological strata. * * *

So many intermediate forms have been discovered between fish and amphibians, between amphibians and reptiles, between reptiles and mammals, and along the primate lines of descent that it often is difficult to identify categorically when the transition occurs from one to another particular species. Actually, nearly all fossils can be regarded as intermediates in some sense; they are life forms that come between the forms that preceded them and those that followed.

The fossil record thus provides consistent evidence of systematic change through time—of descent with modification. From this huge body of evidence, it can be predicted that no reversals will be found in future paleontological studies. That is, amphibians will not appear before fishes, nor mammals before reptiles, and no complex life will occur in the geological record before the oldest eucaryotic cells. This prediction has been upheld by the evidence that has accumulated until now: no reversals have been found.

COMMON STRUCTURES

Inferences about common descent derived from paleontology are reinforced by comparative anatomy. For example, the skeletons of humans, mice, and bats are strikingly similar, despite the different ways of life of these animals and the diversity of environments in which they flourish. The correspondence of these animals, bone by bone, can be observed in every part of the body, including the limbs; yet a person writes, a mouse runs, and a bat flies with structures built of bones that are different in detail but similar in general structure and relation to each other.

Scientists call such structures homologies and have concluded that they are best explained by common descent. Comparative anatomists investigate such homologies, not only in bone structure but also in other parts of the body, working out relationships from degrees of similarity. Their conclusions provide important inferences about the details of evolutionary history, inferences that can be tested by comparisons with the sequence of ancestral forms in the paleontological record.

The mammalian ear and jaw are instances in which paleontology and comparative anatomy combine to show common ancestry through transitional stages. The lower jaws of mammals contain only one bone, whereas those of reptiles have several. The other bones in the reptile jaw are ho-mologous with bones now found in the mammalian ear. Paleontologists have discovered intermediate forms of mammal-like reptiles (Therapsida) with a double jaw joint—one composed of the bones that persist in mam-malian jaws, the other consisting of bones that eventually became the hammer and anvil of the mammalian ear.

THE DISTRIBUTION OF SPECIES

Biogeography also has contributed evidence for descent from common ancestors. The diversity of life is stupendous. Approximately 250,000 spe-cies of living plants, 100,000 species of fungi, and one million species of animals have been described and named, each occupying its own peculiar ecological setting or niche; and the census is far from complete. Some species, such as human beings and our companion the dog, can live under a wide range of environments. Others are amazingly specialized. One spe-cies of a fungus (*Laboulbenia*) grows exclusively on the rear portion of the covering wings of a single species of beetle (*Aphaenops crunei*) found only in some caves of southern France. The larvae of the fly *Drosophila car-cinophila* can develop only in specialized grooves beneath the flaps of the third pair of oral appendages of a land crab that is found only on certain Caribbean islands.

How can we make intelligible the colossal diversity of living beings and the existence of such extraordinary, seemingly whimsical creatures as the fungus, beetle, and fly described above? And why are island groups like the Galápagos so often inhabited by forms similar to those on the nearest mainland but belonging to different species? Evolutionary theory explains that biological diversity results from the descendants of local or migrant predecessors becoming adapted to their diverse environments. This expla-nation can be tested by examining present species and local fossils to see whether they have similar structures, which would indicate how one is derived from the other. Also, there should be evidence that species without an established local ancestry had migrated into the locality.

Wherever such tests have been carried out, these conditions have been confirmed. A good example is provided by the mammalian populations of North and South America, where strikingly different native organisms evolved in isolation until the emergence of the isthmus of Panama ap-proximately 3 million years ago. Thereafter, the armadillo, porcupine, and opossum—mammals of South American origin—migrated north, along with many other species of plants and animals, while the mountain lion and other North American species made their way across the isthmus to the south.

The evidence that Darwin found for the influence of geographical dis-tribution on the evolution of organisms has become stronger with advanc-ing knowledge. For example, approximately 2,000 species of flies belonging to the genus *Drosophila* are now found throughout the world. About one-quarter of them live only in Hawaii. More than a thousand species of snails and other land mollusks also are found only in Hawaii. The biological explanation for the multiplicity of related species in remote localities is that such great diversity is a consequence of their evolution from a few common ancestors that colonized an isolated environment. The Hawaiian Islands are far from any mainland or other islands, and on the basis of geological evidence they never have been attached to other lands. Thus, the few colonizers that reached the Hawaiian Islands found many available ecological niches, where they could over numerous generations, undergo evolutionary change and diversification.

*   *   *

SIMILARITIES DURING DEVELOPMENT

Embryology, the study of biological development from the time of conception, is another source of independent evidence for common descent. Barnacles, for instance, are sedentary crustaceans with little apparent similarity to such other crustaceans as lobsters, shrimps, or copepods. Yet barnacles pass through a free-swimming larval stage in which they look like other crustacean larvae. The similarity of larval stages supports the conclusion that all crustaceans have homologous parts and a common ancestry.

Similarly, a wide variety of organisms from fruit flies to worms to mice to humans have very similar sequences of genes that are active early in development. These genes influence body segmentation or orientation in all these diverse groups. The presence of such similar genes doing similar things across such a wide range of organisms is best explained by their having been present in a very early common ancestor of all of these groups.

NEW EVIDENCE FROM MOLECULAR BIOLOGY

The unifying principle of common descent that emerges from all the foregoing lines of evidence is being reinforced by the discoveries of modern biochemistry and molecular biology.

The code used to translate nucleotide sequences into amino acid sequences is essentially the same in all organisms. Moreover, proteins in all organisms are invariably composed of the same set of 20 amino acids. This unity of composition and function is a powerful argument in favor of the common descent of the most diverse organisms.

In 1959, scientists at Cambridge University in the United Kingdom determined the three-dimensional structures of two proteins that are found in almost every multicelled animal: hemoglobin and myoglobin. Hemoglobin is the protein that carries oxygen in the blood. Myoglobin receives oxygen from hemoglobin and stores it in the tissues until needed. These were the first three-dimensional protein structures to be solved, and they yielded some key insights. Myoglobin has a single chain of 153 amino acids wrapped around a group of iron and other atoms (called "heme") to which oxygen binds. Hemoglobin, in contrast, is made up of four chains: two identical chains consisting of 141 amino acids, and two other identical chains consisting of 146 amino acids. However, each chain has a heme exactly like that of myoglobin, and each of the four chains in the hemoglobin molecule is folded exactly like myoglobin. It was immediately obvious in 1959 that the two molecules are very closely related.

During the next two decades, myoglobin and hemoglobin sequences were determined for dozens of mammals, birds, reptiles, amphibians, fish, worms, and molluscs. All of these sequences were so obviously related that they could be compared with confidence with the three-dimensional structures of two selected standards—whale myoglobin and horse hemoglobin. Even more significantly, the differences between sequences from different organisms could be used to construct a family tree of hemoglobin and myoglobin variation among organisms. This tree agreed completely with observations derived from paleontology and anatomy about the common descent of the corresponding organisms.

Similar family histories have been obtained from the three-dimensional structures and amino acid sequences of other proteins, such as cytochrome c (a protein engaged in energy transfer) and the digestive proteins trypsin and chymotrypsin. The examination of molecular structure offers a new and extremely powerful tool for studying evolutionary relationships. The quantity of information is potentially huge—as large as the thousands of different proteins contained in living organisms, and limited only by the time and resources of molecular biologists.

*   *   *

The evidence for evolution from molecular biology is overwhelming and is growing quickly. In some cases, this molecular evidence makes it possible to go beyond the paleontological evidence. For example, it has long been postulated that whales descended from land mammals that had returned to the sea. From anatomical and paleontological evidence, the whales' closest living land relatives seemed to be the even-toed hoofed mammals (modern cattle, sheep, camels, goats, etc.). Recent comparisons of some milk protein genes (beta-casein and kappa-casein) have confirmed this relationship and have suggested that the closest land-bound living relative of whales may be the hippopotamus. In this case, molecular biology has augmented the fossil record.

CREATIONISM AND THE EVIDENCE FOR EVOLUTION

Some creationists cite what they say is an incomplete fossil record as evidence for the failure of evolutionary theory. The fossil record was incomplete in Darwin's time, but many of the important gaps that existed then have been filled by subsequent paleontological research. Perhaps the most persuasive fossil evidence for evolution is the consistency of the sequence of fossils from early to recent. Nowhere on Earth do we find, for example, mammals in Devonian (the age of fishes) strata, or human fossils coexisting with dinosaur remains. Undisturbed strata with simple unicellular organisms predate those with multicellular organisms, and invertebrates precede vertebrates; nowhere has this sequence been found inverted. Fossils from adjacent strata are more similar than fossils from temporally distant strata. The most reasonable scientific conclusion that can be drawn from the fossil record is that descent with modification has taken place as stated in evolutionary theory.

Special creationists argue that "no one has seen evolution occur." This misses the point about how science tests hypotheses. We don't see Earth going around the sun or the atoms that make up matter. We "see" their consequences. Scientists infer that atoms exist and Earth revolves because they have tested predictions derived from these concepts by extensive observation and experimentation.

Furthermore, on a minor scale, we "experience" evolution occurring every day. The annual changes in influenza viruses and the emergence of antibiotic-resistant bacteria are both products of evolutionary forces. Indeed, the rapidity with which organisms with short generation times, such as bacteria and viruses, can evolve under the influence of their environments is of great medical significance. Many laboratory experiments have shown that, because of mutation and natural selection, such microorganisms can change in specific ways from those of immediately preceding generations.

On a larger scale, the evolution of mosquitoes resistant to insecticides is another example of the tenacity and adaptability of organisms under environmental stress. Similarly, malaria parasites have become resistant to the drugs that were used extensively to combat them for many years. As a consequence, malaria is on the increase, with more than 300 million clinical cases of malaria occurring every year.

Molecular evolutionary data counter a recent proposition called "intelligent design theory." Proponents of this idea argue that structural complexity is proof of the direct hand of God in specially creating organisms as they are today. These arguments echo those of the 18th century cleric William Paley who held that the vertebrate eye, because of its intricate organization, had been specially designed in its present form by an omnipotent Creator. Modern-day intelligent design proponents argue that molecular structures such as DNA, or molecular processes such as the many steps that blood goes through when it clots, are so irreducibly complex that they can function only if all the components are operative at once. Thus, proponents of intelligent design say that these structures and processes could not have evolved in the stepwise mode characteristic of natural selection.

However, structures and processes that are claimed to be "irreducibly" complex typically are not on closer inspection. For example, it is incorrect to assume that a complex structure or biochemical process can function only if all its components are present and functioning as we see them today. Complex biochemical systems can be built up from simpler systems through natural selection. Thus, the "history" of a protein can be traced through simpler organisms. Jawless fish have a simpler hemoglobin than do jawed fish, which in turn have a simpler hemoglobin than mammals.

The evolution of complex molecular systems can occur in several ways. Natural selection can bring together parts of a system for one function at one time and then, at a later time, recombine those parts with other systems of components to produce a system that has a different function.

Genes can be duplicated, altered, and then amplified through natural selection. The complex biochemical cascade resulting in blood clotting has been explained in this fashion.

Similarly, evolutionary mechanisms are capable of explaining the origin of highly complex anatomical structures. For example, eyes may have evolved independently many times during the history of life on Earth. The steps proceed from a simple eye spot made up of light-sensitive retinula cells (as is now found in the flatworm), to formation of individual photo-sensitive units (ommatidia) in insects with light focusing lenses, to the eventual formation of an eye with a single lens focusing images onto a retina. In humans and other vertebrates, the retina consists not only of photoreceptor cells but also of several types of neurons that begin to an-alyze the visual image. Through such gradual steps, very different kinds of eyes have evolved, from simple light-sensing organs to highly complex systems for vision.

Human Evolution

Studies in evolutionary biology have led to the conclusion that human beings arose from ancestral primates. This association was hotly debated among scientists in Darwin's day. But today there is no significant scientific doubt about the close evolutionary relationships among all primates, in-cluding humans.

Many of the most important advances in paleontology over the past century relate to the evolutionary history of humans. Not one but many connecting links—intermediate between and along various branches of the human family tree—have been found as fossils. These linking fossils occur in geological deposits of intermediate age. They document the time and rate at which primate and human evolution occurred.

Scientists have unearthed thousands of fossil specimens representing members of the human family. A great number of these cannot be assigned to the modern human species, *Homo sapiens*. Most of these specimens have been well dated, often by means of radiometric techniques. They reveal a well-branched tree, parts of which trace a general evolutionary sequence leading from ape-like forms to modern humans.

Paleontologists have discovered numerous species of extinct apes in rock strata that are older than four million years, but never a member of the human family at that great age. *Australopithecus*, whose earliest known fossils are about four million years old, is a genus with some features closer to apes and some closer to modern humans. In brain size, *Australopithecus* was barely more advanced than apes. A number of features, including long arms, short legs, intermediate toe structure, and features of the upper limb, indicate that the members of this species spent part of the time in trees. But they also walked upright on the ground, like humans. Bipedal tracks of *Australopithecus* have been discovered, beautifully preserved with those of other extinct animals, in hardened volcanic ash. Most of our *Australo-pithecus* ancestors died out close to two-and-a-half million years ago, while other *Australopithecus* species, which were on side branches of the human tree, survived alongside more advanced hominids for another million years.

Distinctive bones of the oldest species of the human genus, *Homo*, date back to rock strata about 2.4 million years old. Physical anthropologists agree that *Homo* evolved from one of the species of *Australopithecus*. By two million years ago, early members of *Homo* had an average brain size one-and-a-half times larger than that of *Australopithecus*, though still substantially smaller than that of modern humans. The shapes of the pelvic and leg bones suggest that these early *Homo* were not part-time climbers like *Australopithecus* but walked and ran on long legs, as modern humans do. Just as *Australopithecus* showed a complex of ape-like, human-like, and intermediate features, so was early *Homo* intermediate between *Australopithecus* and modern humans in some features, and close to modern humans in other respects. The earliest stone tools are of virtually the same age as the earliest fossils of *Homo*. Early *Homo*, with its larger brain than *Australopithecus*, was a maker of stone tools.

The fossil record for the interval between 2.4 million years ago and the present includes the skeletal remains of several species assigned to the genus *Homo*. The more recent species had larger brains than the older ones. This fossil record is complete enough to show that the human genus first spread from its place of origin in Africa to Europe and Asia a little less than two million years ago. Distinctive types of stone tools are associated with various populations. More recent species with larger brains generally used more sophisticated tools than more ancient species.

Molecular biology also has provided strong evidence of the close relationship between humans and apes. Analysis of many proteins and genes has shown that humans are genetically similar to chimpanzees and gorillas and less similar to orangutans and other primates.

DNA has even been extracted from a well-preserved skeleton of the extinct human creature known as Neanderthal, a member of the genus *Homo* and often considered either as a subspecies of *Homo sapiens* or as a separate species. Application of the molecular clock, which makes use of known rates of genetic mutation, suggests that Neanderthal's lineage diverged from that of modern *Homo sapiens* less than half a million years ago, which is entirely compatible with evidence from the fossil record.

Based on molecular and genetic data, evolutionists favor the hypothesis that modern *Homo sapiens*, individuals very much like us, evolved from more archaic humans about 100,000 to 150,000 years ago. They also believe that this transition occurred in Africa, with modern humans then dispersing to Asia, Europe, and eventually Australasia and the Americas.

Discoveries of hominid remains during the past three decades in East and South Africa, the Middle East, and elsewhere have combined with advances in molecular biology to initiate a new discipline—molecular paleoanthropology. This field of inquiry is providing an ever-growing inventory of evidence for a genetic affinity between human beings and the African apes.

Opinion polls show that many people believe that divine intervention actively guided the evolution of human beings. Science cannot comment on the role that supernatural forces might play in human affairs. But scientific investigations have concluded that the same forces responsible for the evolution of all other life forms on Earth can account for the evolution of human beings.

Conclusion

Science is not the only way of acquiring knowledge about ourselves and the world around us. Humans gain understanding in many other ways, such as through literature, the arts, philosophical reflection, and religious experience. Scientific knowledge may enrich aesthetic and moral perceptions, but these subjects extend beyond science's realm, which is to obtain a better understanding of the natural world.

The claim that equity demands balanced treatment of evolutionary theory and special creation in science classrooms reflects a misunderstanding of what science is and how it is conducted. Scientific investigators seek to understand natural phenomena by observation and experimentation. Scientific interpretations of facts and the explanations that account for them therefore must be testable by observation and experimentation.

Creationism, intelligent design, and other claims of supernatural intervention in the origin of life or of species are not science because they are not testable by the methods of science. These claims subordinate observed data to statements based on authority, revelation, or religious belief. Documentation offered in support of these claims is typically limited to the special publications of their advocates. These publications do not offer hypotheses subject to change in light of new data, new interpretations, or demonstration of error. This contrasts with science, where any hypothesis or theory always remains subject to the possibility of rejection or modification in the light of new knowledge.

No body of beliefs that has its origin in doctrinal material rather than scientific observation, interpretation, and experimentation should be admissible as science in any science course. Incorporating the teaching of such doctrines into a science curriculum compromises the objectives of public education. Science has been greatly successful at explaining natural processes, and this has led not only to increased understanding of the universe but also to major improvements in technology and public health and welfare. The growing role that science plays in modern life requires that science, and not religion, be taught in science classes.

RICHARD DAWKINS

Explaining the Very Improbable (1987)†

We animals are the most complicated things in the known universe. The universe that we know, of course, is a tiny fragment of the actual universe. There may be yet more complicated objects than us on other planets, and some of them may already know about us. But this doesn't alter the point that I want to make. Complicated things, everywhere, deserve a very special kind of explanation. We want to know how they came into existence and why they are so complicated.

* * *

The process by which an airliner came into existence is not fundamentally mysterious to us, because humans built it. The systematic putting together of parts to a purposeful design is something we know and understand, for we have experienced it at first hand, even if only with our childhood Meccano or Erector set.

What about our own bodies? Each one of us is a machine, like an airliner only much more complicated. Were we designed on a drawing board too, and were our parts assembled by a skilled engineer? The answer is no. It is a surprising answer, and we have known and understood it for only a century or so. When Charles Darwin first explained the matter, many people either wouldn't or couldn't grasp it. I myself flatly refused to believe Darwin's theory when I first heard about it as a child. Almost everybody throughout history, up to the second half of the nineteenth century, has firmly believed in the opposite—the Conscious Designer theory. Many people still do, perhaps because the true, Darwinian explanation of our own existence is still, remarkably, not a routine part of the curriculum of a general education. It is certainly very widely misunderstood.

The watchmaker of my title is borrowed from a famous treatise by the eighteenth-century theologian William Paley. His *Natural Theology—or Evidences of the Existence and Attributes of the Deity Collected from the Appearances of Nature*, published in 1802, is the best-known exposition of the 'Argument from Design', always the most influential of the arguments for the existence of a God. It is a book that I greatly admire, for in his own time its author succeeded in doing what I am struggling to do now. He had a point to make, he passionately believed in it, and he spared no effort to ram it home clearly. He had a proper reverence for the complexity of the living world, and he saw that it demands a very special kind of explanation. The only thing he got wrong—admittedly quite a big thing!

† From *The Blind Watchmaker: Why the Evidence of Evolution Reveals a Universe Without Design* (New York, 1987). Copyright © 1996, 1987, 1986 by Richard Dawkins. Reprinted by permission of W. W. Norton & Company, Inc. and Sterling Lord Literistic, Inc. Richard Dawkins (b. 1941) is the Charles Simonyi Professor of the Public Understanding of Science at Oxford University.

—was the explanation itself. He gave the traditional religious answer to the riddle, but he articulated it more clearly and convincingly than anybody had before. The true explanation is utterly different, and it had to wait for one of the most revolutionary thinkers of all time, Charles Darwin.

Paley begins *Natural Theology* with a famous passage:

> In crossing a heath, suppose I pitched my foot against a *stone*, and were asked how the stone came to be there; I might possibly answer, that, for anything I knew to the contrary, it had lain there for ever: nor would it perhaps be very easy to show the absurdity of this answer. But suppose I had found a *watch* upon the ground, and it should be inquired how the watch happened to be in that place, I should hardly think of the answer which I had before given, that for anything I knew, the watch might have always been there.

Paley here appreciates the difference between natural physical objects like stones, and designed and manufactured objects like watches. He goes on to expound the precision with which the cogs and springs of a watch are fashioned, and the intricacy with which they are put together. If we found an object such as a watch upon a heath, even if we didn't know how it had come into existence, its own precision and intricacy of design would force us to conclude

> that the watch must have had a maker: that there must have existed, at some time, and at some place or other, an artificer or artificers, who formed it for the purpose which we find it actually to answer; who comprehended its construction, and designed its use.

Nobody could reasonably dissent from this conclusion, Paley insists, yet that is just what the atheist, in effect, does when he contemplates the works of nature, for:

> every indication of contrivance, every manifestation of design, which existed in the watch, exists in the works of nature; with the difference, on the side of nature, of being greater or more, and that in a degree which exceeds all computation.

Paley drives his point home with beautiful and reverent descriptions of the dissected machinery of life, beginning with the human eye, a favourite example which Darwin was later to use and which will reappear throughout this book. Paley compares the eye with a designed instrument such as a telescope, and concludes that 'there is precisely the same proof that the eye was made for vision, as there is that the telescope was made for assisting it'. The eye must have had a designer, just as the telescope had.

Paley's argument is made with passionate sincerity and is informed by the best biological scholarship of his day, but it is wrong, gloriously and utterly wrong. The analogy between telescope and eye, between watch and living organism, is false. All appearances to the contrary, the only watchmaker in nature is the blind forces of physics, albeit deployed in a very special way. A true watchmaker has foresight: he designs his cogs and springs, and plans their interconnections, with a future purpose in his mind's eye. Natural selection, the blind, unconscious, automatic process which Darwin discovered, and which we now know is the explanation for the existence and apparently purposeful form of all life, has no purpose in mind. It has no mind and no mind's eye. It does not plan for the future. It has no vision, no foresight, no sight at all. If it can be said to play the role of watchmaker in nature, it is the *blind* watchmaker.

*   *   *

The behaviour of a computer can be explained in terms of interactions between semiconductor electronic gates, and the behaviour of these, in turn, is explained by physicists at yet lower levels. But, for most purposes, you would in practice be wasting your time if you tried to understand the behaviour of the whole computer at either of those levels. There are too many electronic gates and too many interconnections between them. A satisfying explanation has to be in terms of a manageably small number of interactions. This is why, if we want to understand the workings of computers, we prefer a preliminary explanation in terms of about half a dozen major subcomponents—memory, processing mill, backing store, control unit, input-output handler, etc. Having grasped the interactions between the half-dozen major components, we then may wish to ask questions about the internal organization of these major components. Only specialist engineers are likely to go down to the level of AND gates and NOR gates, and only physicists will go down further, to the level of how electrons behave in a semiconducting medium.

For those that like '-ism' sorts of names, the aptest name for my approach to understanding how things work is probably 'hierarchical reductionism'. If you read trendy intellectual magazines, you may have noticed that 'reductionism' is one of those things, like sin, that is only mentioned by people who are against it. To call oneself a reductionist will sound, in some circles, a bit like admitting to eating babies. But, just as nobody actually eats babies, so nobody is really a reductionist in any sense worth being against. The nonexistent reductionist—the sort that everybody is against, but who exists only in their imaginations—tries to explain complicated things *directly* in terms of the *smallest* parts, even, in some extreme versions of the myth, as the *sum* of the parts! The hierarchical reductionist, on the other hand, explains a complex entity at any particular level in the hierarchy of organization, in terms of entities only one level down the hierarchy; entities which, themselves, are likely to be complex enough to need further reducing to their own component parts, and so on. It goes without saying—though the mythical, baby-eating reductionist is reputed to deny this—that the kinds of explanations which are suitable at high levels in the hierarchy are quite different from the kinds of explanations which are suitable at lower levels. This was the point of explaining cars in terms of carburettors rather than quarks. But the hierarchical reductionist believes that carburettors are explained in terms of smaller units . . . , which are explained in terms of smaller units . . ., which are ultimately explained in terms of the smallest of fundamental particles. Reductionism, in this sense, is just another name for an honest desire to understand how things work.

* * *

LEWIS THOMAS

On the Uncertainty of Science (1980)†

Puzzlement is an identifying characteristic of the human species, genetically governed, universal, and a central determinant of human behavior. I can go this far with sociobiology, but then, influenced by this human trait, my mind falls away in confusion. Uncertainty, the sure sense that the ground is shifting at every step, is one of the marks of humanity. We keep changing our minds together, in a biological process rather similar, in its outlines, to evolution itself.

The great body of science, built like a vast hill over the past three hundred years, is a mobile, unsteady structure, made up of solid-enough single bits of information, but with all the bits always moving about, fitting together in different ways, adding new bits to themselves with flourishes of adornment as though consulting a mirror, giving the whole arrangement something like the unpredictability and unreliability of living flesh. Human knowledge doesn't stay put, it evolves by what we call trial and error, or, as is more usually the sequence, error and trial.

Other animals differ from us in this respect. Each of them has at least one thing to be very good at, even superlatively skilled, surefooted. Any beetle can live a flawless, impeccable life, infallible in the business of procreating beetles. Not us: we are not necessarily good at anything in particular except language, and using this we tend to get things wrong. It is built into our genes to veer off from the point; somehow we have been selected in evolution for our gift of ambiguity.

This is how we fell into the way of science. The endeavor is not, as is sometimes thought, a way of building a solid, indestructible body of immutable truth, fact laid precisely upon fact in the manner of twigs in an anthill. Science is not like this at all: it keeps changing, shifting, revising, discovering that it was wrong and then heaving itself explosively apart to redesign everything. It is a living thing, a celebration of human fallibility. At its very best, it is rather like an embryo.

Ordinarily scientists do not talk this way about their trade, because there is always in the air the feeling that this time we have it right, this time we are about to come into possession of a finished science, knowing almost everything about everything. Biology has been moving so fast, in just the last few years, that there is some risk of making it seem nearly complete,

† From *The Key Reporter* 46 (Autumn 1980). Reprinted with the permission of Phi Beta Kappa Society. Lewis Thomas (1913–1993) was chancellor of Memorial Sloan-Kettering Cancer Center in New York.

at the very stage in its development when it is, in real life, just getting ready to take off. It is nothing *like* finished, it is only just at its beginning.

We are in trouble whenever persuaded that we know everything. Today, an intellectually fashionable view of man's place in nature is that there is really no great problem: the plain answer is that it makes no sense, no sense at all. The universe is meaningless for human beings: we bumbled our way into the place by a series of random and senseless biological accidents. The sky is not blue: this is an optical illusion—the sky is black. You can walk on the moon if you feel like it, but there is nothing to do there except look at the earth, and when you've seen one earth you've seen them all. The animals and plants of the planet are at hostile odds with one another, each bent on elbowing any nearby neighbor off the earth. Genes, tapes of polymer, are the ultimate adversaries and, by random, the only real survivors.

This grasp of things is sometimes presented as though based on science, with the implication that we already know most of the important knowable matters and this is the way it all turns out. It is the wisdom of the twentieth century, contemplating as its only epiphany the news that the world is an absurd apparatus and we are stuck with it, and in it.

In the circumstance, we would surely have no obligations except to our individual selves, and of course to the genes coding out the selves.

I believe something considerably less than this. I take it as an article of faith that we humans are a profoundly immature species, only now beginning the process of learning how to learn. Our most spectacular biological attribute, which identifies us as our particular sort of animal, is language, and the deep nature of this gift is a mystery. We are aware of our consciousness, but we cannot even make good guesses as to how this awareness arises in our brains—or even, for that matter, that it does arise there for sure. We do not understand how a solitary cell, fused from two, can differentiate into an embryo and then into the systems of tissues and organs that become us, nor do we know how a tadpole accomplished his emergence, or even a flea. We can make up instant myths, transiently satisfying but always subject to abandonment, about the origin of life on the planet. We do not understand why we make music, or dance, or paint, or write poems. We are bewildered, especially in this century, by the pervasive latency of love.

The thing about us that should astonish biologists more than it does is that we are so juvenile a species. By evolutionary standards of time we have only just arrived on the scene, fumbling with our new thumbs, struggling to find our legs under the weight and power of our new brains. We are the newest and most immature of all significant animals, perhaps a million or so years along as the taxonomists would define us, but probably only some thousands of years as communal, speaking creatures, uniquely capable of manufacturing metaphors and therefore recognizable as human.

Our place in the life of the world is still unfathomable because we have so much to learn, but it is surely not absurd. We matter. For a time, anyway, it looks as though we will be responsible for the thinking of the system, which seems to mean, at this stage, the responsibility not to do damage to the rest of life if we can help it. This is in itself an immensely complicated problem, in view of our growing numbers and the demands we feel compelled to make on the planet's resources. There is no hope of thinking our way through the quandary except by learning more, and part of the learning (not all of it, mind you, but a good part) can only be achieved by science, more and better science—not for our longevity or comfort or affluence but for comprehension, without which our long survival is unlikely.

* * *

One major question needing to be examined is the general *attitude* of nature. A century ago there was a consensus about this: nature was "red in tooth and claw," evolution was a record of open warfare among competing species, the fittest were the strongest aggressors, and so forth. Now it begins to look different. The tiniest and most fragile of organisms dominate the life of the earth: the chloroplasts inside the cells of plants, which turn solar energy into food and supply the oxygen for breathing, appear to be the descendants of ancient blue-green algae, living now as permanent lodgers within the cells of "higher" forms; the mitochondria of all nucleated cells, which serve as engines for all the functions of life, are the progeny of bacteria that took to living as cells inside cells long ago. The urge to form partnerships, to link up in collaborative arrangements, is perhaps the oldest, strongest, and most fundamental force in nature. There are no solitary, free-living creatures: every form of life is dependent on other forms. The great successes in evolution, the mutants who have, so to speak, made it, have done so by fitting in with, and sustaining, the rest of life. Up to now we might be counted among the brilliant successes, but flashy and perhaps unstable. We should go warily into the future, looking for ways to be more useful, listening more carefully for the signals, watching our step, and having an eye out for partners.

* * *

Some people believe that we are in trouble because of science, and that we should stop doing science and go back to living in nature, with nature, contemplating nature. It is too late for us to do this, too late by several hundred years, and there are now too many of us—four billion[1] already, with the likelihood of doubling that population and doubling it again within the lifetime of some of us.

What I would like to know most about the developing earth is: Does it already have a mind? Or will it someday gain a mind, and are we part of that? Are we a tissue for the earth's awareness?

I like this thought, even though I cannot take it anywhere, and I must say it embarrasses me. I have that nagging hunch that it is a presumption, a piece of ultimate hubris. A single insect may have only two thoughts, maybe three, but there are a lot of insects. The million blind and almost

---

1. By 1999, the rapidly expanding world population was over six billion. [Editor]

mindless termites in a hill make up in their collective life an intelligence, a kind of brain, now capable of building endless vaulted chambers and turning perfect arches, thinking all the way. I would like to know what whales are thinking about, or dolphins; but if I were hoping to find out how intercommunication really works on this planet, I would study termites.

I am willing to predict, uncertainly, provisionally, that there is one central, universal aspect of human behavior, genetically set by our very nature, biologically governed, driving each of us along. Depending on how one looks at it, it can be defined as the urge to be useful. This urge drives society along, sets our behavior as individuals and in groups, invents all our myths, writes our poetry, composes our music.

This is why it is so hard being a juvenile species, still milling around in groups, trying to construct a civilization that will last. Being useful is easy for an ant; you just wait for the right chemical signal, at the right stage of the construction of the hill, and then you go looking for a twig of exactly the right size for that stage and carry it back, up the flank of the hill, and put it in place, and then you go and do that thing again. An ant can dine out on his usefulness all his life, and never get it wrong.

It is a different problem for us, carrying such risks of doing it wrong, getting the wrong twig, losing the hill, not even recognizing, yet, the outline of the hill. We are beset by strings of DNA, immense arrays of genes, instructing each of us to be helpful, impelling us to try our whole lives to be useful, but never telling us how.

*   *   *

If you are going to make up a story about the earth, based on today's scientific information, it is useful to have a third person to tell the tale. For this role, I summon that sagacious and ubiquitous gentleman known as the Extraterrestrial Visitor. * * * He sees the earth now, but he is one of the older Extraterrestrial Visitors, and has been making periodic detours in our direction since the birth of the structure, the laying down of bone four billion or so years ago, and has been taking time-lapse photographs, close up, every few hundred thousand years. Running the whole film through, say, this year, what sort of impression would he have of us?

I think he would conclude that his lens had caught the gestation, still in progress, of a stupendous embryo, clinging to a warm, round stone by what we call earth, or soil, as though attached all around by a kind of placenta, and turning slowly in the sun. He would have seen this creature starting from a single cell, fertilized by lightning, or ultraviolet light, or cosmic rays, or what-have-you. For two-billion-odd years he would observe the formation of a sort of blastula, a huge cluster of cells multiplying first in the sea and later on land, all pretty much the same kind of primitive, nonnucleated cell. Then the film would show a green tinge here and there; and then, with the appearance of oxygen, and thanks to the sun, an explosive emergence of new forms of life would be seen everywhere, new cells with nuclei, new collections of cells gathering to form tissues, coral

reefs, and finally roses, dolphins, and then at last ourselves, off and running, making metaphors and music, the newest and youngest working parts
of the planet.

I would like to think that we are on our way to becoming an embryonic
central nervous system for the whole system. I even like the notion that
our cities, still primitive, archaic, fragile structures, could turn into the
precursors of ganglia, to be ultimately linked in a network around the
planet. But I do worry, from time to time, about that other possibility: that
we are a transient tissue, replaceable, biologically representing a try at
something needing better means of perfection, and therefore on our way
down under the hill, interesting fossils for contemplation by some other
kind of creature. In my more depressed moments I find this a plausible
form of heartsink. But at better times, remembering how skilled our species
is with language and metaphor, almost from birth, how good we are at
recognizing and recording our mistakes, how spectacularly we excel all
other creatures on this planet, because of the emergence of Johann Se-
bastian Bach as an example of what we can do as a species when we really
try to use our brains, and remembering that nature is by nature parsimonious, tending to hang on to useful things when they really do work, I
have hopes for our survival into maturity, millennia ahead. Perhaps, after
all, we do have a long way to go, but if this is so we have a lot to learn,
and I do like that thought.

NORETTA KOERTGE

Postmodernisms and the Problem
of Scientific Literacy (1998)†

The "House" in our title [A House Built on Sand] refers to interdisciplinary endeavors called Science, Technology, and Society Studies (STS)
or Science and Culture Studies. Within their veritable carnival of approaches and methodologies we find feminists and Marxists of every stripe,
ethnomethodologists, deconstructionists, sociologists of knowledge and
critical theorists—those who find significance in rhetoric and others who
emphasize the role of patronage and the power of empire. One might
expect to find irreconcilable differences between, for example, those who
stress material conditions and those who focus on metaphors, and, indeed,
there are lively debates on such matters. Yet we also find widely shared
convictions and projects. Although it is always hazardous to try to sum-
marize any group's principles and purposes, the following are some noteworthy precepts that appear to be widely shared:

† From "Scrutinizing Science Studies," A House Built on Sand, ed. Noretta Koertge (New York,
1998). Copyright © 1998 by Oxford University Press, Inc. Used by permission of Oxford Unversity
Press, Inc. Noretta Koertge (b. 1935) is professor of the history and philosophy of science of Indiana
University.

- Every aspect of that complex set of enterprises that we call science, including, above all, its content and results, is shaped by and can be understood only in its local historical and cultural context.
- In particular, the products of scientific inquiry, the so-called laws of nature, must always be viewed as social constructions. Their validity depends on the consensus of "experts" in just the same way as the legitimacy of a pope depends on a council of cardinals.
- Although scientists typically succeed in arrogating special epistemic authority to themselves, scientific knowledge is just "one story among many." The more epistemological authority that science has in a given society, the more important it is to unmask its pretensions to be an enterprise dedicated to the pursuit of objective knowledge. Science must be "humbled."
- Since the quest for objective knowledge is a quixotic one, the best way to appraise scientific claims is through a process of political evaluation. Since the "evidence" for a scientific claim is never conclusive and is always open to negotiation, the best way to evaluate scientific results is to ask who stands to benefit if the claim is taken to be true. Thus, for the citizen the key question about a scientific result should not be how well tested the claim is but, rather, Cui bono?
- "Science is politics by other means": the results of scientific inquiry are profoundly and importantly shaped by the ideological agendas of powerful elites.
- There is no univocal sense in which the science of one society is better than that of another. In particular, Euroscience is not objectively superior to the various ethnosciences and shamanisms described by anthropologists or invented by Afrocentrists.
- Neither is there any clear sense in which we can talk about scientific progress within the European tradition. On the contrary, science is characterized chiefly by its complicity in all the most negative and oppressive aspects of modern history: increasingly destructive warfare, environmental disasters, racism, sexism, eugenics, exploitation, alienation, and imperialism.
- Given the impossibility of scientific objectivity, it is futile to exhort scientists and policymakers to try harder to remove ideological bias from the practice of science. Instead, what we need to do is deliberately introduce "corrective biases" and "progressive political values" into science. There is a call for "emancipatory science" and "advocacy research."

Postmodernists pride themselves on their reflexivity, so it is not surprising to find them defending their own approach by proclaiming it to be morally and politically superior to the traditional scientific emphases on disinterestedness, universalism, and empiricism.

*   *   *

Educational policymakers and members of organizations such as the American Association for the Advancement of Science have long been

troubled by indications of scientific illiteracy in our society, such as the
poor performance of U.S. students on standardized tests and the amount
of money spent on extremely dubious alternative health procedures, ranging from the relatively benign old-fashioned homeopathic remedies to new
psychological therapies for "recovered memory syndrome" that can be extremely destructive. There is also concern about the salience of antirational
and pseudoscientific mythologies in our culture (e.g., angel books, astrol-
ogy columns, and TV programs on "unexplained mysteries," as well as the
persistence and success of the "creation science" movement). The history
of science education since *Sputnik* is a story of attempts to ameliorate this
situation.

The postmodern approaches to science studies that figure as major players in the "science wars" also have prescriptions for transforming science
education and redefining scientific literacy. Although they differ on details
and degree, all are intent on radically changing public perceptions of science through an agenda of radical educational reform. In this essay, I show
how these various postmodernist accounts of science are now being un-
critically absorbed into science pedagogy and argue that many of their
proposals are counterproductive.

* * *

Female-Friendly Science

Feminist suggestions for science pedagogy are another mixed bag. Let
us look briefly at one of the seemingly more moderate and systematic
approaches, the "Model for Transforming the Natural Sciences,"[1] proposed by Sue V. Rosser, a former senior program officer at the National
Science Foundation. Although Rosser presents her proposal as a modest
one, it is immediately evident that it is science itself that is to be transformed, not just science education.

The initial recommendations are sensible—one should include the
names of women scientists who have made important discoveries and provide wherever possible hands-on experiences for the students instead of
making them rely on textbook descriptions. Rosser then moves on to the
familiar feminist injunction to "use less competitive models and more
interdisciplinary methods to teach science" (205). (It is anybody's guess
what that might entail, but it sounds innocent enough.)

The last phases of Rosser's planned transformation, however, are explicitly based on culture studies' critiques of science. For example, when Rosser recommends not having laboratory exercises in introductory courses in
which students must kill animals, what is surprising is not the recommen-
dation itself—there has already been a dramatic decrease in the use of
animal subjects—but the reason Rosser gives: "Merchant and Griffin . . .
document the extent to which modern mechanistic science becomes a

---

1. Sue V. Rosser, *Female-Friendly Science* (New York, 1990): 193.

tool men use to dominate both women and animals. Thus many women may particularly empathize with animals" (202).

Rosser goes on to criticize all of modern biology for being reductionistic because of its emphasis on cell and molecular biology. From the beginning, she says, students should be encouraged to develop hypotheses that are "relational, interdependent, and multi-causal rather than hierarchical, reductionistic, and dualistic" (213), and curricula should include "fewer experiments likely to have applications of direct benefit to the military" (194). The goal is to arrive at a new kind of science, one that is "redefined and reconstructed to include us all" (214).

Some of Rosser's proposed reforms show little awareness of the actual practice of science education. Neither I nor my colleagues were able to come up with any examples of student experiments that seemed to be strongly associated with the military. The example Rosser gives, the calculation of trajectories that could be used to describe the motions of bombs and rockets, can equally well be illustrated with space age examples involving *Starship* Captain Kathryn Janeway. And for some time now, the killing of laboratory animals—as opposed to the dissection of them—has been very uncommon in student labs. Other of Rosser's proposals are totally impractical. Since multifactor models are notoriously difficult to evaluate, it hardly seems wise to encourage beginning students to concentrate on them. And the issue of reductionism in modern biology is an extremely complex and contested one. In any case, one can hardly afford not to teach cell biology. * * *

Rosser describes her approach as an application of women's studies, whose central message is that the overall impact of science on the lives of women (and minorities) has been oppressive. Claims that science and technology have eliminated drudgery and many of the dangers of childbirth and provided improved contraceptive devices are said to be outweighed by science's contributions to warfare, the decline of midwifery, and the devaluation of more intuitive, holistic approaches to problem solving.

The methods and values of science are claimed to be intrinsically sexist. Instead of viewing science as an important component of the Enlightenment (a term with positive connotations), many feminists see the rise of modern science as responsible for "the death of nature" (as the historian of science Carolyn Merchant argues in a book with that title). For a variety of reasons (some would posit "womb envy"; others cite the "object relations" successor to Freudian theory), men are seen as more inclined to treat living things as "objects" and to value them only to the extent that they can dissect and control them. Science—with its emphasis on analysis, abstraction, quantification, and prediction—is then viewed, to repeat Mary Daly's terminology, as a paradigm case of patriarchal, phallocratic necrophilia.

It then seems inevitable that the content of science must be sexist. Dozens of books describe cases purporting to show that sexist bias seeps into scientific theorizing. Many of the examples deal with theories of reproduction. Perhaps the most famous one is the saga of the active sperm and passive egg, about which it is claimed that gender stereotypes about human males and females influenced not just the rhetoric of popular accounts of the heroic little sperm valiantly swimming upstream hoping to penetrate the big, fat noncooperative egg but also contributed to the tendency to emphasize research on DNA to the neglect of embryology. * * *

Sophistication versus Cynicism in the Classroom

What unifies the various commentators on science education that I have called post-modern are the convictions that science has too much authority in our society and that there is too much respect for scientific reasoning within the general population. To combat these alleged tendencies toward science worship or science boosterism, these commentators believe that science education must be transformed so as to present students with a less heroic and less idealistic picture of scientific inquiry. Once students learn that scientific knowledge is constructed just like every other segment of our cultural beliefs and once they realize that the results of scientific experiments are the product of social negotiations, just as are the appraised values of the damage caused by a tornado, then, the social constructivists believe, students will grow up to be less admiring of scientific findings and better able to cope as citizens in a complex technological world.

Since allegedly there can be no compelling evidential basis for scientific claims, the discerning citizen needs to ask not whether the claim is well supported but, rather, whose political interests are served by such a claim. Since science supposedly has a long history of oppressing women and minorities, young people in these groups are thought to have a special need for inoculation against a naive belief in the products and procedures of traditional science.

What are we to make of such a program? Even if we reject extreme versions of social constructivism, are there at least some beneficial practical reforms coming out of these critiques? First, we all can agree with the postmodernists—and C. P. Snow—that citizens need to know more about science, but only if what they are told is reasonably accurate and only if it is not presented as a substitute for learning more of the content of science. Of course, students need to learn about scientific controversies like the interesting cases Collins and Pinch discuss in their book.[2] But the study of scientific debates is hardly a novel pedagogical innovation. Old textbooks, such as Holton and Roller and the Harvard Case Histories, gave rich accounts of historical controversies that clearly illustrated the strengths and weaknesses of both positions and the difficulties in settling the matter. The most conventional of the current science books offer alternative accounts of why the dinosaurs became extinct, how the moon was formed, how life began, and how best to model the bonds in benzene. Let us concede to Collins and Pinch, however, that students also need to learn more about professional rivalries in science and the politics of science journalism (more on this later), but the picture must not be reduced to a cynical cartoon of real science. Students must also learn about the role of

2. Harry Collins and Trevor Pinch, *The Golem: What Everyone Should Know about Science* (Cambridge, UK, 1993).

evidence and rational debate in scientific conflict resolution and also successful theory construction and refinement and how they were achieved.

Second, let us agree with the cultural critics of science—and Sir Karl Popper—that students need to learn more about the fallibility of scientific theories. We also freely grant that the hypotheses that spring most readily to the scientist's mind often reflect the commonsense beliefs, metaphysical systems, and ideological predilections of the times. But what we must add to the cultural studies picture and give prominence to is the old Popperian point about the refutability of false scientific theories and the possibility of learning from our mistakes. However obnoxious various outdated scientific theories of reproduction, intelligence, and human differences may be, it still was possible to discredit them through the routine application of the ordinary self-corrective devices of scientific inquiry. These methodological procedures do not always operate as efficiently as we would like, and they also can be subverted by political pressure. But there is no historical warrant for building into the curriculum a cynical, worst-case-scenario view of science.

Third, let us welcome all those who support the proposition that science education at all levels should become more accessible to and welcoming of women and minorities. Professional scientific organizations have long been concerned about the gender gap and racial gaps in scientific literacy. On average, members of these groups are more prone to math anxiety and score lower on standardized math tests, are less likely to take nonrequired science courses in high school, are less inclined to major in science or engineering, and are more liable to drop out if they do choose a science-based career. Sociological studies of attitudes toward science also report interesting gender differences in the patterns of attraction to pseudoscience and belief in paranormal phenomena.[3] In accord with their explicit political commitments, postmodernist commentators on science emphasize the problem of the alienation of such groups from science. But too often their solution is to give each political identity its own special ethnoscience, tailor-made in ontology, methodology, and content to match the ideology and interests of that community. They believe that by denying the transcultural validity of scientific results, they will somehow undermine the power of transnational corporations and military alliances. Somehow feminist science will empower women, and ethnomathematics will improve the lot of the Navajo people.

But here their misunderstanding of the nature of science can have tragic consequences for the very people they want to liberate. It is not easy to generate truth claims about the world, and the scientific process does not always succeed in doing so, but when it does, what wonderful stones they provide for David's sling! To give just one example: I submit that DNA testing—a product of the reductionistic, nonholistic science that cultural critics of science deplore—promotes more justice to rape victims than do the special pleadings of feminist psychologists about the veracity of female plaintiffs. At the same time, DNA testing can promote justice for those

3. Francis B. Harrold and Raymond A. Eve, eds., *Cult Archaeology and Creationism: Understanding Pseudoscientific Beliefs about the Past* (Iowa City, 1995).

African American men who have been falsely accused of rape. The science underlying DNA testing is universal science, not ethnoscience or gendered science, and that is why it can be used to arbitrate disputes between groups in such a manner that the politically less powerful can prevail. What a tragedy to educate members of disadvantaged groups in ersatz science and mathematics, all in the name of multiculturalism. And how dangerous it is to suggest to the powerful in our society that science is part of their rightful patrimony because after all, as Sandra Harding put it, "science is politics by other means." A denigration or subversion of the ideals of science can never be politically progressive in the long run.

It is sometimes tempting to respond to the postmodernists' litany of the fatal flaws in science with a naive defense of science as sacred. Even though I am firmly convinced that the ideals and institutions of science provide the best approach we have for understanding the world, I do not deny for a moment that they are both intrinsically imperfect and subject to improvement. The whole point of science education in a liberal arts tradition is to help students benefit from what has been learned before while simultaneously acquiring the ability to question and improve on the currently received views.

*   *   *

What those who would prioritize the study of the social aspects of science fail to realize is that it is impossible to analyze the functioning of scientific institutions without thoroughly understanding the aims and methods of scientific inquiry. And understanding the process of science in turn requires a detailed knowledge of the structure of some actual scientific theories and of the nature of the specific data-gathering processes that are used to evaluate them and how both the theoretical and experimental components develop over time. It is no use trying to make a virtue out of ignorance by thanking the science teachers we never had or by telling kids that they no longer need to study the content of science but need simply to learn what the sociology of scientific knowledge says about it. *   *   *

RICHARD DAWKINS

Science and Sensibility (1999)†

*   *   *

Many in the academic community *   *   * have discovered a new form of anti-scientific rhetoric, sometimes called the "post-modern critique" of science. The most thorough whistle-blowing on this kind of thing is Paul Gross and Norman Levitt's splendid book, *Higher Superstition: The Aca-*

† From "Science and Sensibility," *Free Inquiry* 19.2 (Spring 1999): 38–42. Reprinted by permission of the author. Richard Dawkins (b. 1941) is Charles Simonyi Professor of the Public Understanding of Science at Oxford University.

demic Left and Its Quarrels with Science. The American anthropologist
Matt Cartmill sums up the basic credo:

> Anybody who claims to have objective knowledge about anything is
> trying to control and dominate the rest of us. . . . There are no
> objective facts. All supposed "facts" are contaminated with theories,
> and all theories are infested with moral and political doctrines. There-
> fore, when some guy in a lab coat tells you that such and such is an
> objective fact . . . he must have a political agenda up his starched
> white sleeve.

There are even a few, but very vocal, fifth columnists within science itself
who hold exactly these views, and use them to waste the time of the rest
of us.

Cartmill's thesis is that there is an unexpected and pernicious alliance
between the know-nothing fundamentalist religious Right, and the sophisticated academic Left. A bizarre manifestation of the alliance is joint opposition to the theory of evolution. The opposition of the fundamentalists
is obvious. That of the left is a compound of hostility to science in general,
of "respect" for tribal creation myths, and various political agendas. Both
these strange bedfellows share a concern for "human dignity" and take
offense at treating humans as "animals." Moreover, in Cartmill's words,
"Both camps believe that the big truths about the world are moral truths.
They view the universe in terms of good and evil, not truth and falsehood.
The first question they ask about any supposed fact is whether it serves the
cause of righteousness."

And there is a feminist angle, which saddens me, for I am sympathetic
to true feminism.

> Instead of exhorting young women to prepare for a variety of technical
> subjects by studying science, logic, and mathematics, Women's Stud-
> ies students are now being taught that logic is a tool of domination
> . . . the standard norms and methods of scientific inquiry are sexist
> because they are incompatible with "women's ways of knowing." The
> authors of the prize-winning book with this title report that the ma-
> jority of the women they interviewed fell into the category of "sub-
> jective knowers," characterized by a "passionate rejection of science
> and scientists." These "subjectivist" women see the methods of logic,
> analysis, and abstraction as "alien territory belonging to men" and
> "value intuition as a safer and more fruitful approach to truth."

That was a quotation from the historian and philosopher of science Noretta
Koertge, who is understandably worried about a subversion of feminism
which could have a malign influence upon women's education. Indeed,
there is an ugly, hectoring streak in this kind of thinking. Barbara Ehrenreich and Janet McIntosh witnessed a woman psychologist speaking at an
interdisciplinary conference. Various members of the audience attacked
her use of the oppressive, sexist, imperialist, and capitalist scientific
method. The psychologist tried to defend science by pointing to its great
discoveries—for example DNA. The retort came back "You believe in
DNA?" Fortunately, there are still many intelligent young women pre-

pared to enter a scientific career, and I should like to pay tribute to their courage in the face of such bullying intimidation.

I have come so far with scarcely a mention of Charles Darwin. His life spanned most of the nineteenth century, and he died with every right to be satisfied that he had cured humanity of its greatest and grandest illusion. Darwin brought life itself within the pale of the explicable. No longer a baffling mystery demanding supernatural explanation, life, with the complexity and elegance that defines it, grows and gradually emerges, by easily understood rules, from simple beginnings. Darwin's legacy to the twentieth century was to demystify the greatest mystery of all.

Legacy and Outlook

Would Darwin be pleased with our stewardship of that legacy, and with what we are now in a position to pass to the twenty-first century? I think he would feel an odd mixture of exhilaration and exasperation. Exhilaration at the detailed knowledge, the comprehensiveness of understanding, that science can now offer, and the polish with which his own theory is being brought to fulfillment. Exasperation at the ignorant suspicion of science, and the air-headed superstition, that still persist.

Exasperation is too weak a word. Darwin might justifiably be saddened, given our huge advantages over himself and his contemporaries, at how little we seem to have done to deploy our superior knowledge in our culture. Late twentieth-century civilization, Darwin would be dismayed to note, though imbued and surrounded by the products and advantages of science, has yet to draw science into its sensibility. Is there even a sense in which we have slipped backwards since Darwin's co-discoverer, Alfred Russel Wallace, wrote *The Wonderful Century*, a glowing scientific retrospective on his era?

Perhaps there was undue complacency in turn-of-century science, about how much had been achieved and how little more advancement could be expected. William Thomson, First Lord Kelvin, president of the Royal Society, pioneered the transatlantic cable—symbol of Victorian progress— and also the second law of thermodynamics—C. P. Snow's litmus of scientific literacy. Kelvin is credited with the following three confident predictions "Radio has no future"; "Heavier than air flying machines are impossible"; "X-rays will prove to be a hoax."

Kelvin also gave Darwin a lot of grief by proving, using all the prestige of the senior science of physics, that the sun was too young to have allowed time for evolution. Kelvin, in effect, said, "Physics argues against evolution" so your biology must be wrong. Darwin could have retorted: "Biology shows that evolution is a fact, so your physics must be wrong." Instead, he bowed to the prevailing assumption that physics automatically trumps biology, and fretted. Twentieth-century physics, of course, showed Kelvin wrong by powers of ten. But Darwin did not live to see his vindication, and he never had the confidence to tell the senior physicist of his day where to get off.

In my attacks on millenarial superstition, I must beware of Kelvinian over-confidence. Undoubtedly there is much that we still don't know. Part of our legacy to the twenty-first century must be unanswered questions, and some of them are big ones. The science of any age must prepare to be superseded. It would be arrogant and rash to claim our present knowledge as all there is to know. Today's commonplaces, such as mobile telephones, would have seemed to previous ages pure magic. And that should be our warning. Arthur C. Clarke, distinguished novelist and evangelist for the limitless power of science, has said, "Any sufficiently advanced technology is indistinguishable from magic." This is Clarke's Third Law.

Maybe, some day in the future, physicists will fully understand gravity, and build an antigravity machine. Levitating people may one day become as commonplace to our descendants as jet planes are to us. So, if someone claims to have witnessed a magic carpet zooming over the minarets, should we believe him, on the grounds that those of our ancestors who doubted the possibility of radio turned out to be wrong? No, *of course* not. But why not?

Clarke's Third Law doesn't work in reverse. Given that "Any sufficiently advanced technology is indistinguishable from magic," it does *not* follow that, "Any magical claim that anybody may make at any time is indistinguishable from a technological advance that will come some time in the future."

Yes, there have been occasions when authoritative skeptics have come away with egg on their pontificating faces. But a far greater number of magical claims have been made and never vindicated. A few things that would surprise us today will come true in the future. But lots and lots of things will not come true in the future. History suggests that the very surprising things that do come true are in a minority. The trick is to sort them out from the rubbish—from claims that will forever remain in the realm of fiction and magic.

It is right that, at the end of our century, we should show the humility that Kelvin, at the end of his did not. But it is also right to acknowledge all that we have learned during the past hundred years. The digital century was the best I could come up with, as a single theme. But it covers only a fraction of what twentieth-century science will bequeath. We now know, as Darwin and Kelvin did not, how old the world is. About 4.6 billion years. We understand—what Alfred Wegener was ridiculed for suggesting—that the shape of geography has not always been the same. South America not only looks as if it might jigsaw neatly under the bulge of Africa. It once did exactly that, until they split apart some 125 million years ago. Madagascar once touched Africa on one side and India on the other. That was before India set off across the widening ocean and crashed into China to raise the Himalayas. The map of the world's continents has a time dimension, and we who are privileged to live in the Plate Tectonic Age know exactly how it has changed, when, and why.

We know roughly how old the universe is, and, indeed, that it *has* an age, which is the same as the age of time itself, and less than 20 billion years. Having begun as a singularity with huge mass and temperature and very small volume, the universe has been expanding ever since. The twenty-first century will probably settle the question whether the expansion is to go on forever, or go into reverse. The *matter* in the cosmos is not homogeneous, but is gathered into some hundred billion galaxies, each averaging a hundred billion stars. We can read the composition of any star in some detail, by spreading its light in a glorified rainbow. Among the stars, our sun is generally unremarkable. It is unremarkable, too, in having planets in orbit, as we know from detecting tiny rhythmic shifts in the spectrums of stars. There is no direct evidence that any other planets house life. If they do, such inhabited islands may be so scattered as to make it unlikely that one will ever encounter another.

We know in some detail the principles governing the evolution of our own island of life. It is a fair bet that the most fundamental principle—Darwinian natural selection—underlies, in some form, other islands of life, if any there be. We know that our kind of life is built of cells, where a cell is either a bacterium or a colony of bacteria. The detailed mechanics of our kind of life depend upon the near-infinite variety of shapes assumed by a special class of molecules called proteins. We know that those all-important three-dimensional shapes are exactly specified by a one-dimensional code, the genetic code, carried by DNA molecules that are replicated through geological time. We understand why there are so many different species, although we don't know *how* many. We cannot predict in detail how evolution will go in the future, but we can predict the general patterns that are to be expected.

Among the unsolved problems we shall bequeath to our successors, physicists such as Steven Weinberg will point to their Dreams of a Final Theory, otherwise known as the Grand Universal Theory, or Theory of Everything. Theorists differ about whether it will ever be attained. Those who think it will would probably date this scientific epiphany somewhere in twenty-first century. Physicists famously resort to religious language when discussing such deep matters. Some of them really mean it. The others are at risk of being taken literally, when really they intend no more than I do when I say "God knows" to mean that I don't.

Biologists will reach their grail of writing down the human genome, early in the next century. They will then discover that it is not so final as some once hoped. The human *embryo* project—working out how the genes interact with their environments, including each other, to build a body—may take at least as long to complete. But it too will probably be finished during the twenty-first century, and artificial wombs built, if these should be thought desirable.

I am less confident about what is for me, as for most biologists, the outstanding scientific problem that remains: the question of how the human brain works, especially the nature of subjective consciousness. The last decade of this century has seen a flurry of big guns take aim at it, including Francis Crick no less, and Daniel Dennett, Steven Pinker, and Sir Roger Penrose. It is a big, profound problem, worthy of minds like these. Obviously I have no solution. If I had, I'd deserve a Nobel Prize. It isn't even clear what *kind* of a problem it is, and therefore what kind of a brilliant idea would constitute a solution. Some people think the problem of consciousness an illusion: there's nobody home, and no problem to be solved. But before Darwin solved the riddle of *life's* provenance, in the last century, I don't think anybody had clearly posed what sort of a problem it was. It was only after Darwin had solved it that most people realized what it had been in the first place. I do not know whether consciousness will prove to be a big problem solved by a genius; or will fritter unsatisfactorily away into a series of small problems and nonproblems.

I am by no means confident that the twenty-first century will solve the human mind. But if it does, there may be an additional by-product. Our successors may even be in a position to understand the paradox of twentieth-century science: On the one hand our century arguably added as much new knowledge to the human store as all previous centuries put together, while on the other hand the twentieth-century ended with approximately the same level of supernatural credulity as the nineteenth, and rather more outright hostility to science. With hope, if not with confidence, I look forward to the twenty-first century and what it may teach us.

THE NEO-DARWINIAN SYNTHESIS
PETER BOWLER

The Evolutionary Synthesis (1984)†

During the early years of the twentieth century, Darwin's theory of natural selection had lost much of its popularity. Field naturalists preserved the original Darwinian emphasis on the role of geographical factors in evolution but were strongly tempted by alternative mechanisms of adaptation, such as Lamarckism. Paleontologists were convinced that evolution is directed along linear paths by either Lamarckism or orthogenesis. The new breed of experimental biologists had gone to the opposite extreme, using genetics to undermine Lamarckism, but refusing to admit any role for adaptation and selection in controlling the flow of new characteristics produced by mutation. In the 1920s the first moves were made toward a reconciliation between the divided branches of biology, and Darwinism emerged from its eclipse to provide the key to a new approach that would solve many outstanding problems. It was realized that the more sophisticated understanding of heredity provided by Mendelism would have to be applied to populations containing a wide range of individual variation and that selection might affect the relative frequencies of the genes. By 1940 many naturalists had come to recognize that their own work could be reconciled with this new form of selectionism, eliminating the need for unsubstantiated alternatives, such as Lamarckism. The resulting "evolutionary synthesis" or "modern synthesis" allowed Darwinism to reemerge as a driving force in biology.

*   *   *

† From *Evolution: The History of an Idea* (Berkeley, Calif., 1984). Copyright © 1984. Reprinted by permission of the University of California Press. Peter Bowler (b. 1944) is professor of social anthropology at Queen's University, Belfast.

Population Genetics

Although many early forms of population genetics ignored vital Darwinian factors, such as geographical isolation, they enabled natural selection to reemerge as a viable mechanism of adaptive evolution. In the period before 1920, geneticists had been convinced that mutation was the only source of new characteristics in evolution; and they did not believe that differences in the adaptive value of new genes would control the extent to which they would spread in a wild population. Laboratory biologists were only too willing to ignore the pressures that might affect an organism living in the wild state. They played down the role of adaptation in evolution at the expense of processes, such as mutation, that could be studied in an artificial environment. The split with field naturalists was exaggerated by antagonisms that sprang up between early Mendelians, such as William Bateson, and the biometrical school, which had tried to preserve the Darwinian approach to the variation of wild populations. Recognizing that the genetical structure of a population is far more complex than had been imagined at first was a crucial step in the resurgence of Darwinism. Only then could it be supposed that selection for adaptive advantage might increase the frequency of some genes within the population at the expense of others. This development arose chiefly from the work of three men: R. A. Fisher and J. B. S. Haldane in Britain and Sewall Wright in America. For all its mathematical sophistication, the work of Fisher and Haldane arose out of what Mayr (1959c) has termed the "beanbag" approach to genetics: selection was supposed to act upon individual genes, each of which could be assigned a fixed adaptive value. Evolution would consist of no more than the addition and subtraction of genes from the "gene pool" of the population. Wright's approach stressed the interactions between genes as a source of additional variability within small, inbreeding populations. This more subtle view of the role played by genetics blended far more easily with the field naturalists' belief that geographical isolation was crucial for speciation. * * *

As early as 1902, G. Udny Yule pointed out that Mendel's laws were not necessarily incompatible with the biometrical approach to the measurement of variation. The Mendelians emphasized discontinuous variation because this was more accessible to their experimental techniques, dismissing continuous variation as of no genetic or evolutionary significance. Yule showed, however, that continuously varying characteristics might be explained by the inheritance of factors obeying Mendel's laws, provided it was assumed that more than a single pair of genetic alternatives could influence the same characteristic. If a series of genetic factors generates small degrees of difference in the same characteristic, the simple Mendelian ratios will be lost in the constant recombination of the factors. The interaction of the many factors will produce, in effect, a continuous range of variation.

Yule's suggestion had immense potential. If the biometricians could accept Mendelian inheritance, Fleeming Jenkin's classic "swamping argument" against the inclusion of mutations in selection would be overthrown. The effect of the new factor would not be halved in each generation by blending; instead it would spread unchanged through the population, especially if it conferred an adaptive benefit. By adopting Yule's point, the biometricians would have gained a valuable advantage and still retained their own techniques for the study of continuous variation.

* * *

The modern synthesis was based upon the alternative, or "balance" hypothesis of population structure. Morgan and Muller repudiated what was to become one of the most important insights of the new population genetics: that a wide range of genes affecting each characteristic already exists in any natural population for selection to act upon. Genetic characteristics produced by mutation continue to circulate within the population at a low frequency even if they confer no advantage, and the species thus builds up a fund of variability that can be exploited by selection when conditions change. Even in a stable environment, "balancing selection" actively helps to maintain the range of genetic variation that will later be exploited in adaptive evolution.

The existence of a wide degree of inheritable variation had been a central tenet of biometrical Darwinism. It was now necessary to interpret this in Mendelian terms through a multiple-factor explanation of continuous variation, and to show that selection had the power to change the frequency of a beneficial gene. * * *

Ronald Aylmer Fisher was trained in mathematics at Cambridge and became interested in Pearson's biometrical techniques. He soon broke with Pearson on the question of Mendelism, although MacKenzie argues that he remained loyal to the biometrical program. Fisher realized that Mendel's laws could solve many of the problems created by Pearson's reliance on blending heredity. Unit characteristics would preserve themselves without blending, and thus would keep up the variability of the population. His first paper on this topic was rejected by the Royal Society of London, so sensitive were the feelings raised by the biometry-Mendelism dispute, and eventually appeared in the transactions of the Royal Society of Edinburgh (1918). Over the next decade, Fisher applied his techniques to study the effect of selection upon a genetically variable population, culminating with the appearance of his classic *Genetical Theory of Natural Selection* (1930).

Fisher made a number of assumptions to arrive at a workable mathematical model. Selection was supposed to act uniformly on a large population in which genetic recombination maximized variability. If a particular gene conferred an advantage resulting in a faster breeding rate, it was possible to calculate how rapidly its frequency would be increased. In Fisher's scheme, selection was a deterministic process, grinding away slowly but surely to increase the frequency of individual genes. Because the model worked with single genes, it was still based on the beanbag approach; although it showed that selection could only reduce the frequency of an unfavored gene, not eliminate it altogether if it were protected by being recessive. Fisher demonstrated that selection could act to maintain the balance between two alleles when the heterozygote is fitter than either homozygote. Most mutations were acknowledged to be deleterious, but because they tended to occur at a fixed rate, this balanced the efforts of selection to reduce their frequency. In a small population, a rare gene could be eliminated by chance. For this reason, Fisher believed that large populations benefited evolution by keeping up variability. A gene that at some point became favorable to the species would immediately begin to increase its frequency. Fisher assumed that new factors fed into the gene pool by mutation were generally very small, so that they became part of the regular variability of the species. Thus although selection made use of discrete mutations, evolution was still a relatively continuous process with no sudden leaps.

J. B. S. Haldane published his first paper of population genetics in 1924 and an important survey of the field in 1932. Like Fisher, he made certain assumptions in order to simplify the mathematics: an infinite population with random mating, perfect Mendelian dominance, and segregation. Again, the emphasis was on selection applied to single genes, but Haldane used practical examples to show that the process could work much more rapidly than Fisher supposed. The best known was the case of industrial melanism in the peppered moth 'Amphidasys' betularia (now renamed Biston betularia). A dark-colored or melanic form of this moth first had been noted in 1848 and had begun to spread in industrial areas of Britain where its color offered protection from predators by concealing it against the soot-covered background. By 1900 the melanic form almost completely replaced the normal gray version of the moth in these areas. Haldane showed that so rapid a spread must indicate a fifty-percent greater production of offspring by the melanic form, a far more intense selective effect than anything imagined by Fisher.

Because Fisher and Haldane both assumed that selection was most effective when it acted on the wide variability of a large population, their theories dealt only with the question of evolution in a continuous, unbranching line. They ignored the field naturalists' interest in speciation, splitting of a population into a number of distinct branches, and were unwilling to concede that geographically isolated populations might play a significant role in evolution. In addition, their use of the beanbag approach treated each gene as an individual unit with a particular adaptive value. This did not take into account the possibility that genes interact with one another, enabling new interactions to extend the variability of a population without the creation of new genes by mutation, and sidestepping Johannsen's claim that the amount of genetic variation is rigidly limited.

* * *

The Modern Synthesis

Few field naturalists could follow the complex mathematics employed by the founders of population genetics. They could only translate the mathematical conclusions into commonsense language and then see if the results offered any insights into their own level of research. A form of population thinking had arisen spontaneously among naturalists who were dealing with geographical variation within and between species. They had realized that the intricate patterns of variation could not be reconciled with a typological view of species in which a basic underlying form was only superficially modified by local conditions. Each local variety or subspecies had to be treated as a distinct breeding population with its own character, reproductively isolated from neighboring groups even where geographical barriers no longer separated them. These naturalists were sure that geographical isolation was crucial for the first splitting up of a once homogeneous population, and that the conditions each subspecies was exposed to had shaped its unique character. Only when this kind of population thinking was fused with mathematical population genetics did the true outlines of the modern synthesis emerge. The techniques used by Fisher and Haldane were less easy to adapt to the naturalists' geographical insights, but even so their work was sufficiently convincing that the majority of biologists now recognized that selection was a powerful mechanism of adaptive evolution. Field naturalists began to abandon their earlier reliance on unsubstantiated alternatives, such as Lamarckism, as news of the mathematicians' conclusions filtered through to them. Not surprisingly, it was Wright's approach that proved easiest to apply to field work, because his emphasis on the role of small, inbreeding populations exactly matched the geographical studies. Theodosius Dobzhansky exploited Wright's conclusions in his highly influential *Genetics and the Origin of Species* (1937), triggering an explosion of activity that initiated the modern synthesis during the 1940s.

* * *

Most influential of all was Julian Huxley, a grandson of T. H. Huxley, who began teaching at Oxford in 1920. Naturally enough, Huxley absorbed his Darwinism from an earlier generation of biologists and began to work for a revival of the theory. He collaborated with H. G. Wells to produce *The Science of Life* (1930), a comprehensive and popular account of the Darwinian view of evolution. His own work on animal behavior fell within the natural history tradition, but he also was interested in embryological growth and kept up with the latest developments in genetics. In 1940 he edited *The New Systematics*, which brought together contributions from all sides of biology, and his own comprehensive survey, *Evolution: the Modern Synthesis*, appeared in 1942. * * *

In 1930 Ernst Mayr came to America from Germany, after several years' field work with birds of New Guinea and the Solomon islands. Mayr was influenced by Bernhard Rensch, who had revived the belief that there was a strong correlation between geographical variation and climate. Rensch and Mayr began with a Lamarckian explanation of this phenomenon, but in the 1930s they both realized that a Darwinian explanation was now possible. Mayr had not read the work of the mathematical geneticists, so that his own experiences form the basis of his claim that a populational view of species was developed independently on the basis of field research.

For Mayr, as for many other naturalists, it was Dobzhansky's *Genetics and the Origin of Species* that pointed the way toward a complete reconciliation by presenting the mathematicians' conclusions in an intelligible form. Mayr's own *Systematics and the Origin of Species* (1942) was one of the founding works of the modern synthesis, emphasizing the role of geographical factors in speciation.

When Theodosius Dobzhansky joined T. H. Morgan's team at Columbia University in 1927, he brought with him the experience of the Russian school's populational approach. He thus was able to appreciate what the field naturalists required from the geneticists, with the result that *Genetics and the Origin of Species* (1937) played a vital role in bridging the gap between the practical experience of the naturalists and the abstract formulations of the experimental and mathematical biologists. In it Dobzhansky summarized the experimental evidence showing the true nature of mutations, emphasizing how small their effects could be and how they built up the natural variability of populations. He also summarized the mathematicians' conclusions, paying particular attention to Wright's work. His own studies of the genetical basis of geographical variation in insects were discussed, along with other demonstrations of the same effect. From 1938 onward, Dobzhansky collaborated with Wright in a series of investigations of the genetics of natural populations. One aim of this research was to show that selection is not just a mechanism of change but can also act to maintain stability through balancing mechanisms, such as that based on superior heterozygote fitness. The widespread existence of such dynamic equilibria is important for modern Darwinism, because it demonstrates that populations do indeed contain substantial reservoirs of genetic variation that can be tapped under new conditions.

Dobzhansky coined the term "isolating mechanism" to denote nongenetic characteristics, such as behavioral differences, that can prevent interbreeding when two related populations come to occupy the same area. Founders of the modern synthesis were convinced that speciation occurred only through an initial phase of geographical isolation, for which Mayr introduced the term "allopatric speciation." With no interbreeding, the various populations could develop their own distinctive characteristics. Isolating mechanisms prevent them from interbreeding even if geographical barriers are subsequently removed; this allows the subspecies to remain distinct and to be driven apart further by selection. The new Darwinism was based on the assumption that speciation did not require special genetic mechanisms; given geographical isolation, natural selection alone can separate one species into many.

The evolutionary synthesis was extended to paleontology chiefly by George Gaylord Simpson, in his *Tempo and Mode in Evolution* (1944). Simpson's task was to demonstrate the plausibility of the claim that macroevolution as revealed by the fossil record took place through the accumulated effect of microevolutionary processes that were now being studied in modern populations. No proof could be offered; but it was possible to show that the available evidence from paleontology was at least consistent with the new theory, despite the anti-Darwinian claims of an earlier generation of biologists. Simpson used a quantitative analysis to show that

major evolutionary developments took place in the irregular and undi-
rected manner predicted by Darwinism. He exposed the weakness of the
evidence that had been used to argue for a linearity of development more
appropriate to Lamarckism or orthogenesis. The evolution of the horse,
for instance, was not a single advance toward the modern, specialized
form; rather it was an irregular tree with many side-branches leading off
to extinction. On the vexing question of the discontinuity of the fossil
sequences, Simpson realized that something more than the imperfection
of the record was involved. Substantial changes could take place through
nonadaptive "quantum evolution," employing Wright's mechanism of genetic drift.

*   *   *

Of the founders of the modern synthesis, Julian Huxley and George
Gaylord Simpson made the greatest effort to extend the new Darwinism
into a general world view. Huxley's *Evolution in Action* (1953) and Simpson's *The Meaning of Evolution* (1949) were intended explicitly to go beyond the technical details of the theory into a broader vision of the nature
and purpose of life. They adopt a positivist philosophy in which science
is the only source of knowledge, and see evolution as the new foundation
of morality, replacing the transcendental source of values invoked by religion. Both writers strove to get away from the mechanistic image of science by stressing the creative, opportunistic aspects of life's development
within the Darwinian scheme. They also conceded that simpleminded
attempts to explain society in terms of human biology were no longer
plausible. It was essential to recognize that man's emergence was not preordained, because Darwinian evolution is not teleological in character;
but the hope was that the process of evolution itself would teach us how
best to meet future challenges. Man has become the dominant form of
life on earth and is now taking charge of his own evolution. Indeed, he
has become responsible for the future of all living things, and his success
will be measured by the extent to which he carries on the creative heritage
of nature. Huxley saw evolution as inherently progressive, leading to successively higher levels of dominant life forms; progress was measured by
an increasing ability to transcend limits imposed by the environment. Freedom to realize the potentialities of life thus was seen as the highest good.
Simpson was more skeptical of the progressionist interpretation but still
saw man as the high point of a tendency for life to develop greater awareness of its surroundings. The drive for knowledge took on an ethical value,
as something man could use for his own benefit and the benefit of all
forms of life for which he is now responsible. * * *

THE HUMAN GENEALOGY

ADAM KUPER

The Chosen Primate (1994)†

To Begin at the Beginning

What makes the human species different from other primates? The
Swedish botanist and explorer Carl Linnaeus pioneered the systematic
classification of natural species. He named the genus *Homo* in 1735, and
classified it alongside apes and monkeys, which he called "Simia," in a
family that he named *Anthropomorpha*. Curiously enough, Linnaeus distinguished the members of this family particularly by the form of the teeth.
He also insisted that they were all quadrupeds—including humans. Man,
as Linnaeus summed him up, "has a mouth made like that of other quadrupeds, and finally four feet, on two of which he goes, and [he] uses the
other two for prehensive purposes."

In 1776 the German anatomist Johann Friedrich Blumenbach protested
that humans were bipeds, and he placed them in a separate class, the
Bimana, or two-handed. Blumenbach insisted that there was a great gulf
between humans and other animals, of which bipedalism was a sign. Linnaeus, in contrast, believed that the differences between people and simians were not great. "Indeed," he admitted, "to speak the truth, as a natural
historian according to the principles of science, up to the present time I
have not been able to discover any character by which man can be distinguished from the ape."

When a colleague remonstrated with him for situating the human species among the *Anthropomorphi*, he replied: "It matters little to me what
name we use; but I demand of you, and of the whole world, that you show
me a generic character—one that is according to generally accepted principles of classification, by which to distinguish between Man and Ape. I
myself most assuredly know of none. I wish someone would indicate one
to me. But, if I had called man an ape, or vice versa, I should have fallen
under the ban of all the ecclesiastics. It may be that as a naturalist I ought
to have done so."

Linnaeus thought that species were fixed. He rejected the vulgar notion
that the human races were significantly different from one another, and
therefore assumed that the genus *Homo* had always contained only one
species, *Homo sapiens*, the modern human type.

Today, two extinct species—*Homo habilis* and *Homo erectus*—are classified as *Homo*, alongside *Homo sapiens*. They are ancestral to modern
humans. It is likely that *Homo sapiens* evolved from *Homo erectus*, which
evolved from *Homo habilis*. The identification of these ancestral human

† From *The Chosen Primate* (Cambridge, Mass., 1994). Reprinted by permission of the publisher:
Harvard University Press, Copyright © 1989 by the President and Fellows of Harvard College.
Adam Kuper (b. 1941) is in the Department of Human Sciences, Brunel University.

species makes it even harder to meet Linnaeus's challenge and to identify one generic principle that would mark off *Homo*. Moreover, Linnaeus only had to worry about the similarities between humans and apes, while we have to accommodate a further extinct genus of near-humans in our debates: *Australopithecus*, which was discovered in 1924. *Australopithecus* was the ancestor of the genus *Homo*, but the boundary line that divides the one from the other is still uncertainly demarcated. Some problematic specimens might be put in either category.

Perhaps the boundary must be moved. It would not be the first time that this has happened. Every time a new species was recognized as *Homo*, the very definition of *Homo* had to be changed to accommodate it. This may seem paradoxical, even somewhat unnerving, but similar uncertainties are inherent in the whole project of evolutionary biology. Every population is changing, and must be transitional between an earlier and a later type. A system of classification has to be devised that captures fluid, diverging characteristics. The old-style definitions of Linnaean biology, which were supposed to fix the unchanging essence of a species, simply became obsolete once evolutionary theory was understood.

What, then, makes us human? Various changes in morphology marked off the human lineage from other primates. Those most commonly cited are the switch to bipedalism, which is associated with the specialization of the hand; changes in the shape and function of the jaw and teeth; and increases in brain size. There are also specifically human skills, notably, perhaps, hunting (which is rare among other primates), tool-making, and language.

Although some purists would prefer to consider morphology and behavior separately, changes in behavior and morphology are usually tied together in evolutionary narratives. Consider one familiar example. Bipedalism is said to have freed the hands for tool use, which enabled humans to hunt stronger and faster animals. As the hominid diet changed, the jaws and teeth went through various adaptations. The cleverer proto-humans must have enjoyed an advantage as toolmakers and hunters. Consequently there would have been selection for higher cranial capacity, which eventually made possible the development of language. And so such narratives go on, constructing human history from a plausible mix of natural and cultural forces.

However complex the narratives they spun, most theorists have assumed that one particular element in the makeup of humans drove the evolutionary process. Linnaeus speculated that the peculiarly human attribute might prove to be the ability to reason: he was, after all, an eighteenth-century man. Darwin naturalized reason. He was particularly impressed by the size of the human brain, and argued that the exceptional growth of the brain in humans had caused the intellectual and moral development that ensured human success.

In a special note contributed as an appendix to chapter 7 of *The Descent of Man*, Huxley compared the brain of humans and that of other primates, and established their structural similarity. The main difference was one of size and, presumably, complexity. "As the various mental faculties gradually developed the brain would almost certainly become larger," Darwin wrote. "No one, I presume, doubts that the large proportion which the size of man's brain bears to his body, compared to the same proportion in the gorilla or orang, is closely connected with his higher mental powers."

Following Darwin and Huxley, cranial capacity became a defining trait of the genus *Homo*. The somewhat dubious assumption was that cranial capacity provided a surrogate for a measure of brain size, and, what was perhaps even more questionable, that brain size would indicate brain power. The volume and weight of the human brain, relative to body size, are some three times greater than might be expected in a primate. The cerebral cortex accounts for three-quarters of total brain weight in humans, which is, again, a uniquely high proportion. Moreover, the development of human cranial capacity is a dramatic feature of the evolutionary story.

* * *

In 1856, workmen in a limestone quarry in the Neander valley near Düsseldorf in Germany discovered some curious fossils. These were identified by Hermann Schaaffhausen, Professor of Anatomy at the University of Bonn, as ancient human remains. He concluded that they represented a barbarous race that had roamed northwestern Europe before the Roman Empire, and he speculated that their repulsive aspect and flashing eyes must have given the first Roman soldiers to penetrate the region rather a nasty shock.

Charles Lyell, the geologist, ordered a plaster cast of the specimens and studied the animal bones that had been found in association with the remains. He concluded that they were very much more ancient than Schaaffhausen had supposed. But although Lyell was a mentor of Darwin, with whom he remained in regular contact, he was reluctant to accept the view that human beings had evolved relatively recently. He identified the fossils as belonging to an extinct species of ape.

Huxley, one of the first Darwinians, was impressed rather by the cranial capacity of the Neanderthals, which fell within the modern human range. This feature persuaded him that the Neanderthals were humans rather than apes. Nevertheless, he judged that they were not directly ancestral to modern humans, since the Neanderthal skull shape was very different from that of living populations.

Other fossils of a similar nature were soon discovered, but the experts could not agree on their interpretation. * * *

In time two incompatible theories crystallized on the Neanderthal question. Gradualists believed that the Neanderthals were immediate ancestors of modern Europeans. Catastrophists argued (as Huxley had done) that the Neanderthals represented a fairly recent "Praesapiens" human which had lived in Europe, become extinct, and left no issue. There was one point, however, on which agreement was soon reached: the Neanderthals were not ancient apelike protohumans who would represent at once the first generation of humanity and the last link with the apes. They had perished long before the Roman legionaries penetrated northern Europe, but nevertheless they had lived too recently, and were too similar to modern humans, to qualify as the elusive "missing link."

The leading Continental advocate of Darwinian theory, Ernst Haeckel, initiated a tradition of research that aimed to identify the missing link between apes and humans, a creature he called *Pithecanthropus* ("Ape-man"). He speculated that it would walk semi-erect but lack the power of speech.

Darwin and Huxley had identified the African apes as the species closest to humans, and Darwin thought it likely that human beings had also evolved in Africa. ("It is therefore probable that Africa was formerly inhabited by extinct apes closely allied to the gorilla and chimpanzee," Darwin wrote, "and as these two species are now man's nearest allies, it is somewhat more probable that our early progenitors lived on the African continent than elsewhere.") Haeckel, however, judged that human evolution began in the East, where the orangutan and gibbon of the Indonesian archipelago might prove to be yet closer kin to ourselves than the African apes.

Inspired by these speculations, a young Dutch doctor, Eugene Dubois, signed up with the colonial army and proceeded to Sumatra. Reports that a curious skull had been found there took him to Java in 1891, but the skulls he was shown were clearly modern. Then he found his own specimens: a skull that appeared to be primitive, in association with a femur which was like that of a modern human. He concluded that he had found an erect but apelike creature, and in 1894 he announced that he had identified the missing link, which he called *Pithecanthropus erectus* ("the erect ape-man").

It was not certain that the skull and femur did indeed belong to the same specimen, or even that they dated from the same period, for the stratigraphy was complex. At the time, however, experts were more concerned that the skullcap seemed more modern than Dubois allowed.

Cheated of his triumph, Dubois retreated in dudgeon to a series of Dutch museums, where he held minor appointments, taking his fossils with him. Eventually, in 1923, he permitted British and American authorities to examine his finds, which they identified as belonging not to an ape or an ape-man, but rather to an archaic but definitely human type. This judgment was vindicated when in 1929 W. C. Pei discovered a skullcap in the Zhoukoudian cave near Peking that closely resembled the Javanese specimens, but was clearly human. Further specimens were uncovered in the following decade. All are less than a million years old, and all are unequivocally human. They are now identified as archaic *Homo sapiens*, or as representatives of another, extinct, species of *Homo*, *Homo erectus*.

* * *

Despite Darwin's deduction that human origins would be traced to Africa, the home of the gorilla and the chimpanzee, for a generation after his death all the important finds had been made in Europe and Asia. Then, in 1925, a young anatomist in South Africa, Raymond Dart, described a fossil hominid infant skull—the "Taung baby"—which had been discovered in a remote quarry in the northern Cape. He claimed that it represented an apelike human ancestor, and named it *Australopithecus africanus*, the "Southern ape."

But while Dubois had been told that his ape-man was really human, Dart's specimen was classified by the London scientists as a fossil ape. Leading the opposition was Sir Arthur Keith, the advocate of a large-brained ancestor, Piltdown Man. The comparatively recent Taung fossil, with its rather human jaw and apelike brain, was virtually a mirror image of Piltdown Man. "What was so unexpected about its structure?" asks Phillip Tobias, Dart's successor as Professor of Anatomy at the University of the Witwatersrand. "The short answer is that Taung was the first of the *small-brained hominids* to be found." It was above all because of its cranial capacity that Keith was not disposed to accept that the Taung specimen could possibly represent an ancestor of modern humans.

Like Dubois, Dart endured decades of isolation without ever doubting his initial intuition, but his case was helped by the discovery of more complete fossils in South African sites, thanks largely to the efforts of another isolated South African scholar, Robert Broom. Broom and other scientists eventually recovered some three hundred specimens of *Australopithecus* from one site alone, the Sterkfontein cave in the Transvaal. Yet for many lonely years Dart and Broom were treated as cranks, as they proclaimed their discoveries in scientific journals and even the popular press. It was only in the late 1940s that one of the leading British scientists in the field, Sir Wilfred Le Gros Clark, visited Dart and was persuaded that the African *Australopithecus* did indeed represent a remote but direct ancestor of *Homo*. Reluctantly, even Sir Arthur Keith was obliged to agree, admitting in a letter to *Nature* that "Professor Dart was right and I was wrong."

*　　*　　*

Apparently Darwin and Huxley had been right after all. The original proto-human beings were neighbors, and kin, to the African apes. For the next generation, the great source of fossil hominids was in Africa, above all eastern Africa, where the Leakey family made a remarkable series of discoveries.

Louis Leakey was born in 1903 in a mission station near Nairobi, where he learned Kikuyu, conceived a passion for collecting Stone Age tools, and grew up with a strong sense of loyalty to his African home. Education in an English public school and at Cambridge University seems only to have confirmed his sense of himself as a colonial outsider (although he did manage to persuade the university authorities that he should be allowed to offer Kikuyu to meet the modern language requirement). He made his career in East Africa, where he was based at the Nairobi Museum. His funding depended on his ability to inspire benefactors (notably the *National Geographic*). He loved to publish his discoveries and speculations in popular papers, and to demonstrate that an undeferential outsider could oblige those in the British establishment to rethink their view of the world.

His second wife, Mary Leakey, was descended from the father of British archaeology, John Frere (1740–1807), but she was more immediately the rebellious daughter of an artist, who had given her a cosmopolitan but wayward upbringing. Adrift on her own as a teenager in London, she had made herself into a good scientific draftsman and become a fervent amateur archaeologist. When she marched into Leakey's life at the age of twenty-two, smoking cigarettes, wearing trousers, beautiful, and devoted to his quest, she brought with her a further and incalculable gift: luck.

Their son, Richard Leakey, was to become—at first reluctantly—the third member of the family team. He showed all of Louis's talent for organization and publicity, and a similar determination; and something too of Louis's sense of himself as a gifted outsider struggling against the entrenched, prejudiced metropolitan specialists. (Richard, like Mary, lacked any formal training.) To all this was added the irreplaceable luck of Mary Leakey.

* * *

The Leakey family had meanwhile discovered yet another candidate for an ancient human forebear. The discoverer was Louis Leakey's youngest son, Jonathan, only nineteen years old and just out of school. Wandering around Olduvai in May 1960, he came upon some bones and teeth that apparently belonged to a large-brained human creature. Geologists were on hand, and they fixed the date of the site at 1.7 million years old. A promising feature was that the fossils were associated with forty-eight stone artifacts.

Phillip Tobias was called in again by the Leakeys, and this time, after another prolonged investigation, and despite initial skepticism, he came down on Louis's side. Here at last was an ancient human tool-maker. In 1964, Leakey, Tobias, and a British anatomist, John Napier, announced the discovery of a new species of the genus *Homo*, which they named *Homo habilis*. It was the third species in the genus, joining *Homo sapiens* and *Homo erectus*. (Represented by Java and Peking Man, *Homo erectus* had been accepted thirty years earlier.)

Leakey was triumphant, but this *Homo habilis* was still too recent for his ultimate purposes. The account of human evolution to which Leakey remained loyal required a very ancient, large-brained ancestor. Leakey's quest was to find a human ancestor older than the australopithecines. And in 1967, once again, a member of his family seemed to have come up with the goods. Richard Leakey had made a promising find at a new site, Koobi Fora, near Lake Turkana in Kenya.

New dating methods were being tried out in California, and these at first yielded a date for the fossils of 3 million years old. There were grounds for supposing that it was *Homo*; its skull was thinner, higher, and rounder than the typical australopithecine skull, and it had a larger cranial capacity. Moreover, stone tools were associated with the finds.

* * *

Richard Leakey had tried to buttress his intuition with the best scientific analysis he could command, but the experimental dating methods used

for the Koobi Fora fossils soon proved to be unreliable. It took several years
to establish a firm date, and then the Koobi Fora specimens turned out
to be less than 2 million years old. The only question that remained was
whether they should be classed as *Australopithecus* or *Homo habilis*.

By now the Leakey family had competition. Scientists flocked to what
a young Leakey collaborator, Glynn Isaac, called the East African Klon-
dike. Among the new wave was a young American, Donald Johanson.

Johanson's parents were immigrants. His father was a barber, his mother
a cleaning-lady. His manner was confident, even brash, his ambition
boundless. And in November 1974, taking part in an expedition at Hadar
in Ethiopia, he and a colleague discovered the most complete hominid
skeleton that had yet been found. The young men were euphoric. "There
was a tape recorder in the camp," Johanson has recalled, "and a tape of
the Beatles song 'Lucy in the Sky with Diamonds' went belting out into
the night sky, and was played at full volume over and over again out of
sheer exuberance." At some stage during the celebrations that evening, the
new fossil was christened Lucy.

Lucy was important because she was virtually intact. This was the only
complete skeleton that had been found of any fossil human older than the
Neanderthals. She had died at the age of about 25, some 3.5 million years
ago. She seemed human, for she walked erect, but she was an odd creature: her brain was in the same range as that of chimpanzees, she was only
36 inches high, and her hands hung down to her knees. If Lucy was an
australopithecine, it was clear that these creatures were similar to apes. If
Lucy had been caught alive, Glynn Isaac remarked, she would have been
put in a zoo.

The Leakey family had to share the limelight now, but Mary Leakey
was making intriguing discoveries in a new site, Laetoli in northern Tanzania. Her most astonishing find was made by accident in 1978–1979,
when she discovered hominid footprints set as if in concrete, preserved in
volcanic-ash layers, and dating to at least 3.6 million years ago. Analysis
of the footprints provided firm proof that early hominids were fully bipedal.

But as the finds piled up they began to raise fresh questions. A rather
diverse set of samples was accumulating within the broad category of *Australopithecus*. Should they be lumped together, or should different types
of *Australopithecus* be distinguished? And how did this increasingly diverse
group of specimens differ from *Homo habilis*?

Homo habilis was the object of much professional skepticism at first,
and recent evidence suggests that it is not easy to distinguish *Homo habilis*
from its close kin. The distinction between *Australopithecus* and *Homo
habilis* depends largely on two features: an increased cranial capacity and
a reduced tooth size. Brain capacity has traditionally been critical to the
definition of the genus *Homo*, but although the cranial capacity of *Homo
habilis* (which was, however, highly variable) could be significantly larger
than that of *Australopithecus*, it did not fall within the accepted human
range. Moreover, the extent of variation between fossils classified as *Homo
habilis* turned out to be disturbingly great. In the end, the main evidence
that a new evolutionary epoch had begun was not so much morphological

as cultural. As its name—"Handyman"—suggests, *Homo habilis* was identified as the first tool-maker.

Ruminating on these uncertainties, Don Johanson teamed up with Tim
White, another American scientist, who was working with Mary Leakey in
Laetoli. In the summer of 1977, they put the Laetoli casts and the Hadar
samples side by side on one table in Johanson's laboratory in Cleveland.
"It was an uncanny experience," Johanson recalls. "One fact came bursting
from the surface of the table: the two sets of fossils were startlingly alike."

But were they australopithecines? They seemed to be quite different
from the South African specimens that were taken to define the type. Two
South African varieties of australopithecines were already recognized, the
robust and the gracile, though anthropologists did not agree which was
the more ancient, and how each fitted into a human genealogy. Now a
third variety was added, dubbed *Australopithecus afarensis*, after the region
in Ethiopia where specimens were first discovered. White and Johanson
suggested in 1981 that *afarensis* was the direct ancestor of *Homo habilis*,
and also of a branching line that led to the other australopithecines.

This solution did not convince everyone, and some scientists began to
suspect that among the fossils found in East and South Africa were representatives of yet more species of both *Australopithecus* and *Homo*. Was
Lucy herself perhaps the representative of another species of *Homo*?

The questions were urgent, and there were spirited public debates between the two stars, Richard Leakey and Don Johanson. Nevertheless, by
this stage much had become clearer. A new synthesis could tentatively be
put together.

The first traces of the primate order in the fossil record have been dated
to some 60 million years ago. This suggests that primates evolved about 5
million years after the catastrophe that brought about the extinction of the
dinosaurs and left the mammals with a decisive comparative advantage in
the struggle for life.

The first fossil remnants of anthropoid apes are dated to some 30 million
years ago. About 12 million years ago, the common ancestors of the hominids and their closest surviving relatives, the African apes, branched off
from the other apes. The human lineage itself—the hominid family—
became differentiated roughly 5 million years ago.

Unfortunately, this crucial period coincides with one of the longest modern gaps in the fossil record, which runs from some 4 to 8 million years
ago. In consequence, there is still no direct evidence for the nature of the
first hominids. We must rely largely on deductions based on the differences
between hominids and other surviving primate species.

Until the hominid branch diverged, all primates were dominantly arboreal creatures, living on a mainly vegetarian diet. Living primates—and
probably their ancestors—are remarkable for the dominance of vision over
the sense of smell, their complex grasping and manipulative skills, and the
possession of a brain that represents a significantly higher proportion of
body weight than is the case for any other mammals. The apes (and humans) are further distinguished by a preference for fruit and plant food

over leaves, their lack of tails, and their generally greater size than the monkeys.

The first distinctive feature of the human lineage to evolve was bipedalism, although the decisive nature of this break should not be exaggerated. Hominids remained well adapted to tree climbing for at least two million years. Nevertheless, all other primates preferred to use their forelimbs to help them move about. The apes generally practice "knuckle-walking," their forepaws bent inward as they brush across the ground. Hominids were the only primates that walked upright for much of the time.

The causes and consequences of the distinctively upright, two-legged human gait have been debated since Darwin. The immediate stimulus for bipedalism was probably the need to adapt to terrestrial living. There was a gradual decline in temperatures. In the tropical regions the forest retreated and savannah spread. Many forest creatures became extinct, including a number of species of ape. The first hominids prospered by adapting to life on the plains. The ability to walk on two legs gave them an edge in making this shift: it permitted them to move about in open country with less effort than the other apes, allowed them to see over the vegetation as they moved, and protected them to some extent from exposure to direct sunlight.

What then were the consequences of bipedalism? Darwin suggested that bipedalism left humans defenseless, and so stimulated the invention of tools and weapons, and that the survival of a bipedal tool-user in this new open environment would also have required the development of intelligence and of those "social qualities which lead him to give and receive aid from his fellow men." Several generations of scientists assumed that there was a close relationship between bipedalism and the development of a human brain, but it is now evident that bipedalism had developed by 4 million years ago, while the rapid evolution of the human brain began only some 2 million years ago. Quite possibly, then, bipedalism was important simply for itself: it enabled early hominids to operate more effectively in open country. Our main physical differences from other apes and from our own distant ancestors have to do with bipedalism, associated shifts in the pelvis and the upper skeleton, modifications of the teeth and jaw, and changes in cranial capacity.

*   *   *

Today some specialists are tempted to reclassify the *Homo habilis* specimens as local varieties of *Australopithecus* and *Homo erectus*. This would leave only two species of *Homo*: *Homoe erectus* and *Homo sapiens*. Others—including Bernard Wood himself and Chris Stringer of London's Natural History Museum—take a very different view. They think it more likely that there are further species of *Homo* still to be identified. *Homo habilis*, perhaps, seems so variable because more than one species has been put into the same category.

Homo erectus evolved 1.8 or 1.7 million years ago. Whether the new hominid species evolved directly from *Homo habilis* or from another hominid contemporary, or even perhaps directly from one of the varieties of *Australopithecus*, is still uncertain. In any case, the earliest *Homo erectus* fossils have all been found in eastern and southern Africa, which was almost certainly once again the place of origin of a new hominid type. About one million years ago, at the start of the main Pleistocene ice age, representatives of *Homo erectus* dispersed to Asia, where they appear in the record most famously as Java Man and Peking Man. They also may have penetrated into Europe. *Homo erectus* was probably the only hominid species on earth for nearly a million years. There was no doubt considerable local variation, but what is most striking is the relative stability of *Homo erectus*, both biologically (as far as can be discovered from fossil remains) and in its behavior over this huge stretch of time.

*   *   *

Beginning with a radical reexamination of the animal bones associated with early *Homo*, [Lewis] Binford brought into question the hunting capability of *Homo erectus*. Soon he began to undermine each of the established claims for the cultural skills of early humans, and young scholars swarmed in to consolidate the work of destruction. By the mid-1980s it seemed that none of the familiar claims could stand up to critical scrutiny.

The implications were formidable. *Homo erectus* had very nearly a modern brain capacity, but apparently very little in the way of human culture to show for it. If human origins are taken to mean the beginnings of a recognizably human culture, then the first 3.5 million of the 4 million years of hominid evolution must be counted still as a period of pre-human history.

IAN TATTERSALL

Out of Africa Again . . . and Again? (1997)†

It all used to seem so simple. The human lineage evolved in Africa. Only at a relatively late date did early humans finally migrate from the continent of their birth, in the guise of the long-known species *Homo erectus*, whose first representatives had arrived in eastern Asia by around one million years ago. All later kinds of humans were the descendants of this species, and almost everyone agreed that all should be classified in our own species, *H. sapiens*. To acknowledge that some of these descendants were strikingly different from ourselves, they were referred to as "archaic *H. sapiens*," but members of our own species they were nonetheless considered to be.

Such beguiling simplicity was, alas, too good to last, and over the past few years it has become evident that the later stages of human evolution

† From "Out of Africa Again . . . and Again?", *Scientific American* 276 (Apr. 1997). Reprinted with permission. Copyright © 1998 by Scientific American, Inc. All rights reserved. Ian Tattersall (b. 1945) is curator in the Department of Anthropology at the American Museum of Natural History in New York City.

have been a great deal more eventful than conventional wisdom for so long had it. This is true for the earlier stages, too, although there is still no reason to believe that humankind's birthplace was elsewhere than in Africa. Indeed, for well over the first half of the documented existence of the hominid family (which includes all upright-walking primates), there is no record at all outside that continent. But recent evidence does seem to indicate that it was not necessarily *H. erectus* who migrated from Africa—and that these peregrinations began earlier than we had thought.

A Confused Early History

Recent discoveries in Kenya of fossils attributed to the new species *Australopithecus anamensis* have now pushed back the record of upright-walking hominids to about 4.2 to 3.9 million years (Myr) ago. More dubious finds in Ethiopia, dubbed *Ardipithecus ramidus*, may extend this to 4.4 Myr ago or so. The *A. anamensis* fossils bear a strong resemblance to the later and far better known species *Australopithecus afarensis*, found at sites in Ethiopia and Tanzania in the 3.9- to 3.0-Myr range and most famously represented by the "Lucy" skeleton from Hadar, Ethiopia.

Lucy and her kind were upright walkers, as the structures of their pelvises and knee joints particularly attest, but they retained many ancestral features, notably in their limb proportions and in their hands and feet, that would have made them fairly adept tree climbers. Together with their ape-size brains and large, protruding faces, these characteristics have led many to call such creatures "bipedal chimpanzees." This is probably a fairly accurate characterization, especially given the increasing evidence that early hominids favored quite heavily wooded habitats. Their preferred way of life was evidently a successful one, for although these primates were less adept arborealists than the living apes and less efficient bipeds than later hominids, their basic "eat your cake and have it" adaptation endured for well over two million years, even as species of this general kind came and went in the fossil record.

It is not even clear to what extent lifestyles changed with the invention of stone tools, which inaugurate our archaeological record at about 2.5 Myr ago. No human fossils are associated with the first stone tools known, from sites in Kenya and Ethiopia. Instead there is a motley assortment of hominid fossils from the period following about 2 Myr ago, mostly associated with the stone tools and butchered mammal bones found at Tanzania's Olduvai Gorge and in Kenya's East Turkana region. By one reckoning, at least some of the first stone toolmakers in these areas were hardly bigger or more advanced in their body skeletons than the tiny Lucy; by another, the first tools may have been made by taller, somewhat larger-brained hominids with more modern body structures. Exactly how many species of early hominids there were, which of them made the tools, and how they walked remains one of the major conundrums of human evolution.

Physically, at least, the picture becomes clearer following about 1.9 Myr ago, when the first good evidence occurs in northern Kenya of a species that is recognizably like ourselves. Best exemplified by the astonishingly complete 1.6-Myr-old skeleton known as the Turkana Boy, discovered in 1984, these humans possessed an essentially modern body structure, indicative of modern gait, combined with moderately large-faced skulls that contained brains double the size of those of apes (though not much above half the modern human average). The Boy himself had died as an adolescent, but it is estimated that had he lived to maturity he would have attained a height of six feet, and his limbs were long and slender, like those of people who live today in hot, arid African climates, although this common adaptation does not, of course, indicate any special relationship. Here at last we have early hominids who were clearly at home on the open savanna.

A long-standing paleoanthropological tradition seeks to minimize the number of species in the human fossil record and to trace a linear, progressive pattern of descent among those few that are recognized. In keeping with this practice, the Boy and his relatives were originally assigned to the species *H. erectus*. This species was first described from a skullcap and thighbone found in Java a century ago. Fossils later found in China—notably the now lost 500,000-year-old (500 Kyr old) "Peking Man"—and elsewhere in Java were soon added to the species, and eventually *H. erectus* came to embrace a wide variety of hominid fossils, including a massive braincase from Olduvai Gorge known as OH9. The latter has been redated to about 1.4 Myr, although it was originally thought to have been a lot younger. All these fossil forms possessed brains of moderate size (about 900 to 1,200 milliliters in volume, compared with an average of around 1,400 milliliters for modern humans and about 400 milliliters for apes), housed in long, low skull vaults with sharp angles at the back and heavy brow ridges in front. The few limb bones known were robust but essentially like our own.

Whether *H. erectus* had ever occupied Europe was vigorously debated, the alternative being to view all early human fossils from that region (the earliest of them being no more than about 500 Kyr old) as representatives of archaic *H. sapiens*. Given that the Javan fossils were conventionally dated in the range of 1 Myr to 700 Kyr and younger and that the earliest Chinese fossils were reckoned to be no more than 1 Myr old, the conclusion appeared clear: *H. erectus* (as exemplified by OH9 and also by the earlier Turkana Boy and associated fossils) had evolved in Africa and had exited that continent not much more than 1 Myr ago, rapidly spreading to eastern Asia and spawning all subsequent developments in human evolution, including those in Europe.

Yet on closer examination the specimens from Kenya turned out to be distinctively different in braincase construction from those of classic eastern Asian *H. erectus*. In particular, certain anatomical features that appear specialized in the eastern Asian *H. erectus* look ancestral in the African fossils of comparable age. Many researchers began to realize that we are dealing with two kinds of early human here, and the earlier Kenyan form is now increasingly placed in its own species, *H. ergaster*. This species makes a plausible ancestor for all subsequent humans, whereas the cranial specializations of *H. erectus* suggest that this species, for so long regarded as the standard-issue hominid of the 1- to 0.5-Myr period, was in fact a local (and, as I shall explain below, ultimately terminal) eastern Asian development.

An Eastern Asian Cul-de-Sac

The plot thickened in early 1994, when Carl C. Swisher of the Berkeley Geochronology Center and his colleagues applied the newish argon/argon dating method to volcanic rock samples taken from two hominid sites in Java. The results were 1.81 and 1.66 Myr: far older than anyone had really expected, although the earlier date did confirm one made many years before. Unfortunately, the fossils from these two sites are rather undiagnostic as to species: the first is a braincase of an infant (juveniles never show all the adult characteristics on which species are defined), and the second is a horrendously crushed and distorted cranium that has never been satisfactorily reconstructed. Both specimens have been regarded by most as *H. erectus*, but more for reasons of convenience than anything else. Over the decades, sporadic debate has continued regarding whether the Javan record contains one or more species of early hominid. Further, major doubt has recently been cast on whether the samples that yielded the older date were actually obtained from the same spot as the infant specimen. Still, these dates do fit with other evidence pointing to the probability that hominids of some kind were around in eastern Asia much earlier than anyone had thought.

Independent corroboration of this scenario comes, for instance, from the site of Dmanisi in the former Soviet republic of Georgia, where in 1991 a hominid lower jaw was found that its describers allocated to *H. erectus*. Three different methods suggested that this jaw was as old as 1.8 Myr; although not everyone has been happy with this dating, taken together the Georgian and new Javan dates imply an unexpectedly early hominid exodus from Africa. And the most parsimonious reading of the admittedly imperfect record suggests that these pioneering emigrants must have been *H. ergaster* or something very much like it.

A very early hominid departure from Africa has the advantage of explaining an apparent anomaly in the archaeological record. The stone tools found in sediments coeval with the earliest *H. ergaster* (just under 2 Myr ago) are effectively identical with those made by the first stone toolmakers many hundreds of thousands of years before. These crude tools consisted principally of sharp flakes struck with a stone "hammer" from small cobbles. Effective cutting tools though these may have been (experimental archaeologists have shown that even elephants can be quite efficiently butchered using them), they were not made to a standard form but were apparently produced simply to obtain a sharp cutting edge. Following about 1.4 Myr ago, however, standardized stone tools began to be made in Africa, typified by the hand axes and cleavers of the Acheulean industry (first identified in the mid-19th century from St. Acheul in France). These were larger implements, carefully shaped on both sides to a tear-drop form. Oddly, stone tool industries in eastern Asia lacked such utensils, which led many to wonder why the first human immigrants to the region had not brought this technology with them, if their ancestors had already wielded it for half a million years. The new dates suggest, however, that the first emigrants had left Africa before the invention of the Acheulean technology, in which case there is no reason why we should expect to find this technology in eastern Asia. Interestingly, a few years ago the archaeologist Robin W. Dennell caused quite a stir by reporting very crude stone tools from Riwat in Pakistan that are older than 1.6 Myr. Their great age is now looking decreasingly anomalous.

Of course, every discovery raises new questions, and in this case the problem is to explain what it was that enabled human populations to expand beyond Africa for the first time. Most scholars had felt it was technological advances that allowed the penetration of the cooler continental areas to the north. If, however, the first emigrants left Africa equipped with only the crudest of stone-working technologies, we have to look to something other than technological prowess for the magic ingredient. And because the first human diaspora apparently followed hard on the heels of the acquisition of more or less modern body form, it seems reasonable to conclude that the typically human wanderlust emerged in concert with the emancipation of hominids from the forest edges that had been their preferred habitat. Of course, the fact that the Turkana Boy and his kin were adapted in their body proportions to hot, dry environments does nothing to explain why *H. ergaster* was able to spread rapidly into the cooler temperate zones beyond the Mediterranean; evidently the new body form that made possible remarkable endurance in open habitats was in itself enough to make the difference.

The failure of the Acheulean ever to diffuse as far as eastern Asia reinforces the notion, consistent with the cranial specializations of *H. erectus*, that this part of the world was a kind of paleoanthropological cul-de-sac. In this region ancient human populations largely followed their own course, independent of what was going on elsewhere in the world. Further datings tend to confirm this view. Thus, Swisher and his colleagues have very recently reported dates for the Ngandong *H. erectus* site in Java that center on only about 40 Kyr ago. These dates, though very carefully obtained, have aroused considerable skepticism; but, if accurate, they have considerable implications for the overall pattern of human evolution. For they are so recent as to suggest that the long-lived *H. erectus* might even have suffered a fate similar to that experienced by the Neanderthals in Europe: extinction at the hands of late-arriving *H. sapiens*. Here we find reinforcement of the gradually emerging picture of human evolution as one of repeated experimentation, with regionally differentiated species, in this case on opposite sides of the Eurasian continent, being ultimately replaced by other hominid lineages that had evolved elsewhere.

At the other end of the scale, an international group led by Huang Wanpo of Beijing's Academia Sinica last year reported a remarkably ancient date for Longgupo Cave in China's Sichuan Province. This site had previously yielded an incisor tooth and a tiny lower jaw fragment with two teeth that were initially attributed to *H. erectus*, plus a few very crude stone artifacts. Huang and his colleagues concluded that the fossils and tools might be as much as 1.9 Myr old, and their reanalysis of the fossils suggested to them a closer resemblance to earliest African *Homo* species than to *H. erectus*.

This latter claim has not gone unexamined. As my colleague Jeffrey H. Schwartz of the University of Pittsburgh and I pointed out, for instance, the teeth in the jaw fragment resemble African *Homo* in primitive features rather than in the specialized ones that indicate a special relationship. What is more, they bear a striking resemblance to the teeth of an orangutan-related hominoid known from a much later site in Vietnam. And although the incisor appears hominid, it is fairly generic, and there is nothing about it that aligns it with any particular human species. Future fossil finds from Longgupo will, with luck, clarify the situation; meanwhile the incisor and stone tools are clear evidence of the presence of humans in China at what may be a very early date indeed. These ancient eastern Asians were the descendants of the first emigrants from Africa, and, whatever the hominids of Longgupo eventually turn out to have been, it is a good bet that Huang and his colleagues are right in guessing that they represent a precursor form to *H. erectus* rather than that species itself.

All this makes sense, but one anomaly remains. If *H. erectus* was an indigenous eastern Asian development, then we have to consider whether we have correctly identified the Olduvai OH9 braincase as belonging to this species. If we have, then *H. erectus* evolved in eastern Asia at quite an early date (remember, OH9 is now thought to be almost 1.4 Myr old), and one branch of the species migrated back to Olduvai in Africa. But if these new Asian dates are accurate, it seems more probable that as we come to know more about OH9 and its kind we will find that they belonged to a different species of hominid altogether.

The opposite end of the Eurasian continent was, as I have hinted, also isolated from the human evolutionary mainstream. As we saw, humans seem to have arrived in Europe fairly late. In this region, the first convincing archaeological sites, with rather crude tools, show up at about 800 Kyr ago or thereabouts (although in the Levant, within hailing distance of Africa, the site of 'Ubeidiya has yielded Acheulean tools dated to around 1.4 Myr ago, just about as early as any found to the south). The problem has been that there has been no sign of the toolmakers themselves.

This gap has now begun to be filled by finds made by Eudald Carbonell of the University of Tarragona in Spain and his co-workers at the Gran Dolina cave site in the Atapuerca Hills of northern Spain. In 1994 excavations there produced numerous rather simple stone tools, plus a number of human fossil fragments, the most complete of which is a partial upper face of an immature individual. All came from a level that was dated to more than 780 Kyr ago. No traces of Acheulean technology were found among the tools, and the investigators noted various primitive traits in the fossils, which they provisionally attributed to *H. heidelbergensis*. This is the species into which specimens formerly classified as archaic *H. sapiens* are increasingly being placed. Carbonell and his colleagues see their fossils as the starting point of an indigenous European lineage that gradually evolved into the Neanderthals. These latter, large-brained hominids are known only from Europe and western Asia, where they flourished in the period between about 200 Kyr and 30 Kyr ago, when they were extinguished in some way by invading H. sapiens.

This is not the only possibility, however. With only a preliminary description of the very fragmentary Gran Dolina fossils available, it is hard to be sure, but it seems at least equally possible that they are the remains of hominids who made an initial foray out of Africa into Europe but failed to establish themselves there over the long term. Representatives of H. heidelbergensis are known in Africa as well, as long ago as 600 Kyr, and this species quite likely recolonized Europe later on. There it would have given rise to the Neanderthals, whereas a less specialized African population founded the lineage that ultimately produced H. sapiens.

* * *

Born in Africa

Every longtime reader of Scientific American will be familiar with the competing models of "regional continuity" and "single African origin" for the emergence of our own species, H. sapiens [see "The Multiregional Evolution of Humans," by Alan G. Thorne and Milford H. Wolpoff, and "The Recent African Genesis of Humans," by Allan C. Wilson and Rebecca L. Cann; April 1992]. The first of these models holds that the highly archaic H. erectus (including H. ergaster) is nothing more than an ancient variant of H. sapiens and that for the past two million years the history of our lineage has been one of a braided stream of evolving populations of this species in all areas of the Old World, each adapting to local conditions, yet all consistently linked by gene exchange. The variation we see today among the major geographic populations of humans is, by this reckoning, simply the latest permutation of this lengthy process.

The other notion, which happens to coincide much better with what we know of evolutionary processes in general, proposes that all modern human populations are descended from a single ancestral population that emerged in one place at some time between about 150 Kyr and 100 Kyr ago. The fossil evidence, thin as it is, suggests that this place of origin was somewhere in Africa (although the neighboring Levant is an alternative possibility); proponents of this scenario point to the support afforded by comparative molecular studies for the notion that all living humans are descended from an African population.

In view of what I have already said about the peripheral roles played in human evolution by early populations both in eastern Asia and Europe, it should come as no surprise that between these two possibilities my strong preference is for a single and comparatively recent origin for H. sapiens, very likely in Africa—the continent that, from the very beginning, has been the engine of mainstream innovation in human evolution. The rise of modern humans is a recent drama that played out against a long and complex backdrop of evolutionary diversification among the hominids, but the fossil record shows that from the earliest times Africa was consistently the center from which new lineages of hominids sprang. Clearly, interesting evolutionary developments occurred in both Europe and eastern Asia, but they involved populations that were not only derived from but also eventually supplanted by emigrants from Africa. In Africa our lineage was born, and ever since its hominids were first emancipated from the forest edges, that continent has pumped out successive waves of emigrants to all parts of the Old World. What we see in the human fossil record as it stands today is without doubt a shadowy reflection at best of what must have been a very complex sequence of events.

Most important, the new dates from eastern Asia show that human population mobility dates right back to the very origins of effectively modern bodily form. Those from Europe demonstrate that although distinctive regional variants evolved there, the history of occupation of that region may itself not have been at all a simple one. As ever, though, new evidence of the remote human past has served principally to underline the complexity of events in our evolution. We can only hope that an improving fossil record will flesh out the details of what was evidently a richly intricate process of hominid speciation and population movement over the past two million years.

STEPHEN JAY GOULD

The Human Difference (1999)†

We can embrace poetical reminders of our connection to the natural world, whether expressed as romantic effusions about oneness, or in the classical meter of Alexander Pope's heroic couplet:

> All are but parts of one stupendous whole,
> Whose body Nature is, and God the soul.

Yet, when we look into the eyes of an ape, our perception of undeniable affinity evokes an eerie fascination that we usually express as laughter or as fear. Our discomfort then increases when we confront the loss of former confidence in our separate and exalted creation "a little lower than the angels . . . crowned . . . with glory and honor" (Psalm 8), and must own the evolutionary alternative, with a key implication stated by Darwin himself (in "The Descent of Man"): "The difference in mind between man and the higher animals, great as it is, certainly is one of degree and not of kind."

We have generally tried to unite our intellectual duty to accept the established fact of evolutionary continuity with our continuing psychological need to see ourselves as separate and superior, by invoking one of our worst and oldest mental habits: dichotomization, or division into two opposite categories, usually with attributions of value expressed as good and bad or higher and lower. We therefore try to define a "golden barrier," a

---

† From "The Human Difference," *The New York Times*, July 2, 1999. Stephen Jay Gould (b. 1941) is Alexander Agassiz Professor of Geology and curator of invertebrate paleontology at the Museum of Comparative Zoology, Harvard University.

firm criterion to mark an unbridgeable gap between the mentality and behavior of humans and all other creatures. We may have evolved from them, but at some point in our advance, we crossed a Rubicon that brooks no passage by any other species.

Thus, we have proposed many varied criteria—and rejected them, one by one. We tried behavior—the use of tools, and upon failure of this broad standard, the use of tools explicitly fashioned for particular tasks. (Chimps, after all, strip leaves off twigs, and then use the naked sticks for extracting termites out of nests.) And we considered distinctive mental attributes— the existence of a moral sense, or the ability to form abstractions. All have failed as absolutes of human uniqueness (while a complex debate contin- ues to surround the meaning and spread of language and its potential rudiments)

The development of "culture"—defined as distinct and complex behav- ior originating in local populations and clearly passed by learning, rather than genetic predisposition—has persisted as a favored candidate for a "golden barrier" to separate humans from animals, but must now be re- jected as well. A study published in a recent issue of the journal Nature proves the existence of complex cultures in chimpanzees. This research proves that chimpanzees learn behaviors through observation and imitation and then pass them on to other chimpanzees. The study represents the cooperative effort of all major research groups engaged in the long-term study of particular groups of chimpanzees in the wild (with Jane Good- all's nearly 40-year study of the Gombé chimps as the flagship of these efforts).

Isolated examples of cultural transmission have long been known—with local "dialects" of songbirds and the potato washing of macaques on a small Japanese island as classical cases. Such rudimentary examples scarcely qualified as arguments against a meaningful barrier between hu- mans and animals. However, the chimpanzee study, summarizing 151 years of observation at seven field sites, found culturally determined, and often quite complex, differences among the sites for 39 behavioral patterns that must have originated in local groups and then spread by learning.

To cite just one example, contrasting the two best studied sites (Ms. Goodall's at Gombé and Toshisada Nishida's in the Mahale Mountains 170 kilometers away, with no recorded contact between the groups), the Mahale chimps clap two hands together over their head as part of the grooming ritual, while no Gombé chimp has ever so behaved. (Grooming itself may be genetically enjoined, but such capricious variations in explicit style must be culturally invented and transmitted.) In the commentary that accompanies the Nature article, Frans B. M. de Waal of the Yerkes Re- gional Primate Research Center in Atlanta summarized the entire study by writing, "The evidence is overwhelming that chimpanzees have a re- markable ability to invent new customs and technologies, and that they pass these on socially rather than genetically."

The conventional commentary on such a conclusion would end here, leaving a far more important issue unaddressed. Why are we so surprised by such a finding? The new documentation is rich and decisive—but why would anyone have doubted the existence of culture in chimps, given well-documented examples in other animals and our expanding knowledge of the far more sophisticated mental lives of chimpanzees?

Our surprise may teach us as much about ourselves as the new findings reveal about chimpanzees. For starters, the basic formulation of them vs. us and the resulting search for a "golden barrier," represents a deep fallacy of human thought. We need not fear Darwin's correct conclusion that we differ from other animals only in degree. A sufficient difference in quantity translates to what we call difference in quality ipso facto. A frozen pond is not the same object as a boiling pool—and New York City does not represent a mere extension of the tree nests at Gombé.

In addition, evolution does provide a legitimate criterion of genuine and principled separation between Homo sapiens and any other species. But the true basis of distinction lies in topology and genealogy, not in any functional attribute marking our superiority. We are linked to chimpanzees (and more distantly to any other species) by complete chains of intermediate forms that proceed backward from our current state into the fossil record until the two lineages meet in a common ancestor. But all these intermediate forms are extinct, and the evolutionary gap between modern humans and chimps therefore stands as absolute and inviolate. In this crucial genealogical sense all humans share equal fellowship as members of Homo sapiens. In biological terms, with species defined by historical and genealogical connection, the most mentally deficient among us is as fully human as Einstein.

If we grasped this fundamental truth of evolution, we might finally make our peace with Alexander Pope's location of human nature on an "isthmus of a middle state"—that is, between bestiality and mental transcendence.

We might also become comfortable with his incisive characterization of our peculiar status as "the glory, jest, and riddle of the world."

PUNCTUATED EQUILIBRIUM

STEPHEN JAY GOULD

[On Punctuated Equilibrium] (1991)†

* * *

Punctuated equilibrium began, as so much else that later looms large in our lives, as a little path that might never have opened. Paleontology, as the study of life's history, should be a jewel among the geological sciences; what subject could be more fascinating? Yet, until recently, it languished with an unjust reputation as a dull exercise in descriptive cataloging. Paleontologists were stereotyped as narrow specialists in mind-numbing particulars of favorite groups, places, and times. *Nature*, the British professional journal of science, editorialized about us in 1969:

† From "Opus 200," *Natural History* (Aug. 1991): 12–18. With permission from *Natural History*. Copyright © the American Museum of Natural History (1991). Stephen Jay Gould (b. 1941) is Alexander Agassiz Professor of Geology and curator of invertebrate paleontology at the Museum of Comparative Zoology, Harvard University.

Scientists in general might be excused for assuming that most geologists are paleontologists and most paleontologists have staked out a square mile as their life's work. A revamping of the geologist's image is badly needed.

During the 1960s, tumultuous for other reasons, a group of young paleontologists (including [Niles] Eldredge and myself, then in that blessed stage of ontogeny) worked hard to reverse this image and to recapture the high reputation merited by more than 3 billion years of evolution. We felt that evolutionary theory provided the context for such a revitalization, and that the exclusively geological training then so traditional for paleontologists had fostered a reputation for dullness by excising the intellectual heart of the subject and leaving only the descriptive task of identifying fossils to tell the age of rocks and the environments of their formation.

We pursued our studies in biology as well and tried to use the latest concepts of evolutionary theory as a new foundation for interpreting life's history. We called our study paleobiology.

* * *

The prevailing opinion of paleontologists was mired in the deepest bias of Darwin's world view. Darwin, following Lyell's lead in geology, preferred to interpret substantial change as the insensibly gradual, incremental building of adaptation, tiny piece by tiny piece, generation by generation. Darwin used a striking metaphor to express his conviction that results of vast scale arise from minor inputs summed over geological immensity; the hero of evolution is time.

> Natural selection is daily and hourly scrutinizing, throughout the world, every variation, even the slightest; rejecting that which is bad, preserving and adding up all that is good; silently and insensibly working. . . . We see nothing of these slow changes in progress until the hand of time has marked the long lapse of ages [*Origin of Species*, 1859].

Beguiled by this vision, most paleontologists envisioned new species as arising by the insensibly slow and steady change of entire populations over long stretches of time, even by geological standards—a notion known as gradualism. Under this model, "*the* species problem in paleontology"—I put the phrase in quotes because it then resounded through our literature as a catechism—centered upon the difficulty of stating where ancestral species A ended and descendant species B began in such a continuously graded transition (the problem, so formulated, has no objective answer, only an arbitrary one).

And yet, while thus stating the issue in general writings, all paleontologists knew that the practical world of fossil collecting rarely imposed such a dilemma. The oldest truth of paleontology proclaimed that the vast majority of species appear fully formed in the fossil record and do not change substantially during the long period of their later existence (average durations for marine invertebrate species may be as high as 5 to 10 million years). In other words, geologically abrupt appearance followed by subsequent stability.

But how could traditional paleontology live with such a striking discordance between a theoretical expectation of gradual transition and the practical knowledge of stability and geologically abrupt appearance as the recorded history of most species? Our colleagues resolved their schizophrenia by taking refuge in a traditional argument, advanced with special ardor by Darwin himself—the gross imperfection of the fossil record. If true history is continuous and gradational, but only one step in a thousand is preserved as geological evidence, then a truly gradual sequence becomes a series of abrupt transitions.

*　*　*

If this argument were sound, then so be it. Catch-22 rears its ugly head in many variations; sometimes you have to admit the intractable and move on to something else. But Niles and I realized that our evolutionary training, then rare for paleontologists, suggested an alternative reading full of fascination for its theoretical implications and promising as an honorable exit from the chill that Darwin's "argument from imperfection" had imposed upon evolutionary studies in the fossil record. (Before I forget, let me record that the ideas came mostly from Niles, with yours truly acting as a sounding board and eventual scribe. I coined the term *punctuated equilibrium* and wrote most of our 1972 paper, but Niles is the proper first author in our pairing of Eldredge and Gould.)

The idea that we eventually called punctuated equilibrium had two sources and one overriding purpose—to provide an exit from the "disabling rescue" of Darwin's argument on imperfection. First, a statement about mode of change: Most new species do not arise by transformation of entire ancestral populations but by the splitting (branching) of a lineage into two populations. Niles and I had learned the standard evolutionary version of speciation by branching—a notion popularized by Ernst Mayr and called by him the allopatric theory. *Allopatric* means "in another place," and the theory argues that new species may arise when a small population becomes isolated at the periphery of the parental geographic range. Isolation can occur by a variety of geological and geographic contingencies—mountains rising, rivers changing course, islands forming. Without geographic isolation, favorable variants will not accumulate in local populations, for breeding with parental forms is a remarkably efficient way to blur and dilute any change that might otherwise become substantial enough to constitute a new species. Most peripherally isolated populations never become new species; they die out or rejoin the larger parental mass. But as species may have no other common means of origin, even a tiny fraction of isolated populations provide more than enough "raw material" for the genesis of evolutionary novelty.

Second, a statement about rate of change. The simple claim that species arise by splitting, and not by transformation of entire ancestral populations, does not guarantee punctuated equilibrium. Suppose that most splitting events divide large populations into two units of roughly equal size, which then change at the conventional gradualistic rate. Splitting events, in this scenario, would yield two examples of gradualism—and the case for punctuated equilibrium would be compromised, not strengthened. Punctuated equilibrium gains its rationale from the idea, also a standard component of the allopatric speciation theory, that most peripherally isolated populations are relatively small and undergo their characteristic changes at a rate that translates into geological time as an instant.

For a variety of reasons, small isolated populations have unusual potential for effective change: for example, favorable genes can quickly spread throughout the population, while the interaction of random change (rarely important in large populations) with natural selection provides another effective pathway for substantial evolution. Even with these possibilities for accelerated change, the formation of a new species from a peripherally isolated population would be glacially slow by the usual standard of our lifetimes. Suppose the process took five to ten thousand years. We might stand in the midst of this peripheral isolate for all our earthly days and see nothing in the way of major change.

But now we come to the nub of punctuated equilibrium. Five to ten thousand years may be an eternity in human time, but such an interval represents an earthly instant in almost any geological situation—a single bedding plane (not a gradual sequence through meters of strata). Moreover, peripheral isolates are small in geographic extent and not located in the larger area where parents are living, dying, and contributing their skeletons to the fossil record.

What then is the expected geological expression of speciation in a peripherally isolated population? The answer is, and must be, punctuated equilibrium. The speciation event occurs in a geological instant and in a region of limited extent at some distance from the parental population. In other words, punctuated equilibrium—and not gradualism—is the expected geological translation for the standard account of speciation in evolutionary theory. Species arise in a geological moment—the punctuation (slow by our standards, abrupt by the planet's). They then persist as large and stable populations on substantial geological watches, usually changing little (if at all) and in an aimless fashion about an unaltered average—the equilibrium.

Most of our paleontological colleagues missed this insight because they had not studied evolutionary theory and either did not know about allopatric speciation or had not considered its translation to geological time. Our evolutionary colleagues also failed to grasp the implication, primarily because they did not think at geological scales. But whatever the theoretical meaning of punctuated equilibrium, Niles and I were most pleased by its practical and heuristic value. We had reinterpreted the fossil record as an accurate reflection of evolution, rather than an embarrassment that made reality (read gradualism) invisible by its imperfections. We gave paleontologists something to do, a way to get hands dirty. Evolution can be studied directly; change by the ordinary route of allopatric speciation is palpable in geological evidence.

*   *   *

Many colleagues thought that we had raised the old anti-Darwinian specter of macromutationism, or truly sudden speciation in a single generation by a large and incredibly lucky mutation. I do not know why this happened; I think that all our articles and public statements were clear in separating human from geological rapidity. The theory, after all, is rooted in this distinction—for punctuated equilibrium is the recognition that gradualism on our mortal measuring rod of three score years and ten translates to suddenness at the planet's temporal scale.   *   *   *

Creationists, with their usual skill in the art of phony rhetoric, cynically distorted punctuated equilibrium for their own ends, claiming that we had virtually thrown in the towel and admitted that the fossil record contains no intermediate forms. (Punctuated equilibrium, on the other hand, is a different theory of intermediacy for evolutionary trends—pushing a ball up an inclined plane for gradualism, climbing a staircase for punctuated equilibrium.) Some of our colleagues, in an all too common and literally perverse reaction, blamed us for this mayhem upon our theory. At least we were able to fight back effectively. Most of my testimony at the Arkansas creationism trial in 1980 centered upon the creationists' distortion of punctuated equilibrium.

*   *   *

On Stasis (Equilibrium)

Niles and I, with some grammatical (but no intellectual) doubt, soon took as the motto of punctuated equilibrium: "Statis is data." We see the world in the light of theories and ideas; as Peter Medawar said, "Innocent, unbiased observation is a myth." My greatest pride in punctuated equilibrium lies in its role in turning the basic fact of paleontology from an unstated embarrassment into a subject of active and burgeoning research. When most of our colleagues defined evolution as gradual change, the stability of species counted as no data—that is, as absence of evolution. All paleontologists recognized the stability of species, but the subject never entered active research. At most, the fact of stability might be noted in the midst of a taxonomic description. Punctuated equilibrium has changed the context. Stasis has become interesting as a central prediction of our theory.

*   *   *

On Punctuation

Punctuated equilibrium has provided a new context for the most important phenomenon of paleontology—evolutionary trends (larger size in horses, more complex sutures in ammonites, bigger brains in humans). Under gradualism, trends arise because natural selection favors some traits over others, and a genealogical continuum builds these features further and further along the path of advantage. Species are arbitrary segments of the resulting continuum—a largely artificial consequence of change. Punctuated equilibrium cleanly reverses this perspective. Species are real units, arising by branching in the first moments of a long and stable existence. A trend arises by the differential success of certain kinds of species. (If large-bodied horses either arise more frequently or live longer than small-bodied horses, then a trend to increased size will permeate the equine bush.) Speciation is the real cause of change, not an arbitrary consequence of artificial division of a continuum. Since the causes of branching are so different from those of continuous transformation, trends must receive a new explanatory apparatus under punctuated equilibrium.

As ordinary human beings with egos and arrogances, scientists love to be right. But we would, I think, all say that to be useful is more important, that is, to propose an idea that gets people excited and suggests fruitful strategies for potential confirmation and disproof. The jury is still out on the relative frequency of punctuated equilibrium (twenty years is a short case in biology), but utility has already been proved in the pudding of practice. * * *

NILES ELDREDGE

The Great Stasis Debate (1995)†

* * *

In his book, *Darwin and His Critics*, philosopher David Hull has reprinted all of the reviews of any consequence of Darwin's first edition of *On the Origin of Species*. Among them are five written by paleontologists. Each of them expresses concern that Darwin does not acknowledge the by then well-known generalization that *once a species appears in the fossil record, it tends to persist with little appreciable change throughout the remainder of its existence.*

Thomas Henry Huxley alluded to this phenomenon of great species stability when he chastised Darwin for stressing the adage "nature does not make jumps" too strenuously. Because species do not, as a rule, grade imperceptibly one into another as we collect fossils up a cliff face, it follows that evolutionary change between species in the fossil record often appears to be rather abrupt. And Darwin himself, in his sixth edition (the usual version available in paperback form), acknowledged the tendency for species to remain stable throughout their duration in the fossil record. This was part of his strenuous and largely effective campaign to mute critics of his earlier editions by answering all their objections. * * *

Evolution does not inevitably and irrevocably transform species as they persist through geological time. To the contrary, species most often seem to go nowhere, evolutionarily speaking. To be sure, some will accrue some evolutionary change over millions of years, but most of them hardly accrue

† From *Reinventing Darwin: The Great Debate at the High Table of Evolutionary Theory* (New York, 1995). Reprinted by permission of John Wiley & Sons. Niles Eldredge (b. 1943) is a curator in the Department of Invertebrates at the American Museum of Natural History, New York.

any change at all. Stasis is now abundantly well documented as the pre-eminent paleontological pattern in the evolutionary history of species. Paleontologist Steven Stanley has labored mightily to establish this point through the 1970s and 1980s, publishing original analyses of marine clam evolution. He emphasizes with great clarity and eloquence the most important point that whatever might underlie the weak and typically vacillating anatomical changes that do show up in the fossil record, the little progressive within-species change we see in the fossil record is simply too slow to account for the great adaptive changes wrought by evolution.

Stasis does not mean that we need an alternative to natural selection. But we do need to understand the circumstances in which natural selection works. On the one hand, how does natural selection keep species stable for long periods of time? And what circumstances obtain when natural selection does effect adaptive change? * * *

The fundamental question in evolution is not how adaptive change occurs (it comes through natural selection), but why adaptive evolutionary change occurs when it does. Understanding why species tend to remain so constant—even in the face of significant environmental change—is an absolute prerequisite to understanding the circumstances in which the vast bulk of adaptive change occurs in evolutionary history.

What Causes Stasis?

George Simpson captured Darwin's original victory perfectly when he exclaimed that natural selection is such a powerful force that it is impossible to imagine how evolution cannot occur. Darwin replaced "evolution is impossible" with "evolution has happened"—to the permanent satisfaction of the rational world.

We naturalists have refocused the picture. Yes, we say, evolution has happened. And, we agree, in the main, evolutionary history is largely a picture of adaptive change that comes through natural selection. But, we add, evolutionary history affirms that, far from being inevitable, adaptive change comes not with the mere passage of time, but seems to be concentrated at particular times and places with the histories of all lineages. Adaptive change more often than not seems to come as discrete events in evolutionary history. If we can understand why species tend to remain so adaptively conservative throughout the vast bulk of their history, perhaps we can shed some light on those very circumstances that seem to allow natural selection to do what we all agree it eventually does do: produce adaptive change in the history of life.

We have already met one key ingredient to understanding stasis: habitat tracking. Traditional Darwinism assumes that adaptive change tracks changing environments, as natural selection modifies features to keep pace with changing conditions. But, as we have seen, species tend to change locale—rather than anatomical features—in response to environmental change. As long as suitable habitat can be found, a species will move rather than stay put and adapt to new environmental regimes.

Darwinians, going back to the grand old man himself, have always acknowledged that evolution proceeds at different rates at different times during the history of a species lineage. Evolution is generally imagined to proceed faster when conditions are changing and more slowly if the environment is relatively stable. Natural selection is the mediator of evolutionary change, whether fast or slow. When conditions change, directional natural selection modifies adaptations in response. When conditions are stable, species will change little if at all—a mode called "stabilizing selection." When times are stable, so goes the Darwinian canon, evolution sets out to perfect, rather than to modify, adaptation.

Stabilizing selection under such circumstances makes perfect sense. We naturalists differ from standard Darwinian expectations, though, when we see environmental change as a medium of stabilizing selection. If populations within a species move as they recognize the appearance of suitable habitat within reach elsewhere, we would expect stabilizing, rather than directional, natural selection. Thus a profound difference emerges between naturalists and traditional Darwinian thinkers. Both camps agree that stable conditions yield little or no adaptive change. But naturalists also see stasis as the most common outcome of environmental change as well: stasis from stabilizing selection even in the face of environmental change. So long as suitable habitats can be recognized and occupied, there is every reason to suppose that stabilizing selection will continue to operate, or at least to predominate.

*   *   *

No idea has excited more interest, sparked more debate, been more widely cited, and been more profoundly misunderstood in the post-1959 annals of evolutionary biology than the notion of "punctuated equilibria" that I published with Stephen Jay Gould in 1972. * * *

Punctuated equilibria itself is a remarkably simple idea. It is a melding, in essence, of the pattern of stasis with the recognition that most evolutionary change seems bound up with the origin of new species—the process of speciation.

*   *   *

I needed to explain why evolution leaves an entirely different sort of pattern in the rock record than Darwin—and his long string of successors, including many paleontologists—had supposed. And I found a very ready source of explanation staring me right in the face. I found it in Dobzhansky's and Mayr's work on species and the nature of the speciation process, specifically the derivation of descendant species from ancestral species through geographic isolation. Thus developed the combination of pattern and process that Steve Gould and I called "punctuated equilibria" in our joint 1972 paper that came hard on the heels of my original 1971 analysis: evolutionary pattern (stasis with its corollary of relatively abrupt evolutionary change—stability *punctuated* by change) plus mechanism (natural selection in the context of speciation). Speciation, the fragmentation of an ancestral species into two or more descendants, is a component of the evolutionary process. It takes speciation, it seems, to break the stranglehold of stasis, providing the context for lasting evolutionary change. Punctuated equilibria is simply the notion of speciation applied as the explanation for evolutionary change interrupting vastly longer periods of monotonous stasis. It should have been noncontroversial. It wasn't.

* * *

Generalizing a bit, Steve and I said that most species of marine invertebrates—that vast bulk of species of the fossil record—last between five and ten million years, a rough estimate that has actually stood up pretty well over the years. Some species last longer, and many become extinct far sooner. Terrestrial animals—of all kinds, including insects, snails, and vertebrates—appear not to last as long as their marine counterparts. Extinction rates are characteristically higher on land. This is testimony to the more immediate and frequent effects of climate change on land when compared to habitats below the waves.

As against five to ten million years of stasis, we claimed that evolutionary change—tied up in speciation events—happens rather quickly. Here we are at the smallest level of resolution of geological time often (but not always) possible with the fossil record. Even tens of thousands of years are usually difficult to decipher in the fossil record. So our estimates of time required for speciation events were much hazier than our estimated average durations of species. I came up with the figure "five to fifty thousand years," which was consistent with some of the events we believed we had some direct data on from our own studies.

The real point, of course, is that "five to fifty thousand years" is in the neighborhood of 1,000 times shorter than the average durations of species. It is the contrast in rates—between vast periods of essentially no change, and brief intervals of actual change—that is most important. What we were saying is that evolution looks instantaneous in the fossil record, but is not.

* * *

Scientists are supposed to hold their theories lightly, to explore all opportunities for knocking them asunder, to "falsify" them. That, it is commonly said, is the way that science progresses: by showing that something is wrong. If an idea squares with the facts (what we think we know to be true), then it might be right. If not, then that beautiful idea is indeed slain by an ugly little fact. We are far more certain when an idea is wrong than when it is right.

That is the nature of things, but no single scientist ever behaves in this proscribed fashion of self-doubt and flagellation. Scientists, being as a rule more or less normal human beings, passionately stick up for their ideas, their pet theories. It's up to someone else to show you are wrong. The scientific enterprise is a true collectivity. Through all the din and shouting, eventually some progress is made in achieving a better—a more accurate, more realistic—picture of nature. * * *

The grand split between what I have been calling ultra-Darwinians and naturalists has its roots in the writings of a single individual: Charles Darwin. Certainly, ever since the advent of genetics nearly 100 years ago, that split has been there in one guise or another. * * * But, within the major factions there are, inevitably, lesser wrangles. Ultra-Darwinians argue among themselves about the nature, meaning, and importance of group selection. They fight over the meaning of sex. We naturalists, on the other hand, argue over the nature, existence of, and significance of species selection. Nor are we unanimous on the causes (even the realities) of mass extinction, or their relevance to subsequent episodes of evolutionary diversification.

Even if some issues are resolved to some degree of general satisfaction, there is no guarantee that they won't arise, phoenix-like, a generation or two down the line, to be reevaluated, fought over again with fresh passion and, no doubt, to a different conclusion—if a conclusion there happens to be.

So, who is right? That cannot be the real question. I do passionately believe that there is a physical reality, a material universe. I do think that it is the job of "science" to describe that universe as accurately as possible. There is, in other words, a correct solution, a right answer. On the road to those answers (which, it seems, we will never fully recognize when and if we get them), all we have is successive approximations—competing claims to truth, always based on different "takes" on the nature of things. If science is always trying to obtain clearer snapshots of that physical reality, scientists are more like painters (or, for that matter, art photographers) whose tastes and objectives are bound to differ. No two painters render the same subject in precisely the same way. And so it inevitably is in science.

The history of evolutionary biology, it seems to me, is a history of successive waves of arriviste painters who claim that they, finally, have the truth. This succession of truth-knowers are most clearly tied (but not restricted) to technological innovation in biology, itself a litany of conversion of biology from the supposed imprecisions of old-fashioned natural history progressively approaching the true Nirvana—the physics model of a real science. In any case, discovery of Mendelian genetics was supposed to have been the death knell of Darwinism. But population genetics eventually sprang up and, eventually, effected a genuine rapprochement between the new "physiological" genetics and the older Darwinian vision. The discovery of the principles of genetics did not, it turns out, make the real phenomena that Darwin so ably described disappear. It seems absurd, in retrospect, that anyone would think that higher-level phenomena somehow would just go away when lower-level phenomena became better known.

Yet the siren song of reductionism will ever, it seems, be heard. Ultra-Darwinians are not molecular biologists. They were, for the most part, all trained in the population genetics tradition, and those molecular biologists who now claim that theirs is the key to the truth annoy ultra-Darwinians no end! But ultra-Darwinians have responded very clearly to the molecular revolution. Ours is the information age, and ultra-Darwinians quite naturally see evolution as a matter of the fate of genetic information. Indeed, we all see evolution in those terms.

The ultra-Darwinian response to the molecular revolution has been to insist that there is a titanic struggle going on—among genes, among organisms, perhaps among groups—to leave more copies of their genetic information to the next generation. I have argued that this represents an inappropriate reversal of the true vector of natural selection. Darwin's original description saw that economic success biases reproductive success, and that such an effect inevitably biases the transmission of heritable features from one generation to the next.

Ultra-Darwinians have flipped the story around. Competition for economic resources only goes on because organisms—or (fide Richard Dawkins) their genes—are locked in a combative, competitive struggle to pass along as many copies of themselves as possible to the next generation. I have suggested that this insistence is part of a seemingly endless progression within evolutionary biology to see itself as a true science. Competitive transmission of genetic information has an active air about it, and science is about the things that exist and what they do. Seeing evolution as the mere passive accumulation, the scorecard recording what worked better than what in the economic arena, seems tame by comparison. And it is evidently not to the tastes of the ultra-Darwinian painters of the evolutionary landscape.

This admittedly rather unflattering picture of ultra-Darwinians sees them as classic reductionists who have tried to inject a pattern of determinative action to a field that is, by its very nature, historical. Their actions have led them to a striking anomaly—one which, I believe, has yet to be fully realized and appreciated. Ultra-Darwinians, led by George Williams, have made the undeniable point that natural selection cannot have "eyes" for the future—meaning that selection can only work on a generation-by-generation basis, recording what worked relatively better among a collection of genetically varying individuals. Selection benefits only organisms, not species.

But what have they replaced it with? Another claim, ostensibly about actions of the present, but one that has direct, conspicuous, and probably equally false claims about the future. Organisms, it is said, are locked in a continual struggle to leave relatively more copies of their genes to the next generation. But how, by doing so, are organisms benefited? The postulate makes a bit more sense when we think, as Dawkins asked us to do with his The Selfish Gene, that the competition is really among variant forms of the genes themselves. But either way, it is a postulate about the future, not the present. Ultra-Darwinians, so it seems to me, have replaced one shopworn, incorrect adage about the supposed ability of evolution to govern the future with another one. I don't see any more sense in the new version than in the old. * * *

Time now to acknowledge what I take to be the main core of good in ultra-Darwinian works; for therein lies the sharpest, most succinct path to revealing our shared vision, as well as the distinctions that divide us naturalists from the ultra-Darwinian camp.

The ultra-Darwinian bailiwick—its base camp—is population genetics. Describing the dynamics of changes in gene frequency under all manner of conditions is the natural province of this branch of evolutionary biology, and progress continues to be made. A reductionist—an ultra-Darwinian—tends to claim that all we need to know about evolution resides here. A naturalist, convinced that other generally larger-scale levels (entities) exist and play important roles in evolution, nonetheless does not deny the existence, or indeed the importance, of population genetics-level processes. That is, after all, the very province of natural selection and genetic drift.

The two traditions of painting the evolutionary landscape are far from symmetrical. Ultra-Darwinians and their immediate predecessors see the existence of genes, chromosomes, organisms, and populations. Rarely do they take the existence of larger-scale entities—species and ecosystems—seriously, or view them as anything more than simple epiphenomena borne out of competition for reproductive success. Naturalists, in upholding the existence and significance of such larger-scale entities, do not reciprocate. To deny the existence or importance of populations would be idle, petulant stupidity.

The result is that we can, and indeed do, appreciate the positive results achieved by ultra-Darwinians when they are applying their concepts and analytic tools to the problems for which they are appropriate. When, for example, the issue is the structure, function, and evolution of a peculiar form of breeding system, their work is often elegant, and their presuppositions are ideally suited to the task at hand.

*   *   *

It comes down to pictures. We naturalists, I am convinced, offer a less assumption ridden, theory laden description of the nature of all manner of biological systems. We absorb what the molecular geneticists have to say about the structure and inner workings of the genome itself. Likewise, as the early architects of the evolutionary synthesis taught us to, we recognize the nature and significance of population-level phenomena. But we also offer descriptions of larger-scale systems: species and higher taxa, avatars, and ecosystems of progressively larger scale. We see these entities as simple outcomes of the dual fact of organismic life: economics and reproduction.

It comes down to this: the competing allure of an essentially reductionist stance—with its charms of apparent simplicity and elegance—versus a partitioning of complexity into component systems—the naturalistic theoretical edifice that, while perhaps not as neat, seems to me a more accurate description of actual biological systems. *   *   *

KEVIN PADIAN

Darwin's Views of Classification (1999)†

* * * Darwin's views on classification have been extensively researched and debated, especially in the decades following the rise of the competing "evolutionary," "phenetic," and "cladistic" schools of systematics. Some scholars have advanced the view that "Darwinian" classification (in theory, in practice, or both) involved dual criteria of genealogy and degree of similarity, at least to some extent. Others have stressed Darwin's insistence on genealogy alone. Most scholars agree that Darwin cannot be regarded simply as an "evolutionary taxonomist" or a cladist, or as a patron saint to any current school. However, issues and terms have shifted so much over the years that it has become both difficult and inappropriate to shoehorn the ideas and language of Victorian science into current debates.

* * *

In this essay I make three points about Darwin's views of classification. First, Darwin advocated and insisted on genealogy as the criterion for classification. He did not connect or correlate it with any other criterion, though he recognized factors such as degree of similarity and correlations in embryological stages as important in *revealing* genealogy (and this is a crucial distinction). He maintained this position in letters from 1843 until after the initial publication of the *Origin of Species* (1859), and through every later edition, as well as in *The Descent of Man* (1871). Second, the argument that Darwin advocated dual criteria of genealogy and degree of similarity is not supported by his writings on how classification should be done, but is rather an interpretation that hinges on a single statement taken out of context that Darwin wrote about another author's work—that he himself does not seem to have fully understood. In fact, on several occasions Darwin denied explicitly that similarity should be the basis for classification. Third, in his work on living and fossil barnacles, Darwin apparently did not follow his own stated theoretical precepts, in the sense that he did not make genealogy a focus of discussion as the basis of classification, and in fact barely referred to it. Nor did he develop in these works any philosophy of classification. However, I suggest that his practical taxonomic work did indeed support his view that classification should be based on genealogy. The difficulty of his taxonomic subjects simply prevented him from achieving his ideal, and have prevented us from understanding why. * * *

For Darwin, the only real difference between traditional systems and

† From "Charles Darwin's Views of Classification in Theory and Practice," *Systematic Biology* 48 (1999): 352–64. Reprinted by permission of the author. Kevin Padian (b. 1951) is professor of integrative biology and curator in the Museum of Paleontology at the University of California at Berkeley.

what he regarded as the proper basis of classification is that descent with modification replaced divine plan or other philosophical considerations. But he still needed a practical way to discover genealogical relationships. He recognized that many of the traditional criteria, such as degree of similarity, embryological resemblances, and so on, reflected genealogical proximity. In these respects, he appreciated that traditional taxonomy had probably been replicating more or less faithfully the pathways of diverging parentage. In one sense evolutionary taxonomy follows Darwin's view, in that it accepts genealogy as the underpinning of most similarity, and only inherited similarity can be a basis for taxonomy. The founders of evolutionary taxonomy explicitly traced this rationale to Darwin's doorstep. It could even be argued that Darwin condoned paraphyletic taxa, a sticking point between the "evolutionary" school and the cladistic school, inasmuch as some of his barnacle taxonomy admitted them. But in the full compass of his writings, Darwin regarded such groups as necessary evils only because the complete genealogy was not known (thanks to differential extinction). Without these gaps, classification would be purely genealogical.

Mayr was correct that Darwin was contemptuous of the Natural System. Darwin traced this system, in its various forms, to Linnaeus and other authors of the 18th and 19th centuries, noting that, at least in its mature form in mid-Victorian England, it incorporated both similarity and divine plan. * * *

Darwin characterized the "Natural System" in a letter to G. R. Waterhouse (emphasis in the original):

> Most authors say it is an endeavour to discover the laws according to which the Creator has willed to produce organized beings—But what empty high-sounding sentences these are—it does not mean order in time of creation, nor propinquity to any one type, as man.—in fact it means just nothing.—According to my opinion, (which I give everyone leave to hoot at . . .) classification consists in grouping beings according to their actual *relationship*, ie their consanguinity, or descent from common stocks.

*   *   *

Fourteen years later, Darwin carried on a similar correspondence with Huxley. Two letters, from 26 September and 3 October 1857, reiterate his views on the Natural System and on genealogy in classification.

> In regard to Classification, & all the endless disputes about the "Natural System["] which no two authors define in same way, I believe it ought, in accordance to my heteredox notions, to be simply genealogical.—But as we have no written pedigrees, you will, perhaps, say this will not help much; but I think it ultimately will, whenever heteredoxy becomes orthodoxy, for it will clear away an immense amount of rubbish about the value of characters &—will make the difference between analogy & homology, clear.—The time will come I believe, though I shall not live to see it, when we shall have very fairly true genealogical trees of each great kingdom of nature.[1]

1. *The Correspondence of Charles Darwin*, Vol. 6, ed. F. Burkhardt and S. Smith (Cambridge, UK, 1985–), p. 456.

* * *

The most crucial passage on classification in the *Origin of Species* (Chapter 13) has been widely cited, but often interpreted out of context. As this passage begins, Darwin has just finished discussing the ideas of various authors (not his own) on criteria for developing classifications (adaptive, inadaptive, reproductive, rudimentary, and embryological characters), and how mutually conflicting these characters can be. He then advances his own view that all of these features can be explained by descent with modification; and hence, if one were to accept this view, "the characters which naturalists consider as showing true affinity between any two or more species, are those which have been inherited from a common parent, and, in so far, all true classification is genealogical." Note that he is not saying that this is how taxonomy was practiced or understood in his day (it was not); he is saying that if the patterns of variation can be explained by descent with modification, then a *true* classification would be strictly genealogical.

Moreover, for Darwin the resemblances that naturalists have been using all along *are* really genealogical. He immediately continues in the same vein (emphasis added): "that community of descent is the hidden bond which naturalists have been unconsciously seeking, and not some unknown plan of creation, or the enunciation of general propositions, and *the mere putting together and separating objects more or less alike.*" Darwin's statement here reveals that similarity is not in itself a criterion for classification, but a means to understand genealogy. In that final phrase, in fact, he could be read as throwing cold water on the idea that degree of difference should have an intrisically important role. Rather, he used similarities in (what we would call) both labile and conservative features, as well as in all stages of embryology, to try to understand genealogical relationships. * * *

Darwin's Barnacle Monographs:
The Conflict between Theory and Practice

Darwin's barnacle monographs (1851–1854) are the only taxonomic works that Darwin ever did, and he spent some 8 years at them (amid other studies). What can they tell us about Darwin's systematic philosophy? It is fruitless to try to read Darwin's practice in these monographs as "evolutionary," "cladistic," or as akin to any 20th-century school. Darwin was a man of his times, though he transcended them, and his taxonomic work must be seen in the context of its times. * * *

The barnacle papers are in most respects characteristic of taxonomic monographs from Darwin's day to this, in that evolution and genealogy are topics subjugated to enumerating, describing, distinguishing, and evaluating characters and taxa, and such judgments have their own reasonable subjectivity and logic. In fact, in the barnacle monographs there is hardly any attempt to document evolution; there is no statement of systematic philosophy; and virtually the only attempt to put any kind of evolutionary perspective to the classification is Darwin's inference that sessile barnacles evolved from stalked ones, because the latter are geologically older. [Michael] Ghiselin masterfully showed how much Darwin transcended most systematic work of his day by introducing considerations of correspondence in larval form, sexual dimorphism, and adaptive modifications to taxonomy, in an effort to reflect evolutionary change; but these considerations were largely inferential and implicit, not explicit. That is, we can read them now if we look for them, but few in Darwin's time would have grasped these subtleties. * * *

His first problem was to determine the point at which cirripedes could be separated from other crustaceans, and so reveal their taxonomic rank. This was difficult, as he showed, because authorities of the time conferred degree of rank based on factors such as species diversity, degree of difference, or "perfection of organs" as being "high" or "low" in relation to a standard type (letters from Darwin to Waterhouse in 1843 express his frustration with this). Darwin wrestled with all these, hoping to offend no one, and finally sided with Dana and against Milne-Edwards (to whom the work was dedicated) in recognizing Cirripedia as a subclass of Crustacea, rather than a subgroup of entomostracan crustaceans. Genealogy, at this point, never explicitly entered the question. Darwin does not *say* that the differences that separate barnacles from other crustaceans reflect their deep genealogical divergence; he simply contrasts their similarities and differences. Yet even a decade earlier he was vehemently stressing to Waterhouse that classification should be based on genealogy alone, and he was still doing it in *The Descent of Man* in 1871. This is the real paradox of the barnacle monographs.

* * *

Visualize an evolving lineage growing upward, and separating as it grows into various branches; transect the tree's upper reaches with a horizontal plane. The plane represents our current slice of time. From this slice, the problem is to trace the divergence of the branches, using only present forms, given that extinction has removed the intermediates. This is how genealogy would have to be discovered. Darwin did not explicitly search for synapomorphies; he searched for any similarities that would reveal genealogy, as taxonomists still do—on the basis of what seem to be valuable characters.

As Ghiselin and [L.] Jaffe noted, Darwin "was formulating a system for his times, and the times were not yet ripe for a strictly genealogical arrangement"—at least one that would have had to be argued as strongly as cladists have argued their philosophy since the 1970s. It is unlikely that Darwin wished to take up that particular cudgel at the time (or could have), given his larger plan. I think, with Ghiselin, that it is a mistake to read too much systematic philosophy into these monographs. For one thing, Darwin never classified any barnacle on the basis of genealogy, which is indisputably regarded as his central criterion—even though, by the 1850s, it clearly underlay his ideas (as his 1843 letters to Waterhouse show). To argue on the basis of the barnacle monographs that Darwin regarded similarity as an equally important criterion, merely because he uses similarities in his taxonomy, makes no sense, because the entire concept of genealogy is suppressed.

Why didn't Darwin bring genealogy more strongly into his barnacle monographs? The simplest explanation, though circumstantial, is consistent with Darwin's long secrecy on many of his views. In order to establish genealogy as the basis of classification for barnacles, he would have had to establish the evidence for the common origin and descent of all living things at the same time. With his great book in a premature stage of gestation, he obviously did not want to let the cat out of the bag too early. Accordingly, he produced a conventional taxonomy that addressed the issues of his day. Recall that he undertook the whole exercise to begin with because of a stray remark in a letter from Hooker, who seemed to suggest that Darwin's own theories might not be taken seriously unless he had himself labored in the taxonomic vineyards. Darwin used similarities not to construct classifications, but to reveal common ancestry on which classifications should be based. His greatest impediments to this were the gaps among living forms, and between living and fossil forms. He used neither primitive nor derived character states on principle; he did not mind what we would call "paraphyletic" taxa if he could not resolve their membership more definitely; and he did not advertise his view that classification should be based on genealogy.

Conclusion

In his book on the fertilization of orchids, Darwin wrote,

> To make a perfect gradation, all the extinct forms which have ever existed, along many lines of descent converging to the common progenitor of the order, would have to be called into life. It is due to their absence, and to the consequent wide gaps in the series, that we are enabled to divide the existing species into definable groups. . . .
> If there had been no extinction, there would still have been great lines, or branches, of special development, . . . but ancient and intermediate forms, very different probably from their present descendants, would have rendered it utterly impossible to separate by distinct characters . . . one great body from [an]other.

Because living things have suffered differential extinction, we have only incomplete series of related forms; because we cannot seriate their entire genealogies, we must rely on their shared similarities to reconstruct that genealogy. This seems to me the closest approach that we can make to Darwin's view of classification.

The preponderance of available evidence indicates that Darwin's only criterion for classification was genealogy, a point that he summarized in the last chapter of the *Origin of Species*, when he was describing the effects that will accrue (again, in a conditional future) to natural history if and when common descent is recognized as the central underlying principle of biological phenomena: "Our classifications will come to be, as far as they can be so made, genealogies; and will then truly give what may be called the plan of creation. The rules for classifying will no doubt become simpler when we have a definite object in view." This last sentence, as the reader will see, recurs to the phrase in the letter he wrote long before to Waterhouse, quoted above. Hence, I conclude, it is difficult to accept Mayr's case for "dual criteria" of genealogy and similarity in Darwin's views on classification. There is certainly enough ambiguity to allow room for interpretation in many of his passages, taken by themselves, but in larger context the argument does not hold up very well. The interpretation that Darwin used similarities to get at genealogy seems to explain more of the available evidence. Moreover, Darwin in taxonomic practice was not particular about what we would call "primitive" and "derived" similarities, nor about paraphyletic groups when strict genealogy could not be discovered. It is not relevant to force Victorian sensibilities into 20th-century modes. Just as Darwin was neither a cladist nor a Linnean, it is not historically faithful to graft the taxonomic philosophies of the Modern Synthesis nor those of phylogenetic systematics onto his ideas and practices.

DAVID L. HULL

Cladistic Analysis (1988)†

*   *   *

Science is supposed to be international, and to some extent it is, but language differences can form very real barriers. In 1950 an East German entomologist, Willi Hennig (1913–76), published a formidable treatise entitled *Grundzüge einer Theorie der Phylogenetischen Systematik*. In this work, Hennig took seriously the claim that phylogenetic classifications are to represent phylogeny. As numerous systematists had noted before him, there is no way that all the details of phylogenetic development can be represented in so simple a system as a traditional hierarchic classification. Instead of opting for a vague reflection of several factors in a classification, Hennig settled on one—the sister-group relation. Two taxa, B and C, are sister groups if they are more closely related to each other than to any third taxon, A. The evidence for this relationship is the presence of characters that B and C exhibit but A lacks. The sister-group relationship is collateral, not ancestor-descendant. B and C must share a more recent common ancestor with each other than either does with A, but none of the taxa mentioned in the statement of a sister-group relation are claimed to be ancestral to any other.

*   *   *

† From *Science as a Process* (Chicago, 1988). Reprinted by permission of the University of Chicago Press. David L. Hull (b. 1935) is professor of philosophy at Northwestern University.

In 1965 Hennig published a short summary of his views in English; a year later, he published *Phylogenetic Systematics* (1966), a translation of an extensive revision of his *Grundzüge.* * * *

In his *Phylogenetic Systematics* Hennig treated three main topics: the species question, inferring phylogenetic relationships, and translating these relationships into classifications. Hennig accepted the gene-pool notion of species so central to the synthetic theory of evolution and the New Systematics. Although he recognized that the limits of particular species are generally inferred indirectly from morphology, he distinguished between the theoretical factors included in the definition of species category (e.g., gene flow) and the evidence that one uses to decide that the theoretically significant criteria have been met (e.g., character distributions). For Hennig, as for Simpson and Mayr, species are the basic units of the evolutionary process. They are the things that evolve as a result of mutation and selection. They are also the basic units in classification. Evolution and classification intersect at the species category. Finally, Hennig insisted that the characters used to infer both species status and phylogenetic relationships must be evolutionary homologies.

*   *   *

Although Hennig found no fault with the synthetic theory of evolution, he was not especially concerned with the evolutionary process in his book. He was more interested in phylogeny reconstruction and the relation of these inferred relationships to classifications. Although he placed much less emphasis on fossils in reconstructing phylogenies than most paleontologists did, the methods he described for reconstructing phylogeny were not especially new. Rather his chief contribution was the clarity with which he set out his principles and the emphasis which he placed on them. According to Hennig, the fundamental relation in phylogenetic systematics is the sister-group relation or, as he usually termed it, the phylogenetic relationship. This relationship can be represented in two ways—either as a hierarchical classification or as a phylogenetic diagram of the sort later to be termed a "cladogram" (see fig. 1).

The important feature of (a) and (b) in figure 1 is that they express precisely the same information. They are isomorphic. They state that B and C are more closely related to each other than either is to A—and that is all. Nothing more should be read into either the classification or cladogram. Because the diagram looks something like a phylogenetic tree, it

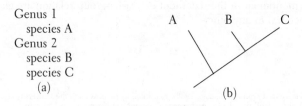

Genus 1
    species A
Genus 2
    species B
    species C
    (a)

Figure 1. Classifications and cladograms.

is easy to think of it as a highly stylized tree (fig. 2), but it is not. In a phylogenetic tree, each line represents a species, the splitting of one line into two represents a stem species splitting into two daughter species, and so on. In both (a) and (b) above none of the letters represent stem species. B and C share a stem species that neither share with C, but that stem species is included in neither the classification nor the diagram.

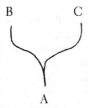

B   C

A

Figure 2. A phylogenetic tree.

*   *   *

The only relation represented in cladograms and their isomorphic classifications are sister-group relations. If a species is considered to go extinct when speciation occurs, then an ancestor species cannot co-exist with its descendant species. No two contemporaneous species can be related by the ancestor-descendant relation. The only relation possible is sister-group. Problems arise when we try to include species at different time horizons in the same classification, as Hennig thought that we can and must. What if by chance we happen on the remains of a species that actually was the immediate common ancestor of two extant species (fig. 2)? Because it appears earlier, it might be a common ancestor, but is it? What character distributions might lead a systematist to recognize it as a common ancestor? Some of the characters of A might have been transformed as part of it evolved into B; others may have been transformed as another part of it evolved into C; or one and the same characters may have evolved differently into the two descendant species.   *   *   *

KEVIN PADIAN AND LUIS M. CHIAPPE

[Cladistics in Action: The Origin of Birds and Their Flight (1998)†]

Until recently, the origin of birds was one of the great mysteries of biology. Birds are dramatically different from all other living creatures. Feathers, toothless beaks, hollow bones, perching feet, wishbones, deep breastbones and stumplike railbones are only part of the combination of

† From "The Origin of Birds and Their Flight," *Scientific American* (Feb. 1998): 28–37. Reprinted with permission. Copyright © 1998 by Scientific American, Inc. All rights reserved. Kevin Padian (b. 1951) is professor of integrative biology and curator at the Museum of Paleontology at the University of California at Berkeley. Luis M. Chiappe (b. 1962) is associate curator at the Natural History Museum of Los Angeles County.

skeletal features that no other living animal has in common with them. How birds evolved feathers and flight was even more imponderable.

In the past 20 years, however, new fossil discoveries and new research methods have enabled paleontologists to determine that birds descend from ground-dwelling, meat-eating dinosaurs of the group known as theropods. The work has also offered a picture of how the earliest birds took to the air.

Scientists have speculated on the evolutionary history of birds since shortly after Charles Darwin set out his theory of evolution in *On the Origin of Species*. In 1860, the year after the publication of Darwin's treatise, a solitary feather of a bird was found in Bavarian limestone deposits dating to about 150 million years ago (just before the Jurassic period gave way to the Cretaceous). The next year a skeleton of an animal that had birdlike wings and feathers—but a very unbirdlike long, bony tail and toothed jaw—turned up in the same region. These finds became the first two specimens of the blue jay-size *Archaeopteryx lithographica*, the most archaic, or basal, known member of the birds.

Archaeopteryx's skeletal anatomy provides clear evidence that birds descend from a dinosaurian ancestor, but in 1861 scientists were not yet in a position to make that connection. A few years later, though, Thomas Henry Huxley, Darwin's staunch defender, became the first person to connect birds to dinosaurs. Comparing the hind limbs of *Megalosaurus*, a giant theropod, with those of the ostrich, he noted 35 features that the two groups shared but that did not occur as a suite in any other animal. He concluded that birds and theropods could be closely related, although whether he thought birds were cousins of theropods or were descended from them is not known.

Huxley presented his results to the Geological Society of London in 1870, but paleontologist Harry Govier Seeley contested Huxley's assertion of kinship between theropods and birds. Seeley suggested that the hind limbs of the ostrich and *Megalosaurus* might look similar just because both animals were large and bipedal and used their hind limbs in similar ways. Besides, dinosaurs were even larger than ostriches, and none of them could fly; how, then, could flying birds have evolved from a dinosaur?

The mystery of the origin of birds gained renewed attention about half a century later. In 1916 Gerhard Heilmann, a medical doctor with a penchant for palcontology, published (in Danish) a brilliant book that in 1926 was translated into English as *The Origin of Birds*. Heilmann showed that birds were anatomically more similar to theropod dinosaurs than to any other fossil group but for one inescapable discrepancy: theropods apparently lacked clavicles, the two collarbones that are fused into a wishbone in birds. Because other reptiles had clavicles, Heilmann inferred that theropods had lost them. To him, this loss meant birds could not have evolved from theropods, because he was convinced (mistakenly, as it turns out) that a feature lost during evolution could not be regained. Birds, he asserted, must have evolved from a more archaic reptilian group that had clavicles. Like Seeley before him, Heilmann concluded that the similarities between birds and dinosaurs must simply reflect the fact that both groups were bipedal.

Heilmann's conclusions influenced thinking for a long time, even though new information told a different story. Two separate findings indicated that theropods did, in fact, have clavicles. In 1924 a published anatomical drawing of the bizarre, parrot-headed theropod *Oviraptor* clearly showed a wishbone, but the structure was misidentified. Then, in 1936, Charles Camp of the University of California at Berkeley found the remains of a small Early Jurassic theropod, complete with clavicles. Heilmann's fatal objection had been overcome, although few scientists recognized it. Recent studies have found clavicles in a broad spectrum of the theropods related to birds.

Finally, a century after Huxley's disputed presentation to the Geological Society of London, John H. Ostrom of Yale University revived the idea that birds were related to theropod dinosaurs, and he proposed explicitly that birds were their direct descendants. In the late 1960s Ostrom had described the skeletal anatomy of the theropod *Deinonychus*, a vicious, sickle-clawed predator about the size of an adolescent human, which roamed in Montana some 115 million years ago (in the Early Cretaceous). In a series of papers published during the next decade, Ostrom went on to identify a collection of features that birds, including *Archaeopteryx*, shared with *Deinonychus* and other theropods but not with other reptiles. On the basis of these findings, he concluded that birds are descended directly from small theropod dinosaurs.

As Ostrom was assembling his evidence for the theropod origin of birds, a new method of deciphering the relations among organisms was taking hold in natural history museums in New York City, Paris and elsewhere. This method—called phylogenetic systematics or, more commonly, cladistics—has since become the standard for comparative biology, and its use has strongly validated Ostrom's conclusions.

Traditional methods for grouping organisms look at the similarities and differences among the animals and might exclude a species from a group solely because the species has a trait not found in other members of the group. In contrast, cladistics groups organisms based exclusively on certain kinds of shared traits that are particularly informative.

This method begins with the Darwinian precept that evolution proceeds when a new heritable trait emerges in some organism and is passed genetically to its descendants. The precept indicates that two groups of animals sharing a set of such new, or "derived," traits are more closely related to each other than they are to groups that display only the original traits but not the derived ones. By identifying shared derived traits, practitioners of cladistics can determine the relations among the organisms they study.

The results of such analyses, which generally examine many traits, can be represented in the form of a cladogram: a treelike diagram depicting the order in which new characteristics, and new creatures, evolved. Each branching point, or node, reflects the emergence of an ancestor that founded a group having derived characteristics not present in groups that evolved earlier. This ancestor and all its descendants constitute a "clade," or closely related group.

Ostrom did not apply cladistic methods to determine that birds evolved from small theropod dinosaurs; in the 1970s the approach was just coming into use. But about a decade later Jacques A. Gauthier, then at the University of California at Berkeley, did an extensive cladistic analysis of birds, dinosaurs and their reptilian relatives. Gauthier put Ostrom's comparisons and many other features into a cladistic framework and confirmed that birds evolved from small theropod dinosaurs. Indeed, some of the closest relatives of birds include the sickle-clawed maniraptoran *Deinonychus* that Ostrom had so vividly described.

Today a cladogram for the lineage leading from theropods to birds shows that the clade labeled Aves (birds) consists of the ancestor of *Archaeopteryx* and all other descendants of that ancestor. This clade is a subgroup of a broader clade consisting of so-called maniraptoran theropods—itself a subgroup of the tetanuran theropods that descended from the most basal theropods. Those archaic theropods in turn evolved from nontheropod dinosaurs. The cladogram shows that birds are not only *descended* from dinosaurs, they *are* dinosaurs (and reptiles)—just as humans are mammals, even though people are as different from other mammals as birds are from other reptiles.

Early Evolutionary Steps to Birds

Gauthier's studies and ones conducted more recently demonstrate that many features traditionally considered "birdlike" actually appeared before the advent of birds, in their preavian theropod ancestors. Many of those properties undoubtedly helped their original possessors to survive as terrestrial dinosaurs; these same traits and others were eventually used directly or were transformed to support flight and an arboreal way of life. The short length of this article does not allow us to catalogue the many dozens of details that combine to support the hypothesis that birds evolved from small theropod dinosaurs, so we will concentrate mainly on those related to the origin of flight.

The birdlike characteristics of the theropods that evolved prior to birds did not appear all at once, and some were present before the theropods themselves emerged—in the earliest dinosaurs. For instance, the immediate reptilian ancestor of dinosaurs was already bipedal and upright in its stance (that is, it basically walked like a bird), and it was small and carnivorous. Its hands, in common with those of early birds, were free for grasping (although the hand still had five digits, not the three found in all but the most basal theropods and in birds). Also, the second finger was longest—not the third, as in other reptiles.

Further, in the ancestors of dinosaurs, the ankle joint had already become hingelike, and the metatarsals, or foot bones, had became elongated. The metatarsals were held off the ground, so the immediate relatives of dinosaurs, and dinosaurs themselves, walked on their toes and put one foot in front of the other, instead of sprawling. Many of the changes in the feet are thought to have increased stride length and running speed, a property that would one day help avian theropods to fly.

The earliest theropods had hollow bones and cavities in the skull; these adjustments lightened the skeleton. They also had a long neck and held their back horizontally, as birds do today. In the hand, digits four and five (the equivalent of the pinky and its neighbor) were already reduced in the first dinosaurs; the fifth finger was virtually gone. Soon it was completely lost, and the fourth was reduced to a nubbin. Those reduced fingers disappeared altogether in tetanuran theropods, and the remaining three (I, II, III) became fused together sometime after *Archaeopteryx* evolved.

In the first theropods, the hind limbs became more birdlike as well. They were long; the thigh was shorter than the shin, and the fibula, the bone to the side of the shinbone, was reduced. (In birds today the toothpicklike bone in the drumstick is all that is left of the fibula.) These dinosaurs walked on the three middle toes—the same ones modern birds use. The fifth toe was shortened and tapered, with no joints, and the first toe included a shortened metatarsal (with a small joint and a claw) that projected from the side of the second toe. The first toe was held higher than the others and had no apparent function, but it was later put to good use in birds. By the time *Archaeopteryx* appeared, that toe had rotated to lie behind the others. In later birds, it descended to become opposable to the others and eventually formed an important part of the perching foot.

More Changes

Through the course of theropod evolution, more features once thought of as strictly avian emerged. For instance, major changes occurred in the forelimb and shoulder girdle; these adjustments at first helped theropods to capture prey and later promoted flight. Notably, during theropod evolution, the arms became progressively longer, except in such giant carnivores as *Carnotaurus*, *Allosaurus* and *Tyrannosaurus*, in which the forelimbs were relatively small. The forelimb was about half the length of the hind limb in very early theropods. By the time *Archaeopteryx* appeared, the forelimb was longer than the hind limb, and it grew still more in later birds. This lengthening in the birds allowed a stronger flight stroke.

The hand became longer, too, accounting for a progressively greater proportion of the forelimb, and the wrist underwent dramatic revision in shape. Basal theropods possessed a flat wristbone (distal carpal) that overlapped the bases of the first and second palm bones (metacarpals) and fingers. In maniraptorans, though, this bone assumed a half-moon shape along the surface that contacted the arm bones. The half-moon, or semilunate, shape was very important because it allowed these animals to flex the wrist sideways in addition to up and down. They could thus fold the long hand, almost as living birds do. The longer hand could then be rotated and whipped forward suddenly to snatch prey.

In the shoulder girdle of early theropods, the scapula (shoulder blade) was long and straplike; the coracoid (which along with the scapula forms the shoulder joint) was rounded, and two separate, S-shaped clavicles connected the shoulder to the sternum, or breastbone. The scapula soon became longer and narrower; the coracoid also thinned and elongated, stretching toward the breastbone. The clavicles fused at the midline and broadened to form a boomerang-shaped wishbone. The sternum, which consisted originally of cartilage, calcified into two fused bony plates in tetanurans. Together these changes strengthened the skeleton; later this strengthening was used to reinforce the flight apparatus and support the flight muscles. The new wishbone, for instance, probably became an anchor for the muscles that moved the forelimbs, at first during foraging and then during flight.

In the pelvis, more vertebrae were added to the hip girdle, and the pubic bone (the pelvic bone that is attached in front of and below the hip socket) changed its orientation. In the first theropods, as in most other reptiles, the pubis pointed down and forward, but then it began to point straight down or backward. Ultimately, in birds more advanced than *Archaeopteryx*, it became parallel to the ischium, the pelvic bone that extends backward from below the hip socket. The benefits derived from these changes, if any, remain unknown, but the fact that these features are unique to birds and other maniraptorans shows their common origin.

Finally, the tail gradually became shorter and stiffer throughout theropod history, serving more and more as a balancing organ during running, somewhat as it does in today's roadrunners. Steven M. Gatesy of Brown University has demonstrated that this transition in tail structure paralleled another change in function: the tail became less and less an anchor for the leg muscles. The pelvis took over that function, and in maniraptorans the muscle that once drew back the leg now mainly controlled the tail. In birds that followed *Archaeopteryx*, these muscles would be used to adjust the feathered tail as needed in flight.

In summary, a great many skeletal features that were once thought of as uniquely avian innovations—such as light, hollow bones, long arms, three-fingered hands with a long second finger, a wishbone, a backward-pointing pelvis, and long hind limbs with a three-toed foot—were already present in theropods before the evolution of birds. Those features generally served different uses than they did in birds and were only later co-opted for flight and other characteristically avian functions, eventually including life in the trees.

Evidence for the dinosaurian origin of birds is not confined to the skeleton. Recent discoveries of nesting sites in Mongolia and Montana reveal that some reproductive behaviors of birds originated in nonavian dinosaurs. These theropods did not deposit a large clutch of eggs all at once, as most other reptiles do. Instead they filled a nest more gradually, laying one or two eggs at a time, perhaps over several days, as birds do. Recently skeletons of the Cretaceous theropod *Oviraptor* have been found atop nests of eggs; the dinosaurs were apparently buried while protecting the eggs in very birdlike fashion. This find is ironic because *Oviraptor*, whose name means "egg stealer," was first thought to have been raiding the eggs of other dinosaurs, rather than protecting them. Even the structure of the eggshell in theropods shows features otherwise seen only in bird eggs. The shells consist of two layers of calcite, one prismatic (crystalline) and one spongy (more irregular and porous).

As one supposedly uniquely avian trait after another has been identified in nonavian dinosaurs, feathers have continued to stand out as a prominent feature belonging to birds alone. Some intriguing evidence, however, hints that even feathers might have predated the emergence of birds.

In 1996 and 1997 Ji Qiang and Ji Shu'an of the National Geological

Museum of China published reports on two fossil animals found in Liaoning Province that date to late in the Jurassic or early in the Cretaceous. One, a turkey-size dinosaur named *Sinosauropteryx*, has fringed, filamentous structures along its backbone and on its body surface. These structures of the skin, or integument, may have been precursors to feathers. But the animal is far from a bird. It has short arms and other skeletal properties indicating that it may be related to the theropod *Compsognathus*, which is not especially close to birds or other maniraptorans.

The second creature, *Protarchaeopteryx*, apparently has short, true feathers on its body and has longer feathers attached to its tail. Preliminary observations suggest that the animal is a maniraptoran theropod. Whether it is also a bird will depend on a fuller description of its anatomy. Nevertheless, the Chinese finds imply that, at the least, the structures that gave rise to feathers probably appeared before birds did and almost certainly before birds began to fly. Whether their original function was for insulation, display or something else cannot yet be determined.

The Beginning of Bird Flight

The origin of birds and the origin of flight are two distinct, albeit related, problems. Feathers were present for other functions before flight evolved, and *Archaeopteryx* was probably not the very first flying theropod, although at present we have no fossils of earlier flying precursors. What can we say about how flight began in bird ancestors?

Traditionally, two opposing scenarios have been put forward. The "arboreal" hypothesis holds that bird ancestors began to fly by climbing trees and gliding down from branches with the help of incipient feathers. The height of trees provides a good starting place for launching flight, especially through gliding. As feathers became larger over time, flapping flight evolved, and birds finally became fully airborne.

This hypothesis makes intuitive sense, but certain aspects are troubling. *Archaeopteryx* and its maniraptoran cousins have no obviously arboreal adaptations, such as feet fully adapted for perching. Perhaps some of them could climb trees, but no convincing analysis has demonstrated how *Archaeopteryx* would have climbed and flown with its forelimbs, and there were no plants taller than a few meters in the environments where *Archaeopteryx* fossils have been found. Even if the animals could climb trees, this ability is not synonymous with arboreal habits or gliding ability. Most small animals, and even some goats and kangaroos, can climb trees, but that does not make them tree dwellers. Besides, *Archaeopteryx* shows no obvious features of gliders, such as a broad membrane connecting forelimbs and hind limbs.

The "cursorial" (running) hypothesis holds that small dinosaurs ran along the ground and stretched out their arms for balance as they leaped into the air after insect prey or, perhaps, to avoid predators. Even rudimentary feathers on forelimbs could have expanded the arm's surface area to enhance lift slightly. Larger feathers could have increased lift incrementally, until sustained flight was gradually achieved. Of course, a leap into the air does not provide the acceleration produced by dropping out of a tree; an animal would have to run quite fast to take off. Still, some small terrestrial animals can achieve high speeds.

The cursorial hypothesis is strengthened by the fact that the immediate theropod ancestors of birds were terrestrial. And they had the traits needed for high liftoff speeds: they were small, active, agile, lightly built, long-legged and good runners. And because they were bipedal, their arms were free to evolve flapping flight, which cannot be said for other reptiles of their time.

Although our limited evidence is tantalizing, probably neither the arboreal nor the cursorial model is correct in its extreme form. More likely, the ancestors of birds used a combination of taking off from the ground and taking advantage of accessible heights (such as hills, large boulders or fallen trees). They may not have climbed trees, but they could have used every available object in their landscape to assist flight.

More central than the question of ground versus trees, however, is the evolution of a flight stroke. This stroke generates not only the lift that gliding animals obtain from moving their wings through the air (as an airfoil) but also the thrust that enables a flapping animal to move forward. (In contrast, the "organs" of lift and thrust in airplanes—the wings and jets—are separate.) In birds and bats, the hand part of the wing generates the thrust, and the rest of the wing provides the lift.

Jeremy M. V. Rayner of the University of Bristol showed in the late 1970s that the down-and-forward flight stroke of birds and bats produces a series of doughnut-shaped vortices that propel the flying animal forward. One of us (Padian) and Gauthier then demonstrated in the mid-1980s that the movement generating these vortices in birds is the same action—sideways flexion of the hand—that was already present in the maniraptorans *Deinonychus* and *Velociraptor* and in *Archaeopteryx*.

As we noted earlier, the first maniraptorans must have used this movement to grab prey. By the time *Archaeopteryx* and other birds appeared, the shoulder joint had changed its angle to point more to the side than down and backward. This alteration in the angle transformed the forelimb motion from a prey-catching one to a flight stroke. New evidence from Argentina suggests that the shoulder girdle in the closest maniraptorans to birds (the new dinosaur *Unenlagia*) was already angled outward so as to permit this kind of stroke.

Recent work by Farish A. Jenkins, Jr., of Harvard University, George E. Goslow of Brown University and their colleagues has revealed much about the role of the wishbone in flight and about how the flight stroke is achieved. The wishbone in some living birds acts as a spacer between the shoulder girdles, one that stores energy expended during the flight stroke. In the first birds, in contrast, it probably was less elastic, and its main function may have been simply to anchor the forelimb muscles. Apparently, too, the muscle most responsible for rotating and raising the wing during the recovery stroke of flight was not yet in the modern position in *Archaeopteryx* or other very early birds. Hence, those birds were probably not particularly skilled fliers; they would have been unable to flap as quickly or as precisely as today's birds can. But it was not long—perhaps just several million years—before birds acquired the apparatus they needed for more controlled flight.

Beyond Archaeopteryx

More than three times as many bird fossils from the Cretaceous period have been found since 1990 than in all the rest of recorded history. These new specimens—uncovered in such places as Spain, China, Mongolia, Madagascar and Argentina—are helping paleontologists to flesh out the early evolution of the birds that followed *Archaeopteryx*, including their acquisition of an improved flying system. Analyses of these finds by one of us (Chiappe) and others have shown that birds quickly took on many different sizes, shapes and behaviors (ranging from diving to flightlessness) and diversified all through the Cretaceous period, which ended about 65 million years ago.

A bird-watching trek through an Early Cretaceous forest would bear little resemblance to such an outing now. These early birds might have spent much of their time in the trees and were able to perch, but there is no evidence that the first birds nested in trees, had complex songs or migrated great distances. Nor did they fledge at nearly adult size, as birds do now, or grow as rapidly as today's birds do. Scientists can only imagine what these animals looked like. Undoubtedly, however, they would have seemed very strange, with their clawed fingers and, in many cases, toothed beaks.

Underneath the skin, though, some skeletal features certainly became more birdlike during the Early Cretaceous and enabled birds to fly quite well. Many bones in the hand and in the hip girdle fused, providing strength to the skeleton for flight. The breastbone became broader and developed a keel down the midline of the chest for flight muscle attachment. The forearm became much longer, and the skull bones and vertebrae became lighter and more hollowed out. The tailbones became a short series of free segments ending in a fused stump (the familiar "parson's nose" or "Pope's nose" of roasted birds) that controlled the tail feathers. And the alula, or "thumb wing," a part of the bird wing essential for flight control at low speed, made its debut, as did a long first toe useful in perching.

Inasmuch as early birds could fly, they certainly had higher metabolic rates than cold-blooded reptiles; at least they were able to generate the heat and energy needed for flying without having to depend on being heated by the environment. But they might not have been as fully warm-blooded as today's birds. Their feathers, in addition to aiding flight, provided a measure of insulation—just as the precursors of feathers could have helped preserve heat and conserve energy in nonavian precursors of birds. These birds probably did not fly as far or as strongly as birds do now.

Bird-watchers traipsing through a forest roughly 50 million years later would still have found representatives of very primitive lineages of birds. Yet other birds would have been recognizable as early members of living groups. Recent research shows that at least four major lineages of living

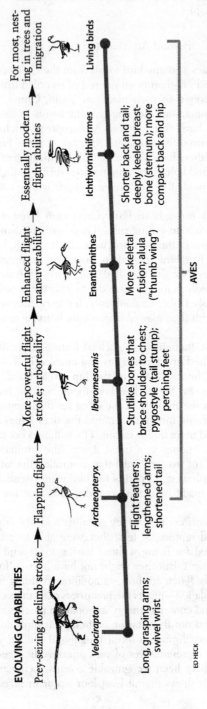

EVOLVING CAPABILITIES

Prey-seizing forelimb stroke → Flapping flight → More powerful flight stroke; arboreality → Enhanced flight maneuverability → Essentially modern flight abilities → For most, nesting in trees and migration

Velociraptor — Long, grasping arms; swivel wrist

Archaeopteryx — Flight feathers; lengthened arms; shortened tail

Iberomesornis — Strutlike bones that brace shoulder to chest; pygostyle (tail stump); perching feet

Enantiornithes — More skeletal fusion; alula ("thumb wing")

Ichthyornithiformes — Shorter back and tail; deeply keeled breastbone (sternum); more compact back and hip

Living birds

AVES

ED HECK

Cladogram of bird evolution indicates that birds (Aves) perfected their flight stroke gradually after they first appeared approximately 150 million years ago. They became arboreal (able to live in trees) relatively early in their history, however. Some of the skeletal innovations that supported their emerging capabilities are listed at the bottom.

birds—including ancient relatives of shorebirds, seabirds, loons, ducks and geese—were already thriving several million years before the end of the Cretaceous period, and new paleontological and molecular evidence suggests that forerunners of other modern birds were around as well.

Most lineages of birds that evolved during the Cretaceous died out during that period, although there is no evidence that they perished suddenly. Researchers may never know whether the birds that disappeared were outcompeted by newer forms, were killed by an environmental catastrophe or were just unable to adapt to changes in their world. There is no reasonable doubt, however, that all groups of birds, living and extinct, are descended from small, meat-eating theropod dinosaurs, as Huxley's work intimated more than a century ago. In fact, living birds are nothing less than small, feathered, short-tailed theropod dinosaurs.

EVOLUTION AS OBSERVABLE FACT

JAMES L. GOULD and WILLIAM T. KEETON with CAROL GRANT GOULD

How Natural Selection Operates (1996)[†]

Adaptation

Every organism is, in a sense, a complex bundle of thousands of *adaptations*. In biology, an adaptation is any genetically controlled characteristic that increases an organism's fitness. *Fitness*, as the term is used in evolutionary biology, is an individual's (or allele's or genotype's) probable genetic contribution to succeeding generations. An adaptation, then, is a characteristic that increases an organism's chances of perpetuating its genes, usually by leaving descendants. Adaptations do not necessarily increase the organism's chances of survival: although it ordinarily enhances prereproductive survival, it need not affect postreproductive survival. In many species it is, in fact, more adaptive for the adults to die soon after they have reproduced.

Adaptations may be structural, physiological, or behavioral. They may be genetically simple or complex. They may involve individual cells or subcellular components, or whole organs or organ systems. They may be highly specific, beneficial only under very limited circumstances, or they may be general and of value under many and varied circumstances.

A population may become adapted to changed environmental conditions very rapidly. W. B. Kemp reported a classic example in 1937. The owner of a pasture in southern Maryland had seeded the pasture with a

† From *Biological Science*, Sixth Edition, by James L. Gould and William T. Keeton. Copyright © 1996, 1993, 1986, 1980, 1979, 1978, 1972, 1967 by W. W. Norton & Company, Inc. Used by permission of W. W. Norton & Company, Inc. James L. Gould (b. 1945) is professor of ecology and evolutionary biology at Princeton University. William T. Keeton (1933–1980) was professor of biological sciences at Cornell University. Carol Grant Gould (b. 1948) is a science writer living in Princeton, N.J.

1. Cryptic coloration of peppered moths
(A) Light and dark morphs of *Biston betularia* at rest on a tree trunk in unpolluted countryside.

mixture of grasses and legumes. Then he divided the pasture into two parts, allowing one to be heavily grazed by cattle, while protecting the other from the livestock and letting it produce hay. Three years after this division, Kemp obtained specimens of blue grass, orchard grass, and white clover from each part of the pasture and planted them in an experimental garden where all the plants were exposed to the same environmental conditions. He found that the specimens of all three species from the heavily grazed half of the pasture exhibited dwarf, rambling growth, while specimens of the same three species from the ungrazed half grew vigorously upright.

In only three years the two populations of each species had become markedly different in their genetically determined growth pattern. The grazing cattle in the one half of the pasture had cropped most of the upright plants, and only plants low enough to be missed had survived and set seed. There had been intense selection against upright growth in this half of the pasture and correspondingly intense selection for the adaptively superior dwarf, rambling growth pattern. In the half of the pasture where there was no grazing, by contrast, upright growth was adaptively superior,

(B) Light and dark morphs on a soot-covered tree trunk. Here the light form is easier to see.

and dwarf plants were unable to compete effectively. Analogous results are observed when animals are subjected to various degrees of predation.

*   *   *

Defensive Adaptations

CRYPTIC APPEARANCE

Many animals blend into their surroundings so well as to be nearly undetectable. Frequently their color matches the background almost perfectly. In some cases animals even have the ability to alter the condition of their own pigment cells and change their appearance to harmonize with their background. Often, rather than match the color of the general background, the animals may resemble inanimate objects commonly found in their habitat, such as leaves or twigs. When the shape or color of an animal offers concealment against its background, it is said to have a *cryptic* appearance.

Cryptic appearance is an adaptive characteristic that helps animals escape predation. * * *

One of the most extensively studied cases of cryptic coloration is the so-called industrial melanism of moths. Since the mid-1880s many species of moths have become decidedly darker in industrial regions. This is actually a case of polymorphism in which the less frequent of two forms has become the more frequent; the originally predominant light form in these species of moths has given way in industrial areas to the dark (melanic) form. In the Manchester area of England, the first black specimens of the species *Biston betularia* were caught in 1848; by 1895 melanics constituted about 98% of the total population in the area. For such a remarkable shift in frequency to have occurred in so short a time, the melanic form must have had at least a 30% advantage over the light form.

The various species of moths exhibiting the rapid shift to melanism, though unrelated to one another, all habitually rest during the day in an exposed position on tree trunks or rocks, being protected from predation only by their close resemblance to their background. In former years the tree trunks and rocks were light colored and often covered with light-colored lichens. Against this background the light forms of the moths were difficult to see, whereas the melanic forms were quite conspicuous (Fig. 1). Under these conditions it seems likely that predators captured melanics far more easily than the cryptically colored light moths. The light forms would thus have been strongly favored, and they would have oc-curred with much higher frequency than melanics. With the advent of extensive industrialization, tree trunks and rocks were blackened by soot, and the lichens, which are particularly sensitive to such pollution, disap-peared. In this altered environment the melanic moths resembled the background more closely than did the light moths. Thus selection should now have favored the melanics, which would explain why they increased in frequency.

This scenario was put to a test in the mid-1950s, when H. B. D. Ket-tlewell released equal numbers of the light and melanic forms of *Biston betularia* onto trees in a rural area in Dorset, England, where the tree trunks were light colored, lichens were abundant, and the wild population of the moth was about 94.6% light colored. Of 190 moths observed to be captured by birds, 164 were melanics and only 26 were light forms. Of hundreds of marked individuals of each form released in another experi-ment, roughly twice as many light moths as melanic moths were recap-tured in traps set up in the woods, an indication that more of the light moths had survived.

Taken alone, however, these experiments did not prove that the factor favoring the light moths over the melanics was their resemblance to their background. Perhaps the birds preferred the melanics because of some difference in flavor. Kettlewell duplicated the experiments under the re-verse environmental conditions—in woods near Birmingham, England, where the tree trunks were blackened with soot, lichens were absent, and the wild population of the moth was about 85% melanic. The results of these experiments were the reverse of those in the Dorset experiments. Now birds captured nearly three times as many light moths as melanics, and roughly twice as many melanics were recaptured in traps. Recently, the imposition of pollution controls has led to a shift back toward the light morph. * * *

PETER R. GRANT

Natural Selection and Darwin's Finches (1991)†

Every year vast numbers of eggs are produced by creatures as small as parasitic nematode worms and as large as salmon and cod. Orchids may disperse a thousand seeds. Other organisms, such as tortoises and coconuts, reproduce much more slowly than this. Yet one demographic feature is common to all: when a population remains at about the same size for a long time, each parent, on average, replaces itself with just one breeding offspring. That ecological simplicity belies a subtle evolutionary complexity. Although the population replaces itself, some parents leave more offspring than others, and this imbalance provides the condition for evolution to occur by natural selection.

Natural selection is differential success. A population of sexually reproducing organisms comprises many different individuals: some are larger, thicker, greener or hairier than others. When some organisms survive or reproduce better than others because they are larger or smaller, or because they are more or less hairy, natural selection occurs.

Charles Darwin devised the concept of natural selection while attempting to explain the evolution of organic diversity. His theory has been elaborated, extended and corrected; it has been founded in physical evidence of which he was unaware, such as DNA and the genes it encodes. The evolutionary mechanism is key to any general understanding of how the world came to be the way it is. Yet it is remarkable that 132 years after the publication of his masterpiece, *On the Origin of Species by Means of Natural Selection*, natural selection is still not widely understood.

There are three reasons for this incomprehension. Natural selection has been discussed in misleading terms, such as "fitness," which are charged with unfortunate meanings. Also, popularizers have confused natural selection with related concepts, such as inheritance. Finally, Darwin himself mistakenly assumed that natural selection necessarily proceeds at a snail's pace and that it therefore cannot be observed but merely deduced. He said as much in a famous passage in *Origin of Species:*

> It may be said that natural selection is daily and hourly scrutinising, throughout the world, every variation, even the slightest; rejecting that which is bad, preserving and adding up all that is good; silently and insensibly working, whenever and wherever opportunity offers, at the improvement of each organic being in relation to its organic and inorganic conditions of life. We see nothing of these slow changes in progress, until the hand of time has marked the long lapses of ages, and then so imperfect is our view into long past geological ages, that we only see that the forms of life are now different from what they formerly were.

† From "Natural Selection and Darwin's Finches," *Scientific American* (Oct. 1991): 82–87. Reprinted with permission. Copyright © 1991 by Scientific American, Inc. All rights reserved. Peter R. Grant (b. 1936) is Class of 1877 Professor of Zoology at Princeton University.

Darwin argued that new species are formed when persistent selection over many generations changes a population so much that its members will no longer breed with individuals from a related population. But if natural selection indeed occurs solely on a historical scale, the study of evolution would be seriously impeded. The subject would not be amenable to scientific observation and experimentation.

Fortunately, this is not the case. John A. Endler of the University of California at Santa Barbara has recently compiled a list of more than 100 studies that have demonstrated natural selection in action. Some of the most easily interpreted cases have been witnessed in environments altered by human activities. Certain grasses, for example, have become tolerant to the high concentrations of lead in mine tailings. The most common and dangerous cases occur when an antibiotic fails to kill all the bacteria infesting a patient because a few of them are naturally resistant to it. In evolutionary terms, the treatment has selected for resistance to the drug. If the surviving microorganisms can pass their resistance on to their daughter cells, a new strain evolves.

Studies of natural selection in natural environments have broader implications, for they help us understand more directly the evolution of organic diversity over the long history of the earth, the problem Darwin tried to solve. The finches named after him provide an unusually clear illustration.

Thirteen species of Darwin's Finches live on the Galápagos Islands, having evolved from a common ancestor, it is believed, in the past one to five million years. The birds are darkly colored and of similar bodily proportions, but they vary in length from about three to six inches (seven to 12 centimeters)—the range between a warbler and a rather fat sparrow—and in the shape of their bills, which reflects their different diets. The common names label their niches and affinities: tree finches, ground finches, cactus finches, a warbler finch, a vegetarian finch, a woodpecker finch and a mangrove finch.

The finches provide a prime example of adaptive radiation, as described in these pages nearly 40 years ago [see "Darwin's Finches," by David Lack; SCIENTIFIC AMERICAN, April, 1953]. Lack noted that the only other group of birds that display a similar pattern, the sicklebills (honeycreeper finches) of Hawaii, also live in an archipelago, and he suggested that many or even most species differentiated in some kind of physical isolation. "What is unique about the Galápagos and Hawaii," he wrote, "is that the birds' evolution there occurred so recently that we can still see the evidence of the differentiations." The evidence is in fact more than recent, it is ongoing: I have seen the finches evolve in response to climatic changes during the past dozen years. These changes can be dramatic. In some years the islands are drenched by rains precipitated by El Niño events; in other years they are parched by drought.

In 1973 I began studying the finches living on Daphne Major, an islet that covers only about 100 acres. This area was small enough to limit the two resident populations—the medium ground finch, *Geospiza fortis*, and the cactus finch, *G. scandens*—to a number that could be studied ex-

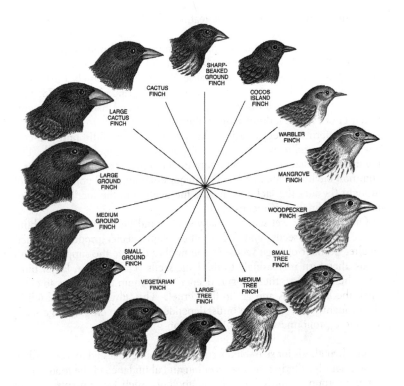

haustively. I have been aided in this endeavor by my wife, Rosemary, and, each year, by two graduate students or other assistants.

We captured the birds in mist nets, so called because their fine filaments are scarcely visible against a dark background. We measured the birds and banded their legs with a numbered metal band and three plastic bands, which allowed us to identify each bird from a distance. Each triplet of colors was coded to correspond to the number on the metal band. By 1977 we had banded more than half of the island's birds, a proportion that passed 90 percent in 1980 and has remained near 100 percent ever since. Thus, from an early stage we were in a position to detect natural selection, if it occurred.

In 1977 it did. In that year Daphne Major had a drought: less than an inch (25 millimeters) of rain fell in the normal wet season. Deciduous plants produced few leaves, and caterpillars were scarce. Some pairs of cactus finches bred, but within three months all their offspring had vanished. Medium ground finches did not even breed. There was a long, dry and unproductive period from the middle of 1976 to early January 1978, when the rains resumed.

During the 18 months, many birds disappeared. Medium ground finches were the hardest hit—only 15 percent remained. Moreover, the winnowing process selected for large size in both species. Although birds of all sizes were reduced in number, the smaller ones were reduced the most. In addition, a conspicuous feature of the survivors was their large beak size.

The missing birds had either died or emigrated. Although the emigration of a few individuals cannot be ruled out, there are two reasons to believe that death was the major cause of the disappearance. First, none of the birds that disappeared in 1976 and 1977 reappeared in 1978. Second, a sample of 38 birds found dead on the island had measurements much closer to the failures than to the successes.

The pattern was repeated in 1982, when there was little rain, scarcely any breeding and heavy mortality, particularly among the small birds. The recurrence of size-selective mortality under similar conditions suggests a common environmental cause. The major environmental consequence of drought (besides the lack of water) is the decline in the food supply. For the ground finch, this means seeds.

During normal wet seasons, many grasses and herbs produce an abundance of small seeds, and a few other plant species produce a much smaller number of large seeds. As the finches deplete the supply of small seeds, they turn increasingly to the large seeds. That is when larger birds have the advantage: their bigger, deeper beaks equip them better to crack open the large seeds and get to the kernels. This advantage would tell in the drought years, when the birds' dependence on the crop of large seeds was more pronounced and prolonged than in other years.

The hypothesis for size-selective mortality could be tested in a controlled experiment by altering the composition and abundance of the food supply for one group of birds but not for another. Such experiments are not feasible in the Galápagos National Park but can be done with other bird species elsewhere. This untested hypothesis is plausible, but it is not the only explanation. Large birds may have survived well because their body size allowed them to dominate other finches in social interactions at restricted sources of food or moisture.

Since body size correlates with beak depth, it is not immediately apparent whether one or the other, or both, played a role in survival. A statistical analysis is needed to isolate the association that each factor, considered separately, has with survival. We used partial regression and found that body size and beak depth each correlated positively—and about equally—with survival. Beak length, on the other hand, did not. Thus, a combination of morphological, behavioral and possibly physiological factors helped to determine which birds survived and which ones succumbed to environmental stress.

Interestingly, Darwin may have witnessed a similar instance of natural selection without noticing it. He estimated that as many as four fifths of the birds in southern England perished during the severe winter of 1854–55. Selection may have been at work, for mortality was similar to what we observed among the medium ground finches in 1977.

I have thus far referred to survival rather than fitness in order to avoid a misunderstanding created more than a century ago by Herbert Spencer. Spencer erroneously equated natural selection with "the survival of the fittest," a catch phrase he coined to popularize Darwin's work. The problem is one of circular reasoning: when the fittest are manifested as such only by surviving, the phrase reduces to the survival of the survivors. Nevertheless, survival of the fittest—or better, the higher frequency of survival among the fittest—does convey part of the essence of natural selection, provided two points are understood. First, some individuals are more fit than others by virtue of their particular traits; second, fitness is ultimately judged by the number of offspring an individual contributes to the next generation.

It is equally essential to avoid confusing selection with genetic variation, that is, with the genes that control variation in the traits on which selection operates. As the British geneticist J.B.S. Haldane emphasized, selection has no effects on the next generation unless it influences traits that are to some degree under genetic control and thus heritable. If the traits are heritable, however, then selection causes a small evolutionary change in the population. Therefore, an important question to ask is whether beak depth and body size in the medium ground finch population are heritable.

The heritability of a trait is a measure of the degree to which the trait varies in a population as a result of the additive effect of genes. Thus, large birds may be large in part because of the particular set of genes they inherit from their parents and in part because of the favorable conditions they experience in early life while growing to their final adult size. Similarly, small birds may be small for a combination of genetic and environmental reasons. The degree to which genes influence body size or beak size can be measured by the average similarity between offspring and their parents. This is accomplished by regressing the average of the offspring measurements on the average of the mother's and father's measurements for as many families as possible, a standard procedure in quantitative genetics. The heritability of the trait is estimated by the slope of the function, which can vary between zero and one.

This technique enabled us to estimate the heritability of beak depth in the medium ground finch population at 0.74. In other words, 74 percent of the variation in beak depth can be attributed to the additive effects of all the relevant genes. The remaining 26 percent is largely attributable to environmental causes. Body size has a somewhat higher heritability, 91 percent. Other morphological traits, including beak length and wing length, have similarly high heritabilities.

Such estimates are subject to the effects of hidden biases, above all the possibility that organisms resemble their parents in part because they grow up in similar environments. Birds might, for example, grow to relatively large adult size in the better territories. If, when seeking their own territories, they outcompete smaller birds for the better territories, they would be able to rear offspring that also reach large adult size. The same self-perpetuating process might work on small birds, leading to an inflated estimate of the genetic contribution to the resemblance between relatives.

One can identify such a bias by randomly exchanging eggs or nestlings among nests in the same population and determining whether final adult size varies between birds raised by true and by foster parents. We have not done this but have preserved the population in an entirely natural state. Where it has been done, with other species of birds, no evidence has been found that the rearing environment distorts the estimation of heritability. Our check was different: we compared birds in food-rich and food-poor territories and looked for a tendency for offspring to breed in the kind of territory in which they were raised. We found no such tendency.

Other small errors may also be present, but there is little doubt that body size and beak depth are highly heritable in this population. Therefore, effects of selection on these two traits are passed on genetically to the next generation, causing evolutionary change in the population.

The change is quantified by selection and heritability factors, the product of which should account for the difference between the mean measurement of a trait before selection occurs and the mean in the next generation. The difference, which is normally expressed in standard deviations, is called the evolutionary response to selection.

If selection occurs but the trait has a heritability of zero, then the offspring should not differ from the parental generation before it underwent selection. In Haldane's words, selection will have been ineffective. On the other hand, if all variation in the trait is genetic and the heritability is one, then there is no discounting: the offspring will have a mean identical to that of their parents. These are the extremes; most cases fall in between.

Evolutionary response to selection becomes more complicated when more than one trait is influenced by selection at the same time, for then the genetic variation of each trait interacts with that of the others. Such genetic covariance affects the response. We can minimize these complications by replacing the several traits with an index, which functions as a single synthetic trait. The index accounts for most of the variation among individuals in all dimensions—body size, beak depth and so forth.

Peter T. Boag, now at Queen's University in Kingston, Ontario, adopted this approach while working as my graduate assistant in the late 1970s. He used the first component from what is called a principal components analysis of morphological variation. This synthetic trait, which has the high heritability of 0.75, is best interpreted as a body-size index. It accounts for 64 percent of the variation in the size of the beak, wing, leg and other body parts of the medium ground finches.

Selection on this synthetic trait produced an evolutionary response of 0.36 standard deviation (SD). This accorded well with the predicted value of 0.40 SD, obtained from the measured selection differential and heritability. Thus, a microevolutionary change took place in this population as a result of natural selection. It amounted to an increase in the average beak depth and body size of about 4 percent.

Studies of natural selection as an observable process help us to understand retrospectively processes of evolution that took millennia to unfold. This is particularly true of the pattern of change involved in speciation. In the case of Darwin's Finches, for example, we can extrapolate the observed microevolutionary change to infer the magnitude, causes and circumstances of changes in the formation of one species from another.

Trevor D. Price, now at the University of California at San Diego, and I attempted to do this by taking into account the genetic variation governing morphological traits and the magnitude of the directional selection that occurred in 1977. The two quantities allowed us to estimate the number of such selection events required to transform the medium ground finch, G. *fortis*, into its close relative, the large ground finch, G. *magnirostris*, which is about 50 percent larger.

The number is surprisingly small: about 20 selection events would have sufficed. If droughts occur once a decade, on average, repeated directional selection at this rate with no selection in between droughts would transform one species into another within 200 years. Even if the estimate is off by a factor of 10, the 2,000 years required for speciation is still very little time in relation to the hundreds of thousands of years the finches have been in the archipelago.

Far more time is needed to form a species differing from its progenitor in shape rather than size, for then selection must work in opposite directions on different traits, in the face of positive correlations between them. The transformation of the medium ground finch into the cactus finch, for example, would require a relative increase in beak length but a relative decrease in beak depth and in body mass—a process we estimate would take six times longer than the transformation into the large ground finch.

An alternative to this scheme of speciation occurring on a single island is one involving the colonization of several islands in the archipelago. One species becomes transformed into another through the cumulative effects of selection, predominantly or solely in one direction, on not one but a series of islands. That suggestion is plausible because, as our field studies have shown, each island has a distinctive constellation of types of food for the finches, so in dispersing from one island to another they encounter a different food supply.

In each case, selection will drive the traits of newly established populations fairly rapidly toward the optimal attainable form. Stabilizing selection will then hold the population near that optimum until the environment changes, causing an alteration in diets, perhaps as a result of a rise or decline in the number of competing organisms.

Most species observed in nature appear to have attained stable forms and behaviors. One might conclude, then, that Darwin's Finches on Daphne Major constitute an exception, in that the population is currently heading in the direction of becoming a larger species. This hunch may be right, but I doubt it; other factors are also at play.

Effects of the droughts of 1977 and 1982 were approximately offset by selection in the opposite direction—toward smaller body size—in 1984–85. A relative scarcity of large seeds, together with an ample supply of small ones, favored small finches. Because the food supply on this island changes in composition and size from year to year, the optimal beak form for a finch is shifting in position, and the population, subjected to natural selection, is oscillating back and forth with every shift. Whether or not there is a net directional trend toward larger size, like an arrow through the oscillations, is unclear and could be determined only by a much longer study. Such a trend may come to pass, if human-induced global warming increases the incidence of drought in the Pacific.

We have observed fluctuations of a somewhat different kind in the pop-

ulation of the large cactus finch, G. *conirostris*, on Genovesa, 55 miles to
the northeast of Daphne Major. In this case, the foods provided by cactus
bushes changed as a result of extremely wet conditions produced by El
Niño in 1983. In the next year long-billed birds were at a disadvantage
because the food they are best equipped to exploit, cactus flowers and
fruits, declined drastically. In 1985, a drought year, the birds had little to
eat except the arthropods living under the bark of trees and in the tough
pads of cactus bushes. Under these changed circumstances, the finches
with strong, deep beaks were best equipped to extract the arthropods. As
a result of this advantage, they had the highest rate of survival.

Oscillating direction selection may furnish a general model for what
happens elsewhere—and not just to populations of birds. Annual variation
in environmental conditions is pronounced, as we know from the summers
in the U.S. during the past decade. We also know that many populations
of animals, from insects to mammals, fluctuate greatly in numbers under
the influence of a varying climate. Most of these populations live in the
temperate zone, but even the inhabitants of tropical rain forests are not as
stable in numbers as was once assumed.

When a population fluctuates, gene frequencies are likely to change as
a result of random processes, especially when the population declines to
low numbers. The unanswered question is whether, in addition to this
process, demographic fluctuations in a wide variety of organisms are accompanied by microevolutionary changes in phenotypic traits as a result
of natural selection. My guess is that they often are, but proof will require
detailed studies of individually recognizable members of a population. If
oscillating selection is indeed widespread and not just a peculiarity experienced by Darwin's Finches and a few other organisms, then the model
will constitute a powerful tool to help us achieve Darwin's goal: the explanation of the causes of organic diversity.

JOHN A. ENDLER

Natural Selection in the Wild (1986)†

* * *

It is the purpose of this book to describe natural selection clearly, show
that it is neither a tautology nor a metaphysical exercise, discuss the problems of its demonstration and measurement, present the critical evidence
for its existence, and place it in perspective.

* * *

Direct Demonstrations of Natural Selection in the Wild

The literature contains a very large number of studies on natural selection. They vary greatly in quality as well as in kinds of species and traits. * * *

Of historical interest, the earliest example is an experiment that was performed inadvertently on humans, and it actually shows unequivocal evidence for natural selection. In the seventeenth century the Dutch slave traders introduced people from a single area of West Africa (Gold Coast) at random in Surinam and Curaçao. Curaçao has no malaria but Surinam does. The descendants of these people in Surinam today have a high frequency of sickle-cell trait, while those in Curaçao have a very low frequency.

Another early example is that of Weldon (1899) on crabs. He observed a significant long-term change in frontal breadth of *Carcinus moenas* near an estuary that was becoming progressively more polluted with clay silt and sewage. To test the suggested causal relationship he kept large numbers of crabs in running clear sea water, sea water with clay silt, and sea water with silt and sewage. He showed, by following cohorts, that crabs with smaller frontal breadth survived better than the others, and the major source of mortality was silt. The reason is problematic but might be a function of the relationship between frontal breadth and efficiency of water circulation past the gills; but this was never tested. Although there are major problems with the design, including inadequate controls, this is a good early example of an attempt to use a laboratory study to test a hypothesis suggested by field correlations.

* * *

[In the following pages, Endler lists more than a hundred studies that demonstrate natural selection in action, identifying the traits examined, the method of demonstration, the selective agent, and source materials. (Editor)]

Demonstrations of natural selection are widely distributed among a great diversity of animal and plant taxa; there is no evidence that any particular group is more likely to be represented than another. More animal species are represented than plants, but this probably is an artifact; until recently, studies of natural selection have been primarily done by zoologists. This is rapidly changing, and there seems to be nothing inherently more difficult about detecting selection in either kingdom. Within animals, vertebrates and invertebrates are about equally represented. Since there are more invertebrate species, this might suggest that selection is more common in vertebrates; but once again, this is probably the result of greater interest by vertebrate biologists. I hope this book will encourage correction of the inbalance.

It would be interesting to ask whether or not genera that are currently undergoing rapid radiation are more likely to show detectable natural selection than, say, species-poor genera. Unfortunately, there are insufficient data to address this question at present; it would repay further study. It would be especially interesting to study intensively natural selection of a few traits in a species-rich and a species-poor genus living in the same habitat.

Of the various components of fitness, mortality is the most commonly demonstrated, perhaps because many researchers have not looked for differences in fertility, mating ability, and other components. Yet the others are by no means rare. It is impossible to say which forms of selection are more common because the number of unpublished studies with insignificant results is unknown. (This problem also applies to the other patterns discussed in this section.) However, since about 1982 there has been much interest in mate choice and sexual selection, and this aspect of fitness has only just begun to be explored seriously.

*   *   *

Summary

One's opinion on the importance of natural selection depends upon one's relative interests in a variety of aspects of evolution. Different viewpoints emphasize the relative importance of natural selection, mutation, genetic drift, and constraints to variation, as well as their influence on the direction and rate of evolution. The fundamental mechanisms of evolution are the molecular mechanisms leading to new genetic variants, the expression of those variants through the genetic and developmental systems, and constraints to the appearance and function of those variants. Natural selection and genetic drift are mechanisms that cause only frequency changes in populations. Certainly all components are important in evolution, but for different reasons. The tempo of evolution may be most strongly influenced by mutation and genetic drift, and the mode of evolution by natural selection within the constraints of the developmental and genetic systems, which themselves are subject to the same processes. Which aspect of evolution one studies reflects one's interests, and not its relative importance, just as a student of geomorphology must consider erosion, orogeny, and geological structure and history, although he may choose to study only a subset of those phenomena. Increased collaboration among ecologists, geneticists, organismal and developmental biologists is required to cover all aspects of evolution in the same organisms. We are most remarkably ignorant about the ecological aspects of natural selection, and there are at least six major gaps in our knowledge: (1) Why does natural selection occur? (2) How does it occur? (3) What kinds of traits are most likely to be affected? (4) What are the effects of simultaneous natural selection of many traits and of the interactions among them? (5) What are the evolutionary dynamics of selected traits? (6) Are genera that are most prone to exhibit natural selection also those that are currently radiating most rapidly?

PART VI
DARWINIAN PATTERNS IN
SOCIAL THOUGHT

Just as Darwin discovered the law of evolution in organic nature, so Marx discovered the law of evolution in human history.

—Friedrich Engels, 1883

A struggle is inevitable and it is a question of the survival of the fittest.

—Andrew Carnegie, 1900

The fortunes of railroad companies are determined by the law of the survival of the fittest.

—James J. Hill, 1910

The growth of a large business is merely the survival of the fittest.

—John D. Rockefeller, c. 1900

God gave me my money.

—John D. Rockefeller, 1915

History warns us * * * that it is the customary fate of new truths to begin as heresies and to end as superstitions.

—Thomas Henry Huxley, 1880

"BLACK-FOOTED FERRET ENDANGERED"†

The taste in our mouths
is the feeding of tigers.
We're killing off eagles, too,
and whales.
How it all began: the way
our thumbs slowly came round
to grab for the throat, our toes
flattened for stalking, more than animal
cunning
swelling the skull—and then
the clever tools, the hand-ax,
the motor, more dangerous
than tigers.
It was only a matter of time
till the tools were a part of us
like glands, a million years of murder
creating this:
the pitiless face of the tiger
is our own face grinning
with gears.

—Philip Appleman, 1984

Competition and Cooperation

RICHARD HOFSTADTER

The Vogue of Spencer (1955)†

As it seems to me, we have in Herbert Spencer not only the profound-
est thinker of our time, but the most capacious and most powerful
intellect of all time. Aristotle and his master were no more beyond
the pygmies who preceded them than he is beyond Aristotle. Kant,
Hegel, Fichte, and Schelling are gropers in the dark by the side of
him. In all the history of science, there is but one name which can
be compared to his, and that is Newton's * * *

—F. A. P. Barnard

I am an ultra and thoroughgoing American. I believe there is great
work to be done here for civilization. What we want are ideas—large,
organizing ideas—and I believe there is no other man whose thoughts
are so valuable for our needs as yours are.

—Edward Livingston Youmans to Herbert Spencer

I

"The peculiar condition of American society," wrote Henry Ward
Beecher to Herbert Spencer in 1866, "has made your writings far more
fruitful and quickening here than in Europe."[1] Why Americans were disposed to open their minds to Spencer, Beecher did not say; but there is
much to substantiate his words. Spencer's philosophy was admirably suited
to the American scene. It was scientific in derivation and comprehensive
in scope. It had a reassuring theory of progress based upon biology and
physics. It was large enough to be all things to all men, broad enough to
satisfy agnostics like Robert Ingersoll and theists like Fiske and Beecher.
It offered a comprehensive world-view, uniting under one generalization
everything in nature from protozoa to politics. Satisfying the desire of
"advanced thinkers" for a world-system to replace the shattered Mosaic
cosmogony, it soon gave Spencer a public influence that transcended

† From Chapter 2 of *Social Darwinism in American Thought* (Boston, 1955). Copyright © 1944,
1955 by the American Historical Association. Reprinted by permission of Beacon Press, Boston.
Richard Hofstadter (1916–1970) was professor of history at Columbia University.
1. David Duncan, *The Life and Letters of Herbert Spencer* (London, 1908), p. 128.

Darwin's. Moreover it was not a technical creed for professionals. Presented in language that tyros in philosophy could understand,[2] it made Spencer the metaphysician of the homemade intellectual, and the prophet of the cracker-barrel agnostic. Although its influence far outstripped its merits, the Spencerian system serves students of the American mind as a fossil specimen from which the intellectual body of the period may be reconstructed. Oliver Wendell Holmes hardly exaggerated when he expressed his doubt that "any writer of English except Darwin has done so much to affect our whole way of thinking about the universe."[3] * * *

II

Herbert Spencer and his philosophy were products of English industrialism. It was appropriate that this spokesman of the new era should have trained to be a civil engineer, and that the scientific components of his thought—the conservation of energy and the idea of evolution—should have been indirectly derived from earlier observations in hydrotechnics and population theory. Spencer's was a system conceived in and dedicated to an age of steel and steam engines, competition, exploitation, and struggle. * * *

The aim of Spencer's synthesis was to join in one coherent structure the latest findings of physics and biology. While the idea of natural selection had been taking form in the mind of Darwin, the work of a series of investigators in thermodynamics had also yielded an illuminating generalization. Joule, Mayer, Helmholtz, Kelvin, and others had been exploring the relations between heat and energy, and had brought forth the principle of the conservation of energy which Helmholtz enunciated most clearly in his *Die Erhaltung der Kraft* (1847). The concept won general acceptance along with natural selection, and the convergence of the two discoveries upon the nineteenth-century mind was chiefly responsible for the enormous growth in the prestige of the natural sciences. Science, it was believed, had now drawn the last line in its picture of a self-contained universe, in which matter and energy were never destroyed but constantly changing form, whose varieties of organic life were integral, intelligible products of the universal economy. Previous philosophies paled into obsolescence much as pre-Newtonian philosophies had done in the eighteenth century. * * *

The conservation of energy—which Spencer preferred to call "the persistence of force"—was the starting point of his deductive system. The life process is essentially evolutionary, embodying a continuous change from incoherent homogeneity, illustrated by the lowly protozoa, to coherent heterogeneity, manifested in man and the higher animals. * * *

The final result of this process, in an animal organism or society, is the

---

2. Spencer, wrote William James, "is the philosopher whom those who have no other philosopher can appreciate." *Memories and Studies*, p. 126.
3. M. De Wolfe Howe, ed., *Holmes-Pollock Letters* (Cambridge, 1941), I, 57–58. "Spencer," wrote Parrington, "laid out the broad highway over which American thought traveled in the later years of the century." *Main Currents in American Thought*, III, 198.

achievement of a state of equilibrium—a process Spencer called "equilibration." The ultimate attainment of equilibration is inevitable, because
the evolutionary process cannot go on forever in the direction of increasing
heterogeneity. "Evolution has an impassable limit."[4] Here the pattern of
universal rhythm comes into play: dissolution follows evolution, disintegra-
tion follows integration. In an organism this phase is represented by death
and decay, built in society by the establishment of a stable, harmonious,
completely adapted state, in which "evolution can end only in the establishment of the greatest perfection and the most complete happiness."[5]

This imposing positivistic edifice might have been totally unacceptable
in America, had it not also been bound up with an important concession
to religion in the form of Spencer's doctrine of the Unknowable. The great
question of the day was whether religion and science could be reconciled.
Spencer gave not only the desired affirmative answer, but also an assurance
for all future ages that, whatever science might learn about the world, the
true sphere of religion—worship of the Unknowable—is by its very nature
inviolable.[6] * * *

III

Spencer's supposition that a general law of evolution could be formulated led him to apply the biologic scheme of evolution to society. The
principles of social structure and change, if the generalizations of his system were valid, must be the same as those of the universe at large. In
applying evolution to society, Spencer, and after him the social Darwinists,
were doing poetic justice to its origins. The "survival of the fittest" was a
biological generalization of the cruel processes which reflective observers
saw at work in early nineteenth-century society, and Darwinism was a
derivative of political economy. The miserable social conditions of the
early industrial revolution had provided the data for Malthus' *Essay on The
Principle of Population*, and Malthus' observations had been the matrix of
natural-selection theory.

* * *

Fundamental to all ethical progress, Spencer believed, is the adaptation
of human character to the conditions of life. The root of all evil is the
"non-adaption of constitution to conditions." Because the process of adaptation, founded in the very nature of the organism, is constantly at work,
evil tends to disappear. While the moral constitution of the human race
is still ridden with vestiges of man's original predatory life which demanded
brutal self-assertion, adaptation assures that he will ultimately develop a
new moral constitution fitted to the needs of civilized life. Human perfection is not only possible but inevitable:

4. "The Instability of the Homogeneous," *First Principles* (4th Amer. ed., 1900), p. 476.
5. *Ibid.*, p. 530.
6. *Ibid.*, pp. 99, 103–4.

The ultimate development of the ideal man is logically certain—as certain as any conclusion in which we place the most implicit faith; for instance that all men will die. . . . Progress, therefore, is not an accident, but a necessity. Instead of civilization being artificial, it is a part of nature; all of a piece with the development of the embryo or the unfolding of a flower.[7]

Despite its radicalism on incidental themes—the injustice of private land ownership, the rights of women and children, and a peculiar Spencerian "right to ignore the state" which was dropped from his later writings—the main trend of Spencer's book was ultra-conservative. His categorical repudiation of state interference with the "natural," unimpeded growth of society led him to oppose all state aid to the poor. They were unfit, he said, and should be eliminated. "The whole effort of nature is to get rid of such, to clear the world of them, and make room for better." Nature is as insistent upon fitness of mental character as she is upon physical character, "and radical defects are as much causes of death in the one case as in the other." He who loses his life because of his stupidity, vice, or idleness is in the same class as the victims of weak viscera or malformed limbs. Under the nature's laws all alike are put on trial. "If they are sufficiently complete to live, they *do* live, and it is well they should live. If they are not sufficiently complete to live, they die, and it is best they should die."[8]

Spencer deplored not only poor laws, but also state-supported education, sanitary supervision other than the suppression of nuisances, regulation of housing conditions, and even state protection of the ignorant from medical quacks.[9] He likewise opposed tariffs, state banking, and government postal systems.

* * *

The great task of sociology, as Spencer envisioned it, is to chart "the normal course of social evolution," to show how it will be affected by any given policy, and to condemn all types of behavior that interfere with it.[1] Social science is a practical instrument in a negative sense. Its purpose is not to guide the conscious control of societal evolution, but rather to show that such control is an absolute impossibility, and that the best that organized knowledge can do is to teach men to submit more readily to the dynamic factors in progress. Spencer referred to the function of a true theory of society as a lubricant but not a motive power in progress: it can grease the wheels and prevent friction but cannot keep the engine moving.[2] "There cannot be more good done," he said, "than that of letting social progress go on unhindered; yet an immensity of mischief may be done in the way of disturbing, and distorting and repressing, by policies carried out

---

7. *Social Statics*, pp. 79–80.
8. *Ibid.*, pp. 414–15.
9. *Ibid.*, pp. 325–444.
1. *The Study of Sociology*, chap i, pp. 70–71.
2. Duncan, *op. cit.*, p. 367.

in pursuit of erroneous conceptions."[3] Any adequate theory of society, Spencer concluded, will recognize the "general truths" of biology and will refrain from violating the selection principle by "the artificial preservation of those least able to take care of themselves."[4]

IV

With its rapid expansion, its exploitative methods, its desperate competition, and its peremptory rejection of failure, post-bellum America was like a vast human caricature of the Darwinian struggle for existence and survival of the fittest. Successful business entrepreneurs apparently accepted almost by instinct the Darwinian terminology which seemed to portray the conditions of their existence.[5] Businessmen are not commonly articulate social philosophers, but a rough reconstruction of their social outlook shows how congenial to their thinking were the plausible analogies of social selection, and how welcome was the expansive evolutionary optimism of the Spencerian system. In a nation permeated with the gospel of progress, the incentive of pecuniary success appealed even to many persons whose ethical horizons were considerably broader than those of business enterprise. "I perceive clearly," wrote Walt Whitman in *Democratic Vistas*, "that the extreme business energy, and this almost maniacal appetite for wealth prevalent in the United States, are parts of amelioration and progress, indispensably needed to prepare the very results I demand. My theory includes riches, and the getting of riches . . ." No doubt there were many to applaud the assertion of the railroad executive Chauncey Depew that the guests at the great dinners and public banquets of New York City represented the survival of the fittest of the thousands who came there in search of fame, fortune, or power, and that it was "superior ability, foresight, and adaptability" that brought them successfully through the fierce competitions of the metropolis.[6] James J. Hill, another railroad magnate, in an essay defending business consolidation, argued that "the fortunes of railroad companies are determined by the law of the survival of the fittest," and implied that the absorption of smaller by larger roads represents the industrial analogy of the victory of the strong.[7] And John D.

---

3. Spencer, *op. cit.*, pp. 401–2.
4. *Ibid.*, pp. 343–46.
5. "It would be strange," wrote a sociologist in 1896, "if the 'captain of the industry' did not sometimes manifest a militant spirit, for he has risen from the ranks largely because he was a better fighter than most of us. Competitive commercial life is not a flowery bed of ease, but a battle field where the 'struggle for existence' is defining the industrially 'fittest to survive.' In this country the great prizes are not found in Congress, in literature, in law, in medicine, but in industry. The successful man is praised and honored for his success. The social rewards of business prosperity, in power, in praise, and luxury, are so great as to entice men of the greatest intellectual faculties. Men of splendid abilities find in the career of a manufacturer or merchant an opportunity for the most intense energy. The very perils of the situation have a fascination for adventurous and inventive spirits. In this fierce, though voiceless contest, a peculiar type of manhood is developed, characterized by vitality, energy, concentration, skill in combining numerous forces for an end, and great foresight into the consequence of social events." C. R. Henderson. "Business Men and Social Theorists," *American Journal of Sociology*, I (1896), 385–86.
6. *My Memories of Eighty Years* (New York, 1922), pp. 383–84.
7. *Highways of Progress* (New York, 1910), p. 126; cf. also p. 137.

Rockefeller, speaking from an intimate acquaintance with the methods of competition, declared in a Sunday-school address:

> The growth of a large business is merely a survival of the fittest. . . . The American Beauty rose can be produced in the splendor and fragrance which bring cheer to its beholder only by sacrificing the early buds which grow up around it. This is not an evil tendency in business. It is merely the working-out of a law of nature and a law of God.[8]

The most prominent of the disciples of Spencer was Andrew Carnegie, who sought out the philosopher, became his intimate friend, and showered him with favors. In his autobiography, Carnegie told how troubled and perplexed he had been over the collapse of Christian theology, until he took the trouble to read Darwin and Spencer.

> I remember that light came as in a flood and all was clear. Not only had I got rid of theology and the supernatural, but I had found the truth of evolution. "All is well since all grows better," became my motto, my true source of comfort. Man was not created with an instinct for his own degradation, but from the lower he had risen to the higher forms. Nor is there any conceivable end to his march to perfection. His face is turned to the light; he stands in the sun and looks upward.[9]

* * *

Conservatism and Spencer's philosophy walked hand in hand. The doctrine of selection and the biological apology for laissez faire, preached in Spencer's formal sociological writings and in a series of shorter essays, satisfied the desire of the select for a scientific rationale. Spencer's plea for absolute freedom of individual enterprise was a large philosophical statement of the constitutional ban upon interference with liberty and property without due process of law. Spencer was advancing within a cosmic framework the same general political philosophy which under the Supreme Court's exegesis of the Fourteenth Amendment served so brilliantly to turn back the tide of state reform. It was this convergence of Spencer's philosophy with the Court's interpretation of due process which finally inspired Mr. Justice Holmes (himself an admirer of Spencer) to protest that "the fourteenth Amendment does not enact Mr. Herbert Spencer's Social Statics."[1]

The social views of Spencer's popularizers were likewise conservative. Youmans took time from his promotion of science to attack the eight-hour strikers in 1872. Labor, he urged in characteristic Spencerian vein, must "accept the spirit of civilization, which is pacific, constructive, controlled by reason, and slowly ameliorating and progressive. Coercive and violent measures which aim at great and sudden advantages are sure to prove illusory." He suggested that, if people were taught the elements of political economy and social science in the course of their education, such mistakes

---

8. Quoted in William J. Ghent, *Our Benevolent Feudalism*, p. 29.
9. *Autobiography of Andrew Carnegie* (Boston, 1920), p. 327.
1. Lochner v. New York, 198 U.S. 45 (1905).

might be avoided.[2] Youmans attacked the newly founded American Social Science Association for devoting itself to unscientific reform measures instead of a "strict and passionless study of society from a scientific point of view." Until the laws of social behavior are known, he declared, reform is blind; the Association might do better to recognize a sphere of natural, self-adjusting activity, with which government intervention usually wreaks havoc.[3] There was precious little scope for meliorist activities in the outlook of one who believed with Youmans that science shows "that we are born well, or born badly, and that whoever is ushered into existence at the bottom of the scale can never rise to the top because the weight of the universe is upon him."[4]

Acceptance of the Spencerian philosophy brought with it a paralysis of the will to reform. One day, some years after the publication of *Progress and Poverty*, Youmans in Henry George's presence denounced with great fervor the political corruption of New York and the selfishness of the rich in ignoring or promoting it when they found it profitable to do so. "What do you propose to do about it?" George asked. Youmans replied, "Nothing! You and I can do nothing at all. It's all a matter of evolution. We can only wait for evolution. Perhaps in four or five thousand years evolution may have carried men beyond this state of things."[5]

Spencer's doctrines were imported into the Republic long after individualism had become a national tradition. Yet in the expansive age of our industrial culture he became the spokesman of that tradition, and his contribution materially swelled the stream of individualism if it did not change its course. If Spencer's abiding impact on American thought seems impalpable to later generations, it is perhaps only because it has been so thoroughly absorbed.[6] His language has become a standard feature of the folklore of individualism. "You can't make the world all planned and soft," says the businessman of Middletown. "The strongest and best survive— that's the law of nature after all—always has been and always will be."[7]

2. Youmans, "The Recent Strike," *Popular Science Monthly*, III (1872), 623–24. See also R. G. Eccles, "The Labor Question," *ibid.*, XI (1877), 606–11; *Appleton's Journal*, N. S., V (1878), 473–75.
3. "The Social Science Association," *Popular Science Monthly*, V (1874), 267–69. See also *ibid.*, VII (1875), 365–67.
4. "On the Scientific Study of Human Nature," reprinted in Fiske, *op. cit.*, p. 482. For other statements of the conservative Spencerian viewpoint, see Erastus B. Bigelow. "The Relations of Capital and Labor," *Atlantic Monthly*, XLII (1878), 475–87; G. F. Parsons, "The Labor Question," *ibid.*, LVIII (1886), 97–113. Also "Editor's Table," *Appleton's Journal*, N. S., V (1878), 473–75.
5. Henry George, *A Perplexed Philosopher*, pp. 163–64 n. Fiske shared Youman's conservatism, but was less alarmed at the menace of radicalism to the American future. See Fiske, *op. cit.*, pp. 381–82n. For the social outlook of an American thinker thoroughly influenced by Spencer, see Henry Holt, *The Civic Relations* (Boston, 1907), and *Garrulities of an Octogenarian Editor*, pp. 374–88.
6. See Thomas C. Cochran, "The Faith of Our Fathers," *Frontiers of Democracy*, VI (1939), 17–19.
7. Robert S. and Helen M. Lynd, *Middletown in Transition* (New York, 1937), p. 500.

ANDREW CARNEGIE

The Gospel of Wealth (1900)†

* * *

The price which society pays for the law of competition, like the price it pays for cheap comforts and luxuries, is also great; but the advantages of this law are also greater still than its cost—for it is to this law that we owe our wonderful material development, which brings improved conditions in its train. But, whether the law be benign or not, we must say of it, as we say of the change in the conditions of men to which we have referred: It is here, we cannot evade it; no substitutes for it have been found; and while the law may be sometimes hard for the individual, it is best for the race, because it insures the survival of the fittest in every department. We accept and welcome, therefore, as conditions to which we must accommodate ourselves, great inequality of environment; the concentration of business, industrial and commercial, in the hands of a few; and the law of competition between these, as being not only beneficial, but essential to the future progress of the race. * * *

Objections to the foundations upon which society is based are not in order, because the condition of the race is better with these than it has been with any other which has been tried. Of the effect of any new substitutes proposed we cannot be sure. The Socialist or Anarchist who seeks to overturn present conditions is to be regarded as attacking the foundation upon which civilization itself rests, for civilization took its start from the day when the capable, industrious workman said to his incompetent and lazy fellow, "If thou dost not sow, thou shalt not reap," and thus ended primitive Communism by separating the drones from the bees. One who studies this subject will soon be brought face to face with the conclusion that upon the sacredness of property civilization itself depends—the right of the laborer to his hundred dollars in the savings-bank, and equally the legal right of the millionaire to his millions. Every man must be allowed "to sit under his own vine and fig-tree, with none to make afraid," if human society is to advance, or even to remain so far advanced as it is. To those who propose to substitute Communism for this intense Individualism, the answer therefore is: The race has tried that. All progress from that barbarous day to the present time has resulted from its displacement. Not evil, but good, has come to the race from the accumulation of wealth by those who have had the ability and energy to produce it. But even if we admit for a moment that it might be better for the race to discard its present foundation, Individualism,—that it is a nobler ideal that man should labor, not for himself alone, but in and for a brotherhood of his fellows, and share with them all in common, realizing Swedenborg's idea

---

† From Chapter 2 of *The Gospel of Wealth and Other Timely Essays* (New York, 1900). Andrew Carnegie (1835–1919), American industrialist and philanthropist, wrote extensively on business and social problems.

of heaven, where, as he says, the angels derive their happiness, not from laboring for self, but for each other,—even admit all this, and a sufficient answer is, This is not evolution, but revolution. It necessitates the changing of human nature itself—a work of eons, even if it were good to change it, which we cannot know. ____ _Profitable._

It is not (practicable) in our day or in our age. Even if desirable theoretically, it belongs to another and long-succeeding sociological stratum. Our duty is with what is practicable now—with the next step possible in our day and generation. It is criminal to waste our energies in endeavoring to uproot, when all we can profitably accomplish is to bend the universal tree of humanity a little in the direction most favorable to the production of good fruit under existing circumstances. We might as well urge the destruction of the highest existing type of man because he failed to reach our ideal as to favor the destruction of Individualism, Private Property, the Law of Accumulation of Wealth, and the Law of Competition; for these are the highest result of human experience, the soil in which society, so far, has produced the best fruit. Unequally or unjustly, perhaps, as these laws sometimes operate, and imperfect as they appear to the Idealist, they are, nevertheless, like the highest type of man, the best and most valuable of all that humanity has yet accomplished. * * *

It were better for mankind that the millions of the rich were thrown into the sea than so spent as to encourage the slothful, the drunken, the unworthy. Of every thousand dollars spent in so-called charity to-day, it is probable that nine hundred and fifty dollars is unwisely spent—so spent, indeed, as to produce the very evils which it hopes to mitigate or cure. A well-known writer of philosophic books admitted the other day that he had given a quarter of a dollar to a man who approached him as he was coming to visit the house of his friend. He knew nothing of the habits of this beggar, knew not the use that would be made of this money, although he had every reason to suspect that it would be spent improperly. This man professed to be a disciple of Herbert Spencer; yet the quarter-dollar given that night will probably work more injury than all the money will do good which its thoughtless donor will ever be able to give in true charity. He only gratified his own feelings, saved himself from annoyance—and this was probably one of the most selfish and very worst actions of his life, for in all respects he is most worthy.

In bestowing charity, the main consideration should be to help those who will help themselves; to provide part of the means by which those who desire to improve may do so; to give those who desire to rise the aids by which they may rise; to assist, but rarely or never to do all. Neither the individual nor the race is improved by almsgiving. Those worthy of assistance, except in rare cases, seldom require assistance. * * *

Time was when the words concerning the rich man entering the kingdom of heaven were regarded as a hard saying. To-day, when all questions are probed to the bottom and the standards of faith receive the most liberal interpretations, the startling verse has been relegated to the rear, to await the next kindly revision as one of those things which cannot be quite understood, but which, meanwhile, it is carefully to be noted, are not to be understood literally. But is it so very improbable that the next stage of thought is to restore the doctrine in all its pristine purity and force, as being in perfect harmony with sound ideas upon the subject of wealth and poverty, the rich and the poor, and the contrasts everywhere seen and deplored? In Christ's day, it is evident, reformers were against the wealthy. It is none the less evident that we are fast recurring to that position to-day; and there will be nothing to surprise the student of sociological development if society should soon approve the text which has caused so much anxiety: "It is easier for a camel to enter the eye of a needle than for a rich man to enter the kingdom of heaven." Even if the needle were the small casement at the gates, the words betoken serious difficulty for the rich. It will be but a step for the theologian from the doctrine that he who dies rich dies disgraced, to that which brings upon the man punishment or deprivation hereafter.

The gospel of wealth but echoes Christ's words. It calls upon the millionaire to sell all that he hath and give it in the highest and best form to the poor by administering his estate himself for the good of his fellows, before he is called upon to lie down and rest upon the bosom of Mother Earth. So doing, he will approach his end no longer the ignoble hoarder of useless millions; poor, very poor indeed, in money, but rich, very rich, twenty times a millionaire still, in the affection, gratitude, and admiration of his fellow-men, and—sweeter far—soothed and sustained by the still, small voice within, which, whispering, tells him that, because he has lived, perhaps one small part of the great world has been bettered just a little. This much is sure: against such riches as these no bar will be found at the gates of Paradise.

PETER KROPOTKIN

Mutual Aid (1902)†

Introduction

Two aspects of animal life impressed me most during the journeys which I made in my youth in Eastern Siberia and Northern Manchuria. One of them was the extreme severity of the struggle for existence which most species of animals have to carry on against an inclement Nature; the enormous destruction of life which periodically results from natural agencies; and the consequent paucity of life over the vast territory which fell under my observation. And the other was, that even in those few spots where animal life teemed in abundance, I failed to find—although I was eagerly looking for it—that bitter struggle for the means of existence, *among animals belonging to the same species*, which was considered by

---

† From the Introduction and chapter 2 of *Mutual Aid* (London, 1902). Peter Kropotkin (1842–1921) was a Russian prince who spent much of his mature life in anarchist-nihilist activities. As a young man, however, he held a variety of military and diplomatic posts in Siberia and led geographical survey expeditions in Manchuria, where he observed some of the phenomena he described in *Mutual Aid*.

most Darwinists (though not always by Darwin himself) as the dominant characteristic of struggle for life, and the main factor of evolution.

The terrible snow-storms which sweep over the northern portion of Eurasia in the later part of the winter, and the glazed frost that often follows them; the frosts and the snow-storms which return every year in the second half of May, when the trees are already in full blossom and insect life swarms everywhere; the early frosts and, occasionally, the heavy snowfalls in July and August, which suddenly destroy myriads of insects, as well as the second broods of the birds in the prairies; the torrential rains, due to the monsoons, which fall in more temperate regions in August and September—resulting in inundations on a scale which is only known in America and in Eastern Asia, and swamping, on the plateaus, areas as wide as European States; and finally, the heavy snowfalls, early in October, which eventually render a territory as large as France and Germany, absolutely impracticable for ruminants, and destroy them by the thousand— these were the conditions under which I saw animal life struggling in Northern Asia. They made me realize at an early date the overwhelming importance in Nature of what Darwin described as "the natural checks to overmultiplication," in comparison to the struggle between individuals of the same species for the means of subsistence, which may go on here and there, to some limited extent, but never attains the importance of the former. Paucity of life, under-population—not overpopulation—being the distinctive feature of that immense part of the globe which we name Northern Asia, I conceived since then serious doubts—which subsequent study has only confirmed—as to the reality of that fearful competition for food and life within each species, which was an article of faith with most Darwinists, and, consequently, as to the dominant part which this sort of competition was supposed to play in the evolution of new species.

On the other hand, wherever I saw animal life in abundance, as, for instance, on the lakes where scores of species and millions of individuals came together to rear their progeny; in the colonies of rodents; in the migrations of birds which took place at that time on a truly American scale along the Usuri; and especially in a migration of fallow-deer which I witnessed on the Amur, and during which scores of thousands of these intelligent animals came together from an immense territory, flying before the coming deep snow, in order to cross the Amur where it is narrowest —in all these scenes of animal life which passed before my eyes, I saw Mutual Aid and Mutual Support carried on to an extent which made me suspect in it a feature of the greatest importance for the maintenance of life, the preservation of each species, and its further evolution.

And finally, I saw among the semi-wild cattle and horses in Transbaikalia, among the wild ruminants everywhere, the squirrels, and so on, that when animals have to struggle against scarcity of food, in consequence of one of the above-mentioned causes, the whole of that portion of the species which is affected by the calamity, comes out of the ordeal so much impoverished in vigour and health, that *no progressive evolution of the species can be based upon such periods of keen competition.*

Consequently, when my attention was drawn, later on, to the relations between Darwinism and Sociology, I could agree with none of the works and pamphlets that had been written upon this important subject. They all endeavoured to prove that Man, owing to his higher intelligence and knowledge, *may* mitigate the harshness of the struggle for life between men; but they all recognized at the same time that the struggle for the means of existence, of every animal against all its congeners, and of every man against all other men, was "a law of Nature." This view, however, I could not accept, because I was persuaded that to admit a pitiless inner war for life within each species, and to see in that war a condition of progress, was to admit something which not only had not yet been proved, but also lacked confirmation from direct observation.

On the contrary, a lecture "On the Law of Mutual Aid," which was delivered at a Russian Congress of Naturalists, in January 1880, by the well-known zoologist, Professor Kessler, the then Dean of the St. Petersburg University, struck me as throwing a new light on the whole subject. Kessler's idea was, that besides the *law of Mutual Struggle* there is in Nature *the law of Mutual Aid*, which, for the success of the struggle for life, and especially for the progressive evolution of the species, is far more important than the law of mutual contest. This suggestion—which was, in reality, nothing but a further development of the ideas expressed by Darwin himself in *The Descent of Man*—seemed to me so correct and of so great an importance, that since I became acquainted with it (in 1883) I began to collect materials for further developing the idea. * * *

To reduce animal sociability to *love* and *sympathy* means to reduce its generality and its importance, just as human ethics based upon love and personal sympathy only have contributed to narrow the comprehension of the moral feeling as a whole. It is not love to my neighbour—whom I often do not know at all—which induces me to seize a pail of water and to rush towards his house when I see it on fire; it is a far wider, even though more vague feeling or instinct of human solidarity and sociability which moves me. So it is also with animals. It is not love, and not even sympathy (understood in its proper sense) which induces a herd of ruminants or of horses to form a ring in order to resist an attack of wolves; not love which induces wolves to form a pack for hunting; not love which induces kittens or lambs to play, or a dozen of species of young birds to spend their days together in the autumn; and it is neither love nor personal sympathy which induces many thousand fallow-deer scattered over a territory as large as France to form into a score of separate herds, all marching towards a given spot, in order to cross there a river. It is a feeling infinitely wider than love or personal sympathy—an instinct that has been slowly developed among animals and men in the course of an extremely long evolution, and which has taught animals and men alike the force they can borrow from the practice of mutual aid and support, and the joys they can find in social life.

The importance of this distinction will be easily appreciated by the student of animal psychology, and the more so by the student of human ethics. Love, sympathy and self-sacrifice certainly play an immense part in the progressive development of our moral feelings. But it is not love and not even sympathy upon which Society is based in mankind. It is the conscience—be it only at the stage of an instinct—of human solidarity. It is the unconscious recognition of the force that is borrowed by each man from the practice of mutual aid; of the close dependency of every one's happiness upon the happiness of all; and of the sense of justice, or equity, which brings the individual to consider the rights of every other individual as equal to his own. Upon this broad and necessary foundation the still higher moral feelings are developed. * * *

After having discussed the importance of mutual aid in various classes of animals, I was evidently bound to discuss the importance of the same factor in the evolution of Man. This was the more necessary as there are a number of evolutionists who may not refuse to admit the importance of mutual aid among animals, but who, like Herbert Spencer, will refuse to admit it for Man. For primitive Man—they maintain—war of each against all was *the* law of life. * * *

Chapter II. Mutual Aid among Animals (continued)

* * *

I have to say yet a few words about the societies of monkeys, which acquire an additional interest from their being the link which will bring us to the societies of primitive men.

It is hardly needful to say that those mammals, which stand at the very top of the animal world and most approach man by their structure and intelligence, are eminently sociable. Evidently we must be prepared to meet with all varieties of character and habits in so great a division of the animal kingdom which includes hundreds of species. But, all things considered, it must be said that sociability, action in common, mutual protection, and a high development of those feelings which are the necessary outcome of social life, are characteristic of most monkeys and apes. From the smallest species to the biggest ones, sociability is a rule to which we know but a few exceptions. The nocturnal apes prefer isolated life; the capuchins (*Cebus capucinus*), the monos, and the howling monkeys live but in small families; and the orang-outans have never been seen by A. R. Wallace otherwise than either solitary or in very small groups of three or four individuals, while the gorillas seem never to join in bands. But all the remainder of the monkey tribe—the chimpanzees, the sajous, the sakis, the mandrills, the baboons, and so on—are sociable in the highest degree. They live in great bands, and even join with other species than their own. Most of them become quite unhappy when solitary. The cries of distress of each one of the band immediately bring together the whole of the band, and they boldly repulse the attacks of most carnivores and birds of prey. Even eagles do not dare attack them. They plunder our fields always in bands—the old ones taking care for the safety of the commonwealth. The little tee-tees, whose childish sweet faces so much struck Humboldt, embrace and protect one another when it rains, rolling their tails over the necks of their shivering comrades. Several species display the greatest solicitude for their wounded, and do not abandon a wounded comrade during a retreat till they have ascertained that it is dead and that they are helpless to restore it to life. Thus James Forbes narrated in his *Oriental*

Memoirs a fact of such resistance in reclaiming from his hunting party the dead body of a female monkey that one fully understands why "the witnesses of this extraordinary scene resolved never again to fire at one of the monkey race."[1] In some species several individuals will combine to overturn a stone in order to search for ants' eggs under it. The hamadryas not only post sentries, but have been seen making a chain for the transmission of the spoil to a safe place; and their courage is well known. Brehm's description of the regular fight which his caravan had to sustain before the hamadryas would let it resume its journey in the valley of the Mensa, in Abyssinia, has become classical.[2] The playfulness of the tailed apes and the mutual attachment which reigns in the families of chimpanzees also are familiar to the general reader. And if we find among the highest apes two species, the orang-outan and the gorilla, which are not sociable, we must remember that both—limited as they are to very small areas, the one in the heart of Africa, and the other in the two islands of Borneo and Sumatra—have all the appearance of being the last remnants of formerly much more numerous species. The gorilla at least seems to have been sociable in olden times, if the apes mentioned in the *Periplus* really were gorillas.

We thus see, even from the above brief review, that life in societies is no exception in the animal world; it is the rule, the law of Nature, and it reaches its fullest development with the higher vertebrates. Those species which live solitary, or in small families only, are relatively few, and their numbers are limited. Nay, it appears very probable that, apart from a few exceptions, those birds and mammals which are not gregarious now, were living in societies before man multiplied on the earth and waged a permanent war against them, or destroyed the sources from which they formerly derived food. "On ne s'associe pas pour mourir,"[3] was the sound remark of Espinas; and Houzeau, who knew the animal world of some parts of America when it was not yet affected by man, wrote to the same effect.

Association is found in the animal world at all degrees of evolution; and, according to the grand idea of Herbert Spencer, so brilliantly developed in Perrier's *Colonies Animales*, colonies are at the very origin of evolution in the animal kingdom. But, in proportion as we ascend the scale of evolution, we see association growing more and more conscious. It loses its purely physical character, it ceases to be simply instinctive, it becomes reasoned. With the higher vertebrates it is periodical, or is resorted to for the satisfaction of a given want—propagation of the species, migration, hunting, or mutual defence. It even becomes occasional, when birds associate against a robber, or mammals combine, under the pressure of exceptional circumstances, to emigrate. In this last case, it becomes a voluntary deviation from habitual moods of life. The combination sometimes appears in two or more degrees—the family first, then the group, and

1. Romanes's *Animal Intelligence*, p. 472.
2. Brehm, i. 82; Darwin's *Descent of Man*, ch. iii. The Kozloff expedition of 1899–1901 have also had to sustain in Northern Thibet a similar fight.
3. "You don't team up in order to die."

finally the association of groups, habitually scattered, but uniting in case of need, as we saw it with the bisons and other ruminants. It also takes higher forms, guaranteeing more independence to the individual without depriving it of the benefits of social life. With most rodents the individual has its own dwelling, which it can retire to when it prefers being left alone; but the dwellings are laid out in villages and cities, so as to guarantee to all inhabitants the benefits and joys of social life. And finally, in several species, such as rats, marmots, hares, etc., sociable life is maintained notwithstanding the quarrelsome or otherwise egotistic inclinations of the isolated individual. Thus it is not imposed, as is the case with ants and bees, by the very physiological structure of the individuals; it is cultivated for the benefits of mutual aid, or for the sake of its pleasures. * * *

MARTIN A. NOWAK, ROBERT M. MAY, AND KARL SIGMUND

The Arithmetics of Mutual Help (1995)†

The principle of give and take pervades our society. It is older than commerce and trade. All members of a household, for example, are engaged in a ceaseless, mostly unconscious bartering of services and goods. Economists have become increasingly fascinated by these exchanges. So have biologists, who have documented many comparable instances in groups of chimpanzees and other primates. Charles Darwin himself was well aware of the role of cooperation in human evolution. In *Descent of Man* he wrote that "the small strength and speed of man, his want of natural weapons, & c., are more than counterbalanced by his . . . social qualities, which lead him to give and receive aid from his fellow-men."

Obviously, this is a far cry from the savage human existence that the philosopher Thomas Hobbes described as "solitary, poor, nasty, brutish, and short." Nevertheless, a number of Darwin's early followers emphasized the ferocious aspects of the "struggle for survival" to such an extent that the Russian prince Kropotkin felt compelled to write a book to refute them. In *Mutual Aid*, hailed by the London *Times* as "possibly the most important book of the year" (1902), he drew a vast fresco of cooperation acting among Siberian herds, Polynesian islanders and medieval guilds. Kropotkin was a famous ideologue of anarchism, but his dabbling in natural history was no mere hobby; for someone bent on getting rid of the State, it was essential to show that human cooperation was not imposed from an iron-fisted authority but had its origins rooted in natural conditions.

In a way, his arguments have succeeded far beyond what Kropotkin could ever have foreseen. A wealth of studies in anthropology and pri-

† From "The Arithmetics of Mutual Help," *Scientific American* (June 1995): pp. 76–81. Reprinted with permission. Copyright © 1995 by Scientific American, Inc. All rights reserved. Martin A. Nowak (b. 1965) is professor of theoretical biology at the Institute for Advanced Study, Princeton, N.J. Robert M. May (b. 1936) is Royal Society research professor at Oxford University and at Imperial College, London. Karl Sigmund (b. 1945) is a professor at the Institute of Mathematics, University of Vienna.

matology point to the overwhelming role of reciprocal help in early hominid societies. Textbooks on animal behavior are filled with examples of mutual aid: grooming, feeding, teaching, warning, helping in fights and joint hunting. In ecology, symbiotic associations are increasingly seen as fundamental. Biologists find examples of cooperation at the level of cells, organelles and even prebiotic molecules.

But at the same time, the ubiquity of cooperation seems to have become ever more paradoxical. The Russian anarchist had failed to see how threatened it is by exploitation. What prevents mutualists from turning into parasites? Why should anyone share in a common effort rather than cheat the others? Natural selection puts a premium on individual reproductive success. How can this mechanism shape behavior that is altruistic in the sense that it benefits others at the expense of one's own progeny?

There are two main approaches to this question that go under the headings of kin selection and reciprocal aid. These concepts are not mutually exclusive, but they are sharply distinct. Kin selection is rooted in genetics. If a gene helps in promoting the reproductive success of close relatives of its bearer, it helps in promoting copies of itself. Within a family, a good turn is its own reward. But a good turn to an unrelated fellow being has to be returned in order to pay off. Reciprocal aid—the trading of altruistic acts in which benefit exceeds cost—is essentially an economic exchange. It works less directly than kin selection and is therefore more vulnerable to abuse.

Two parties can strike a mutually profitable bargain, but each could gain still more by withholding its contribution. In modern society an enormous apparatus of law and enforcement makes the temptation to cheat resistible. But how can reciprocal altruism work in the absence of those authoritarian institutions so despised by Kropotkin's anarchists? This difficult question is best answered by first considering simple, idealized systems.

The Prisoner's Dilemma

To demonstrate the conundrum, Robert L. Trivers, a sociobiologist (and, fittingly, a former lawyer), now at the University of California at Santa Cruz, borrowed a metaphor from game theory known as the Prisoner's Dilemma. As originally conceived in the early 1950s, each of two prisoners is asked whether the other committed a crime; their level of punishment depends on whether one, both or neither indicates the other's guilt. This situation can be viewed as a simple game. The two players engaged in it have only to decide whether they wish to cooperate with each other or not. In one illustration of the Prisoner's Dilemma, if both choose to cooperate, they get a reward of three points each. If both defect (by not cooperating), they get only one point each. But if one player defects and the other cooperates, the defector receives five points, whereas the player who chose to cooperate receives nothing.

Will they cooperate? If the first player defects, the second who cooperates will end up with nothing. Clearly, the second player ought to have defected. In fact, even if the first player cooperates, the second should defect, because this combination gives five points instead of three. No matter what the first player does, the second's best option is to defect. But the first player is in exactly the same position. Hence, both players will choose to defect and receive only one point each. Why didn't they cooperate?

The prisoners' decisions highlight the difference between what is best from an individual's point of view and from that of a collective. This conflict endangers almost every form of cooperation, including trade and mutual aid. The reward for mutual cooperation is higher than the punishment for mutual defection, but a one-sided defection yields a temptation greater than the reward, leaving the exploited cooperator with a loser's payoff that is even worse than the punishment. This ranking—from temptation through reward and punishment down to the loser's payoff—implies that the best move is always to defect, irrespective of the opposing player's move. The logic leads inexorably to mutual defection.

Most people feel uneasy with this conclusion. They do often cooperate, in fact, motivated by feelings of solidarity or selflessness. In business dealings, defection is also relatively rare, perhaps from the pressure of society. Yet such concerns should not affect a game that encapsulates life in a strictly Darwinian sense, where every form of payoff (be it calories, mates or safety from predators) is ultimately converted into a single currency: offspring.

Virtual Tournaments

One can conceive a thought experiment in which an entire population consists of programmed players. Each of these automata is firmly wedded to a fixed strategy and will either always cooperate or always defect. They engage in a round-robin tournament of the Prisoner's Dilemma. For each contestant, the total payoff will depend on the other players encountered and therefore on the composition of the population. A defector will, however, always achieve more than a cooperator would earn in its stead. At the end of the imaginary tournament, the players reproduce, creating progeny of their own kind (defectors or cooperators). The next generation will, again, engage in a round-robin competition and get paid in offspring, and so on. In this caricature of biological evolution, where the payoff is number of offspring and strategies are inherited, the outcome is obvious: defectors will steadily increase from one generation to the next and will eventually swamp the population.

There are several ways to escape from this fate. In many societies the same two individuals interact not just once but frequently. Each participant will think twice about defecting if this move makes the other player defect on the next occasion. So the strategy for the repeated game can change in response to what happened in previous rounds.

In contrast to a single instance of the Prisoner's Dilemma, where it is always better to defect, countless strategies for the repeated version exist, and none serves as a best reply against all opponents. If the opposite player, for instance, decides always to cooperate, then you will do best by always defecting. But if your adversary decides to cooperate until you defect and then never to cooperate again, you will be careful not to spoil your partnership: the temptation to cheat in one round and grab five points instead of three will be more than offset by the expected loss in the subsequent rounds where you cannot hope to earn more than one point.

The absence of a best choice is crucial. There is no hard-and-fast recipe for playing the repeated Prisoner's Dilemma. Success will depend on the other player's strategy, which one does not know beforehand. A strategy that does well in certain environments can fail miserably in others.

In the late 1970s the political scientist Robert Axelrod, at the University of Michigan, conducted round-robin tournaments of the repeated Prisoner's Dilemma on his computer. The contestants—programs submitted by colleagues—were quite sophisticated, but it turned out that the simplest entry ultimately won. This strategy is aptly called Tit-for-Tat. It starts with a cooperative response and then always repeats the opposing player's previous move.

Remarkably, a player applying Tit-for-Tat is never ahead at any stage of the repeated game, being always last to defect. The Tit-for-Tat player can nonetheless win the whole tournament, because the Prisoner's Dilemma is not a zero-sum game: it is possible to make points without taking them away from others. By its transparency Tit-for-Tat frequently persuades opponents that it pays to cooperate. In Axelrod's tournaments the Tit-for-Tat strategy (entered by the game theorist Anatol Rapoport) elicited many rewarding rounds of cooperation, whereas other players, among themselves, were apt to get bogged down in long runs of defection.

By winning the round-robin tournament, Tit-for-Tat obtained more representatives among the next generation than did other strategies. Moreover, those players who had cooperated tended also to receive more offspring than those who had not. With each generation Tit-for-Tat shaped a more congenial environment. The strategies that ruthlessly exploited cooperators succeeded only in depleting their own resources.

Unpredictable Adversaries

We recently performed computer simulations with an extended set of strategies that base their next move on the result of the previous round rather than just the opponent's previous move (as does Tit-for-Tat). A strategy based on prior outcome must determine the response for each of four eventualities: temptation, reward, punishment or loss. Two possible responses for each of four prior outcomes give 16 possible types of players.

We further allowed for "stochastic" strategies that respond to the four possible outcomes by changing only their statistical propensity to cooperate. Such strategies are not obliged to respond always in the same way to a given outcome. One form of stochastic player might, for example, cooperate 90 percent of the time after experiencing the reward. Such uncertainty simulates the inevitable mistakes that occur during real interactions.

The addition of stochastic responses resulted in a huge array of possibilities. Our computer searched for the most successful of these players by simulating the forces of natural selection, adding to every hundredth generation some small amount of a new, randomly selected stochastic strategy. We followed many such mutation-selection rounds for millions of generations, not because the emergence of cooperation needed so many iterations but because this span allowed us to test a very large number of possible strategies. In spite of the rich diversity displayed in these chronicles, they led us invariably to some simple, clear results. The first is that the average payoff in the population can change suddenly. Indeed, the behavior we found is a showpiece for punctuated equilibria in biological evolution. Most of the time, either almost all members of the population cooperate, or almost all defect. The transitions between these two regimes are usually rare and abrupt, taking just a few generations. We found that later in the run, quiescent periods tended to last longer. And there was a definite trend toward cooperation. The longer the system was allowed to evolve, the greater the likelihood for a cooperative regime to blossom. But the threat of a sudden collapse always remained. * * *

Innate Cooperation

One can safely conclude that the emergence and persistence of cooperative behavior are not at all unlikely, provided the participants meet repeatedly, recognize one another and remember the outcomes of past encounters. These circumstances may seem familiar from daily life in the home or office, but among the larger world of living things, such requirements demand a high degree of sophistication. And yet we observe cooperation even among simple organisms that do not possess such abilities. Furthermore, the strategies discussed will work only if benefits from future encounters are not significantly discounted as compared with present gains. Again this expectation may be reasonable for many of the activities humans conduct, but for most simpler organisms delayed payoffs in the form of future reproductive success may count for little: if life is short and unpredictable, there is scant evolutionary pressure to make long-term investments.

But what of the creatures, such as many invertebrates, that seem to exhibit forms of reciprocal cooperation, even though they often cannot recognize individual players or remember their actions? Or what if future payoffs are heavily discounted? How can altruistic arrangements be established and maintained in these circumstances? One possible solution is that these players find a fixed set of fellow contestants and make sure the game is played largely with them. In general, this selectivity will be hard to attain. But there is one circumstance in which it is not only easy, it is automatic. If the players occupy fixed sites, and if they interact only with close neighbors, there will be no need to recognize and remember, because the other players are fixed by the geometry. Whereas in many of our simulations players always encounter a representative sample of the population, we have also looked specifically at scenarios in which every player interacts only with a few neighbors on a two-dimensional grid. Such "spatial games" are very recent. They give an altogether new twist to the Prisoner's Dilemma.

Fixed in Flatland

It should come as no surprise that cooperation is easier to maintain in a sedentary population: defectors can thrive in an anonymous crowd, but mutual aid is frequent among neighbors. That concept is clear enough. But in many cases, territorially structured interactions promote cooperation, even if no follow-up encounter is expected. This result favors cooperation even for the seemingly hopeless single round of the Prisoner's Dilemma. * * *

Nature and Nurture

EDWARD O. WILSON

Sociobiology: The New Synthesis (1975)†

The Morality of the Gene

Camus said that the only serious philosophical question is suicide. That is wrong even in the strict sense intended. The biologist, who is concerned with questions of physiology and evolutionary history, realizes that self-knowledge is constrained and shaped by the emotional control centers in the hypothalamus and limbic system of the brain. These centers flood our consciousness with all the emotions—hate, love, guilt, fear, and others—that are consulted by ethical philosophers who wish to intuit the standards of good and evil. What, we are then compelled to ask, made the hypo-thalamus and limbic system? They evolved by natural selection. That simple biological statement must be pursued to explain ethics and ethical philosophers, if not epistemology and epistemologists, at all depths. Self-existence, or the suicide that terminates it, is not the central question of philosophy. The hypothalamic-limbic complex automatically denies such logical reduction by countering it with feelings of guilt and altruism. In this one way the philosopher's own emotional control centers are wiser than his solipsist consciousness, "knowing" that in evolutionary time the individual organism counts for almost nothing. In a Darwinist sense the organism does not live for itself. Its primary function is not even to repro-duce other organisms; it reproduces genes, and it serves as their temporary carrier. Each organism generated by sexual reproduction is a unique, ac-cidental subset of all the genes constituting the species. Natural selection is the process whereby certain genes gain representation in the following generations superior to that of other genes located at the same chromo-some positions. When new sex cells are manufactured in each generation, the winning genes are pulled apart and reassembled to manufacture new organisms that, on the average, contain a higher proportion of the same genes. But the individual organism is only their vehicle, part of an elab-orate device to preserve and spread them with the least possible biochem-ical perturbation. Samuel Butler's famous aphorism, that the chicken is

† From chapters 1 and 27 of *Sociobiology: The New Synthesis* (Cambridge, Mass., 1975). Reprinted by permission of the publisher from *Sociobiology: The New Synthesis* by E. O. Wilson, Cambridge, Mass.: Harvard University Press. Copyright © 1975 by the President and Fellows of Harvard College. Edward O. Wilson (b. 1929) is Pellegrino University research professor and honorary curator in entomology at the Museum of Comparative Zoology, Harvard University.

only an egg's way of making another egg, has been modernized: the organism is only DNA's way of making more DNA. More to the point, the hypothalamus and limbic system are engineered to perpetuate DNA.

In the process of natural selection, then, any device that can insert a higher proportion of certain genes into subsequent generations will come to characterize the species. One class of such devices promotes prolonged individual survival. Another promotes superior mating performance and care of the resulting offspring. As more complex social behavior by the organism is added to the genes' techniques for replicating themselves, altruism becomes increasingly prevalent and eventually appears in exaggerated forms. This brings us to the central theoretical problem of sociobiology: how can altruism, which by definition reduces personal fitness, possibly evolve by natural selection? The answer is kinship: if the genes causing the altruism are shared by two organisms because of common descent, and if the altruistic act by one organism increases the joint contribution of these genes to the next generation, the propensity to altruism will spread through the gene pool. This occurs even though the altruist makes less of a solitary contribution to the gene pool as the price of its altruistic act.

To his own question, "Does the Absurd dictate death?" Camus replied that the struggle toward the heights is itself enough to fill a man's heart. This arid judgment is probably correct, but it makes little sense except when closely examined in the light of evolutionary theory. The hypothalamic-limbic complex of a highly social species, such as man, "knows," or more precisely it has been programmed to perform as if it knows, that its underlying genes will be proliferated maximally only if it orchestrates behavioral responses that bring into play an efficient mixture of personal survival, reproduction, and altruism. Consequently, the centers of the complex tax the conscious mind with ambivalences whenever the organisms encounter stressful situations. Love joins hate; aggression, fear; expansiveness, withdrawal; and so on; in blends designed not to promote the happiness and survival of the individual, but to favor the maximum transmission of the controlling genes.

The ambivalences stem from counteracting pressures on the units of natural selection. Their genetic consequences will be explored formally later in this book. For the moment suffice it to note that what is good for the individual can be destructive to the family; what preserves the family can be harsh on both the individual and the tribe to which its family belongs; what promotes the tribe can weaken the family and destroy the individual; and so on upward through the permutations of levels of organization. Counteracting selection on these different units will result in certain genes being multiplied and fixed, others lost, and combinations of still others held in static proportions. According to the present theory, some of the genes will produce emotional states that reflect the balance of counteracting selection forces at the different levels.

I have raised a problem in ethical philosophy in order to characterize the essence of sociobiology. Sociobiology is defined as the systematic study of the biological basis of all social behavior. For the present it focuses on animal societies, their population structure, castes, and communication, together with all of the physiology underlying the social adaptations. But the discipline is also concerned with the social behavior of early man and the adaptive features of organization in the more primitive contemporary human societies. Sociology *sensu stricto*, the study of human societies at all levels of complexity, still stands apart from sociobiology because of its largely structuralist and nongenetic approach. It attempts to explain human behavior primarily by empirical description of the outermost phenotypes and by unaided intuition, without reference to evolutionary explanations in the true genetic sense. It is most successful, in the way descriptive taxonomy and ecology have been most successful, when it provides a detailed description of particular phenomena and demonstrates first-order correlations with features of the environment. Taxonomy and ecology, however, have been reshaped entirely during the past forty years by integration into neo-Darwinist evolutionary theory—the "Modern Synthesis," as it is often called—in which each phenomenon is weighed for its adaptive significance and then related to the basic principles of population genetics. It may not be too much to say that sociology and the other social sciences, as well as the humanities, are the last branches of biology waiting to be included in the Modern Synthesis.

*   *   *

It is part of the conventional wisdom that virtually all cultural variation is phenotypic rather than genetic in origin. This view has gained support from the ease with which certain aspects of culture can be altered in the space of a single generation, too quickly to be evolutionary in nature. The drastic alteration in Irish society in the first two years of the potato blight (1846–1848) is a case in point. Another is the shift in the Japanese authority structure during the American occupation following World War II. Such examples can be multiplied endlessly—they are the substance of history. It is also true that human populations are not very different from one another genetically. When Lewontin[1] analyzed existing data on nine blood-type systems, he found that 85 percent of the variance was composed of diversity within populations and only 15 percent was due to diversity between populations. There is no a priori reason for supposing that this sample of genes possesses a distribution much different from those of other, less accessible systems affecting behavior.

The extreme orthodox view of environmentalism goes further, holding that in effect there is no genetic variance in the transmission of culture. In other words, the capacity for culture is transmitted by a single human genotype. Dobzhansky[2] stated this hypothesis as follows: "Culture is not inherited through genes, it is acquired by learning from other human beings . . . In a sense, human genes have surrendered their primacy in human evolution to an entirely new, nonbiological or superorganic agent, culture. However, it should not be forgotten that this agent is entirely

1. R. C. Lewontin, "The Apportionment of Human Diversity," *Evolutionary Biology*, 6 (1972), 381–398.
2. Theodosius Dobzhansky, "Anthropology and the Natural Sciences—the Problem of Human Evolution," *Current Anthropology*, 4 (1963), 138, 146–148.

dependent on the human genotype." Although the genes have given away most of their sovereignty, they maintain a certain amount of influence in at least the behavioral qualities that underlie variations between cultures. Moderately high heritability has been documented in introversion-extroversion measures, personal tempo, psychomotor and sports activities, neuroticism, dominance, depression, and the tendency toward certain forms of mental illness such as schizophrenia.[3] Even a small portion of this variance invested in population differences might predispose societies toward cultural differences. At the very least, we should try to measure this amount. It is not valid to point to the absence of a behavioral trait in one or a few societies as conclusive evidence that the trait is environmentally induced and has no genetic disposition in man. The very opposite could be true.

In short, there is a need for a discipline of anthropological genetics. In the interval before we acquire it, it should be possible to characterize the human biogram by two indirect methods. First, models can be constructed from the most elementary rules of human behavior. Insofar as they can be tested, the rules will characterize the biogram in much the same way that ethograms drawn by zoologists identify the "typical" behavioral repertories of animal species. The rules can be legitimately compared with the ethograms of other primate species. Variation in the rules among human cultures, however slight, might provide clues to underlying genetic differences, particularly when it is correlated with variation in behavioral traits known to be heritable. * * *

The other indirect approach to anthropological genetics is through phylogenetic analysis. By comparing man with other primate species, it might be possible to identify basic primate traits that lie beneath the surface and help to determine the configuration of man's higher social behavior. This approach has been taken with great style and vigor in a series of popular books by Konrad Lorenz (*On Aggression*), Robert Ardrey (*The Social Contract*), Desmond Morris (*The Naked Ape*), and Lionel Tiger and Robin Fox (*The Imperial Animal*). Their efforts were salutary in calling attention to man's status as a biological species adapted to particular environments. The wide attention they received broke the stifling grip of the extreme behaviorists, whose view of the mind of man as a virtually equipotent response machine was neither correct nor heuristic. But their particular handling of the problem tended to be inefficient and misleading. They selected one plausible hypothesis or another based on a review of a small sample of animal species, then advocated the explanation to the limit. * * *

The correct approach using comparative ethology is to base a rigorous phylogeny of closely related species on many biological traits. Then social behavior is treated as the dependent variable and its evolution deduced from it. When this cannot be done with confidence (and it cannot in man) the next best procedure is [to] establish the lowest taxonomic level at which each character shows significant intertaxon variation. Characters

3. P. A. Parsons, *The Genetic Analysis of Behaviour* (London, 1967); I. M. Lerner, *Heredity, Evolution, and Society* (San Francisco, 1968).

that shift from species to species or genus to genus are the most labile. We cannot safely extrapolate them from the cercopithecoid monkeys and apes to man. In the primates these labile qualities include group size, group cohesiveness, openness of the group to others, involvement of the male in parental care, attention structure, and the intensity and form of territorial defense. Characters are considered conservative if they remain constant at the level of the taxonomic family or throughout the order Primates, and they are the ones most likely to have persisted in relatively unaltered form into the evolution of *Homo*. These conservative traits include aggressive dominance systems, with males generally dominant over females; scaling in the intensity of responses, especially during aggressive interactions; intensive and prolonged maternal care, with a pronounced degree of socialization in the young; and matrilineal social organization. This classification of behavioral traits offers an appropriate basis for hypothesis formation. It allows a qualitative assessment of the probabilities that various behavioral traits have persisted into modern *Homo sapiens*.

✳ ✳ ✳

Ethics

Scientists and humanists should consider together the possibility that the time has come for ethics to be removed temporarily from the hands of the philosophers and biologicized. The subject at present consists of several oddly disjunct conceptualizations. The first is *ethical intuitionism*, the belief that the mind has a direct awareness of true right and wrong that it can formalize by logic and translate into rules of social action. The purest guiding precept of secular Western thought has been the theory of the social contract as formulated by Locke, Rousseau, and Kant. In our time the precept has been rewoven into a solid philosophical system by John Rawls.[4] His imperative is that justice should be not merely integral to a system of government but rather the object of the original contract. The principles called by Rawls "justice as fairness" are those which free and rational persons would choose if they were beginning an association from a position of equal advantage and wished to define the fundamental rules of the association. In judging the appropriateness of subsequent laws and behavior, it would be necessary to test their conformity to the unchallengeable starting position.

The Achilles heel of the intuitionist position is that it relies on the emotive judgment of the brain as though that organ must be treated as a black box. While few will disagree that justice as fairness is an ideal state for disembodied spirits, the conception is in no way explanatory or predictive with reference to human beings. Consequently, it does not consider the ultimate ecological or genetic consequences of the rigorous prosecution of its conclusions. Perhaps explanation and prediction will not be needed for the millennium. But this is unlikely—the human genotype and the ecosystem in which it evolved were fashioned out of extreme unfair-

4. John Rawls, *A Theory of Justice* (Cambridge, Mass., 1971).

ness. In either case the full exploration of the neural machinery of ethical judgment is desirable and already in progress. One such effort, constituting the second mode of conceptualization, can be called *ethical behaviorism*. Its basic proposition, which has been expanded most fully by J. F. Scott,[5] holds that moral commitment is entirely learned, with operant conditioning being the dominant mechanism. In other words, children simply internalize the behavioral norms of the society. * * * The difference between ethical behaviorism and the current version of developmental-genetic analysis is that the former postulates a mechanism (operant conditioning) without evidence and the latter presents evidence without postulating a mechanism. No great conceptual difficulty underlies this disparity. The study of moral development is only a more complicated and less tractable version of the genetic variance problem (see Chapters 2 and 7). With the accretion of data the two approaches can be expected to merge to form a recognizable exercise in behavioral genetics.

Even if the problem were solved tomorrow, however, an important piece would still be missing. This is the *genetic evolution of ethics*. In the first chapter of this book I argued that ethical philosophers intuit the deonto-logical canons of morality by consulting the emotive centers of their own hypothalamic-limbic system. This is also true of the developmentalists, even when they are being their most severely objective. Only by interpreting the activity of the emotive centers as a biological adaptation can the meaning of the canons be deciphered. Some of the activity is likely to be outdated, a relic of adjustment to the most primitive form of tribal organization. Some of it may prove to be *in statu nascendi*, constituting new and quickly changing adaptations to agrarian and urban life. The resulting confusion will be reinforced by other factors. To the extent that unilaterally altruistic genes have been established in the population by group selection, they will be opposed by allelomorphs favored by individual selection. The conflict of impulses under their various controls is likely to be widespread in the population, since current theory predicts that the genes will be at best maintained in a state of balanced polymorphism (Chapter 5). Moral ambivalency will be further intensified by the circumstance that a schedule of sex- and age-dependent ethics can impart higher genetic fitness than a single moral code which is applied uniformly to all sex-age groups. * * *

If there is any truth to this theory of innate moral pluralism, the requirement for an evolutionary approach to ethics is self-evident. It should also be clear that no single set of moral standards can be applied to all human populations, let alone all sex-age classes within each population. To impose a uniform code is therefore to create complex, intractable moral dilemmas—these, of course, are the current condition of mankind. * * *

5. J. F. Scott, *Internalization of Norms: A Sociological Theory of Moral Commitment* (New York, 1971).

STEPHEN JAY GOULD

Biological Potentiality vs.
Biological Determinism (1977)†

*   *   *

The statement that humans are animals does not imply that our specific patterns of behavior and social arrangements are in any way directly determined by our genes. *Potentiality* and *determination* are different concepts.

The intense discussion aroused by E. O. Wilson's *Sociobiology* (Harvard University Press, 1975) has led me to take up this subject. Wilson's book has been greeted by a chorus of praise and publicity. I, however, find myself among the smaller group of its detractors. Most of *Sociobiology* wins from me the same high praise almost universally accorded it. For a lucid account of evolutionary principles and an indefatigably thorough discussion of social behavior among all groups of animals, *Sociobiology* will be the primary document for years to come. But Wilson's last chapter, "From Sociobiology to Sociology," leaves me very unhappy indeed. After twenty-six chapters of careful documentation for the nonhuman animals, Wilson concludes with an extended speculation on the genetic basis of supposedly universal patterns in human behavior. Unfortunately, since this chapter is his statement on the subject closest to all our hearts, it has also attracted more than 80 percent of all the commentary in the popular press.

We who have criticized this last chapter have been accused of denying altogether the relevance of biology to human behavior, of reviving an ancient superstition by placing ourselves outside the rest of "the creation." Are we pure "nurturists?" Do we permit a political vision of human perfectibility to blind us to evident constraints imposed by our biological nature? The answer to both statements is no. The issue is not universal biology vs. human uniqueness, but biological potentiality vs. biological determinism.

Replying to a critic of his article in the *New York Times Magazine* (October 12, 1975), Wilson wrote:

> There is no doubt that the patterns of human social behavior, including altruistic behavior, are under genetic control, in the sense that they represent a restricted subset of possible patterns that are very different from the patterns of termites, chimpanzees and other animal species.

If this is all that Wilson means by genetic control, then we can scarcely disagree. Surely we do not do all the things that other animals do, and

† From chapter 32 of *Ever Since Darwin* (New York, 1977). With permission from *Natural History*, May 1976. Copyright © 1976 the American Museum of Natural History. Stephen Jay Gould (b. 1941) is Alexander Agassiz Professor of Geology and curator of invertebrate paleontology at the Museum of Comparative Zoology, Harvard University.

just as surely, the range of our potential behavior is circumscribed by our biology. We would lead very different social lives if we photosynthesized (no agriculture, gathering, or hunting—the major determinants of our social evolution) or had life cycles like those of the gall midges discussed in essay 10. (When feeding on an uncrowded mushroom, these insects reproduce in the larval or pupal stage. The young grow within the mother's body, devour her from inside, and emerge from her depleted external shell ready to feed, grow the next generation, and make the supreme sacrifice.)

But Wilson makes much stronger claims. Chapter 27 is not a statement about the range of potential human behaviors or even an argument for the restriction of that range from a much larger total domain among all animals. It is, primarily, an extended speculation on the existence of genes for specific and variable traits in human behavior—including spite, aggression, xenophobia, conformity, homosexuality, and the characteristic behavioral differences between men and women in Western society. Of course, Wilson does not deny the role of nongenetic learning in human behavior; he even states at one point that "genes have given away most of their sovereignty." But, he quickly adds, genes "maintain a certain amount of influence in at least the behavioral qualities that underlie variations between cultures." And the next paragraph calls for a "discipline of anthropological genetics."

Biological determinism is the primary theme in Wilson's discussion of human behavior; chapter 27 makes no sense in any other context. Wilson's primary aim, as I read him, is to suggest that Darwinian theory might reformulate the human sciences just as it previously transformed so many other biological disciplines. But Darwinian processes can not operate without genes to select. Unless the "interesting" properties of human behavior are under specific genetic control, sociology need fear no invasion of its turf. By interesting, I refer to the subjects sociologists and anthropologists fight about most often—aggression, social stratification, and differences in behavior between men and women. If genes only specify that we are large enough to live in a world of gravitational forces, need to rest our bodies by sleeping, and do not photosynthesize, then the realm of genetic determinism will be relatively uninspiring.

What is the direct evidence for genetic control of specific human social behavior? At the moment, the answer is none whatever. (It would not be impossible, in theory, to gain such evidence by standard, controlled experiments in breeding, but we do not raise people in *Drosophila* bottles, establish pure lines, or control environments for invariant nurturing.) Sociobiologists must therefore advance indirect arguments based on plausibility. Wilson uses three major strategies: universality, continuity, and adaptiveness.

1. Universality: If certain behaviors are invariably found in our closest primate relatives and among humans themselves, a circumstantial case for common, inherited genetic control may be advanced. Chapter 27 abounds with statements about supposed human universals. For example, "Human beings are absurdly easy to indoctrinate—they *seek* it." Or, "Men would rather believe than know." I can only say that my own experience does not correspond with Wilson's.

When Wilson must acknowledge diversity, he often dismisses the uncomfortable "exceptions" as temporary and unimportant aberrations. Since Wilson believes that repeated, often genocidal warfare has shaped our genetic destiny, the existence of nonaggressive peoples is embarrassing. But he writes: "It is to be expected that some isolated cultures will escape the process for generations at a time, in effect reverting temporarily to what ethnographers classify as a pacific state."

In any case, even if we can compile a list of behavioral traits shared by humans and our closest primate relatives, this does not make a good case for common genetic control. Similar results need not imply similar causes; in fact, evolutionists are so keenly aware of this problem that they have developed a terminology to express it. Similar features due to common genetic ancestry are "homologous"; similarities due to common function, but with different evolutionary histories, are "analogous" (the wings of birds and insects, for example—the common ancestor of both groups lacked wings). I will argue below that a basic feature of human biology supports the idea that many behavioral similarities between humans and other primates are analogous, and that they have no direct genetic specification in humans.

2. Continuity: Wilson claims, with ample justice in my opinion, that the Darwinian explanation of altruism in W. D. Hamilton's 1964 theory of "kin selection" forms the basis for an evolutionary theory of animal societies. Altruistic acts are the cement of stable societies, yet they seem to defy a Darwinian explanation. On Darwinian principles, all individuals are selected to maximize their own genetic contribution to future generations. How, then, can they willingly sacrifice or endanger themselves by performing altruistic acts to benefit others?

The resolution is charmingly simple in concept, although complex in technical detail. By benefiting relatives, altruistic acts preserve an altruist's genes even if the altruist himself will not be the one to perpetuate them. For example, in most sexually reproducing organisms, an individual shares (on average) one-half the genes of his sibs and one-eighth the genes of his first cousins. Hence, if faced with a choice of saving oneself alone or sacrificing oneself to save more than two sibs or more than eight first cousins, the Darwinian calculus favors altruistic sacrifice; for in so doing, an altruist actually increases his own genetic representation in future generations.

Natural selection will favor the preservation of such self-serving altruist genes. But what of altruistic acts toward nonrelatives? Here sociobiologists must invoke a related concept of "reciprocal altruism" to preserve a genetic explanation. The altruistic act entails some danger and no immediate benefit, but if it inspires a reciprocal act by the current beneficiary at some future time, it may pay off in the long run: a genetic incarnation of the age-old adage: you scratch my back and I'll scratch yours (even if we're not related).

The argument from continuity then proceeds. Altruistic acts in other animal societies can be plausibly explained as examples of Darwinian kin selection. Humans perform altruistic acts and these are likely to have a similarly direct genetic basis. But again, similarity of result does not imply identity of cause (see below for an alternate explanation based on biological potentiality rather than biological determinism).

3. Adaptiveness: Adaptation is the hallmark of Darwinian processes. Natural selection operates continuously and relentlessly to fit organisms to their environments. Disadvantageous social structures, like poorly designed morphological structures, will not survive for long.

Human social practices are clearly adaptive. Marvin Harris has delighted in demonstrating the logic and sensibility of those social practices in other cultures that seem most bizarre to smug Westerners (*Cows, Pigs, Wars, and Witches*. Random House, 1974). Human social behavior is riddled with altruism; it is also clearly adaptive. Is this not a prima facie argument for direct genetic control? My answer is definitely "no," and I can best illustrate my claim by reporting an argument I recently had with an eminent anthropologist.

My colleague insisted that the classic story of Eskimos on ice floes provides adequate proof for the existence of specific altruist genes maintained by kin selection. Apparently, among some Eskimo peoples, social units are arranged as family groups. If food resources dwindle and the family must move to survive, aged grandparents willingly remain behind (to die) rather than endanger the survival of their entire family by slowing an arduous and dangerous migration. Family groups with no altruist genes have succumbed to natural selection as migrations hindered by the old and sick lead to the death of entire families. Grandparents with altruist genes increase their own fitness by their sacrifice, for they enhance the survival of close relatives sharing their genes.

The explanation by my colleague is plausible, to be sure, but scarcely conclusive since an eminently simple, nongenetic explanation also exists: there are no altruist genes at all, in fact, no important genetic differences among Eskimo families whatsoever. The sacrifice of grandparents is an adaptive, but nongenetic, cultural trait. Families with no tradition for sacrifice do not survive for many generations. In other families, sacrifice is celebrated in song and story; aged grandparents who stay behind become the greatest heroes of the clan. Children are socialized from their earliest memories to the glory and honor of such sacrifice.

I cannot prove my scenario, any more than my colleague can demonstrate his. But in the current context of no evidence, they are at least equally plausible. Likewise, reciprocal altruism undeniably exists in human societies, but this provides no evidence whatever for its genetic basis. As Benjamin Franklin said: "We must all hang together, or assuredly we shall all hang separately." Functioning societies may require reciprocal altruism. But these acts need not be coded into our consciousness by genes; they may be inculcated equally well by learning.

*   *   *

We are both ordinary and special. The central feature of our biological uniqueness also provides the major reason for doubting that our behaviors are directly coded by specific genes. That feature is, of course, our large brain. *   *   *

Why imagine that specific genes for aggression, dominance, or spite have any importance when we know that the brain's enormous flexibility permits us to be aggressive or peaceful, dominant or submissive, spiteful or generous? Violence, sexism, and general nastiness *are* biological since they represent one subset of a possible range of behaviors. But peacefulness, equality, and kindness are just as biological—and we may see their influence increase if we can create social structures that permit them to flourish. Thus, my criticism of Wilson does not invoke a nonbiological "environmentalism"; it merely pits the concept of biological potentiality— a brain capable of the full range of human behaviors and rigidity predisposed toward none—against the idea of biological determinism—specific genes for specific behavioral traits.

But why is this academic issue so delicate and explosive? There is no hard evidence for either position, and what difference does it make, for example, whether we conform because conformer genes have been selected or because our general genetic makeup permits conformity as one strategy among many?

The protracted and intense debate surrounding biological determinism has arisen as a function of its social and political message. As I argue in the preceding set of essays, biological determinism has always been used to defend existing social arrangements as biologically inevitable—from "for ye have the poor always with you" to nineteenth-century imperialism to modern sexism. Why else would a set of ideas so devoid of factual support gain such a consistently good press from established media throughout the centuries? This usage is quite out of the control of individual scientists who propose deterministic theories for a host of reasons, often benevolent.

I make no attribution of motive in Wilson's or anyone else's case. Neither do I reject determinism because I dislike its political usage. Scientific truth, as we understand it, must be our primary criterion. We live with several unpleasant biological truths, death being the most undeniable and ineluctable. If genetic determinism is true, we will learn to live with it as well. But I reiterate my statement that no evidence exists to support it, that the crude versions of past centuries have been conclusively disproved, and that its continued popularity is a function of social prejudice among those who benefit most from the status quo. * * *

We are both similar to and different from other animals. In different cultural contexts, emphasis upon one side or the other of this fundamental truth plays a useful social role. In Darwin's day, an assertion of our similarity broke through centuries of harmful superstition. Now we may need to emphasize our difference as flexible animals with a vast range of potential behavior. Our biological nature does not stand in the way of social reform. We are, as Simone de Beauvoir said, "l'être dont l'être est de n'être pas"—the being whose essence lies in having no essence.

BARBARA EHRENREICH AND JANET McINTOSH

The New Creationism: Biology under Attack (1997)†

When social psychologist Phoebe Ellsworth took the podium at a recent interdisciplinary seminar on emotions, she was already feeling rattled. Colleagues who'd presented earlier had warned her that the crowd was tough and had little patience for the reduction of human experience to numbers or bold generalizations about emotions across cultures. Ellsworth had a plan: She would pre-empt criticism by playing the critic, offering a social history of psychological approaches to the topic. But no sooner had the word "experiment" passed her lips than the hands shot up. Audience members pointed out that the experimental method is the brainchild of white Victorian males. Ellsworth agreed that white Victorian males had done their share of damage in the world but noted that, nonetheless, their efforts had led to the discovery of DNA. This short-lived dialogue between paradigms ground to a halt with the retort: "You believe in DNA?"

More grist for the academic right? No doubt, but this exchange reflects a tension in academia that goes far deeper than spats over "political correctness." Ellsworth's experience illustrates the trend—in anthropology, sociology, cultural studies and other departments across the nation—to dismiss the possibility that there are any biologically based commonalities that cut across cultural differences. This aversion to biological or, as they are often branded, "reductionist" explanations commonly operates as an informal ethos limiting what can be said in seminars, asked at lectures, or incorporated into social theory. Extreme anti-innatism has had formal institutional consequences as well. At some universities like the University of California, Berkeley, the biological subdivision of the anthropology department has been relocated to another building—a spatial metaphor for an epistemological gap.

Although some of the strongest rejections of the biological have come from scholars with a left or feminist perspective, antipathy toward innatist theories does not always score neatly along political lines. Consider a recent review essay by centrist sociologist Alan Wolfe in *The New Republic*. Wolfe makes quick work of Frank Sulloway's dodgy Darwinist claims (in *Born to Rebel: Birth Order, Family Dynamics, and Creative Lives*) about the influence of birth order on personality, but can't resist going on to impugn the motives of anyone who would apply biology to the human condition. In general, he asserts, "the biologizing of human beings is not only bad humanism, but also bad science."

For many social theorists, innate biology can be let in only as a constraint—"a set of natural limits on human functioning," as anthropol-

† From "The New Creationism: Biology under Attack," *The Nation* (June 9, 1997): 11–16. Reprinted with permission from the June 9, 1997 issue of *The Nation*. Barbara Ehrenreich (b. 1941) is an associate fellow with the New York Institute of the Humanities. Janet McIntosh (b. 1969) is a graduate student in ethnology at the University of Michigan and teaches writing at Harvard University.

ogist Marshall Sahlins has written. It has, from this point of view, no positive insights to offer into how humans think, act or arrange their cultures. For others, the study of innate human properties is not merely uninteresting but deeply misguided. Stanford philosopher of science John Dupré, for example, argues that it is "essentialist" even to think that we are a biological species in the usual sense—that is, a group possessing any common tendencies or "universal properties" that might shed some light on our behavior. As feminist theorist Judith Butler puts it, "The very category of the universal has begun to be exposed for its own highly ethnocentric biases."

But the notion that humans have no shared biologically based "nature" constitutes a theory of human nature itself. No one, after all, is challenging the idea that chimpanzees have a chimpanzee nature—that is, a set of genetically scripted tendencies and potential responses that evolved along with the physical characteristics we recognize as chimpanzee-like. To set humans apart from even our closest animal relatives as the one species that is exempt from the influences of biology is to suggest that we do indeed possess a defining "essence," and that it is defined by our unique and miraculous freedom from biology. The result is an ideological outlook eerily similar to that of religious creationism. Like their fundamentalist Christian counterparts, the most extreme antibiologists suggest that humans occupy a status utterly different from and clearly "above" that of all other living beings. And, like the religious fundamentalists, the new academic creationists defend their stance as if all of human dignity—and all hope for the future—were at stake.

The new secular creationism emerged as an understandable reaction to excess. Since the nineteenth century, conservatives have routinely deployed supposed biological differences as immutable barriers to the achievement of a more egalitarian social order. Darwinism was quickly appropriated as social Darwinism—a handy defense of economic inequality and colonialism. In the twentieth century, from the early eugenicists to *The Bell Curve*, pseudo-biology has served the cause of white supremacy. Most recently, evolutionary psychology has become, in some hands, a font of patriarchal social prescriptions. Alas, in the past few years such simplistic biological reductionism has tapped a media nerve, with the result that, among many Americans, schlock genetics has become the default explanation for every aspect of human behavior from homosexuality to male promiscuity, from depression to "criminality."

Clearly science needs close and ongoing scrutiny, and in the past decade or two there has been a healthy boom in science studies and criticism. Scholars such as Evelyn Fox Keller, Sandra Harding, Emily Martin and Donna Haraway have offered useful critiques of the biases and ethnocentric metaphors that can skew everything from hypothesis formation to data collection techniques. Feminists (one of the authors included) have deconstructed medicine and psychology for patriarchal biases; left-leaning biologists such as Stephen Jay Gould, Richard Lewontin and Ruth Hubbard have exposed misapplications of biology to questions of social policy. However, contemporary antibiologists decry a vast range of academic pursuits coming from very different theoretical corners—from hypotheses about the effects of genes and hormones, to arguments about innate cognitive modules and grammar, to explorations of universal ritual form and patterns of linguistic interaction. All these can be branded as "essentialist," hence wrongheaded and politically mischievous. Paradoxically, assertions about universal human traits and tendencies are usually targeted just as vehemently as assertions about differences: There are no differences between groups, seems to be the message, but there is no sameness among them either.

Within anthropology, the social science traditionally friendliest to biology and now the one most bitterly divided over it, nineteenth-century claims about universal human nature were supplanted in the early twentieth century by Franz Boas and colleagues, who conducted detailed studies of particular cultures. By the mid-1960s, any role for biological commonalities in cultural anthropology was effectively foreclosed when Clifford Geertz remarked that "our ideas, our values, our acts, even our emotions are, like our nervous system itself, cultural products."

As neo-Marxist and behaviorist theories of the tabula rasa human gained ground over the next decade, other disciplines followed anthropology's lead. So completely was sociology purged of biology that when Nicholas Petryszak analyzed twenty-four introductory sociology textbooks in 1979, he found that all assumed that "any consideration of biological factors believed to be innate to the human species is completely irrelevant in understanding the nature of human behavior and society." In general, by the seventies, antibiologism had become the rallying cry of academic liberals and feminists—and the apparent defense of human freedom against the iron chains of nature.

It was only with the arrival of the intellectual movements lumped under the term "postmodernism" that academic antibiologism began to sound perilously like religious creationism. Postmodernist perspectives go beyond a critique of the misuses of biology to offer a critique of biology itself, extending to all of science and often to the very notion of rational thought. In the simplified form it often takes in casual academic talk, postmodernism can be summed up as a series of tenets that include a wariness of meta-narratives (meaning grand explanatory theories), a horror of essentialism (extending to the idea of any innate human traits) and a fixation on "power" as the only force limiting human freedom—which at maximum strength precludes claims about any universal human traits while casting doubt on the use of science to study our species or anything at all. Glibly applied, postmodernism portrays evolutionary theory as nothing more than a sexist and racist storyline created by Western white men.

The deepest motives behind this new secular version of creationism are understandable. We are different from other animals. Language makes us more plastic and semiotically sophisticated, and renders us deeply susceptible to meanings and ideas. As for power, Foucault was right: It's everywhere, and it shapes our preferences and categories of thought, as well as our life chances. Many dimensions of human life that feel utterly "natural" are in fact locally constructed, a hard-earned lesson too easy to forget and too important not to publicize. The problem is that the combined vigor of antibiologism and simplified postmodernism has tended to obliterate the possibility that human beings have anything in common, and to silence efforts to explore this domain. Hence we have gone, in the space of a decade or two, from what began as a healthy skepticism about the misuses of biology to a new form of dogma.

As a biologically oriented researcher who has made controversial innatist claims, Rutgers social theorist Robin Fox notes with irony that secular creationist academics seem to have replaced the church as the leading opponents of Darwinism: "It's like they're responding to heresy." Stephen Jay Gould, who has devoted much of his career to critiquing misuses of biology, also detects parallels between religious and academic creationist zeal. While holding that many aspects of human life are local and contingent, he adds, "Some facts and theories are truly universal (and true)— and no variety of cultural traditions can change that . . . we can't let a supposedly friendly left-wing source be exempt from criticism for anti-intellectual positions."

The new creationism is not simply a case of well-intended politics gone awry; it represents a grave misunderstanding of biology and science generally. Ironically, the creationists invest the natural sciences with a determinative potency no thoughtful scientist would want to claim. Biology is rhetorically yoked to "determinism," a concept that threatens to clip our wings and lay waste to our utopian visions, while culture is viewed as a domain where power relations with other humans are the only obstacle to freedom.

But these stereotypes of biological determinism and cultural malleability don't hold up under scrutiny. For one thing, biology is not a dictatorship— genes work probabilistically, and their expression depends on interaction with their environment. As even Richard Dawkins, author of *The Selfish Gene* and a veritable Antichrist to contemporary creationists of both the secular and Christian varieties, makes clear: "It is perfectly possible to hold that genes exert a statistical influence on human behaviour while at the same time believing that this influence can be modified, overridden or reversed by other influences." And if biology is not a dictatorship, neither is culture a realm of perfect plasticity. The accumulated lessons of ethnography—and, paradoxically, postmodern theories of power themselves—suggest that even in the absence of biological constraints, it is not easy to remold human cultures to suit our utopian visions. In fact, in the extreme constructivist scenario borrowed by secular creationists, it's hard to imagine who would have the will or the ability to orchestrate real change: the people in power, who have no motivation to alter the status quo, or the oppressed, whose choices, preferences and sentiments have been so thoroughly shaped by the cultural hegemony of the elite? Judged solely as a political stance, secular creationism is no less pessimistic than the biologism it seeks to uproot.

Milder versions of the "nature/nurture" debate begat a synthesis: "There is no biology that is not culturally mediated." But giving biology its due while taking cultural mediation into account requires inclusive and complex thinking—as Phoebe Ellsworth puts it: "You need a high tolerance of ambiguity to believe both that culture shapes things and that we have a lot in common." Despite the ham-fisted efforts of early sociobiologists, many (probably most) biologically based human universals are not obvious to the naked eye or accessible to common sense.

Finally, many secular creationists are a few decades out of date on the kind of "human nature" that evolutionary biology threatens to impose on us. Feminists and liberal academics were perhaps understandably alarmed by the aggressive "man the hunter" image that prevailed in the sixties and seventies; and a major reason for denying the relevance of evolution was a horror of the nasty, brutish cavemen we had supposedly evolved from. But today, evolutionary theory has moved to a more modest assessment of the economic contribution of big-game hunting (as opposed to gathering and scavenging) and a new emphasis on the cooperative—even altruistic —traits that underlie human sociality and intelligence. We don't have to like what biology has to tell us about our ancestors, but the fact is that they have become a lot more likable than they used to be.

In portraying human beings as pure products of cultural context, the secular creationist standpoint not only commits biological errors but defies common sense. In the exaggerated postmodernist perspective appropriated by secular creationists, no real understanding or communication is possible between cultures. Since the meaning of any human practice is inextricable from its locally spun semiotic web, to pluck a phenomenon such as "ritual" or "fear" out of its cultural context is, in effect, to destroy it. Certainly such categories have different properties from place to place, and careful contextualization is necessary to grasp their local implications. But as Ellsworth asks: "At the level of detail of 'sameness' that postmodernists are demanding, what makes them think that two people in the same culture will understand each other?" The ultimate postmodern retort would be, of course, that we do not, but this nihilism does not stand up to either common sense or deeper scrutiny. We manage to grasp things about each other—emotions, motives, nuanced (if imperfect) linguistic meanings— that couldn't survive communicative transmission if we didn't have some basic emotional and cognitive tendencies in common.

The creationist rejection of innate human universals threatens not only an intellectual dead end but a practical one. In writing off any biologically based human commonality, secular creationists undermine the very bedrock of the politics they claim to uphold. As Barbara Epstein of the History of Consciousness Program at the University of California, Santa Cruz, remarks: "If there is no human nature outside social construction, no needs or capacities other than those constructed by a particular discourse, then there is no basis for social criticism and no reason for protest or rebellion." In fact, tacit assumptions of human similarity are embedded in the theories of even such ostensible social constructionists as Marx, whose theory of alienation assumes (in some interpretations, anyway) that there are authentic human needs that capitalism fails to meet.

Would it really be so destructive to our self-esteem as a species to acknowledge that we, like our primate relatives, are possessed of an inherited repertory of potential responses and mental structures? Would we forfeit all sense of agency and revolutionary possibility if we admitted that we, like our primate relatives, are subject to the rules of DNA replication (not to mention the law of gravity)? In their horror of "determinism," academic creationists seem to forget postmodernism's finest insight: that, whatever else we may be, we are indeed creatures of symbol and "text." We may be, in many ways, constrained by our DNA, but we are also the discoverers of DNA—and, beyond that, the only living creature capable of representing its biological legacy in such brilliant and vastly condensed symbols as "DNA."

The good news is that a break may be coming. In spite of the nose-thumbing inspired by the Alan Sokal/*Social Text* hoax, constructive debates and conversations between scientists and social theorists have been initiated in newsletters, journals and conferences across the country. A few anthropology departments, including those at Northwestern, Penn State and Emory, are encouraging communication between their cultural and biological subfields. And although interactionist work has not had adequate space to flourish, achievements so far suggest that regardless of creationist disclaimers, biological and cognitive universals may be acutely relevant to social theory. Ann Stoler, an anthropologist, historian and scholar of Foucault at the University of Michigan, agrees. By failing to take our innate cognitive tendencies seriously, she writes, social constructionists may be dodging the "uncomfortable question" as to whether oppressive ideologies like racism and sexism "acquire the weight . . . they do . . . because of the ways in which they feed off and build upon [universal] categories of the mind." As Ellsworth says, the meeting of human universals and culture is "where the interesting questions begin."

But for the time being it takes more than a nuanced mind to deal with the interface of culture and biology. It takes courage. This climate of intolerance, often imposed by scholars associated with the left, ill suits an academic tradition rhetorically committed to human freedom. What's worse, it provides intellectual backup for a political outlook that sees no real basis for common ground among humans of different sexes, races and cultures.

Evolution and Gender

ELIZABETH CADY STANTON

The Woman's Bible (1898)†

* * *

I have been deeply impressed with the difficulty of substituting reason for superstition in minds once perverted by a false faith. Women have been taught by their religious guardians that the Bible, unlike all other books, was written under the special inspiration of the Great Ruling Intelligence of the Universe. Not conversant with works on science and higher criticism, which point out its fabulous pretensions, they cling to it with an unreasoning tenacity, like a savage to his fetich. Though it is full of contradictions, absurdities and impossibilities, and bears the strongest evidence in every line of its human origin, and in moral sentiment is below many of the best books of our own day, they blindly worship it as the Word of God.

When you point out what in plain English it tells us God did say to his people in regard to woman, and there is no escape from its degrading teaching as to her position, then they shelter themselves under false translations, interpretations and symbolic meanings. It does not occur to them that men learned in the languages have revised the book many times, but made no change in woman's position. Though familiar with "the designs of God," trained in Biblical research and higher criticism, interpreters of signs and symbols and Egyptian hieroglyphics, learned astronomers and astrologers, yet they cannot twist out of the Old or New Testaments a message of justice, liberty or equality from God to the women of the nineteenth century!

The real difficulty in woman's case is that the whole foundation of the Christian religion rests on her temptation and man's fall, hence the necessity of a Redeemer and a plan of salvation. As the chief cause of this dire calamity, woman's degradation and subordination were made a necessity. If, however, we accept the Darwinian theory, that the race has been a gradual growth from the lower to a higher form of life, and that the story of the fall is a myth, we can exonerate the snake, emancipate the woman, and reconstruct a more rational religion for the nineteenth century, and thus escape all the perplexities of the Jewish mythology as of no more importance than those of the Greek, Persian and Egyptian.

† From the Appendix to *The Woman's Bible*, Part 2 (1898), reprinted in *Women without Superstition*, ed. Annie Laurie Gaylor (Madison, Wis., 1997). Elizabeth Cady Stanton (1815–1902), American feminist, was a pioneer reformer for women's rights and the first president of the National Woman Suffrage Association.

NANCY MAKEPEACE TANNER

On Becoming Human (1981)†

* * *

Despite vast changes in biological evolutionary thought since Darwin, he still stands as a giant figure in intellectual history. His monumental work on speciation was exemplary in terms of scientific investigation, and his proposal of change through natural and sexual selection formed the basis for *the* new paradigm within which the biological sciences have operated for the past century. But, in Darwin's day, at least equally important was the immense influence of social evolutionary theory on Western folk beliefs.

* * *

After Darwin, the search for origins shifted from priests and philosophers to geologists and biologists, whose solutions were often no less naive than those of their predecessors. First, Social Darwinism and, more recently, a spate of pseudobiological tracts have become the functional equivalents of origin myths for Western man. From the time of Spencer and Darwin to the present, the evolutionary writings that have captured the popular imagination—regardless of whether they were serious scholarly works or popularized formulations—have utilized metaphors that keyed into cultural themes of long standing. Sometimes these metaphors have rested on powerful poetic imagery; sometimes they have been merely catchy and essentially trite. What they have in common is that, given our culture, they have been quite effective. Recall, for example, evolutionary slogans such as "survival of the fittest"; "nature red in tooth and claw" put forward in a poem by Tennyson (1850) and still extant over a century later; popular titles from the 1960s and 1970s such as "the imperial animal," "the naked ape," "men in groups," or a sociobiological metaphor, "the selfish gene." Thematically, many such metaphors bear a striking resemblance to images promulgated by the entertainment industry—also a product of Western culture. Twentieth century evolutionary myths, like Social Darwinism in the nineteenth century, are often no more than backward projections of features of our own culture. They thus serve to interpret and justify aspects of the Western economic system and some of Western society's particularly chauvinistic, hierarchical, and warlike characteristics.

* * *

† From *On Becoming Human* (Cambridge, UK, 1981). Reprinted with the permission of Cambridge University Press. Nancy M. Tanner (1933–1989) was professor of anthropology at the University of California at Santa Cruz.

Female behavior and the behavior of the young—in whom, for example, the early development of intelligence and the evolution of crying, smiling, and gurgling may well have been important bases for survival—were, until this last quarter of the twentieth century, largely neglected. Women's reproductive role, of course, had been acknowledged, but their part in subsistence, protection, play, communication, and tool making had been almost ignored. Gathering plants for subsistence, an activity far more certain of result than predation on or hunting of animals, is of such basic importance in the food quest that it is simply amazing that there has been so little inquiry into its invention, development, and effects for the evolving hominids. One thing seems clear: Plant gathering was and is an arena in which females exercised their ingenuity and expended their energy.

* * *

Although others have mentioned that early hominids probably gathered much of their food, until quite recently the prevailing idea underlying reconstructions of social behavior has been that *Australopithecus* was primarily a hunter. There are, however, considerable data that are anomalous from a hunting perspective. For their small size, all australopithecines— even the early basal hominids and the so-called gracile line—had powerful chewing and grinding capacities. This kind of chewing apparatus is best understood as an adaptation to a diet including a high proportion of tough, uncooked plant food. Further, given their small size and still very simple technology, it is improbable that they pursued, captured, and killed large dangerous animals with tools. The data on size, tools, and teeth do not fit a hunting model but make a great deal of sense when viewed within a gathering context.

There has been a misemphasis on hunting—that is, using tools to stop and kill moving animals—at this early stage of hominid evolution. Along with the premature emphasis on hunting has come a plethora of dubious assumptions: for example, the supposition of male-male bonding, assumed to have been developed for cooperation in hunting and in defense; similarly, the belief that males provided meat for and protection to females with whom they had fathered offspring, and so to their own young. The presumption that females did not provide a significant degree of food or protection for themselves and their offspring apparently then followed. Reconstructions largely fail to make note of females in these contexts.

With the supposition that males were the providers of meat and were the defenders of females and young in the face of danger, the idea of a pair bond became intimately interwoven into the evolutionary saga, with our earliest hominid female forebears—much like American women of the 1940s and 1950s—relegated to a passive role in sexual, economic, technological, protective, and even most social behaviors. Here is the evolutionist version of the Adam and Eve story: a pair-bond mating system, with coterminous economic and mating units.

Male tool use related to hunting and protection frequently is referred to in popular and scholarly writing alike; female tool use has seldom been mentioned. Yet it seems highly probable that early hominid females made and used tools for digging up vegetable food, knocking down fruit and nuts, collecting insects and their products such as honey, and dividing plant and animal food. They also may have invented a simple container for carrying gathered food and a device for supporting infants. And it is very likely indeed that both sexes used tools for protection and eventually some butchering and that neither males nor females used tools in extensive big game hunting.

* * *

Intelligence usually has been discussed relative to hunting—in turn assumed to be a male activity. By implication, then, there is no selection pressure for female intelligence. The list could go on and on, but that is hardly necessary. The point is not to dwell on all the gaps in past reconstructions but to develop a model that corrects the imbalance. Even now, when a role for gathering is often acknowledged, the far-reaching implications of this major innovation are rarely explored.

The approach taken here obviously is not without assumptions: The perspective is evolutionary. From this it follows that selection operated on all ages and both sexes for effective behaviors. As a corollary, females as well as males were intelligent and active. They were not so encumbered by being pregnant or carrying a young child that they were prevented from tool making and using, thinking about where to find food, gathering it, or defending themselves and their children. Indeed, it is assumed that there was selection for all adult females to possess these capacities and consistently utilize their abilities. The children with the best survival chances were those whose mothers most effectively exercised such capabilities.

* * *

WHAT WERE EARLY HOMINID COMMUNITIES LIKE?

If plant gathering was the basis of the australopithecine adaptation and if mothers were the most regular gatherers, then the basic unit of australopithecine society, as for the transitional population, was probably a mother and one to several offspring. Sometimes this genealogical unit may have been three generational, including an old mother, adult daughter(s) and her infant or juvenile offspring, plus the old mother's adult son(s), and adolescent offspring of both sexes. As generations were short, and life not long, units of more than three generations would be extremely unlikely. These units would not be large; with lengthy nursing a female might bear only four or so children during her childbearing years, and not all would survive. This mother-centered genealogical unit was the most stable group; these individuals might often travel and gather together, with two or three going off to look for meat sporadically. Several of these genealogical units, especially those that were descendants of sisters, may have met frequently and camped with some regularity around well-known water sources.

Adult australopithecine males would have had stronger social bonds with adult females, especially but not exclusively with their mothers and sisters, than is true for living chimpanzees. There was an even longer and more intense association with the mother and with siblings than for the ancestral and transitional populations. Further incorporation of adult males into group life was made possible by increased sociability and decreased disruptiveness of the males (related both to the longer period of maternal care and socialization and to the probable decrease in sexual dimorphism, particularly in canine height). This relatively relaxed incorporation of males into the group was perhaps also reinforced by male contributions to defense and meat acquisition and by male help in bringing raw materials for tool manufacture from some distance to the campsite.

* * *

Summary: the generic adaptation

Australopithecus is precisely the sort of early hominid one would expect, given (1) a chimpanzee-like ancestral population and (2) the * * * transition to regular utilization of the mosaic savanna. * * * Early hominid anatomy, compared with the ancestral population, was modified for new behaviors: changes in the pelvis, legs, and feet for bipedal locomotion; developing hand skills for tool use; large grinding molars and premolars with reduced canines for effective chewing of savanna plant foods; minimal sexual dimorphism because of selection for a common behavioral adaptation for both females and males; brain expansion and reorganization for their developing memory, conceptualization, problem solving, innovativeness, and more sophisticated communication, as well as for increased hand skills; and the expansion of the brain and reduced sexual dimorphism, in turn, interrelated with the social and technological aspects of the new adaptation.

All of the foregoing are related to gathering plant food on the savanna as the primary adaptation. Females were innovators in gathering. Because of nutritional requirements of pregnancy and nursing and overt demands from hungry children, women had more motivation for technological inventiveness, for creativity in dealing with the environment, for learning about plants, and for developing tools to increase productivity and save time. Males continued to forage for plants without tools as did the ape ancestors and probably also borrowed some of the gathering technology. Selection was for increasingly efficient, time-saving, energy-saving ways of getting food: "Necessity is the mother of invention." Vegetation from the savanna and the woodlands that border streams and lakes was the primary food resource; but meat eating also was increasing somewhat. Inventions, especially of digging and cutting tools, were associated with gathering and sharing. A technology of butchering perhaps had also begun to develop toward the end of *Australopithecus*'s tenure, but there was not yet a technology of hunting. Bipedalism, combined with increasing use of hands and tools, was fundamental to the new way of life.

The ability to communicate social and environmental information was enhanced and formed the basis for hominid communities. Social organization was flexible and perhaps relatively complex; groups could vary in size because sufficient protection was provided by object use, rather than by anatomical specializations such as large canines. The social organization was one of dispersion and aggregation occurring according to situation. With larger aggregations not having a regular or stable membership, everyday communication might become more elaborate in order to deal with a fairly large number of individuals that are not all equally well known or seen in any regular sequence.

A steady food supply was obtained through a flexible social organization, effective communication, anatomical structures appropriate to the new adaptation, and the use of tools. Gathering many kinds of plants and a few types of insects with tools, killing some small game by hand, and, later on, perhaps occasionally butchering large immobile animals together provided a regular omnivorous diet. Objects were used successfully for protection in the environment in which the food was found. Tools were made and used for obtaining and, subsequently, for preparing the food itself. This highly successful adaptation worked for a very long time; it lasted for some 2 million years.

* * *

Chapter 11. Conclusion: Becoming Human

The search for origins is an insistent and particularly human quest. In times past—and in many parts of the world yet today—it has found expression in origin myths. More recently in the West, with the development of a "scientific" view of the world, understanding and explanation of human origins have been sought from that vast jigsaw puzzle called evolution. We all want to know who our ancestors were, how we came to be, and, in a very real sense, what sort of creatures we have become. The origins, development, and very nature of our humanness is at the same time one of the most intriguing and most enigmatic of evolutionary riddles.

In this reconstruction of early human lifeways my objective has been to construct a sequential model that builds in, as fundamental to the model itself, the probable ranges of behavior and the social and cultural contributions of both sexes. * * *

WHAT KIND OF ANCESTOR?

Recent studies have demonstrated that the African apes are far more closely related to humans than once imagined. Anatomically, common and pygmy chimpanzees provide an excellent model of what the generalized ancestral ape population may have been like. The other African ape, the gorilla, which is also closely related to us, provides a much less useful model because gorilla anatomy and adaptation are far more specialized. For example, there is a great deal more size difference between males and females in gorillas than occurs in chimpanzees or humans. Although chimpanzees provide an excellent anatomical model for what the generalized ancestral apes might have looked like, this is not the primary reason they are such a superb model for the ancestral population. It is the study of chimpanzee behavior that has proved particularly instructive. Of special interest are: chimpanzee intelligence, communication, and sociability; the flexibility and variability, with structure, apparent in chimpanzee groups; the durability of mother-child and sibling relationships; bipedal and manipulatory capacities; the surprising extent of object modification and tool use; the heavy reliance on plant food combined with insect collecting and some predation; a chimpanzee's immaturity at birth, the extended period of contact with its mother and the significance of this extended contact for learning both relational and technical skills; extensive food sharing by mothers; and the important roles that social tradition and environmental context play in patterns of social interaction, diet, and the use of tools. All these features make *Pan* unusually interesting in the attempt to postulate the capacities and behaviors that could have provided a base for the hominid divergence from an ape ancestor.

When we look at humans living today, there is one fact that especially stands out. Humans have many cultures with social and economic systems ranging from small communities of gatherer-hunters or horticulturalists to ancient, agriculturally based states and the recent industrial nations. All humans today are members of just one biological species, *Homo sapiens sapiens*. Culturally, however, we are a most various species. Language, clothing styles, rituals, art forms, values, beliefs, kinship arrangements, community size and organization, the personal characteristics considered masculine or feminine, the role of the aged, and many other features vary from society to society. Furthermore, our ecological adaptations differ enormously from one society to the next. Humans are unique in having such an enormous adaptive range. Biologically speaking, we are able to utilize many extremely different ecological niches, from the Sahara to the Arctic, as well as to create and destroy niches.

Our species' exceptional reliance on culture is what makes this extraordinary adaptive range possible. It is this human uniqueness—the fundamental role of culture in our species' adaptation—that must be understood if we are to reconstruct the behavioral capacities of the ancestral population. Chimpanzee intelligence, tool use, sociability, flexible social organization, effective nonverbal communication, minimal sexual dimorphism, the importance of mother—offspring ties, nurturing, and the social context of learning for the young indicate what sorts of behavioral bases may have existed for evolution of the human capacity for culture, just as dietary omnivorousness and locomotor patterns that include occasional bipedalism help us understand how our earliest bipedal, savanna-living ancestors could have physically evolved from early apes.

* * *

Natural selection—the fitness of the individual (e.g., surviving long enough to reproduce) and, especially, the survival and fitness of the progeny—is of course a prime feature in human evolution. The intelligence to gather (i.e., to learn, improve upon, and teach this crucial innovation) and the sociability to share with offspring doubtless were enhanced by natural selection just as were anatomical changes related to bipedalism and skilled use of the hands. These changes enhanced the survival of the mothers themselves and of their children.

In addition, sexual selection may have contributed to similar ends. In many species, the number of ova released, fetuses carried, live births, and children who survive are all infinitesimally small compared to sperm produced and available. In addition, among mammals (and especially primates where single births are the rule), the physical and other input of the female into her progeny is enormous; it far exceeds that of the male. For both these reasons, the female and her ova are the "limiting resources." Most sperm will not fertilize ova. If some males have a better chance than others of having their sperm fertilize an ovum, then we say sexual selection is occurring.

Sexual selection has two components: (1) the direct selection by the female of the male(s) with whom she chooses to copulate and (2) competition among the males for opportunity to copulate. Darwin discussed both aspects in *The Descent of Man and Selection in Relation to Sex* (1871). Strangely, however, since Darwin almost all attention has been directed to the second component; the former—the sexual choice of males by females—has been largely ignored. The present model incorporates the possible impact of this first aspect during the hominid divergence.

After gathering became common, the mother's contribution to the life chances of her offspring increased dramatically as compared to that of the pongid ancestor. At the time of the initial divergence, when the earliest hominids still resembled the ape-like ancestor in many features, it is extremely unlikely that social fatherhood had yet been invented. In other words, the increase in maternal contribution through gathering was not counterbalanced at that time by any like increase in paternal "investment." This provided a genetic and social context for an increase in female sexual selectivity. Let us suppose for a moment that female choice was, in fact, heightened during the divergence. If females chose males who—like themselves—were intelligent and sociable, adept with their hands, and comparatively effective bipeds, then natural and sexual selection could reinforce each other. With gathering, the maternal contribution to a surviving offspring was intensified. A corresponding intensification of sexual selection, combined with the increased natural selection consequent to gathering, makes probable a rapid transition from ancestral ape to early hominid.

This fits very well with the appearance of a few hominid-like fossils in eastern Africa some 6 million to 4 million years ago, followed by the sudden appearance of fairly plentiful early hominid remains (*Australopithecus*) there after about 3.5 million years ago. This fossil record is also consistent with the evidence from molecular evolution for a particularly close relationship between apes and humans, and for a comparatively recent pongid-hominid divergence.

The evolutionary result is ourselves—creatures in which bipedalism, hand-eye coordination with effective manipulatory ability, tool making and use, intelligence, the ability to symbol, a multifaceted communication system, extended infant dependence on the mother, and extensive reliance on learning are characteristic of both sexes. This provides some evidence that natural and sexual selection did indeed work to the same ends.

* * *

EVELLEEN RICHARDS

Darwin and the Descent of Woman (1983)†

A growing number of social historians and sociologists of science have come to think of scientific knowledge as a 'contingent cultural product, which cannot be separated from the social context in which it is produced', and they have begun to explore the possibility of there being direct 'external' or what are generally regarded as 'non-scientific' influences on the content of what scientists consider to be genuine knowledge.[1] In their view, scientific assertions are 'socially created and not directly given by the physical world as previously supposed'.[2] This is not to assert that science is merely a matter of convention—that the external world does not constrain scientific conclusions—but rather that scientific knowledge 'offers an account of the physical world which is mediated through available cultural resources; and these resources are in no way definitive'.[3] This view undercuts the special epistemological status generally accorded to scientific knowledge, whereby it is assumed to be value-free and politically and socially neutral. In this revised view of science, the basis of the traditional distinction between scientific and social thought is eliminated, and as a consequence, the customary contrast between "internal" intellectual and 'external' social factors in the history of science loses its significance. It becomes possible to consider scientific knowledge as socially contingent and an understanding of the socially derived perspectives of the knowers and their purposes becomes essential to coherent historical explanation of scientific knowledge. This paper is an attempt to examine and explain Charles Darwin's conclusions on the biological and social evolution of women in the light of this revised view of scientific knowledge.

† From *The Wider Domain of Evolutionary Thought*, ed. David Oldroyd and Ian Langham (Dordrecht, Holland, 1983). Reprinted with kind permission from Kluwer Academic Publishers. Evelleen Richards (b. 1941) is Honorary Visiting Professor in the School of Science and Technology Studies at the University of New South Wales, Australia.

1. M. Mulkay, *Science and the Sociology of Knowledge* (London, Boston, Sydney, 1979), p. 79. See also B. Barnes and S. Shapin (eds), *Natural Order: Historical Studies of Scientific Culture* (Beverly Hills, London, 1979), pp. 9–13; R. M. Macleod, 'Changing Perspectives in Social History of Science' in *Science, Technology and Society: A Cross-Disciplinary Perspective* eds I. Spiegel-Rosing and D. de Solla Price (Beverly Hills, London, 1977), pp. 189–95; R. Johnston, 'Contextual Knowledge: A Model for the Overthrow of the Internal/External Dichotomy', *Australian and New Zealand Journal of Sociology* XII, 1976, pp. 193–203.
2. M. Mulkay, *op. cit.* (Note 1, p. xxx), p. 62.
3. *Ibid.* p. 60.

The Darwinian theory of evolution is the subject of a large and growing literature, but most historians have treated its content and its reception as independent of the social context in which it was conceived and accepted into the body of scientific knowledge. With few exceptions, Darwin is presented as the young naturalist of the 'Beagle', subsequent pigeon breeder and barnacle dissector and, above all, detached and objective observer and theoretician—remote from the political concerns of his fellow Victorians who misappropriated his scientific concepts to rationalize *their* imperialism, laissez-faire economics, and racism. The congruence of his writings, especially *The Descent of Man*, with the flourishing Social Darwinism of the late Victorian period, is either ignored or tortuously explained away and Darwin himself absolved of political and social intent and his theoretical constructs of ideological taint.[4]

The handful of Darwin studies like those of Young and Gale[5] which does not conform to this historical orthodoxy but has been concerned to depict Darwin's evolutionary theory as embedded in an ideological context, has focussed on the concept of natural selection and the associated themes of struggle and adaptation. As far as I am aware, no similar 'contextualist' or 'naturalistic'[6] study has been made of Darwin's concept of sexual selection and his related conclusions on the biological and social evolution of women. In fact, these have received scant attention from more orthodox scholars, who have also focussed on natural selection.

*   *   *

It has been left to feminist scholars * * * to explore the social dimensions of Darwin's writings on the biological and social evolution of women. They are unanimous in their categorization of them as catering to and supporting a prejudiced and discriminatory view of women's abilities and potential—one unsupported by evidence and based upon Victorian sexist ideology.[7] The small section of the appropriately named *Descent of Man*, where Darwin deduced the natural and innate inferiority of women from

4. For a perceptive analysis of historiographic representations of Darwin's relation to Social Darwinism, see S. Shapin and B. Barnes, 'Darwin and Social Darwinism: Purity and History' in *Natural Order, op. cit.* (Note 1, p. xxx), p. 125–142.
5. R. M. Young, 'Malthus and the Evolutionists: The Common Context of Biological and Social Theory', *Past and Present* XLIII, 1969, pp. 109–145; R. M. Young, 'Darwin's Metaphor: Does Nature Select?', *The Monist* LV, 1971, pp. 442–503; R. M. Young, 'Evolutionary Biology and Ideology—Then and Now', *Science Studies* 1, 1971, pp. 177–206; R. M. Young, 'The Historiographic and Ideological Contexts of the Nineteenth Century Debate on Man's Place in Nature' in *Changing Perspectives in the History of Science* eds M. Teich and R. M. Young (London, 1973); G. Gale, 'Darwin and the Concept of Struggle for Existence: A Study in the Extrascientific Origins of Scientific Ideas', *Isis* LXIII, 1972, pp. 321–344.
6. 'Contextualism' is the term adopted by Young and Johnston to describe the sociocultural history of scientific knowledge they advocate, and is to be preferred to that of 'naturalism' adopted by Barnes and Shapin for the same purpose. See Notes 1 (p. xxx) and 5 (p. xxx).
7. See R. Hubbard, 'Have Only Men Evolved?', in *Women Look at Biology Looking at Women* ed. R. Hubbard *et al.* (Boston, 1979), pp. 7–35; see also the Introduction, p. xv. Darwin's views on the inferiority of women are also discussed by S. Sleeth Mosedale, 'Science Corrupted: Victorian Biologists Consider "The Woman Question" ', *Journal of the History of Biology* XI, 1978, pp. 1–55; and by F. Alaya, 'Victorian Science and the "Genius" of Woman', *Journal of the History of Ideas* XXXVIII, 1977, pp. 261–280. See also J. H. Crooke, 'Darwinism and the Sexual Politics of Primates', *Social Science Information* XII, 1973, pp. 7–28.

his theory of evolution by natural and sexual selection, is fast becoming notorious in feminist literature.

The most extensive feminist critique of Darwin has been undertaken by Ruth Hubbard, Professor of Biology at Harvard. Hubbard has been readily able to point to passages in Darwin's writings to support her charge of 'blatant sexism'.[8] She places late-Victorian scientific sexism and its contemporary re-emergence in ethology and sociobiology squarely at Darwin's door. Contemporary ethologists and sociobiologists she asserts, are conducting their arguments within the context of nineteenth-century anthropological and biological speculation. Nineteenth-century anthropology and biology were dominated by Darwin, whose *Origin of Species* and *Descent of Man* provided the theoretical framework within which anthropologists and biologists have ever since been able to endorse the social inequality of the sexes.

* * *

While I agree with Hubbard that Darwin's concept of sexual selection and his application of it to human evolution were contingent upon his socially derived perceptions of feminine characteristics and abilities, I argue in this paper that it is not only historically incorrect to impute an anti-feminist motive to Darwin, but unnecessary.

It is historically incorrect, because Darwin's conclusions on the biological and social evolution of women were as much constrained by his commitment to a naturalistic or scientific explanation of human mental and moral characteristics as they were by his socially derived assumptions of the innate inferiority and domesticity of women, as I argue in Section I. It is unnecessary, because in order to demonstrate that Darwin's reconstruction of human evolution was pervaded by Victorian sexist ideology, one has only to examine his lived experience as Victorian bourgeois husband and father, as I do in Section II of this paper, and relate it to his theoretical arguments. Generally, the domestic relations of Charles and Emma Darwin have been of interest to historians only in so far as Charles' deference to Emma's religious beliefs offers a ready-made explanation of the twenty year delay between the inception of his theory of evolution and its publication. However, I argue that his relations with Emma had a more fundamental and enduring effect on his theory of evolution than this. Just as contextualists have argued that Darwin's concepts of artificial and natural selection were not directly based on biological phenomena, but were in some degree taken over from the practical activities of the plant and animal breeders with whom he associated and whose commercial criteria and interests he absorbed,[9] so I argue that Darwin's experience of women and his practical activities of husband and father entered into his concept of sexual selection and his associated interpretations of human evolution.

8. R. Hubbard, 'Have Only Men Evolved?', *op. cit.* (Note 7, p. xxx), p. 16.
9. M. Mulkay, *Science and the Sociology of Knowledge*, *op. cit.* (Note 1, p. xxx), pp. 100–108; A. Sandow, 'Social Factors in the Origin of Darwinism', *Quarterly Review of Biology* XIII, 1938, pp. 315–326. See also R. M. Young, *op. cit.* (Note 5, p. xxx, 1971).

To this end I demonstrate in Section II that Darwin's domestic relations in no way called into question Victorian sexual stereotypes but entirely conformed with them.

In Section III I carry this analysis further and locate both the content of Darwin's theory of human evolution and his domestic relations in the larger context of Victorian society. Here, both feminism and Darwinism are related to the nineteenth-century naturalist movement, which was concerned with bringing the whole of nature and society under the sway of natural law and improving the social standing of science. In the process, naturalism was brought into opposition to the traditional authority and status of religion and into line with those of the newly-powerful bourgeoisie, whose interests it promoted and rationalized under the universality and inevitability of natural law. Darwin's *Origin of Species* and *Descent of Man* and the intense public debate they engendered in the mid-Victorian period, are viewed as central to this transition and were shaped and constrained by it. When the bourgeois social order began to perceive the growing feminist movement as a threat, late-Victorian Darwinism was brought into conflict with feminism and imposed naturalistic scientific limits to the claims by women for political and social equality.

＊   ＊   ＊

Darwin had briefly discussed sexual selection in *The Origin*, and carefully distinguished it from natural selection:

> [Sexual selection] depends, not on a struggle for existence, but on a struggle between the males for possession of the females; the result is not death to the unsuccessful competitor, but few or no offspring. Sexual selection is, therefore, less rigorous than natural selection. Generally, the most vigorous males, those which are best fitted for their places in nature, will leave most progeny. But in many cases, victory will depend not on general vigour, but on having special weapons, confined to the male sex.[1]

Apart from male combat for possession of the females, Darwin recognized another aspect of sexual selection—female choice. This occurred especially among birds, where the males competed with one another in brilliance of plumage, song, etc., in their wooing of the female during courtship. Sexual selection could be invoked to explain a great deal that otherwise seemed inexplicable in terms of natural selection, such as the bright plumage of many male birds that renders them more conspicuous to predators, or the disadvantageously long, curved horns of an antelope. Such structures did not confer any advantage in the struggle for existence, but they were advantageous in the struggle for mates and thus gave their possessors a better chance of reproducing themselves, of leaving more offspring than other less well-endowed males. As Darwin succinctly expressed it in *The Origin*:

---

1. C. Darwin, *The Origin of Species*, Reprint of First Edition, ed. J. W. Burrow (Harmondsworth, 1968), p. 136.

[W]hen the males and females of any animal have the same general habits of life, but differ in structure, colour, or ornament, such differences have been mainly caused by sexual selection; that is, individual males have had, in successive generations, some slight advantage over other males, in their weapons, means of defence, or charms; and have transmitted these advantages to their male offspring.[2]

Sexual selection was vital to Darwin's defence of natural selection against the established theory of special creation. Apart from its importance in explaining the persistence of seemingly disadvantageous or useless characteristics, it enhanced the action of natural selection by ensuring that the fittest males ('the most vigorous males, those which are best fitted for their places in nature') were reproduced. The accumulation of advantageous variation would therefore be all the more probable. Thus, although so little space was given to sexual selection in *The Origin*, it was of considerable importance to Darwin's theory of evolution.

At this stage, it should be noted that in Darwin's initial presentation of sexual selection, attention is focussed on the *males* who compete actively with one another for the females. Even in cases of female choice, males compete to display before the females 'which standing by as spectators, at last choose the most attractive partner'; though of a 'more peaceful character' it is still a contest and it is the males who play the active rôle, who 'struggle', female choice being depicted as passive. In *The Origin* sexual selection is a process whereby males compete with other males by means of weapons or charms to reproduce themselves. The female rôle is merely one of submission to and transmission of these male characteristics. As a description of sex roles in reproduction, it is undeniably androcentric.[3]

* * *

Darwin initially introduced sexual selection in *The Descent* at the close of Part I, as an explanation of racial differences such as skin colour, hair, shape of skull, proportions of the body, etc., which he assumed to be of no evident benefit and not to correlate with climate and racial habits and customs. However, like natural selection, sexual selection took on a much wider role in human evolution. Darwin summed up its effects in the General Conclusion:

He who admits the principle of sexual selection will be led to the remarkable conclusion that the nervous system not only regulates most of the existing functions of the body, but has indirectly influenced the progressive development of various bodily structures and of certain mental qualities. Courage, pugnacity, perseverence, strength and size of body, weapons of all kinds, musical organs, both vocal and instrumental, bright colours and ornamental appendages, have all been indirectly gained by the one sex or the other through the exertion of choice, the influence of love and jealousy, and the appreciation of the beautiful in sound, colour or form; and these

2. *Ibid.* pp. 137–138.
3. Male-centred or sexist. See R. Hubbard, *op. cit.* (Note 7, p. xxx), p. 16.

powers of the mind manifestly depend on the development of the brain.[4]

Thus, apart from its primary function of explaining the persistence of seemingly non-beneficial human racial and sexual physical differences, sexual selection explained the utility of the aesthetic sense, and accounted for its high human development. It also accounted for the evolution of other uniquely human traits such as speech and music, for Darwin argued that these derived from the courtship behaviour of our 'ape-like progenitors', females for instance, having acquired sweeter voices to attract the male; human speech having arisen from the probable effects of the long-continued use of the vocal organs of the male under the excitement of love, rage and jealousy. Sexual selection also of course accounted for the social inequality of the sexes.

* * *

As for the mental differences between the sexes, here Darwin was aware that he was venturing on a contentious issue. He had read *The Subjection of Women* where Harriet Taylor and John Stuart Mill had argued that such differences as could be ascertained were culturally conditioned, not innate.[5] But, consistent with his earlier opposition to Mill on the heritability of the 'moral faculties', Darwin insisted that the 'differences in the mental powers of the two sexes' (and he emphasized considerable differences) were biologically based. Again he invoked the analogy with lower animals:

> I am aware that some writers doubt whether there is any such inherent difference; but this is at least probable from the analogy of the lower animals which present other secondary sexual characters. No-one disputes that the bull differs in disposition from the cow, the wild-boar from the sow, the stallion from the mare, and, as is well

4. C. Darwin, *The Descent of Man, and Selection in Relation to Sex*, 2nd ed. (London, 1889), p. 617.
5. Mill wrote: 'I consider it presumption in any one to pretend to decide what women are or are not, can or cannot be, by natural constitution. They have always hitherto been kept, as far as regards spontaneous development, in so unnatural a state, that their nature cannot but have been greatly distorted and disguised; and no one can safely pronounce that if women's nature were left to choose its direction as freely as men's, and if no artificial bent were attempted to be given to it except that required by the conditions of human society, and given to both sexes alike, there would be any material difference, or perhaps any difference at all, in the character and capacities which would unfold themselves. I shall presently show, that even the least contestable differences which now exist, are such as may very well have been produced merely by circumstances, without any difference of natural capacity'. 'The Subjection of Women', in *Essays on Sex Equality*, ed. A. S. Rossi (Chicago and London, 1970), p. 190. See M. T. Ghiselin, *The Economy of Nature and the Evolution of Sex* (Berkeley, Los Angeles, London, 1974). Darwin referred to *The Subjection of Women* in a footnote to this section (*The Descent of Man, op. cit.* [Note 4, p. xxx], p. 564): 'J. Stuart Mill remarks (*The Subjection of Women*, 1869, p. 122), "The things in which man most excels woman are those which require most plodding, and long hammering at single thoughts". What is this but energy and perseverance?'. Compare this with Darwin's description of his own 'mental qualities' where he attributed his success as a 'man of science' to, among other qualities, 'unbounded patience in long reflecting over any subject—industry in observing and collecting facts'. N. Barlow (ed.), *The Autobiography of Charles Darwin: with original omissions restored* (New York, 1969), pp. 139–145. See also his letter to Francis Galton of 1870, where he stressed the importance of 'zeal and hard work' in intellectual achievement.

known to the keepers of menageries, the males of the larger apes from the females.[6]

On this basis Darwin proceeded to assert the instinctive maternal traits of the human female and the human male's innate aggressive and competitive characteristics. Woman's maternal instincts lead her to be generally more tender and altruistic than man whose 'natural and unfortunate birthright' is to be competitive, ambitious and selfish. But above all man is more intelligent than woman:

> The chief distinction in the intellectual powers of the two sexes is shewn by man's attaining to a higher eminence in whatever he takes up, than can woman — whether requiring deep thought, reason, or imagination, or merely the use of the senses and hands.[7]

For Darwin, the intellectual differences between the sexes were entirely predictable on the basis of a consideration of the long-continued action of natural and sexual selection, reinforced by use-inheritance. Male intelligence would have been consistently sharpened through the struggle for possession of the females, through hunting and other male activities such as defence of the females and young.

* * *

From the 1870s on, it became possible for those who found it expedient, to look to evolution rather than religion for the corroboration of their social values. The more theologically minded could make a 'subtle accommodation with the theory . . . adopting an attendant natural theology which, while it made God remote from nature, made his rule grander', thus securing at a stroke the double ratification of God and science.[8] It was a double ideological ratification that also appealed strongly to American 'robber barons', reaching its apotheosis in the well-known Sunday School Address by J. D. Rockefeller, where he defended the morality of the monopolistic practices of Standard Oil as 'not an evil tendency in business' but 'merely the working-out of a law of nature and a law of God'.[9]

Contradictory as it may seem, in certain respects (as a number of scholars have stressed)[1] Darwinism represents not so much a revolutionary break as an underlying continuity with natural theology, which, by the time *The Origin* burst on the scene, had made its own accommodation with Malthusian social theory and the ideology of progress and was moving cautiously towards a more naturalistic or scientific interpretation of earth's history. As suggested above, Darwinism was simply one aspect of a much

6. C. Darwin, *op. cit.* (Note 4, p. xxx), p. 563.
7. *Ibid.* p. 564.
8. R. M. Young, 'The Impact of Darwin on Conventional Thought' in *The Victorian Crisis of Faith*, ed. A. Symondson (London, 1974), p. 23.
9. Cited in R. Hofstadter, *Social Darwinism in American Thought* (first published in 1944, Revised Edition, Boston, 1955), p. 45.
1. W. F. Cannon, 'The Bases of Darwin's Achievement: A Revaluation', *Victorian Studies* V, 1961, pp. 109–134; R. M. Young, *op. cit.* (Note 5, p. xxx, 1969); R. M. Young, *op. cit.* (Note 8, p. xxx); P. J. Bowler, 'Darwinism and the Argument from Design: Suggestions for a Re-evaluation', *Journal of the History of Biology* X, 1977, pp. 29–43.

broader movement that can be traced back to the end of the eighteenth century, and embraced not only directly evolutionary writings, such as those of Erasmus Darwin and Robert Chambers, but the population theory of Malthus, utilitarianism and laissez-faire doctrine, feminism and natural theology. All aimed at reinterpreting more naturalistically, traditional views of nature and society, while assuming a basically theistic view of both. Where they differed was in where to draw the line, the evolutionists insisting that *all* of nature including humanity, and mind was under the domain of natural law and therefore a legitimate object of scientific inquiry, the natural theologians disputing the inclusion of humanity, or at least mind, in the course of material nature. Viewed in this light, the Darwinian controversy becomes a 'demarcation dispute within natural theology',[2] and the ability of theology ultimately to accommodate Darwinism, when faced with the necessity for doing so, becomes explicable.

This interpretation also helps us to understand why, having triumphed and made men's and women's minds subject to natural law, many leading Darwinians became so rigidly determinist in their views on human social and economic arrangements.

*   *   *

By the 1870s, feminism was beginning to be perceived as a direct threat to the bourgeois family. Nineteenth-century feminism, from Mary Wollstonecraft on, was thoroughly bourgeois in its derivation and aspirations. Its demands for women's suffrage, higher education and entrance to middle-class professions and occupations grew out of that progressive middle-class liberalism for which John Stuart Mill was the leading spokesman. By 1870, not only had Mill's powerful voice been raised in the service of feminism, but women were already attending courses at London and Cambridge (although not as official members of the universities). A few had even managed with great difficulty to gain entrance to medicine and qualify as doctors, while many others were being prepared to compete with boys for the university lower examinations. In 1870, Oxford University decided to open its lower examinations to women also. It seemed only a matter of time before middle-class women not only gained the franchise, but would be able to take out degrees and compete professionally with men, thus acquiring not only intellectual but economic and political independence of the family.[3] Moreover the possibility of family limitation was discreetly beginning to be raised by some feminists—a prospect that struck at the heart of a growing middle-class concern with its reproductive potential versus that of the teeming, irresponsible and potentially insurrectionary lower orders. Inevitably, in the context of a general hardening of attitudes, the increasing intensity and urgency of the demands of feminism fostered a strong reaction against the gains it had made during the confident and prosperous '50s and '60s.

2. R. M. Young, *op. cit.* (Note n. 8, p. xxx), p. 24.
3. See J. N. Burstyn, 'Education and Sex: The Medical Case Against Higher Education for Women in England, 1870–1900', *Proceedings of the American Philosophical Society* CXVII, 1973, pp. 79–89.

The traditional sexual division of labour which had been characteristic of the pre-industrial and pre-capitalist period, where women had a clearly defined domestic rôle, was accentuated by the new organization of labour demanded by industrial capitalism. This was particularly so for bourgeois women:

> For them the division between public life and the private world of the home was absolute, and most became mere symbols by which their husband's financial and social status was evaluated. They were embodiments of conspicuous consumption and remained in their homes to provide their husbands and children with the tenderness, sensitivity and devotion to the arts which was so conspicuously lacking in the factories and mines of Victorian industry . . . Women worked inside the home and men outside it, and this strict differentiation between the spheres of men and women lay at the heart of Victorian society.[4]

It was woman's responsibility to guard the values inherent in the 'family' and the 'home', where her maternal virtues of love, patience and compassion were to temper the savagery of capitalist competition. The feminists' demand for their liberal 'rights' was thoroughly at odds with this renewed emphasis on the sexual division of labour. As in other areas of social concern, during the 1870s science was increasingly invoked to reinforce the traditional religion-sanctioned belief in the essential domesticity of women. With the timely appearance of The Descent at the beginning of the decade, Darwin's growing authority and prestige were pitted against the claims by women for intellectual and social equality.

*   *   *

Darwin's consideration of human sexual differences in The Descent was not motivated by the contemporary wave of anti-feminism (as can be said of most late-Victorian biologists who dealt so exhaustively with the attributes of women), but was central to his naturalistic explanation of human evolution. It was his theoretically directed contention that human mental and moral characteristics had arisen by natural evolutionary processes which predisposed him to ground these characteristics in nature rather than nurture—to insist on the biological basis of mental and moral differences as the raw material on which natural and sexual selection might operate. This brought him into opposition with Mill and others who argued for an environmental or cultural explanation of such differences, and into line with the biological determinism of Galton, Vogt, Spencer and others, whose related but more explicit social and political conceptions he borrowed and built into The Descent. In return he proffered additional support and the prestige of his name which entered into social theory as 'Social Darwinism' and was widely used to endorse late-Victorian assumptions of white middle-class male supremacy. In this fash-

---

4. L. Doyal, The Political Economy of Health (London, 1979), p. 151.

ion, Darwin endorsed the anti-feminist arguments of those 'Darwinians' like Huxley, Spencer, Romanes, Geddes and Thomson, who drew biological limitations to woman's political and social potentiality. His own foray into social justification and prescription in *The Descent* was a specific contribution by Darwin to the scientific anti-feminism that characterized this period.

Further, through his concept of sexual selection, Darwin promoted an androcentric account of human evolution which rationalized Victorian conceptions of male dominance and importance and confirmed Victorian sexual stereotypes. An examination of his early Notebook entries demonstrates that Darwin consistently held to these values and by a process of circularity fed them into his conceptions of human biological and social evolution.

Darwin's feminist critics are therefore correct in asserting the bias at the root of Darwin's characterization of women as innately domestic and intellectually inferior to men, and in pointing to the cultural and social values implicit in his concept of sexual selection. They are also correct in asserting the political effects of Darwin's argument for woman's continuing inferiority in the contemporary struggle by feminists for higher education, and the general political rôle of Darwinism in scientifically endorsing anti-feminism through late nineteenth-century biology and anthropology.

However, to do Darwin historical justice, it must be acknowledged that Darwin's personal experience did not lead him to question Victorian sexual stereotypes and the sexual division of labour, and his bourgeois class position reinforced them. Nor was he primarily motivated by anti-feminism, but by the defence of his theory of evolution. Apart from the social and political constraints within which Darwin operated, there were powerful intellectual ones which led not only Darwin but many feminists into biological determinism in their joint effort to replace traditional theological modes of explanation with scientific ones.

* * *

There are dangers in the wholesale extrapolation of nineteenth-century events to the twentieth, and vice versa. The attribution of Victorian values to twentieth-century biologists is not only historically incorrect but politically meaningless. Twentieth-century biologists are patently *not* conducting their arguments in a late Victorian social, political and intellectual context, but very much in the present, and only a thorough analysis of the present context can clarify the ideological rôle of such biological arguments in our society and lay bare their political ramifications.

Similarly, Darwin cannot be personally judged by twentieth-century yardsticks any more than his work can be assessed by twentieth-century standards and concepts. To label him a sexist may be technically correct and emotionally satisfying to those who oppose all manifestations of sexual discrimination, but is mere rhetoric in the context of a society in which almost everyone was a sexist—who held discriminatory views of woman's nature and social rôle. Those men and women who managed to transcend these socially-induced conventions to live their personal lives and locate their theoretical constructs outside them were rare indeed.

* * *

JAMES ELI ADAMS

Woman Red in Tooth and Claw (1989)†

One can easily imagine Tennyson's satisfaction at the fate of his phrase, "Nature, red in tooth and claw": a mere six words have been vested by historians with power to sum up nothing less than the impact of evolutionary thought on Christian humanism. But of course the transformation of poetry into a slogan has its costs. Tennyson's phrase has been profoundly diminished by the effacement of its original context—in particular, by the neglect of the fundamental poetic device within which the phrase functions. Tennyson's "Nature," so commonly invoked as a transparent scientific concept, appears in the famous sections 55 and 56 of *In Memoriam* (1850) as a personification—an extended, strikingly elaborate personification of the world-image Tennyson derived from contemporary science. Curiously, this fact is almost never remarked upon by commentators. Perhaps the feature seems unremarkable, since the idea of Nature is so deeply engrained in Western culture and its languages as a feminine agent with volition and purpose. Yet the very point of Tennyson's personification is to unsettle this traditional figuration. His Nature remains feminine, to be sure, yet his night thoughts on modern science are focused by the dread that the character of this feminine being has changed utterly—that "Mother Nature" has become a mocking, savage oxymoron.

Tennyson's personification of nature, so often cited to illustrate the impact of science on religious faith, thus suggests that evolutionary speculation also rendered newly problematic a deeply traditional and comforting archetype of womanhood. In registering this disturbance, the "scientific" sections of *In Memoriam* suggest an important relation between science and gender not only in Tennyson's poetry but throughout early Victorian discourse. It is a relation articulated by Darwin (albeit more obliquely) when he, too, acknowledges new pressures on traditional figurations of Nature. Responding to critics who complained of his figurative language in *The Origin of Species*, Darwin protested, "It is hard to avoid personifying the word Nature"—a somewhat impatient objection, it might seem, but one which goes to the heart of debates about the very concept of nature.[1]

---

† From "Woman Red in Tooth and Claw: Nature and the Feminine in Tennyson and Darwin," *Victorian Studies* 33 (Autumn 1989): 7–13. Reprinted by permission of Indiana University Press. James Eli Adams (b. 1955) is associate professor of English at Cornell University.
1. The remark was inserted in the third edition (1861): Charles Darwin, *The Origin of Species: A Variorum Edition*, ed. Morse Peckham (Philadelphia: University of Pennsylvania Press, 1959), p. 165. Further references to the *Origin* will be to the text of the first edition (1859), in the Pelican edition edited by J. R. Burrow (Harmondsworth: Penguin, 1968).

Darwin's theory ostensibly dealt a final blow to anthropomorphic understandings of the natural world—and hence to personifications of Nature
—yet in the famous work setting forth that theory Darwin clearly and
persistently depicts the natural world as a feminine, nurturing being. To
be sure, anthropomorphism had been logically suspect at least since the
rise of Baconian empiricism, which rejected the notion of final cause in
scientific explanation, and Darwin was hardly the first scientist to fail to
live up to the descriptive norms of a thoroughgoing positivism. Yet in light
of the growing authority of this skeptical tradition—of which the *Origin* is
in some respects a culmination—personifications of Nature increasingly
come to represent a reactionary, even archaic mode of discourse. Tennyson's trope in particular can be viewed as a desperate effort to humanize
the results of science by envisioning nature even in its bleakest aspects as
a conscious, designing being, however perverse. In representing an older,
anthropocentric worldview, however, the personification also allowed Tennyson to contemplate the destruction of that older view as a transformation
in conceptions of gender. To question the nature of "Nature" as *In Memoriam* does is inescapably to question the nature of woman. More precisely, it is to ask what has become of those conventionally feminine
attributes that have so long distinguished "Mother Nature."[2]

Throughout history, of course, the "conventionally feminine" has been
constructed antithetically. There is no figurative image of woman, Simone
de Beauvoir has contended, that does not immediately evoke its opposite.[3]
Indeed, the archetypal doubleness of the feminine (and hence of Nature)
clearly informs a work by one of Tennyson's contemporaries that may well
have suggested the figure of "Nature, red in tooth and claw." In the chapter of *Past and Present* (1843) entitled "The Sphinx," Carlyle proclaimed
that

> Nature, like the Sphinx, is of womanly celestial loveliness and ten-
> derness: the face and bosom of a goddess, but ending in claws and
> the body of a lioness. There is in her a celestial beauty . . . but there
> is also a darkness, a ferocity, fatality, which are infernal. . . . Answer
> her riddle, it is well with thee. Answer it not, pass on regarding it not,
> it will answer itself; the solution is a thing of teeth and claws.[4]

By virtue of the desire invested in the image of nature as a maternal
agency, the image always holds in reserve a terrible double associated with
the withdrawal of that agency. But such doubleness (and duplicity) seems
to have become an especially urgent and threatening reality in early Victorian discourse, which shaped the long gestations of both *In Memoriam*

---

2. For a brief historical survey of the concept of Mother Nature, see Carolyn Merchant, *The Death
of Nature: Woman, Ecology, and the Scientific Revolution* (San Francisco: Harper and Row, 1983),
pp. 1–41. Merchant locates "The death of Nature" conceived as a nurturing mother in the seventeenth century, when an organic theory of the earth gave way to a mechanistic model. Yet the
appeal within scientific discourse to a maternal Nature persists at least into the early Victorian
period: see Susan Gliserman, "Early Victorian Science Writers and Tennyson's *In Memoriam*: A
Study in Cultural Exchange," *Victorian Studies* 18 (1975), 277–308 and 437–460.
3. Simone de Beauvoir, *The Second Sex*, trans. and ed. H. M. Parshley (Harmondsworth: Penguin,
1973), p. 218.
4. Thomas Carlyle, *Past and Present*, ed. Richard D. Altick (New York: New York University Press,
1977), p. 13.

and *The Origin of Species*, as well as the feverish production of *Past and Present*. On the one hand, during the 1830s and '40s, conservative voices in the debate over woman's place—such as Sarah Ellis, author of the immensely popular *Women of England* (1837)—were codifying an ideal of womanhood as a quasi-redemptive agency that operated almost entirely within the sphere of maternity and domestic life. Woman's very being, it seemed, was constituted by her role of tending to the physical and emotional needs of men and children.[5] This is precisely the maternal ideal which Tennyson's Nature confounds—and from which that figure would have drawn a special power to disturb its original audience. Of course the very fervor with which motherhood is celebrated in this period makes plain the role of the ideal as a response to a wealth of adversarial forces.[6] But Tennyson's poetry, like Darwin's science, reminds us that the maternal ideal assumes its urgency in Victorian culture at the same moment that the claims of science are finally undermining one of the culture's most powerful icons of maternity: the very conception of nature as Mother Nature. Hence it is that Tennyson's poetry can articulate a direct and substantial bond between evolutionary science and an image that, in its subversion of the domestic ideal of womanhood, haunts the Victorian consciousness: the figure of the femme fatale or demonic woman.[7] In personifying nature, Tennyson envisions the subversion of the maternal archetype as an act of feminine betrayal. When Nature's maternal solicitude gives way to indifference, the male poet regards the withdrawal as an act of open hostility toward mankind.

*　*　*

I

Darwin's response to critics of his figurative language—"It is difficult to avoid personifying the word Nature"—appeals to the inherently figurative character of language itself. But the rejoinder, as many commentators have

5. "The angel in the house" was not one half of a simple dualism. In *The Woman Question: Society and Literature in Britain and America, 1837–1883*, 3 vols. (New York: Garland, 1983), III, xiv–xv, Elizabeth Helsinger, Robin Lauterbach Sheets, and William Veeder distinguish at least four "myths" of the feminine: 1) the Angel in the House; 2) the Angel out of the House (the model of which would become Florence Nightingale); 3) an "apocalyptic" feminism, which looked to woman's nature for a redemption of the world; 4) the model of complete equality. For my purposes, however, it is important that the second and third models can be seen as in large part a simple extension of the domestic ideal to a wider sphere, within which woman remains distinguished as a nurturing being; the radical model of equality, as the authors point out, played a much smaller role in the debate.

6. The mere fact that it seemed necessary to spell out a position like that of Ellis, as Ray Strachey pointed out in *The Cause* (1928), in itself reveals undercurrents of resistance to "the duty of female submissiveness which before had been entirely taken for granted" (quoted in Wendell Stacy Johnson, *Sex and Marriage in Victorian Poetry* [Ithaca: Cornell University Press, 1975], p. 28).

7. The two terms are notoriously elusive, as is the phenomenon they are invoked to describe. Broadly speaking, I use the two terms interchangeably to denote an image of a woman who repudiates the nurturing, maternal qualities of the domestic ideal of femininity ("the angel in the house") and thereby strikes the male observer as enigmatic and profoundly "unnatural" but also hostile; moreover, her hostility betrays a powerful erotic fascination she exerts on the male observer.

objected, hardly explains Darwin's reluctance to surrender his intricate and emphatic personifications of Nature:[8]

> As man can produce and certainly has produced a great result by his methodical and unconscious means of selection, what may not nature effect? Man can act only on external and visible characters: nature cares nothing for appearances, except in so far as they may be useful to any being. She can act on every internal organ, on every shade of constitutional difference, on the whole machinery of life. Man selects only for his own good; Nature only for that of the being which she tends. Every selected character is fully exercised by her; and the being is placed under well-suited conditions of life.
>
> (*Origin*, p. 132).

Darwin's crucial analogy between natural and artificial selection is thus presented in a form that defies the explanatory norms enforced by a rigorous positivism. As recent Darwin scholars have pointed out, however, his metaphors generally perform what Edward Manier has called "a full job of scientific work." This particular personification, Manier argues, has a crucial function as a heuristic device that enabled Darwin to outline his theoretical framework in some detail, even though he could not precisely specify the mechanisms that would account for natural selection. Ironically, this "logic of possibility"—like Darwin's image of nature as a conscious agent—is deeply indebted to the discourse of natural theology. Indeed, in Darwin's earlier drafts of his theory nature seems to verge on divinity: in the *Sketch* of 1842, it is "a being infinitely more sagacious than man," in the *Essay* of 1844 "a Being with penetration sufficient to perceive differences quite imperceptible to man."[9] But why, then, should Darwin in the *Origin* present nature's sagacity as an emphatically feminine wisdom?

It is not entirely surprising that Darwin's central analogy between natural and human selection would articulate an ideology of gender, since the analogy is so readily associated with the dualism of nature and culture, which in turn is almost universally aligned with a cultural opposition between male and female attributes.[1] Yet the particular attributes Darwin assigns to Nature are revealing. The leading characteristic of this female agent is not the sheer fecundity one might associate with Mother Nature, but rather a peculiarly domestic femininity, an attribute closely identified with rearing offspring and ministering to the needs of individuals. The activity of man's selection is, by comparison, rather crude, shortsighted

8. As Robert Young remarks, "Even by the loose standards of biological explanation, it is surprising to find such rank anthropomorphism at the heart of the most celebrated unifying theory in biology" (*Darwin's Metaphor: Nature's Place in Victorian Culture* [Cambridge: Cambridge University Press, 1985], p. 93).
9. Edward Manier, *The Young Darwin and His Cultural Circle* (Dordrecht: Reidel, 1978), pp. 150 –186. The literature on Darwin's relation to the discourse of natural theology is vast and growing; for a recent development of Manier's views, see John Healy Brooke, "The Relation Between Darwin's Science and His Religion," in John Durant, ed., *Darwinism and Divinity: Essays on Evolution and Religious Belief* (Oxford: Blackwell, 1985), pp. 40–75.
1. For an anthropological account, see Sherry B. Ortner, "Is Female to Male as Nature Is to Culture?" in Michelle Z. Rosaldo, ed., *Woman, Culture, and Society* (Palo Alto: Standford University Press, 1974), pp. 67–87.

(governed solely by external characteristics), and selfish: man selects only with an eye to what benefits man. But Nature is more discerning and more generous. She has an intuitive grasp of, and can minister to, subtleties of inner being that elude the coarser sensibility. She is careful, vigilant, disinterested, even selfless in her responsibility for "the being which she tends."[2] Clearly this personification responds to and underscores Darwin's apprehension of nature as a marvel of intricate adjustment to changing conditions. The special aptitude with which species seem to have adapted (or been adapted) to those conditions suggests an agency whose attentiveness to the individual needs of each being is distinctively feminine. Moreover, the personification offers a speculative balm which anticipates the anxieties of Darwin's audience, and perhaps responds to those of Darwin himself. As forbiddingly impersonal and inhuman as evolution might seem, the fact that natural selection might be plausibly presented as a constructive, nurturing power implied that the process need not be profoundly alien to human aspirations and desires (Manier, p. 186, notes this hint of consolation).

* * *

That gesture of consolation, however, is most clearly apparent in its incapacity to disarm another, more plausible inference to be drawn from Darwin's theory. In personifying Nature as a nurturing mother, Darwin indulges in a reassuring ambiguity of the term "being." As that term is employed in the *Origin*, it most often denotes, not a particular individual, but a particular *variety* or species. In retaining the traditional model of Mother Nature, Darwin resists a central feature of his theory, a feature that aligns it with much nineteenth-century radical speculation: the subordination of individual needs to the dynamics of a group. Within the dynamics of these larger *types* of being, the "good" can no longer be adjusted to the demands of a particular individual: it is whatever enables a particular species to become established and to survive—invariably at the expense of some of its own members—within an intricate, dynamic biological equilibrium. We must "keep steadily in mind," Darwin urges, "that each organic being is striving to increase at a geometrical ratio; that each at some period of its life . . . has to struggle for life, and to suffer great destruction. When we reflect on this struggle, we may console ourselves with the full belief, that the war of nature is not incessant, that no fear is felt, that death is generally prompt, and that the vigorous, the healthy, and the happy survive and multiply" (p. 129). It taxes scientific logic to con-

2. In *Darwin's Plots* (London: Ark, 1984), Gillian Beer also notes the alignment of man/nature with male/female (pp. 68–74). The typology is more explicitly outlined in *The Descent of Man*: "Woman seems to differ from man in mental disposition, chiefly in her greater tenderness and less selfishness. . . . Woman, owing to her maternal instincts, displays these qualities towards her infants in an eminent degree; therefore it is likely that she would often extend them towards her fellow-creatures. Man is the rival of other men; he delights in competition, and this leads to ambition which passes too easily into selfishness. . . . It is generally admitted that with women the powers of intuition, of rapid perception, and perhaps of imitation, are more strongly marked than in man" (2 vols., [London: John Murray, 1871], II, 326). This is a rather different and far more precise image of woman than that which Nina Auerbach discovers when she claims that Darwin incorporates in his personifications "his century's 'myth' " of women as "mysteriously, boundlessly metamorphic creatures" (*Woman and the Demon* [New York: Columbia, 1982], p. 52).

ceive of an amoeba or a lichen as "happy," save in the weak sense of "fortunate." But there is more than a hint of straining for consolation here, and in the context Darwin can hardly personify nature as a nurturing mother. At best one might imagine a being rather like Florence Nightingale, a nurse who eases the pain of the dying. Yet the vision of incessant struggle also invites a more somber image of nature: not a nurse, but an angel of death, a monstrous agent that rigidly and impersonally lays waste its own dependents.

Ten years before the publication of the *Origin of Species*, Tennyson in *In Memoriam* had imagined just such a sinister Nature. Like Darwin, Tennyson personifies Nature as a female being whose characteristics clearly owe much to the domestic norms of Victorian femininity. Tennyson's Nature, however, acknowledges those norms by defying them. Whereas Darwin conceives of nature as a marvel of intricate adaptation— adaptation that suggests the activity of a feminine agent attentive to individual needs—Tennyson is most deeply engaged by the idea of a nature indifferent to its own creatures, a nature which fails to display the maternal character that even Darwin is anxious to preserve.

*   *   *

Evolution and Other Disciplines

EDWARD O. WILSON

[On Consilience] (1998)†

Consilience, a term introduced by the English theologian and polymath William Whewell in his 1840 masterwork *The Philosophy of the Inductive Sciences*, means the alignment (literally, the "jumping together") of knowledge from different disciplines. Exotic as its origins sound, the idea is neither an abstruse philosophical concept nor a mere plaything of intellectuals. It is the mother's milk of the natural sciences.

Since Whewell's time, physics, chemistry, and biology have been connected by a web of causal explanation organized by induction-based theories that telescope into one another. The entire known universe, from the smallest subatomic particles to the reach of the farthest known galaxies, together spanning more than 40 orders of magnitude (a magnification of one followed by more than 40 zeros), is encompassed by consilient explanation. Thus, quantum theory underlies atomic physics, which is the foundation of reagent chemistry and its specialized offshoot biochemistry, which interlock with molecular biology—essentially, the chemistry of organic macromolecules—and thence, through successively higher levels of organization, cellular, organismic, and evolutionary biology. This sequence of causal explanation proceeds step by step from more general phenomena to the increasingly complex and specific phenomena arising from them. Such is the unifying and highly productive understanding of the world that has evolved in the natural sciences. Its success testifies to a fortunate combination of three circumstances: the surprising orderliness of the universe, the possible intrinsic consilience of all knowledge concerning it, and the ingenuity of the human mind in comprehending both.

On the horizon are the social sciences and the humanities. Ever since the decline of the Enlightenment in the late 18th century—and, with it, confidence in the unity of knowledge—it has been customary to speak of these second and third great branches of learning as intellectually independent. They are separated, conventional wisdom has it, by an epistemological discontinuity, in particular by possession of different categories of truth, autonomous ways of knowing, and languages largely untranslatable into those of the natural sciences.

† From "Resuming the Enlightenment Quest," *The Wilson Quarterly* 22 (1998): 16–27. Reprinted by permission of the author. Copyright © 1998 Edward O. Wilson. Edward O. Wilson (b. 1929) is Pellegrino University Research Professor and honorary curator in entomology of the Museum of Comparative Zoology, Harvard University.

Now, however, the expansion of consilient cause-and-effect explanation outward from the natural sciences toward the social sciences and humanities is calling the traditional division of knowledge into question. What most of the academy still takes to be a discontinuity is starting to look like something entirely different, a broad and largely unexplored terrain of phenomena bound up with the material origins and functioning of the human brain. The study of this terrain, rooted in biology, appears increasingly available as a new foundational discipline of the social sciences and humanities. The discontinuity, it now seems, is neither an intrinsic barrier between the great branches of learning nor a Hadrian's Wall protecting humanistic studies and high culture from reductionistic barbarians, but rather a subject of extraordinary potential awaiting cooperative exploration from both sides.

At the heart of this borderland is the shifting concept of culture and its hitherto puzzling relation to human nature—and thence to the general inherited properties of individual behavior. In the spirit of the natural sciences, the matter can be expressed, I believe, as a problem to be solved. It is as follows: Compelling evidence shows that all culture is learned. But its invention and transmission are biased by innate properties of the sensory system and the brain. These developmental biases, which we collectively call human nature, are themselves prescribed by genes that evolved or were sustained over hundreds of thousands of years in primarily cultural settings. Hence, genes and culture have coevolved; they are linked. What then, is the nature of gene-culture coevolution, and how has it affected the human condition today? That, in my opinion, is the central intellectual question of the social sciences and humanities. It is also one of the most important remaining problems of the natural sciences.

Confidence in the unity of knowledge—universal consilience—rests ultimately on the hypothesis that all mental activity is material in nature and occurs in a manner consistent with the causal explanations of the natural sciences. During the past several decades, that hypothesis has gained considerable support from four disciplines that succeed partially in connecting the great branches of learning. The first is cognitive neuroscience, also known as the brain sciences—the once but no longer "quiet" revolution of neuroscience—which is physically mapping the mental process. The second is human behavioral genetics, now in the early stages of teasing apart the hereditary basis of the process, including the biasing influence of the genes on mental development. The third bridging discipline is evolutionary biology (including human sociobiology, often referred to as evolutionary psychology), which attempts to reconstruct the evolution of brain and mind. The last is environmental science, which describes the physical environment to which humanity is genetically and culturally adapted.

The natural sciences are best understood as humanity's way of correctly perceiving the real world, as opposed to the way the human brain perceives that same world unaided by instruments and verifiable fact and theory. The brain, it is becoming increasingly clear, evolved as an instrument of survival. It did not evolve as a device to understand itself, much less the underlying principles of physics, chemistry, and biology. Under the circumstances of physical environment and culture prevailing from one generation to the next during the long haul of prehistory, natural selection built a brain that conferred the highest rates of survival and reproduction. The jury-rigged quality of our perceptual and cognitive apparatus, the legacy of genetic evolution, is part of the reason social scientists have such a hard time grappling with human nature, why so much of the history of philosophy can be fairly said to consist of failed models of the brain, and why people generally understand automobiles better than their own minds.

Consider the matter of vision. What we intuitively believe to be the "real world" is what we see. But what we see is only an infinitesimal slice of the electromagnetic spectrum, comprising wavelengths of 400 to 700 billionths of a meter. With instrumentation, we are now able to observe the remainder of the spectrum that rains down on our bodies, from gamma waves trillions of times shorter than visible light to radio waves trillions of times longer. Many animals see a part of the spectrum outside our range. Insects, for example, depend heavily on ultraviolet light at wavelengths shorter than the human visible spectrum. Color in the visible spectrum also deceives us. We intuitively think that the rainbow is a natural phenomenon existing apart from the human mind, but it is not. Its palette is a product of the way the visual system and brain break the continuously varying wavelength of sunlight into the seemingly discrete segments we call colors. Such hereditary filtering and self-deception occur in all of the other senses. And some capabilities present in other organisms are totally absent from our uninstrumented minds. We have, for example, no organs to monitor the electric fields that some species of fish use to guide themselves through dark water, or the magnetic field by which migratory birds navigate across clouded night skies.

Why are human beings, supposedly the summum bonum of creation, so handicapped? The simplest and most thoroughly verifiable answer has been provided by the natural sciences, and most particularly the borderland disciplines of cognitive neuroscience and evolutionary biology. Outside our heads there is freestanding reality. Only lunatics and a sprinkling of constructivist philosophers doubt its existence. Inside our heads is a reconstruction of reality based on sensory input and the self-assembly of symbol-based concepts. Scenarios based on these concepts, rather than an independent executive entity in the brain—the "ghost in the machine," in philosopher Gilbert Ryle's famous derogation—appear to constitute the mind. The scenarios of conscious thought move constantly back and forth through time. As these configurations fly by, driven by stimuli and drawing upon memories of prior scenarios, they are weighted and guided by emotion, which is the modification of neural activity that animates and focuses mental activity.

Emotion, as now understood, is not something separate and distinct from thinking, as the Romantics fancied. Rather, it is an active partner of ratiocination and a crucial component of human thought. Emotion operates through physiological processes that select certain streams of information over others, shifting the body and mind to higher or lower degrees

of activity, agitating the neural circuits that create scenarios, and selecting
for ones that end in certain ways. The winning scenarios, those that match
goals preprogrammed by instinct and the reinforcing satisfactions of prior
experience, determine focus and decision.

In this view, which represents a consensus of many investigators in cognitive neuroscience, what we call *meaning* is the linkage among the neural
networks created by the spreading excitation that enlarges imagery and
engages emotion. The competitive selection among scenarios is what we
call *decision making*. The outcome, in terms of the match of the winning
scenarios to instinctive or learned favorable states, sets the kind and intensity of subsequent emotion. The *self*, by virtue of the physical location of
the brain in the body and the programs of emotional response, is the
necessary central player in the scenarios. The persistent form and intensity
of emotions is called *mood*. The ability of the brain to generate novel
scenarios and settle upon the most effective among them is called *creativity*. The persistent production of scenarios lacking reality and survival value
is called *insanity*.

The alignment of outer existence with its inner representation has been
distorted by the idiosyncrasies of human evolution, the hundred-millen-
nium process directed primarily by the struggle to survive rather than the
pursuit of self-understanding. The brain, although a magnificent instrument, is still rooted in the deep genetic history of the Paleolithic Age,
when most or all of human evolution occurred. Introspection alone cannot
disclose the sensory and psychophysiological distortions it creates, which
are usually beneficent but sometimes catastrophic. To diagnose and correct the misalignment is the proper task of the natural sciences and—one
can reasonably hope—the social sciences and humanities as well. To explore the borderland between the great branches of learning would seem
to lead to a better understanding of the human condition than the various
skeptical and relativistic accounts of "socially constructed" realities supplied by intellectuals who have lost faith in the original Enlightenment
quest for unified knowledge.

Much of the new understanding will hinge on an inquiry into the exact
manner by which genetic evolution and cultural evolution have been
joined to create the mind. The key to the linkage can be found in the
properties of human nature. This diagnostic core of Homo sapiens is not
the genes, which prescribe it, nor culture, which is its product. Human
nature is the ensemble of epigenetic rules of mental development, the
hereditary regularities in the growth of individual minds and behavior.
Following are some of the examples that researchers in the natural and
social sciences have identified, proceeding from the relatively simple to
the complex:

• The smile, which appears in infants from the ages of two to four
months, invariably evokes affection from adults and reinforces bonding
between caregiver and infant. In all cultures and throughout life, smiling
is used to signal friendliness, approval, and a sense of pleasure. Each culture molds its meaning into nuances determined by form and the context
in which it is displayed. There is no doubt that smiling is hereditary. It

appears on schedule in deaf-blind children and even in thalidomide-deformed children who are not only deaf and blind but crippled so badly they cannot touch their own faces.

• Phobias are aversions powerful enough to engage the autonomic nervous system. They can evoke panic, cold sweat, and nausea; are easily acquired, often from a single frightening experience; and are notoriously difficult to eradicate. The most common phobias are directed at the ancient perils of humankind, including snakes, spiders, dogs (thus, wolves), heights, closed spaces, crowds of strangers, and running water. They rarely focus on the far more dangerous objects of modern life, such as automobiles, electric sockets, knives, and firearms. It is reasonable to suppose that such selective avoidance is an inherited predisposition that reflects the long history of natural selection during which the human brain formed. In other words, the ancient dangers are "remembered" in the epigenetic programs, while the modern ones have not existed long enough for aversions to them to be hereditarily installed in the same manner.

• Color vision, one of the important sensory determinants of culture, has been relatively well tracked all the way from genes to neurons. The chemistry of the three protein cone pigments of the retina, both the amino acids of which they are composed and the shapes into which the molecular chains are folded, is fully known. So is the sequence of base pairs in the genes on the X-chromosome that prescribe them, as well as the sequence of the mutations that cause color blindness, the triggering of the cone neurons by light-induced changes in the pigments, the coding used by the optic nerve to distinguish wavelength, and the pathways leading from the optic nerve cells to the higher integrating centers of the visual cortex in the rear of the brain.

By inherited molecular processes, the human sensory and nervous systems break continuously varying wavelengths of light into colors. We perceive, in proceeding from the short-wavelength end to the long-wavelength end of the spectrum, first a broad band of blue, then green, then yellow, and finally red. The array is arbitrary in an ultimately biological sense. That is, it is only one of many arrays that might have evolved over the past millions of years. But it is not arbitrary in a cultural sense. Having evolved genetically, it cannot be altered by learning or by conscious internal construction of new color codes.

All of culture involving color is derived ultimately from these molecular and cellular processes. Color terms independently invented by societies around the world are faithfully clustered in the least ambiguous wavelength zones of the four elementary colors. Cultures tend to avoid the ambiguous intermediate zones. Each society uses from two to 11 basic linguistic terms drawn from within the favored zones. The maximum 11 are black, white, red, yellow, green, blue, brown, purple, pink, orange, and gray. At one extreme, the Dani of New Guinea, for example, use only two of the terms, and at the other extreme, English speakers use all 11. From societies with simple classifications to those with complex classifications, the combinations of basic color terms generally grow in a hierarchical fashion, as follows:

Languages with two basic color terms distinguish black and white.
Languages with three terms have words for black, white, and red.
Languages with four terms have words for black, white, red, and either green or yellow.
Languages with five terms have words for black, white, red, green, *and* yellow.
Languages with six terms have words for black, white, red, green, yellow, and blue.
Languages with seven terms have words for black, white, red, green, yellow, blue, and brown.
No such precedence occurs among the remaining four basic colors, purple, pink, orange, and gray, when these have been added to the first seven.

If basic patterns were invented and combined at random from the 11 basic colors, the vocabularies of different societies would be drawn helter-skelter from among 2,036 mathematically possible combinations. The evidence indicates that, on the contrary, they are drawn primarily from only 22. This constraint can be reasonably interpreted as an epigenetic rule in addition to that of color vision itself. Unlike those of basic color vision, however, its genetic and neurobiological bases remain unknown.

• Incest avoidance, the focus of so many cultural conventions, also springs from a hereditary epigenetic rule. The rule is called the Westermarck effect, after the Finnish anthropologist Edward A. Westermarck, who first reported it in 1891. Recent anthropological research has refined it as follows: when a boy and girl are brought together before one or the other is 30 months of age, and then the pair are raised in proximity (they use the same potty, so to speak), they are later devoid of sexual interest in each other; indeed, the very thought of its arouses aversion. This emotional incapacity, fortified in many societies by a rational understanding of the consequence of inbreeding, has led to the cultural incest taboos—whose origins Sigmund Freud explained differently, and erroneously, as barriers against strong innate urges to commit incest. The Darwinian advantage of the epigenetic rule is overwhelming. The mortality rate among children born of incest—mating of full siblings or parents and offspring—is about twice that of outbred children, and among those who survive, genetic defects such as dwarfism, heart deformities, deaf-mutism, and severe mental retardation are 10 times more common.

Human incest avoidance is obedient to the following general rule in animals and plants: almost all species vulnerable to moderate or severe inbreeding depression use some biologically programmed method to avoid incest. Homo sapiens not only conforms to this rule but does so in the same manner as our closest evolutionary relatives. Among the apes, monkeys, and other nonhuman primates, resistance to incest consists of two barriers. In the first, young individuals of all 19 social species whose mating patterns have been studied practice the equivalent of human exogamy: before reaching full adult size, they leave the group in which they were born and join another. The second barrier is the Westermarck effect. In all species whose sexual development has been carefully studied, including marmosets and tamarins of South America, Asian macaques, baboons, and chimpanzees, adults avoid mating with individuals who were intimately known to them in early life. In as many as a third of human societies there exists in addition a third, cultural barrier: incest is proscribed due to the direct recognition that children with congenital disabilities are a frequent product of incestuous unions. Thus, the incest taboos and myths that pervade cultures everywhere appear likely to have arisen from the Westermarck effect, but also, in a minority of societies, from a direct perception of the destructive effects of inbreeding.

Epigenetic rules, the true combinatorial elements of human nature, evidently shape the development of mind and social interaction through most, if not all, categories of behavior. While the full causal sequences into which the rules fit, which run from genes to cells to sensory organs to behavior to culture, are still poorly understood, they appear clearly to be the key link between the evolution of genes and the evolution of culture.

The process of gene-culture coevolution itself is also still in an early stage of research, but a broad outline of the process in theory is possible. I believe the following account represents a consensus of the small number of investigators working on the subject.

Culture is created by the communal mind, this view holds, and each mind in turn is the product of the genetically structured human sensory system and brain. Genes and culture are therefore inseparably linked. But the linkage is flexible, to a degree still mostly unmeasured. The linkage is also tortuous: genes prescribe epigenetic rules, which are the inherited neural pathways and regularities in cognitive development by which the mind assembles itself. The mind grows by learning those parts of the environment and surrounding culture available to it. Mental development is a selective absorption process, one that is unavoidably biased by the epigenetic rules.

As part of gene-culture coevolution, culture is reconstructed collectively in the minds of individuals each generation. When oral tradition is supplemented by writing and the arts, it can grow indefinitely large (example: five million patents to the present time in the United States alone), and it can even skip generations. But the biasing influence of the epigenetic rules, being genetic and ineradicable, remains the same across all societies and generations.

The epigenetic rules nevertheless vary genetically in degree among individuals within populations. Some individuals have always inherited epigenetic rules in different strengths from others, degrees of expression which, in past evolutionary time at least, enabled them to survive and reproduce better in the surrounding environment and culture. By this means, over many generations, the more successful epigenetic rules spread, along with the genes that prescribe them. As a consequence, the human species has evolved by natural selection in the developmental biases of mind and behavior, hence in human nature, just as it has in the anatomy and physiology of the body.

To outline the theory of the coevolution of genes and culture in this way is not to claim that particular forms of culture are genetically determined. Certain cultural norms can survive and reproduce better than others, even when guided by exactly the same epigenetic biases as competing norms, causing culture to evolve in a track parallel to and usually much faster than genetic evolution. The quicker the pace of cultural evolution, the weaker the connection between genes and culture, although the connection is never completely broken. Culture allows a rapid adjustment to changes in the environment by finely tuned adaptations invented and transmitted without correspondingly precise, matching genetic prescription. In this respect, human beings differ fundamentally from all other animal species. Particular cultures can also be maladaptive in the long term, causing the destruction of individuals and societies that contrived them. But the linkage between genes and culture is unbreakable; culture can never have a life entirely on its own. Nor, I believe, should we wish it otherwise. Human nature is what defines our species and binds it together.

The consilient view of the human condition that I have outlined only briefly here, and which I elaborate in *Consilience: The Unity of Knowledge*, is predicated on the well-supported assumption that Homo sapiens is a biological species, having evolved for the most part in the same manner as the remainder of life, and conservatively enough that the humanity-defining traits of language and culture retain a residue of their deeper, genetic history. While still very sketchy in detail, the emerging factual picture of the epigenetic rules lends support to consilience and, for the time being at least, to the theory of gene-culture coevolution. It also suggests in broad outline an important part of the terrain between the great branches of learning that can be fruitfully explored.

Such an extension of consilient explanation from the natural sciences to the social sciences and humanities may be faulted as reductionistic, and for that reason unsuited to the hypercomplex realities of human social life. But reductionism is the driving wedge of the natural sciences, by which they have already broken apart many hypercomplex systems. Reductionistic analysis typically proceeds from more complex and specific phenomena and the disciplines addressing them to underlying phenomena that are less complex and specific. For example, the living cell has been opened to clear view by biochemistry and molecular biology, and mental processes are beginning to yield to cellular biology and neurophysiology. Both are among the hypercomplex phenomena that have so far proved congenial to consilient explanation, and both are directly relevant to human social behavior. There is no obvious reason why the social sciences and humanities, except by degree of their specificity and complexity (and, granted, these are important distinctions), should prove resistant to the same approach.

Moreover, the scientific method is equally concerned with synthesis, and thereby holism. The most successful research has always been cyclical. It begins with the description of a complex entity or process. It proceeds by reduction to the main components, then reassembly of the components in vitro or by abstract modeling to the original whole, followed by correction through testing, further reduction, and reassembly. And so on around, until understanding is considered satisfactory by even the most demanding critics.

It may be further argued that attempts at such an extension are merely a return to the failed program of logical positivism, a variation on general positivism that attempted to define the essence of scientific statements by means of rigorous logic and the analysis of language. But logical positivism, whose influence peaked among philosophers from the 1920s to the early 1940s, lacked cognitive neuroscience, human genetics, evolutionary biology, and environmental science. None of these bridging disciplines were mature enough to shed light on the linkage between biology and culture. Logical positivism was also argued from the top down in a largely abstract framework. That is, its proponents set out to identify freestanding criteria against which scientific knowledge can be judged. Every symbol, they argued, should denote something real. It should be consistent with the total structure of established facts and theories, with no revelations or freeflight generalizing allowed. Theory must follow in lockstep with facts, during which process the informational content of language is carefully distinguished from its emotional content. Finally, verification, the logical positivists argued, is all-important; scientific statements should clearly imply the methods and reasoning used to verify the conclusions drawn. If these guidelines are progressively refined and followed, they concluded, we can hope to close in on objective truth.

The fatal flaw in logical positivism was in the semantic linchpin of the system: its creators and followers could not agree on the basic distinctions between fact and concept, between generalization and mathematical truth, or between theory and speculation. Stalled by the combination of these fog-shrouded dichotomies, they were unable to arrive at an invariant and fundamental difference between scientific and nonscientific statements.

The shortcoming of logical positivism was ignorance of how the brain works, and why. That, in my opinion, is the whole story. Neither philosophers nor scientists who attacked the problem could explain the physical acts of observation and reasoning in other than highly subjective terms. None could track material phenomena of the outer world through the labyrinth of causal processes in the inner mental world, and thus precisely map outer material phenomena onto the inner material phenomena of conscious activity. But there is every reason to suppose that such a feat can be accomplished. Such is the means by which symbols and concepts might in time be exactly defined, and objective truth more precisely triangulated.

In short, the canonical criterion of objective truth so ardently sought by the logical positivists is not a philosophical problem, and it cannot be attained, as many had expected, by logical and semantical analysis. It is an empirical problem solvable only by a continuing investigation of the physical basis of the mind itself. In time, like so many philosophical searches of the past, it will be transformed into the description of a material process.

Meanwhile, the search for universal consilience begun in the Enlightenment is gaining in factual substance. The borderland domain between the great branches of learning appears at last to be coming into focus. If successful, its exploration offers the prospect of a full disciplinary foundation of the social sciences, by extending analysis to the deeper levels of biological organization that underlie human behavior and the origins of culture. By this means, I believe, can the social sciences expect to create a true and more powerful body of theory. Through similar explanatory connections to the natural sciences, the exploration of aesthetics and the creative process offers a comparable foundation for interpretation of the arts. And not least, consilient explanation will shed much-needed new light on the material origins of ethical precepts and religious belief.

RANDOLPH M. NESSE AND GEORGE C. WILLIAMS

Evolution and the Origins of Disease (1998)†

Thoughtful contemplation of the human body elicits awe—in equal measure with perplexity. The eye, for instance, has long been an object of wonder, with the clear, living tissue of the cornea curving just the right amount, the iris adjusting to brightness and the lens to distance, so that the optimal quantity of light focuses exactly on the surface of the retina. Admiration of such apparent perfection soon gives way, however, to consternation. Contrary to any sensible design, blood vessels and nerves traverse the inside of the retina, creating a blind spot at their point of exit.

The body is a bundle of such jarring contradictions. For each exquisite heart valve, we have a wisdom tooth. Strands of DNA direct the development of the 10 trillion cells that make up a human adult but then permit his or her steady deterioration and eventual death. Our immune system can identify and destroy a million kinds of foreign matter, yet many bacteria can still kill us. These contradictions make it appear as if the body was designed by a team of superb engineers with occasional interventions by Rube Goldberg.

In fact, such seeming incongruities make sense but only when we investigate the origins of the body's vulnerabilities while keeping in mind the wise words of distinguished geneticist Theodosius Dobzhansky: "Nothing in biology makes sense except in the light of evolution." Evolutionary biology is, of course, the scientific foundation for all biology, and biology is the foundation for all medicine. To a surprising degree, however, evo-

† From "Evolution and the Origins of Disease," *Scientific American* 279 (November 1998): 86–93. Reprinted by permission of *Scientific American*. Randolph M. Nesse (b. 1948) is professor of psychiatry at the University of Michigan. George C. Williams (b. 1926) is professor emeritus of ecology and evolution at the State University of New York at Stony Brook.

lutionary biology is just now being recognized as a basic medical science. The enterprise of studying medical problems in an evolutionary context has been termed Darwinian medicine. Most medical research tries to explain the causes of an individual's disease and seeks therapies to cure or relieve deleterious conditions. These efforts are traditionally based on consideration of proximate issues, the straightforward study of the body's anatomic and physiological mechanisms as they currently exist. In contrast, Darwinian medicine asks why the body is designed in a way that makes us all vulnerable to problems like cancer, atherosclerosis, depression and choking, thus offering a broader context in which to conduct research.

The evolutionary explanations for the body's flaws fall into surprisingly few categories. First, some discomforting conditions, such as pain, fever, cough, vomiting and anxiety, are actually neither diseases nor design defects but rather are evolved defenses. Second, conflicts with other organisms—*Escherichia coli* or crocodiles, for instance—are a fact of life. Third, some circumstances, such as the ready availability of dietary fats, are so recent that natural selection has not yet had a chance to deal with them. Fourth, the body may fall victim to trade-offs between a trait's benefits and its costs; a textbook example is the sickle cell gene, which also protects against malaria. Finally, the process of natural selection is constrained in ways that leave us with suboptimal design features, as in the case of the mammalian eye.

Evolved Defenses

Perhaps the most obviously useful defense mechanism is coughing; people who cannot clear foreign matter from their lungs are likely to die from pneumonia. The capacity for pain is also certainly beneficial. The rare individuals who cannot feel pain fail even to experience discomfort from staying in the same position for long periods. Their unnatural stillness impairs the blood supply to their joints, which then deteriorate. Such pain free people usually die by early adulthood from tissue damage and infections. Cough or pain is usually interpreted as disease or trauma but is actually part of the solution rather than the problem. These defensive capabilities, shaped by natural selection, are kept in reserve until needed.

Less widely recognized as defenses are fever, nausea, vomiting, diarrhea, anxiety, fatigue, sneezing and inflammation. Even some physicians remain unaware of fever's utility. No mere increase in metabolic rate, fever is a carefully regulated rise in the set point of the body's thermostat. The higher body temperature facilitates the destruction of pathogens. Work by Matthew J. Kluger of the Lovelace Institute in Albuquerque, N.M., has shown that even cold-blooded lizards, when infected, move to warmer places until their bodies are several degrees above their usual temperature. If prevented from moving to the warm part of their cage, they are at increased risk of death from the infection. In a similar study by Evelyn Satinoff of the University of Delaware, elderly rats, who can no longer achieve the high fevers of their younger lab companions, also instinctively sought hotter environments when challenged by infection.

A reduced level of iron in the blood is another misunderstood defense mechanism. People suffering from chronic infection often have decreased levels of blood iron. Although such low iron is sometimes blamed for the illness, it actually is a protective response: during infection, iron is sequestered in the liver, which prevents invading bacteria from getting adequate supplies of this vital element.

Morning sickness has long been considered an unfortunate side effect of pregnancy. The nausea, however, coincides with the period of rapid tissue differentiation of the fetus, when development is most vulnerable to interference by toxins. And nauseated women tend to restrict their intake of strong-tasting, potentially harmful substances. These observations led independent researcher Margie Profet to hypothesize that the nausea of pregnancy is an adaptation whereby the mother protects the fetus from exposure to toxins.

* * *

Conflicts with Other Organisms

Natural selection is unable to provide us with perfect protection against all pathogens, because they tend to evolve much faster than humans do. E. coli, for example, with its rapid rates of reproduction, has as much opportunity for mutation and selection in one day as humanity gets in a millennium. And our defenses, whether natural or artificial, make for potent selection forces. Pathogens either quickly evolve a counterdefense or become extinct. Amherst College biologist Paul W. Ewald has suggested classifying phenomena associated with infection according to whether they benefit the host, the pathogen, both or neither. Consider the runny nose associated with a cold. Nasal mucous secretion could expel intruders, speed the pathogen's transmission to new hosts or both [see "The Evolution of Virulence," by Paul W. Ewald; Scientific American, April 1993]. Answers could come from studies examining whether blocking nasal secretions shortens or prolongs illness, but few such studies have been done.

Humanity won huge battles in the war against pathogens with the development of antibiotics and vaccines. Our victories were so rapid and seemingly complete that in 1969 U.S. Surgeon General William H. Stewart said that it was "time to close the book on infectious disease." But the enemy, and the power of natural selection, had been underestimated. The sober reality is that pathogens apparently can adapt to every chemical researchers develop. ("The war has been won," one scientist more recently quipped. "By the other side.")

Antibiotic resistance is a classic demonstration of natural selection. Bacteria that happen to have genes that allow them to prosper despite the presence of an antibiotic reproduce faster than others, and so the genes that confer resistance spread quickly. As shown by Nobel laureate Joshua Lederberg of the Rockefeller University, they can even jump to different species of bacteria, borne on bits of infectious DNA. Today some strains of tuberculosis in New York City are resistant to all three main antibiotic treatments; patients with those strains have no better chance of surviving than did TB patients a century ago. Stephen S. Morse of Columbia University notes that the multidrug-resistant strain that has spread throughout the East Coast may have originated in a homeless shelter across the street from Columbia-Presbyterian Medical Center. Such a phenomenon would indeed be predicted in an environment where fierce selection pressure quickly weeds out less hardy strains. The surviving bacilli have been bred for resistance.

Many people, including some physicians and scientists, still believe the outdated theory that pathogens necessarily become benign after long association with hosts. Superficially, this makes sense. An organism that kills rapidly may never get to a new host, so natural selection would seem to favor lower virulence. Syphilis, for instance, was a highly virulent disease when it first arrived in Europe, but as the centuries passed it became steadily more mild. The virulence of a pathogen is, however, a life history trait that can increase as well as decrease, depending on which option is more advantageous to its genes.

For agents of disease that are spread directly from person to person, low virulence tends to be beneficial, as it allows the host to remain active and in contact with other potential hosts. But some diseases, like malaria, are transmitted just as well—or better—by the incapacitated. For such pathogens, which usually rely on intermediate vectors like mosquitoes, high virulence can give a selective advantage. This principle has direct implications for infection control in hospitals, where health care workers' hands can be vectors that lead to selection for more virulent strains.

In the case of cholera, public water supplies play the mosquitoes' role. When water for drinking and bathing is contaminated by waste from immobilized patients, selection tends to increase virulence, because more diarrhea enhances the spread of the organism even if individual hosts quickly die. But, as Ewald has shown, when sanitation improves, selection acts against classical *Vibrio cholerae* bacteria in favor of the more benign El Tor biotype. Under these conditions, a dead host is a dead end. But a less ill and more mobile host, able to infect many others over a much longer time, is an effective vehicle for a pathogen of lower virulence. In another example, better sanitation leads to displacement of the aggressive *Shigella flexneri* by the more benign *S. sonnei*.

Such considerations may be relevant for public policy. Evolutionary theory predicts that clean needles and the encouragement of safe sex will do more than save numerous individuals from HIV infection. If humanity's behavior itself slows HIV transmission rates, strains that do not soon kill their hosts have the long-term survival advantage over the more virulent viruses that then die with their hosts, denied the opportunity to spread. Our collective choices can change the very nature of HIV.

*　*　*

Coping with Novelty

Making rounds in any modern hospital provides sad testimony to the prevalence of diseases humanity has brought on itself. Heart attacks, for example, result mainly from atherosclerosis, a problem that became widespread only in this century and that remains rare among hunter-gatherers. Epidemiological research furnishes the information that should help us prevent heart attacks: limit fat intake, eat lots of vegetables, and exercise hard each day. But hamburger chains proliferate, diet foods languish on the shelves, and exercise machines serve as expensive clothing hangers throughout the land. The proportion of overweight Americans is one third and rising. We all know what is good for us. Why do so many of us continue to make unhealthy choices?

Our poor decisions about diet and exercise are made by brains shaped to cope with an environment substantially different from the one our species now inhabits. On the African savanna, where the modern human design was fine-tuned, fat, salt and sugar were scarce and precious. Individuals who had a tendency to consume large amounts of fat when given the rare opportunity had a selective advantage. They were more likely to survive famines that killed their thinner companions. And we, their descendants, still carry those urges for foodstuffs that today are anything but scarce. These evolved desires—inflamed by advertisements from competing food corporations that themselves survive by selling us more of whatever we want to buy—easily defeat our intellect and willpower. How ironic that humanity worked for centuries to create environments that are almost literally flowing with milk and honey, only to see our success responsible for much modern disease and untimely death.

* * *

Trade-offs and Constraints

Compromise is inherent in every adaptation. Arm bones three times their current thickness would almost never break, but *Homo sapiens* would be lumbering creatures on a never-ending quest for calcium. More sensitive ears might sometimes be useful, but we would be distracted by the noise of air molecules banging into our eardrums.

Such trade-offs also exist at the genetic level. If a mutation offers a net reproductive advantage, it will tend to increase in frequency in a population even if it causes vulnerability to disease. People with two copies of the sickle cell gene, for example, suffer terrible pain and die young. People with two copies of the "normal" gene are at high risk of death from malaria. But individuals with one of each are protected from both malaria and sickle cell disease. Where malaria is prevalent, such people are fitter, in the Darwinian sense, than members of either other group. So even though the sickle cell gene causes disease, it is selected for where malaria persists. Which is the "healthy" allele in this environment? The question has no answer. There is no one normal human genome—there are only genes.

* * *

Because evolution can take place only in the direction of time's arrow, an organism's design is constrained by structures already in place. As noted, the vertebrate eye is arranged backward. The squid eye, in contrast, is free from this defect, with vessels and nerves running on the outside, penetrating where necessary and pinning down the retina so it cannot detach. The human eye's flaw results from simple bad luck; hundreds of millions of years ago, the layer of cells that happened to become sensitive to light in our ancestors was positioned differently from the corresponding layer in ancestors of squids. The two designs evolved along separate tracks, and there is no going back.

Such path dependence also explains why the simple act of swallowing can be life-threatening. Our respiratory and food passages intersect because in an early lungfish ancestor the air opening for breathing at the surface was understandably located at the top of the snout and led into a common space shared by the food passageway. Because natural selection cannot start from scratch, humans are stuck with the possibility that food will clog the opening to our lungs.

* * *

Evolution of Darwinian Medicine

Despite the power of the Darwinian paradigm, evolutionary biology is just now being recognized as a basic science essential for medicine. Most diseases decrease fitness, so it would seem that natural selection could explain only health, not disease. A Darwinian approach makes sense only when the object of explanation is changed from diseases to the traits that make us vulnerable to diseases. The assumption that natural selection maximizes health also is incorrect—selection maximizes the reproductive success of genes. Those genes that make bodies having superior reproductive success will become more common, even if they compromise the individual's health in the end.

Finally, history and misunderstanding have presented obstacles to the acceptance of Darwinian medicine. An evolutionary approach to functional analysis can appear akin to naive teleology or vitalism, errors banished only recently, and with great effort, from medical thinking. And, of course, whenever evolution and medicine are mentioned together, the specter of eugenics arises. Discoveries made through a Darwinian view of how all human bodies are alike in their vulnerability to disease will offer great benefits for individuals, but such insights do not imply that we can or should make any attempt to improve the species. If anything, this approach cautions that apparent genetic defects may have unrecognized adaptive significance, that a single "normal" genome is nonexistent and that notions of "normality" tend to be simplistic.

The systematic application of evolutionary biology to medicine is a new enterprise. Like biochemistry at the beginning of this century, Darwinian medicine very likely will need to develop in several incubators before it can prove its power and utility. If it must progress only from the work of scholars without funding to gather data to test their ideas, it will take decades for the field to mature. Departments of evolutionary biology in medical schools would accelerate the process, but for the most part they do not yet exist. If funding agencies had review panels with evolutionary expertise, research would develop faster, but such panels remain to be created. We expect that they will.

The evolutionary viewpoint provides a deep connection between the states of disease and normal functioning and can integrate disparate avenues of medical research as well as suggest fresh and important areas of inquiry. Its utility and power will ultimately lead to recognition of evolutionary biology as a basic medical science.

STEVEN PINKER

How the Mind Works (1997)†

Reverse-Engineering the Psyche

*   *   *

The mind is a system of organs of computation, designed by natural selection to solve the kinds of problems our ancestors faced in their foraging way of life, in particular, understanding and outmaneuvering objects, animals, plants, and other people. The summary can be unpacked into several claims. The mind is what the brain does; specifically, the brain processes information, and thinking is a kind of computation. The mind is organized into modules or mental organs, each with a specialized design that makes it an expert in one arena of interaction with the world. The modules' basic logic is specified by our genetic program. Their operation was shaped by natural selection to solve the problems of the hunting and gathering life led by our ancestors in most of our evolutionary history. The various problems for our ancestors were subtasks of one big problem for their genes, maximizing the number of copies that made it into the next generation.

On this view, psychology is engineering in reverse. In forward-engineering, one designs a machine to do something; in reverse-engineering, one figures out what a machine was designed to do. *   *   *

In the seventeenth century William Harvey discovered that veins had valves and deduced that the valves must be there to make the blood circulate. Since then we have understood the body as a wonderfully complex machine, an assembly of struts, ties, springs, pulleys, levers, joints, hinges, sockets, tanks, pipes, valves, sheaths, pumps, exchangers, and filters. Even today we can be delighted to learn what mysterious parts are for. Why do we have our wrinkled, asymmetrical ears? Because they filter sound waves coming from different directions in different ways. The nuances of the sound shadow tell the brain whether the source of the sound is above or below, in front of or behind us. The strategy of reverse-engineering the body has continued in the last half of this century as we have explored the nanotechnology of the cell and of the molecules of life. The stuff of

† From *How the Mind Works* (New York, 1997). Copyright © 1997 by Steven Pinker. Reprinted by permission of W. W. Norton & Company, Inc. Steven Pinker (b. 1954) is professor and director of the Center for Cognitive Neuroscience at the Massachusetts Institute of Technology.

life turned out to be not a quivering, glowing, wondrous gel but a contraption of tiny jigs, springs, hinges, rods, sheets, magnets, zippers, and trapdoors, assembled by a data tape whose information is copied, downloaded, and scanned.

The rationale for reverse-engineering living things comes, of course, from Charles Darwin. He showed how "organs of extreme perfection and complication, which justly excite our admiration" arise not from God's foresight but from the evolution of replicators over immense spans of time. As replicators replicate, random copying errors sometimes crop up, and those that happen to enhance the survival and reproduction rate of the replicator tend to accumulate over the generations. Plants and animals are replicators, and their complicated machinery thus appears to have been engineered to allow them to survive and reproduce.

Darwin insisted that his theory explained not just the complexity of an animal's body but the complexity of its mind. "Psychology will be based on a new foundation," he famously predicted at the end of *The Origin of Species*. But Darwin's prophecy has not yet been fulfilled. More than a century after he wrote those words, the study of the mind is still mostly Darwin-free, often defiantly so. Evolution is said to be irrelevant, sinful, or fit only for speculation over a beer at the end of the day. The allergy to evolution in the social and cognitive sciences has been, I think, a barrier to understanding. The mind is an exquisitely organized system that accomplishes remarkable feats no engineer can duplicate. How could the forces that shaped that system, and the purposes for which it was designed, be irrelevant to understanding it? Evolutionary thinking is indispensable, not in the form that many people think of—dreaming up missing links or narrating stories about the stages of Man—but in the form of careful reverse-engineering. * * *

Only in the past few years has Darwin's challenge been taken up, by a new approach christened "evolutionary psychology" by the anthropologist John Tooby and the psychologist Leda Cosmides. Evolutionary psychology brings together two scientific revolutions. One is the cognitive revolution of the 1950s and 1960s, which explains the mechanics of thought and emotion in terms of information and computation. The other is the revolution in evolutionary biology of the 1960s and 1970s, which explains the complex adaptive design of living things in terms of selection among replicators. The two ideas make a powerful combination. Cognitive science helps us to understand how a mind is possible and what kind of mind we have. Evolutionary biology helps us to understand *why* we have the kind of mind we have.

The evolutionary psychology of this book is, in one sense, a straightforward extension of biology, focusing on one organ, the mind, of one species, *Homo sapiens*. But in another sense it is a radical thesis that discards the way issues about the mind have been framed for almost a century. The premises of this book are probably not what you think they are. Thinking is computation, I claim, but that does not mean that the computer is a good metaphor for the mind. The mind is a set of modules, but the modules are not encapsulated boxes or circumscribed swatches on the surface of the brain. The organization of our mental modules comes from our genetic program, but that does not mean that there is a gene for every trait or that learning is less important than we used to think. The mind is an adaptation designed by natural selection, but that does not mean that everything we think, feel, and do is biologically adaptive. We evolved from apes, but that does not mean we have the same minds as apes. And the ultimate goal of natural selection is to propagate genes, but that does not mean that the ultimate goal of people is to propagate genes. Let me show you why not.

This book is about the brain, but I will not say much about neurons, hormones, and neurotransmitters. That is because the mind is not the brain but what the brain does, and not even everything it does, such as metabolizing fat and giving off heat. The 1990s have been named the Decade of the Brain, but there will never be a Decade of the Pancreas. The brain's special status comes from a special thing the brain does, which makes us see, think, feel, choose, and act. That special thing is information processing, or computation.

Information and computation reside in patterns of data and in relations of logic that are independent of the physical medium that carries them. When you telephone your mother in another city, the message stays the same as it goes from your lips to her ears even as it physically changes its form, from vibrating air, to electricity in a wire, to charges in silicon, to flickering light in a fiber optic cable, to electromagnetic waves, and then back again in reverse order. In a similar sense, the message stays the same when she repeats it to your father at the other end of the couch after it has changed its form inside her head into a cascade of neurons firing and chemicals diffusing across synapses. Likewise, a given program can run on computers made of vacuum tubes, electromagnetic switches, transistors, integrated circuits, or well-trained pigeons, and it accomplishes the same things for the same reasons.

This insight, first expressed by the mathematician Alan Turing, the computer scientists Alan Newell, Herbert Simon, and Marvin Minsky, and the philosophers Hilary Putnam and Jerry Fodor, is now called the computational theory of mind. It is one of the great ideas in intellectual history, for it solves one of the puzzles that make up the "mind-body problem": how to connect the ethereal world of meaning and intention, the stuff of our mental lives, with a physical hunk of matter like the brain. Why did Bill get on the bus? Because he wanted to visit his grandmother and knew the bus would take him there. No other answer will do. If he hated the sight of his grandmother, or if he knew the route had changed, his body would not be on that bus. For millennia this has been a paradox. Entities like "wanting to visit one's grandmother" and "knowing the bus goes to Grandma's house" are colorless, odorless, and tasteless. But at the same time they are *causes* of physical events, as potent as any billiard ball clacking into another.

The computational theory of mind resolves the paradox. It says that beliefs and desires are *information*, incarnated as configurations of symbols. The symbols are the physical states of bits of matter, like chips in a computer or neurons in the brain. They symbolize things in the world because they are triggered by those things via our sense organs, and because of what they do once they are triggered. If the bits of matter that constitute a symbol are arranged to bump into the bits of matter constituting another symbol in just the right way, the symbols corresponding to one belief can give rise to new symbols corresponding to another belief logically related to it, which can give rise to symbols corresponding to other beliefs, and so on. Eventually the bits of matter constituting a symbol bump into bits of matter connected to the muscles, and behavior happens. The computational theory of mind thus allows us to keep beliefs and desires in our explanations of behavior while planting them squarely in the physical universe. It allows meaning to cause and be caused.

*　*　*

Our organs of computation are a product of natural selection. The biologist Richard Dawkins called natural selection the Blind Watchmaker; in the case of the mind, we can call it the Blind Programmer. Our mental programs work as well as they do because they were shaped by selection to allow our ancestors to master rocks, tools, plants, animals, and each other, ultimately in the service of survival and reproduction.

Natural selection is not the only cause of evolutionary change. Organisms also change over the eons because of statistical accidents in who lives and who dies, environmental catastrophes that wipe out whole families of creatures, and the unavoidable by-products of changes that *are* the product of selection. But natural selection is the only evolutionary force that acts like an engineer, "designing" organs that accomplish improbable but adaptive outcomes.

*　*　*

The human mind is a product of evolution, so our mental organs are either present in the minds of apes (and perhaps other mammals and vertebrates) or arose from overhauling the minds of apes, specifically, the common ancestors of humans and chimpanzees that lived about six million years ago in Africa. Many titles of books on human evolution remind us of this fact: *The Naked Ape, The Electric Ape, The Scented Ape, The Lopsided Ape, The Aquatic Ape, The Thinking Ape, The Human Ape, The Ape That Spoke, The Third Chimpanzee, The Chosen Primate*. Some authors are militant that humans are barely different from chimpanzees and that any focus on specifically human talents is arrogant chauvinism or tantamount to creationism. For some readers that is a reductio ad absurdum of the evolutionary framework. If the theory says that man "at best is only a monkey shaved," as Gilbert and Sullivan put it in *Princess Ida*, then it fails to explain the obvious fact that men and monkeys have different minds.

We *are* naked, lopsided apes that speak, but we also have minds that differ considerably from those of apes. The outsize brain of *Homo sapiens sapiens* is, by any standard, an extraordinary adaptation. It has allowed us to inhabit every ecosystem on earth, reshape the planet, walk on the moon, and discover the secrets of the physical universe. Chimpanzees, for all their vaunted intelligence, are a threatened species clinging to a few patches of forest and living as they did millions of years ago. Our curiosity about this difference demands more than repeating that we share most of our DNA with chimpanzees and that small changes can have big effects. Three hundred thousand generations and up to ten megabytes of potential genetic information are enough to revamp a mind considerably. Indeed, minds are probably easier to revamp than bodies because software is easier to modify than hardware. We should not be surprised to discover impressive new cognitive abilities in humans, language being just the most obvious one.

None of this is incompatible with the theory of evolution. Evolution is a conservative process, to be sure, but it can't be all *that* conservative or we would all be pond scum. Natural selection introduces differences into descendants by fitting them with specializations that adapt them to different niches.   *   *   *

To say that the mind is an evolutionary adaptation is not to say that all behavior is adaptive in Darwin's sense. Natural selection is not a guardian angel that hovers over us making sure that our behavior always maximizes biological fitness. Until recently, scientists with an evolutionary bent felt a responsibility to account for acts that seem like Darwinian suicide, such as celibacy, adoption, and contraception. Perhaps, they ventured, celibate people have more time to raise large broods of nieces and nephews and thereby propagate more copies of their genes than they would if they had their own children. This kind of stretch is unnecessary, however. The reasons, first articulated by the anthropologist Donald Symons, distinguish evolutionary psychology from the school of thought in the 1970s and 1980s called sociobiology (though there is much overlap between the approaches as well).

First, selection operates over thousands of generations. For ninety-nine percent of human existence, people lived as foragers in small nomadic bands. Our brains are adapted to that long-vanished way of life, not to brand-new agricultural and industrial civilizations. They are not wired to cope with anonymous crowds, schooling, written language, government, police, courts, armies, modern medicine, formal social institutions, high technology, and other newcomers to the human experience. Since the modern mind is adapted to the Stone Age, not the computer age, there is no need to strain for adaptive explanations for everything we do.   *   *   *

Second, natural selection is not a puppetmaster that pulls the strings of behavior directly. It acts by designing the generator of behavior: the package of information-processing and goal-pursuing mechanisms called the mind. Our minds are designed to generate behavior that would have been adaptive, on average, in our ancestral environment, but any particular deed done today is the effect of dozens of causes. Behavior is the outcome of an internal struggle among many mental modules, and it is played out on the chessboard of opportunities and constraints defined by *other* people's behavior.

*   *   *

Though the process of natural selection itself has no goal, it evolved entities that (like the automobile) are highly organized to bring about certain goals and subgoals. To reverse-engineer the mind, we must sort them out and identify the ultimate goal in its design. Was the human mind ultimately designed to create beauty? To discover truth? To love and to work? To harmonize with other human beings and with nature?

The logic of natural selection gives the answer. The ultimate goal that the mind was designed to attain is maximizing the number of copies of the genes that created it. Natural selection cares only about the long-term fate of entities that replicate, that is, entities that retain a stable identity across many generations of copying. It predicts only that replicators whose effects tend to enhance the probability of their own replication come to predominate. When we ask questions like "Who or what is supposed to benefit from an adaptation?" and "What is a design in living things a design *for?*" the theory of natural selection provides the answer: the long-term stable replicators, genes. Even our bodies, our selves, are not the ultimate beneficiary of our design. As [Stephen Jay] Gould has said, "What is the 'individual reproductive success' of which Darwin speaks? It cannot be the passage of one's body into the next generation—for, truly, you can't take it with you in this sense above all!" The criterion by which genes get selected is the quality of the bodies they build, but it is the genes making it into the next generation, not the perishable bodies, that are selected to live and fight another day.

* * *

Psychological Correctness

The evolutionary psychology of this book is a departure from the dominant view of the human mind in our intellectual tradition, which Tooby and Cosmides have dubbed the Standard Social Science Model (SSSM). The SSSM proposes a fundamental division between biology and culture. Biology endows humans with the five senses, a few drives like hunger and fear, and a general capacity to learn. But biological evolution, according to the SSSM, has been superseded by cultural evolution. Culture is an autonomous entity that carries out a desire to perpetuate itself by setting up expectations and assigning roles, which can vary arbitrarily from society to society. Even the reformers of the SSSM have accepted its framing of the issues. Biology is "just as important as" culture, say the reformers; biology imposes "constraints" on behavior, and all behavior is a mixture of the two.

The SSSM not only has become an intellectual orthodoxy but has acquired a moral authority. When sociobiologists first began to challenge it, they met with a ferocity that is unusual even by the standards of academic invective. The biologist E. O. Wilson was doused with a pitcher of ice water at a scientific convention, and students yelled for his dismissal over bullhorns and put up posters urging people to bring noisemakers to his lectures. Angry manifestos and book-length denunciations were published by organizations with names like Science for the People and The Campaign Against Racism, IQ, and the Class Society. In *Not in Our Genes*, Richard Lewontin, Steven Rose, and Leon Kamin dropped innuendos about Donald Symons' sex life and doctored a defensible passage of Richard Dawkins' into an insane one. (Dawkins said of the genes, "They created us, body and mind"; the authors have quoted it repeatedly as "They *control* us, body and mind.") When *Scientific American* ran an article on behavior genetics (studies of twins, families, and adoptees), they entitled it "Eugenics Revisited," an allusion to the discredited movement to improve the human genetic stock. When the magazine covered evolutionary psychology, they called the article "The New Social Darwinists," an allusion to the nineteenth-century movement that justified social inequality as part of the wisdom of nature. Even one of sociobiology's distinguished practitioners, the primatologist Sarah Blaffer Hrdy, said, "I question whether sociobiology should be taught at the high school level, or even the undergraduate level. . . . The whole message of sociobiology is oriented toward the success of the individual. It's Machiavellian, and unless a student has a moral framework already in place, we could be producing social monsters by teaching this. It really fits in very nicely with the yuppie 'me first' ethos."

Entire scholarly societies joined in the fun, passing votes on empirical issues that one might have thought would be hashed out in the lab and the field. Margaret Mead's portrayal of an idyllic, egalitarian Samoa was one of the founding documents of the SSSM, and when the anthropologist Derek Freeman showed that she got the facts spectacularly wrong, the American Anthropological Association voted at its business meeting to denounce his finding as unscientific. In 1986, twenty social scientists at a "Brain and Aggression" meeting drafted the Seville Statement on Violence, subsequently adopted by UNESCO and endorsed by several scientific organizations. The statement claimed to "challenge a number of alleged biological findings that have been used, even by some in our disciplines, to justify violence and war":

> It is *scientifically incorrect* to say that we have inherited a tendency to make war from our animal ancestors.
>
> It is *scientifically incorrect* to say that war or any other violent behavior is genetically programmed into our human nature.
>
> It is *scientifically incorrect* to say that in the course of human evolution there has been a selection for aggressive behavior more than for other kinds of behavior.
>
> It is *scientifically incorrect* to say that humans have a "violent brain."
>
> It is *scientifically incorrect* to say that war is caused by "instinct" or any single motivation. . . . We conclude that biology does not condemn humanity to war, and that humanity can be freed from the bondage of biological pessimism and empowered with confidence to undertake the transformative tasks needed in the International Year of Peace and in the years to come.

What moral certainty could have incited these scholars to doctor quotations, censor ideas, attack the ideas' proponents ad hominem, smear them with unwarranted associations to repugnant political movements, and mobilize powerful institutions to legislate what is correct and incorrect? The certainty comes from an opposition to three putative implications of an innate human nature.

First, if the mind has an innate structure, different people (or different classes, sexes, and races) could have different innate structures. That would justify discrimination and oppression.

Second, if obnoxious behavior like aggression, war, rape, clannishness, and the pursuit of status and wealth are innate, that would make them "natural" and hence good. And even if they are deemed objectionable, they are in the genes and cannot be changed, so attempts at social reform are futile.

Third, if behavior is caused by the genes, then individuals cannot be held responsible for their actions. If the rapist is following a biological imperative to spread his genes, it's not his fault.

Aside perhaps from a few cynical defense lawyers and a lunatic fringe who are unlikely to read manifestos in the *New York Review of Books*, no one has actually drawn these mad conclusions. Rather, they are thought to be extrapolations that the untutored masses *might* draw, so the dangerous ideas must themselves be suppressed. In fact, the problem with the three arguments is not that the conclusions are so abhorrent that no one should be allowed near the top of the slippery slope that leads to them. The problem is that there is no such slope; the arguments are non sequiturs. To expose them, one need only examine the logic of the theories and separate the scientific from the moral issues.

My point is not that scientists should pursue the truth in their ivory tower, undistracted by moral and political thoughts. Every human act involving another living being is both the subject matter of psychology and the subject matter of moral philosophy, and both are important. But they are not the same thing. The debate over human nature has been muddied by an intellectual laziness, an unwillingness to make moral arguments when moral issues come up. Rather than reasoning from principles of rights and values, the tendency has been to buy an off-the-shelf moral package (generally New Left or Marxist) or to lobby for a feel-good picture of human nature that would spare us from having to argue moral issues at all.

* * *

So what about the three supposed implications of an innate human nature? The first "implication"—that an innate human nature implies innate human differences—is no implication at all. The mental machinery I argue for is installed in every neurologically normal human being. The differences among people may have nothing to do with the design of that machinery. They could very well come from random variations in the assembly process or from different life histories. Even if the differences were innate, they could be quantitative variations and minor quirks in equipment present in all of us (how fast a module works, which module prevails in a competition inside the head) and are not necessarily any more pernicious than the kinds of innate differences allowed in the Standard

Social Science Model (a faster general-purpose learning process, a stronger sex drive).

A universal structure to the mind is not only logically possible but likely to be true. Tooby and Cosmides point out a fundamental consequence of sexual reproduction: every generation, each person's blueprint is scrambled with someone else's. That means we must be qualitatively alike. If two people's genomes had designs for different kinds of machines, like an electric motor and a gasoline engine, the new pastiche would not specify a working machine at all. Natural selection is a homogenizing force within a species; it eliminates the vast majority of macroscopic design variants because they are not improvements. Natural selection does depend on there having been variation in the past, but it feeds off the variation and uses it up. That is why all normal people have the same physical organs, and why we all surely have the same mental organs as well. There are, to be sure, microscopic variations among people, mostly small differences in the molecule-by-molecule sequence of many of our proteins. But at the level of functioning organs, physical and mental, people work in the same ways. Differences among people, for all their endless fascination to us as we live our lives, are of minor interest when we ask how the mind works. The same is true for differences—whatever their source—between the averages of entire groups of people, such as races.

The sexes, of course, are a different matter. The male and female reproductive organs are a vivid reminder that qualitatively different designs *are* possible for the sexes, and we know that the differences come from the special gadget of a genetic "switch," which triggers a line of biochemical dominoes that activate and deactivate families of genes throughout the brain and body. I will present evidence that some of these effects cause differences in how the mind works. In another of the ironies that run through the academic politics of human nature, this evolution-inspired research has proposed sex differences that are tightly focused on reproduction and related domains, and are far less invidious than the differences proudly claimed by some schools of feminism. Among the claims of "difference feminists" are that women do not engage in abstract linear reasoning, that they do not treat ideas with skepticism or evaluate them through rigorous debate, that they do not argue from general moral principles, and other insults.

But ultimately we cannot just look at who is portrayed more flatteringly; the question is what to make of any group differences we do stumble upon. And here we must be prepared to make a moral argument. Discrimination against individuals on the basis of their race, sex, or ethnicity is wrong. The argument can be defended in various ways that have nothing to do with the average traits of the groups. One might argue that it is unfair to deny a social benefit to individuals because of factors they cannot control, or that a victim of discrimination experiences it as a uniquely painful sting, or that a group of victims is liable to react with rage, or that discrimination tends to escalate into horrors like slavery and genocide. (Those who favor affirmative action could acknowledge that reverse discrimination is wrong but argue that it undoes an even greater wrong.) None of these arguments is affected by anything any scientist will ever claim to discover. The final word on the political non-implications of group differences must go to Gloria Steinem: "There are really not many jobs that actually require a penis or a vagina, and all the other occupations should be open to everyone."

The fallacy of the second supposed implication of a human nature—that if our ignoble motives are innate, they can't be so bad after all—is so obvious it has been given a name: the naturalistic fallacy, that what happens in nature is right. Forget the romantic nonsense in wildlife documentaries, where all creatures great and small act for the greater good and the harmony of the ecosystem. As Darwin said, "What a book a devil's chaplain might write on the clumsy, wasteful, blundering, low, and horribly cruel works of nature!" A classic example is the ichneumon wasp, who paralyzes a caterpillar and lays eggs in its body so her hatchlings can slowly devour its living flesh from the inside.

Like many species, *Homo sapiens* is a nasty business. Recorded history from the Bible to the present is a story of murder, rape, and war, and honest ethnography shows that foraging peoples, like the rest of us, are more savage than noble. The !Kung San of the Kalahari Desert are often held out as a relatively peaceful people, and so they are, compared with other foragers: their murder rate is only as high as Detroit's. A linguist friend of mine who studies the Wari in the Amazon rainforest learned that their language has a term for edible things, which includes anyone who isn't a Wari. Of course humans don't have an "instinct for war" or a "violent brain," as the Seville Statement assures us, but humans don't exactly have an instinct for peace or a nonviolent brain, either. We cannot attribute all of human history and ethnography to toy guns and superhero cartoons.

Does that mean that "biology condemns man to war" (or rape or murder or selfish yuppies) and that any optimism about reducing it should be snuffed out? No one needs a scientist to make the moral point that war is not healthy for children and other living things, or the empirical point that some places and periods are vastly more peaceable than others and that we should try to understand and duplicate what makes them so. And no one needs the bromides of the Seville Statement or its disinformation that war is unknown among animals and that their dominance hierarchies are a form of bonding and affiliation that benefits the group. What could not hurt is a realistic understanding of the psychology of human malevolence. For what it's worth, the theory of a module-packed mind allows both for innate motives that lead to evil acts and for innate motives that can avert them. Not that this is a unique discovery of evolutionary psychology; all the major religions observe that mental life is often a struggle between desire and conscience.

When it comes to the hopes of changing bad behavior, the conventional wisdom again needs to be inverted: a complex human nature may allow *more* scope for change than the blank slate of the Standard Social Science Model. A richly structured mind allows for complicated negotiations inside the head, and one module could subvert the ugly designs of another one. In the SSSM, in contrast, upbringing is often said to have an insidious and irreversible power. "Is it a boy or a girl?" is the first question we ask about a new human being, and from then on parents treat their sons and daughters differently: they touch, comfort, breast-feed, indulge, and talk to boys and girls in unequal amounts. Imagine that this behavior has long-term consequences on the children, which include all the documented sex differences *and* a tendency to treat *their* children differently from birth. Unless we stationed parenting police in the maternity ward, the circle would be complete and irrevocable. Culture would condemn women to inferiority, and we would be enslaved to the bondage of cultural pessimism, disempowered by self-doubt from undertaking transformative tasks.

Nature does not dictate what we should accept or how we should live our lives. Some feminists and gay activists react with fury to the banal observations that natural selection designed women in part for growing and nursing children and that it designed both men and women for heterosexual sex. They see in those observations the sexist and homophobic message that only traditional sexual roles are "natural" and that alternative lifestyles are to be condemned. For example, the novelist Mary Gordon, mocking a historian's remark that what all women have in common is the ability to bear children, wrote, "If the defining quality of being a woman is the ability to bear children, then not bearing children (as, for instance, Florence Nightingale and Greta Garbo did not) is somehow a failure to fulfill your destiny." I'm not sure what "the defining quality of being a woman" and "fulfilling your destiny" even *mean*, but I do know that happiness and virtue have nothing to do with what natural selection designed us to accomplish in the ancestral environment. They are for us to determine. In saying this I am no hypocrite, even though I am a conventional straight white male. Well into my procreating years I am, so far, voluntarily childless, having squandered my biological resources reading and writing, doing research, helping out friends and students, and jogging in circles, ignoring the solemn imperative to spread my genes. By Darwinian standards I am a horrible mistake, a pathetic loser, not one iota less than if I were a card-carrying member of Queer Nation. But I am happy to be that way, and if my genes don't like it, they can go jump in the lake.

Finally, what about blaming bad behavior on our genes? The neuroscientist Steven Rose, in a review of a book by E. O. Wilson in which Wilson wrote that men have a greater desire for polygamy than women, accused him of really saying, "Don't blame your mates for sleeping around, ladies, it's not their fault they are genetically programmed." The title of Rose's own book with Lewontin and Kamin, *Not in Our Genes*, is an allusion to *Julius Caesar*:

> Men at some time are masters of their fates:
> The fault, dear Brutus, lies not in our stars,
> But in ourselves . . .

For Cassius, the programming that was thought to excuse human faults was not genetic but astrological, and that raises a key point. *Any* cause of behavior, not just the genes, raises the question of free will and responsibility. The difference between explaining behavior and excusing it is an ancient theme of moral reasoning, captured in the saw "To understand is not to forgive."

In this scientific age, "to understand" means to try to explain behavior as a complex interaction among (1) the genes, (2) the anatomy of the brain, (3) its biochemical state, (4) the person's family upbringing, (5) the way society has treated him or her, and (6) the stimuli that impinge upon the person. Sure enough, *every one* of these factors, not just the stars or the genes, has been inappropriately invoked as the source of our faults and a claim that we are not masters of our fates.

* * *

As science advances and explanations of behavior become less fanciful, the Specter of Creeping Exculpation, as [Daniel] Dennett calls it, will loom larger. Without a clearer moral philosophy, any cause of behavior could be taken to undermine free will and hence moral responsibility. Science is guaranteed to appear to eat away at the will, *regardless* of what it finds, because the scientific mode of explanation cannot accommodate the mysterious notion of uncaused causation that underlies the will. If scientists wanted to show that people had free will, what would they look for? Some random neural event that the rest of the brain amplifies into a signal triggering behavior? But a random event does not fit the concept of free will any more than a lawful one does, and could not serve as the long-sought locus of moral responsibility. We would not find someone guilty if his finger pulled the trigger when it was mechanically connected to a roulette wheel, why should it be any different if the roulette wheel is inside his skull? The same problem arises for another unpredictable cause that has been suggested as the source of free will, chaos theory, in which, according to the cliché, a butterfly's flutter can set off a cascade of events culminating in a hurricane. A fluttering in the brain that causes a hurri-cane of behavior, if it were ever found, would still be a cause of behavior and would not fit the concept of uncaused free will that underlies moral responsibility.

Either we dispense with all morality as an unscientific superstition, or we find a way to reconcile causation (genetic or otherwise) with respon-sibility and free will. I doubt that our puzzlement will ever be completely assuaged, but we can surely reconcile them in part. Like many philoso-phers, I believe that science and ethics are two self-contained systems played out among the same entities in the world, just as poker and bridge are different games played with the same fifty-two-card deck. The science game treats people as material objects, and its rules are the physical proc-esses that cause behavior through natural selection and neurophysiology. The ethics game treats people as equivalent, sentient, rational, free-willed agents, and its rules are the calculus that assigns moral value to behavior through the behavior's inherent nature or its consequences.

* * *

The confusion of scientific psychology with moral and political goals, and the resulting pressure to believe in a structureless mind, have rippled per-niciously through the academy and modern intellectual discourse. Many of us have been puzzled by the takeover of humanities departments by the doctrines of postmodernism, poststructuralism, and deconstructionism, according to which objectivity is impossible, meaning is self-contradictory, and reality is socially constructed. The motives become clearer when we consider typical statements like "Human beings have constructed and used gender—human beings can deconstruct and stop using gender," and "The heterosexual/homosexual binary is not in nature, but is socially constructed, and therefore deconstructable." Reality is denied to categories, knowledge, and the world itself so that reality can be denied to stereotypes of gender, race, and sexual orientation. The doctrine is basically a convoluted way of getting to the conclusion that oppression of women, gays, and minorities is bad. And the dichotomy between "in nature" and "socially constructed" shows a poverty of the imagination, because it omits a third alternative: that some categories are products of a complex mind designed to mesh with what is in nature.

* * *

STEVE JONES

The Set within the Skull (1997)†

* * *

How the Mind Works is * * * an ambitious attempt to explain how we act, think, and feel in terms of cognitive science. Steven Pinker believes that the voyage of discovery is more or less complete; or, at least, we have got about as far as we will. In spite of an escape clause of the kind familiar to consumers of health foods ("We don't understand how the mind works"), his agenda is clear. It is presented in the forceful manner expected of the author of *The Language Instinct*. The mind works in a particular way, he says, because of evolution.

* * *

Pinker treats the mind as other biologists treat the kidney. His thesis is clear: "The mind is a system of organs of computation designed by natural selection to solve the problems faced by our ancestors in their foraging way of life." Perhaps it is, but to treat thought as an upbeat version of making water run uphill runs into the problems that haunt those who work on less pretentious organs. Evolution has a grammar of its own which applies to whatever structure is being studied. Any argument that is—like Pinker's—based on comparing different creatures must defer to it.

His book makes much of the fact that the mind works in a certain way because for 99 percent of our evolution we were hunter-gatherers. That

† From "The Set within the Skull," *New York Review of Books* (November 6, 1997). Reprinted by permission of the author. Steve Jones (b. 1944) is professor of genetics at University College London.

seems fair but is not, because when speculating about the past you have to know which 99 percent to choose. At one point in *How the Mind Works*, a female student interjects into a tutorial on sex roles the heartfelt statement that "Men are slime!" Well, for 99 percent of their evolution they —and women, and ostriches, and cacti—were. Our pedigree began not a hundred thousand years ago when one lineage was defined to be human, but at the origin of life four thousand million years before that. Why pick on the hunter-gatherers? Without other evidence one could as well say that human evolution began with the appearance of the cell membrane or the printing press and fit a hypothesis around those milestones instead.

To understand how far a body part—a kidney, perhaps—has come, one needs to know where it started from. For the mind that is not possible. It is for cell membranes, for kidneys, gills, breasts, or opposable thumbs, because some creatures have them and some do not. Their pattern—shared by groups who descend from a common ancestor and not by others—is a map through the past. "Shared derived characters," as they are known, untangle the hierarchy of evolution.

The mind is different. * * * From a Chinese speaker's point of view, Welsh and English are just dialects of each other, both equally easy or difficult to understand. As members of the Indo-European family of languages, all descended from a common ancestor, this is of course true. Although English tourists find Welsh impenetrable (which is why it stays alive), the only way of testing how different it really is is to put the language into evolutionary context, with Chinese as an "outgroup" with which Welsh and its presumed relative can be compared. This shows that, bizarre though it might sound to those who cannot speak it, there is nothing special about Welsh. The pattern of shared derived characters proves that the language broke away from what became English long after Chinese separated from the Ursprache. The romantic languages split off even later (to Dumas, after all, English was just French badly pronounced). Literary fragments—fossil speech—and a few daring assumptions about the rate at which words change with time can date the separation of what became each of those tongues. But what if there were only one world language— how would we know when it began? It would be impossible. That is the trouble with the mind. You can guess when it appeared but evolution won't tell you; there is no outgroup, no creature possessing measurably more or less mind than us available for comparison. Did it start before the chimps broke off from the human lineage (on the way losing what little mind they had), or with the first ground-dwellers, the hunter-gatherers, the first to speak, the inventors of the printing press, or (ask any teenager) with television itself? Without an outgroup with which to compare ourselves we * * * cannot know.

It took a long time for biology to wake up to that dilemma. Now it has a statistical machine to sort it out, based on the objective measurement of the affinities of different creatures. Cladistics, as it is called, has come up with some suprises. It shows that a group such as "reptiles" is unnatural: it contains lizards and crocodiles, but crocodiles are closer to birds than to their supposed companions. Shared features in cows and worms prove that the great forms of life supposed to have burst into existence during the Cambrian Explosion five and a half million years ago were born long before that. The mind, though, has no relatives and leaves no fossils. It may look like the sort of mind that would be useful to a hunter-gatherer, but without the evidence we cannot be sure. There is another problem with the argument from evolution. Darwin's key phrase is that "the present is the key to the past"; that the events of today—mutation, natural selection, accidental change—explain the course of biological history. That is why the first pages of *The Origin* are not about universals but about pigeons. * * *

Darwin's interest came from the fact that different breeds could be seen to descend from a shared ancestor through the daily efforts of fanciers. That present process could, he thought, explain not just the origin of pigeon stocks but how the birds themselves began.

There is a great snare awaiting those who use Darwinism to understand the modern world: that of reversing his formula. It is fatally easy to assume that the past must be the key to the present. That is simply not true, for the mind or anything else. Most evolutionary arguments turn on events which are enormously powerful over vast lengths of time but cannot be measured or even perceived over the instant in which we live our lives. I once released a million fruit flies into Death Valley in the hope of measuring the difference in fitness between two forms of a certain enzyme. The idea was absurd. To see any real effect needed hundreds of times as many flies for perhaps thousands of generations.

Evolution has a speedometer. It is read in Darwins, a measure of the rate of change over time. In fossil mammals, one of the most rapidly evolving of all groups, the average velocity over the past few million years was at a Darwin or so. A tiny average difference in fitness—the length of a giraffe's neck changing by a fraction of a millimeter a generation—led to the vast diversity of mammals that surrounds us. To look for such differences among living giraffes would be a waste of time. Not to find them would say little about why they have long necks (or, for that matter, philosophers great minds). The mind, like the neck, may have evolved through something quite invisible to experimental science.

There is a matching problem. It arises from the fact that evolution has wonderful tactics but no strategy. Although there may be a long-term trend, the driver of the Darwinian machine often throws his charge into reverse. The direction in which it travels at any instant says little about what it might do in the future. What is advantageous over centuries may be harmful on a scale of decades.

Take the famous finches of the Galapagos. Fossils show that each species, with its characteristic large or small beak, has persisted more or less unchanged for thousands of years. That makes evolutionary sense since the islands have not changed much either. Experiments with marked birds, though, show that at any moment there is within each species strong selection—at a thousand Darwins and more—for one extreme of beak size or the other. In dry years (such as those that follow El Niño, the climatic shift that leads to drought and is about to break out again) birds with large beaks do better since they can crack the hard seeds that survive. In wet years, those with slender bills are favored. In most years, one form or its opposite is at a great advantage and the hopeful biologist is sure to find a difference between them. In the long term, though, as the fossils show, that is quite irrelevant and everything stays the same. A calm (or at least inconsistent) past is no key to the evolutionary turbulence of today.

For "big beak," substitute "rape" or "cognitive thinking." At any moment in history rape may have been biologically advantageous and cognitive thinking a disaster (or vice versa). However, this moment is not that. Even if in past ages either practice made a difference to the job of passing on the genes, that fact tells us almost nothing about their value now. We may be—we are—in an El Niño of the soul, a time against the trend, when what was once good is now bad. What once explained human behavior in evolutionary terms simply need not apply to the modern world.

* * *

PART VII
DARWINIAN INFLUENCES
ON PHILOSOPHY
AND ETHICS

Intellectual progress usually occurs through sheer abandonment of
questions. * * * We do not solve them; we get over them.

—John Dewey, 1909

Darwin threw down a challenge to the old rigidities, and his doctrine
of evolution made everything a matter of degree, obliterating the ab-
soluteness of white-and-black, right-and-wrong. * * * It seemed that
everything, instead of being so or not so, as in the logic books, was
only more so or less so. And in this mush of compromise all the old
splendid certainties dissolved.

—Bertrand Russell, 1949

Today we know that we are not entirely the masters of our fate, certainly not the captains of our souls, but neither are we innocent and
passive bystanders. Many factors in nature interact to cause and direct
our evolution, but our understanding of evolution has itself become
one of the factors.

—Conway Zirkle, 1958

THE ANT†

The ant, Darwin reminded us,
defies all simple-mindedness.
Take nothing (says the ant) on faith,
and never trust a simple truth.
The PR men of bestiaries
eulogized for centuries
this busy little paragon,
nature's proletarian—
but look here, Darwin said: some ants
make slaves of smaller ants, and end
exploiting in their peonages
the sweating brows of their tiny drudges.
Thus the ant speaks out of both
sides of its mealy little mouth:
its example is extolled
to the workers of the world,
but its habits also preach
the virtues of the idle rich.

—Philip Appleman, 1984

JOHN DEWEY

The Influence of Darwin on Philosophy (1909)†

I

That the publication of the "Origin of Species" marked an epoch in the development of the natural sciences is well known to the layman. That the combination of the very words origin and species embodied an intellectual revolt and introduced a new intellectual temper is easily overlooked by the expert. The conceptions that had reigned in the philosophy of nature and knowledge for two thousand years, the conceptions that had become the familiar furniture of the mind, rested on the assumption of the superiority of the fixed and final; they rested upon treating change and origin as signs of defect and unreality. In laying hands upon the sacred ark of absolute permanency, in treating the forms that had been regarded as types of fixity and perfection as originating and passing away, the "Origin of Species" introduced a mode of thinking that in the end was bound to transform the logic of knowledge, and hence the treatment of morals, politics, and religion.

No wonder, then, that the publication of Darwin's book, a half century ago, precipitated a crisis. The true nature of the controversy is easily concealed from us, however, by the theological clamor that attended it. The vivid and popular features of the anti-Darwinian row tended to leave the impression that the issue was between science on one side and theology on the other. Such was not the case—the issue lay primarily within science itself, as Darwin himself early recognized. The theological outcry he discounted from the start, hardly noticing it save as it bore upon the "feelings of his female relatives." But for two decades before final publication he contemplated the possibility of being put down by his scientific peers as a fool or as crazy; and he set, as the measure of his success, the degree in which he should affect three men of science: Lyell in geology, Hooker in botany, and Huxley in zoology.

Religious considerations lent fervor to the controversy, but they did not provoke it. Intellectually, religious emotions are not creative but conservative. They attach themselves readily to the current view of the world and consecrate it. They steep and dye intellectual fabrics in the seething vat of emotions; they do not form their warp and woof. There is not, I think, an instance of any large idea about the world being independently generated by religion. Although the ideas that rose up like armed men against Darwinism owed their intensity to religious associations, their origin and meaning are to be sought in science and philosophy, not in religion.

† Originally a lecture given at Columbia University in 1909. John Dewey (1859–1952), noted American philosopher, included this essay in his *The Influence of Darwin on Philosophy and Other Essays in Contemporary Thought* (New York, 1910).

II

Few words in our language foreshorten intellectual history as much as does the word species. The Greeks, in initiating the intellectual life of Europe, were impressed by characteristic traits of the life of plants and animals; so impressed indeed that they made these traits the key to defining nature and to explaining mind and society. And truly, life is so wonderful that a seemingly successful reading of its mystery might well lead men to believe that the key to the secrets of heaven and earth was in their hands. The Greek rendering of this mystery, the Greek formulation of the aim and standard of knowledge, was in the course of time embodied in the word species, and it controlled philosophy for two thousand years. To understand the intellectual face-about expressed in the phrase "Origin of Species," we must, then, understand the long dominant idea against which it is a protest.

Consider how men were impressed by the facts of life. Their eyes fell upon certain things slight in bulk, and frail in structure. To every appearance, these perceived things were inert and passive. Suddenly, under certain circumstances, these things—henceforth known as seeds or eggs or germs—begin to change, to change rapidly in size, form, and qualities. Rapid and extensive changes occur, however, in many things—as when wood is touched by fire. But the changes in the living thing are orderly; they are cumulative; they tend constantly in one direction; they do not, like other changes, destroy or consume, or pass fruitless into wandering flux; they realize and fulfil. Each successive stage, no matter how unlike its predecessor, preserves its net effect and also prepares the way for a fuller activity on the part of its successor. In living beings, changes do not happen as they seem to happen elsewhere, any which way; the earlier changes are regulated in view of later results. This progressive organization does not cease till there is achieved a true final term, a τελὸs, a completed, perfected end. This final form exercises in turn a plenitude of functions, not the least noteworthy of which is production of germs like those from which it took its own origin, germs capable of the same cycle of self-fulfilling activity.

But the whole miraculous tale is not yet told. The same drama is enacted to the same destiny in countless myriads of individuals so sundered in time, so severed in space, that they have no opportunity for mutual consultation and no means of interaction. As an old writer quaintly said, "things of the same kind go through the same formalities"—celebrate, as it were, the same ceremonial rites.

This formal activity which operates throughout a series of changes and holds them to a single course; which subordinates their aimless flux to its own perfect manifestation; which, leaping the boundaries of space and time, keeps individuals distant in space and remote in time to a uniform type of structure and function: this principle seemed to give insight into the very nature of reality itself. To it Aristotle gave the name, εῖδος. This term the scholastics translated as *species*.

The force of this term was deepened by its application to everything in the universe that observes order in flux and manifests constancy through change. From the casual drift of daily weather, through the uneven recurrence of seasons and unequal return of seed time and harvest, up to the majestic sweep of the heavens—the image of eternity in time—and from this to the unchanging pure and contemplative intelligence beyond nature lies one unbroken fulfillment of ends. Nature as a whole is a progressive realization of purpose strictly comparable to the realization of purpose in any single plant or animal.

The conception of εἶδος, species, a fixed form and final cause, was the central principle of knowledge as well as of nature. Upon it rested the logic of science. Change as change is mere flux and lapse; it insults intelligence. Genuinely to know is to grasp a permanent end that realizes itself through changes, holding them thereby within the metes and bounds of fixed truth. Completely to know is to relate all special forms to their one single end and good: pure contemplative intelligence. Since, however, the scene of nature which directly confronts us is in change, nature as directly and practically experienced does not satisfy the conditions of knowledge. Human experience is in flux, and hence the instrumentalities of sense-perception and of inference based upon observation are condemned in advance. Science is compelled to aim at realities lying behind and beyond the processes of nature, and to carry on its search for these realities by means of rational forms transcending ordinary modes of perception and inference.

There are, indeed, but two alternative courses. We must either find the appropriate objects and organs of knowledge in the mutual interactions of changing things; or else, to escape the infection of change, we *must* seek them in some transcendent and supernal region. The human mind, deliberately as it were, exhausted the logic of the changeless, the final, and the transcendent, before it essayed adventure on the pathless wastes of generation and transformation. We dispose all too easily of the efforts of the schoolmen to interpret nature and mind in terms of real essences, hidden forms, and occult faculties, forgetful of the seriousness and dignity of the ideas that lay behind. We dispose of them by laughing at the famous gentleman who accounted for the fact that opium put people to sleep on the ground it had a dormitive faculty. But the doctrine, held in our own day, that knowledge of the plant that yields the poppy consists in referring the peculiarities of an individual to a type, to a universal form, a doctrine so firmly established that any other method of knowing was conceived to be unphilosophical and unscientific, is a survival of precisely the same logic. This identity of conception in the scholastic and anti-Darwinian theory may well suggest greater sympathy for what has become unfamiliar as well as greater humility regarding the further unfamiliarities that history has in store.

Darwin was not, of course, the first to question the classic philosophy of nature and of knowledge. The beginnings of the revolution are in the physical science of the sixteenth and seventeenth centuries. When Galileo said: "It is my opinion that the earth is very noble and admirable by reason of so many and so different alterations and generations which are incessantly made therein," he expressed the changed temper that was coming over the world; the transfer of interest from the permanent to the changing.

When Descartes said: "The nature of physical things is much more easily conceived when they are beheld coming gradually into existence, than when they are only considered as produced at once in a finished and perfect state," the modern world became self-conscious of the logic that was henceforth to control it, the logic of which Darwin's "Origin of Species" is the latest scientific achievement. Without the methods of Copernicus, Kepler, Galileo, and their successors in astronomy, physics, and chemistry, Darwin would have been helpless in the organic sciences. But prior to Darwin the impact of the new scientific method upon life, mind, and politics, had been arrested, because between these ideal or moral interests and the inorganic world intervened the kingdom of plants and animals. The gates of the garden of life were barred to the new ideas; and only through this garden was there access to mind and politics. The influence of Darwin upon philosophy resides in his having conquered the phenomena of life for the principle of transition, and thereby freed the new logic for application to mind and morals and life. When he said of species what Galileo had said of the earth, *e pur se muove*, he emancipated, once for all, genetic and experimental ideas as an organon of asking questions and looking for explanations.

III

The exact bearings upon philosophy of the new logical outlook are, of course, as yet, uncertain and inchoate. We live in the twilight of intellectual transition. One must add the rashness of the prophet to the stubbornness of the partizan to venture a systematic exposition of the influence upon philosophy of the Darwinian method. At best, we can but inquire as to its general bearing—the effect upon mental temper and complexion, upon that body of half-conscious, half-instinctive intellectual aversions and preferences which determine, after all, our more deliberate intellectual enterprises. In this vague inquiry there happens to exist as a kind of touchstone a problem of long historic currency that has also been much discussed in Darwinian literature. I refer to the old problem of design *versus* chance, mind *versus* matter, as the causal explanation, first or final, of things.

As we have already seen, the classic notion of species carried with it the idea of purpose. In all living forms, a specific type is present directing the earlier stages of growth to the realization of its own perfection. Since this purposive regulative principle is not visible to the senses, it follows that it must be an ideal or rational force. Since, however, the perfect form is gradually approximated through the sensible changes, it also follows that in and through a sensible realm a rational ideal force is working out its own ultimate manifestation. These inferences were extended to nature: (*a*) She does nothing in vain; but all for an ulterior purpose. (*b*) Within natural sensible events there is therefore contained a spiritual causal force, which as spiritual escapes perception, but is apprehended by an enlightened reason. (*c*) The manifestation of this principle brings about a subordination of matter and sense to its own realization, and this ultimate fulfillment is the goal of nature and of man. The design argument thus operated in two directions. Purposefulness accounted for the intelligibility of nature and the possibility of science, while the absolute or cosmic character of this purposefulness gave sanction and worth to the moral and religious endeavors of man. Science was underpinned and morals authorized by one and the same principle, and their mutual agreement was eternally guaranteed.

This philosophy remained, in spite of sceptical and polemic outbursts, the official and the regnant philosophy of Europe for over two thousand years. The expulsion of fixed first and final causes from astronomy, physics, and chemistry had indeed given the doctrine something of a shock. But, on the other hand, increased acquaintance with the details of plant and animal life operated as a counterbalance and perhaps even strengthened the argument from design. The marvelous adaptations of organisms to their environment, of organs to the organism, of unlike parts of a complex organ—like the eye—to the organ itself; the foreshadowing by lower forms of the higher; the preparation in earlier stages of growth for organs that only later had their functioning—these things were increasingly recognized with the progress of botany, zoology, paleontology, and embryology. Together, they added such prestige to the design argument that by the late eighteenth century it was, as approved by the sciences of organic life, the central point of theistic and idealistic philosophy.

The Darwinian principle of natural selection cut straight under this philosophy. If all organic adaptations are due simply to constant variation and the elimination of those variations which are harmful in the struggle for existence that is brought about by excessive reproduction, there is no call for a prior intelligent causal force to plan and preordain them. Hostile critics charged Darwin with materialism and with making chance the cause of the universe.

Some naturalists, like Asa Gray, favored the Darwinian principle and attempted to reconcile it with design. Gray held to what may be called design on the installment plan. If we conceive the "stream of variations" to be itself intended, we may suppose that each successive variation was designed from the first to be selected. In that case, variation, struggle, and selection simply define the mechanism of "secondary causes" through which the "first cause" acts; and the doctrine of design is none the worse off because we know more of its *modus operandi*.

Darwin could not accept this mediating proposal. He admits or rather he asserts that it is "impossible to conceive this immense and wonderful universe including man with his capacity of looking far backwards and far into futurity as the result of blind chance or necessity."[1] But nevertheless he holds that since variations are in useless as well as useful directions, and since the latter are sifted out simply by the stress of the conditions of struggle for existence, the design argument as applied to living beings is unjustifiable; and its lack of support there deprives it of scientific value as applied to nature in general. If the variations of the pigeon, which under

1. "Life and Letters," Vol. I., p. 282; cf. 285.

artificial selection give the pouter pigeon, are not preordained for the sake of the breeder, by what logic do we argue that variations resulting in natural species are pre-designed?[2]

IV

So much for some of the more obvious facts of the discussion of design *versus* chance, as causal principles of nature and of life as a whole. We brought up this discussion, you recall, as a crucial instance. What does our touchstone indicate as to the bearing of Darwinian ideas upon philosophy? In the first place, the new logic outlaws, flanks, dismisses—what you will—one type of problems and substitutes for it another type. Philosophy forswears inquiry after absolute origins and absolute finalities in order to explore specific values and the specific conditions that generate them.

Darwin concluded that the impossibility of assigning the world to chance as a whole and to design in its parts indicated the insolubility of the question. Two radically different reasons, however, may be given as to why a problem is insoluble. One reason is that the problem is too high for intelligence; the other is that the question in its very asking makes assumptions that render the question meaningless. The latter alternative is unerringly pointed to in the celebrated case of design *versus* chance. Once admit that the sole verifiable or fruitful object of knowledge is the particular set of changes that generate the object of study together with the consequences that then flow from it, and no intelligible question can be asked about what, by assumption, lies outside. To assert—as is often asserted—that specific values of particular truth, social bonds and forms of beauty, if they can be shown to be generated by concretely knowable conditions, are meaningless and in vain; to assert that they are justified only when they and their particular causes and effects have all at once been gathered up into some inclusive first cause and some exhaustive final goal, is intellectual atavism.

*   *   *

In anticipating the direction of the transformations in philosophy to be wrought by the Darwinian genetic and experimental logic, I do not profess to speak for any save those who yield themselves consciously or unconsciously to this logic. No one can fairly deny that at present there are two effects of the Darwinian mode of thinking. On the one hand, there are many sincere and vital efforts to revise our traditional philosophic conceptions in accordance with its demands. On the other hand, there is as definitely a recrudescence of absolutistic philosophies; an assertion of a type of philosophic knowing distinct from that of the sciences, one which opens to us another kind of reality from that to which the sciences give access; an appeal through experience to something that essentially goes beyond experience. This reaction affects popular creeds and religious

---

2. "Life and Letters," Vol. II, pp. 146, 170, 245; Vol. I., pp. 283–84. See also the closing portion of his "Variations of Animals and Plants under Domestication."

movements as well as technical philosophies. The very conquest of the biological sciences by the new ideas has led many to proclaim an explicit and rigid separation of philosophy from science.

Old ideas give way slowly; for they are more than abstract logical forms and categories. They are habits, predispositions, deeply engrained attitudes of aversion and preference. Moreover, the conviction persists—though history shows it to be a hallucination—that all the questions that the human mind has asked are questions that can be answered in terms of the alternatives that the questions themselves present. But in fact intellectual progress usually occurs through sheer abandonment of questions together with both of the alternatives they assume—an abandonment that results from their decreasing vitality and a change of urgent interest. We do not solve them: we get over them. Old questions are solved by disappearing, evaporating, while new questions corresponding to the changed attitude of endeavor and preference take their place. Doubtless the greatest dissolvent in contemporary thought of old questions, the greatest precipitant of new methods, new intentions, new problems, is the one effected by the scientific revolution that found its climax in the "Origin of Species."

DANIEL C. DENNETT

Darwin's Dangerous Idea: Natural Selection as an Algorithmic Process (1995)†

What limit can be put to this power, acting during long ages and rigidly scrutinising the whole constitution, structure, and habits of each creature,—favouring the good and rejecting the bad? I can see no limit to this power, in slowly and beautifully adapting each form to the most complex relations of life.

—CHARLES DARWIN, *The Origin of Species*

[Darwin] presents his principle as deducible by a formal argument—*if* the conditions are met, a certain outcome is *assured*.[1] Here is the summary again, with some key terms in boldface.

If, during the long course of ages and under varying conditions of life, organic beings vary at all in the several parts of their organization, and I think this cannot be disputed; if there be, owing to the high geometric powers of increase of each species, at some age, season, or

† From chapter 2 of *Darwin's Dangerous Idea: Evolution and the Meanings of Life* (New York, 1995). Reprinted with the permission of Simon & Schuster, Inc. Copyright © 1995 by Daniel C. Dennett. Daniel C. Dennett (b. 1942) is Distinguished Arts and Sciences Professor of Philosophy and director of the Center for Cognitive Studies at Tufts University.

1. The ideal of a deductive (or "nomologico-deductive") science, modeled on Newtonian or Galilean physics, was quite standard until fairly recently in the philosophy of science, so it is not surprising that much effort has been devoted to devising and criticizing various axiomatizations of Darwin's theory—since it was presumed that in such a formalization lay scientific vindication. The idea, introduced in this section, that Darwin should be seen, rather, as postulating that evolution is an algorithmic process, permits us to do justice to the undeniable *a priori* flavor of Darwin's thinking without forcing it into the Procrustean (and obsolete) bed of the nomologico-deductive model.

year, a severe struggle for life, and this certainly cannot be disputed; **then**, considering the infinite complexity of the relations of all organic beings to each other and to their conditions of existence, causing an infinite diversity in structure, constitution, and habits, to be advantageous to them, **I think it would be a most extraordinary fact if no variation ever had occurred useful to each being's own welfare**, in the same way as so many variations have occurred useful to man. But **if** variations useful to any organic being do occur, **assuredly** individuals thus characterized will have the best chance of being preserved in the struggle for life; and from the strong principle of inheritance they will tend to produce offspring similarly characterized. This principle of preservation, I have called, for the sake of brevity, Natural Selection. [*Origin*, p. 127 (facs. ed. of 1st ed.).]

The basic deductive argument is short and sweet, but Darwin himself described *Origin of Species* as "one long argument." That is because it consists of two sorts of demonstrations: the logical demonstration that a certain *sort* of process would necessarily have a certain sort of outcome, and the empirical demonstration that the requisite conditions for that sort of process had in fact been met in nature. He bolsters up his logical demonstration with thought experiments—"imaginary instances" (*Origin*, p. 95)—that show *how* the meeting of these conditions *might* actually account for the effects he claimed to be explaining, but his whole argument extends to book length because he presents a wealth of hard-won empirical detail to convince the reader that these conditions have been met over and over again.

*   *   *

The theoretical power of Darwin's abstract scheme was due to several features that Darwin quite firmly identified, and appreciated better than many of his supporters, but lacked the terminology to describe explicitly. Today we could capture these features under a single term. Darwin had discovered the power of an *algorithm*. An algorithm is a certain sort of formal process that can be counted on—logically—to yield a certain sort of result whenever it is "run" or instantiated. Algorithms are not new, and were not new in Darwin's day. Many familiar arithmetic procedures, such as long division or balancing your checkbook, are algorithms, and so are the decision procedures for playing perfect tic-tac-toe, and for putting a list of words into alphabetical order. What is relatively new—permitting us valuable hindsight on Darwin's discovery—is the theoretical reflection by mathematicians and logicians on the nature and power of algorithms in general, a twentieth-century development which led to the birth of the computer, which has led in turn, of course, to a much deeper and more lively understanding of the powers of algorithms in general.

The term *algorithm* descends, via Latin (*algorismus*) to early English (*algorisme* and, mistakenly therefrom, *algorithm*), from the name of a Persian mathematician, Mûusâ al-Khowârizm, whose book on arithmetical procedures, written about 835 A.D., was translated into Latin in the twelfth century by Adelard of Bath or Robert of Chester. The idea that an algorithm is a foolproof and somehow "mechanical" procedure has been present for centuries, but it was the pioneering work of Alan Turing, Kurt Gödel, and Alonzo Church in the 1930s that more or less fixed our current understanding of the term. Three key features of algorithms will be important to us, and each is somewhat difficult to define. Each, moreover, has given rise to confusions (and anxieties) that continue to beset our thinking about Darwin's revolutionary discovery, so we will have to revisit and reconsider these introductory characterizations several times before we are through:

1. *substrate neutrality:* The procedure for long division works equally well with pencil or pen, paper or parchment, neon lights or skywriting, using any symbol system you like. The power of the procedure is due to its *logical* structure, not the causal powers of the materials used in the instantiation, just so long as those causal powers permit the prescribed steps to be followed exactly.

2. *underlying mindlessness:* Although the overall design of the procedure may be brilliant, or yield brilliant results, each constituent step, as well as the transition between steps, is utterly simple. How simple? Simple enough for a dutiful idiot to perform—or for a straightforward mechanical device to perform. The standard textbook analogy notes that algorithms are *recipes* of sorts, designed to be followed by *novice* cooks. A recipe book written for great chefs might include the phrase "Poach the fish in a suitable wine until almost done," but an algorithm for the same process might begin, "Choose a white wine that says 'dry' on the label; take a corkscrew and open the bottle; pour an inch of wine in the bottom of a pan; turn the burner under the pan on high; . . ."—a tedious breakdown of the process into dead-simple steps, requiring no wise decisions or delicate judgments or intuitions on the part of the recipe-reader.

3. *guaranteed results:* Whatever it is that an algorithm does, it always does it, if it is executed without misstep. An algorithm is a foolproof recipe.

It is easy to see how these features made the computer possible. *Every computer program is an algorithm,* ultimately composed of simple steps that can be executed with stupendous reliability by one simple mechanism or another. Electronic circuits are the usual choice, but the power of computers owes nothing (save speed) to the causal peculiarities of electrons darting about on silicon chips. The very same algorithms can be performed (even faster) by devices shunting photons in glass fibers, or (much, much slower) by teams of people using paper and pencil. And as we shall see, the capacity of computers to run algorithms with tremendous speed and reliability is now permitting theoreticians to explore Darwin's dangerous idea in ways heretofore impossible, with fascinating results.

✳ ✳ ✳

Algorithms don't have to have points or purposes. In addition to all the useful algorithms for alphabetizing lists of words, there are kazillions of algorithms for reliably *mis*alphabetizing words, and they work perfectly every time (as if anyone would care). Just as there is an algorithm (many, actually) for finding the square root of any number, so there are algorithms for finding the square root of any number except 18 or 703. Some algorithms do things so boringly irregular and pointless that there is no succinct way of saying what they are *for*. They just do what they do, and they do it every time.

We can now expose perhaps the most common misunderstanding of Darwinism: the idea that Darwin showed that evolution by natural selection is a procedure *for* producing Us. Ever since Darwin proposed his theory, people have often misguidedly tried to interpret it as showing that we are the destination, the goal, the point of all that winnowing and competition. * * * This confusion has been fostered by evolution's friends and foes alike, and it is parallel to the confusion of the coin-toss tournament winner who basks in the misconsidered glory of the idea that since the tournament had to have a winner, and since he is the winner, the tournament had to produce him as the winner. Evolution can be an algorithm, and evolution can have produced us by an algorithmic process, without its being true that evolution is an algorithm for producing us. The main conclusion of Stephen Jay Gould's *Wonderful Life: The Burgess Shale and the Nature of History* (1989) is that if we were to "wind the tape of life back" and play it again and again, the likelihood is infinitesimal of Us being the product on any other run through the evolutionary mill. This is undoubtedly true (if by "Us" we mean the particular variety of *Homo sapiens* we are: hairless and upright, with five fingers on each of two hands, speaking English and French and playing tennis and chess). Evolution is not a process that was designed to produce us, but it does not follow from this that evolution is not an algorithmic process that has in fact produced us.

Evolutionary algorithms are manifestly interesting algorithms—interesting to us, at least—not because what they are guaranteed to do is interesting to us, but because what they are guaranteed to *tend* to do is interesting to us. They are like tournaments of skill in this regard. The power of an algorithm to yield something of interest or value is not at all limited to what the algorithm can be mathematically proven to yield in a foolproof way, and this is especially true of evolutionary algorithms. Most of the controversies about Darwinism, as we shall see, boil down to disagreements about just how powerful certain postulated evolutionary processes are—could they actually do all this or all that in the time available? These are typically investigations into what an evolutionary algorithm *might* produce, or *could* produce, or is *likely* to produce, and only indirectly into what such an algorithm would *inevitably* produce. Darwin himself sets the stage in the wording of his summary: his idea is a claim about what "assuredly" the process of natural selection will "tend" to yield.

* * *

Here, then, is Darwin's dangerous idea: the algorithmic level *is* the level that best accounts for the speed of the antelope, the wing of the eagle, the shape of the orchid, the diversity of species, and all the other occasions for wonder in the world of nature. It is hard to believe that something as mindless and mechanical as an algorithm could produce such wonderful things. No matter how impressive the products of an algorithm, the underlying process always consists of nothing but a set of individually mindless steps succeeding each other without the help of any intelligent supervision; they are "automatic" by definition: the workings of an automaton. They feed on each other, or on blind chance—coin flips, if you like—and on nothing else. Most algorithms we are familiar with have rather modest products: they do long division or alphabetize lists or figure out the income of the Average Taxpayer. Fancier algorithms produce the dazzling computer-animated graphics we see every day on television, transforming faces, creating herds of imaginary ice-skating polar bears, simulating whole virtual worlds of entities never seen or imagined before. But the actual biosphere is much fancier still, by many orders of magnitude. Can it really be the outcome of nothing but a cascade of algorithmic processes feeding on chance? And if so, who designed that cascade? Nobody. It is itself the product of a blind, algorithmic process. As Darwin himself put it, in a letter to the geologist Charles Lyell shortly after publication of *Origin*, "I would give absolutely nothing for the theory of Natural Selection, if it requires miraculous additions at any one stage of descent. . . . If I were convinced that I required such additions to the theory of natural selection, I would reject it as rubbish . . ."

According to Darwin, then, evolution is an algorithmic process. Putting it this way is still controversial. One of the tugs-of-war going on within evolutionary biology is between those who are relentlessly pushing, pushing, pushing towards an algorithmic treatment, and those who, for various submerged reasons, are resisting this trend. It is rather as if there were metallurgists around who were disappointed by the algorithmic explanation of annealing. "You mean that's all there is to it? No submicroscopic Superglue specially created by the heating and cooling process?" Darwin has convinced all the scientists that evolution, like annealing, *works*. His radical vision of *how* and *why* it works is still somewhat embattled, largely because those who resist can dimly see that their skirmish is part of a larger campaign. If the game is lost in evolutionary biology, where will it all end?

MICHAEL RUSE

Darwinian Epistemology (1998)†

The Darwinian theory of evolution through natural selection, taken literally, throws important light on the status of knowledge. By this I mean that it can advance us in the kinds of concerns about knowledge that have traditionally absorbed philosophers. I take scientific knowledge as my par-

---

† From *Taking Darwin Seriously* (Amherst, N.Y.: Prometheus Books, 1998). Copyright 1998. Reprinted by permission of the publisher. Michael Ruse (b. 1940) is professor of philosophy and zoology at the University of Guelph.

adigm; but I expect my conclusions to have consequences for knowledge of all kinds.

*   *   *

The Nature of Science

The chief distinguishing mark of science is the attempt to understand through *law*, that is through unbroken empirical regularity. Science shows that things fall into place, because of laws. Thus, building on the work of Kepler and Galileo, Newton persuaded us that the motions of moving bodies follow certain fixed rules—things do not fly about randomly, without rhyme or reason. Furthermore, he showed that things down here on Earth follow laws—the same laws—as do the heavenly bodies. Analogically, Darwin's great achievement was to show that organisms are no less subject to law than is the inanimate world, and that the consequence of such laws is evolution.

It is important to note that the laws of science are not just happenstance contingencies. It is thought that the regularities *must* hold. It is not purely chance that any two bodies are attracting with a force inversely proportional to the square of the distance between them. Because of Newton's law of gravity, this is something which had to be. Thus laws support counter-factuals—'I know that the pressure on this gas isn't 2 lb. per square inch, because if it were its volume would be 5 cubic feet.' More on this 'nomic' necessity in a moment.

In all of the emphasis on law, we have the starkest contrast with non-science. Creationists openly appeal to events outside of law, that is to say to miracles. The first appearance of matter itself, the arrival of man, the start of Noah's flood—all of these things supposedly stand without and beyond law.

> The simple fact of the matter is that one cannot have *any* kind of a Genesis Flood without acknowledging the presence of supernatural elements . . .
>
> That God intervened in a supernatural way to gather the animals into the Ark and to keep them under control during the year of the Flood is explicitly stated in the text of Scripture. Furthermore, it is obvious that the opening of the 'windows of heaven' in order to allow 'the waters which were above the firmament' to fall upon the earth, and the breaking up of 'all the fountains of the great deep' were supernatural acts of God.[1]

This may be good theology. (As it happens, I do not think it is.) It is certainly not science.

Laws do not exist in splendid isolation. Science aims to bind them together, into theories. There is much debate about the nature of this binding, but generally (and to a first approximation) it involves showing that some laws follow deductively from other laws. Kepler's laws of plan-

---

1. J. C. Whitcomb and H. M. Morris, *The Genesis Flood* (Philadelphia, 1961): 76.

etary motion and Galileo's laws of terrestrial motion follow from Newton's three fundamental laws of motion, together with his law of gravitational attraction. Arguably, the ultimate ideal is a full-blooded axiom system, with everything following rigorously from just a few premises. But, obviously, most scientists most of the time (i.e. in their everyday work) are not aiming for massive overarching theories, deducing one fundamental law from another, producing systems readily applicable wherever and whenever. Rather, against a known background, scientists specify certain peculiar conditions, which they feel (or hope) obtain at certain times and places, and then try to build limited law-networks around them. Often these 'models' include simplications of reality, in order to avoid unmanageable complexity. You get many examples of models in population genetics.

How are theories or models brought into contact with empirical reality? Through prediction, explanation, and testing. You use science to try to predict and explain particular phenomena, like the motions of individual planets, or the peculiar distribution of a certain set of organisms, or the presence of volcanoes in one part of the earth and not another. This involves showing how the phenomena under study follow from your science. They are proven to be consequences of the laws of your theory or models. In other words, from the science you aim to infer specified empirical phenomena. At least, you aim usually to make such inferences from the science as seen in conjunction with other specified empirical phenomena, so-called 'initial conditions'.

The difference between explanation and prediction is essentially formal.[2] In explanation, you probably know full well just what you are inferring. In fact, that being explained is often the stimulus for the whole enquiry. In prediction, you are going on to infer new things. In common talk, 'prediction' usually means inference of expected future phenomena. Scientific usage is somewhat broader—from the known to the unknown. A palaeontologist might predict that a newly-discovered fossil should have certain as yet undescribed features.

These inferences all give us a way of checking our ideas, and of correcting as needed. If our science leads us to predict conclusions which simply are not true, then there must be something wrong with the science. It needs scrapping or at least revising. This process of testing scientific ideas against the evidence is at the heart of Karl Popper's well-known criterion of demarcation between science and non-science. According to Popper and his school, a genuinely scientific theory must expose itself to the real world. It must be *falsifiable*. But, although this property is obviously fundamental to the essence of science, it is clear that there is more to what we usually think of as *good* science. Amongst other things, in good science you look for a certain elegance or simplicity. In other words, good science cuts through the surface complexities of the world, showing that all can be explained by a few powerful laws.

And closely connected to this (indeed, some have argued, the other side of the same coin), the best science tries to bind together different areas of

---

2. I must emphasize that I am only giving a rough characterization of science—a *very* rough characterization, my fellow philosophers of science would say.

investigation into one unified whole. It shows how the same idea can explain different things, and conversely how the different things point to the genuineness of the thing explaining. Newton's genius was to subsume so much—the world of our earthly experience and the mysterious domain of the heavenly bodies—beneath but a few powerful laws. As we have seen, this mark of good science, what the Victorian man of science William Whewell (1840) called a 'consilience of inductions', was also at the heart of Darwinian evolutionary theory. And, as we have also seen, this was not fortuitous. Darwin modelled his thinking on Whewell's vision of Newtonian mechanics. Today, the selfsame criterion of excellence continues to function powerfully. Plate tectonics is a contemporary theory which succeeds because, beyond all else, it is consilient.

Whewell argued that what lies at the centre of a consilience is a *vera causa*, or true cause. This is the power or force or some such thing which makes other things (effects) occur. Given the cause, then the effect simply must follow. * * *

Talk of causation leads straight to a related aspect of science. Observation of any kind, even the crudest, tends to occur in the context of various ideas or thoughts or enquiries, of one sort or another. Nevertheless, much of the content of science refers to the world of relatively raw experience, the world of sensation. It is about colours and shapes and sounds, about prisms and pendulums and plants. However, as science develops and produces more and more subtle theories, as you go up through the framework which the scientist has created, to the highest-level claims—finally, unto the very premises themselves—the talk tends to become increasingly abstract, theoretical, divorced from immediate experience. One hears mention of forces, and electrons, and genes, and the like. Often, indeed, one is dealing with microentities, invisible to the unaided human eye—things which are never (nor very soon likely to be) experienced.

I doubt that anyone today would claim that there is an absolute sharp distinction in science between reference to observables and unobservables (or however else you label them); but there does seem to be a difference nevertheless. Picking up on what was said just previously about causes, there is an obvious conclusion which many draw, namely that real causal understanding necessarily requires reference to the unseen ultimates, occurring in the highest level of science. For instance, to understand what is going on in chemistry, say when you mix an acid and an alkali and get a salt, you simply have to know about the underlying protons and electrons and so forth.

* * *

Taking the common-sense approach (which will be scrutinized before the chapter is over), I assume here that science presupposes and justifies a fairly robust sense of reality. If something is at the focus of a consilience, say a sub-atomic particle, it really is strained to pretend that we might not be talking about anything at all, or that our talk says nothing about the true nature of that about which we talk. After all, to recall a favourite analogy of mine, we use consiliences constantly in courts of law, when we convict on circumstantial evidence. Does anyone truly believe that we always hang people for fictions? In short, progress in science consists in ever increasing knowledge of what the world is really like. The only people who seem to have genuine doubts about this are those impressed by modern physics, and by its assertions about such funny entities as electrons, which (apparently) have contradictory properties. I shall speak later to these concerns.

As a corollary to the common-sense approach just endorsed, I would argue that even though we believe the key unseen entities of science to be truly real, this is no good reason to claim that the world of phenomena is totally unreal. After all, granting the solidity of the marbles in the bag is not to downgrade the reality of the bag, or of the bag-of-marbles taken as a whole. Thanks to science, we have different ways of looking at things. Of course, this is not to deny that, at the phenomenal level, claims are more prone to the vagaries of individual perception.

* * *

Scientific Reasoning

Our enquiry is about the true nature and status of science. * * * Whatever else science may be, it is a human product. It may be the aim of the scientist to mirror reality—an aim which may or may not be realizable—but the science itself is a product of human intentions and powers and thought processes. The science results from human reasoning ability. The ways in which we think and argue and infer are those things which constrain and mould the product. This is so whether you think that reason is some peculiarly human phenomenon, or something ultimately with a distinctively extra-human status and validity.

In other words, in order to understand why science is as it is—why laws, why predictions, why falsifiability, why consiliences—we need to look at the principles of scientific reasoning or methodology. And as I am sure you now realize, what I argue is that these principles have their being and only justification in their Darwinian value, that is in their adaptive worth to us humans—or, at least, to our proto-human ancestors. In short, I argue that the principles which guide and mould science are rooted in our biology, as mediated by our epigenetic rules.

* * *

Taking our cue, therefore, from the work of others, it is generally agreed that science is the product of roughly two kinds of reasoning: deductive and inductive. Beginning with deduction, we find the scientist constrained and guided by inference of a formal kind, where conclusions follow necessarily from premises. An important branch of such formal reasoning is (deductive) *logic*, where the scientist is bound, or (if you like) *qua* scientist agrees to be bound, by certain basic logical principles, together with fixed laws or rules of inference.

* * *

Logic alone is not enough for the scientist. His/her concern is with the world around us. The very essence of a scientific system is to bind together empirical claims about this world. But, logic constrains and informs the scientist's work. Logic sets up boundary conditions within which the scientist must work. He/she cannot afford to be illogical. Thus, for instance, the law of non-contradiction is crucially important. You must not permit contradictory claims within your system.

* * *

Logic is vitally important to the scientist. Its only rival in this respect is *mathematics*. Arithmetic, algebra, geometry, calculus, and much more— all are absolutely crucial to science, particularly the well-articulated, sophisticated parts of modern science. You need the premises of mathematics, and you need the inferences of mathematics. One is tempted, indeed, to say that progress is a direct function of mathematization. Certainly, the two go hand in hand. We see this very clearly in the development of evolutionary theory itself. Darwin used little mathematics, although that which he did use was crucial. (The struggle for existence follows from the Malthusian fact that food supplies have a potential arithmetic rate of increase, and population numbers have a potential geometric rate of increase, and the latter is greater than the former.) Today, population genetics—the very heart of the modern evolutionary enterprise—relies very heavily on algebra, calculus, statistics, and other tools of the mathematician's kit-bag. There can be no doubt that, without such a form of reasoning, little could be done in science.

Moving now from the more formal aspects of science to its more empirical side, it is here that we encounter the results of what we might think of as inductive argumentation in its broadest sense. One important kind of inductive argument is *analogy*, where we compare two similar (although different) things, trying to draw conclusions about one on the basis of the other. * * *

Even more crucial than analogy is the mode of thought whereby we pick up particular instances and mould them together into general statements—statements which we do not just think happen to be true, but rather which in some important sense have to be true. I refer, of course, to the scientist's penchant for binding his/her particulars into *laws*, the very key to the scientific enterprise. * * *

This, as we have seen, is all very much bound up with our tendency to think in terms of *causes*—indeed, perhaps (as noted) all laws are themselves causal laws, or the consequences of causal laws. The scientist believes that things do not just follow on from each other in a random fashion, but are connected because some things—causes—make other things—effects— occur. * * *

Laws and causal thinking are at the heart of science. But we know now that, at the non-formal level, there is more to scientific methodology. Most importantly, questions of *simplicity* or elegance govern the work of the scientist. * * *

And also, bound up with causality and with simplicity, we have the urge towards *consilience*. Scientists aim to gather their ideas beneath one or two sweeping, all-powerful hypotheses. When they can do this, they feel happy. And when they can do this between widely disparate areas, perhaps even using the new theory to push into new and surprising areas—making predictions which might have been thought false, but which prove to be true—they feel satisfied that they have captured some important facet of reality.

*   *   *

The Case for a Biological Backing

As a philosopher, I am pushing biology out from its established boundaries, trying to understand the nature of knowledge. I argue that the methodology presented in the last section, leading to the science sketched in the first section, is produced by Darwinian-selected epigenetic rules. There are rules for approval of *modus ponens* and consiliences, no less than there is a rule setting up incest barriers. This is the hypothesis.

Nevertheless, despite all the talk of incompleteness, you are surely entitled to a little more than a flat assertion that the principles of scientific reason have their being in human Darwinian needs, that their foundation is no more (and no less) than a bed of epigenetic rules. Supposing now that you accept the description of scientific methodology just given, why should you go on to take the crucial step which I urge? Why should you accept that *modus ponens* and the drive to consilience are produced by epigenetic rules? The following points are pertinent.

First, we are not now operating in a vacuum. We know a great deal about humans, which can properly be regarded as relevant background. In particular, we know from the discussion of the last chapter that humans are the product of evolution through natural selection, and that this mechanism reaches right up into the distinctively human area of culture.

*   *   *

We may now reasonably presume that Darwinian advantage reaches through science like bones through a vertebrate. And this, despite the other concession, that ultimately in its highest reaches, science pushes to the limits of culture where direct adaptive advantage sits lightly.

Second, following straight on the first point, the requirements of methodology given above certainly presuppose highly plausible candidates for full epigenetic-rule status. They demand just the sorts of directives one would expect to find valuable in the ongoing struggle for survival and reproduction. Consider two would-be human ancestors, one with elementary logical and mathematical skills, and the other without very much in that direction. One can think of countless situations, many of which must have happened in real life, where the former proto-human would have been at great selective advantage over the other. A tiger is seen entering a cave that you and your family usually use for sleeping. No one has seen the tiger emerge. Should you seek alternative accommodation for this night at least? How else does one achieve a happy end to this story, other than by an application of those laws of logic that we try to uncover for our students in elementary logic classes?

Analogously for mathematics. Two tigers were seen going into the cave. Only one came out. Is the cave now safe? Again: you have to travel across a plain to get to your hunting grounds. You can only walk a limited distance in this heat. Should you set off now? Should you wait until tomorrow? Should you plan to camp out for the night? And so forth. The proto-human who had an innate disposition to take seriously the law of excluded middle, and who avoided contradictions, survived and reproduced better than he/she who did not. The proto-human who innately preferred '2 + 2 = 4' to '2 + 2 = 5' was at a selective advantage over his/ her less discriminating cousin.

* * *

Incidentally, here we surely have the answer to certain inane paradoxes which have much absorbed post-war philosophers of science. Formally, on known evidence, you cannot decide between the statements, 'All emeralds are green' and 'All emeralds are grue', where 'grue' is defined as 'green before time t and blue after time t', and t is some point in the future. Any emerald studied confirms its grueness, no less than its greenness. Obviously, the caveman who filled his head with grue-type predicates rather heroically sacrificed the needs of day-to-day life for the joys of philosophical discourse. By the time he had puzzled out that what stands before him is a 'tigamb', namely a 'tiger before time t and a lamb after time t', and that t is not yet in the past, he would have been eaten.

* * *

Finally, pointing to the plausibility of the epigenetic-rule status of the sorts of things my position demands, let me make brief mention of the biological value of consilience. One hominid arrives at the water-hole, finding tiger-like footprints at the edge, blood-stains on the ground, growls and snarls and shrieks in the nearby undergrowth, and no other animals in sight. She reasons: 'Tigers! Beware!' And she flees. The second hominid arrives at the water, notices all of the signs, but concludes that since all of the evidence is circumstantial nothing can be proven. 'Tigers are just a theory, not a fact.' He settles down for a good long drink. Which of these two hominids was your ancestor?

The pointers, therefore, are that those rules which I have identified as lying behind science are precisely the inclinations which would prove to be of maximum selective value. If we wanted the best possible candidates for epigenetic-rule status, we could not do better than turn to these rules. The proto-human who ignored such rules underlying science would be in a real mess. Conversely, if selection is going to make anything innate, it would do well to start here.

* * *

THOMAS HENRY HUXLEY

Evolution and Ethics (1893)†

* * *

The propounders of what are called the 'ethics of evolution', when the 'evolution of ethics' would usually better express the object of their speculations, adduce a number of more or less interesting facts and more or less sound arguments, in favour of the origin of the moral sentiments, in the same way as other natural phenomena, by a process of evolution. I have little doubt, for my own part, that they are on the right track; but as the immoral sentiments have no less been evolved, there is, so far, as much natural sanction for the one as the other. The thief and the murderer follow nature just as much as the philanthropist. Cosmic evolution may teach us how the good and the evil tendencies of man may have come about; but, in itself, it is incompetent to furnish any better reason why what we call good is preferable to what we call evil than we had before. Some day, I doubt not, we shall arrive at an understanding of the evolution of the æsthetic faculty; but all the understanding in the world will neither increase nor diminish the force of the intuition that this is beautiful and that is ugly.

There is another fallacy which appears to me to pervade the so-called 'ethics of evolution'. It is the notion that because, on the whole, animals and plants have advanced in perfection of organization by means of the struggle for existence and the consequent 'survival of the fittest'; therefore men in society, men as ethical beings, must look to the same process to help them towards perfection. I suspect that this fallacy has arisen out of the unfortunate ambiguity of the phrase 'survival of the fittest'. 'Fittest' has a connotation of 'best'; and about 'best' there hangs a moral flavour. In cosmic nature, however, what is 'fittest' depends upon the conditions. Long since,[1] I ventured to point out that if our hemisphere were to cool again, the survival of the fittest might bring about, in the vegetable kingdom, a population of more and more stunted and humbler and humbler organisms, until the 'fittest' that survived might be nothing but lichens, diatoms, and such microscopic organisms as those which give red snow its colour; while, if it became hotter, the pleasant valleys of the Thames and Isis might be uninhabitable by any animated beings save those that flourish in a tropical jungle. They, as the fittest, the best adapted to the changed conditions, would survive.

Men in society are undoubtedly subject to the cosmic process. As among other animals, multiplication goes on without cessation, and involves severe competition for the means of support. The struggle for existence tends to eliminate those less fitted to adapt themselves to the circumstances of

---

† The Romanes lecture for 1893; it is reprinted in Thomas Henry Huxley and Julian Huxley, *Touchstone for Ethics* (New York, 1947): 67–112. Thomas Henry Huxley (1825–1895), Fellow of the Royal Society, was one of Darwin's firmest advocates.
1. 'Criticisms on the Origin of Species,' 1864. *Collected Essays*, vol. ii, p. 91. [1894].

their existence. The strongest, the most self-assertive, tend to tread down the weaker. But the influence of the cosmic process on the evolution of society is the greater the more rudimentary its civilization. Social progress means a checking of the cosmic process at every step and the substitution for it of another, which may be called the ethical process; the end of which is not the survival of those who may happen to be the fittest, in respect of the whole of the conditions which obtain, but of those who are ethically the best.[2]

As I have already urged, the practice of that which is ethically best—what we call goodness or virtue—involves a course of conduct which, in all respects, is opposed to that which leads to success in the cosmic struggle for existence. In place of ruthless self-assertion it demands self-restraint; in place of thrusting aside, or treading down, all competitors, it requires that the individual shall not merely respect, but shall help his fellows; its influence is directed, not so much to the survival of the fittest, as to the fitting of as many as possible to survive. It repudiates the gladiatorial theory of existence. It demands that each man who enters into the enjoyment of the advantages of a polity shall be mindful of his debt to those who have laboriously constructed it; and shall take heed that no act of his weakens the fabric in which he has been permitted to live. Laws and moral precepts are directed to the end of curbing the cosmic process and reminding the individual of his duty to the community, to the protection and influence of which he owes, if not existence itself, at least the life of something better than a brutal savage.

It is from neglect of these plain considerations that the fanatical individualism[3] of our time attempts to apply the analogy of cosmic nature to society. Once more we have a misapplication of the stoical injunction to follow nature; the duties of the individual to the State are forgotten, and his tendencies to self-assertion are dignified by the name of rights. It is seriously debated whether the members of a community are justified in using their combined strength to constrain one of their number to contribute his share to the maintenance of it; or even to prevent him from doing his best to destroy it. The struggle for existence, which has done such admirable work in cosmic nature, must, it appears, be equally beneficent in the ethical sphere. Yet if that which I have insisted upon is true; if the cosmic process has no sort of relation to moral ends; if the

2. Of course, strictly speaking, social life, and the ethical process in virtue of which it advances towards perfection, are part and parcel of the general process of evolution, just as the gregarious habit of innumerable plants and animals, which has been of immense advantage to them, is so. A hive of bees is an organic polity, a society in which the part played by each member is determined by organic necessities. Queens, workers, and drones are, so to speak, castes, divided from one another by marked physical barriers. Among birds and mammals, societies are formed, of which the bond in many cases seems to be purely psychological; that is to say, it appears to depend upon the liking of the individuals for one another's company. The tendency of individuals to over self-assertion is kept down by fighting. Even in these rudimentary forms of society, love and fear come into play, and enforce a greater or less renunciation of self-will. To this extent the general cosmic process begins to be checked by a rudimentary ethical process, which is, strictly speaking, part of the former, just as the 'governor' in a steam-engine is part of the mechanism of the engine.

3. See 'Government: Anarchy or Regimentation'. *Collected Essays*, vol. i. pp. 413–418. It is this form of political philosophy to which I conceive the epithet of 'reasoned savagery' to be strictly applicable. [1894.]

imitation of it by man is inconsistent with the first principles of ethics; what becomes of this surprising theory?

Let us understand, once for all, that the ethical progress of society depends, not on imitating the cosmic process, still less in running away from it, but in combating it. It may seem an audacious proposal thus to pit the microcosm against the macrocosm and to set man to subdue nature to his higher ends; but I venture to think that the great intellectual difference between the ancient times with which we have been occupied and our day, lies in the solid foundation we have acquired for the hope that such an enterprise may meet with a certain measure of success. * * *

JULIAN HUXLEY

Evolutionary Ethics (1943)†

I. T. H. Huxley's Antithesis Between Ethics and Evolution

* * *

For T. H. Huxley, fifty years ago, there was a fundamental contradiction between the ethical process and the cosmic process. By the former, he meant the universalist ethics of the Victorian enlightenment, bred by nineteenth-century humanitarianism out of traditional Christian ethics, and in him personally tinged by a noble but stern puritanism and an almost fanatical devotion to scientific truth and its pursuit. And the cosmic process he restricted almost entirely to biological evolution and to the selective struggle for existence on which it depends. 'The ethical progress of society'—this was the main conclusion of his Romanes lecture—'consists, not in imitating the cosmic process, still less in running away from it, but in combating it'.

Today, that contradiction can, I believe, be resolved—on the one hand by extending the concept of evolution both backward into the inorganic and forward into the human domain, and on the other by considering ethics not as a body of fixed principles, but as a product of evolution, and itself evolving. In both cases, the intellectual tool which has given us new insight is that of developmental analysis—the scientific study of change, of becoming, of the production of novelty, whether of life from not-life, of a baby from an ovum and a man from a baby, of ants and swallows and tigers out of ancestral protozoa, of civilized societies out of barbarism and barbarism out of the dim beginnings of social life. * * *

† The Romanes Lecture for 1943; it is reprinted in Thomas Henry Huxley and Julian Huxley, *Touchstone for Ethics* (New York, 1947): 113–166. Julian Huxley (1887–1975) the grandson of Thomas Henry Huxley, was a distinguished zoologist and man of letters.

V. Evolutionary Levels and Directions

During the thousand million years of organic evolution, the degree of organization attained by the highest forms of life increased enormously. And with this there increased also the possibilities of control, of independence, of inner harmony and self-regulation, of experience. Compared with what a protozoan or a polyp can show, the complexity of later forms of life, like bee or swallow or antelope, is stupendous, their capacity for self-regulation almost miraculous, their experience so much richer and more varied as to be different in kind.

And finally there is, in certain types of animals, an increase in consciousness or mind. Whether mind be a sudden emergent or, as biologists prefer to think, a gradual development of some universal property of the world-stuff, mind of the same general nature as ours is clearly present on the higher organizational levels of life, and at least in the birds and mammals we can trace its steady evolution towards greater capacities for feeling, knowing, willing, and understanding.

There is thus one direction within the multifariousness of evolution which we can legitimately call progress. It consists in the capacity to attain a higher degree of organization, but without closing the door to further advance. In the organic phase of evolution, this depends on all-round improvement as opposed to the limited improvement or one-sided specialization which, it can be demonstrated, automatically leads sooner or later to a dead end, after which no true advance is possible, but only minor variations on an already existent theme. Insects appear to have reached an evolutionary dead end over 30 million years ago; birds a little later; and all the main lines of higher mammals except the primates—carnivores, ungulates, whales, bats, rodents, and so forth—at least no later than the early Pliocene. Most evolutionary lines or trends are specializations which either thus come to a stop or are extinguished; true progress or the unlimited capacity for advance is rare.

However, the details of biological evolution need not concern us overmuch, since during the last half-million years or so a new and more comprehensive type of order of organization has arisen; and on this new level, the world-stuff is once more introduced to altogether new possibilities, and has quite new methods of evolutionary operation at its disposal. Biological or organic evolution has at its upper end been merged into and largely succeeded by conscious or social evolution.

Just as biological evolution was rendered both possible and inevitable when material organization became self-reproducing, so conscious evolution was rendered both possible and inevitable when social organization became self-reproducing. This occurred when the evolving world-stuff, in the form of ancestral man, became capable of true speech and conceptual thought. For just as animal organization, however elaborate, had been transmissible across the generation by the vehicle of the chromosomes and genes, so from then on conscious experience could be transmitted down the stream of time on the vehicle of words and other symbols and representations. And somewhat as sexual fusion made possible the pooling of individual mutations, so reason made possible the pooling of individual experiences. For the first time in evolution, tradition and education became continuous and cumulative processes.

With this, a new type of organization came into being—that of self-reproducing society. So long as man survives as a species (and there is no reason for thinking he will not) there seems no possibility for any other form of life to push up to this new organizational level. Indeed there are grounds for suspecting that biological evolution has come to an end, so far as any sort of major advance is concerned. Thus further large-scale evolution has once again been immensely restricted in extent, being now it would seem confined to the single species man; but at the same time again immensely accelerated in its speed, through the operation of the new mechanisms now available.

In any case, it is only through social evolution that the world-stuff can now realize radically new possibilities. Mechanical interaction and natural selection still operate, but have become of secondary importance. For good or evil, the mechanism of evolution has in the main been transferred onto the social or conscious level. Part of the blind struggle for existence between separate individuals or groups is transposed into conflict in consciousness, either within the individual mind or within the tradition which is the vehicle of pooled social consciousness. The slow methods of variation and heredity are outstripped by the speedier processes of acquiring and transmitting experience. New tools of living originated *ex post facto* as biological adaptations or unconscious adjustments become increasingly unimportant compared with the tools deliberately produced by human design. Physical trial and error can be more and more transposed to the sphere of thought.

And in so far as the mechanism of evolution ceases to be blind and automatic and becomes conscious, ethics can be injected into the evolutionary process. Before man that process was merely amoral. After his emergence onto life's stage it became possible to introduce faith, courage, love of truth, goodness—in a word moral purpose—into evolution. It became possible, but the possibility has been and is too often unrealized. It is the business of an enlightened ethics to help in its realization.

*   *   *

In the broadest possible terms evolutionary ethics must be based on a combination of a few main principles: that it is right to realize ever new possibilities in evolution, notably those which are valued for their own sake; that it is right both to respect human individuality and to encourage its fullest development; that it is right to construct a mechanism for further social evolution which shall satisfy these prior conditions as fully, efficiently, and as rapidly as possible.

*   *   *

If desirable direction of evolution provides the most comprehensive (though also the least specific) external standard for our ethics, then one very important corollary at once follows: namely that social organization should be planned, not to prevent change, nor merely to permit it, but to encourage it. Thus a static stability is undesirable, and a complete or static certitude of ethical belief itself becomes unethical. * * *

Furthermore, the rate as well as the direction of change is important. Theoretically, there must be an optimum rate of change, above which stability is endangered and the sacrifices of the present are excessive, below which advance is so slow that the welfare of future generations is needlessly impaired. Thus anything which retards advance below this optimum, even if it be moving in the same right direction, is wrong.

Next we have the guidance derived from an understanding of the workings of human societies. In the first place, it is clear on evolutionary grounds that the individual is in a real sense higher than the State or the social organism. The possibilities which are of value for their own sake, and whose realization must be one of our primary aims, are not experienced by society as a unit, but by some or all of the human beings which compose it.

All claims that the State has an intrinsically higher value than the individual are false. They turn out, on closer scrutiny, to be rationalizations or myths aimed at securing greater power or privilege for a limited group which controls the machinery of the State.

On the other hand the individual is meaningless in isolation, and the possibilities of development and self-realization open to him are conditioned and limited by the nature of the social organization. The individual thus has duties and responsibilities as well as rights and privileges, or if you prefer it, finds certain outlets and satisfactions (such as devotion to a cause, or participation in a joint enterprise) only in relation to the type of society in which he lives. * * *

With this we are brought into the area of the individual. The human individual is not merely inherently higher than the State, but the rightly-developed individual is, and will continue to be, the highest product of evolution, even though he needs the proper organization of society to achieve his welfare and realize his development.

The phrase *rightly-developed* begs a question. I would suggest that it includes not only the full, all-round development of potentialities, but also the one-sided development of particular possibilities or special talents, provided always that these restrict the development or interfere with the welfare of other individuals or groups as little as possible. * * *

If the right development of the individual is an evolutionary end in itself, then it is right that there should be universal equality of opportunity for development, and to the fullest degree. The reciprocal of this is the rightness of unselfishness and kindness, as the necessary means for realizing general well-being. Thus individual ethics will always in large measure be concerned with the conflict between the claims of self-expression and self-sacrifice, and their best reconciliation through love.

The Golden Rule, as various philosophers have pointed out, is an impossible ideal; it cannot ever be put into practice, not merely because of the imperfections of human nature, but also because it does not provide a real basis on which to make practical ethical decisions. However, it is the hyperbole beyond a perfectly practical ideal—the extension of more opportunity of fuller life to more human beings. Psychologically, this can be promoted by extending the child's love and sympathy to an ever-widening circle, and linking the idea of any and all avoidable suffering and stunting of development with his personal sense of wrong. And it can be promoted institutionally by the rational acceptance of certain moral principles, and then by laws and practical measures designed to give effect to those principles.

To accept this view is to give a new content to that sector of ethics concerned with justice.

＊   ＊   ＊

But man is not only the heir of the past and the victim of the present: he is also the agent through whom evolution may unfold its further possibilities. Here, it seems, is the solution of our riddle of ethical relativity: the ultimate guarantees for the correctness of our labels of rightness and wrongness are to be sought for among the facts of evolutionary direction. Here, too, is to be found the reconciliation of T. H. Huxley's antithesis between the ethical and the cosmic process: for the cosmic process, we now perceive, is continued into human affairs. Thus man can impose moral principles upon ever-widening areas of the cosmic process, in whose further slow unfolding he is now the protagonist. He can inject his ethics into the heart of evolution.

MICHAEL RUSE AND EDWARD O. WILSON

The Evolution of Ethics (1985)†

Attempts to link evolution and ethics first sprang up in the middle of the last century, as people turned to alternative foundations in response to what they perceived as the collapse of Christianity. If God does not stand behind the Sermon on the Mount, then what does? Such attempts at evolutionary ethicising became known collectively as "social Darwinism," although they owed less to Charles Darwin and more to that quintessentially Victorian man of ideas, Herbert Spencer. Finding worth in what he perceived to be the upward progress of evolution from amoeba to human, from savage to *Homo britannicus*, Spencer argued that right conduct lies in the cherishing of the evolutionary process, in order that the best or fittest be able to survive and the inadequate be rigorously eliminated.

While Spencer's ideas attracted strong support in some quarters, for example the North American barons of industry, evolutionary ethics in this mode never really caught fire. On the one hand, social Darwinism seems so immoral! Right conduct surely cannot entail stamping on widows and babies. And no amount of tinkering by revisionists, such as Prince Peter

† From "The Evolution of Ethics" in *New Scientist*, October 1985. Used by permission of *New Scientist*. Michael Ruse (b. 1940) is professor of philosophy and zoology at the University of Guelph. Edward O. Wilson (b. 1929) is Pellegrino University Research Professor and Honorary Curator in Entomology of the Museum of Comparative Zoology at Harvard University.

Kropotkin in the last century and Sir Julian Huxley and C. H. Waddington in this, changes the fact. On the other hand, the very basis of a Spencerian-type approach is shaky. There is no progress to evolution. In a purely Darwinian sense, an amoeba is as good as a person.

Most people, therefore, have happily agreed with the 18th-century philosopher David Hume that there is an impassible gulf between matters of fact (for example, evolution) and matters of morality (disinterested help of others). To use phrasing made popular in this century by the Cambridge philosopher G. E. Moore, evolutionary ethics commits "the naturalistic fallacy" by trying to translate *is* into *ought*.

It is true that past efforts to create an evolutionary ethics have come to very little. Yet to revert to the opposite conclusion, that evolution and ethics have nothing to say to each other, is altogether too quick. Recent advances in evolutionary theory have cast a new light on the matter, giving substance to the dreams of the old theorisers, although not in the way or for the reasons they thought.

Our starting point is with the science. Two propositions appear to have been established beyond any reasonable doubt. First, the social behaviour of animals is firmly under the control of the genes, and has been shaped into forms that give reproductive advantages. Secondly, humans are animals. Darwin knew that the first claim was true, and a multitude of recent studies, from fruit flies to frogs, have affirmed it repeatedly. Darwin knew also that the second claim is true, and positive evidence continues to pour in from virtually every biological discipline. Genetically, we are a sibling species to the chimpanzee, having evolved with them for more than 3½ billion years, parting a mere 6 million or so years ago.

What do these facts have to do with morality? A chain of reasoning leads us to a distinctly human but still biologically based ethical sense. First, note that we are not just talking about behaviour, but about *social* behaviour. Today's students of this subject, sociobiologists, know that it is often in an individual's biological self-interest to cooperate with its fellows, rather than (as traditional evolutionary ethicists thought) to fight flat out. After all, a loaf shared is better than a whole loaf, if the latter carries the risk of being killed or seriously hurt.

Secondly, and less obviously, there are ways in which nature can bring about "altruism," in the sense of self-sacrifice for the benefit of others. If those benefited are relatives, the altruist is still favouring genes identical to his own, even if he dies without leaving any direct offspring. Thus we say that the individual is altruistic but his genes are "selfish." Note that such behaviour implies nothing about good intentions or other ways of being "nice." To get altruism you can go the way of the ants. They are genetically hardwired, performing their duties in perfect cooperative harmony. They have no thoughts, at least of a human kind, only actions. Alternatively, you could go to the other extreme, and evolve super-brains, where every possible action is first weighed and assessed, and a policy of rationally assessed self-interest is always followed.

Neither of these options has proved attractive to animals like humans, and we have avoided both. If we had become hardwired in the course of evolution, we could never deviate from our course. Were something untoward to happen, we would be stuck with maladaptive behaviour. Worker ants are relatively cheap to produce, so this rigidity matters relatively little to their colonies. Humans require a great deal of parental investment, and it would be stupid in the literal sense of the word if we were to go wrong at the slightest environmental quiver. Alternatively, if we possessed super-brains, we would require even more resources than we do now; such as parental care stretched over many more years. Additionally, like those chess machines that survey every move, we would be forever making up our minds. Crises would be upon us, and we would still be thinking.

Nature's Moral Imperative

How then has nature made humans "altruistic"? The clue lies in the chess machines we just mentioned. The new breed, those that can beat grandmasters, forgo omnipotence for utility. They follow certain strategies that have proved successful. So with humans. Our minds are not tabulae rasae, but moulded according to certain innate dispositions. These dispositions, known technically as "epigenetic rules," incline us to particular courses of action, such as learning rapidly to fear heights and snakes, although they certainly do not lock us, ant-like, into undeviating behaviour.

The best studied epigenetic rules, such as those affecting fears or the avoidance of incest, appear to have been put into place because of their biological virtues. Although altruism is less well documented (there is some evidence, for example, that varying degrees of its expression have a genetic component), such behaviour is also adaptive—at least when directed in appropriate measure toward kin and allies. We need to be altruistic. Thus, we have rules inclining us to such courses of behaviour. The key question is then: how are these rules expressed in our conscious awareness? We need something to spur us against our usual selfish dispositions. Nature, therefore, has made us (via the rules) believe in a disinterested moral code, according to which we *ought* to help our fellows. Thus, we are inclined to go out and work with our fellows. In short, to make us altruistic in the adaptive, biological sense, our biology makes us altruistic in the more conventionally understood sense of acting on deeply held beliefs about right and wrong.

Such is the modern scientific account of morality; at least the one most consistent with biology. But, what has any of this to do with the concerns of the traditional evolutionary ethicist? Even if the explanation were proved to be entirely true, it does not reveal whether in some ultimate, absolute sense, evolution stands behind morality. Does the sociobiological scenario just sketched justify the same moral code that religionists believe to be decreed by God? Or that some philosophers believe to exist apart from humanity, like a mathematical theorem?

It used to be thought, in the bad old days of social Darwinism when evolution was poorly understood, that life is an uninterrupted struggle— "nature red in tooth and claw." But this is only one side of natural selection. What we have just seen is that the same process also leads to altruism and reciprocity in highly social groups. Thus the human species has evolved genuine sentiments of obligation, of the duty to be loving and kind. In no way does this materialist explanation imply that we are hypocrites consciously trying to further our biological ends and paying lip-service to ethics. We function better because we believe. In this sense, evolution is consistent with conventional views of morality.

On the other hand, the question of ultimate foundations requires a different and more subtle answer. As evolutionists, we see that no justification of the traditional kind is possible. Morality, or more strictly our belief in morality, is merely an adaptation put in place to further our reproductive ends. Hence the basis of ethics does not lie in God's will—or in the metaphorical roots of evolution or any other part of the framework of the Universe. In an important sense, ethics as we understand it is an illusion fobbed off on us by our genes to get us to cooperate. It is without external grounding. Ethics is produced by evolution but not justified by it, because, like Macbeth's dagger, it serves a powerful purpose without existing in substance.

In speaking thus of illusion, we are not saying that ethics is nothing, and should now be thought of as purely dreamlike. Unlike Macbeth's dagger, ethics is a *shared* illusion of the human race. If it were not so, it would not work. The moral ones among us would be outbred by the immoral. For this reason, since all human beings are dependent on the "ethics game," evolutionary reasoning emphatically does not lead to moral relativism. Human minds develop according to epigenetic rules that distinguish between proper moral claims like "Be kind to children" and crazy imperatives like "Treat cabbages with the respect you show your mother."

Ethical codes work because they drive us to go against our selfish day-to-day impulses in favour of long-term group survival and harmony and thus, over our lifetimes, the multiplication of our genes many times. Furthermore, the way our biology enforces its ends is by making us think that there is an objective higher code, to which we are all subject. If we thought ethics to be no more than a question of personal desires, we would tend to ignore it. Why should we base our life's plan on your love of French cuisine? Because we think that ethics is objectively based, we are inclined to obey moral rules. We help small children because it is right even though it is personally inconvenient to us.

If this perception of human evolution is correct, it provides a new basis for moral reasoning. Ethics is seen to have a solid foundation, not in divine guidance or pure moral imperatives, but in the shared qualities of human nature and the desperate need for reciprocity. The key is the deeper, more objective study of human nature, and for this reason we need to turn ethical philosophy into an applied science.

Some philosophers have argued that even if ethics could be explained wholly in such a materialist fashion, this alone would not eliminate the possibility that moral imperatives exist, sitting apart like mathematical truths. Perhaps human evolution is moving toward such celestial perfection, and the apprehension of such truths. There are biological reasons for seeing and hearing the moving train, but it still exists!

Unfortunately, the cases of mathematical principles, material objects and ethics are not parallel. Natural selection is above all opportunistic. Suppose that, instead of evolving from savannah-dwelling primates, we had evolved in a very different way. If, like the termites, we needed to dwell in darkness, eat each other's faeces and cannibalise the dead, our epigenetic rules would be very different from what they are now. Our minds would be strongly prone to extol such acts as beautiful and moral. And we would find it morally disgusting to live in the open air, dispose of body waste and bury the dead. Termite ayatollahs would surely declare such things to be against the will of God. Termite social theorists would surely argue for a stricter caste system.

Ethics does not have the objective foundation our biology leads us to think it has. But this is no negative conclusion. Human beings face incredible social problems, primarily because their biology cannot cope with the effects of their technology. A deeper understanding of this biology is surely a first step towards solving some of these pressing worries. Seeing morality for what it is, a legacy of evolution rather than a reflection of eternal, divinely inspired verities, is part of this understanding.

FRANS DE WAAL

Good Natured: The Origin of Right and Wrong in Humans and Other Animals (1996)†

* * *

The sociobiological idiom is almost derisive in its characterization of animals. Given the image of biologists as nature buffs, it may be shocking for outsiders to learn that the current scientific literature routinely depicts animals as "suckers," "grudgers," and "cheaters" who act "spitefully," "greedily," and "murderously." There is really nothing lovable about them! If animals do show tolerance or altruism, these terms are often placed in quotation marks lest their author be judged hopelessly romantic or naive. To avoid an overload of quotation marks, positive inclinations tend to receive negative labels. Preferential treatment of kin, for instance, instead of being called "love for kin," is sometimes known as "nepotism."

As noted by economist Robert Frank (referring to a problem common to the behavioral sciences):

> The flint-eyed researcher fears no greater humiliation than to have called some action altruistic, only to have a more sophisticated colleague later demonstrate that it was self-serving. This fear surely helps account for the extraordinary volume of ink behavioral scientists have spent trying to unearth selfish motives for seemingly self-sacrificing acts.

As a student of chimpanzee behavior, I myself have encountered resistance to the label "reconciliation" for friendly reunions between former adversaries. Actually, I should not have used the word "friendly" either,

† From *Good Natured* (Cambridge: Harvard University Press, 1996). Reprinted by permission of the publisher. Frans de Waal (b. 1948) is C. H. Candler Professor of Primate Behavior at Emory University and director of the Living Links Center at the Yerkes Regional Primate Research Center.

"affiliative" being the accepted euphemism. More than once I was asked whether the term "reconciliation" was not overly anthropomorphic. Whereas terms related to aggression, violence, and competition never posed the slightest problem, I was supposed to switch to dehumanized language as soon as the affectionate aftermath of a fight was the issue.

*   *   *

Animals, particularly those close to us, show an enormous spectrum of emotions and different kinds of relationships. It is only fair to reflect this fact in a broad array of terms. If animals can have enemies they can have friends; if they can cheat they can be honest, and if they can be spiteful they can also be kind and altruistic. Semantic distinctions between animal and human behavior often obscure fundamental similarities; a discussion of morality will be pointless if we allow our language to be distorted by a denial of benign motives and emotions in animals.

*   *   *

Ethology and Ethics

In the 1940s a special label became necessary to distinguish the study of animal behavior in nature from the laboratory experiments of behaviorists on white rats and other domesticated animals. The chosen name was *ethology*, and its most famous representative became the Austrian zoologist Konrad Lorenz. * * *

The term "ethology" comes from the Greek *ethos*, which means character, both in the sense of what is characteristic of a person or animal and in the sense of moral qualities. * * * When ethology later reached Great Britain, the term gained its current status in Webster's as "the scientific study of the characteristic behavior patterns of animals" (although most ethologists would probably change "scientific" to "naturalistic").

Early ethology stressed instinct—suggesting purely inborn behavior—yet was by no means blind to other influences. In fact, one of its strongest contributions was the study of imprinting, a learning process. Ducklings and goslings are not born with any detailed knowledge of their species; they acquire information in the first hours of their life. Normally, they do so by watching and following their mother, but they may take cues from any moving object encountered during the sensitive period.

*   *   *

Human morality shares with language that it is far too complex to be learned through trial and error, and far too variable to be genetically programmed. Some cultures permit the killing of newborns, whereas others debate abortion of the unborn. Some cultures disapprove of premarital sex, whereas others encourage it as part of a healthy sexual education. The gravest error of biologists speculating about the origin of morality has been to ignore this variability, and to downplay the learned character of ethical principles.

Possibly we are born, not with any specific social norms, but with a learning agenda that tells us which information to imbibe and how to organize it. We could then figure out, understand, and eventually internalize the moral fabric of our native society. Because a similar learning agenda seems to regulate language acquisition, I will speak of *moral ability* as a parallel to language ability. In a sense, we are imprinted upon a particular moral system through a process that, though hundreds of times more complicated than the imprinting of birds, may be just as effective and lasting.

*   *   *

Virtually every existing moral principle has by now been biologically explained, a dubious genre of literature going back to Ernest Seton's *Natural History of the Ten Commandments*, published in 1907. * * *

Much of this literature assumes that the world is waiting for biologists to point out what is Normal and Natural, hence worth being adopted as ideal. Attempts to derive ethical norms from nature are highly problematic, however. Biologists may tell us how things are, perhaps even analyze human nature in intricate detail, yet there is no logical connection between the typical form and frequency of a behavior (a statistical measure of what is "normal") and the value we attach to it (a moral decision). * * *

Known as the *naturalistic fallacy*, the problem of deriving norms from nature is very old indeed. It has to do with the impossibility of translating "is" language (how things are) into "ought" language (how things ought to be). * * *

To put the issue of ethics back into ethology in a more successful manner, we need to take note of the chorus of protest against previous attempts. Philosophers tell us that there is an element of rational choice in human morality, psychologists say that there is a learning component, and anthropologists argue that there are few if any universal rules. The distinction between right and wrong is made by people on the basis of how they would like their society to function. It arises from interpersonal negotiation in a particular environment, and derives its sense of obligation and guilt from the internalization of these processes. Moral reasoning is done by *us*, not by natural selection.

At the same time it should be obvious that human morality cannot be infinitely flexible. Of our own design are neither the tools of morality nor the basic needs and desires that form the substance with which it works. Natural tendencies may not amount to moral imperatives, but they do figure in our decision-making. Thus, while some moral rules reinforce species-typical predispositions and others suppress them, none blithely ignore them.

Evolution has produced the requisites for morality: a tendency to develop social norms and enforce them, the capacities of empathy and sympathy, mutual aid and a sense of fairness, the mechanisms of conflict resolution, and so on. Evolution also has produced the unalterable needs and desires of our species: the need of the young for care, a desire for high status, the need to belong to a group, and so forth. How all of these factors are put together to form a moral framework is poorly understood, and current theories of moral evolution are no doubt only part of the answer.

* * *

Warm Blood in Cold Waters

Reports of leviathan care and assistance go back to the ancient Greeks. Dolphins are said to save companions by biting through harpoon lines or by hauling them out of nets in which they have gotten entangled. Whales may interpose themselves between a hunter's boat and an injured conspecific or capsize the boat. * * *

But am I justified in using the term "sympathy," which after all is a venerated human concept with very special connotations? Let us for the moment simply speak of *succorant behavior*, defined as helping, caregiving, or providing relief to distressed or endangered individuals other than progeny. Thus, the dog staying protectively close to a crying child shows succorance, whereas the same dog responding to the yelps of her puppies shows nurturance. In reviewing the succorant behavior of animals we will pay special attention to characteristics it might share with human sympathy, the most important being empathy—that is, the ability to be vicariously affected by someone else's feelings and situation. Psychologists and philosophers consider this capacity so central that "empathy" has gradually replaced "sympathy," "compassion," "sorrow," and "pity" in much of their writings. * * *

This blurring is unfortunate, for it ignores the distinction between the ability to recognize someone else's pain and the impulse to do something about it. * * * As neatly summed up by the psychologist Lauren Wispé: "The object of empathy is understanding. The object of sympathy is the other person's well-being."

Whether based on empathy or not, animal succorance is the functional equivalent of human sympathy, expected only in species that know strong attachment. I am not speaking here of anonymous aggregations of fish or butterflies, but the individualized bonding, affection, and fellowship of many mammals and birds.

* * *

To this day, those who see our species as part of the animal kingdom continue to lock horns with those who see us as separate. Even authors with a distinctly evolutionary perspective often cannot resist searching for the one BIG difference, the one trait that sets us apart—whether it is opposable thumbs, toolmaking, cooperative hunting, humor, pure altruism, sexual orgasm, the incest taboo, language, or the anatomy of the larynx.

* * *

As a separate species, humans do possess distinct traits, yet the overwhelming majority of our anatomical, physiological, and psychological characteristics are part of an ancient heritage. Holding the magnifying glass over a few beauty spots (our distinct traits are invariably judged advanced and superior) is a much less exciting enterprise, it seems to me, than trying to get a good look at the human animal as a whole.

In this broader perspective, peculiarly human traits are juxtaposed with the obvious continuity with the rest of nature. Included are both our most noble traits and the ones of which we are less proud, such as our genocidal and destructive tendencies. Even if we like to blame the latter on our progenitors (as soon as people hack each other to pieces they are said to be "acting like animals") and claim the former for ourselves, it is safe to assume that both run in our extended family.

There is no need to launch probes into space in order to compare ourselves with other intelligent life: there is plenty of intelligent life down here. It is infinitely more suitable to elucidate the working of our minds than those of whatever extraterrestrial forms might exist. In order to explore earthly intelligences, we need breathing room in the study of animal cognition: freedom from traditional constraints that tell us that nothing is there, or that *if* anything is there, we will never be able to catch even a glimpse.

* * *

Even if animals other than ourselves act in ways tantamount to moral behavior, their behavior does not necessarily rest on deliberations of the kind we engage in. It is hard to believe that animals weigh their own interests against the rights of others, that they develop a vision of the greater good of society, or that they feel lifelong guilt about something they should not have done.

What Does It Take to Be Moral?

Members of some species may reach tacit consensus about what kind of behavior to tolerate or inhibit in their midst, but without language the principles behind such decisions cannot be conceptualized, let alone debated. To communicate intentions and feelings is one thing; to clarify what is right, and why, and what is wrong, and why, is quite something else. Animals are no moral philosophers.

But then, how many *people* are? We have a tendency to compare animal behavior with the most dizzying accomplishments of our race, and to be smugly satisfied when a thousand monkeys with a thousand typewriters do not come close to William Shakespeare. Is this a reason to classify ourselves as smart, and animals as stupid? Are we not much of the time considerably less rational than advertised? People seem far better at explaining their behavior after the fact than at considering the consequences beforehand. There is no denying that we are creatures of intellect; it is also evident that we are born with powerful inclinations and emotions that bias our thinking and behavior.

A chimpanzee stroking and patting a victim of attack or sharing her food with a hungry companion shows attitudes that are hard to distinguish from those of a person picking up a crying child, or doing volunteer work in a soup kitchen. To classify the chimpanzee's behavior as based on instinct and the person's behavior as proof of moral decency is misleading, and probably incorrect. First of all, it is uneconomic in that it assumes different processes for similar behavior in two closely related species. Second, it ignores the growing body of evidence for mental complexity in the chimpanzee, including the possibility of empathy. I hesitate to call the members of any species other than our own "moral beings," yet I also believe that many of the sentiments and cognitive abilities underlying human morality antedate the appearance of our species on this planet.

The question of whether animals have morality is a bit like the question of whether they have culture, politics, or language. If we take the full-blown human phenomenon as a yardstick, they most definitely do not. On the other hand, if we break the relevant human abilities into their component parts, some are recognizable in other animals.

> *Culture*: Field primatologists have noticed differences in tool use and communication among populations of the same species. Thus, in one chimpanzee community all adults may crack nuts with stones, whereas another community totally lacks this technology. Group-specific signals and habits have been documented in bonobos as well as chimpanzees. Increasingly, primatologists explain these differences as learned traditions handed down from one generation to the next.
>
> *Language*: For decades apes have been taught vocabularies of hand signals (such as American Sign Language) and computerized symbols. Koko, Kanzi, Washoe, and several other anthropoids have learned to effectively communicate their needs and desires through this medium.
>
> *Politics*: Tendencies basic to human political systems have been observed in other primates, such as alliances that challenge the status quo, and tit-for-tat deals between a leader and his supporters. As a result, status struggles are as much popularity contests as physical battles.

In each of these domains, nonhuman primates show impressive intelligence yet do not integrate information quite the way we do. The utterances of language-trained apes, for example, show little if any evidence of grammar. The transmission of knowledge from one generation to the next is rarely, if ever, achieved through active teaching. And it is still ambiguous how much planning and foresight, if any, go into the social careers of monkeys and apes.

Despite these limitations, I see no reason to avoid labels such as "primate culture," "ape language," or "chimpanzee politics" as long as it is understood that this terminology points out fundamental similarities without in any way claiming *identity* between ape and human behavior. Such terms serve to stimulate debate about how much or little animals share with us. To focus attention on those aspects in which we differ—a favorite tactic of the detractors of the evolutionary perspective—overlooks the critical importance of what we have in common. Inasmuch as shared characteristics most likely derive from the common ancestor, they probably laid the groundwork for much that followed, including whatever we claim as uniquely ours. To disparage this common ground is a bit like arriving at the top of a tower only to declare that the rest of the building is irrelevant, that the precious concept of "tower" ought to be reserved for the summit.

While making for good academic fights, semantics are mostly a waste of time. Are animals moral? Let us simply conclude that they occupy a number of floors of the tower of morality. Rejection of even this modest proposal can only result in an impoverished view of the structure as a whole.

*   *   *

Conscience is not some disembodied concept that can be understood only on the basis of culture and religion. Morality is as firmly grounded in neurobiology as anything else we do or are. Once thought of as purely spiritual matters, honesty, guilt, and the weighing of ethical dilemmas are traceable to specific areas of the brain. It should not surprise us, therefore, to find animal parallels. The human brain is a product of evolution. Despite its larger volume and greater complexity, it is fundamentally similar to the central nervous system of other mammals.

We seem to be reaching a point at which science can wrest morality from the hands of philosophers. That this is already happening—albeit largely at a theoretical level—is evident from recent books by, among others, Richard Alexander, Robert Frank, James Q. Wilson, and Robert Wright. The occasional disagreements within this budding field are far outweighed by the shared belief that evolution needs to be part of any satisfactory explanation of morality.

Gardener and garden are one and the same. The fact that the human moral sense goes so far back in evolutionary history that other species show signs of it plants morality firmly near the center of our much-maligned nature. It is neither a recent innovation nor a thin layer that covers a beastly and selfish makeup.

It takes up space in our heads, it reaches out to fellow human beings, and it is as much a part of what we are as the tendencies that it holds in check.

MATT RIDLEY

The Origins of Virtue (1997)†

*   *   *

In 1888, balding, bearded, bespectacled, rotund and kindly, [Peter] Kropotkin was living the life of an impoverished freelance writer in Harrow, on the outskirts of London, still patiently expecting the revolution in his

† From *The Origins of Virtue: Human Instincts and the Evolution of Cooperation* (Penguin UK, 1996; New York: Viking Penguin, 1997). British zoologist Matt Ridley (b. 1958) is a research fellow of the Institute of Economic Affairs.

native land. That year, stung by an essay of Thomas Henry Huxley's with which he disagreed, the anarchist began work on what was to prove his enduring legacy, the chief thing for which he is now remembered. It became a book, called *Mutual Aid: A Factor in Evolution*, and it is a prophetic work, though now largely forgotten.

Huxley argued that nature was an arena for pitiless struggle between self-interested creatures. This placed him in a long tradition, going back through Malthus, Hobbes, Machiavelli and St Augustine to the Sophist philosophers of Greece, which viewed human nature as essentially selfish and individualistic unless tamed by culture. Kropotkin appealed to a different tradition, derived from Godwin, Rousseau, Pelagius and Plato, that man was born virtuous and benevolent, but was corrupted by society.

Kropotkin argued that the emphasis Huxley placed upon the 'struggle for existence' simply did not accord with what he observed in the natural world, let alone in the world of men. Life was not a bloody free-for-all, or (in Huxley's paraphrase of Thomas Hobbes) 'a war of each against all', but was characterized as much by cooperation as by competition. The most successful animals, indeed, seemed to be the most cooperative. If evolution worked by pitting individuals against each other, it also worked by designing them to seek mutual benefit.[1]

Kropotkin refused to accept that selfishness was an animal legacy and morality a civilized one. He saw cooperation as an ancient, animal tradition with which man, like other animals, was endowed. 'But if we resort to an indirect test, and ask Nature "Who are the fittest: those [species] who are continually at war with each other, or those who support one another?" we at once see that those animals which acquire habits of mutual aid are undoubtedly the fittest.' He could not stomach the idea that life was a ruthless struggle of selfish beings. Had he not been sprung from prison by a dozen faithful friends at great risk to their own lives? Where in Huxley's struggle could he explain such altruism? Parrots are superior to other birds, he suggested, because they are more sociable and therefore more intelligent. And among people, cooperation is just as pronounced among primitive tribes as it is among civilized citizens. From a common meadow in a rural village to the structure of a medieval guild, Kropotkin argued, the more people helped each other, the more the community thrived.

> The sight of a Russian commune mowing a meadow—the men rivalling each other in their advance with the scythe, while the women turn the grass over and throw it up into heaps—is one of the most awe-inspiring sights; it shows what human work might be and ought to be.

Kropotkin's was not a mechanistic theory of evolution, like Darwin's. He could not explain how mutual aid gained such a foothold, except by the selective survival of sociable species and groups in competition with less sociable ones—which was just to remove competition and natural selection

---

1. Woodcock, George and Avakumovic, Ivan. 1950. *The Anarchist Prince: A Biographical Study of Peter Kropotkin.* T. V. Boardman and Co. London; Kropotkin, Peter. 1902/1972. *Mutual Aid: A Factor in Evolution.* Allen Lane, London.

one step, to the group rather than the individual. But he had posed a question that reverberates through economics, politics and biology a century later. If life is a competitive struggle, why is there so much cooperation about? And why, in particular, are people such eager cooperators? Is humankind instinctively an anti-social or a pro-social animal? That is my quest in this book: the roots of human society. I shall demonstrate that Kropotkin was half right and those roots lie much deeper than we think. Society works not because we have consciously invented it, but because it is an ancient product of our evolved predispositions. It is literally in our nature.[2]

Original Virtue

This is a book about human nature, and in particular the surprisingly social nature of the human animal. We live in towns, work in teams, and our lives are spiders' webs of connections—linking us to relatives, colleagues, companions, friends, superiors, inferiors. We are, misanthropes notwithstanding, unable to live without each other. Even on a practical level, it is probably a million years since any human being was entirely and convincingly self-sufficient: able to survive without trading his skills for those of his fellow humans. We are far more dependent on other members of our species than any other ape or monkey. We are more like ants or termites who live as slaves to their societies. We define virtue almost exclusively as pro-social behaviour, and vice as anti-social behaviour. Kropotkin was right to emphasize the huge role that mutual aid plays in our species, but wrong and anthropomorphic to assume that therefore it applied to other species as well. One of the things that marks humanity out from other species, and accounts for our ecological success, is our collection of hyper-social instincts.

Yet to most people instincts are animal things, not human. The conventional wisdom in the social sciences is that human nature is simply an imprint of an individual's background and experience. But our cultures are not random collections of arbitrary habits. They are canalized expressions of our instincts. That is why the same themes crop up in all cultures—themes such as family, ritual, bargain, love, hierarchy, friendship, jealousy, group loyalty and superstition. That is why, for all their superficial differences of language and custom, foreign cultures are still immediately comprehensible at the deeper level of motives, emotions and social habits. Instincts, in a species like the human one, are not immutable genetic programmes; they are predispositions to learn. And to believe that human beings have instincts is no more determinist than to believe they are the products of their upbringings.

It is the claim of this book that the answer to an old question—how is society possible?—is suddenly at hand, thanks to the insights of evolutionary biology. Society was not invented by reasoning men. It evolved as part of our nature. It is as much a product of our genes as our bodies are. To understand it we must look inside our brains at the instincts for creating

2. Kropotkin. *Mutual Aid. op. cit.*

and exploiting social bonds that are there. We must also look at other animals to see how the essentially competitive business of evolution can sometimes give rise to cooperative instincts. This book is on three levels. It is about the billion-year coagulation of our genes into cooperative teams, the million-year coagulation of our ancestors into cooperative societies, and the thousand-year coagulation of ideas about society and its origins.

※ ※ ※

The Selfish Gene

There was a revolution in biology in the mid 1960s, pioneered especially by two men, George Williams and William Hamilton. This revolution is best known by Richard Dawkins's phrase 'the selfish gene', and at its core lies the idea that individuals do not consistently do things for the good of their group, or their families, or even themselves. They consistently do things that benefit their genes, because they are all inevitably descended from those that did the same. None of your ancestors died celibate.

※ ※ ※

This idea emerged from two directions. First, it came out of theory. Given that genes are the replicating currency of natural selection, it is an inevitable, algorithmic certainty that genes which cause behavior that enhances the survival of such genes must thrive at the expense of genes that do not. It is just a simple consequence of the fact of replication. The insight also came out of observation and experiment. All sorts of behaviour that had seemed puzzling when seen through the lens of the individual or the species, suddenly became clear when seen through a gene-focused lens. In particular, as Hamilton triumphantly showed, the social insects, by helping their sisters to breed, left more copies of their genes in the next generation than by trying to breed themselves. From the gene's point of view, therefore, the astonishing altruism of the worker ant was purely, unambiguously selfish. The selfless cooperation of the ant colony was an illusion: each worker ant was striving for genetic eternity through its brothers and sisters, the queen's royal offspring, rather than through its own offspring, but it was doing so with just as much gene-selfishness as any human being elbowing aside his rivals on the way up the corporate ladder. The ants and termites might, as Kropotkin had said, have 'renounced the Hobbesian war' as individuals, but their genes had not.[3]

The mental impact of this revolution in biology for those close to it was dramatic. Like Copernicus and Darwin, Williams and Hamilton dealt a humiliating blow to human self-importance. Not only was the human being just another animal, but it was also the disposable plaything and tool of a committee of self-interested genes. Hamilton himself recalls the moment when it dawned upon him that his body and his genome were more like a society than a machine. 'There had come the realization that

3. Hamilton, W. D. 1964. The genetical evolution of social behaviour. I, II. *Journal of Theoretical Biology* 7:1–52.

the genome wasn't the monolithic data bank plus executive team devoted to one project—keeping oneself alive, having babies—that I had hitherto imagined it to be. Instead, it was beginning to seem more a company boardroom, a theatre for a power struggle of egotists and factions . . . I was an ambassador ordered abroad by some fragile coalition, a bearer of conflicting orders from the uneasy masters of a divided empire."[4]

Richard Dawkins, coming upon the same ideas as a young scientist, was equally stunned: 'We are survival machines—robot vehicles blindly programmed to preserve the selfish molecules known as genes. This is a truth which still fills me with astonishment. Though I have known it for years, I never seem to get fully used to it."[5]

*   *   *

Some philosophers have argued that there cannot be such a thing as animal altruism, because altruism must imply a generous motive rather than a generous act. Even St Augustine wrestled with this question; alms giving, he said, must be done for the motive of love of God, not out of pride. A similar question divided Adam Smith from his teacher, Francis Hutcheson, who argued that benevolence motivated by vanity or self-interest was not benevolence. Smith thought this too extreme. A man may do a good deed, even if he does it out of vanity. More recently, the economist Amartya Sen, echoing Kant, has written:

> If the knowledge of torture of others makes you sick, it is a case of sympathy . . . It can be argued that behaviour based on sympathy is in an important sense egoistic, for one is oneself pleased at others' pleasure and pained at others' pain, and the pursuit of one's own utility may thus be helped by sympathetic action.[6]

In other words, the more you truly feel for people in distress, the more selfish you are being in alleviating that distress. Only those who do good out of cold, unmoved conviction are 'true' altruists.

Yet what matters to society is whether people are likely to be nice to each other, not their motives. If I am setting out to raise money for a charity, I am not going to return the cheques of companies and celebrities on the grounds that they are motivated more by the search for good publicity than by the cause itself. Likewise, when Hamilton developed the theory of kin selection, he did not for one moment interpret the worker ant as selfish, rather than selfless, because it remained sterile. He merely interpreted its selfless behaviour as a consequence of selfish genes.

*   *   *

Our minds have been built by selfish genes, but they have been built to be social, trustworthy and cooperative. That is the paradox this book has tried to explain. Human beings have social instincts. They come into

4. Hamilton, W. D. 1996. *Narrow Roads of Gene Land. Vol. I: Evolution and Social Behaviour.* W. H. Freeman/Spektrum, Oxford.
5. Dawkins, R. 1976. *The Selfish Gene.* Oxford University Press, Oxford.
6. Sen, A. K. 1977. Rational fools: a critique of the behavioral foundations of economic theory. *Philosophy and Public Affairs* 6:317–44. See also Hirshleifer, J. 1985. The expanding domain of economics. *American Economic Review* 75:53–68.

the world equipped with predispositions to learn how to cooperate, to discriminate the trustworthy from the treacherous, to commit themselves to be trustworthy, to earn good reputations, to exchange goods and information, and to divide labour. In this we are on our own. No other species has been so far down this evolutionary path before us, for no species has built a truly integrated society except among the inbred relatives of a large family such as an ant colony. We owe our success as a species to our social instincts; they have enabled us to reap undreamt benefits from the division of labour for our masters—the genes. They are responsible for the rapid expansion of our brains in the past two million years and thence for our inventiveness. Our societies and our minds evolved together, each reinforcing trends in the other. Far from being a universal feature of animal life, as Kropotkin believed, this instinctive cooperativeness is the very hallmark of humanity and what sets us apart from other animals.

The evolutionary perspective is a long one. This book has in passing tried to nail some myths about when we adopted our cultured habits. I have argued that there was morality before the Church; trade before the state; exchange before money; social contracts before Hobbes; welfare before the rights of man; culture before Babylon; society before Greece; self-interest before Adam Smith; and greed before capitalism. These things have been expressions of human nature since deep in the hunter-gatherer Pleistocene. Some of them have roots in the missing links with other primates. Only our supreme self-importance has obscured this so far.

But self-congratulation is premature. We have as many darker as lighter instincts. The tendency of human societies to fragment into competing groups has left us with minds all too ready to adopt prejudices and pursue genocidal feuds. Also, though we may have within our heads the capacity to form a functioning society, we patently fail to use it properly. Our societies are torn by war, violence, theft, dissension and inequality. We struggle to understand why, variously apportioning blame to nature, nurture, government, greed or gods. The dawning self-awareness that this book has chronicled ought—indeed must—have some practical use. Knowing how evolution arrived at the human capacity for social trust, we can surely find out how to cure its lack. Which human institutions generate trust and which ones dissipate it?

*   *   *

Thomas Hobbes was Charles Darwin's direct intellectual ancestor. Hobbes (1651) begat David Hume (1739), who begat Adam Smith (1776), who begat Thomas Robert Malthus (1798), who begat Charles Darwin (1859). It was after reading Malthus that Darwin shifted from thinking about competition between groups to thinking about competition between individuals, a shift Smith had achieved in the century before. The Hobbesian diagnosis—though not the prescription—still lies at the heart of both economics and modern evolutionary biology (Smith begat Friedman; Darwin begat Dawkins). At the root of both disciplines lies the notion that, if the balance of nature was not designed from above but emerged from below, then there is no reason to think it will prove to be a harmonious whole. John Maynard Keynes would later describe *The Origin of Species* as 'simply Ricardian economics couched in scientific language', and Stephen Jay Gould has said that natural selection 'was essentially Adam Smith's economics read into nature'. Karl Marx made much the same point: 'It is remarkable,' he wrote to Friedrich Engels in June 1862, 'how Darwin recognises among beasts and plants his own English society with its division of labour, competition, opening up of new markets, "inventions," and the Malthusian struggle for existence. It is Hobbes' *bellum omnium contra omnes*.'[7]

Darwin's disciple, Thomas Henry Huxley, chose exactly the same quotation from Hobbes to illustrate his argument that life is a pitiless struggle. For primitive man, he said, 'life was a continual free fight, and beyond the limited and temporary relations of the family, the Hobbesian war of each against all was the normal state of existence. The human species, like others, plashed and floundered amid the general stream of evolution, keeping its head above the water as it best might, and thinking neither of whence nor whither.' It was this essay that provoked Kropotkin to write *Mutual Aid*.

*   *   *

I am not going to fall into the trap of pretending that our dim and misty understanding of the human social instinct can be instantly translated into a political philosophy. For a start, it teaches us that Utopia is impossible, because society is an uneasy compromise between individuals with conflicting ambitions, rather than something designed directly by natural selection itself.

None the less, the new 'gene-tilitarian' understanding of human instincts that this book has explored leads to a few simple precepts for avoiding mistakes. Human beings have some instincts that foster the greater good and others that foster self-interested and anti-social behaviour. We must design a society that encourages the former and discourages the latter.

Consider, for example, a glaring paradox of free enterprise. If we declare that Smith, Malthus, Ricardo, Friedrich Hayek and Milton Friedman are right, and that man is basically motivated by self-interest, do we not by that very declaration encourage people to be more selfish? By recognizing the inevitability of greed and self-interest, we seem to approve it.

The essayist William Hazlitt certainly believed so, fulminating in his 'Reply to Malthus' that:

> It is neither generous nor just to come to the aid of the narrow prejudices and hard-heartedness of mankind, with metaphysical distinctions and the cobwebs of philosophy. The balance inclines too much on that side already, without the addition of false weights.[8]

In other words, the reason we must not say that people are nasty is that it is true.

*   *   *

7. The war of all against all. [Editor]
8. Hazlitt, W. 1902. A reply to the essay on population by the Rev. T. R. Malthus. *The Collected Works of William Hazlitt. Vol. 4*. J. M. Dent, London.

So the first thing we should do to create a good society is to conceal the truth about humankind's propensity for self-interest, the better to delude our fellows into thinking that they are noble savages inside. It is a distasteful idea for those of us who think the truth is more interesting than lies, however white. But the distaste need not worry us for long, because the white-lying is already happening. As we have repeatedly encountered in this book, propagandists always exaggerate the niceness of people, partly to flatter them and partly because the message is more palatable. People wish to believe in noble savages. As Robert Wright has argued:

> The new [selfish gene] paradigm strips self-absorption of its noble raiment. Selfishness, remember, seldom presents itself to us in naked form. Belonging as we do to a species (*the* species) whose members justify their actions morally, we are designed to think of ourselves as good and our behaviour as defensible, even when these propositions are objectively dubious.[9]

*   *   *

9. Wright. *The Moral Animal*. New York, 1994.

PART VIII
EVOLUTIONARY THEORY
AND RELIGIOUS THEORY

The assumed instinctive belief in God has been used by many persons as an argument for His existence. But this is a rash argument, as we should thus be compelled to believe in the existence of many cruel and malignant spirits . . . for the belief in them is far more general than in a beneficent Deity. The idea of a universal and beneficent Creator does not seem to arise in the mind of man, until he has been elevated by long-continued culture.

—Charles Darwin, 1871

Ignorance more frequently begets confidence than does knowledge.

—Charles Darwin, 1871

CREATION†

for the discoverer of the Grotte de Lascaux
Marcel Ravidat, 1923–1995

On all the living walls
of this dim cave,
soot and ochre, acts of will,
come down to us to say:

This is who we were.
We foraged here in an age of ice,
and, warmed by the fur of wolves,
felt the pride of predators
going for game.
Here we traced the strength of bulls,
the grace of deer, turned life into art,
and left this testimony on our walls.
Explorers of the future, see how,
when our dreams reach forward,
your wonder reaches back, and we embrace.
When we are long since dust,
and false prophets come,
then don't forget that *we* were your creators.
So build your days
on what you know is real, and remember
that nothing will keep your lives alive
but art—the black and ochre visions
you draw inside your cave
will honor your lost tribe
when explorers in some far future
marvel at the paintings on *your* walls.

—Philip Appleman, 1996

† From *New and Selected Poems, 1956–1996*, by Philip Appleman. Reprinted by permission of The University of Arkansas Press. Copyright © 1996 by Philip Appleman.

Mainstream Religious Support for Evolution

POPE JOHN PAUL II

Message to the Pontifical Academy of Sciences (1996)†

* * *

1. In celebrating the 60th anniversary of the Academy's refoundation, I would like to recall the intentions of my predecessor Pius XI, who wished to surround himself with a select group of scholars, relying on them to inform the Holy See in complete freedom about developments in scientific research, and thereby to assist him in his reflections.

* * *

2. I am pleased with the first theme you have chosen, that of the origins of life and evolution, an essential subject which deeply interests the Church, since Revelation, for its part, contains teaching concerning the nature and origins of man. How do the conclusions reached by the various scientific disciplines coincide with those contained in the message of Revelation? And if, at first sight, there are apparent contradictions, in what direction do we look for their solution? We know, in fact, that truth cannot contradict truth (cf. Leo XIII, Encyclical *Providentissimus Deus*). Moreover, to shed greater light on historical truth, your research on the Church's relations with science between the 16th and 18th centuries is of great importance.

During this plenary session, you are undertaking a "reflection on science at the dawn of the third millennium", starting with the identification of the principal problems created by the sciences and which affect humanity's future. With this step you point the way to solutions which will be beneficial to the whole human community. In the domain of inanimate and animate nature, the evolution of science and its applications gives rise to new questions. The better the Church's knowledge is of their essential aspects, the more she will understand their impact.

* * *

In his Encyclical *Humani generis* (1950), my predecessor Pius XII had already stated that there was no opposition between evolution and the

---

† First published in *L'Osservatore Romano*, October 30, 1996. John Paul II (b. 1920), pope of the Roman Catholic Church (1978–).

doctrine of the faith about man and his vocation, on condition that one did not lose sight of several indisputable points.

* * *

4. Taking into account the state of scientific research at the time as well as of the requirements of theology, the Encyclical *Humani generis* considered the doctrine of "evolutionism" a serious hypothesis, worthy of investigation and in-depth study equal to that of the opposing hypothesis. * * *

Today, almost half a century after the publication of the Encyclical, new knowledge has led to the recognition of more than one hypothesis in the theory of evolution. [*Editor's note: On 19 November 1996, Father Robert Dempsey, editor of the English-language edition of* L'Osservatore Romano, *stated that the newspaper had published an overly literal translation of the French-language message that "obscures the real meaning of the text." He said that the pope's real meaning was that it is now possible to recognize that the theory of evolution is more than a hypothesis* (Catholic News Service, 19 November 1996, p 14; and CRUX of the News, 2 December 1996, p 6).] It is indeed remarkable that this theory has been progressively accepted by researchers, following a series of discoveries in various fields of knowledge.

* * *

By means of it a series of independent data and facts can be related and interpreted in a unified explanation. A theory's validity depends on whether or not it can be verified; it is constantly tested against the facts; wherever it can no longer explain the latter, it shows its limitations and unsuitability. It must then be rethought.

Furthermore, while the formulation of a theory like that of evolution complies with the need for consistency with the observed data, it borrows certain notions from natural philosophy.

And, to tell the truth, rather than *the* theory of evolution, we should speak of *several* theories of evolution. On the one hand, this plurality has to do with the different explanations advanced for the mechanism of evolution, and on the other, with the various philosophies on which it is based.

* * *

But even more, man is called to enter into a relationship of knowledge and love with God himself, a relationship which will find its complete fulfilment beyond time, in eternity. All the depth and grandeur of this vocation are revealed to us in the mystery of the risen Christ (cf. *Gaudium el spes*, n. 22). It is by virtue of his spiritual soul that the whole person possesses such a dignity even in his body. Pius XII stressed this essential point: if the human body takes its origin from pre-existent living matter, the spiritual soul is immediately created by God.

* * *

From the Vatican, 22 October 1996

CENTRAL CONFERENCE OF AMERICAN RABBIS

On Creationism in School Textbooks (1984)†

Whereas the principles and concepts of biological evolution are basic to understanding science; and

Whereas students who are not taught these principles, or who hear "creationism" presented as a scientific alternative, will not be receiving an education based on modern scientific knowledge; and

Whereas these students' ignorance about evolution will seriously undermine their understanding of the world and the natural laws governing it, and their introduction to other explanations described as "scientific" will give them false ideas about scientific methods and criteria.

Therefore be it resolved that the Central Conference of American Rabbis commend the Texas State Board of Education for affirming the constitutional separation of Church and State, and the principle that no group, no matter how large or small, may use the organs of government, of which the public schools are among the most conspicuous and influential, to foist its religious beliefs on others;

Be it further resolved that we call upon publishers of science textbooks to reject those texts that clearly distort the integrity of science and to treat other explanations of human origins for just what they are—beyond the realm of science;

Be it further resolved that we call upon science teachers and local school authorities in all states to demand quality textbooks that are based on modern, scientific knowledge and that exclude "scientific" creationism;

Be it further resolved that we call upon parents and other citizens concerned about the quality of science education in the public schools to urge their Boards of Education, publishers, and science teachers to implement these needed reforms.

UNITED PRESBYTERIAN CHURCH IN THE U. S. A.

Evolution and Creationism (1982)‡

Whereas, The Program Agency of the United Presbyterian Church in the USA notes with concern a concerted effort to introduce legislation and other means for the adoption of a public school curriculum variously known as "Creationism" or "Creation Science,"

† Adopted at the ninety-fifth annual convention of the Central Conference of American Rabbis, June 18–21, 1984. Reprinted in *Voices for Evolution* (Berkeley, Calif., 1995): 88. Reprinted by permission of the National Center for Science Education. This volume was originated by Dr. Kenneth Saladin of Georgia College; the first edition was edited by Betty McCollister, the second edition by Molleen Matsumura.
‡ Resolution adopted by the General Assembly, 1982. Reprinted in *Voices for Evolution* (Berkeley, Calif., 1995): 107–08. Reprinted by permission of the National Center for Science Education.

Whereas, over several years, fundamentalist church leadership, resourced by the Creation Science Research Center and the Institute for Creation Research, has prepared legislation for a number of states calling for "balanced treatment" for "creation-science" and "evolution-science," requiring that wherever one is taught the other must be granted a comparable presentation in the classroom;

Whereas, this issue represents a new situation, there are General Assembly policies on Church and State and Public Education which guide us to assert once again that the state cannot legislate the establishment of religion in the public domain;

Whereas, the dispute is not really over biology or faith, but is essentially about Biblical interpretation, particularly over two irreconcilable viewpoints regarding the characteristics of Biblical literature and the nature of Biblical authority:

Therefore, the Program Agency recommends to the 194th General Assembly (1982) the adoption of the following affirmation:

Affirms that, despite efforts to establish "creationism" or "creation-science" as a valid science, it is teaching based upon a particular religious dogma as agreed by the court (*McLean vs Arkansas Board of Education*);

Affirms that, the imposition of a fundamentalist viewpoint about the interpretation of Biblical literature—where every word is taken with uniform literalness and becomes an absolute authority on all matters, whether moral, religious, political, historical or scientific—is in conflict with the perspective on Biblical interpretation characteristically maintained by Biblical scholars and theological schools in the mainstream of Protestantism, Roman Catholicism and Judaism. Such scholars find that the scientific theory of evolution does not conflict with their interpretation of the origins of life found in Biblical literature.

Affirms that, academic freedom of both teachers and students is being further limited by the impositions of the campaign most notably in the modification of textbooks which limits the teaching about evolution but also by the threats to the professional authority and freedom of teachers to teach and students to learn;

Affirms that, required teaching of such a view constitutes an establishment of religion and a violation of the separation of church and state, as provided in the First Amendment to the Constitution and laws of the United States;

Affirms that, exposure to the Genesis account is best sought through the teaching about religion, history, social studies and literature, provinces other than the discipline of natural science, and

Calls upon Presbyterians, and upon legislators and school board members, to resist all efforts to establish any requirements upon teachers and schools to teach "creationism" or "creation science."

THE LUTHERAN WORLD FEDERATION

[Statement on Evolution] (1965)†

Symbolic of the prominence of the evolutionary idea in contemporary thought is the occurrence of "evolved" as the last word of the famous closing paragraph of Darwin's *The Origin of Species*, 1859. While not original with the emergence of Darwinism, evolution has nevertheless been intimately associated with it and has in the intervening century become one of the most comprehensive concepts of the modern mind. Consequently the issue cannot be stated in terms of the restricted alternative whether any one phase of evolution (especially the biological) is still "only a scientific theory" or long since "an established fact." Neither is it a matter of holding out the hope that if only enough fault can be found with Darwin the church's doctrine of creation will automatically be accepted and religion can then be at peace with science.

Rather, the evolutionary dynamisms of today's world compel a more realistic confrontation. One area of reality after another has been analyzed and described on the basis of some kind of progressive change until the whole may be viewed as a single process. The standpoint of the one who views this unitary development may be avowedly atheistic in the sense of ruling out the supernatural (Sir Julian Huxley) or just as avowedly Christian in the sense of finding in evolution an infusion of new life into Christianity, with Christianity alone dynamic enough to unify the world with God (Teilhard de Chardin).

In whatever way the process may be ultimately explained, it has come about that an idea which has been most thoroughly explored in the field of biology (lower forms of life evolving into higher) has by means of organismic analogy found universal application. Phenomena thus accounted for range from physical realities (evolution of the atoms and expanding galaxies) to man and his social experience (the evolution of cultural values) including his understanding of time and history (the evolutionary vision of scientific eschatology). Hence there is posited a movement of cumulative change in the organic and the inorganic; in the evolution of life and of man, of social institutions and political constitutions, of emerging races and nations, of language and art forms, of school systems and educational methods, of religion and doctrine; and of science and of the theory of evolution itself.

* * *

With biological evolution (ostensibly a matter of pure science) thereby becoming a metaphysics of evolution it needs to be determined whether religion's proper quarrel is with the science which permits itself such dogmatic extension or whether the misgivings are primarily with the particular

† From the *Encyclopedia of the Lutheran Church*, vol. 1 (Minneapolis, 1965). Reprinted in *Voices for Evolution* (Berkeley, Calif., 1995): 95–96. Reprinted by permission of the National Center for Science Education.

philosophical interpretation involved. To the evolutionary concept in general there are however (in spite of innumerable variations) basically two religious reactions.

1. As in the days of the Scopes trial all evolution may still be denied on the grounds of a literalistic interpretation of the Bible, especially Genesis 1–11. Not content with the commitment of faith in the Creator expressed in the First Article of the Apostles' Creed this interpretation may demand a specific answer also to the questions of when creation occurred and how long it took. * * *

2. On the other hand there are those who can no more close their eyes to the evidence which substantiates some kind of lengthy evolutionary process in the opinion of the vast majority of those scientists most competent to judge than they could deny the awesome reality of God's presence in nature and their own experience of complete dependence upon the creative and sustaining hand of God revealed in the Scriptures. * * *

An assessment of the prevailing situation makes it clear that evolution's assumptions are as much around us as the air we breathe and no more escapable. At the same time theology's affirmations are being made as responsibly as ever. In this sense both science and religion are here to stay, and the demands of either are great enough to keep most (if not all) from daring to profess competence in both. To preserve their own integrity both science and religion need to remain in a healthful tension of respect toward one another and to engage in a searching debate which no more permits theologians to pose as scientists than it permits scientists to pose as theologians.

THE GENERAL CONVENTION OF THE EPISCOPAL CHURCH

Resolution on Evolution and Creationism (1982)†

Whereas, the state legislatures of several states have recently passed so-called "balanced treatment" laws requiring the teaching of "Creation-science" whenever evolutionary models are taught; and

Whereas, in many other states political pressures are developing for such "balanced treatment" laws; and

Whereas, the terms "Creationism" and "Creation-science" as understood in these laws do not refer simply to the affirmation that God created the Earth and Heavens and everything in them, but specify certain methods and timing of the creative acts, and impose limits on these acts which are neither scriptural nor accepted by many Christians; and

† Adopted by the sixty-seventh general convention of the Episcopal Church, 1982. Reprinted in *Voices for Evolution* (Berkeley, Calif., 1995): 92. Reprinted by permission of the National Center for Science Education.

Whereas, the dogma of "Creationism" and "Creation-science" as understood in the above contexts has been discredited by scientific and theologic studies and rejected in the statements of many church leaders; and

Whereas, "Creationism" and "Creation-science" is not limited to just the origin of life, but intends to monitor public school courses, such as biology, life science, anthropology, sociology, and often also English, physics, chemistry, world history, philosophy, and social studies; therefore be it

Resolved, that the 67th General Convention affirm the glorious ability of God to create in any manner, whether men understand it or not, and in this affirmation reject the limited insight and rigid dogmatism of the "Creationist" movement, and be it further

Resolved, that we affirm our support of the sciences and educators and of the Church and theologians in their search for truth in this Creation that God has given and entrusted to us; and be it further

Resolved, that the Presiding Bishop appoint a Committee to organize Episcopalians and to cooperate with all Episcopalians to encourage actively their state legislators not to be persuaded by arguments and pressures of the "Creationists" into legislating any form of "balanced treatment" laws or any law requiring the teaching of "Creation-science."

UNITARIAN UNIVERSALIST ASSOCIATION

Resolution Opposing "Scientific Creationism" (1982)†

Whereas, the constitutional principles of religious liberty and the separation of church and state that safeguards liberty, and the ideal of a pluralistic society are under increasing attack in the Congress of the United States, in state legislatures, and in some sectors of the communications media by a combination of sectarian and secular special interests;

Be it resolved: That the 1982 General Assembly of UUA reaffirms its support for these principles and urges the Board of Trustees and President of the Association, member societies, and Unitarian-Universalists in the United States to: . . . 2. Uphold religious neutrality in public education, oppose all government mandated or sponsored prayers, devotional observances, and religious indoctrination in public schools; and oppose efforts to compromise the integrity of public school teaching by the introduction of sectarian religious doctrines, such as "scientific creationism," and by exclusion of educational materials on sectarian grounds . . .

---

† Passed at the twenty-first annual general assembly of the Unitarian Universalist Association, June 1992. Reprinted in *Voices for Evolution* (Berkeley, Calif., 1995): 99. Reprinted by permission of the National Center for Science Education.

Fundamentalist Creationism

EUGENIE C. SCOTT

Antievolution and Creationism
in the United States (1997)†

Introduction

According to a 1996 poll of adult Americans conducted by the National Science Board, only 44% agreed with the statement, "Human beings, as we know them today, developed from earlier species of animals" (National Science Board). Forty percent disagreed, and 16% answered "don't know." The same survey showed that 52% of American adults either agreed or didn't know that "[t]he earliest humans lived at the same time as the dinosaurs" (32% agreed, 20% didn't know).

And yet, the National Academy of Sciences states unequivocally that:

> Evolution pervades all biological phenomena. To ignore that it occurred or to classify it as a form of dogma is to deprive the student of the most fundamental organizational concept in the biological sciences. No other biological concept has been more extensively tested and more thoroughly corroborated than the evolutionary history of organisms (National Academy of Sciences 1984).

There is a gap between the acceptance of evolution in the scientific community and its acceptance among the general public. It appears that among well-accepted scientific theories (heliocentrism, cell theory, atomic theory, plate tectonics), evolution alone is rejected by nonscientists. In a poll by the American Museum of Natural History, for example, 78% of adult Americans accepted the theory of continental drift ("continents gradually change their positions") (American Museum of Natural History 1994).

A significant variable in understanding antievolutionism is the degree to which a literal interpretation of holy texts is considered essential to theology. Thus Biblical-literalist Christians, ultraconservative Jews, and Koranic-literalist Muslims object to evolution. Because the number of Jews and Muslims in the United States is small compared with Christians, and because the most active antievolutionists are Christian, I focus on Christians in this review. * * *

† From the *Annual Review of Anthropology*, 26 (1997): 263–89. With permission, from the *Annual Review of Anthropology*, Volume 26, Copyright © 1997, by Annual Reviews. Eugenie C. Scott (b. 1945) is executive director of the National Center for Science Education in Berkeley, California.

Religious opposition to evolution propels antievolutionism. Although antievolutionists pay lip service to supposed scientific problems with evolution, what motivates them to battle its teaching is apprehension over the implications of evolution for religion. Conservative Christians who are strongly literalist in their views fear that if their children learn evolution, they will cease to believe in God. Without God to guide them, children will grow up to be bad people. In the words of Henry R Morris, a prominent creationist, "Evolution is at the foundation of communism, fascism, Freudianism, social darwinism, behaviorism, Kinseyism, materialism, atheism, and in the religious world, modernism and neo-orthodoxy."[1] Conservative Christians also believe that the child who loses faith in God also is lost to salvation. Clearly, antievolutionists' motives for opposing the teaching of evolution to their children are strong. As shown below, however, the strict literalist view is not universally held by the majority of Christians in the United States.

Rejecting evolution has a long history in America. Antievolutionism has been a political and social movement in this country for most of this century. In this review, I define terms and issues critical to an understanding of the movement and briefly discuss the history, motivations, and evolution of antievolutionism. I argue that antievolutionism has evolved from the purely religious opposition of the Scopes era to creation science, and to the present neocreationism period. The academic response to creationism has been an unusual mixture of scholarship and activism. An explosion of books and articles from the mid-1970s through the late 1980s was motivated less by scholarly interest than by efforts to oppose antievolutionists in their attempts to legally impose their views on the public education system. * * *

Definitions

EVOLUTION

"Evolution" in its most basic sense is a simple idea: Change through time has taken place. The universe has a history: The present is different from the past. Physical and chemical evolution include the formation of elements in the nuclear blast furnaces of evolving stars, the formation of galaxies, and the formation of star systems with planets. The earth has changed greatly in the past four billion years; the present is different from the past.

Darwin's "descent with modification" is the most useful definition of biological evolution. Darwinism is a specific kind of evolution: Living things descend with modification from ancestors through natural selection. In the 1940s and 1950s, classical natural selection theory coupled with genetic theory became known as the synthetic theory of evolution, or neo-Darwinism. Late-twentieth-century explanations of the rate and manner of biological evolution include Eldredge and Gould's theory of "punctuated equilibria," speculations about natural selection above (species selection)

1. J. C. Whitcomb and H. M. Morris, *The Genesis Flood* (Phillipsburg, N.J., 1963): 24.

and below (selfish genes) the level of organism or population, and non-selective mechanisms bringing about evolutionary change (neutralism or non-Darwinian evolution). The relationship between evolution and developmental biology is an active area of research. Evolutionary biological theory has progressed beyond classical Darwinism and even neo-Darwinism, although the current consensus is that neo-Darwinism explains much, if not most, of biological evolution.

CREATIONISM

Creationism generally refers to the idea that a supernatural entity(s) created the universe and humankind. Creation stories are extensively studied in comparative religion and in the anthropology of religion.

* * *

Special Creationists can be divided into two groups: Young Earth Creationists and Old Earth Creationists.

YOUNG EARTH CREATIONISM

Young Earth Creationists (YECs) are Special Creationists who believe that the universe came into being only a few thousand years ago. The most conservative YECs are Flat Earthers, who accept little of the modern scientific consensus. Charles K. Johnson, head of the International Flat Earth Society, headquartered in Lancaster, California, believes seriously that earth is as the ancients perceived it: circular and flat, not spherical.

* * *

Geocentrists are somewhat more liberal YECs. They accept that the planet is a sphere but deny that the sun is the center of the solar system. Like Flat Earthers, they reject virtually all of modern physics and chemistry as well as biology. * * *

Flat Earthers and Geocentrists believe in a universe and planet that are only a few thousand years old, much as did Bishop Ussher and John Lightfoot. Technically, they are YECs, but within antievolutionist circles the term YEC is usually reserved for the followers of Henry Morris, founder and recently retired director of the Institute for Creation Research (ICR) and arguably the most influential creationist of the late twentieth century. * * *

YEC AND THE INSTITUTE FOR CREATION RESEARCH

Henry Morris can be said to have defined antievolutionism in its modern form. In 1963, he and John C Whitcomb published *The Genesis Flood* (Whitcomb & Morris 1963), a seminal work that outlined a scientific rationale for Young Earth Creationism. As the title suggests, the authors accept Genesis literally, including not just the special, separate creation of human beings and all other species, but the historicity of Noah's Flood. * * *

Very little actual research is performed by ICR faculty. Publications are almost entirely on Christian apologetics. In a review of the ICR graduate school, a visiting committee of scientists concluded that "no member of the resident faculty of the ICR has continued an active and published research program since arrival at the ICR. The Institute for Creation Research can therefore not be considered to be a scientific research institution."

* * *

During the early 1980s, a series of bills promoting equal time for the teaching of creation science was introduced in at least 26 state legislatures, some more than once. Most of them were clones of a model bill developed by a South Carolina respiratory therapist, Paul Elwanger, which was influenced by an ICR model resolution for equal time. The bills defined creation science as including the ideas of "a worldwide flood" and other YEC mainstays, including the special creation of human beings. If so-called evolution science was taught, then creation science, its proposed parallel, must be taught as well. Arkansas and Louisiana each passed similar Elwanger-type bills, and both bills were taken to court.

ARKANSAS AND LOUISIANA

Arkansas's equal time law was declared unconstitutional in 1982 after a full trial dubbed "Scopes II." Opposing the law were leaders of many religious organizations. Joining the lead plaintiff, Methodist Rev. Bill Mc-Lean, were the bishops or other leaders of Roman Catholic, Episcopalian, African Methodist Episcopal, Presbyterian, and Southern Baptist churches, and Reform Jews. The ACLU arranged pro bono representation by a leading New York law firm and assembled an all-star cast of witnesses from the fields of science, philosophy of science, education, and theology. The *McLean* v. *Arkansas* decision was a rousing victory for the anticreationists: Federal District Judge Overton not only struck down the law but declared that creation science failed as science. Having lost badly, the state did not appeal.

The failure of the Arkansas equal time law slowed but did not halt the effort to pass legislation. At virtually the same time as the Arkansas decision was being issued, Louisiana passed a similar equal time law which was challenged by both proponents and opponents: one side suing to immediately implement the law and the other requesting an injunction. The lawsuits took a long time to wend their ways through the courts, and there was no full trial as there had been in Arkansas. Finally, in 1987, the Supreme Court decided in *Edwards* v. *Aguillard* that equal time laws like Louisiana's violated the establishment clause of the First Amendment of the Constitution because they promoted an inherently religious idea: creationism.

The Scholarly Response

The scientific community was appalled at the proliferation of such laws, and in 1980–1981 a loose coalition of scientists and teachers formed Committees of Correspondence in most of the states. Led by biologist Wayne Moyer, then-director of the National Association of Biology Teachers, and retired high-school biology teacher Stanley Weinberg, this coalition evolved by 1983 into the National Center for Science Education (NCSE), which remains an organization consisting primarily of scientists who support the teaching of evolution in the public schools and oppose creation science and other religiously based attacks on evolution.

*   *   *

Scientists, many of them associated with Weinberg's Committees of Correspondence network, testified against equal time laws in their state legislatures, helping to persuade legislators not to pass such bills. The role of scientists was critical: If creationism could indeed be made scientific, then it would deserve a place in the curriculum. Scientists were the only ones qualified to judge whether creationism was in fact scientific and whether it was good scholarship. When equal time provisions were suggested in local school-board meetings, teachers greatly appreciated the input of scientists. Typical of the combined activism and scholarship of the period, one publication documented the obvious: that creation science articles were not being published in refereed journals. The authors argued that documenting the missing scholarly foundation to creation science was necessary to blunt the claims being made at school boards and in court that creation science was a legitimate scientific alternative to evolution.

*   *   *

After the defeat of YEC-type equal time laws, it was minimally necessary to devise new terms, if not new strategies. I refer to this period of anti-evolutionism after *Edwards* as Neocreationism. Equal time for creation science is still being pushed, although in the 1990s it occurs more often at the local school-board level than in the state legislatures.

*   *   *

Evolution as Theory or Fact

In 1996, the State of Tennessee debated and narrowly defeated a bill that would have made teachers who taught evolution as a fact—rather than as a theory—subject to dismissal for insubordination. In late 1995, Alabama passed a state science curriculum that required that evolution be taught "as theory rather than fact." These are not the first such cases; NCSE has records of school-board controversies or individual teachers' complaints concerning pressure to teach evolution as a theory and not fact from Alabama, Arkansas, California, Florida, Georgia, Louisiana, Pennsylvania, Texas, and Wisconsin, among other places.

The problem is that "theory" and "fact" are used differently in science and among the public. In science, a theory is a logical construct of facts, hypotheses, and laws that explains a natural phenomenon. To the general public, however, a theory is not an explanation, but a hunch or guess. To teach evolution as a theory in this sense is to teach it as something students don't have to take seriously. The State Senator in Tennessee who proposed the 1996 legislation described theories as "whims." Many a school-board meeting has erupted over evolution being presented dogmatically as fact, and letters to editors regularly fulminate with outrage over children being "forced" to "believe" in evolution.

More than one factor contributes to this vehemence. One cause is the underlying, if usually unspoken, fear many nonscientists have that "evolution means you can't believe in God." There has been no pressure for teachers to present the theories of heliocentrism, gravitation, the cell, the atom, or relativity nondogmatically, but these theories do not have consequences for some religions. People react as though they believe that when evolution is presented as a fact, it must be believed in and that students will then have to give up their faith. Most Americans do not seem to understand that Catholicism, mainline Protestantism, and all but ultraorthodox Judaism have accommodated evolution into their theologies. There are concerns about parental control as well: If parents can't control something as basic as the religious beliefs of their children, what is left?

Intelligent Design

In 1989, shortly after the *Edwards* Supreme Court decision, *Of Pandas and People*, a supplemental textbook for high-school biology was published (Davis & Kenyon 1989). Its publication signified the increasing OEC influence in the neocreationist movement and introduced the term Intelligent Design (ID). ID is promoted primarily by university-based antievolutionists who tend to be PCs [Progressive Creationists] rather than YECs. Dean Kenyon, for example, a tenured professor of biology at San Francisco State University, and Percival Davis, who teaches at Hillsborough Community College, in Tampa, Florida, advocate ID.

ID is a lineal descendent of William Paley's Argument from Design, which held that God's existence could be proved by examining his works. Paley used a metaphor: He claimed that if one found an intricately contrived watch, it was obvious that such a thing could not have come together by chance. The existence of a watch implied a watchmaker who had designed the watch with a purpose in mind. Similarly, because there is order, purpose, and design in the world, naturally there is an omniscient designer. The existence of God was proven by the presence of order and intricacy.

The vertebrate eye was Paley's classic example, well known to educated people of the nineteenth century, of design in nature. Darwin deliberately used the example of the vertebrate eye in *The Origin of Species* to demonstrate how complexity and intricate design could come about through natural selection, which of course is not a chance phenomenon. In creationist literature, evolution is synonymous with chance. In scientific accounts, there are random or chance elements in the generation of genetic variation, but natural selection, acting upon this genetic variation, is the antithesis of chance. In the PC tradition, ID allows for a fair amount of microevolution, but supporters deny that mutation and natural selection are adequate to explain the evolution of one "kind" to another, such as chordates from echinoderms, or human beings from apes. These and the origin of life are considered too complex to be explained naturally, thus ID demands that a role be left for the intelligent designer, God.

*   *   *

ANTIEVOLUTION AT THE UNIVERSITY

One of the leading exponents of ID is Phillip Johnson, who holds an endowed chair at Boalt Hall School of Law, University of California, Berkeley. Johnson appeared on the anticreationist scene in 1991 with the publication of his book, *Darwin on Trial*. Because of Johnson's academic credentials, and because he ignored arguments about the age of the earth and was even faintly contemptuous of YEC, the book was perceived as different from traditional creation science, even though no new arguments were presented. *Darwin on Trial* was reviewed by people and in journals that would never have reviewed a publication by Morris. All concluded that Johnson lacked a solid grounding in the theory and factual basis of evolutionary science.

*   *   *

In 1996, Michael Behe, a biochemist at Lehigh University, published the most scholarly and scientific ID book to date, *Darwin's Black Box* (Behe 1996), which offers little comfort to typical antievolutionists. Behe accepts that natural selection produces most of the complex structural adaptations of plants and animals, and he even accepts that modern living things descended with modification from common ancestors. In a debate with Kenneth Miller, a biologist at Brown University, during the summer of 1995, Behe accepted that human beings and chimps share a common ancestor. Still, Behe asserted that there are things that can't be explained through natural processes. He claims that at the level of cell biochemistry lie "irreducibly complex" processes and structures, such as the blood-clotting cascade and the rotor motor of a microorganism's flagellum. Such structures cannot be broken down into component parts, says Behe, and therefore cannot be explained through the incremental activity of natural selection. They therefore could not have evolved, and because they could not have evolved they must have been specially created. Behe argues, as did Paley, that complexity is proof that there must be an intelligent designer, but his examples of complexity are biochemical.

Because Behe is a research scientist with a track record of legitimate publications (though not in evolutionary biology), his book has been reviewed with more seriousness than Johnson's *Darwin on Trial*. Although Behe claimed in *Darwin's Black Box* that his views would sweep the scientific world in a manner comparable to the discoveries of "Newton and Einstein, Lavoisier and Schroedinger, Pasteur, and Darwin," the response from the scientific community thus far has been decidedly tepid. Reviewers were quick to point out flaws both in reasoning and in factual and conceptual understanding.

ID proponents are not Luddites, objecting to science and its technological fruits, but they do not like naturalistic evolution. Like all conservative Christians, they insist on a significant explanatory role for God, and in life having a divinely directed purpose and meaning. * * *

Old Earth, ID publications by Behe, Johnson, and others will have a more profound effect on antievolutionism than creation science publications because they are being discussed at the university and college level, where the far more numerous publications of Morris are regarded primarily as curiosities. Articles and books by more moderate antievolutionists tend to be used not in science courses, but in "science studies," social problems, or philosophy courses taught by social scientists or philosophers less familiar with the facts and theory of evolution than are science faculty.

* * *

Faculty in fields with a historical component, which include astronomy, geology, biology, and anthropology, need to be explicit in their treatment of evolution so that members of the educated public understand this important scientific concept. Scientists in these fields recognize that evolution is an organizing principle in their disciplines but often fail to make this explicit to students. Biologists will, for example, teach principles of systematics and taxonomy without mentioning that the genus/species classification of organisms is possible because the splitting and branching process of evolution generates hierarchy. Astronomers will discuss galaxy formation and not use the "e-word." It is impossible to teach a physical anthropology course (or any introductory anthropology course) without teaching evolution, thus ironically it may be that most students who learn about evolution do so in departments classified as "social science" rather than natural science. This places an important responsibility upon anthropologists, who may by default be the major purveyors of evolutionary theory at the college level. We may need to spend even more time in our classes on principles of evolution than we perhaps have in the past. As members of a field that also includes the consideration of religion as part of the human way of life, anthropologists may in fact be the scientists best able to cope with the myriad aspects of the creation/evolution controversy.

The scientific establishment itself is not going to give up on evolution any more than it is going to give up on the periodic table of elements, but the amount of public support for evolution, including financial support for evolution-oriented research from federally funded organizations such as the National Science Foundation and the National Institutes of Health, may well dwindle even further if evolution loses yet more support among the general public.

CIRCUIT COURT, TENNESSEE

The Scopes Trial (1925)†

GEN. STEWART—[*Reading:*] State of Tennessee, County of Rhea. Circuit Court. July Special Term, 1925.

The grand jurors for the state aforesaid, being duly summoned, elected, empanelled, sworn, and charged to inquire for the body of the county aforesaid, upon their oaths present:

That John Thomas Scopes, heretofore on the 24th day of April, 1925, in the county aforesaid, then and there, unlawfully did willfully teach in the public schools of Rhea County, Tennessee, which said public schools are supported in part and in whole by the public school fund of the state, a certain theory and theories that deny the story of the divine creation of man as taught in the Bible, and did teach instead thereof that man has descended from a lower order of animals, he, the said John Thomas Scopes, being at the time, and prior thereto, a teacher in the public schools of Rhea County, Tennessee, aforesaid, against the peace and dignity of the State.

THE COURT—What is your plea, gentlemen?

* * *

MR. NEAL—[*Reading:*] The defendant moves the court to quash the indictment in this case for the following reasons:

First—(A) Because the act which is the basis of the indictment, and which the defendant is charged with violating, is unconstitutional and void in that it violates * * * Section 3, Article I of the constitution of Tennessee:

> Section 3. Right of Worship Free—That all men have a natural and indefeasible right to worship Almighty God according to the dictates of his own conscience; * * * and that no preference

† In 1925, the Tennessee legislature passed the "Butler Act," forbidding the teaching of evolution in the public schools of that state. In May, John Thomas Scopes, a science teacher at Dayton High School, consented to be the defendant in a court test of the law. He was indicted by a grand jury and stood trial on July 10–21, 1925. Defended by the American Civil Liberties Union, Scopes was represented by (among others) the noted trial lawyer Clarence Darrow; the prosecution was assisted by William Jennings Bryan, thrice-defeated presidential candidate. These men broadened the case from an investigation of a simple issue of law to a forum for the debate of a highly controversial issue: whether science (particularly evolution) and religion (particularly fundamentalism) could coexist.

In the wake of excitement following the Scopes trial, there was a nationwide flurry of antievolutionary activity, led by fundamentalist religious groups. In 1926 and 1927, laws similar to the Butler Act were passed by the legislatures of Mississippi and Arkansas, and these, together with the Butler Act, survived for decades. The Butler Act was finally repealed in 1967, and in 1968 the United States Supreme Court declared the Arkansas law unconstitutional—thus in effect nullifying the last remaining antievolutionary law.

The text is from the official stenographic transcript of the trial: *State of Tennessee* vs. *John Thomas Scopes*, Nos. 5231 and 5232, in the Circuit Court of Rhea County, Tennessee. Besides Scopes, Darrow, and Bryan, others mentioned in the transcript are Attorney General A. T. Stewart, counsel for the state, and John R. Neal, Dudley Field Malone, and Arthur Garfield Hays, all counsel for the defendant.

shall ever be given, by law, to any religious establishment or mode of worship.

* * *

MR. DARROW— * * * The part we claim is that last clause, "no preference shall ever be given, by law, to any religious establishment or mode of worship."

* * *

MR. DARROW—That is the part we claim is affected.

GEN. STEWART—In what wise?

MR. DARROW—Giving preference to the Bible.

GEN. STEWART— * * * If your Honor please, the St. James Version of the Bible is the recognized one in this section of the country. The laws of the land recognize the Bible; the laws of the land recognize the law of God and Christianity as a part of the common law.

MR. MALONE—Mr. Attorney General, may I ask a question?

GEN. STEWART—Certainly.

MR. MALONE—Does the law of the land or the law of the state of Tennessee recognize the Bible as part of a course in biology or science?

GEN. STEWART—I do not think the law of the land recognizes them as confusing one another in any particular.

* * *

MR. NEAL—It does not mention the Bible?

GEN. STEWART—Yes, it mentions the Bible. The legislature, according to our laws, in my opinion, would have the right to preclude the teaching of geography. That is—

MR. NEAL—Does not it prefer the Bible to the Koran?

GEN. STEWART—It does not mention the Koran.

MR. MALONE—Does not it prefer the Bible to the Koran?

GEN. STEWART—We are not living in a heathen country.

MR. MALONE—Will you answer my question? Does not it prefer the Bible to the Koran?

GEN. STEWART—We are not living in a heathen country, so how could it prefer the Bible to the Koran? * * *

MR. MALONE— * * * I would say to base a theory set forth in any version of the Bible to be taught in the public school is an invasion of the rights of the citizen, whether exercised by the police power or by the legislature.

GEN. STEWART—Because it imposes a religious opinion?

MR. MALONE—Because it imposes a religious opinion, yes. What I mean is this: If there be in the state of Tennessee a single child or young man or young woman in your school who is a Jew, to impose upon any course of science a particular view of creation from the Bible is interfering, from our point of view, with his civil rights under our theory of the case. That is our contention.

* * *

MR. DARROW— * * * This case we have to argue is a case at law, and hard as it is for me to bring my mind to conceive it, almost impossible as it is to put my mind back into the sixteenth century, I am going to argue it as if it was serious, and as if it was a death struggle between two civilizations.

* * *

Here, we find today as brazen and as bold an attempt to destroy learning as was ever made in the Middle Ages, and the only difference is we have not provided that they shall be burned at the stake, but there is time for that, your Honor; we have to approach these things gradually.

* * *

The statute should be comprehensible. It should not be written in Chinese anyway. It should be in passing English, as you say, so that common, human beings would understand what it meant, and so a man would know whether he is liable to go to jail when he is teaching, not so ambiguous as to be a snare or a trap to get someone who does not agree with you. It should be plain, simple and easy. Does this statute state what you shall teach and what you shall not? Oh, no! Oh, no! Not at all. Does it say you cannot teach the earth is round, because Genesis says it is flat? No. Does it say you cannot teach that the earth is millions of ages old, because the account in Genesis makes it less than six thousand years old? Oh, no. It doesn't state that. If it did you could understand it. It says you shan't teach any theory of the origin of man that is contrary to the divine theory contained in the Bible.

Now let us pass up the word "divine"! No legislature is strong enough in any state in the Union to characterize and pick any book as being divine. Let us take it as it is. What is the Bible? * * * The Bible is not one book. The Bible is made up of sixty-six books written over a period of about one thousand years, some of them very early and some of them comparatively late. It is a book primarily of religion and morals. It is not a book of science. Never was and was never meant to be. Under it there is nothing prescribed that would tell you how to build a railroad or a steamboat or to make anything that would advance civilization. It is not a textbook or a text on chemistry. It is not big enough to be. It is not a book on geology; they knew nothing about it. It is not a work on evolution; that is a mystery to them. It is not a work on astronomy. The man who looked out at the universe and studied the heavens had no thought but that the earth was the center of the universe. But we know better than that. We know that the sun is the center of the solar system. And that there are an infinity of other systems around about us. They thought the sun went around the earth and gave us light and gave us night. We know better. We know the earth turns on its axis to produce days and nights. They thought the earth was 4,004 years before the Christian Era. We know better. They told it the best they knew.

* * *

Ignorance and fanaticism is ever busy and needs feeding. Always it is feeding and gloating for more. Today it is the public school teachers, tomorrow the private. The next day the preachers and the lecturers, the magazines, the books, the newspapers. After a while, your Honor, it is the setting of man against man and creed against creed, until with flying banners and beating drums we are marching backward to the glorious ages of the sixteenth century, when bigots lighted fagots to burn the men who dared to bring any intelligence and enlightenment and culture to the human mind. * * *

MR. BRYAN — Did he [Darrow] tell you where life began? Did he tell you that back of all these that there was a God? Not a word about it. Did he tell you how life began? Not a word, and not one of them can tell you how life began. The atheists say it came some way without a God; the agnostics say it came in some way, they know not whether with a God or not. And the Christian evolutionists say we came away back there somewhere, but they do not know how far back—they do not give you the beginning—not that gentleman that tried to qualify as an expert; he did not tell you whether it began with God or how. No, they take up life as a mystery that nobody can explain, and they want you to let them commence there and ask no questions. They want to come in with their little padded up evolution that commences with nothing and ends nowhere. They do not dare to tell you that it began with God and . . . ended with God. They come here with this bunch of stuff that they call evolution, that they tell you that everybody believes in, but do not know that everybody knows as a fact, and nobody can tell how it came, and they do not explain the great riddle of the universe—they do not deal with the problems of life—they do not teach the great science of how to live—and yet they would undermine the faith of these little children in that God who stands back of everything and whose promise we have that we shall live with Him forever bye and bye. They shut God out of the world. They do not talk about God. Darwin says the beginning of all things is a mystery unsolvable by us. He does not pretend to say how these things started. * * *

And your Honor asked me whether it has anything to do with the principle of the virgin birth. Yes, because this principle of evolution disputes the miracle; there is no place for the miracle in this train of evolution, and the Old Testament and the New are filled with miracles, and if this doctrine is true, this logic eliminates every mystery in the Old Testament and the New, and eliminates everything supernatural; and that means they eliminate the virgin birth—that means that they eliminate the resurrection of the body—that means that they eliminate the doctrine of atonement. And they believe man has been rising all the time, that man never fell; that when the Savior came there was not any reason for His coming; * * *

Your Honor, we first pointed out that we do not need any experts in science. . . . And, when it comes to Bible experts, every member of the jury is as good an expert on the Bible as any man that they could bring, or that we could bring. The one beauty about the Word of God is, it does not take an expert to understand it.

* * *

MR. HAYS—The Defense desires to call Mr. Bryan as a witness, and, of course, since the only question here is whether Mr. Scopes taught what these children said he taught, we recognize what Mr. Bryan says as a witness would not be very valuable. We think there are other questions involved, and we should want to take Mr. Bryan's testimony for the purposes of our record, * * *

Q [MR. DARROW]—You have given considerable study to the Bible, haven't you, Mr. Bryan?

A [MR. BRYAN]—Yes, sir, I have tried to.

* * *

Q—Do you claim that everything in the Bible should be literally interpreted?

A—I believe everything in the Bible should be accepted as it is given there; some of the Bible is given illustratively. For instance: "Ye are the salt of the earth." I would not insist that man was actually salt, or that he had flesh of salt, but it is used in the sense of salt as saving God's people.

Q—But when you read that Jonah swallowed the whale—or that the whale swallowed Jonah—excuse me please—how do you literally interpret that?

A—When I read that a big fish swallowed Jonah—it does not say whale.

Q—Doesn't it? Are you sure?

A—That is my recollection of it. A big fish, and I believe it; and I believe in a God who can make a whale and can make a man and make both do what He pleases.

Q—Mr. Bryan, doesn't the New Testament say a whale?[1]

A—I am not sure. My impression is that it says fish; but it does not make so much difference; I merely called your attention to where it says fish— it does not say whale.

Q—But in the New Testament it says whale, doesn't it?

A—That may be true; I cannot remember in my own mind what I read about it.

A—Now, you say, the big fish swallowed Jonah, and he there remained how long? three days? and then he spewed him upon the land. You believe that the big fish was made to swallow Jonah?

A—I am not prepared to say that; the Bible merely says it was done.

A—You don't know whether it was the ordinary run of fish, or made for that purpose?

A—You may guess; you evolutionists guess.

Q—But when we do guess, we have a sense to guess right.

A—But do not do it often.

Q—You are not prepared to say whether that fish was made especially to swallow a man or not?

1. Matthew 12:40 says "whale"; Jonah 1:17 and 2:10 say "fish" and "great fish," respectively. [Editor]

A—The Bible doesn't say, so I am not prepared to say.

Q—You don't know whether that was fixed up specially for the purpose?

A—No, the Bible doesn't say.

Q—But you do believe He made them—that He made such a fish and that it was big enough to swallow Jonah?

A—Yes, sir. Let me add: one miracle is just as easy to believe as another.

Q—It is for me.

A—It is for me.

Q—Just as hard?

A—It is hard to believe for you, but easy for me. A miracle is a thing performed beyond what man can perform. What you get beyond what man can do, you get within the realm of miracles; and it is just as easy to believe the miracle of Jonah as any other miracle in the Bible.

Q—Perfectly easy to believe that Jonah swallowed the whale?

A—If the Bible said so; the Bible doesn't make as extreme statements as evolutionists do.

MR. DARROW—That may be a question, Mr. Bryan, about some of those you have known.

A—The only thing is, you have a definition of fact that includes imagination.

Q—And you have a definition that excludes everything but imagination.

GEN. STEWART—I object to that as argumentative.

THE WITNESS—You—

MR. DARROW—The witness must not argue with me, either.

Q—Do you consider the story of Jonah and the whale a miracle?

A—I think it is.

Q—Do you believe Joshua made the sun stand still?

A—I believe what the Bible says. I suppose you mean that the earth stood still?

Q—I don't know. I am talking about the Bible now.

A—I accept the Bible absolutely.

Q—The Bible says Joshua commanded the sun to stand still for the purpose of lengthening the day, doesn't it? and you believe it?

A—I do.

Q—Do you believe at that time the entire sun went around the earth?

A—No, I believe that the earth goes around the sun.

Q—Do you believe that men who wrote it thought that the day could be lengthened or that the sun could be stopped?

A—I don't know what they thought.

Q—You don't know?

A—I think they wrote the fact without expressing their own thoughts.

* * *

MR. DARROW—Have you an opinion as to whether—whoever wrote the book, I believe it is, Joshua, the Book of Joshua, thought the sun went around the earth or not?

A—I believe that he was inspired.

MR. DARROW—Can you answer my question?

A—When you let me finish the statement.

Q—It is a simple question, but finish it.

THE WITNESS—You cannot measure the length of my answer by the length of your question.

[*Laughter in the courtyard.*]

MR. DARROW—No, except that the answer be longer.

[*Laughter in the courtyard.*]

A—I believe that the Bible is inspired, an inspired author, whether one who wrote as he was directed to write understood the things he he was writing about, I don't know.

Q—Whoever inspired it? Do you think whoever inspired it believed that the sun went around the earth?

A—I believe it was inspired by the Almighty, and He may have used language that could be understood at that time.

Q—Was—

THE WITNESS—Instead of using language that could not be understood until Mr. Darrow was born.

[*Laughter and applause in the courtyard.*]

* * *

Q—You believe the story of the flood to be a literal interpretation?

A—Yes, sir.

Q—When was that flood?

A—I would not attempt to fix the date. The date is fixed, as suggested this morning.

Q—About 4004 B.C.?

A—That has been the estimate of a man that is accepted today. I would not say it is accurate.

* * *

MR. DARROW—How long ago was the flood, Mr. Bryan?

* * *

THE WITNESS—Oh, I would put the estimate where it is, because I have no reason to vary it. But I would have to look at it to give you the exact date.

Q—I would, too. Do you remember what book the account is in?

A—Genesis.

MR. HAYES—Is that the one in evidence?

MR. NEAL—That will have it; that is the King James Version.

MR. DARROW—The one in evidence has it.

THE WITNESS—It is given here, as 2348 years B.C.

Q—Well, 2348 years B.C. You believe that all the living things that were not contained in the ark were destroyed.

A—I think the fish may have lived.

* * *

Q—Don't you know that the ancient civilizations of China are 6,000 or 7,000 years old, at the very least?

A—No; but they would not run back beyond the creation, according to the Bible, 6,000 years.

Q—You don't know how old they are, is that right?

A—I don't know how old they are, but probably you do. [*Laughter in the courtyard.*] I think you would give preference to anybody who opposed the Bible, and I give the preference to the Bible.

Q—I see. Well, you are welcome to your opinion. * * *

THOMAS McIVER

Orthodox Jewish Creationists (2000)†

* * *

Many orthodox Jews oppose evolution, now often using creation-science arguments from Protestant sources. * * *

In an intricately bizarre tome, *Genesis: Mother of Sciences* (1953), Pincas Dov claimed discovery of a "new science" through his "decoding" of Genesis in which each Hebrew letter corresponds to a cluster of physical, physiological, and metaphysical concepts. Adam translated the "hisses" and vibrations of nature into words—the Book of Genesis—by "mentally fondling" them, thereby revealing, for instance, that argon (Hebrew letter *kh*) is the basis of life. Life, created hundreds of millions of years ago, developed through "evolutionary creationism"—a kind of continuing spontaneous generation—not Darwinism. Animals arose from "nitrogen ooze," and fishes turned directly into birds. Humans are not descended from lower forms. Adam, who coalesced from biogenetic materials such as "pre-pollens" in the atmosphere and cosmic ingredients from meteors and comets, hatched from an egg as a bird-man with no visceral organs. The Fall triggered an explosion which reversed Earth's rotation, catapulting the Nephilim from Moon to Earth where they ate human females. Animals and humans then cross-bred. Evolutionists are completely wrong in claiming human descent from apes, as most animals, apes included, are adulterated human-animal hybrids.

* * *

Many ultra-orthodox Jews in America and Israel reject evolution completely. Some 20% of Israeli students attend private religious schools, and the ultra-orthodox often reject evolution—they have attacked Israel's Education Minister for opposing teaching of creationism. Shamir, an Israeli-based organization of fundamentalist Jewish scientists and professionals from former communist nations, publishes creationist articles in its journal *B'or Ha' Torah*. *Science in the Light of the Torah* is a collection of these articles. Yaacov Hanoka, a Boston-area physicist with Mobil and Shamir's

---

† From *Ever Since Genesis* (2000). Printed by permission of the author. Thomas McIver (b. 1951) is an anthropologist and librarian.

U.S. representative, argues that science supports the traditional Jewish date of creation of 3761 BC.

Moshe Trop, a chemist at Ben Gurion University in Israel and former visiting professor at Rutgers, wrote a book in Hebrew called *Creation: Origin of Life* (1982), which he describes as showing the "scientific alternatives to evolution." Trop, active in Shamir, has also published articles in the *Creation Research Society Quarterly* (1974). One, "Is the Archaeopteryx a Fake?," (1983) defended Lee Spetner's claim that this celebrated transitional fossil is a hoax. Spetner, who taught applied physics at Johns Hopkins University and Bar Ilan University in Israel, studied the British Museum's specimen and reported that it was "probably false and counterfeit" at a 1980 meeting of orthodox Jewish scientists.

* * *

American, British, and Israeli Orthodox Jews support creationism in *Challenge: Torah Views on Science and Its Problems*, including Rabbi Menachem Schneerson (d. 1994), leader of the ultra-orthodox Lubavitch Hassidim, who affirmed the creation date of 3761 BC, and suggested that fossils may have been created as such. Aranoff Sanford, a research scientist with the Israeli Defense Department with a Ph.D. in theoretical physics from NYU, says that alleged contradictions between the Torah and science are "meaningless" because scientific laws were not valid at creation. Adam, for instance, could count tree-rings indicating great age, though the trees were created fully-formed only days before. In "How Old Is the Universe?," Rabbi Simon Schwab hypothesized that time was compressed during the Six Days of creation; the Earth rotated much faster and all other processes were similarly speeded up, so that God's "Cosmic Days" of creation lasted billions of years according to our human frame of reference.

The Israeli organization Arachim published the strongly creationist *Pathways to the Torah*; a 1985 edition was prepared by the staff of Aish Ha'Torah in Los Angeles. The section "Science and Torah—Evolution" is an extended collage of anti-evolution quotes. "Codes of the Torah" describes hidden patterns and "clusterings" (statistically unusual distributions of words) proving divine origin. Daniel Michelson, a UCLA professor in the 1980s affiliated with Aish Ha'Torah, is an expert in this type of analysis. Statistical results of his computer studies, and those of his Israeli colleagues, show millions-to-one odds against chance occurrence of these patterns; they also contain predictions about Zionism, the Holocaust, and Armageddon (forecast for 1988). "Computerized gematria" is a specialty of members of the Association of Orthodox Jewish Scientists. It involves discovery of significant mathematical patterns and relationships by manipulating and adding up biblical words and phrases, with each letter of the alphabet assigned a number. Computerized searches for "equidistant letter sequences" in which significant words are found by trying out every nth letter in the Hebrew text (with n any number, and starting from any character and going in any direction) has been developed by a number of Jewish scientists and researchers. This method has been enthusiastically praised by Protestant creationists Grant Jeffrey (1996) and Henry Morris, and popularized in the books *The Bible Code* and *Cracking the Bible Code*.

Jews for Jesus, a San Francisco-based organization of "saved" Jews who have accepted Jesus as Messiah, condemn evolution as "devil-ution" (1980s). They are led by Moishe Rosen, a member of the International Council on Biblical Inerrancy.

One of the editors of the landmark booklet series *The Fundamentals*, Louis Meyer, was a "Christian Jew." The Christian Jew Foundation of San Antonio, Texas (still active), published creationist radio sermons by Wayne Carver. Zola Levitt, a born-again "Hebrew Christian" televangelist concerned with Bible prophecy, satanic UFOs, and other fundamentalist topics, said he "secretly believed in evolution" until he met creationist John N. Moore, whom he featured in *Creation: A Scientist's Choice* (1976). Levitt is now a committed creationist.

Meir Ben Uri, who has published in the *Creation Research Society Quarterly*, is an Israeli religious artist and architect who reconstructs biblical objects based on biblical descriptions. His model of Noah's Ark—a prismatic bamboo rhomboid (Noah assembled the original from prefabricated triangular sections), has been displayed at Solomon's Palace in Jerusalem and is cited admiringly by many creationists.

* * *

HARUN YAHYA

[Islamic Creationism] (1997)†

Cultural Hegemony

When we look at political science, * * * we come across some interesting theories. One of these is the "hegemony theory" developed by some political scientists in this century.

According to this theory, the powers dominating modern societies do not control the masses they take under their hegemony by using power. They use a more effective method than power: Persuasion. This persuasion process is effected in a quite indirect way. The directed masses learn to evaluate the world through the criteria and measures of their directors. This learning process is realized by some mechanism set up by the directors. The theory takes this formation it calls "cultural hegemony" to be the most important substructure of political hegemony.

* * *

Counting on this, we can say that the basic characteristic of the present world system is its secularism, that is, its anti-religionism. Because, as we will analyze in the following chapters in detail, this world system was

† From *The Evolution Deceit* (Istanbul: *Vural Yayincilik*, 1997). Reprinted by permission of the author. Harun Yahya is the pseudonym of Adnan Oktar.

established by fighting against the religious authorities. Its subsistence depends on the fact that these authorities should be kept under control. The moral order it owns is a morals which is non-religious or abstracted from certain aspects of religion. The most important characteristic that makes the world system itself is its non-religionism.

So, the most important aspect of the cultural hegemony this world system tries to establish on the masses should be non-religionism.

*   *   *

One of the most important propaganda means employed to attack religion indirectly is the theory of evolution. The theory is imposed on the whole world by the two important means of the cultural hegemony, namely the intellectuals (scientists) and the media.

Well, but what does this theory have to do with religion? What is it that makes this theory one of the most important elements of the indirect war waged against religion?

Creation and Evolution

In Europe, until the beginning of the 19th century, a common answer was given to the question of how this nature existed: The emergence of the living things was like it was written in the Providential books: that all was created by God who has created the whole universe from nothing in a conscious and wise way. God first created the heavens and earth, and then placed the living things on the earth one by one. And all this creation was completed in 6 days. This fact, believed in by the Christians and the Jews, was also described in the last Providential book, the Kor'an. As God emphasized the creation of the universe in six days in the Kor'an, He addressed the people as follows:

> "Your Lord is Allah, Who created the heavens and the earth in six days, and is firmly established on the throne (of authority): He draweth the night as a veil o'er the day, each seeking the other in rapid succession: He created the sun, the moon, and the stars, (all) governed by laws under His command. Is it not His to create and to govern? Blessed be Allah, the Cherisher and Sustainer of the worlds!"

In short, the creation of the heavens, the earth, that is, the whole universe and all the living things in the earth by God was the common belief of the three Providential religions. Europe, as we mentioned above, protected this belief dating from the 4th. century when she had accepted Christianity. *   *   *

But on the other hand, there was a developing opposition as well. Some people did not want to admit that the universe and the living things were created. And more, they brought an alternative explanation to this. The efforts in this direction had their first substantial outcome in the theories developed by Georges de Buffon, Erasmus Darwin, Jean Baptiste Lamarck, and similar biologists. The theory which was advanced *   *   * that the living things had sprung from each other as a result of coincidences, was at last taken up by Charles Darwin and developed in detail. Darwin's book named *Origin of Species* took its place in history as the main source of evolution.

By the communication of Darwin's theory, the positivist and atheist trends, which dominated the 19th century, attained a great acceleration. All the religion-oppositioned ideologists thought that a big blow was struck against religion and congratulated Darwin incessantly.

After these dates, the theory of evolution was used as a master card in each war waged against religion. First in the Christian societies, then in the Islamic world, it became the indispensable means of support of each combat pursued against religion.

The ones who organized this war were the dominators of the world system, as we have stressed at the beginning. They wanted to secure a justification for the non-religious system they had established. And for this end, they had to find a model (a cosmology) which brought an anti-religionist explanation to the whole universe. Darwinism and all the other versions of the theory of evolution were important because they made up a great part of this cosmology.

The scientists who put forward the theory of evolution and developed it were "the intellectuals at the service of the dominators" mentioned in the cultural hegemony theory. They had adopted the secular culture owned by the dominators of the world system, and then devoted themselves to developing it.

* * *

The theory of evolution is nothing but a deception imposed on us by the dominators the world system, deception they have organized to establish a "cultural hegemony" over us and to make us adopt their own secular world-view.

SWAMI ŚRĪLA PRABHUPĀDA

[A Hare Krishna on Darwinian Evolution] (1977)†

What follows is a conversation between His Divine Grace A. C. Bhaktive-danta Swami Prabhupāda and one of his disciples, Dr. Thoudam Damodar Singh. It took place during an early morning walk on Los Angeles's Venice Beach.

Dr. Singh: Your Divine Grace, are all the species of life created simultaneously?

Śrīla Prabhupāda: Yes. The species already exist, and the living entity simply transfers himself from one womb to the next, just as a man transfers himself from one apartment to another. Suppose a person comes from a

† From "Śrīla Prabhupāda Speaks out on Darwinian Evolution," *Back to Godhead*, 12 (1977): 16. Copyright © The Bhaktivedanta Book Trust International, 1999. Reprinted by permission of the publisher. Swami Prabhupāda (1896–1977) was the founder of *Back to Godhead* and the International Society for Krishna Consciousness.

lower-class apartment to a first-class apartment. The person is the same, but now, according to his capacity for payment—according to his *karma* —he is able to occupy a higher-class apartment. Evolution does not mean physical development, but development of consciousness. Do you follow?

Dr. Singh: I think so. Do you mean that evolution is actually the soul's transmigration from the lower species of life up to the higher species?

Śrīla Prabhupāda: Yes. As you get more money you can move to a better apartment. Similarly, as your consciousness develops, you move up to a higher species of life. The species already exist, however. It is not that the lower species become higher species—that is Darwin's nonsensical theory.

Dr. Singh: And each living entity is made to live in a particular type of body according to his desires?

Śrīla Prabhupāda: Yes. God knows the various desires of all the living entities in the material world. Therefore, to accommodate all the conditioned souls, He creates the 8,400,000 species of life from the very beginning.

Dr. Singh: Śrīla Prabhupāda, what is the difference between the transmigration of souls in animal bodies and the transmigration of human souls?

Śrīla Prabhupāda: Animals transmigrate only in one direction— upward—but human beings can transmigrate to either a higher or a lower form of life. By nature's law, the lower species are coming up from animal forms to the higher, human forms. But once you come to the human form, if you don't cultivate Kṛṣṇa consciousness, you may return to the body of a cat or dog.

Dr. Singh: The scientists have no information that evolution can operate in either direction.

Śrīla Prabhupāda: Therefore, I say they are fools and rascals. They have no knowledge, yet they still claim to be scientists.

Dr. Singh: One of the prominent scientific arguments is that before Darwin's biophysical type of evolution could take place, there had to be something they call "prebiotic chemistry," or "chemical evolution."

Śrīla Prabhupāda: But from what have the chemicals evolved? The term "chemical evolution" implies that chemicals have an origin. And we know from the Vedic science that the origin is spirit, or life. For example, a lemon tree produces citric acid. Also, our bodies produce many chemicals through our urine, blood, and bodily secretions. So there are many examples of how life produces chemicals, but there are no instances where chemicals have produced life.

Dr. Singh: A Russian biologist in 1920 developed the idea of chemical evolution. He demonstrated that before biochemical evolution, the earth's atmosphere was composed mostly of hydrogen, with very little oxygen. Then, in due course. . .

Śrīla Prabhupāda: This is a side study. First of all, where did the hydrogen come from? The scientists simply study the middle of the process —they do not study the origin. You must know the beginning. There is an airplane [Śrīla Prabhupāda points to an airplane appearing on the horizon]. Would you say the origin of that machine is the sea? A foolish person might say that all of a sudden a light appeared in the sea, and that's how the airplane was created. But is that a scientific explanation? The scientists' theories are just like that. They say, "*This* existed, and then all of a sudden, simply by chance, *that* occured." This is not real science. Real science must explain the original cause.

Dr. Singh: What you have been saying completely contradicts Darwin's theory of evolution. Darwin and his supporters say that life started from matter and evolved from unicellular organisms to multicellular organisms. They believe higher species like animals and men didn't exist at the beginning of creation.

Śrīla Prabhupāda: Darwin and his followers are rascals. If the higher species have evolved from the lower species, then why do the lower species still exist? At the present moment we see both the human species, with its advanced intelligence, and the foolish ass. Why do both these entities exist simultaneously? Why hasn't the ass form simply evolved into a higher species and thus become extinct? Darwin thought that human beings evolved from the monkeys. But why do we never see a monkey giving birth to a human being?

The Darwinists' theory that human life began in such-and-such an era is nonsense. The *Bhagavad-gītā* says that on leaving this present body you can directly transmigrate to any species of life, according to your karma. Sometimes I travel to America, sometimes to Australia, and sometimes to Africa. The countries already exist; I am simply traveling through them. It is not that because I have come to America I have *created* or *become* America. And there are many countries I have not yet seen. Does that mean they do not exist? Any scientist who supports Darwin is unintelligent. The *Bhagavad-gītā* clearly says that all the species of life exist simultaneously, and that you can go to any of them—that will depend on your consciousness at the time of death. If you become Kṛṣṇa conscious, you can even go up to the kingdom of God. Lord Kṛṣṇa explains all this very clearly in the *Bhagavad-gītā*.

INSTITUTE FOR CREATION RESEARCH

Tenets of Creationism (1998)†

The Institute for Creation Research Graduate School has a unique statement of faith for its faculty and students, incorporating most of the basic Christian doctrines in a creationist framework, organized in terms of two parallel sets of tenets, related to God's created world and God's inspired Word, respectively. * * *

---

† From ICR *Tenets of Creationism* (El Cajon, Calif., 1998). Reprinted by permission of the Institute for Creation Research.

ICR Educational Philosophy

The programs and curricula of the Graduate School, as well as the activities of other ICR divisions, while similar in factual content to those of other graduate colleges, are distinctive in one major respect. The Institute for Creation Research bases its educational philosophy on the foundational truth of a personal Creator-God and His authoritative and unique revelation of truth in the Bible, both Old and New Testaments.

* * *

TENETS OF SCIENTIFIC CREATIONISM

- The physical universe of space, time, matter, and energy has not always existed, but was supernaturally created by a transcendent personal Creator who alone has existed from eternity.
- The phenomenon of biological life did not develop by natural processes from inanimate systems but was specially and supernaturally created by the Creator.
- Each of the major kinds of plants and animals was created functionally complete from the beginning and did not evolve from some other kind of organism. Changes in basic kinds since their first creation are limited to "horizontal" changes (variation) within the kinds, or "downward" changes (e.g., harmful mutations, extinctions).
- The first human beings did not evolve from an animal ancestry, but were specially created in fully human form from the start. Furthermore, the "spiritual" nature of man (self-image, moral consciousness, abstract reasoning, language, will, religious nature, etc.) is itself a supernaturally created entity distinct from mere biological life.
- The record of earth history, as preserved in the earth's crust, especially in the rocks and fossil deposits, is primarily a record of catastrophic intensities of natural processes, operating largely within uniform natural laws, rather than one of gradualism and relatively uniform process rates. There are many scientific evidences for a relatively recent creation of the earth and the universe, in addition to strong scientific evidence that most of the earth's fossiliferous sedimentary rocks were formed in an even more recent global hydraulic cataclysm.
- Processes today operate primarily within fixed natural laws and relatively uniform process rates but, since these were themselves originally created and are daily maintained by their Creator, there is always the possibility of miraculous intervention in these laws or processes by their Creator. Evidences for such intervention should be scrutinized critically, however, because there must be clear and adequate reason for any such action on the part of the Creator.
- The universe and life have somehow been impaired since the completion of creation, so that imperfections in structure, disease, aging, extinctions, and other such phenomena are the result of "negative"

changes in properties and processes occurring in an originally-perfect created order.

- Since the universe and its primary components were created perfect for their purposes in the beginning by a competent and volitional Creator, and since the Creator does remain active in this now-decaying creation, there do exist ultimate purposes and meanings in the universe. Teleological considerations, therefore, are appropriate in scientific studies whenever they are consistent with the actual data of observation, and it is reasonable to assume that the creation presently awaits the consummation of the Creator's purpose.
- Although people are finite and scientific data concerning origins are always circumstantial and incomplete, the human mind (if open to the possibility of creation) is able to explore the manifestations of that Creator rationally and scientifically, and to reach an intelligent decision regarding one's place in the Creator's plan.

* * *

HENRY M. MORRIS

Scientific Creationism (1985)†

Variation and Selection

When Charles Darwin first published his theory of the origin of species by natural selection, it was his idea that the continual small variations between individuals of a species, that are observed in nature, would confer differing degrees of advantage or disadvantage in the struggle for existence. Those with significant advantages would be favored by natural selection and thus would survive longer to transmit these characteristics by inheritance to their descendants. Thus, gradually, completely new and higher types of organisms would emerge.

Normal variations were later found to be subject to the rigid Mendelian laws of inheritance, representing nothing really novel but only characters already latent within the genetic system. Modern molecular biology, with its penetrating insight into the remarkable genetic code implanted in the DNA system, has further confirmed that normal variations operate only within the range specified by the DNA for the particular type of organism, so that no truly novel characteristics, producing higher degrees of order or complexity, can appear. Variation is horizontal, not vertical!

* * *

† From *Scientific Creationism* (El Cajon, Calif., 1985) Reprinted by permission of the Institute for Creation Research. Henry M. Morris (b. 1918) is the founder of the Institute for Creation Research.

Similarities and Differences

In the organic realm, there are many similarities between different kinds of plants and animals, and evolutionists have interpreted these as evidence of common ancestry. Creationists, on the other hand, interpret the same similarities as evidence of common creative planning and design. The evolutionist has to assume all such characteristics have developed by chance mutations and natural selection. Creationists explain them as structures designed by the Creator for specific purposes, so that when similar purposes were involved, similar structures were created.

One might write this issue off as an impasse, since similarities are expected in both the evolution and creation models. However, we also have *differences* to account for!

For example, cats and dogs are somewhat similar, but they have many differences as well. The creation model says that similar structures on both were created for similar functions for both, and that different structures were created for their different functions.

The evolution model, on the other hand, encounters a real problem. If the cat and dog evolved from a common ancestor in the same environment by the same process, how did they ever get to be different? It would seem there ought rather to be an integrated series of animals between cats and dogs, so that one could never tell where "cats" stop and "dogs" begin.

*   *   *

The evolution model implies that all organisms have come from a common ancestor. Since they all live in a continuity of environments in the same world and have developed by the same natural processes, the primary prediction from the evolution model must be that of a continuum of organisms, rather than distinct kinds separated by gaps. To explain the gaps, numerous secondary assumptions have to be introduced into the model.

In view of the foregoing facts, it is strange that evolutionists constantly place such strong emphasis on similarities as evidence of evolution. In every case the similarities are better explained by creation and the differences are predicted by creation.

*   *   *

Now that we have mentioned DNA, it is noteworthy that even this has been offered as evidence of evolution. That is, the fact that the DNA molecule is basic in the reproductive mechanisms for all kinds of organisms is assumed to suggest common ancestry. The infinitely more significant fact that each specific kind of organism has its *own* DNA molecular structure, different from that of every other kind, is ignored. The tremendous complexity of DNA molecules has already been discussed; such a system could never have evolved itself by chance. Neither could one type of DNA evolve into the DNA for another type of organism; its structure is designed to prevent that very thing. It is hard to imagine a more solid evidence for special creation than the mere existence and function of DNA.

Other chemicals in living organisms have likewise been studied on a comparative basis, especially such proteins as gamma globulin, insulin, cytochrome C, hemoglobin and others. Various techniques have been used to test these molecules on a comparative basis for a wide variety of organisms. In general (though with a great many exceptions) the respective similarities in these biochemical systems align themselves in about the same way as do the more traditional similarities based on anatomical and other gross morphological features.

This, of course, is exactly what would be expected on the basis of the creation model, so it certainly cannot be used as legitimate evidence for evolution. These studies in *molecular taxonomy* can actually prove helpfully supplemental to older studies in *morphological taxonomy*, with a view to eventual determination of the true boundaries of the original created kinds, beyond which variation and mutation cannot go.

4. SIMILARITIES IN BEHAVIOR

Occasionally, similarities in animal behavior have been cited as evidence of relationship. Examples are difficult to find, however, and the much more typical situation is that of different behavior patterns. Even closely related kinds are often found to have drastically divergent habits or instincts. Once again, such similarities in behavior as may actually exist can be well explained in a creationist context.

5. DECEPTIVE SIMILARITIES

There are many cases of what appear to be striking similarities which even evolutionists do not believe came from a common ancestor. They attribute these either to convergence or mimicry.

Convergence, or parallelism, is the assumed parallel and independent evolutionary development of similar features in unrelated animals. Wings, for example, are believed to have evolved completely independently four different times (in insects, flying reptiles, birds and bats) from four different non-winged ancestors. The eye of the squid is believed to have been evolved independently from the eye of the fish, even though both types of eyes are structurally very similar. The whale is believed to have evolved from a land mammal, even though its shape is like that of a fish. There are numerous other examples of convergence.

Mimicry is a phenomenon in which one type of organism appears as though it were imitating another type—for example, in coloration—in order to achieve the same type of environmental protection. The main examples of mimicry are found among insects.

Evolutionists use the explanations of either convergence or mimicry to explain superficial similarities which, for some reason (usually other more significant similarities—e.g., the mammalian features of the whale) do not lend themselves to the direct evolutionary explanation.

The point is, however, if there are actually numerous similarities among organisms which cannot be attributed to common ancestry, how then can we be sure which, if any, similarities *are* due to common ancestry?

The creation model, remember, does not encounter such problems. It suggests an array of similarities and differences, so that similarities simply suggest similar purposes (e.g., both birds and bats needed to fly, so the Creator created wings for both of them). This concept would apply equally well to so-called convergent evolution and cases of mimicry. All were created as distinct kinds, with similar structures for similar purposes and different structures for different purposes.

* * *

The Message of the Fossils

In the preceding chapter, we have shown that the regular and systematic gaps in the fossil record are inconsistent with the evolution model of earth history. But if the fossils do not teach evolution, then what exactly is their message? How and when were formed the tremendous beds of sedimentary rocks which contain those fossils?

This question immediately raises the issue of uniformitarianism or catastrophism.

* * *

Now the evolution model is usually associated with uniformitarianism and the creation model with catastrophism. This association does not preclude the possibility that *local* catastrophes can occur within the broad framework of evolutionary uniformitarianism. Nor does it suggest that catastrophism rejects the normal uniform operation of natural laws and processes during most of earth history. Creationists believe in general uniformitarianism as an evidence of the Creator's providential maintenance of the laws He created in the beginning.

* * *

We should first establish that the standard order of the geologic column is indeed the order predicted from the cataclysmic model. The order is not at all uniquely a prediction of evolution.

The creation model postulates that all the organisms of the fossil record were originally created contemporaneously by the Creator during the creation period. They thus lived together in the same world, just as the equivalent plants and animals all live together in the present world. However, they lived in ecologic communities, just as is true in the present world. Man would not live with dinosaurs and trilobites, for example, any more than he now lives with crocodiles and starfish.

Visualize, then, a great hydraulic cataclysm bursting upon the present world, with currents of waters pouring perpetually from the skies and erupting continuously from the earth's crust, all over the world, for weeks on end, until the entire globe was submerged, accompanied by outpourings of magma from the mantle, gigantic earth movements, landslides, tsunamis, and explosions. The uniformitarian will of course question how such a cataclysm could be caused, and this will be considered shortly, but for the moment simply take it as a model and visualize the expected results if it should happen today.

Sooner or later all land animals would perish. Many, but not all, marine animals would perish. Human beings would swim, run, climb, and attempt to escape the floods but, unless a few managed to ride out the cataclysm in unusually strong watertight sea-going vessels, they would eventually all drown or otherwise perish.

Soils would soon erode away and trees and plants be uprooted and carried down toward the sea in great mats on flooding streams. Eventually the hills and mountains themselves would disintegrate and flow down-stream in great landslides and turbidity currents. Slabs of rock would crack and bounce and gradually be rounded into boulders and gravel and sand. Vast seas of mud and rock would flow downriver, trapping many animals and rafting great masses of plants with them.

On the ocean bottom, upwelling sediments and subterranean waters and magmas would entomb hordes of invertebrates. The waters would undergo rapid changes in heat and salinity, great slurries would form, and immense amounts of chemicals would be dissolved and dispersed throughout the seaways.

Eventually, the land sediments and waters would commingle with those in the ocean. Finally the sediments would settle out as the waters slowed down, dissolved chemicals would precipitate out at times and places where the salinity and temperature permitted, and great beds of sediment, soon to be cemented into rock, would be formed all over the world.

The above of course is only the barest outline of the great variety of phenomena that would accompany such a cataclysm. The very complexity of the model makes it extremely versatile in its ability to explain a wide diversity of data (although, admittedly, this makes it difficult to test).

The immediate point under discussion, however, is what it would imply with respect to the order of the fossils in the geologic column. A little consideration will quickly yield the following obvious predictions.

1. As a rule, there would be many more marine invertebrate animals trapped and buried in the sediments than other types, since there are many more of them and, being relatively immobile, they would usually be unable to escape.

2. Animals caught and buried would normally be buried with others living in the same region. In other words, fossil assemblages would tend to represent ecological communities of the pre-cataclysmic world.

3. In general, animals living at the lowest elevations would tend to be buried at the lowest elevations, and so on, with elevations in the strata thus representing relative elevations of habitat or eco-logical zones.

*   *   *

10. Mammals and birds would be found in general at higher eleva-tions than reptiles and amphibians, both because of their habitat

and because of their greater mobility. However, few birds would be found at all, only occasional exhausted birds being trapped and buried in sediments.

*   *   *

13. Very few human fossils or artifacts would be found at all. Men would escape burial for the most part and, after the waters receded, their bodies would lie on the ground until decomposed.

*   *   *

The Antiquity of Man

Heretofore in this chapter, our primary concern has been evidence of the earth's age, and of the various geologic formations which supposedly antedate man's arrival. In this section, we wish to deal mainly with evidence related to the time of man's origin.

Although written records made by early man go back only several thousand years, evolutionists generally believe that man and the apes diverged from their unknown common ancestor about 30 to 70 million years ago, and that true modern man had arrived at least one million years ago, possibly more than three million years ago.

The fossil evidence associated with the hypothetical evolutionary history of man will be discussed in the next chapter. The dates attached to these fossils have been derived mostly by the potassium-argon and other similar methods. The fallacies in these methods have already been discussed. The creation model would tend to place them all within the chronologic framework suggested by, say, the decay of the earth's magnetic field; in other words, within the past six to ten thousand years.

In this case, however, we must also reckon with the radiocarbon method, which has been widely used in the past 25 years to date cultural artifacts of man back to about 50,000 years. We also shall find that a study of human population statistics gives significant chronologic data on man's origin.

*   *   *

The radiocarbon dating method seems very useful and won for its inventor, Willard Libby, a Nobel prize. It has been checked with fair accuracy against known historical dates back to about 3000 years ago, although with considerable scatter and uncertainty.

Despite its high popularity, it involves a number of doubtful assumptions, some of which are sufficiently serious to make its results for all ages exceeding about 2000 to 3000 years, in serious need of revision.

*   *   *

2. POPULATION STATISTICS

Another process that bears interestingly on the subject of human antiquity is that of the growth of population. The "population explosion" is, of course, a topic of much current interest, both to professional ecologists and to children, and teachers should help place it in proper perspective. If man has indeed been dwelling on this planet for a million years or more, it is strange that only in recent years has population become a problem.

*　　*　　*

The creation model of human chronology fits the facts very well and is, in fact, quite conservative. There is more than enough room in the model to allow long periods of time when, because of war or pestilence, the population growth rates were far below the required averages.

The evolution model, on the other hand, with its million-year history of man, has to be strained to the breaking point. It is essentially incredible that there could have been 25,000 generations of men with a resulting population of only 3.5 billion. *　*　*

Although it is true that the evolution model can be modified by various secondary assumptions to fit the known data of population statistics, it is also true that the creation model fits the data directly, without such modifications. Even if the population were assumed to grow so slowly that it would only reach 3.5 billion in a million years, it is still true that at least a total of 3000 billion people would have lived and died on the earth in the past million years. Therefore, it is incredible that today there would be so little fossil or cultural evidence of ancient man preserved as is actually the case.

*　　*　　*

Summary of the Biblical Model

In summary, the Biblical model of earth history centers around three great worldwide events: (1) a period of six days of special creation and formation of all things, the completion and permanence of which are now manifest in the Law of Conservation of Energy; (2) the rebellion of man and the resultant Curse of God on all man's dominion, formalized now in the Law of Increasing Entropy; and (3) the world-destroying Flood in the days of Noah, leaving the new world largely under the domain of natural uniformity.

This framework does not, of course, preclude the occurrence of later events of worldwide implications, such as the confusion of tongues at Babel, the long day of Joshua and the midday darkness at the crucifixion of Christ. The Flood itself occupied only a year, but the after-effects were felt all over the world for many centuries.

The main key, however, to the true interpretation of the physical data relating to earth history, must lie in full recognition of the effects of creation, the Curse and the Flood.

* * *

The vast complex of godless movements spawned by the pervasive and powerful system of evolutionary uniformitarianism can only be turned back if their foundation can be destroyed, and this requires the re-establishment of special creation, on a Biblical and scientific basis, as the true foundation of knowledge and practice in every field. This therefore must be a primary emphasis in Christian schools, in Christian churches and in all kinds of institutions everywhere.

* * *

THOMAS J. WHEELER

Review of Morris (1992)†

This book * * * represents the ICR's basic textbook of its so-called "scientific" creationism model, supposedly backed by scientific evidence but in reality based on a literal reading of Genesis: creation of the entire universe and all "kinds" of life only a few thousand years ago, with most of Earth's geology and fossil record created in a worldwide flood. * * *

The book attempts to cover a broad spectrum of scientific disciplines (physics, astronomy, chemistry, geology, paleontology, anthropology, etc.). However, its treatment of scientific knowledge in all of these is flawed. Rather than presenting the consensus of scientific experts in various disciplines, as we expect in a science textbook, Morris presents a mixture of nonexpert or minority viewpoints, obsolete or discredited data, and other types of invalid information and conclusions. The experts have examined numerous claims made in this and other creationist works, and, as documented in many books and articles, have found them to be without scientific merit.

There are several types of errors and deficiencies in this book, which I will list along with only a few of the many possible examples:

Misunderstanding of the nature of science. While modern science does not claim to *prove* ideas, but rather to *support* them with evidence, Morris attacks evolution because it "cannot be proved" (pp. 5–6).[1] However, evolution is accepted by science because it is extremely well supported by evidence. Thus, acceptance of evolution is not "faith" similar to religious faith (p. 69). Nor is evolution equivalent to a "religion, with its

† From *Reviews of Creationist Books*, ed. Liz Rank Hughes (Berkeley, Calif., 1992). Reprinted by permission of the National Center for Science Education. Thomas J. Wheeler (b. 1951) is professor of biochemistry and molecular biology at the University of Louisville.
1. Page numbers refer to the 1985 edition of Morris's *Scientific Creationism*. [Editor]

own system of ethics, values, and ultimate meanings," as claimed on page 196; science, including evolution, does not deal with these issues.

Appeal to religious prejudice. Morris attempts to prejudice his readers by stating that Christianity, Judaism, and Islam are "inherently creationist" (even though many believers in these religions also accept evolution), while Eastern religions, atheism, and humanism are linked to evolution (p. 16). He then goes on to group Marxists, Nazis (p. 16) and racists (pp. 179–180) among the believers in evolution.

Straw men. In many places Morris attributes to evolutionists ideas which they do not actually hold ("straw men"), and then refutes these ideas, as if this argues against evolution. Although a basic principle of science is that natural laws are constant, he claims (p. 18) that evolution predicts that these laws (such as the law of gravity) also evolve! Evolution recognizes that while mutations occasionally will be beneficial, they are more likely to be harmful; Morris claims that the "basic prediction" of evolution is that they will be beneficial, and proposes (p. 57) that evolutionists should favor increased mutations (such as from nuclear testing) in order to advance evolution. He devotes an extensive section (pp. 40–43) to refuting arguments supposedly offered for why the Second Law of Thermodynamics does not apply to evolution. But evolutionists do not make such arguments; there is no reason to, since experts in thermodynamics agree that evolution does not violate the Second Law.[2] On pages 22 and 72, Morris suggests that according to evolution, we should expect a continuum of living things *in the present*, and thus be unable to classify organisms by their similarities and differences. However, evolution proposes that living things diverged *in the past*; with time, the differences have grown such that today we can observe distinct groups. Pages 59–62 are devoted to showing that the "probability of a complex system arising instantly by chance" is negligible, but scientists involved in origin of life research propose that complex systems arose step by step, not instantly. (Subsequent calculations [pp. 63–69] have other flaws, such as assuming that any failure destroys all progress; they are irrelevant to a scientific evaluation of whether life could have arisen by natural means.)

Misrepresentation of scientific knowledge. The text misrepresents the state of scientific understanding in several areas. On page 26, Morris states that "it is obvious by definition" that the Big Bang theory has no "observational basis." However, the theory was *based on* the observation that galaxies are receding in all directions at rates proportional to their distances; it predicted the cosmic microwave background radiation, which was later observed. On page 79, it is stated that "There is no evidence that there have ever been transitional forms" between basic "kinds." This is merely Morris's opinion; paleontologists believe that there is plenty of such evidence. On page 95, he says "The assumption of evolution is the basis upon which fossils are used to date the rocks." However, geology provides methods for determining the *relative* order of rock layers, and for using

2. Patterson, John W. 1983. "Thermodynamics and Evolution." In: L. R. Godfrey, ed., *Scientists Confront Creationism*, pp. 99–116. New York: W.W. Norton & Co.

fossils to *correlate* layers of the same age in different locations. These do not require the assumption of evolution, and indeed were developed and applied by creationist geologists before Darwin's theory.[3] *Absolute* ages are provided by radiodating, a later development which also involves no assumptions of evolution. On page 174, Morris suggests that the evidence for *Homo erectus* is "equivocal" for reasons such as the disappearance of the original Peking Man bones. However, numerous other specimens were known by the 1970s. (The revision of the book added a description of the 1984 discovery of a nearly complete *Homo erectus* skeleton, but left the earlier passage unchanged.)

Out-of-date material. The book's description of scientific knowledge, inadequate in 1974, has grown worse with time. Despite the many scientific advances from 1974 to 1985, the revised edition made minimal changes; new material was inserted where convenient (e.g., as footnotes or at ends of chapters), but very little of the text was rewritten. For example, while many precambrian animal fossils were known by 1985, Morris (p. 81) retained his reference (supported by quotes from the 1950s and 1960s) to the "tremendous gap" between one-celled organisms and Cambrian invertebrates. The evidence for continental drift has grown steadily stronger in recent decades, but a sentence expressing doubt about the evidence and stating that "the pendulum may be starting to swing back again" against the idea (p. 126) was left unchanged in the revised edition.

Since 1985, many new discoveries in various areas lend further support to evolution and refute the ICR's young-Earth and worldwide flood model, making the book even more out of date. For example, there has been an explosive growth in biochemical data (protein and gene sequences) supporting evolution. Morris (pp. 73–4) dismisses this type of evidence, claiming that it may illuminate "the true boundaries of the original created kinds," but in fact the data reveal the evolutionary unity of all living things.

Deceptive use of "catastrophism." Chapter V attempts to mislead the reader into thinking that the occurrence of catastrophic events supports creationism rather than conventional geology. Geologists have long recognized that catastrophic events were important in Earth's history; increasing attention to such events in recent years is not, as the book implies (p. 130), a consequence of "the rapid growth of the creation movement," but rather is the natural result of continuing research. Morris' catastrophism (which really involves just *one* catastrophic period, the worldwide flood and events in the subsequent centuries) bears little resemblance to that recognized by geologists, who have found evidence for numerous catastrophes over the 4.5-billion-year history of Earth.

Religious content. While the book supposedly uses only scientific arguments (except in the final chapter of the General Edition), it actually contains several theological arguments and thinly-disguised Bible stories. Morris comments on "the Creator's providential maintenance of the laws He created in the beginning" (p. 91), on why it would be inappropriate for the Creator to "waste aeons of time in essentially meaningless caretak-

---

3. Schafersman, Steven D. 1983. "Fossils, Stratigraphy, and Evolution: Consideration of a Creationist Argument." In: L. R. Godfrey, ed., *op. cit.*, pp. 219–244.

ing" (p. 136), and on the consequences of belief in "a personal Creator who had a specific purpose in his creation" (p. 178). A worldwide flood, which is based solely on the story of Noah and is refuted by the evidence of geology, is introduced in Chapter V to explain catastrophic geological events; by page 123, Morris discusses the "Flood" (capitalized) as if it were an established event. In Chapter VII we find the story of the Tower of Babel. While linguists, anthropologists, and archaeologists have no problem explaining the dispersal of humans around the Earth and the evolution of languages in terms of natural mechanisms, Morris claims (p. 185) that "there really seems no way to explain the different languages except in terms of the special creative purpose of the Creator," and on pages 187–8 reveals that this came about among descendants of "a remnant that survived the worldwide flood" as a result of "the Creator's direct creative restructuring of their common language into many languages."

Omission of opposing lines of evidence. Morris's treatment is also flawed by the omission of lines of evidence which argue against creationism. The area of biogeography (the geographical distribution of living and fossil organisms), which is considered one of the strongest areas of support for evolution, is not mentioned—perhaps because the data cannot be explained by the creationist post-flood dispersal.[4] In discussing the supposed creation of Earth's geology in the worldwide flood, the book omits numerous features which cannot possibly have been formed in such a flood (e.g., fossil beaches and deserts; the layers of fossil forests in Yellowstone National Park; the Green River shales, where millions of annual layers of sediments can be observed).[5] The chapter on the age of the Earth does not mention the abundant astronomical evidence that the universe is very old (such as starlight that has been travelling for billions of years to reach us).

Double standards. In several cases the book applies far more rigorous standards to mainstream science than to creation "science." The pattern seen in the fossil record does not even remotely resemble that predicted by Morris's "cataclysmic model," and he admits (p. 120) that the model "would also admit of many exceptions in every case." However, he claims that "it is the exceptions that are inimical to the evolution model," even though science proposes reasonable explanations for exceptions such as those he cites. On page 129, Morris describes the handful of creationist scientists who have not yet had time to deal with the mass of geological evidence, as if we should admit "flood geology" into science classes based on our sympathy rather than on its scientific merits. The principles of carbon dating are well-supported, and the method can be calibrated against both historical evidence and tree-ring data, but Morris dismisses the latter because it "is highly subjective," and says that "it need not be considered further in this connection" (p. 193). However, he uses his own types of "corrections," which are not scientifically justified, to adjust radiocarbon ages of 8000–9000 B.C. to about 3000–4000 B.C. (pp. 192–3).

4. Cracraft, Joel 1983. "Systematics, Comparative Biology, and the Case Against Creationism." In: L. R. Godfrey, ed., *op. cit.*, pp. 163–191.
5. Weber, Christopher G. 1980. "The Fatal Flaws of Flood Geology." *Creation/Evolution* 1:24–37.

Absurd conclusions. On page 117, Morris describes the worldwide flood as "a great hydraulic cataclysm . . . accompanied by outpourings of magma from the mantle, gigantic earth movements, landslides, tsunamis, and explosions." Nevertheless, we are supposed to believe that in such turbulent and chaotic conditions, alternating flows of plant material and mud (p. 108) could neatly lay down the layers of coal seams—even a series of 50 to 60 cycles of sandstone, shale, and coal (p. 109). Morris concludes that his explanation is "much more realistic" than that proposed by geologists.

* * *

Silly calculations. Perhaps the most absurd parts of the book are the calculations which purport to show that the Earth is young. Dividing the concentrations of chemicals in the ocean by the rate at which they enter from rivers (pp. 153–4) is an invalid method for determining the age of the Earth, since it ignores processes which remove the chemicals, and also assumes constant rates of influx.[6] It is obvious that the method is flawed because the calculated "ages" are all different, and some are as small as 100 years! On pages 167–9, Morris assumes a constant growth rate for the human population to show that it could have reached its present level in just 4000 years, and that humans could not have existed for one million years. However, it is well known that the growth rate has increased dramatically in recent centuries. Moreover, calculations such as this generate ridiculously low numbers of people for ancient times.[7]

* * *

Summary

Because of these many flaws, *Scientific Creationism* cannot be recommended for use in public school science classes, or indeed for anyone interested in learning science; it is essentially religious propaganda masquerading as science. It is, however, a valuable reference for anyone interested in studying the phenomenon of creationism.

6. Dalrymple, G. Brent 1984. "How Old is the Earth? A Reply to 'Scientific' Creationism." In: F. Awbrey and W.M. Thwaites, eds., *Evolutionists Confront Creationists. Proceedings of the Annual Meeting, Pacific Division, American Association for the Advancement of Science* 1:66–131.
7. Milne, David H. 1984. "Creationist, Population Growth, Bunnies, and the Great Pyramid." *Creation/Evolution* 14:1–5.

RICHARD D. SJOLUND AND
BETTY McCOLLISTER

Evolution at the Grass Roots (1998)

Richard D. Sjolund

[CREATIONISM VERSUS BIOTECHNOLOGY] (1998)†

* * *

In a few weeks, Eastern Iowa will be full of fields planted with genetically engineered crops. A very real search for evidence of evolution is about to take place in those fields—a hunt for insects that evolve resistance to the Bt toxin, and weeds that evolve resistance to a herbicide.

Your local physician and your hospital are also watching evolution in action: the mutation of bacterial genes that confer resistance to antibiotics, and the sharing of those genes with other species of microbes.

If Eastern Iowa parents expect their sons and daughters to live and work in the real world, their children had better be preparing to understand the molecular basis of evolution, and to contribute to the biochemical engineering of the inserted genes that will stay one step ahead of the rapid evolution of bacteria, bugs, and weeds. A student currently in a public school could found a whole new industry based on that quest—or not.

Are your children learning what they need to know to contribute to the 21st century of biotechnology, medicine and agriculture? Eastern Iowa industries, present and future, rely on the products of living organisms. They need well-educated graduates who understand modern science. Those industries won't need the victims of indoctrination by zealots who are in denial.

Imagine for a moment a group of parents who were religiously persuaded to teach their children that 2 plus 3 equals 6, and who were upset that the public schools taught otherwise. And consider, for a moment, under the guise of "family values" and "local control of schools," that a group of such parents might gain sufficient clout to demand that all students be taught that the answer is 6, and not 5. You can probably predict that no graduate of such a school would ever be hired by any firm.

The scientific basis of evolution is as real as 2+3=5. Your child will live in a world of work based on understanding DNA, as forensic evidence, in gene therapy, and in the engineering of crops that must feed a world that in your child's lifetime may hold 6 billion more people than it does today, but that will see no increase in the amount of farm land or available water.

If you have a child graduating from a local high school, do this test. Ask him or her to answer two questions: 1) Describe the structure of a DNA molecule, including the nature and significance of its chemical bonds, and 2) Describe how a mutation in the sequence of nucleotides in

† From the Cedar Rapids (Iowa) *Gazette*, April 20, 1998. Reprinted by permission of the author. Richard D. Sjolund (b. 1941) is professor of biological sciences at the University of Iowa.

a segment of DNA results in the alteration of the amino acid sequence in the protein encoded by that gene.

If your child is clueless, then your school has failed. * * *

[The Politics of Creationism] (1998)†

Betty McCollister

Darwin's magnificent "Origin of Species" burst on the world 140 years ago. It wove all life into an intricately connected whole and opened dazzling vistas for countless new discoveries in biology and other sciences, some of which didn't arise until after his death.

Disgracefully, Americans are scientifically illiterate on this most profound, most vital, most relevant to our species finding. If you doubt it, ask University of Iowa botany professor Richard Sjolund. He asks his incoming students to describe (a) the structure of a DNA molecule and (b) how a mutation in a DNA nucleotide sequence alters the amino acid sequence in the protein encoded by that gene.

This information reached the public domain 40 years ago, but few students have assimilated it. Sjolund's findings confirm the dismal results of a National Science Foundation poll which three out of four respondents flunked. Less than half were clear that the earth circles the sun only once a year, or that humans and dinosaurs didn't co-exist. Only 9 percent could define a molecule and only 21 percent could explain DNA. On evolution, polls for decades have disclosed that almost half of Americans don't believe it ever occurred.

Reacting to this appalling scientific illiteracy, the National Academy of Science has issued a clarion call for teaching evolution as the core of biology, and has distributed a manual to help high school teachers do just that.

What accounts for this extensive ignorance?

Scientists themselves are partly to blame, those who write arcane monographs in professional jargon for each other and arrogantly disdain writers like Carl Sagan and Stephen Jay Gould, whose lucid and eloquent expositions make science accessible and contagiously exciting to lay people.

But most of the blame falls on fundamentalist Christian sectarians who still, astonishingly, cling like barnacles to belief in ancient myths which our ancestors dreamed up millennia before science made its recent entrance. Convinced that their faith stands or falls on taking the Bible literally, they consider Genesis a science and history textbook whose tales of Adam and Eve in Eden and Noah's Ark describe real events. Why does this mulish, irrational denial of well-established biology persist?

It's because, as William Allman argues convincingly in "The Stone Age Present," the knowledge and technology which have altered so much haven't altered our species or eradicated our Stone Age propensities, one

---

† From *The Daily Iowan* (Iowa City), May 4, 1998. Reprinted by permission of the author. Betty McCollister (b. 1920) is a founder of the Iowa Committee of Correspondence on Evolution.

of which is our commitment to religion. Writes sociobiology maven Edward O. Wilson: "The human mind evolved to believe in the gods. It did not evolve to believe in biology."

Arguing against evolution, creationist Walter Brown, Jr. maintains, "If evolution happened, then a tremendous amount of death occurred before man evolved. But if death preceded man, and was not a result of Adam's sin, then sin is a fiction. If sin is a fiction, then we have no need of a Savior."

Creationist Henry Morris put it more succinctly: "No Adam, no fall, no atonement; no atonement, no Savior. Accepting Evolution, how can we believe in a fall?"

Drawing on funding as boundless as their zeal, creationists have seriously eroded public school biology teaching. They have pressured publishers to put out dumbed-down texts, aimed at the lucrative Bible belt market, which barely mention the e-word. Regarding the public schools as their biggest mission field (and never mind the Constitution), they have insinuated their people onto school boards and into teaching positions.

*　*　*

Our young people are being shortchanged. They are not learning that science is a high intellectual adventure. It is not about memorizing a laundry list of disparate facts. It is about observing and discovering and deducing and connecting and concluding. As Sjolund exclaims enthusiastically, "These are wonderful times for biology! We've learned more about the nature of life in the last 40 years than in the previous 400."

On a more cautionary note, he says that among students in his biology class for non-majors, "Scientific literacy is abysmal. If they have any knowledge at all, the can't put it together in a meaningful way . . ."

Scott Goodman, who fought creationists in British Columbia and won, warned in a recent National Center for Science Education *Reports*, "Anti-scientific, anti-enlightenment sentiments are growing throughout the world. From New Age mumbo-jumbo to Christian evangelical zeal, science and knowledge in general are being attacked and vilified as the root of all of society's ills. A return to ignorance and superstition is being urged that many are heeding."

For tens or perhaps hundreds of thousands of years, religion has been a potent factor in human experience. It will retain its consequential place in the human psyche. But that place is in churches, homes and hearts, not in biology classes.

MOLLEEN MATSUMURA

What Do Christians *Really* Believe about Evolution? (1998)†

What Do Christians Believe?

While a number of recent surveys give us some information on how many Americans express beliefs compatible with literal interpretations of the Bible, they don't tell us whether such beliefs are, in fact, required of Christians by their denominations. Even though the numbers of those polled in the US who say that they accept evolution is about equal with those who accept special creation of humans, the majority of Americans professing to be Christians belong to denominations that accept evolution.

[The] table [p. 573] is adapted from a 1998 article released by the Religion News Service and lists the twelve largest denominations in the US in order of size. It also shows which denominations have in some manner officially supported the teaching of evolution in public schools. The percentages listed in the second column represent the percentage of that denomination's members in relation to the total membership of those listed in the table (not in relation to all Christian denominations). A mark in the column entitled "Voices" indicates that the leaders of this denomination have contributed an official statement which we have published in NCSE's *Voices for Evolution.*

Some denominations have subsequently issued additional statements. The column headed "Joint Statement" shows which denominations endorsed "Religion in the Public Schools: A Joint Statement of Current Law," an interfaith statement that declares:

> 5. Students may be taught about religion, but public schools may not teach religion. . . .

> 6. These same rules apply to the recurring controversy surrounding theories of evolution. Schools may teach about explanations of life on earth, including religious ones (such as "creationism"), in comparative religion or social studies classes. In science class, however, they may present only genuinely scientific critiques of, or evidence for, any explanation of life on earth, but not religious critiques (beliefs unverifiable by scientific methodology)

* * *

Finally, official representatives of some denominations were plaintiffs in the famous *McLean v Arkansas* case. Official denominational opposition to the law requiring the teaching of "creation science" is recorded in the column headed *"McLean."*

† From the National Center for Science Education *Reports* 18 (March–April 1998): 8–9. Reprinted by permission of the publisher. Molleen Matsumura (b. 1948) is network project director of the National Center for Science Education.

Membership and Acceptance of Evolution in 12 Largest US Christian Denominations

Denomination	Membership (millions)	Percent	Voices	Joint Statement	McLean
Roman Catholic Church	61.2	49.0	•		•
Southern Baptist Convention	15.7	12.6			•
United Methodist Convention	8.5	6.8		○	•
National Baptist Convention USA	8.2	6.6	•	○	
Church of God in Christ	5.5	4.4			
Evangelical Lutheran Church in America	5.2	4.2		*	
Church of Jesus Christ of Later-Day Saints (Mormons)	4.8	3.8			
Presbyterian Church (USA)	3.5	2.8	•	*	•
National Baptist Convention of America	3.5	2.8		○	•
African Methodist Episcopal Church	3.5	2.8		○	
Lutheran Church-Missouri Synod	2.6	2.1			
The Episcopal Church	2.5	2.0	•	○	•

• Indicates statement issued by official body of this denomination.

○ Indicates statement signed by the National Council of Churches of which this denomination is a member.

* Indicates that this denomination was listed as an "endorsing organization."

[The] table demonstrates that of Americans in the 12 largest Christian denominations, 89.6% belong to churches that support evolution education! Indeed, many of the statements in *Voices* insist quite strongly that evolution must be included in science education and "creation science" must be excluded. Even if we subtract the Southern Baptist Convention, which has changed its view of evolution since *McLean v Arkansas* and might take a different position now, the percentage those in denominations supporting evolution is still a substantial 77%.

*   *   *

NATIONAL CENTER FOR SCIENCE EDUCATION

Seven Significant Court Decisions Regarding Evolution/ Creation Issues (1998)†

1. In 1968, in *Epperson v. Arkansas*, the United States Supreme court invalidated an Arkansas statute that prohibited the teaching of evolution. The Court held the statute unconstitutional on grounds that the First Amendment to the U.S. Constitution does not permit a state to require that teaching and learning must be tailored to the principles or prohibitions of any particular religious sect or doctrine. (*Epperson v. Arkansas* (1968) 393 U.S. 97, 37 U.S. Law Week 4017, 89 S. Ct. 266, 21 L. Ed 228)

2. In 1981, in *Segraves v. State of California* the Court found that the California State Board of Education's *Science Framework*, as written and as qualified by its anti-dogmatism policy, gave sufficient accommodation to the views of Segraves, contrary to his contention that class discussion of evolution prohibited his and his children's free exercise of religion. The anti-dogmatism policy provided that class discussions of origins should emphasize that scientific explanations focus on "how," not "ultimate cause," and that any speculative statements concerning origins, both in texts and in classes, should be presented conditionally, not dogmatically. The court's ruling also directed the Board of education to widely disseminate the policy, which in 1989 was expanded to cover all areas of science, not just those concerning issues of origins. (*Segraves v. California (1981)* Sacramento Superior Court #278978)

3. In 1982, in *McLean v. Arkansas Board of Education*, a federal court held that a "balanced treatment" statute violated the Establishment Clause of the U.S. Constitution. The Arkansas statute required public schools to give balanced treatment to "creation-science" and "evolution-science." In a decision that gave a detailed definition of the term "science," the court declared that "creation science" is not in fact a science. The court also

† From the National Center for Science Education, Berkeley, Calif., 1998. Reprinted by permission of the publisher.

found that the statute did not have a secular purpose, noting that the statute used language peculiar to creationist literature in emphasizing origins of life as an aspect of the theory of evolution. While the subject of life's origins is within the province of biology, the scientific community does not consider the subject as part of evolutionary theory, which assumes the existence of life and is directed to an explanation of how life evolved after it originated. The theory of evolution does not presuppose either the absence or the presence of a creator. (*McLean v. Arkansas Board of Education* (1982) 529 F. Supp. 1255, 50 U.S. Law Week 2412)

4. In 1987, in *Edwards v. Aguillard,* the U.S. Supreme Court held unconstitutional Louisiana's "Creationism Act." This statute prohibited the teaching of evolution in public schools, except when it was accompanied by instruction in "creation science." The Court found that, by advancing the religious belief that a supernatural being created humankind, which is embraced by the term *creation science,* the act impermissibly endorses religion. In addition, the Court found that the provision of a comprehensive science education is undermined when it is forbidden to teach evolution except when creation science is also taught. (*Edwards v. Aguillard* (1987) 482 U.S. 578)

5. In 1990, in *Webster v. New Lenox School District,* the Seventh Circuit Court of Appeals found that a school district may prohibit a teacher from teaching creation science, in fulfilling its responsibility to ensure that the First Amendment's establishment clause is not violated, and religious beliefs are not injected into the public school curriculum. The court upheld a district court finding that the school district had not violated Webster's free speech rights when it prohibited him from teaching "creation science," since it is a form of religious advocacy. (*Webster v. New Lenox School District #122,* 917 F. 2d 1004)

6. In 1994, in *Peloza v. Capistrano School District,* the Ninth Circuit Court of Appeals upheld a district court finding that a teacher's First Amendment right to free exercise of religion is not violated by a school district's requirement that evolution be taught in biology classes. Rejecting plaintiff Peloza's definition of a "religion" of "evolutionism," the Court found that the district had simply and appropriately required a science teacher to teach a scientific theory in biology class. (*John E. Peloza v. Capistrano Unified School District,* (1994) 37 F. 3rd 517)

7. In 1997, in *Freiler v. Tangipahoa Parish Board of Education,* the United States District Court for the Eastern District of Louisiana rejected a policy requiring teachers to read aloud a disclaimer whenever they taught about evolution, ostensibly to promote "critical thinking." Noting that the policy singled out the theory of evolution for attention, that it specifically stated that the only "concept" from which students were not to be "dissuaded" was "the Biblical concept of Creation," and that students were already urged in all their classes to engage in critical thinking, the Court wrote that, "In mandating this disclaimer, the School Board is endorsing religion by disclaiming the teaching of evolution in such a manner as to convey the message that evolution is a religious viewpoint that runs counter

to . . . other religious views." Besides addressing disclaimer policies, the decision is noteworthy for recognizing that curriculum proposals for "intelligent design" are equivalent to proposals for teaching "creation science." (*Freiler v Tangipahoa Board of Education*, No. 94-3577 (E.D. La. Aug. 8, 1997).[1]

1. On June 19, 2000, the U.S. Supreme Court refused to hear an appeal of the lower court's ruling, thus leaving it in place. [Editor]

Personal Incredulity and Antievolutionism

RICHARD DAWKINS

[The Argument from Personal Incredulity] (1987)†

Natural selection is the blind watchmaker, blind because it does not see ahead, does not plan consequences, has no purpose in view. Yet the living results of natural selection overwhelmingly impress us with the appearance of design as if by a master watchmaker, impress us with the illusion of design and planning.

* * *

Nowadays theologians aren't quite so straightforward as Paley. They don't point to complex living mechanisms and say that they are self-evidently designed by a creator, just like a watch. But there is a tendency to point to them and say 'It is impossible to believe' that such complexity, or such perfection, could have evolved by natural selection. Whenever I read such a remark, I always feel like writing 'Speak for yourself' in the margin. There are numerous examples (I counted 35 in one chapter) in a recent book called *The Probability of God* by the Bishop of Birmingham, Hugh Montefiore. I shall use this book for all my examples in the rest of this chapter, because it is a sincere and honest attempt, by a reputable and educated writer, to bring natural theology up to date. When I say honest, I mean honest. Unlike some of his theological colleagues, Bishop Montefiore is not afraid to state that the question of whether God exists is a definite question of fact. He has no truck with shifty evasions such as 'Christianity is a way of life. The question of God's *existence* is eliminated: it is a mirage created by the illusions of realism'. Parts of his book are about physics and cosmology, and I am not competent to comment on those except to note that he seems to have used genuine physicists as his authorities. Would that he had done the same in the biological parts. Unfortunately, he preferred here to consult the works of Arthur Koestler, Fred Hoyle, Gordon Rattray-Taylor and Karl Popper! The Bishop believes in evolution, but cannot believe that natural selection is an adequate explanation for the course that evolution has taken (partly because, like many

† From *The Blind Watchmaker* (New York, 1987). Reprinted by permission of Sterling Lord Literistic, Inc. Copyright by Richard Dawkins. Richard Dawkins (b. 1941) is Charles Simonyi Professor of the Public Understanding of Science at Oxford University.

others, he sadly misunderstands natural selection to be 'random' and 'meaningless').

He makes heavy use of what may be called the Argument from Personal Incredulity. In the course of one chapter we find the following phrases, in this order:

> . . . there seems no explanation on Darwinian grounds . . . It is no easier to explain . . . It is hard to understand . . . It is not easy to understand . . . It is equally difficult to explain . . . I do not find it easy to comprehend . . . I do not find it easy to see . . . I find it hard to understand . . . it does not seem feasible to explain . . . I cannot see how . . . neo-Darwinism seems inadequate to explain many of the complexities of animal behavior . . . it is not easy to comprehend how such behavior could have evolved solely through natural selection . . . It is impossible . . . How could an organ so complex evolve? . . . It is not easy to see . . . It is difficult to see . . .

The Argument from Personal Incredulity is an extremely weak argument, as Darwin himself noted. In some cases it is based upon simple ignorance. For instance, one of the facts that the Bishop finds it difficult to understand is the white colour of polar bears.

> As for camouflage, this is not always easily explicable on neo-Darwinian premises. If polar bears are dominant in the Arctic, then there would seem to have been no need for them to evolve a white-coloured form of camouflage.

This should be translated:

> I personally, off the top of my head sitting in my study, never having visited the Arctic, never having seen a polar bear in the wild, and having been educated in classical literature and theology, have not so far managed to think of a reason why polar bears might benefit from being white.

In this particular case, the assumption being made is that only animals that are preyed upon need camouflage. What is overlooked is that predators also benefit from being concealed from their prey. Polar bears stalk seals resting on the ice. If the seal sees the bear coming from far-enough away, it can escape. I suspect that, if he imagines a dark grizzly bear trying to stalk seals over the snow, the Bishop will immediately see the answer to his problem.

The polar bear argument turned out to be almost too easy to demolish but, in an important sense, this is not the point. Even if the foremost authority in the world can't explain some remarkable biological phenomenon, this doesn't mean that it is inexplicable. Plenty of mysteries have lasted for centuries and finally yielded to explanation. For what it is worth, most modern biologists wouldn't find it difficult to explain every one of the Bishop's 35 examples in terms of the theory of natural selection, although not all of them are quite as easy as the polar bears. But we aren't testing human ingenuity. Even if we found one example that we *couldn't* explain, we should hesitate to draw any grandiose conclusions from the fact of our own inability. Darwin himself was very clear on this point.

There are more serious versions of the argument from personal incredulity, versions which do not rest simply upon ignorance or lack of ingenuity. One form of the argument makes direct use of the extreme sense of wonder which we all feel when confronted with highly complicated machinery, like the detailed perfection of the echolocation equipment of bats. The implication is that it is somehow self-evident that anything so wonderful as this could not possibly have evolved by natural selection. The Bishop quotes, with approval, G. Bennett on spider webs:

> It is impossible for one who has watched the work for many hours to have any doubt that neither the present spiders of this species nor their ancestors were ever the architects of the web or that it could conceivably have been produced step by step through random variation; it would be as absurd to suppose that the intricate and exact proportions of the Parthenon were produced by piling together bits of marble.

It is not impossible at all. That is exactly what I firmly believe, and I have some experience of spiders and their webs.

The Bishop goes on to the human eye, asking rhetorically, and with the implication that there is no answer, 'How could an organ so complex evolve?' This is not an argument, it is simply an affirmation of incredulity. The underlying basis for the intuitive incredulity that we all are tempted to feel about what Darwin called organs of extreme perfection and complication is, I think, twofold. First we have no intuitive grasp of the immensities of time available for evolutionary change. Most sceptics about natural selection are prepared to accept that it can bring about minor changes like the dark coloration that has evolved in various species of moth since the industrial revolution. But, having accepted this, they then point out how small a change this is. As the Bishop underlines, the dark moth is not a *new species*. I agree that this is a small change, no match for the evolution of the eye, or of echolocation. But equally, the moths only took a hundred years to make their change. One hundred years seems like a long time to us, because it is longer than our lifetime. But to a geologist it is about a thousand times shorter than he can ordinarily measure!

Eyes don't fossilize, so we don't know how long our type of eye took to evolve its present complexity and perfection from nothing, but the time available is several hundred million years. Think, by way of comparison, of the change that man has wrought in a much shorter time by genetic selection of dogs. In a few hundreds, or at most thousands, of years we have gone from wolf to Pekinese, Bulldog, Chihuahua and Saint Bernard. Ah, but they are still *dogs* aren't they? They haven't turned into a different *'kind'* of animal? Yes, if it comforts you to play with words like that, you can call them all dogs. But just think about the time involved. Let's represent the total time it took to evolve all these breeds of dog from a wolf, by one ordinary walking pace. Then, on the same scale, how far would you have to walk, in order to get back to Lucy and her kind, the earliest human fossils that unequivocally walked upright? The answer is about

2 miles. And how far would you have to walk, in order to get back to the start of evolution on Earth? The answer is that you would have to slog it out all the way from London to Baghdad. Think of the total quantity of change involved in going from wolf to Chihuahua, and then multiply it up by the number of walking paces between London and Baghdad. This will give some intuitive idea of the amount of change that we can expect in real natural evolution.

The second basis for our natural incredulity about the evolution of very complex organs like human eyes and bat ears is an intuitive application of probability theory. Bishop Montefiore quotes C. E. Raven on cuckoos. These lay their eggs in the nests of other birds, which then act as unwitting foster parents. Like so many biological adaptations, that of the cuckoo is not single but multiple. Several different facts about cuckoos fit them to their parasitic way of life. For instance, the mother has the habit of laying in other birds' nests, and the baby has the habit of throwing the host's own chicks out of the nest. Both habits help the cuckoo succeed in its parasitic life. Raven goes on:

> It will be seen that each one of this sequence of conditions is essential for the success of the whole. Yet each by itself is useless. The whole *opus perfectum* must have been achieved simultaneously. The odds against the random occurrence of such a series of coincidences are, as we have already stated, astronomical.

Arguments such as this are in principle more respectable than the argument based on sheer, naked incredulity. Measuring the statistical improbability of a suggestion is the right way to go about assessing its believability. Indeed, it is a method that we shall use in this book several times. But you have to do it right! There are two things wrong with the argument put by Raven. First, there is the familiar, and I have to say rather irritating, confusion of natural selection with 'randomness'. Mutation is random; natural selection is the very opposite of random. Second, it just isn't *true* that 'each by itself is useless'. It isn't true that the whole perfect work must have been achieved simultaneously. It isn't true that each part is essential for the success of the whole. A simple, rudimentary, half-cocked eye/ear/echolocation system/cuckoo parasitism system, etc., is better than none at all. Without an eye you are totally blind. With half an eye you may at least be able to detect the general direction of a predator's movement, even if you can't focus a clear image. And this may make all the difference between life and death. * * *

PHILLIP E. JOHNSON

Darwin on Trial (1991)†

Natural Selection as a Philosophical Necessity

The National Academy of Sciences told the Supreme Court that the most basic characteristic of science is "reliance upon naturalistic explanations," as opposed to "supernatural means inaccessible to human understanding." In the latter, unacceptable category contemporary scientists place not only God, but also any non-material vital force that supposedly drives evolution in the direction of greater complexity, consciousness, or whatever. If science is to have any explanation for biological complexity at all it has to make do with what is left when the unacceptable has been excluded. Natural selection is the best of the remaining alternatives, probably the only alternative.

In this situation some may decide that Darwinism simply *must* be true, and for such persons the purpose of any further investigation will be merely to explain how natural selection works and to solve the mysteries created by apparent anomalies. For them there is no need to test the theory itself, for there is no respectable alternative to test it against. Any persons who say the theory itself is inadequately supported can be vanquished by the question "Darwin's Bulldog" T. H. Huxley used to ask the doubters in Darwin's time: What is your alternative?

I do not think that many scientists would be comfortable accepting Darwinism solely as a philosophical principle, without seeking to find at least some empirical evidence that it is true. But there is an important difference between going to the empirical evidence to test a doubtful theory against some plausible alternative, and going to the evidence to look for confirmation of the only theory that one is willing to tolerate. * * *

If positive confirmation of the creative potency of natural selection is not required, there is little danger that the theory will be disproved by negative evidence. Darwinists have evolved an array of subsidiary concepts capable of furnishing a plausible explanation for just about any conceivable eventuality. For example, the living fossils, which have remained basically unchanged for millions of years while their cousins were supposedly evolving into more advanced creatures like human beings, are no embarrassment to Darwinists. They failed to evolve because the necessary mutations didn't arrive, or because of "developmental constraints," or because they were already adequately adapted to their environment. In short, they didn't evolve because they didn't evolve.

Some animals give warning signals at the approach of predators, apparently reducing their own safety for the benefit of others in the herd. How does natural selection encourage the evolution of a trait for self-sacrifice? Some Darwinists attribute the apparent anomaly to "group selection." Hu-

---

† From *Darwin on Trial* (Washington D.C., 1991). Copyright © 1991 by Regnery Publishing. All rights reserved. Reprinted by special permission of Regnery Publishing, Inc. Washington, D.C. Phillip E. Johnson (b. 1940) is professor of law at the University of California at Berkeley.

man nations benefit if they contain individuals willing to die in battle for their country, and likewise animal groups containing self-sacrificing individuals may have an advantage over groups composed exclusively of selfish individuals.

Other Darwinists are scornful of group selection and prefer to explain altruism on the basis of "kinship selection." By sacrificing itself to preserve its offspring or near relations an individual promotes the survival of its genes. Selection may thus operate at the genetic level to encourage the perpetuation of genetic combinations that produce individuals capable of altruistic behavior. By moving the focus of selection either up (to the group level) or down (to the genetic level), Darwinists can easily account for traits that seem to contradict the selection hypothesis at the level of individual organisms.

Potentially the most powerful explanatory tool in the entire Darwinist armory is *pleiotropy*, the fact that a single gene has multiple effects. This means that any mutation which affects one functional characteristic is likely to change other features as well, and whether or not it is advantageous depends upon the net effect. Characteristics which on their face appear to be maladaptive may therefore be presumed to be linked genetically to more favorable characteristics, and natural selection can be credited with preserving the package.

I am not implying that there is anything inherently unreasonable in invoking pleiotropy, or kinship selection, or developmental constraints to explain why apparent anomalies are not necessarily inconsistent with Darwinism. If we assume that Darwinism is basically true then it is perfectly reasonable to adjust the theory as necessary to make it conform to the observed facts. The problem is that the adjusting devices are so flexible that in combination they make it difficult to conceive of a way to test the claims of Darwinism empirically. Apparently maladaptive features can be attributed to pleiotropy, or to our inability to perceive the advantage that may be there, or when all else fails simply to "chance."

* * *

Biologists before and after Darwin have generally sensed that in classifying they were not merely forcing creatures into arbitrary categories, but discovering relationships that are in some sense real. Some pre-Darwinian taxonomists expressed this sense by saying that whales and bats are superficially like fish and birds but they are *essentially* mammals—that is, they conform in their "essence" to the mammalian "type." Similarly, all birds are essentially birds, whether they fly, swim, or run. The principle can be extended up or down the scale of classification: St. Bernards and dachshunds are essentially dogs, despite the visible dissimilarity, and sparrows and elephants are essentially vertebrates.

Essentialism did not attempt to explain the cause of natural relationships, but merely described the pattern in the language of Platonic philosophy. The essentialists knew about fossils and hence were aware that different kinds of creatures had lived at different times. The concept of evolution did not make sense to them, however, because it required the existence of numerous intermediates—impossible creatures that were somewhere in transition from one essential state to another. Essentialists therefore attributed the common features linking each class not to inheritance from common ancestors, but to a sort of blueprint called the "Archetype," which existed only in some metaphysical realm such as the mind of God.

Darwin proposed a naturalistic explanation for the essentialist features of the living world that was so stunning in its logical appeal that it conquered the scientific world even while doubts remained about some important parts of his theory. He theorized that the discontinuous groups of the living world were the descendants of long-extinct common ancestors. Relatively closely related groups (like reptiles, birds, and mammals) shared a relatively recent common ancestor; all vertebrates shared a more ancient common ancestor; and all animals shared a still more ancient common ancestor.

*   *   *

Descent with modification could be something much more substantial than a tautology or a semantic trick. It could be a testable scientific hypothesis. If common ancestors and chains of linking intermediates once existed, fossil studies should be able, at least in some cases, to identify them. If it is possible for a single ancestral species to change by natural processes into such different forms as a shark, a frog, a snake, a penguin, and a monkey, then laboratory science should be able to discover the mechanism of change.

If laboratory science cannot establish a mechanism, and if fossil studies cannot find the common ancestors and transitional links, then Darwinism fails as an empirical theory. But Darwinists suppress consideration of that possibility by invoking a distinction between the "fact" of evolution and Darwin's particular theory. Objections based upon the fossil record and the inadequacy of the Darwinist mechanism go only to the theory, they argue. Evolution itself (the logical explanation for relationships) remains a fact, by which they seem to mean it is an inescapable deduction from the fact of relationship. Stephen Jay Gould's influential article, "Evolution as Fact and Theory" explains the distinction by citing the fact and theory of gravity:

> Facts are the world's data. Theories are structures of ideas that explain and interpret facts. Facts do not go away while scientists debate rival theories for explaining them. Einstein's theory of gravitation replaced Newton's, but apples did not suspend themselves in mid-air pending the outcome. And human beings evolved from ape-like ancestors whether they did so by Darwin's proposed mechanism or by some other, yet to be identified.

The analogy is spurious. We observe directly that apples fall when dropped, but we do not observe a common ancestor for modern apes and humans. What we *do* observe is that apes and humans are physically and biochemically more like each other than they are like rabbits, snakes, or trees. The ape-like common ancestor is a hypothesis in a *theory*, which purports to explain how these greater and lesser similarities came about.

The theory is plausible, especially to a philosophical materialist, but it may nonetheless be false. The true explanation for natural relationships may be something much more mysterious.

*   *   *

Gould's second argument, and the centerpiece of his case for the "fact" of evolution, is the argument from imperfection:

> The second argument—that the imperfection of nature reveals evolution—strikes many people as ironic, for they feel that evolution should be most elegantly displayed in the nearly perfect adaptation expressed by some organisms—the camber of a gull's wing, or butterflies that cannot be seen in ground litter because they mimic leaves so precisely. But perfection could be imposed by a wise creator or evolved by natural selection. Perfection covers the tracks of past history. And past history—the evidence of descent—is the mark of evolution.
>
> Evolution lies exposed in the imperfections that record a history of descent. Why should a rat run, a bat fly, a porpoise swim, and I type this essay with structures built of the same bones unless we all inherited them from a common ancestor? An engineer, starting from scratch, could design better limbs in each case. Why should all the large native mammals of Australia be marsupials, unless they descended from a common ancestor on this island continent? Marsupials are not "better," or ideally suited for Australia; many have been wiped out by placental animals imported by man from other continents. . . .

Gould here merely repeats Darwin's explanation for the existence of natural groups—the theory for which we are seeking confirmation—and gives it a theological twist. A proper Creator should have designed each kind of organism from scratch to achieve maximum efficiency. This speculation is no substitute for scientific evidence establishing the reality of the common ancestors. It also does nothing to confirm the natural process by which the transformation from ancestral to descendant forms supposedly occurred. It is Darwin, after all, who banished speculation about the "unknown plan of creation" from science.

Douglas Futuyma also leans heavily on the "God wouldn't have done it" theme, citing examples from vertebrate embryology:

> Why should species that ultimately develop adaptations for utterly different ways of life be nearly indistinguishable in their early stages? How does God's plan for humans and sharks require them to have almost identical embryos? Why should terrestrial salamanders, if they were not descended from aquatic ancestors, go through a larval stage entirely within the egg, with gills and fins that are never used, and then lose these features before they hatch?

These are rhetorical questions, but they point to legitimate starting points for investigation. The features Futuyma cites may exist because a Creator employed them for some inscrutable purpose; or they may reflect inheritance from specific common ancestors; or they may be due to some as yet unimagined process which science may discover in the future.

* * *

If an omnipotent Creator exists He might have created things instantaneously in a single week or through gradual evolution over billions of years. He might have employed means wholly inaccessible to science, or mechanisms that are at least in part understandable through scientific investigation. * * *

The essential point of creation has nothing to do with the timing or the mechanism the Creator chose to employ, but with the element of design or purpose. In the broadest sense, a "creationist" is simply a person who believes that the world (and especially mankind) was *designed*, and exists for a *purpose*. With the issue defined that way, the question becomes: Is mainstream science opposed to the possibility that the natural world was designed by a Creator for a purpose? If so, on what basis?

* * *

Theistic or "guided" evolution has to be excluded as a possibility because Darwinists identify science with a philosophical doctrine known as *naturalism*. Naturalism assumes the entire realm of nature to be a closed system of material causes and effects, which cannot be influenced by anything from "outside." Naturalism does not explicitly deny the mere existence of God, but it does deny that a supernatural being could in any way influence natural events, such as evolution, or communicate with natural creatures like ourselves. *Scientific* naturalism makes the same point by starting with the assumption that science, which studies only the natural, is our only reliable path to knowledge. A God who can never do anything that makes a difference, and of whom we can have no reliable knowledge, is of no importance to us.

Naturalism is not something about which Darwinists can afford to be tentative, because their science is based upon it. As we have seen, the positive evidence that Darwinian evolution either can produce or has produced important biological innovations is nonexistent. Darwinists know that the mutation-selection mechanism can produce wings, eyes, and brains not because the mechanism can be observed to do anything of the kind, but because their guiding philosophy assures them that no other power is available to do the job. The absence from the cosmos of any Creator is therefore the essential starting point for Darwinism.

* * *

To cite an example from my personal experience, it is pointless to try to engage a scientific naturalist in a discussion about whether the neo-Darwinist theory of evolution is *true*. The reply is likely to be that neo-Darwinism is the best scientific explanation we have, and that *means* it is our closest approximation to the truth. Naturalists will usually concede that any theory can be improved, and that our understanding of naturalistic evolution may one day be much greater than it is now. To question whether naturalistic evolution itself is "true," on the other hand, is to talk nonsense. Naturalistic evolution is the only conceivable explanation for life, and so the fact that life exists proves it to be true.

It is easy to see why scientific naturalism is an attractive philosophy for scientists. It gives science a virtual monopoly on the production of knowledge, and it assures scientists that no important questions are in principle beyond scientific investigation. The important question, however, is whether this philosophical viewpoint is merely an understandable professional prejudice or whether it is *the* objectively valid way of understanding the world. That is the real issue behind the push to make naturalistic evolution a fundamental tenet of society, to which everyone must be converted.

* * *

EUGENIE C. SCOTT

Review of Johnson (1992)†

* * *

Like many conservative Christians, Johnson is concerned with the implications of evolution. Although he states in his book that theistic evolution (evolution that is God-directed) is possible, he doubts it. He is not a young-earth creationist, and in fact, is almost contemptuous of their point of view. He accepts that the earth is old, but rejects evolution, thus he is perhaps describable as an old-earth creationist. His concern with evolution is primarily religious: if evolution by natural selection (Darwinism) really happened, then it is not possible for life to have purpose and for the universe and Earth to have been designed by an omnipotent, personal God. He feels that life would have no meaning, and moral and ethical systems would have no foundation. Thus his goal in *Darwin on Trial* is to demonstrate that Darwinian natural selection is impossible; therefore evolution didn't take place; therefore his theological views are preserved. He stresses that Darwinism is inherently an atheistic, naturalistic philosophy.

Out of His Element

Let me stress that my objections to *Darwin on Trial* are not because its author lacks a Ph.D. in science. Science is not a secret activity that can be performed or understood only by priests in white coats—I've argued long and hard to try to make science explicable to nonscientists, and to demystify science as a way of knowing. But if one wishes to step out of one's area of expertise, scientist or nonscientist, it behooves one to make a careful study of the new area, and carefully weigh one's pronouncements.

† From *Creation/Evolution* 13 (1992): 36–47. Reprinted by permission of the National Center for Science Education. Eugenie C. Scott (b. 1945) is executive director of the National Center for Science Education in Berkeley, Calif.

If I were to critique the newest developments on astrophysics, or medieval art history, or patent law, I would have to first acquaint myself with not only the fundamentals of physics, art history, or law, but also *astrophysics*, *medieval* art history, or *patent* law. Similarly, it behooves Johnson to study not only science, but that particular and complicated science known as evolution.

Johnson has grasped the general picture of evolutionary biology, and even some of the details, but he lacks the deep understanding that is required to make the criticisms he makes. A deep understanding of a field comes from careful study of relevant literature, including primary sources, and communication with specialists in the field. Indeed, Darwinism has been critiqued by evolutionary biologists, but there is a clear difference in quality and nuance between their criticisms and those parroted by Johnson. Perhaps this is because he got most of his information from a suspect source: the criticisms of evolution he offers are immediately recognizable as originating with the "scientific" creationists, (although Johnson disdains young-earth creationism, and speaks disparagingly of Biblical literalism).

We find the usual "gaps in the fossil record," "natural selection is a tautology," "there are no transitional fossils," "mutations are harmful," "natural selection is not creative," "microevolution does not explain macroevolution," "natural selection only produces variation within the kind," and the vertebrate eye and the argument from design, just as in any standard Institute for Creation Research tract.

* * *

As a result of his reliance on creationist sources, Johnson makes a lot of flat-out mistakes. *Archaeopteryx* is not mostly bird; the British Museum did not prevent the inspection of the Piltdown fossils; Zuckerman studied pre-1970 Australopithecines, so his comments on early human evolution are essentially irrelevant; most mutations are not harmful. But mostly the problems in his book reflect subtle misunderstanding of how science works—and knowing or unknowing misstatements of theory in evolutionary biology.

Johnsonian science assumes that something that is not currently fully understood is perhaps un-understandable. He concludes, for example, that the Cambrian fossil explosion, the origin of the first replicating molecule, and the evolution of whales or bats are "difficult problem(s)" for evolution, as if the fact that we don't know all the details of evolution somehow proves evolution didn't take place.

This ignores the consilience factor: the vast amount of detail from natural history that is compatible (only) with the idea that evolution actually took place. If we don't know every link in the fossil phylogeny of bats, why would this make us give up on the idea of evolution, when so many other sources of data support it? We have evidence that evolution occurred from comparative anatomy, geology, biogeography, biochemistry, astronomy— all shouting that change has taken place during the history of the universe. * * * This entire monument is not about to be disassembled because we don't know exactly how bats evolved from primitive insectivores.

Consilience is a phenomenon that creationists seem to have great difficulty with, so they ignore it. So does Johnson.

* * *

Perhaps his greatest misunderstanding of evolution is his expectation of what a "transitional form" should be like. His goal, of course, is to discredit his version of Darwinism, which stresses slow, gradual evolution. (Johnson sometimes means Darwinism, and sometimes means Neo-Darwinism, but that is another issue.) Like the ICR's Duane Gish, Johnson will not accept evolution unless a lineage can be recreated showing every individual specimen from A to Z. If mammals arose from reptiles, for example (which technically, they didn't, but from a tetrapod common ancestor), then to "prove" this, evolutionists would have to show them a fossil that is 25% mammal and 75% reptile, then one that is 50:50, and one that is 25% reptile and 75% mammal—and then kindly fill in the gaps, please. What great confidence this shows in the fossil record! Futuyma puts it best, "The creationist argument that if evolution were true we should have an abundance of intermediate fossils is built by exaggerating the richness of paleontological collections, by denying the transitional series that exist, and by distorting, or misunderstanding, the genetical theory of evolution."

The way Darwin expected the fossil record to look is irrelevant to modern evolutionary theory; Darwin died 112 years ago. We can reasonably expect theory to change in a century. To quote Futuyma again, "The supposition that evolution proceeds very slowly and gradually, and so should leave thousands of fossil intermediates of any species in its wake, has not been part of evolutionary theory for more than thirty years." But Johnson flogs the gradualist horse because it serves his purpose to discredit evolution.

Modern evolutionists, on the other hand, are more concerned with tracing the *pattern* of evolution, rather than tracing a specific lineage down to the gnat's eyelash. The pattern of evolution is more likely to be shown across a broad series of lineages within an evolving taxon. Transitional structures are sought, rather than individual specimens showing precise intermediacy in all anatomical structures. Evolutionists consider a transitional structure to be one that shows characteristics of more than one taxon. Thus a number of fossils sometimes called reptile-like mammals show characteristics of mammals and also of more primitive tetrapods. These characteristics are especially clear in the skull, and particularly the lower jaw.

It would take a very long essay to criticize all or even most of the misleading, or just plain wrong, statements Johnson makes about evolutionary biology. For example, "Darwinists do not in principle deny the fundamental discontinuity of the living world, but they explain it as being due to the extinction of vast numbers of intermediates that once linked the discrete groups to their remote common ancestors" (p. 87).[1] Wrong. First of all, the discontinuity of modern groups is not something embarrassing to "Darwinists" which they are trying to deny. Discontinuity exists, and it

---

1. Page numbers refer to the 1991 edition of Johnson's *Darwin on Trial*. [Editor]

exists because of the process of speciation, which produces reproductively isolated groups of organisms through a number of well-understood processes of heredity. The hierarchy of taxa produced by evolution would be discrete regardless of whether we had examples of every intermediate species. It is just how we expect evolution to work, but Johnson does not understand this. As one reads the book, one stops over and over to say, "No, that's not quite right." It is as if Johnson is talking about a familiar topic, but he gives it a spin that requires careful reading—sort of like discussing a zebra as a horse-like quadruped distinguished by a stiff mane and black and red stripes.

* * *

Evolution Is Not Evolutionism

First, Johnson defines evolution as if it were an ideology: evolution*ism*. Evolutionism to him is a philosophy that excludes the possibility of divine intervention occurring during evolution. Some individuals *have* made an ideology out of evolution, but Johnson errs in assuming that therefore evolution itself is an incorrect explanation of the history of the universe.

The quality or usefulness of a scientific idea is independent of the philosophical implications one may or may not draw from it. The fact that one can take a scientific idea and make an ideology out of it does not mean that every treatment of this idea will require an ideological treatment. If a high school teacher someplace should decide that photosynthesis is the foundation for a new religion, that doesn't mean that other teachers should cease teaching photosynthesis. Yet Johnson worries greatly that children will learn evolution*ism* rather than "just" evolution, and then lose their faith in there being a purpose for life. In this regard, let me reassure Johnson that in speaking with hundreds of teachers all over the country, I have found that when evolution is taught, evolution is taught, not evolution*ism*. Most teachers appear to be strongly (and conventionally) religious. I know of no recent national survey, but a recent survey of Texas teachers shows a high degree of church attendance (80%).

Science Is Not Philosophical Naturalism

Johnson protests that Darwinism cannot be extricated from atheistic, materialist philosophy. Evolution is defined in *Darwin on Trial* as "fully naturalistic evolution,—meaning evolution that is not directed by any purposeful intelligence" (p. 4). In this he errs, as do many "scientific" creationists, in conflating the necessary methodological materialism of science with philosophical materialism or naturalism. Naturalism is a philosophy stating that God does not have anything to do with the universe, about which science, as a non-theistic (rather than anti-theistic) enterprise, can say nothing. Like the more familiar ICR creationists, Johnson doesn't want to allow science to be a purely naturalistic, materialist exercise; he insists on the right to retain the possibility of divine intervention or guidance.

Unfortunately, for him, that is just not the way science operates in the late 20th century, and for good reason. Naturalistic explanations have been found to be far more fruitful in the explanation of natural phenomena than supernatural ones. The problem with supernatural explanations is that, correct or incorrect, they cannot be rejected, and science proceeds by rejecting explanations rather than "proving" them true. If you want to know whether the earth goes around the sun or the sun goes around the earth, you'll get a lot farther if you posit testable, natural explanations rather than untestable ones from supernatural revelation. The Hare Krishnas, based on their understanding of the Vedas, believe that the sun is closer to the earth than is the moon. Do you want revelation or empiricism to determine where to send the Apollo mission?

Evolution Is Not the Same As Darwinism

Johnson conflates evolution and Darwinism, believing that by disproving Darwinism, he can demonstrate evolution could not have occurred.

Evolution is a statement about the history of the universe: that the universe has a past. The message of evolution essentially is that change has occurred, as opposed to special creation's view that all the galaxies, solar systems, planets, and organisms in the universe were specially created all at one time. The difference between an evolutionist and a creationist is not "Did God create?" but "What is the history of the universe?" Did everything we see today occur all at one time, or is the universe of today different than it was in the past? Also, evolution refers to a very broad spectrum of natural phenomena: from galaxies and stars and solar systems, to geological phenomena, to organic life.

Darwinism is a mechanism by which part of this spectrum of history may be explained, in whole or in part. Darwinism attempts to explain organic evolution, at least in major part, by natural selection. But Darwinism is only one possible explanation for the history of life. If Darwinism were to be discovered not to explain organic evolution, this would have nothing in the universe (literally) to do with whether stellar or galactic evolution took place—or even whether organic evolution took place. Johnson does not recognize that by trying to disprove organic evolution by natural selection, he leaves untouched the explanation of organic evolution by other mechanisms. But he really doesn't care. His main concern is whether *human* evolution, one small component of this great sweeping theory, is adequately explained by natural causes, or requires supernatural purpose and design.

The Origin of Life Is Not the Same as Evolution
The Big Bang Is Not the Same as Evolution

Like the scientific creationists, Johnson confuses the origin of life and the Big Bang (the origin of the universe) with evolution. This is rather like confusing starting up the car's engine with driving away. It is necessary to start the engine to go anywhere, but there is nothing inherent about starting the car that tells you whether you are going to work, or to the corner store, or just idling in the driveway. The origin of life and the Big

Bang are both interesting scientific problems, and, as they do with any scientific problem, scientists are attempting to explain them with natural rather than supernatural explanations. Clearly, there is much more to be learned about both, but it appears as if it is *possible* to explain these phenomena naturally. This possibility is offensive to creationists, who demand that supernatural forces must be invoked. Still, logically, whether the origin of the universe and the production of the first replicating molecule are ever fully explained with naturalistic explanations has nothing to do with what happened subsequently. Did evolution take place, or not?

Just as the ICR's Duane Gish in his debates shifts smoothly to the origin of life when his debate opponents are sufficiently knowledgeable to defend the fossil record, so Johnson apparently thinks the incompleteness of explanations for the origin of life/Big Bang appear to the general public as soft underbellies of evolution.

Materialism, Religion, and Darwinism

Johnson presents a narrow view of science, an inaccurate view of evolution/Darwinism, and even a narrow theology. In a 1992 speech Johnson remarked:

> Our discussion today is over whether belief in Darwinism is compatible with a meaningful theism. When most people ask that question, they take the Darwinism for granted and ask whether the theism has to be discarded. I think it is more illuminating to approach the question from the other side. Is there any reason that a person who believes in a real, personal God should believe Darwinist claims that biological creation occurred through a fully naturalistic evolutionary process? The answer is clearly "no."

Applying the lawyer's "cold, dispassionate eye for logic and proof" as touted on his book's dustjacket, Johnson manages to set up another strawman that does not accurately reflect the real relationship between evolution and religion. Evolution is presented as a "fully naturalistic process," implying an antithesis between evolution and the supernatural. This certainty is not the position of the majority of Christians in the US today, neither Catholic nor main-line Protestants.

Johnson confuses the necessary *methodological* materialism (or naturalism) of science with philosophical materialism/naturalism. Science neither denies nor opposes the supernatural, but *ignores* the supernatural for methodological reasons. The history of science has shown that progress comes from logical and empirical study rather than reference to revelation or to inner psychological states. That's how we play our game; his basketball won't work on our baseball field. The essence of science is empiricism and control of variables, and if there is an omnipotent God, it certainly can't be controlled like temperature or humidity. Science has made a little deal with itself: because you can't put God in a test tube (or keep it out of one), science acts as if the supernatural did not exist. This methodological materialism is the cornerstone of modern science.

Materialism also is the cornerstone of mathematics. It may be the case that God caused 2+2 to equal 4, but ultimate cause is irrelevant to the mathematical applications that can be made to 2+2 = 4. Scientists no more accept supernatural explanations for phenomena than mathematicians would accept a solution to a mathematical problem based on revelation. Yet no one claims mathematics is antireligious. Neither is science.

Johnson fails to recognize the necessity for methodological materialism, because of his concern for philosophical materialism's attack on his theology. The *process* of evolutionary change, like any scientific process, *must* be studied without reference to the supernatural. Johnson is certainly welcome to criticize *philosophical* materialism if he wishes to, but such a criticism is irrelevant to science.

*   *   *

Summary

Darwin on Trial attacks evolution by natural selection in an attempt to bolster a theology based on a personal God who created humankind for a reason, and gave us a purpose. It does this by trying to convince the reader that evolution did not occur, and that Darwinism, as a mechanism, is inadequate to explain how descent with modification could have occurred. The arguments are recycled arguments from the discredited "scientific" creationists, although they are presented with style and persuasiveness.

The book fails to disprove evolution, but the spirit behind it deserves to be recognized by all scientists. Johnson reflects the anguish expressed by many conservative Christians who believe that something terribly important is lost if evolution is true, and especially if the way things changed is through the wasteful and unattractive mechanism of natural selection. To someone who is serious about religion, Darwinian evolution needs to be coped with, and it may not be psychologically easy. Unfortunately, the job of a science teacher is to teach state of the art science, and that means evolution. Students who do not understand evolution cannot be said to be scientifically literate.

*   *   *

MICHAEL BEHE

Darwin's Black Box (1996)†

Irreducible Complexity and the Nature of Mutation

Darwin knew that his theory of gradual evolution by natural selection carried a heavy burden:

† From *Darwin's Black Box* (New York, 1996). Reprinted with the permission of The Free Press, a Division of Simon and Schuster, Inc. Copyright © 1996. Michael Behe (b. 1952) is professor of biochemistry at Lehigh University.

> If it could be demonstrated that any complex organ existed which could not possibly have been formed by numerous, successive, slight modifications, my theory would absolutely break down.

It is safe to say that most of the scientific skepticism about Darwinism in the past century has centered on this requirement. From Mivart's concern over the incipient stages of new structures to Margulis's dismissal of gradual evolution, critics of Darwin have suspected that his criterion of failure had been met. But how can we be confident? What type of biological system could not be formed by "numerous, successive, slight modifications"?

Well, for starters, a system that is irreducibly complex. By *irreducibly complex* I mean a single system composed of several well-matched, interacting parts that contribute to the basic function, wherein the removal of any one of the parts causes the system to effectively cease functioning. An irreducibly complex system cannot be produced directly (that is, by continuously improving the initial function, which continues to work by the same mechanism) by slight, successive modifications of a precursor system, because any precursor to an irreducibly complex system that is missing a part is by definition nonfunctional. An irreducibly complex biological system, if there is such a thing, would be a powerful challenge to Darwinian evolution. Since natural selection can only choose systems that are already working, then if a biological system cannot be produced gradually it would have to arise as an integrated unit, in one fell swoop, for natural selection to have anything to act on.

Even if a system is irreducibly complex (and thus cannot have been produced directly), however, one can not definitively rule out the possibility of an indirect, circuitous route. As the complexity of an interacting system increases, though, the likelihood of such an indirect route drops precipitously. And as the number of unexplained, irreducibly complex biological systems increases, our confidence that Darwin's criterion of failure has been met skyrockets toward the maximum that science allows.

In the abstract, it might be tempting to imagine that irreducible complexity simply requires multiple simultaneous mutations—that evolution might be far chancier than we thought, but still possible. This is essentially Goldschmidt's hopeful-monster theory. Such an appeal to brute luck can never be refuted. Yet it is an empty argument. One may as well say that the world luckily popped into existence yesterday with all the features it now has. Luck is metaphysical speculation; scientific explanations invoke causes. It is almost universally conceded that such sudden events would be irreconcilable with the gradualism Darwin envisioned. Richard Dawkins explains the problem well:

> Evolution is very possibly not, in actual fact, always gradual. But it must be gradual when it is being used to explain the coming into existence of complicated, apparently designed objects, like eyes. For if it is not gradual in these cases, it ceases to have any explanatory power at all. Without gradualness in these cases, we are back to miracle, which is simply a synonym for the total absence of explanation.

The reason why this is so rests in the nature of mutation.

In biochemistry, a mutation is a change in DNA. To be inherited, the change must occur in the DNA of a reproductive cell. The simplest mutation occurs when a single nucleotide (nucleotides are the "building blocks" of DNA) in a creature's DNA is switched to a different nucleotide. Alternatively, a single nucleotide can be added or left out when the DNA is copied during cell division. Sometimes, though, a whole region of DNA—thousands or millions of nucleotides—is accidentally deleted or duplicated. That counts as a single mutation, too, because it happens at one time, as a single event. Generally a single mutation can, at best, make only a small change in a creature—even if the change impresses us as a big one. For example, there is a well-known mutation called *antennapedia* that scientists can produce in a laboratory fruit fly: the poor mutant creature has legs growing out of its head instead of antennas. Although that strikes us as a big change, it really isn't. The legs on the head are typical fruit-fly legs, only in a different location.

An analogy may be useful here: Consider a step-by-step list of instructions. A mutation is a change in *one* of the lines of instructions. So instead of saying, "Take a ¼-inch nut," a mutation might say, "Take a ⅜-inch nut." Or instead of "Place the round peg in the round hole," we might get "Place the round peg in the square hole." Or instead of "Attach the seat to the top of the engine," we might get "Attach the seat to the handlebars" (but we could only get this if the nuts and bolts could be attached to the handlebars). What a mutation *cannot* do is change all the instructions in one step—say, to build a fax machine instead of a radio.

Thus, to go back to the bombardier beetle and the human eye, the question is whether the numerous anatomical changes can be accounted for by many small mutations. The frustrating answer is that *we can't tell*. Both the bombardier beetle's defensive apparatus and the vertebrate eye contain so many molecular components (on the order of tens of thousands of different types of molecules) that listing them—and speculating on the mutations that might have produced them—is currently impossible. Too many of the nuts and bolts (and screws, motor parts, handlebars, and so on) are unaccounted for. For us to debate whether Darwinian evolution could produce such large structures is like nineteenth century scientists debating whether cells could arise spontaneously. Such debates are fruitless because not all the components are known.

We should not, however, lose our perspective over this; other ages have been unable to answer many questions that interested them. Furthermore, because we can't yet evaluate the question of eye evolution or beetle evolution does not mean we can't evaluate Darwinism's claims for any biological structure. When we descend from the level of a whole animal (such as a beetle) or whole organ (such as an eye) to the molecular level, then in many cases we *can* make a judgment on evolution because all of the parts of many discrete molecular systems *are* known. In the next five chapters we will meet a number of such systems—and render our judgment.

Now, let's return to the notion of irreducible complexity. At this point in our discussion *irreducible complexity* is just a term whose power resides mostly in its definition. We must ask how we can recognize an irreducibly complex system. Given the nature of mutation, when can we be sure that a biological system is irreducibly complex?

The first step in determining irreducible complexity is to specify both the function of the system and all system components. An irreducibly complex object will be composed of several parts, all of which contribute to the function. To avoid the problems encountered with extremely complex objects (such as eyes, beetles, or other multicellular biological systems) I will begin with a simple mechanical example: the humble mousetrap.

The function of a mousetrap is to immobilize a mouse so that it can't perform such unfriendly acts as chewing through sacks of flour or electrical cords, or leaving little reminders of its presence in unswept corners. The mousetraps that my family uses consist of a number of parts: (1) a flat wooden platform to act as a base; (2) a metal hammer, which does the actual job of crushing the little mouse; (3) a spring with extended ends to press against the platform and the hammer when the trap is charged; (4) a sensitive catch that releases when slight pressure is applied, and (5) a metal bar that connects to the catch and holds the hammer back when the trap is charged. (There are also assorted staples to hold the system together.)

The second step in determining if a system is irreducibly complex is to ask if all the components are required for the function. In this example, the answer is clearly yes. Suppose that while reading one evening, you hear the patter of little feet in the pantry, and you go to the utility drawer to get a mousetrap. Unfortunately, due to faulty manufacture, the trap is missing one of the parts listed above. Which part could be missing and still allow you to catch a mouse? If the wooden base were gone, there would be no platform for attaching the other components. If the hammer were gone, the mouse could dance all night on the platform without becoming pinned to the wooden base. If there were no spring, the hammer and platform would jangle loosely, and again the rodent would be unimpeded. If there were no catch or metal holding bar, then the spring would snap the hammer shut as soon as you let go of it; in order to use a trap like that you would have to chase the mouse around while holding the trap open.

* * *

The Cascade

The body commonly stores enzymes (proteins that catalyze a chemical reaction, like the cleavage of fibrinogen) in an inactive form for later use. The inactive forms are called proenzymes. When a signal is received that a certain enzyme is needed, the corresponding proenzyme is activated to give the mature enzyme. As with the conversion of fibrinogen to fibrin, proenzymes are often activated by cutting off a piece of the proenzyme that is blocking a critical area. The strategy is commonly used with digestive enzymes. Large quantities can be stored as inactive proenzymes, then quickly activated when the next good meal comes along.

Thrombin initially exists as the inactive form, prothrombin. Because it is inactive, prothrombin can't cleave fibrinogen, and the animal is saved from death by massive, inappropriate clotting. Still, the dilemma of control remains. If the cartoon saw were inactivated, the telephone pole would not fall at the wrong time. If nothing switches on the saw, however, then it would never cut the rope; the pole wouldn't fall even at the right time. If fibrinogen and prothrombin were the only proteins in the blood-clotting pathway, again our animal would be in bad shape. When the animal was cut, prothrombin would just float helplessly by the fibrinogen as the animal bled to death. Because prothrombin cannot cleave fibrinogen to fibrin, something is needed to activate prothrombin. Perhaps the reader can see why the blood-clotting system is called a *cascade*—a system where one component activates another component, which activates a third component, and so on. * * *

A protein called Stuart factor cleaves prothrombin, turning it into active thrombin that can then cleave fibrinogen to fibrin to form the blood clot. Unfortunately, as you may have guessed, if Stuart factor, prothrombin, and fibrinogen were the only blood-clotting proteins, then Stuart factor would rapidly trigger the cascade, congealing all the blood of the organism. So Stuart factor also exists in an inactive form that must first be activated.

At this point there's a little twist to our developing chicken-and-egg scenario. Even activated Stuart factor can't turn on prothrombin. Stuart factor and prothrombin can be mixed in a test tube for longer than it would take a large animal to bleed to death without any noticeable production of thrombin. It turns out that another protein, called accelerin, is needed to increase the activity of Stuart factor. The dynamic duo—accelerin and activated Stuart factor—cleave prothrombin fast enough to do the bleeding animal some good. So in this step we need two separate proteins to activate one proenzyme.

Yes, accelerin also initially exists in an inactive form, called proaccelerin (sigh). And what activates it? Thrombin! But thrombin, as we have seen, is further down the regulatory cascade than proaccelerin. So thrombin regulating the production of accelerin is like having the granddaughter regulate production of the grandmother. Nonetheless, due to a very low rate of cleavage of prothrombin by Stuart factor, it seems there is always a trace of thrombin in the bloodstream. Blood clotting is therefore *autocatalytic*, because proteins in the cascade accelerate the production of more of the same proteins.

We need to back up a little at this point because, as it turns out, prothrombin as it is initially made by the cell can't be transformed into thrombin, even in the presence of activated Stuart factor and accelerin. Prothrombin must first be modified by having ten specific amino acid residues, called glutamate (Glu) residues, changed to γ-carboxyglutamate (Gla) residues. The modification can be compared to placing a lower jaw onto the upper jaw of a skull. The completed structure can bite and hang on to the bitten object; without the lower jaw, the skull couldn't hang on. In the case of prothrombin, Gla residues "bite" (or bind) calcium, allowing prothrombin to stick to the surfaces of cells. Only the intact, modified calcium-prothrombin complex, bound to a cell membrane, can be cleaved by activated Stuart factor and accelerin to give thrombin.

The modification of prothrombin does not happen by accident. Like virtually all biochemical reactions, it requires catalysis by a specific enzyme. In addition to the enzyme, however, the conversion of Glu to Gla needs another component: vitamin K. Vitamin K is not a protein; rather, it is a small molecule, like the 11-cis-retinal that is necessary for vision. Like a gun that needs bullets, the enzyme that changes Glu to Gla needs vitamin K to work. One type of rat poison is based on the role that vitamin K plays in blood coagulation. The synthetic poison, called "warfarin" (for the Wisconsin Alumni Research Fund, which receives a cut of the profits from its sale), was made to look like vitamin K to the enzyme that uses it. In the presence of warfarin the enzyme is unable to modify prothrombin. When rats eat food poisoned with warfarin, prothrombin is neither modified nor cleaved, and the poisoned animals bleed to death.

But it still seems we haven't made much progress—now we have to go back and ask what activates Stuart factor. It turns out that it can be activated by two different routes, called the *intrinsic* and the *extrinsic* pathways. In the intrinsic pathway, all the proteins required for clotting are contained in the blood plasma; in the extrinsic pathway, some clotting proteins occur on cells. Let's first examine the intrinsic pathway.

When an animal is cut, a protein called Hageman factor sticks to the surface of cells near the wound. Bound Hageman factor is then cleaved by a protein called HMK to yield activated Hageman factor. Immediately the activated Hageman factor converts another protein, called prekallikrein, to its active form, kallikrein. Kallikrein helps HMK speed up the conversion of more Hageman factor to its active form. Activated Hageman factor and HMK then together transform another protein, called PTA, to its active form. Activated PTA in turn, together with the activated form of another protein called convertin, switch a protein called Christmas factor to its active form. Finally, activated Christmas factor, together with antihemophilic factor (which is itself activated by thrombin in a manner similar to that of proaccelerin) changes Stuart factor to its active form.

Like the intrinsic pathway, the extrinsic pathway is also a cascade. The extrinsic pathway begins when a protein called proconvertin is turned into convertin by activated Hageman factor and thrombin. In the presence of another protein, tissue factor, convertin changes Stuart factor to its active form. Tissue factor, however, only appears on the outside of cells that are usually not in contact with blood. Therefore, only when an injury brings tissue into contact with blood will the extrinsic pathway be initiated. (A cut plays a role similar to that of Foghorn Leghorn picking up the dollar. It is the initiating event—something outside of the cascade mechanism itself.)

The intrinsic and extrinsic pathways cross over at several points. Hageman factor, activated by the intrinsic pathway, can switch on proconvertin of the extrinsic pathway. Convertin can then feed back into the intrinsic pathway to help activated PTA activate Christmas factor. Thrombin itself can trigger both branches of the clotting cascade by activating antihemo-

philic factor, which is required to help activated Christmas factor in the
conversion of Stuart factor to its active form, and also by activating proconvertin.

Slogging through a description of the blood-clotting system makes a
fellow yearn for the simplicity of a cartoon Rube Goldberg machine.

*   *   *

To a person who does not feel obliged to restrict his search to unintelligent causes, the straightforward conclusion is that many biochemical systems were designed. They were designed not by the laws of nature, not by
chance and necessity; rather, they were *planned*. The designer knew what
the systems would look like when they were completed, then took steps to
bring the systems about. Life on earth at its most fundamental level, in its
most critical components, is the product of intelligent activity.

The conclusion of intelligent design flows naturally from the data
itself—not from sacred books or sectarian beliefs. Inferring that biochemical systems were designed by an intelligent agent is a humdrum process
that requires no new principles of logic or science. It comes simply from
the hard work that biochemistry has done over the past forty years, combined with consideration of the way in which we reach conclusions of
design every day.

*   *   *

What Will Science Do?

The discovery of design expands the number of factors that must be
considered by science when trying to explain life. What will be the effect
of the awareness of intelligent design on different branches of science?
Biologists who are working at the cellular level or above can continue their
research without paying much attention to design, because above the cellular level organisms are black boxes, and design is difficult to prove. So
those who labor in the fields of paleontology, comparative anatomy, population genetics, and biogeography should not invoke design until the
molecular sciences show that design has an effect at those higher levels.
Of course, the possibility of design should cause researchers in biology to
hesitate before claiming that a particular biological feature has been produced substantially by another mechanism, such as natural selection or
transposition. Instead, detailed models should be produced to justify the
assertion that a given mechanism produced a given biological feature.

Unlike Darwinian evolution, the theory of intelligent design is new to
modern science, so there are a host of questions that need to be answered
and much work lies ahead. For those who work at the molecular level,
the challenge will be to rigorously determine which systems were designed
and which might have arisen by other mechanisms. To reach a conclusion
of design will require the identification of the components of an interacting molecular system and the roles they play, as well as a determination
that the system is not a composite of several separable systems. To reach

a strong presumption of nondesign will require the demonstration that a system is not irreducibly complex or does not have much specificity between its components. To decide borderline cases of design will require the experimental or theoretical exploration of models whereby a system might have developed in a continuous manner, or a demonstration of points where the development of the system would necessarily be discontinuous.

Future research could take several directions. Work could be undertaken to determine whether information for designed systems could lie dormant for long periods of time, or whether the information would have to be added close to the time when the system became operational. Since the simplest possible design scenario posits a single cell—formed billions of years ago—that already contained all information to produce descendant organisms, other studies could test this scenario by attempting to calculate how much DNA would be required to code the information (keeping in mind that much of the information might be implicit). If DNA alone is insufficient, studies could be initiated to see if information could be stored in the cell in other ways—for example, as positional information. Other work could focus on whether larger, compound systems (containing two or more irreducibly complex systems) could have developed gradually or whether there are compounded irreducibilities.

The preceding are just the obvious questions that flow from a theory of design. Undoubtedly, more and better-formed questions will be generated as more and more scientists grow curious about design. The theory of intelligent design promises to reinvigorate a field of science grown stale from a lack of viable solutions to dead-end problems. The intellectual competition created by the discovery of design will bring sharper analysis to the professional scientific literature and will require that assertions be backed by hard data. The theory will spark experimental approaches and new hypotheses that would otherwise be untried. A rigorous theory of intelligent design will be a useful tool for the advancement of science in an area that has been moribund for decades.

*　　*　　*

The knowledge we now have of life at the molecular level has been stitched together from innumerable experiments in which proteins were purified, genes cloned, electron micrographs taken, cells cultured, structures determined, sequences compared, parameters varied, and controls done. Papers were published, results checked, reviews written, blind alleys searched, and new leads fleshed out.

The result of these cumulative efforts to investigate the cell—to investigate life at the molecular level—is a loud, clear, piercing cry of "*design!*" The result is so unambiguous and so significant that it must be ranked as one of the greatest achievements in the history of science. The discovery rivals those of Newton and Einstein, Lavoisier and Schrödinger, Pasteur, and Darwin. The observation of the intelligent design of life is as momentous as the observation that the earth goes around the sun or that disease is caused by bacteria or that radiation is emitted in quanta. The magnitude of the victory, gained at such great cost through sustained effort over the course of decades, would be expected to send champagne corks flying in labs around the world. This triumph of science should evoke cries of "Eureka!" from ten thousand throats, should occasion much hand-slapping and high-fiving, and perhaps even be an excuse to take a day off.

But no bottles have been uncorked, no hands slapped. Instead, a curious, embarrassed silence surrounds the stark complexity of the cell. When the subject comes up in public, feet start to shuffle, and breathing gets a bit labored. In private people are a bit more relaxed; many explicitly admit the obvious but then stare at the ground, shake their heads, and let it go at that.

Why does the scientific community not greedily embrace its startling discovery? Why is the observation of design handled with intellectual gloves? The dilemma is that while one side of the elephant is labeled intelligent design, the other side might be labeled God.

A non-scientist might ask the obvious question: so what? The idea that a being such as God exists is not unpopular—far from it. Polls show that more than 90 percent of Americans believe in God, and that about half attend religious services regularly. Politicians invoke the name of God with great regularity (more often around election time). Many football coaches pray with their teams before games, musicians compose hymns, artists paint pictures of religious events, organizations of businessmen gather for prayers. Hospitals and airports have chapels; the army and Congress employ chaplains. As a country we honor people, such as Martin Luther King, whose actions were deeply rooted in a belief in God. With all of this public affirmation, why should science find it difficult to accept a theory that supports what most people believe anyway?

* * *

Curiouser and Curiouser

The reluctance of science to embrace the conclusion of intelligent design that its long, hard labors have made manifest has no justifiable foundation. Scientific chauvinism is an understandable emotion, but it should not be allowed to affect serious intellectual issues. The history of skirmishes between religion and science is regrettable and has caused bad feelings all around. Inherited anger, however, is no basis for making scientific judgments. The philosophical argument (made by some theists) that science should avoid theories which smack of the supernatural is an artificial restriction on science. Their fear that supernatural explanations would overwhelm science is unfounded. Further, the example of the Big Bang theory shows that scientific theories with supernatural ramifications can be quite fruitful. The philosophical commitment of some people to the principle that nothing beyond nature exists should not be allowed to interfere with a theory that flows naturally from observable scientific data. The rights of those people to avoid a supernatural conclusion should be scrupulously respected, but their aversion should not be determinative.

As we reach the end of this book, we are left with no substantive defense against what feels to be a strange conclusion: that life was designed by an intelligent agent.

✻   ✻   ✻

ROBERT DORIT

Review of Behe (1997)†

"Will you honestly tell me (and I should be really much obliged) whether you believe that the shape of my nose was ordained and 'guided by an intelligent cause?' " In exasperation, but not without humor, Charles Darwin posed this question to Charles Lyell in 1860, the year Darwin dealt with the maelstrom unleashed by the publication of *The Origin of Species*. In both the popular and the scientific press, Darwin had to contend with the wrath of those for whom the notion of a living world based on accident, time and natural selection was simply too disquieting. Look around, Darwin's critics argued, and see the evidence of design. And where there is design, there must be a designer.

One hundred thirty-six years later, this argument makes a reappearance in Michael Behe's *Darwin's Black Box*. Adorned this time around with the language of molecular biology, spiced up with charges of a conspiracy of scientists, masquerading as an appeal for truth and not for theology, it is nonetheless the same old thing: There cannot be design without a designer. Although I do not doubt the sincerity of the author, nor scoff at his unease with a world apparently lacking purpose, the case for intelligent design put forth in *Darwin's Black Box* is built on some deep misunderstandings about evolution, molecular organization and, ultimately, about the nature of scientific inquiry. Because of these misperceptions, not a blow is landed on the central, radical claim of Darwinian thinking: Biological order and design emerge from the workings of the evolutionary process and not from the hand of a designer.

This book will, no doubt, find its defenders. Those who are uneasy with a materialist explanation of the living world will welcome this attack on the Darwinian worldview. But as a practicing biologist, and a card-carrying molecular evolutionist, I cannot but find the premise of this book—that molecular discoveries have plunged a wooden stake through the heart of Darwinian logic—ludicrous. This book tells me that the field of molecular evolution has "grown stale from a lack of viable solutions to dead end problems." Worse yet, it appears that the endeavor "has been moribund for decades" and that "molecular evolution is not based on scientific authority . . . the assertion of Darwinian molecular evolution is merely bluster." And all this time I have been thinking that this is probably the golden

† From *American Scientist* 85 (1997): 474–75. Reprinted with the permission of the *American Scientist*. Robert Dorit (b. 1957) is associate professor of ecology and evolutionary biology at Yale University.

age of evolutionary biology (although 1860 and the early years of the Modern Synthesis in the 1940s were probably not bad, either). For the first time we have molecular methods that allow the generation of massive amounts of detailed data relevant to a host of evolutionary questions. We have techniques that allow us to follow the control and expression of single genes in living organisms. We can now move genes from one species to another to test their function in a novel genetic context. Computational power now allows us to compare tens of thousands of DNA sequences to one another in search for conserved motifs, shared functions and common ancestry. We can carry out simulations of complex biological phenomena and find solutions to quantitative problems that seem to defy analytic solutions. Not bad at all, I thought.

What then is Behe's argument? The central point of *Darwin's Black Box* is not always easy to spot, but it appears to rely on Behe's notion of irreducible complexity. Molecular systems, defined to include both linked sets of biochemical reactions (the clotting cascade) and aspects of cellular organization (cilia and flagella), for example, are apparently "irreducibly complex": They only work when all the pieces are in place and finely tuned. Any single component, on its own, is useless. If there is a single missing piece, the whole apparatus ceases to function, like a mousetrap without a spring. Such complex mechanisms, argues Behe, could not have arisen "in a Darwinistic manner." Their complexity shows an intelligent designer at work. But this is a conclusion reached only by stacking misunderstandings of the evolutionary process upon misrepresentations of the practice of evolutionary biology. I emphasize six fallacies inherent in Behe's claim, although there are many others where these came from.

Fallacy one: There is a boundary between the molecular world and other levels of biological organization.

By the author's own admission, the Darwinian argument appears to suffice in accounting for design at visible levels of organization—bird flight or the hydrodynamic design of aquatic organisms. Only at the molecular level does the argument somehow fail. But, in fact, there is no fundamental discontinuity between the molecular and the supramolecular level in biology. The traditions, tools and approaches of the molecular biologist may differ radically from those of the functional morphologist, but the fabric of living systems is seamless. There is nothing that makes design at the molecular level any more special than design or organization at any other level in biology. If anything, molecular design may be somewhat easier to account for, because the components of molecular machines are frequently the products of identifiable genes.

Fallacy two: The current utility of a given feature (molecular or otherwise) explains "why" the feature originally evolved.

By this logic, if a particular protein is part of a complex system—say, the eye—that protein must have arisen to play a role in the incipient eye. But we know this is not the case. Many of the proteins in the eye lens, for example, begin their careers doing something completely different and unrelated to vision. Evolution is a creative scavenger, taking what is available and putting it to new use. The correct metaphor for the Darwinian process is not that of a First World engineer, but that of the Third World auto mechanic who will get your car running again, but only if parts already lying around can be used for the repair. Ironically, it is at the molecular level that this recycling of available parts is most apparent. My current favorite example (of many available) is the discovery that a gene complex originally involved in specifying the pattern of segmentation in insects has now been found to assist in the proper development of the vertebrate hindbrain (a structure that has no counterpart in segmented insects). This homeotic complex of genes is an exquisite piece of molecular machinery, precisely of the sort that the author finds so imponderable in a Darwinian world. Once the origin and the current role of the homeotic complex are disentangled, the problem vexing Behe—". . . biochemical systems cannot be built up by natural selection working on mutations: no direct gradual route exists to these irreducibly complex systems"—simply disappears. Then we can see that just as the aging home-run hitter is drafted to be the designated hitter, the homeotic complex that helps guide the development of the vertebrate hindbrain predates the vertebrates by hundreds of millions of years. The homeotic complex did not evolve to regulate hindbrain development, it was recruited. In fact, homeotic complexes have been recruited over and over again wherever delicate control of gene expression is required. Design-from-scratch and direct routes are not luxuries afforded to the evolutionary process.

Fallacy three: Unless we can identify advantages for each imaginary gradual step leading to a contemporary bit of biochemistry, we cannot invoke a Darwinian explanation.

There has always been a version of popular evolution that consists of identifying some curious feature of the living world, speculating on why that feature might be "good for the organism" and imagining how that feature may have come to pass. Any one of us can come up with multiple, plausible stories concerning the evolution of a given biological feature. But plausibility is about the weakest criterion one can apply to an evolutionary hypothesis. Evolutionary biology may finally be coming of age precisely because we are moving away from particularistic, speculative scenarios—the just-so stories. The rigorous testing of evolutionary hypotheses depends on the use of comparative data, on an understanding of mechanism and, increasingly, on the experimental manipulation of components of the system. It does not (see fallacy two) depend on inventing an "advantage" for a partially evolved flagellar motor. In a narrow sense, Behe is correct when he argues that we do not yet fully understand the evolution of the flagellar motor or of the clotting cascade. Unsolved questions, however, are the hallmark of an exciting science.

Fallacy four: Molecular evolution: "a lot of sequences, some math, and no answers."

In a peculiar quest for an article or book that "tells us how specific biochemical structures came to be," Behe has made glancing contact with the literature of my field. What he has found apparently dismays him. The basic tools of the trade—the comparative analysis of sequences and structures, the mathematical modeling of the evolutionary process and the experimental generation of biologically relevant molecules in abiotic systems—are summarily dismissed. What then is left? Would the accumulating evidence that myriad novel molecular functions for proteins and nucleic acids can be evolved (not engineered) *in vitro* count as evidence against intelligent design? How about the observation in real time of the acquisition of antibiotic resistance by bacteria? Drug resistance by viruses? Herbicide resistance by weeds? I suspect that in the end nothing would cause the author to abandon his commitment to intelligent design.

Fallacy five: There is a conspiracy of silence among scientists concerning the failure of Darwinian explanation.

Anyone who has ever attended a scientific meeting will find the notion of a conspiracy of silence—well, unlikely. The meetings I go to are usually characterized by N scientists voicing at least N+1 opinions on the topic at hand. When Behe reviews the indices of several major biochemistry textbooks and finds that fewer than one percent of the entries deal with evolution, I fear he may be onto something: Molecular biologists and biochemists often have no training in evolution. Given my conference experience, however, that does not always stop them from voicing a personal opinion about the evolutionary process. But like my personal opinions about the analysis of detailed crystallographic data, such opinions should not be mistaken for expertise.

Fallacy six: The evolution of complexity is unaddressed and unexplained.

The very definition of complexity, and the rules that govern its emergence, are indeed critical issues in evolutionary biology. But the problem becomes deeply uninteresting if the only legitimate approach to solving it is the demonstration of "a direct, gradual route [leading to] irreducibly complex systems." We are still deciding how to measure complexity, debating whether the history of life shows a tendency toward increased complexity, and arguing about whether biological organization is but a subset of the larger problem of order and complexity. We do not as yet know what form the answers will take, but mathematical models, computational simulations and, increasingly, experimental results suggest that complexity and organization may be inexorable outcomes in multicomponent systems. If our hypotheses about complexity are to be of any use, however, they will have to be materialist explanations grounded in material cause.

I've often wondered why the argument from design so appeals to engineers and chemists. I suspect that the problem derives from the day-to-day experience of these professions. Engineers and chemists know that they do not get a desired outcome—stable bridge or purified compound—from random inputs, time and a statistical principle for differential representation. In these professions, there is no design without a designer, no desired outcome without careful and intelligent planning. But personal experience is not always the best guide.

Behe's argument for intelligent design ultimately fails because it is a belief and not a potential explanation. The hand of God may well be all around us, but it is not, nor can it be, the task of science to dust for fingerprints.

MICHAEL RUSE

Darwin's New Critics on Trial (1998)†

* * *

Creationism, the belief that the Bible is literally true and that one must conclude that the earth and its denizens were created miraculously some six thousand years ago, in six days of twenty-four-hour duration, that humans appeared last, and that at some later point the earth was totally submerged by water, is an American invention of the past century. Scorned by members of mainline churches as well as by scientists, it has nevertheless shown considerable staying power. In the 1960s, thanks to the efforts of a Bible scholar John C. Whitcomb and a hydraulic engineer Henry M. Morris, authors of *Genesis Flood* (1961), Creationism took on a whole new life, leading eventually to court trials as certain states of the American South tried to insist that the children in their public schools be taught Creationism as a viable alternative alongside evolution. Beaten back in this attempt, it seemed that perhaps Creationism was at last defeated, but, phoenix-like, it has arisen again, and as the century comes to an end is perhaps showing more life—certainly more respectability—than at any time previously.

The new Creationists are wary of indiscriminate labelling. Most of them do admit to religious beliefs, but they are much aware of the ridicule that has been heaped on those who deny physics to the extent of claiming the falsity of an earth of more than a few thousand years of age. I suspect that most of these people are not in fact 'young earthers'; but whatever the minutiae of their beliefs, one finds that inasmuch as these new arrivals accept the name of 'Creationist', it is usually defined in such a broad way as to be compatible with a great deal of science, even a little bit of evolution, if one is so inclined. In fact, one particularly significant point is that these new arrivals, whether from conviction or expediency, have tended—at least, until recently—to stay very carefully away from explications of their own positions. The effort expended has been very much in the direction of the sins of Darwinism rather than in the direction of the virtues of any alternative.

It is with this critique that I am concerned in this section, and since it is he who has led the way and shown the path to others, my main concern is with the case made by Berkeley professor of law Phillip Johnson, author of *Darwin on Trial* (1991). * * *

I begin with the most striking thing about Johnson's work and the others following in its footsteps: given the intention to trash one of the most prominent branches of science, the attack is curiously one-sided. Perhaps a horizontal metaphor is better than a vertical one: the attack is curiously shallow. * * * One searches in vain in the writings of Johnson and his

† From *Taking Darwin Seriously: A Naturalistic Approach to Philosophy* (Amherst, N.Y.: Prometheus Books, 1998). Copyright 1998. Reprinted by permission of the publisher. Michael Ruse (b. 1940) is professor of philosophy and zoology at the University of Guelph.

fellow new Creationists for any of the exciting discoveries and theories of today that make evolution such a vibrant area of research: the findings of molecular evolutionists thanks to brilliant work by Richard Lewontin in discerning variations in proteins, for instance, or the work of the socio-biologists following up the ideas of William Hamilton on kin selection as applied to the *Hymenoptera* (ants, bees, and wasps), or John Maynard Smith using models drawn from game theory. There is nothing on the ways in which, using modern thinking about natural selection, students of the social insects have been able to tease apart the relationships among workers, queens, and drones. This is a sin of omission rather than com-mission, but it is glaring and heinous for all that. As Thomas Kuhn and other students of the theory of science have rightly stressed repeatedly, in judging a theory or paradigm or new area of science, one must ask as much about the new directions it uncovers as about problems one might have with foundations. Great achievements look forwards as much as backwards.

What of the science that is actually discussed? Again, there is a reluc-tance to engage evolutionary ideas on level terms—at least, there is no interest in taking seriously (acknowledging even) the kinds of simple points which I (following professional evolutionists) make at the beginning of [this book]. Most particularly, there is a constant confusing of the *fact* of evolution with the *path* or paths of evolution, and then with the *cause* or mechanisms of evolution. A point is made about one of these items and then suddenly one finds oneself drawing a conclusion about another of the items. * * *

We must not be bullied by the Creationists' strategy. They may ignore it but let us continue to be guided by the three-fold division of fact, path, and cause. What has Johnson (and his fellows) to say about the fact of evolution? I showed at the beginning of [this book] that the key to under-standing the evolutionist's conviction of the fact of evolution lies in the total-evidence-appealing consilience at its heart—the very same kind of consilience which is at the heart of legal practice, as prosecutors try to pin guilt on defendants through circumstantial evidence. There is nothing on this method of argumentation: a curious omission, especially given that Johnson is an academic lawyer specializing in criminal law. One conse-quence of this omission is that Johnson and others can avoid talking about all of the evidence, quite ignoring such crucial planks in the evolutionist's case as biogeography: again, a great help in the negative case.

* * *

How does Johnson treat the other branches of the evolutionary family? Instinct is conspicuous by its absence, as is systematics. Embryology does get discussed, although the main focus seems to be on nineteenth-century thinkers rather than workers today: a bit like judging the big bang theory by reference to Copernicus and Galileo. What of the really important matter of comparative anatomy? What of homology—the similarities that occur among disparate species and are attributed to common ancestors?

* * *

Most remarkable of all is Johnson's treatment of that old chestnut, the gaps in the record. Expectedly, *Archaeopteryx*—the reptile-bird—gets short shrift. None of the intermediate features gets an airing. At best, it shows the inadequacy of the rest of the record: 'Persons who come to the fossil evidence as convinced Darwinists will see a stunning confirmation, but sceptics will see only a lonely exception to a consistent pattern of fossil disconfirmation. If we are testing Darwinism rather than simply looking for a confirming example or two, then a single good candidate for ancestor status is not enough to save a theory which posits a worldwide history of evolutionary transformation'. Heads, I win. Tails, you lose.

It is, of course, just not true that *Archaeopteryx* is the only bridging fossil known to evolutionists. Take a favourite argument of the Creationists: the lack of transitional fossils between the land animals and the marine animals, like whales. Now these gaps are being filled. Proto-whales have been discovered. We really do have fossil marine mammals with rudimentary limbs, on the way to the organisms of today but not yet there. Do not, however, expect an apology and a retraction. 'Even the vestigial limbs [of supposed whale ancestors] present problems. By what Darwinian process did useful hind limbs wither away to vestigial proportions, and at what stage in the transformation from rodent to sea monster did this occur? Did rodent forelimbs transform themselves by gradual adaptive stages into whale flippers? We hear nothing of the difficulties because to Darwinists unsolvable problems are not important'. In any case, can we be sure that these supposed limbs really were connected with the proto-whales? Perhaps they were just lying nearby.

I will treat this kind of argumentation with the silent contempt that it merits—although I would love to know where Johnson got the idea that whales are descended from rodents.

* * *

Irreducible Complexity

* * * Perhaps encouraged by their self-awarded success, the new Creationists have recently started to break from their strategy of unrelenting attack. Thanks to biochemist Michael J. Behe, author of *Darwin's Black Box: The Biochemical Challenge to Evolution* (1996), they have started to lift the veil from their own beliefs about origins *qua* science. * * *

It is Behe's claim that there are facts of organic nature whose origin cannot be evolutionary. In fact, they cannot be natural at all, meaning the consequence of regular unguided law. These facts, marked by irreducible complexity, have to be the product of a designer, however construed.

* * *

Behe's case for the impossibility of a small-step natural origin of biological complexity has been trampled upon contemptuously by the scientists working in the field. It is not just that they disagree, but that they think his grasp of the pertinent science is weak and his knowledge of the literature curiously (although conveniently) outdated. Particularly censorious are those scientists whose work has been used by Behe, against them, to support his position. Russell Doolittle, the world's expert on the evolution of blood clotting, is a case in point. In a 1997 lecture discussing the phenomenon of blood clotting, which involves a kind of 'cascade' as first one biochemical reaction occurs and then this triggers another and so forth, he uses the notions (drawn from ancient Chinese science) of yin and yang. First one thing (yin) happens, and then another (yang) in reaction, and so on down the line.

About this Behe writes:

> Doolittle's scenario implicitly acknowledges that the clotting cascade is irreducibly complex, but it tries to paper over the dilemma with a hail of metaphorical references to yin and yang. The bottom line is that clusters of proteins have to be inserted *all at once* into the cascade. This can be done only by postulating a 'hopeful monster' who luckily gets all of the proteins at once, or by the guidance of an intelligent agent.

Doolittle's response is that Behe's science is simply out of date. Far from the evolution of clotting being a mystery, the past three decades of work by Doolittle himself and others have thrown significant light on the ways in which clotting came into being. More than this, it can be shown that the clotting mechanism does not have to be a one-step phenomenon with everything already in place and functioning. One step in the cascade involves fibrinogen, required for clotting, and another, plaminogen, required for clearing clots away. Doolittle writes:

> It has become possible during the last decade to 'knock out' genes in experimental organisms. 'Knock out mice' are now a common (but expensive) tool in the armamentarium of those scientists anxious to cure the world's ills. Recently the gene for plaminogen was knocked out of mice and, predictably, those mice had thrombotic complications because fibrin clots could not be cleared away. Not long after that, the same workers knocked out the gene for fibrinogen in another line of mice. Again, predictably, those mice were ailing, although in this case hemorrhage was the problem. And what do you think happened when these two lines of mice were crossed? For all practical purposes the mice lacking both genes were normal. Contrary to claims about irreducible complexity, the entire ensemble of proteins is *not* needed. Music and harmony can arise from a smaller orchestra.

Behe's knowledge of evolution is suspect. His knowledge of his own area of science is suspect. And the same is true when he moves into philosophy and theology. The common complaint about evolutionary theory is that it cannot be properly checked. The critics claim that it is too flabby to yield testable predictions: it is in some sense unfalsifiable. But whether or not this is true (I do not happen to think it is), such a complaint must certainly be made of Behe's theory. How can you tell when irreducible complexity can be explained by evolution and when it must be explained by something else (or Something Else)? Behe himself admits there is no sharp line and he gives no real answers to this problem. Newton and Einstein and those other great scientists to whom he likens himself produced work that did lead to quantification and to measurement and prediction. As it stands, Behe's ideas can simply be protected against any counter-evidence. You can explain some phenomenon through evolution? Then, either the phenomenon was not irreducibly complex or it was not complex enough. You cannot explain some phenomenon through evolution? Then either the phenomenon is too complex for an evolutionary explanation or you will later find such an explanation. Once again, heads, I win; tails, you lose.

And in any case—and here I will bring to an end my discussion of Behe—suppose you accept his conclusion about the existence of a Designer. What precisely is the role of this Designer? *Qua* scientist, Behe is careful not to identify it with the Christian God. But let us suppose such a Designer does exist and is at work producing irreducibly complex organisms. Who then is responsible when things go wrong? What about mal-mutations causing such awful things as Tay-Sachs disease and sickle-cell anemia? Is this just the fault of no one, or do we blame evolution? Why does the Designer not step in here? It (let us not pre-judge its sex) is pretty clever and could surely fix just one bad move—the whole point is that It can produce the irreducibly complex. So why not the not-very-complex-but-absolutely-dreadful? Behe says that raising this problem is raising the problem of evil—How can an all-powerful, all-good God allow pain?—which is so. But labelling the problem does not make it go away.

There are some standard arguments against the problem of evil—that it is a function of human free will, for instance—which may or may not work. My point now is simply that Behe himself gives no reason to think that the problem can be solved or will vanish. He is in as much trouble in the realm of philosophical theology as he was in the realm of biological science. He has offered us a freshened-up version of the old 'God of the gaps' argument for the deity's existence: a Supreme Being must be invoked to explain those phenomena for which I cannot offer a natural explanation. But such an argument proves only one's own ignorance and inadequacy. It tells us nothing of beings beyond science. In the words of the Christian theologian and martyr Dietrich Bonhoeffer, 'We are to find God in what we know, not in what we don't know'.

* * *

The real problem with Darwinism for the new Creationists lies not in its status as science. I doubt these critics would ever be truly happy with Darwinism as science, but that would not drive them to write books and articles attacking it in every possible way. The real objection is to Darwinism as religion. To the new Creationists, Darwinism is a wolf in sheep's clothing—secular religion in the clothing of empirical science. It is truly a religion of modernism: a system with all of the lax moral attitudes and beliefs that plague our society today. Darwinism is based on a philosophy—the philosophy of 'naturalism'—and not only does this make something like homology self-confirming of the position, but we are now on the straight road leading to the claims and belief systems that we properly call 'religious'. 'Darwinist evolution is an imaginative story about who we are and where we came from, which is to say a creation myth. As such it is an obvious starting point for speculation about how we ought to live and what we ought to value'. From here it is but a short step to sex, drugs, and contempt for capitalism.

> If God is merely a projection of human desires—or worse, a concept invented by patriarchal authorities to rationalize their oppressive rule—then the death of God is like being released from a prison. All the rules promulgated in the name of the illusion that deprived us of our freedom lose their authority when the illusion is exposed. Some elements of the prison moral code might be retained in the new situation: a ban on polygamy, for example, might be kept as a protection for gender equality. But the outlook on family morality as a whole rightly becomes entirely different once the death of God becomes fully assimilated as knowledge.[1]

At one level, we evolutionists can answer this objection rapidly and decisively. First one draws a distinction between fact and value. Facts are statements about the way things are: they are objective, independent of human experience. Science aims to be about facts: descriptions and understandings. This applies to Darwinian evolutionary theory. Values are about the way things ought to be: they are more subjective, they refer to human feelings and senses of obligation or judgement. Science is free of values, for these belong more in the realms of philosophy and religion and politics and the like. Johnson therefore has to be wrong—in principle—when he complains that Darwinism promotes promiscuity and much more of that ilk. This is simply an impossibility, for Darwinism promotes nothing. You cannot get blood from a stone or values from facts.

Moreover, one can point out that even if it were true that there is a connection between fact and value, between Darwinism and people's systems of value, it is far from obvious that this has to be one of freedom and permissiveness, of sexual laxity and of personal autonomy. There have been Darwinians of the political and moral and religious right of a kind to make Johnson and his fellows look like escapees from the 1960s. Sir Ronald Fisher, for example, is certainly the most distinguished theoretical biologist in the history of evolutionary thought. A fanatical Darwinian, his *Genetical Theory of Natural Selection* (1930) is a formidable demonstration of mathematical technique and a work which quite transformed our understanding of the evolutionary process. He was also a Christian, a member of the Church of England, a conservative, a member of the British Establishment, and one whose social views were somewhere to the right of Louis XIV. There simply must be something wrong with the claim that Darwinism leads straight to the *Playboy* philosophy.

It is not difficult to see precisely what has gone wrong. Look beyond *Darwin on Trial*, towards the follow-up book Johnson wrote on the implications of Darwinism, *Reason in the Balance: The Case against Naturalism in Science, Law and Education* (1995). Johnson draws a distinction between 'methodological naturalism', the attitude of the scientist that one

1. Phillip E. Johnson, *Reason in the Balance* (1995): 31–32.

should explain as far as is possible in terms of natural unbroken laws, and 'metaphysical naturalism', the belief that unbroken-law-governed material is all there is to existence. Unfortunately, argues Johnson, the scientist starts off down the path of methodological naturalism and ends up with metaphysical naturalism. And this spells atheism, which in turn leads to complete moral license.

Fleshing out this argument—and now he is out of the realm of science, far more willing to speak of his own beliefs—Johnson describes himself as a 'theistic realist'. This is someone who accepts God as creator and who thinks that God's existence makes a difference to the way that the world is and functions: 'many important questions, including the origin of genetic information and human consciousness—may not be explicable in terms of unintelligent causes, just as a computer or a book cannot be explained that way'. In Johnson's opinion, when methodological naturalism meets theistic realism, the former always hardens into metaphysical naturalism and conflict arises: 'experience leads me to predict that any compromise position will turn out to be M[ethodological] N[aturalism] when the chips are down'.

So much for Johnson's argument. Against it, let me say that what he claims is simply not so and even if it were, the moral consequences drawn by Johnson do not obtain. The fact is that there are people who are fully committed to methodological naturalism, believing that evolution is true, and who yet are theists in as meaningful a sense as one could ever wish. The present pope—a man, incidentally, who is notoriously tough on such things as sexuality—is precisely such a person. Recently, the pope has come out four-square in favor of evolution and yet he reserves to God His traditional full power of action. How can this be? Two moves are made. On the one hand, a theist like John Paul II does not take all manifestations of God's miraculous powers to be in conflict with science working according to law. Transubstantiation, the miraculous turning of the bread and wine into the body and blood of Christ, is a case in point. You will not see something physical happening to the bread and wine, however hard you may look. Likewise the act through which God gave humans immortal souls. On the other hand, the theist argues (or feels free to argue) that at some points God simply overrides laws. The resurrection of Christ is surely such an event. And far from this being an impossibility or betrayal of earlier commitments, it is the position of many theists that it is precisely the working of law which makes the miraculous miraculous!

> Science had pushed the deist's God farther and farther away, and at the moment when it seemed as if He would be thrust out altogether, Darwinism appeared, and, under the guise of a foe, did the work of a friend. It has conferred upon philosophy and religion an inestimable benefit, by showing us that we must choose between two alternatives. Either God is everywhere present in nature, or He is nowhere. He cannot be here, and not there. He cannot delegate his power to demigods called 'second causes'. In nature everything must be His work or nothing. We must frankly return to the Christian view of direct Divine agency, the immanence of Divine power from end to end,

the belief in a God in Whom not only we, but all things have their being, or we must banish him altogether.[2]

Finishing the argument against Johnson, the evolutionist notes that his moral worries are no more well taken than his fears for theism. Even if Darwinism were to imply atheism, there is no logical reason to think that such a person would thereby be committed to moral nihilism. In the last century, although people like Thomas Henry Huxley described themselves as agnostics, they were certainly atheistic with respect to Johnson's kind of God. Yet they were moral—boringly and obsessively moral—in a very conventional manner. Huxley met and admired George Eliot, but, given that she lived openly with a man to whom she was not married, he would not invite her to his own house to meet his wife and children.

❊ ❊ ❊

2. A. Moore, *The Christian Doctrine of a God* (1890): 99–100.

Scientists' Opposition to Creationism

AMERICAN ASSOCIATION FOR THE ADVANCEMENT OF SCIENCE

Forced Teaching of Creationist Beliefs in Public School Science Education (1982)†

Whereas it is the responsibility of the American Association for the Advancement of Science to preserve the integrity of science, and

Whereas science is a systematic method of investigation based on continuous experimentation, observation, and measurement leading to evolving explanations of natural phenomena, explanations which are continuously open to further testing, and

Whereas evolution fully satisfies these criteria, irrespective of remaining debates concerning its detailed mechanisms, and

Whereas the Association respects the right of people to hold diverse beliefs about creation that do not come within the definitions of science, and

Whereas Creationist groups are imposing beliefs disguised as science upon teachers and students to the detriment and distortion of public education in the United States

Therefore be it resolved that because "Creationist Science" has no scientific validity it should not be taught as science, and further, that the AAAS views legislation requiring "Creationist Science" to be taught in public schools as a real and present threat to the integrity of education and the teaching of science, and

Be it further resolved that the AAAS urges citizens, educational authorities, and legislators to oppose the compulsory inclusion in science education curricula of beliefs that are not amenable to the process of scrutiny, testing, and revision that is indispensable to science.

---

† From *Science* 215 (1982): 1072. Resolution passed by the AAAS Board of Directors on January 4, 1982; passed by the AAAS Council as a joint resolution on January 7, 1982. Reprinted by permission from *Voices for Evolution* (Berkeley, Calif., 1995): 25.

AMERICAN INSTITUTE OF BIOLOGICAL SCIENCES

Resolution Opposing Creationism in Science Courses (1999)†

The AIBS Executive Committee passed a resolution in 1972 deploring efforts by Biblical literalists to interject creationism and religion into science courses. It is very troubling that more than 20 years later, there is an urgent need to reaffirm AIBS's earlier position. Despite rulings by the Supreme Court declaring it unconstitutional to promote a religious perspective in public school education, such attempts by creationists continue in a variety of guises.

The theory of evolution is the only scientifically defensible explanation for the origin of life and development of species. A theory in science, such as the atomic theory in chemistry and the Newtonian and relativity theories in physics, is not a speculative hypothesis, but a coherent body of explanatory statements supported by evidence. The theory of evolution has this status. The body of knowledge that supports the theory of evolution is ever growing: fossils continue to be discovered that fill gaps in the evolutionary tree and recent DNA sequence data provide evidence that all living organisms are related to each other and to extinct species. These data, consistent with evolution, imply a common chemical and biological heritage for all living organisms and allow scientists to map branch points in the evolutionary tree.

Biologists may disagree about the details of the history and mechanisms of evolution. Such debate is a normal, healthy, and necessary part of scientific discourse and in no way negates the theory of evolution. As a community, biologists agree that evolution occurred and that the forces driving the evolutionary process are still active today. This consensus is based on more than a century of scientific data gathering and analysis.

Because creationism is based * * * on religious dogma stemming from faith rather than demonstrable facts, it does not lend itself to the scientific process. As a result, creationism should not be taught in any science classroom.

Therefore, AIBS reaffirms its 1972 resolution that explanations for the origin of life and the development of species that are not supportable on scientific grounds should not be taught as science.

† AIBS Board Resolution, 1994, as amended and reconfirmed by the Executive Committee of the AIBS in 1999. From *Voices for Evolution* (Berkeley, Calif., 1995): 33. Reprinted with permission of the American Institute of Biological Sciences.

NATIONAL ASSOCIATION OF BIOLOGY TEACHERS

Statement on Teaching Evolution (1998)†

As stated in *The American Biology Teacher* by the eminent scientist Theodosius Dobzhansky (1973), "Nothing in biology makes sense except in the light of evolution." This often-quoted assertion accurately illuminates the central, unifying role of evolution in nature, and therefore in biology. Teaching biology in an effective and scientifically honest manner requires classroom discussions and laboratory experiences on evolution.

Modern biologists constantly study, ponder and deliberate the patterns, mechanisms and pace of evolution, but they do not debate evolution's occurrence. The fossil record and the diversity of extant organisms, combined with modern techniques of molecular biology, taxonomy and geology, provide exhaustive examples and powerful evidence for genetic variation, natural selection, speciation, extinction and other well-established components of current evolutionary theory. Scientific deliberations and modifications of these components clearly demonstrate the vitality and scientific integrity of evolution and the theory that explains it.

This same examination, pondering and possible revision have firmly established evolution as an important natural process explained by valid scientific principles, and clearly differentiate and separate science from various kinds of nonscientific ways of knowing, including those with a supernatural basis such as creationism. Whether called "creation science," "scientific creationism," "intelligent-design theory," "young-earth theory" or some other synonym, creation beliefs have no place in the science classroom. Explanations employing nonnaturalistic or supernatural events, whether or not explicit reference is made to a supernatural being, are outside the realm of science and not part of a valid science curriculum. Evolutionary theory, indeed all of science, is necessarily silent on religion and neither refutes nor supports the existence of a deity or deities.

Accordingly, the National Association of Biology Teachers, an organization of science teachers, endorses the following tenets of science, evolution and biology education:

- The diversity of life on earth is the outcome of evolution: an unpredictable and natural process of temporal descent with genetic modification that is affected by natural selection, chance, historical contingencies and changing environments.
- Evolutionary theory is significant in biology, among other reasons, for its unifying properties and predictive features, the clear empirical testability of its integral models and the richness of new scientific research it fosters.

† Statement adopted by the board of the NABT, March 15, 1995 (amended May 4, 1998). From *Voices for Evolution* (Berkeley, Calif., 1995): 140–44, with later amendments incorporated. Reprinted with permission of the National Association of Biology Teachers.

- The fossil record, which includes abundant transitional forms in diverse taxonomic groups, establishes extensive and comprehensive evidence for organic evolution.
- Natural selection, the primary mechanism for evolutionary changes, can be demonstrated with numerous, convincing examples, both extant and extinct.
- Natural selection—a differential, greater survival and reproduction of some genetic variants within a population under an existing environmental state—has no specific direction or goal, including survival of a species.
- Adaptations do not always provide an obvious selective advantage. Furthermore, there is no indication that adaptations—molecular to organismal—must be perfect: adaptations providing a selective advantage must simply be good enough for survival and increased reproductive fitness.
- The model of punctuated equilibrium provides another account of the tempo of speciation in the fossil record of many lineages: it does not refute or overturn evolutionary theory, but instead adds to its scientific richness.
- Evolution does not violate the second law of thermodynamics: producing order from disorder is possible with the addition of energy, such as from the sun.
- Although comprehending deep time is difficult, the earth is about 4.5 billion years old. *Homo sapiens* has occupied only a minuscule moment of that immense duration of time.
- When compared with earlier periods, the Cambrian explosion evident in the fossil record reflects at least three phenomena: the evolution of animals with readily-fossilized hard body parts; Cambrian environment (sedimentary rock) more conducive to preserving fossils; and the evolution from pre-Cambrian forms of an increased diversity of body patterns in animals.
- Radiometric and other dating techniques, when used properly, are highly accurate means of establishing dates in the history of the planet and in the history of life.
- In science, a theory is not a guess or an approximation but an extensive explanation developed from well-documented, reproducible sets of experimentally-derived data from repeated observations of natural processes.
- The models and the subsequent outcomes of a scientific theory are not decided in advance, but can be, and often are, modified and improved as new empirical evidence is uncovered. Thus, science is a constantly self-correcting endeavor to understand nature and natural phenomena.
- Science is not teleological: the accepted processes do not start with a conclusion, then refuse to change it, or acknowledge as valid only those data that support an unyielding conclusion. Science does not base theories on an untestable collection of dogmatic proposals. Instead, the processes of science are characterized by asking questions, proposing hypotheses, and designing empirical models and conceptual frameworks for research about natural events.
- Providing a rational, coherent and scientific account of the taxo-

nomic history and diversity of organisms requires inclusion of the mechanisms and principles of evolution.

- Similarly, effective teaching of cellular and molecular biology requires inclusion of evolution.
- Specific textbook chapters on evolution should be included in biology curricula, and evolution should be a recurrent theme throughout biology textbooks and courses.
- Students can maintain their religious beliefs and learn the scientific foundations of evolution.
- Teachers should respect diverse beliefs, but contrasting science with religion, such as belief in creationism, is not a role of science. Science teachers can, and often do, hold devout religious beliefs, accept evolution as a valid scientific theory, and teach the theory's mechanisms and principles.
- Science and religion differ in significant ways that make it inappropriate to teach any of the different religious beliefs in the science classroom. * * *

NATIONAL ACADEMY OF SCIENCES

Frequently Asked Questions about Evolution and the Nature of Science (1998)†

Definitions

WHAT IS EVOLUTION?

Evolution in the broadest sense explains that what we see today is different from what existed in the past. Galaxies, stars, the solar system, and earth have changed through time, and so has life on earth.

Biological evolution concerns changes in living things during the history of life on earth. It explains that living things share common ancestors. Over time, evolutionary change gives rise to new species. Darwin called this process "descent with modification," and it remains a good definition of biological evolution today.

WHAT IS "CREATION SCIENCE"?

The ideas of "creation science" derive from the conviction that God created the universe—including humans and other living things—all at once in the relatively recent past. However, scientists from many fields have examined these ideas and have found them to be scientifically insupportable. For example, evidence for a very young earth is incompatible with many different methods of establishing the age of rocks. Furthermore, because the basic proposals of creation science are not subject to test and

---

† From *Teaching about Evolution and the Nature of Science* (Washington, D.C., 1998). Copyright © 1998 by the National Academy of Sciences. Courtesy of the National Academy Press, Washington, D.C.

verification, these ideas do not meet the criteria for science. Indeed, U.S. courts have ruled that ideas of creation science are religious views and cannot be taught when evolution is taught.

The Supporting Evidence

HOW CAN EVOLUTION BE SCIENTIFIC WHEN NO ONE WAS THERE TO SEE IT HAPPEN?

This question reflects a narrow view of how science works. Things in science can be studied even if they cannot be directly observed or experimented on. Archaeologists study past cultures by examining the artifacts those cultures left behind. Geologists can describe past changes in sea level by studying the marks ocean waves left on rocks. Paleontologists study the fossilized remains of organisms that lived long ago.

Something that happened in the past is thus not "off limits" for scientific study. Hypotheses can be made about such phenomena, and these hypotheses can be tested and can lead to solid conclusions. Furthermore, many key aspects of evolution occur in relatively short periods that can be observed directly—such as the evolution in bacteria of resistance to antibiotics.

ISN'T EVOLUTION JUST AN INFERENCE?

No one saw the evolution of one-toed horses from three-toed horses, but that does not mean that we cannot be confident that horses evolved. Science is practiced in many ways besides direct observation and experimentation. Much scientific discovery is done through indirect experimentation and observation in which inferences are made, and hypotheses generated from those inferences are tested.

For instance, particle physicists cannot directly observe subatomic particles because the particles are too small. They must make inferences about the weight, speed, and other properties of the particles based on other observations. A logical hypothesis might be something like this: If the weight of this particle is Y, when I bombard it, X will happen. If X does not happen, then the hypothesis is disproved. Thus, we can learn about the natural world even if we cannot directly observe a phenomenon—and that is true about the past, too.

In historical sciences like astronomy, geology, evolutionary biology, and archaeology, logical inferences are made and then tested against data. Sometimes the test cannot be made until new data are available, but a great deal has been done to help us understand the past. For example, scorpionflies (*Mecoptera*) and true flies (*Diptera*) have enough similarities that entomologists consider them to be closely related. Scorpionflies have four wings of about the same size, and true flies have a large front pair of wings but the back pair is replaced by small club-shaped structures. If *Diptera* evolved from *Mecoptera*, as comparative anatomy suggests, scientists predicted that a fossil fly with four wings might be found—and in 1976 this is exactly what was discovered. Furthermore, geneticists have found that the number of wings in flies can be changed through mutations in a single gene.

Evolution is a well-supported theory drawn from a variety of sources of data, including observations about the fossil record, genetic information, the distribution of plants and animals, and the similarities across species of anatomy and development. Scientists have inferred that descent with modification offers the best scientific explanation for these observations.

IS EVOLUTION A FACT OR A THEORY?

The theory of evolution explains how life on earth has changed. In scientific terms, "theory" does not mean "guess" or "hunch" as it does in everyday usage. Scientific theories are explanations of natural phenomena built up logically from testable observations and hypotheses. Biological evolution is the best scientific explanation we have for the enormous range of observations about the living world.

Scientists most often use the word "fact" to describe an observation. But scientists can also use fact to mean something that has been tested or observed so many times that there is no longer a compelling reason to keep testing or looking for examples. The occurrence of evolution in this sense is a fact. Scientists no longer question whether descent with modification occurred because the evidence supporting the idea is so strong.

WHY ISN'T EVOLUTION CALLED A LAW?

Laws are generalizations that *describe* phenomena, whereas theories *explain* phenomena. For example, the laws of thermodynamics describe what will happen under certain circumstances; thermodynamics theories explain why these events occur.

Laws, like facts and theories, can change with better data. But theories do not develop into laws with the accumulation of evidence. Rather, theories are the goal of science.

DON'T MANY FAMOUS SCIENTISTS REJECT EVOLUTION?

No. The scientific consensus around evolution is overwhelming. Those opposed to the teaching of evolution sometimes use quotations from prominent scientists out of context to claim that scientists do not support evolution. However, examination of the quotations reveals that the scientists are actually disputing some aspect of *how* evolution occurs, not *whether* evolution occurred. For example, the biologist Stephen Jay Gould once wrote that "the extreme rarity of transitional forms in the fossil record persists as the trade secret of paleontology." But Gould, an accomplished paleontologist and eloquent educator about evolution, was arguing about *how* evolution takes place. He was discussing whether the rate of change of species is constant and gradual or whether it takes place in bursts after long periods when little change occurs—an idea known as punctuated equilibrium. As Gould writes in response, "This quotation, although accurate as a partial citation, is dishonest in leaving out the following explanatory material showing my true purpose—to discuss rates of evolutionary change, not to deny the fact of evolution itself."

Gould defines punctuated equilibrium as follows:

> Punctuated equilibrium is neither a creationist idea nor even a non-Darwinian evolutionary theory about sudden change that produces a new species all at once in a single generation. Punctuated equilibrium accepts the conventional idea that new species form over hundreds or thousands of generations and through an extensive series of intermediate stages. But geological time is so long that even a few thousand years may appear as a mere "moment" relative to the several million years of existence for most species. Thus, rates of evolution vary enormously and new species may appear to arise "suddenly" in geological time, even though the time involved would seem long, and the change very slow, when compared to a human lifetime.

ISN'T THE FOSSIL RECORD FULL OF GAPS?

Though significant gaps existed in the fossil record in the 19th century, many have been filled in. In addition, the consistent pattern of ancient to modern species found in the fossil record is strong evidence for evolution. The plants and animals living today are not like the plants and animals of the remote past. For example, dinosaurs were extinct long before humans walked the earth. We know this because no human remains have ever been found in rocks dated to the dinosaur era.

Some changes in populations might occur too rapidly to leave many transitional fossils. Also, many organisms were very unlikely to leave fossils, either because of their habitats or because they had no body parts that could easily be fossilized. However, in many cases, such as between primitive fish and amphibians, amphibians and reptiles, reptiles and mammals, and reptiles and birds, there are excellent transitional fossils.

CAN EVOLUTION ACCOUNT FOR NEW SPECIES?

One argument sometimes made by supporters of "creation science" is that natural selection can produce minor changes within species, such as changes in color or beak size, but cannot generate new species from pre-existing species. However, evolutionary biologists have documented many cases in which new species have appeared in recent years. Among most plants and animals, speciation is an extended process, and a single human observer can witness only a part of this process. Yet these observations of evolution at work provide powerful confirmation that evolution forms new species.

IF HUMANS EVOLVED FROM APES, WHY ARE THERE STILL APES?

Humans did not evolve from modern apes, but humans and modern apes shared a common ancestor, a species that no longer exists. Because we shared a recent common ancestor with chimpanzees and gorillas, we have many anatomical, genetic, biochemical, and even behavioral similarities with the African great apes. We are less similar to the Asian apes —orangutans and gibbons—and even less similar to monkeys, because we shared common ancestors with these groups in the more distant past.

Evolution is a branching or splitting process in which populations split off from one another and gradually become different. As the two groups become isolated from each other, they stop sharing genes, and eventually genetic differences increase until members of the groups can no longer interbreed. At this point, they have become separate species. Through time, these two species might give rise to new species, and so on through millennia.

DOESN'T THE SUDDEN APPEARANCE OF ALL THE "MODERN GROUPS" OF ANIMALS DURING THE CAMBRIAN EXPLOSION PROVE CREATIONISM?

During the Cambrian explosion, primitive representatives of the major phyla of invertebrate animals appeared—hard-shelled organisms like mollusks and arthropods. More modern representatives of these invertebrates appeared gradually through the Cambrian and the Ordovician periods. "Modern groups" like terrestrial vertebrates and flowering plants were not present. It is not true that "all the modern groups of animals" appeared during this period.

Also, Cambrian fossils did not appear spontaneously. They had ancestors in the Precambrian period, but because these Precambrian forms were soft-bodied, they left fewer fossils. A characteristic of the Cambrian fossils is the evolution of hard body parts, which greatly improved the chance of fossilization. And even without fossils, we can infer relationships among organisms from biochemical information.

Religious Issues

CAN A PERSON BELIEVE IN GOD AND STILL ACCEPT EVOLUTION?

Many do. Most religions of the world do not have any direct conflict with the idea of evolution. Within the Judeo-Christian religions, many people believe that God works through the process of evolution. That is, God has created both a world that is ever-changing and a mechanism through which creatures can adapt to environmental change over time.

At the root of the apparent conflict between some religions and evolution is a misunderstanding of the critical difference between religious and scientific ways of knowing. Religions and science answer different questions about the world. Whether there is a purpose to the universe or a purpose for human existence are not questions for science. Religious and scientific ways of knowing have played, and will continue to play, significant roles in human history.

No one way of knowing can provide all of the answers to the questions that humans ask. Consequently, many people, including many scientists, hold strong religious beliefs and simultaneously accept the occurrence of evolution.

AREN'T SCIENTIFIC BELIEFS BASED ON FAITH AS WELL?

Usually "faith" refers to beliefs that are accepted without empirical evidence. Most religions have tenets of faith. Science differs from religion because it is the nature of science to test and retest explanations against the natural world. Thus, scientific explanations are likely to be built on and modified with new information and new ways of looking at old information. This is quite different from most religious beliefs.

Therefore, "belief" is not really an appropriate term to use in science, because testing is such an important part of this way of knowing. If there is a component of faith to science, it is the assumption that the universe operates according to regularities—for example, that the speed of light will not change tomorrow. Even the assumption of that regularity is often tested—and thus far has held up well. This "faith" is very different from religious faith.

Science is a way of knowing about the natural world. It is limited to explaining the natural world through natural causes. Science can say nothing about the supernatural. Whether God exists or not is a question about which science is neutral.

Legal Issues

WHY CAN'T WE TEACH CREATION SCIENCE IN MY SCHOOL?

The courts have ruled that "creation science" is actually a religious view. Because public schools must be religiously neutral under the U.S. Constitution, the courts have held that it is unconstitutional to present creation science as legitimate scholarship.

In particular, in a trial in which supporters of creation science testified in support of their view, a district court declared that creation science does not meet the tenets of science as scientists use the term (*McLean v. Arkansas Board of Education*). The Supreme Court has held that it is illegal to require that creation science be taught when evolution is taught (*Edwards v. Aguillard*). In addition, district courts have decided that individual teachers cannot advocate creation science on their own (*Peloza v. San Juan Capistrano School District* and *Webster v. New Lennox School District*).

Teachers' organizations such as the National Science Teachers Association, the National Association of Biology Teachers, the National Science Education Leadership Association, and many others also have rejected the science and pedagogy of creation science and have strongly discouraged its presentation in the public schools. In addition, a coalition of religious and other organizations has noted in "A Joint Statement of Current Law" that "in science class, [schools] may present only genuinely scientific critiques of, or evidence for, any explanation of life on earth, but not religious critiques (beliefs unverifiable by scientific methodology)."

Some argue that "fairness" demands the teaching of creationism along with evolution. But a science curriculum should cover science, not the religious views of particular groups or individuals.

Educational Issues

IF EVOLUTION IS TAUGHT IN SCHOOLS, SHOULDN'T CREATIONISM BE GIVEN EQUAL TIME?

Some religious groups deny that microorganisms cause disease, but the science curriculum should not therefore be altered to reflect this belief. Most people agree that students should be exposed to the best possible scholarship in each field. That scholarship is evaluated by professionals and educators in those fields. In science, scientists as well as educators have concluded that evolution—and only evolution—should be taught in science classes because it is the only *scientific* explanation for why the universe is the way it is today.

Many people say that they want their children to be exposed to creationism in school, but there are thousands of different ideas about creation among the world's people. Comparative religions might comprise a worthwhile field of study but not one appropriate for a science class. Furthermore, the U.S. Constitution states that schools must be religiously neutral, so legally a teacher could not present any particular creationist view as being more "true" than others.

WHY SHOULD TEACHERS TEACH EVOLUTION WHEN THEY ALREADY HAVE SO MANY THINGS TO TEACH AND CAN COVER BIOLOGY WITHOUT MENTIONING EVOLUTION?

Teachers face difficult choices in deciding what to teach in their limited time, but some ideas are of central importance in each discipline. In biology, evolution is such an idea. Biology is sometimes taught as a list of facts, but if evolution is introduced early in a class and in an uncomplicated manner, it can tie many disparate facts together. Most important, it offers a way to understand the astonishing complexity, diversity, and activity of the modern world. Why are there so many different types of organisms? What is the response of a species or community to a changing environment? Why is it so difficult to develop antibiotics and insecticides that are useful for more than a decade or two? All of these questions are easily discussed in terms of evolution but are difficult to answer otherwise.

A lack of instruction about evolution also can hamper students when they need that information to take other classes, apply for college or medical school, or make decisions that require a knowledge of evolution.

*   *   *

Fundamentalist Creationism and the Value of Satire

Immediately after the publication of the *Origin of Species* in 1859, the clergy began to lampoon evolution. In a famous Oxford debate about evolution in 1860, Bishop Samuel Wilberforce, playing to the audience, challenged Thomas Henry Huxley, Darwin's defender, with the question, "Do you claim descent from a monkey on your grandfather's or your grandmother's side?" The endless permutations of that sarcasm include a Victorian preacher's gibe, "Oh, leave me my Father in heaven, and I will gladly leave you yours in the zoological garden," and a favorite taunt of present-day evangelists: "*You* might have sprung from a monkey, but *I* sure didn't!" And so on.

It should come as no surprise then, that as a matter of fair play, evolutionists sometimes respond to the creationists' bludgeon of sarcasm with the rapier of satire. Encouraged, no doubt, by its ancient and distinguished pedigree, evolutionists are using satire for the traditional reasons: to expose folly and to bring enlightenment through humor. Religion posing as science is exactly the kind of folly that satire is meant to correct.

History, reason, and logic should convince any rational person that the biblical tale of creation was the product of a primitive people who, lacking hard evidence, had to fall back on imagination, and simply made things up. Mainstream Christian and Jewish groups have accepted this common-sense view, and regard the creation stories in Genesis as metaphorical rather than literal.

Despite this broad religious consensus, however, the fundamentalist minority obstinately goes on insisting, against all evidence, that the ancient biblical tales are factual and "scientific"; that Noah's ark was real; that it could actually hold seven "clean" or two "unclean" specimens of every species of animal in the entire world; and that the Genesis flood constitutes a "scientific" explanation of the observable geological succession of stratified rocks and the worldwide, consistent sequence of fossil distribution. Unfortunately, those same religious fundamentalists have, by political means, managed to induce many state and local school boards and other authorities to abolish evolution from the teaching of high school biology, or to label it a "mere" theory, or to give equal time in science classes to *un*scientific creationism.

Because the creationists are constantly increasing their political activities and because, in regard to evolution, many people seem impervious to logic or evidence, perhaps satire is the most effective way to demonstrate that the would-be creationist emperor has no clothes at all. The following are two recent examples of satire doing its traditional job: exposing folly and serving reason.

P. A.

MICHAEL SHERMER

Genesis Revisited: A Scientific Creation Story (1998)†

In the beginning—specifically on October 23, 4004 BCE at noon—out of quantum foam fluctuation God created Big Bang inflationary cosmology. He saw that the Big Bang was VERY big, too big for creatures that could worship him, so He created the earth. And darkness was upon the face of the deep, so He commanded hydrogen atoms (which He created out of Quarks and other subatomic goodies) to fuse and become helium atoms and in the process release energy in the form of light. And the light maker he called the sun, and the process He called fusion. And He saw the light was good because now He could see what He was doing. And the evening and the morning were the first day.

And God said, Let there be lots of fusion light makers in the sky. Some of these fusion makers appear to be more than 4004 light years from Earth. In fact, some of the fusion makers He grouped into collections He called galaxies, and these appeared to be millions and even billions of light years from Earth, so He created tired light so that the 4004 BCE creation would be preserved. And created He wondrous splendors such as Red Giants, White Dwarfs, Quasars, Pulsars, Nova and Supernova, worm holes, and even Black Holes out of which nothing can escape. But since God cannot be constrained by nothing, He created Hawking radiation through which information can escape from Black Holes. This made God even more tired than tired light, and the evening and the morning were the second day.

And God said, Let the waters under the heavens be gathered together unto one place, and let the continents drift apart by plate tectonics. He decreed sea floor spreading would create zones of emergence, and He caused subduction zones to build mountains and cause earthquakes. In weak points in the crust God created volcanic islands, where the next day He would place organisms that were similar to but different from their relatives on the mainlands so that still later created creatures called humans would mistake them for evolved descendants. And in the land God placed fossil fuels, natural gas, and other natural resources for humans to exploit, but not until after Day Six. And the evening and the morning were the third day.

And God saw that the land was lonely, so He created animals bearing their own kind, declaring, "Thou shalt not evolve into new species, and thy equilibrium shall not be punctuated." And God placed into the land's strata fossils that appeared older than 4004 BCE. And the sequence resembled descent with modification. And the evening and morning were the fourth day.

And God said, Let the waters bring forth abundantly the moving creatures that have life, the fishes. And God created great whales whose skeletal

† From *Skeptic* 6 (1998): 21. Copyright © 1998 by Michael Shermer and *Skeptic Magazine*. Reprinted by permission of the publisher and author. Michael Shermer (b. 1954) is adjunct professor of the history of science at Occidental College and publisher of *Skeptic* magazine.

structure and physiology were homologous with the land mammals He would create later that day. Since this caused confusion in the valley of the shadow of doubt God brought forth abundantly all creatures, great and small, declaring that microevolution was permitted, but not macroevolution. And God said, *Natura non facit saltum*—Nature shall not make leaps. And the evening and morning were the fifth day.

And God created the pongids and hominids with 98% genetic similarity, naming two of them Adam and Eve, who were anatomically fully modern humans. And in the ground placed He in abundance teeth, jaws, skulls, and pelvises of transitional fossils from pre-Adamic creatures. One He chose as his special creation He named Lucy. And God realized this was confusing, so He created paleoanthropologists to sort it out. And just as He was finishing up the loose ends of the creation, such as putting the pit in avocados, God realized that Adam's immediate descendants would not understand inflationary cosmology, global general relativity, quantum mechanics, astrophysics, biochemistry, paleontology, and the other ologies, so he created creation myths. But there were so many creation stories throughout the world God realized this was confusing, so he created anthropologists, folklorists, and mythologists to sort it out. But confusion still reigned in the valley of the shadow of doubt, so God became angry, so angry that God lost His temper and cursed the first humans, telling them to go forth and multiply themselves. But they took God literally and 6,000 years later there are six billion humans. And the evening and morning were the sixth day. So God said, Thank me its Friday, and He made the weekend. And He saw that it was a good idea.

PHILIP APPLEMAN

Darwin's Ark (1984)†

[Noah and his sons, Shem, Ham, and Japheth—and their wives—
having managed to build an ark, prepare for the flood.]

* * *

So finally they have themselves an ark,
and God says, "Good work, Noah, now
get the animals—clean beasts, seven of a kind,
unclean, just two, but make sure
they're male and female, you got that straight?"

* * *

Think of it—they're living out there
in that gritty wilderness, and all of a sudden
they're supposed to come up with two elephants.
Or is it more?
"Shem," Japheth calls. "Is the elephant
a clean or an unclean animal?
If it's clean, that means seven of them
and the ark is in trouble. And how
about rhinos? And hippos? What do we do
about the dinosaurs? How do we get a brontosaurus
up the gangplank?" Japheth
loves raising problems that Noah
hasn't thought of at all. "Oh, by the way, Dad,
how are we going to keep the lions
away from the lambs?"

It's not just a headache, it's a nightmare.
Just think of poor Ham, after all of his angst
and sweat getting the ark assembled, and then
having to trudge off to the Congo and the Amazon,
to round up all those tricky
long-tailed leapers, there in the jungle greenery—
gibbons, orangutans, gorillas, baboons, chimps,
howler monkeys, capuchins, mandrills, tamarins . . .

And Shem, dutiful Shem, in charge
of the other mammals—the giraffes,
the horses, zebras, quaggas, tapirs, bison,

† From the title poem in *Darwin's Ark* (Bloomington, Ind., 1984). In this version, Darwin dreams
that he is Noah. Subsequently published as "Noah" in Philip Appleman, *New and Selected Poems,
1956–1996* (Fayetteville, Ark., 1996). Reprinted with permission of the University of Arkansas
Press. Copyright 1996 by Philip Appleman.

the pumas, bears, shrews, raccoons, weasels—
thousands of species of mammals . . .

And Japheth out there on the cliffs and treetops
trying to snare the birds—the eagles, condors,
hawks, buzzards, vultures—thousands upon thousands
of hyperkinetic birds . . .

Well, it's pretty clear, isn't it,
that there's a space problem here: a boat
only four hundred fifty feet long, already
buzzing and bleating and squeaking and mooing
and grunting and mewing and hissing and cooing
and croaking and roaring and peeping and howling
and chirping and snarling and clucking and growling—
and the crocodiles aren't back from the Nile
yet, or the iguanas from the islands,
or the kangaroos or koalas,
or the thirty different species of rattlesnakes,
or the tortoises, salamanders, centipedes, toads . . .

It takes some doing, all that,
but Ham comes back with them.
And wouldn't you know,
it's Japheth who opens up, so to speak,
the can of worms. "Dad, there are thousands
of species of worms! Who's
going digging for them? And oh, yes,
how about the insects?"
"Insects!" Shem rebels at last,
"Dad, do we have to save *insects*?" Noah,
faithful servant, quotes the Word:
"Every living thing."

                        *   *   *

Japheth ticks away at his roster. "So far
we've got dragonflies, damselflies, locusts, and aphids,
grasshoppers, mantises, crickets, and termites . . .
Wait a minute—termites?
We're going to save termites, in a wooden boat?"
But Japheth knows that arguing with Noah
is like driving a nail into chicken soup. He shrugs
and carries on. "Dad,
we haven't even scratched the surface.
There must be a million species
of insects out there.
Even if we unload all the other animals,
the insects alone will sink the ark!"

Ah, but the ark was not floating on fact,
it was floating on faith—that is to say,
on fiction. And in fiction, the insects
went aboard—*and* a year's supply
of hay for the elephants, a year's bananas
for the monkeys, and so on.
"Well, that's that," Japheth says,
"but you still haven't answered my question—
what will the meat-eaters eat?"
"We'll cross that bridge when we come to it,"
Noah replies, in history's
least appropriate trope,
"All aboard now, it's starting
to sprinkle."

              *   *   *

Twelve hard months that strange menagerie lived
in the ark, the sixteen thousand hungry birds
lusting for the two million insects,
and the twelve thousand snakes and lizards
nipping at the seven thousand mammals,
and everyone slipping and sliding around
on the sixty-four thousand worms
and the one hundred thousand spiders—
and Noah driving everyone buggy, repeating
every morning, as if he'd just thought of it,
"Well, we're all in the same boat."

It was a long, long year
for those weary men and their bedraggled wives,
feeding the gerbils and hamsters, cleaning
the thousands of cages, keeping the jaguars
away from the gazelles, the grizzlies away
from the cottontails—everything aboard, after all,
was an endangered species.
But finally the waters subsided,
the dove fluttered off and never returned,
the gangplank slid down to Ararat,
and the animals scampered out to the muddy,
corpse-ridden earth.

And Noah, burning a lamb on his altar
under that mocking rainbow, cannot forget
that he rescued the snakes and spiders, but
he let Enoch and Jubal
and Cainan and Lamech and
their wives and innocent children
go to a soggy grave.

And Noah knows, in his tired bones,
that now he will have to be fruitful once more,
and multiply, and replenish the earth
with a pure new race of people who
would never, *never* sin again,
for if they did,
all that killing would be for nothing,
a terrible embarrassment
to God.

PART IX
DARWIN AND THE
LITERARY MIND

Evolution ever climbing after some ideal good,
And reversion ever dragging Evolution in the mud.
—Alfred Tennyson, 1886

The theater is much older than the doctrine of evolution, but its one faith, asseverated again and again for every age and every year, is a faith in evolution, in the reaching and the climb of man toward distant goals, glimpsed but never seen, perhaps never achieved, or achieved only to be passed impatiently on the way to a more distant horizon.
—Maxwell Anderson, 1947

One of the most famous passages of [Darwin's] *Autobiography* starts out, "My mind seems to have become a kind of machine for grinding general laws out of large collections of facts . . ." Many an historian has seized and reproduced the passage as triumphant proof that Darwin's poetic senses "atrophied" in later life. Little did they notice that the passage chosen made such good copy because it was itself poetic.
—Frederick B. Churchill, 1982

Scientists, awake and held responsible for what they say while awake, have not found postmodernism useful.
—Edward O. Wilson, 1998

Darwin's Literary Sensibility

CHARLES DARWIN

Autobiography (1876)†

* * *

I have said that in one respect my mind has changed during the last twenty or thirty years. Up to the age of thirty, or beyond it, poetry of many kinds, such as the works of Milton, Gray, Byron, Wordsworth, Coleridge, and Shelley, gave me great pleasure, and even as a schoolboy I took intense delight in Shakespeare, especially in the historical plays. I have also said that formerly pictures gave me considerable, and music very great delight. But now for many years I cannot endure to read a line of poetry: I have tried lately to read Shakespeare, and found it so intolerably dull that it nauseated me. I have also almost lost any taste for pictures or music.— Music generally sets me thinking too energetically on what I have been at work on, instead of giving me pleasure. I retain some taste for fine scenery, but it does not cause me the exquisite delight which it formerly did. On the other hand, novels which are works of the imagination, though not of a very high order, have been for years a wonderful relief and pleasure to me, and I often bless all novelists. A surprising number have been read aloud to me, and I like all if moderately good, and if they do not end unhappily—against which a law ought to be passed. A novel, according to my taste, does not come into the first class unless it contains some person whom one can thoroughly love, and if it be a pretty woman all the better.

This curious and lamentable loss of the higher aesthetic tastes is all the odder, as books on history, biographies and travels (independently of any scientific facts which they may contain), and essays on all sorts of subjects interest me as much as ever they did. My mind seems to have become a kind of machine for grinding general laws out of large collections of facts, but why this should have caused the atrophy of that part of the brain alone, on which the higher tastes depend, I cannot conceive. A man with a mind more highly organised or better constituted than mine, would not I suppose have thus suffered; and if I had to live my life again I would have made a rule to read some poetry and listen to some music at least once every week; for perhaps the parts of my brain now atrophied could thus have been kept active through use. The loss of these tastes is a loss of

† From *The Autobiography of Charles Darwin, 1809–1882*, ed. Nora Barlow (New York, 1969). Written, Darwin said, for his children and grandchildren, his autobiography was published posthumously. Lady Nora Barlow was Darwin's granddaughter.

happiness, and may possibly be injurious to the intellect, and more probably to the moral character, by enfeebling the emotional part of our nature.

* * *

L. ROBERT STEVENS

Darwin's Humane Reading (1982)†

In his *Autobiography* Charles Darwin overstated the extent of his rejection of humane literature. The recent publication of his reading lists affords a new source from which to see that the common theory that Darwin became an "anaesthetic man" masks the true breadth of his mind.[1]

Darwin is the principle witness against himself, and it is upon his own testimony that Darwinists have come to think of him as anaesthetic. * * * Donald Fleming's article on the Darwinian anaesthesis offers the explanation that Darwin dissociated himself from art because he identified art with religion and thought of religion as an ideological justification for pain.[2] Certain other Darwinists, sensing a contradiction between the achievement of Darwin and the picture of an anaesthetic man, have written around the difficulty. Howard Gruber and Paul Barrett, for example, confess that "we have not attempted a study of Darwin's personality, although we have grown skeptical of a common psychoanalytically oriented picture of him as the neurotic victim of a tyrannical father, timid, reclusive, compulsive, and afflicted with a psychological malady."[3] One conclusion to be drawn from Darwin's reading lists is that Gruber and Barrett's intuitive skepticism is well-grounded in relation at least to the claims that Darwin was an aesthetically thwarted man. Even though there was a diminishment in Darwin's reading of poetry (interpreted broadly to include drama), there was not an anaesthesis. The autobiographical evidence which has generated such terms as "bland," "colorless," "anaesthetic," and "dessication," as descriptions of Charles Darwin, are now supplemented by more exact autobiographical materials which moderate the general view of his reading in humanistic subjects and show that the stark terms listed above are not apt.

It is time to alter the claim that Darwin was an anaesthetic specialist getting on with his job in an intellectual vacuum. His reading notebooks give documentary evidence that he did stop reading poetry at about age thirty-six (not thirty), but only after reading a great deal of very good work. Even then he continued virtually every other form of humane reading,

† From "Darwin's Humane Reading: The Anaesthetic Man Reconsidered," *Victorian Studies* 26 (1982): 51–63 (Bloomington: Indiana University Press, 1982). Used by permission of Indiana University Press. L. Robert Stevens (b. 1932) is professor emeritus of English at the University of North Texas.

1. Peter J. Vorzimmer, "The Darwin Reading Notebooks (1838–1869)," *Journal of the History of Biology*, 10 (1977), 107–153.
2. Donald Fleming, "Charles Darwin, The Anaesthetic Man," *Victorian Studies*, 4 (1961), 219–236.
3. Howard Gruber and Paul Barrett, *Darwin on Man* (New York: E. P. Dutton and Co., 1974), pp. xvi–xvii.

that is, the literary essay, philosophy, biography, and the novel at least to age fifty-one, when the notebooks ceased, and probably—it is certainly so with novels—to the end of his life. Darwin's illness did obstruct his reading of poetry, which he deeply regretted. But it now seems likely that he simply thought too lowly of essays and novels as forms of art, and therefore he has judged himself too modestly. Darwin entered well over 1,600 titles in the twenty-two years he kept his list.[4] Of course scientific titles are easily more common, and, as might be expected, the most frequently listed authors are naturalists—Owen (twelve times), Isidore Geoffrey St. Hilaire (nine), Humboldt (eight), Temminck (eight), Lyell and Decandolle (seven), for example. Still, Carlyle and Shakespeare are cited ten times each, and in sections of the list where a count of titles is possible—as for 1842 and 1857—the ratio of humane to scientific books is as high as one-third. This ratio is not constant, and poetry had disappeared well before the end of the notebook, but the list does not show a vacuum. Darwin was a man enormously interested in matters of the mind and enormously well-read.

Although there is a certain truth in Darwin's disclaimer, his diminished sense of the aesthetic was not so broad, nor did it come so early as his own testimony has led biographers to believe. After Darwin's graduation as a moderately successful university student, he continued for fifteen years to provide himself with a wide reading of some of the most enduring texts in our culture. After virtually giving up poetry by age thirty-six, he continued to read philosophy, literary essays, and biographies at least to 1860 and quite probably longer (*Autobiography*, p. 139). His reading surpasses in its humane content that of many an able and intelligent graduate who has finished formal training. Among scientists Darwin has left one of the clearest records of his reading known to the history of science. It is neither a narrow nor a dreary list.

So long as the *Autobiography* is used as the principle source of information about Darwin's reading, the view of his biographers seems accurate. There he tells us that "I took much delight in Wordsworth's and Coleridge's poetry, and can boast that I read the *Excursion* twice through. Formerly Milton's *Paradise Lost* had been my favorite, and in my excursions during the voyage of the *Beagle*, when I could take only a single small volume, I always chose Milton."

*   *   *

4. An exact count of the titles Darwin read even though recorded in the notebooks is not possible. He occasionally enters an indeterminate note, such as "Some of Shelley's Poems" or "many novels." It is more difficult still to get an exact count of them by the categories of scientific and humane reading. Darwin expressly tells us that he read travel books "independently of any scientific facts which they may contain" (*Autobiography*, p. 139); that is, he read them both for science and for their human interest. There are over 130 travels and memoirs listed. It is also difficult to count titles because in his list of books "To Be Read" for 1852–1860, that is, in the part of notebook number 128 which Vorzimmer does not transcribe, a great many are subsequently marked "read" by Darwin. But not all of them are so marked even when external evidence indicates that he did in fact read a given title. I concur in Vorzimmer's view that caution must be used in making assumptions about Darwin's reading of the books in this section of the list when they are not expressly marked. My figure of 1,600 includes those read and those "to be read"; it also includes the pages of the notebook not transcribed by Vorzimmer.

I

The list identifies eight specific plays by Shakespeare which Darwin read (*Julius Caesar* was "good," *Richard II* "bad"). Elsewhere another "several plays" are shown and it should be remembered that this is a second, not a schoolboy reading of Shakespeare. He also read Shakespeare's sonnets. He read the minor poems of Milton and the poems of Alexander Pope. He read "part of" Dante, Gray's poems, tried and failed at Dryden, read all of Wordsworth, skimmed Burns, read Shelley's poems, and also Campbell's. He read Byron's *Childe Harold, Manfred, Cain,* and *The Giaour.* The last entries Darwin makes for poetry are Southey's *Thalaba* and Cowper's translation of the *Iliad.* Both are for the year 1845; in the following year, at thirty-six, Darwin began his time-consuming work of classifying barnacles.

Of literary essays—and again, my count is indicative, not definitive—Darwin records at least thirty volumes. They include Burke's speeches, Joshua Reynolds's *Discourses,* Tocqueville's *Democracy,* Bacon's nonscientific works (Darwin lists *The Advancement of Learning* and *Novum Organum* separately), Thackeray's *Lectures on English Poets,* five books by Thomas Carlyle, three by Harriet Martineau, and Emerson's essays. In the twentieth century, perhaps, the prose essay has been devalued as an art form. Thomas DeQuincey believed that it had already happened in the nineteenth, and Martin Svaglic thinks that the devaluation of "rhetoric," at least, goes as far back as the seventeenth century. But Darwin was undeniably concerned with the prose accounts of topics which are habitually thought to be of interest to the quickened intellect. The formal essay is indeed a high art, and at its best, a humane one. Darwin read John Henry Newman's *On the Soul,* and *Phases of Faith,* which he thought excellent. He read Pepys's *Diary* and Chesterton's *Prison Life*—both listed after the date 1860, the last year of his notebook, when Darwin was fifty-one.

Even by his own account, Darwin never lost interest in biography. What now appears from his reading list, however, is that he read more lives of literary than of scientific figures. Perhaps it should be assumed that great figures in science were less commonly written about at the time; Darwin did read the lives of Newton, Kepler, Galileo, Buffon, Lavater, Priestly, Hutton, and I. G. St. Hilaire. But the fact remains that he read a great many more of the lives of literary figures. During the twenty-two years he kept his list, Darwin read at least 100 biographies. The lives of the following literary figures appear on Darwin's list: Montaigne, Bunyan, Byron (both Lockhart's and Moore's), Goldsmith, Brontë, Collins, Southey, Scott, Samuel Johnson (Boswell's), Swift, Burns, Dryden, Sydney Smith, and Goethe. There are numerous others. In addition to these personalities who might be thought of as literary in the most narrow sense, Darwin also read the lives of Beethoven, Haydn, Mozart, and Constable. He read collections of "lives" too: the "Lives of the Chancellors," for example, and of "Great artists and Great Anatomists." The last biography of a writer of imaginative literature is Sheridan's, which appears in the last year of the list. Thus as late as 1860 Darwin was still reading the lives of literary figures, if not their works.

Unlike this professed turning away from poetry, Darwin claimed a continuing love for novels. That love, as all Darwinists readily acknowledge, continued to the end of his life.

*   *   *

Darwin's criteria for a good novel show, it is true, no special sophistication, as almost every biographer has made plain. He asked that a novel "not end unhappily" and contain "some person whom one can thoroughly love, and if it be a pretty woman, all the better." Culler takes this as another instance of Darwin's having "no aesthetic sense." But such a novel as Darwin describes is not necessarily a poor one and might refer to Anthony Trollope's *The Warden* (which Darwin read in 1855) or to Dickens's *Oliver Twist*. Among the numerous novels Darwin read during the twenty years covered by the notebooks, the following works appear along with the purely sentimental ones: *Don Quixote, The Vicar of Wakefield, Mansfield Park, Sense and Sensibility, Northanger Abbey, Gulliver's Travels, Robinson Crusoe, Martin Chuzzlewit, Jane Eyre, Quentin Durward, Villette,* and perhaps *Barnaby Rudge*. He also read novels by Thackeray, Mrs. Oliphant, Fanney Burney, and possibly George Sand.

There is a practical result to all of this humane reading—although we need not ask that there should be. In his book *The Expression of the Emotions of Men and Animals* (1872), Darwin cites Dickens, Maria Edgeworth, Gaskell, Lessing, Oliphant, and Shakespeare (in eight different plays) as authorities on human expression. In *The Descent of Man* (1871), he cites Walter Bagehot, Hume, Kant, Malthus, John Stuart Mill, Jean Paul Richter, Friederich Schlegel, Adam Smith, and Tennyson. In *The Variation of Plants and Animals Under Domestication*, Pliny, Aristophanes, Goethe, and Macaulay are among those cited.

My point, however, is not that Darwin used these literary sources in his science, but that he knew them. Without having read a luxuriance of imaginative literature, he would not have had such ready access to the concrete instances which rose to mind when needed; that is, the data arise from a life-long habit of reading both scientific books and books not especially aimed at scientific uses.

*   *   *

Darwin's disclaimer is, of course, plain enough: "I cannot endure to read a line of Poetry . . . I have found it so intolerably dull that it nauseated me." But the poetry is not the cause of the nausea, rather the nausea—that is, the whole of his forty-year malaise—is the cause of the lessening in his "intense delight" in poetry. Darwin also finally became unable to dine with Hooker and Huxley because of his nervous indisposition, but no one thinks of him as having become "unfriendly." Why should he then be thought, as West thinks of him, as a "fragmentary man"? He was educated in the classical tradition, translating Greek and Latin texts virtually every school day for many years—Caesar, Cicero, Virgil, Plato, Pliny. He taught himself to read French and German, and although he used these acquired languages almost exclusively for scientific reading, the work of learning them is generally considered humanistic. He lists forty-three

German and one-hundred-fifty French titles. He read nearly every major English poet from Shakespeare to his own day, continuing his reading for fourteen years after leaving college. He read belles-lettres and philosophy at least to age fifty-one and probably to the end of his life. He read novels as long as he lived. The wonder is not that he stopped reading poetry, but that he read so much of it before he did, and that he wished he had not ceased. The picture of Darwin as a "dessicated" or "atrophied" man merely serves to aggravate the sense of a split between two cultures, whether such a split actually exists or not. It creates the image, false in Darwin's case, of a plodding dullard, uninterested in the imaginative and creative work of artists. Darwin was grievously ill in the last decades of his life. It is not remarkable that his illness suppressed his reading of poetry. It is remarkable that his mind was full and rich, that he regretted any intellectual losses he suffered, and that he may have been one of the most complete scientists of the nineteenth century as his reading notebooks now abundantly show.

* * *

Darwin enlarged his experience of life through his lifelong commitment to reading which was varied in subject matter, prodigious in quantity. It was humane and philosophical as well as scientific. As though he were his own Boswell, Darwin took account of this enlarged life by transforming his experience into language. He cultivated the acquaintance of creative writers—Gaskell, Eliot, Ruskin, and Carlyle, for example. He may have thought of himself as one of them, reading their works and occasionally exchanging observations with them, as with Harriet Martineau. His sixteen books—or twenty, depending on how they are counted—required him for forty years to give constant attention to the authorial uses of language. He worked at this requirement, as most good writers do, by reading what good writers have written.

Charles Darwin was a plain and honest man who lived the life of the mind with a singleness of vision which it has been difficult to credit. As an old man, he modestly disclaimed ability in the arts, and that disclaimer has evolved into a modern legend. * * *

The legend which originated in Darwin's own statements about his life is incorrect. The history of ideas suffers a loss in thinking that so brilliant a theory emerged from so placid an intellect, in thinking of this great scientific figure as something less than he was: enormously well-read in the best traditions of our literature, patiently self-taught in two modern languages, fascinated by music even though it enlivened him to a state of nervous anxiety. Darwin was a man who lived the life of the mind fully and without dissimulation, who gave deference to literary and art critics even when he stubbornly resisted their judgments and stayed true to his own tastes, in whom the service of the imagination was brilliantly adapted to the service of science. Darwin's adult life was the living-out of a powerful expressive urge. He took daily notes on a lively parade of plants and animals, kept a personal journal, and wrote his own life's story; he kept up a worldwide correspondence, made notes on his impressions of each piece of his favorite music—a whole man, if an ill one, whose mind was daily quickened by the wonders of a natural world which never failed to surprise and fascinate him.

*   *   *

GEORGE LEVINE

Darwin and Pain: Why Science Made Shakespeare Nauseating (1995)†

*   *   *

Near the end * * * of his life, Darwin famously lamented his loss of feeling for art or poetry: "Now for many years I cannot endure to read a line of poetry: I have tried lately to read Shakespeare, and found it so intolerably dull that it nauseated me."

*   *   *

The nausea Darwin felt in reading Shakespeare embarrassed him because he was convinced this was his failure, not Shakespeare's. Science may in fact have been the source of Darwin's revulsion from poetry but poetry was part of what made him a scientist and science could only work its antipoetic effects on him because he was steeped in poetry. So by looking a bit at aspects of Darwin's life and theory I want now to speculate about this paradox and, perhaps, on its implications for the false antithesis between science and the humanities.

*   *   *

In the cramped quarters of the *Beagle* on which the young Darwin began his world-historical five-year voyage as ship's naturalist, he could take very few books. Famously, one of those books was, sensibly enough, Charles Lyell's *Principles of Geology*, from which Darwin learned how to look at geological phenomena. But, as he also indicates, "in my excursions during the voyage of the 'Beagle,' when I could take only a single small volume, I always chose Milton." I call that loving poetry.

But what was Milton, that most famous of creationists, doing in the hands of the incipient evolutionist? Feeding his imagination, satisfying his need for the beautiful and for order and at the same time encouraging his sense, as Gillian Beer argues, of multiplicity, profusion, abundance.

*   *   *

But somewhere, either during the voyage or in reflection upon it afterward, his accumulating knowledge of nature seems to have begun to create

† From *Raritan* 15, no. 2 (Fall 1995): 97–114. Copyright © 1995 by *Raritan*. Reprinted by permission from *Raritan: A Quarterly Review*. George Levine (b. 1931) is Kenneth Burke Professor of English and director of the Center for the Critical Analysis of Contemporary Culture at Rutgers University.

tension between the hardness of the natural fact and the imaginative satisfactions of emotion recollected in tranquility. Despite rumors to the contrary, romantic passion has never been incompatible with "fact," and
Darwin seems virtually to have lived on facts, as he crammed his pages
with them. *The Voyage of the Beagle* has the kind of factual density that
marks virtually every page of *The Origin of Species*, a book that differs in
this respect primarily because the facts are there organized to make, as
Darwin put it, one long argument. What, he might have questioned, has
poetry to do with the rough and inhuman landscapes of a nature that
seemed not to care about consciousness, memory, or desire?

* * *

Seeing the world self-consciously from the perspective of what he knew
and what he had read seduced him into longing for what was not like
home; "sterile" landscapes were suddenly sublime for him. His evolutionary theory, "Descent by variation through Natural Selection," notoriously
decentered the human. Evolution doesn't happen "for" human beings but
works impersonally and inhumanly, unintentionally, without "design."
This is familiar to us; but that decentering—another aspect of his modesty,
through which he decentered himself and refused to make proud claims
for himself or for his species—was an aspect of virtually every part of his
life and work.

* * *

One of his great virtues as naturalist on the *Beagle* was that everything
he observed, and he seems to have observed everything, offered itself to
him as a question. Where did this come from? How did it get here? What
is it composed of? The questions are never cosmic, never transcendental,
and the answers are always material.

The startlingly new visions of worlds that might, as he noted, be on
another planet, were only partly domesticated by Darwin's experience of
literature. Wordsworth had found consciousness in nature, the mind and
memory turning the material into humanly significant life. Increasingly,
Darwin lost the power to imagine that humanization. When he did find
consciousness in nature, as he did in worms, the effect is not to provide a
satisfying domestication of the apparently inhuman but to shake the assumptions of readers about the uniqueness of human consciousness. Tracing living matter back through its history, he found himself further and
further from the consolations of consciousness and of poetic meaning. His
imagination leaped ahead—or behind—to strip matter of its accrued spir-
ituality and find a true wilderness. And when, fifteen years after the *Beagle*
voyage, his beloved daughter Annie died, the world, for Darwin, would
indeed be stripped of life and meaning.

* * *

Darwin's "Dangerous Idea," as Daniel Dennett's new book describes it,
is not friendly to traditional human interests in design, consciousness, and
meaning, and it creates a paradox in the middle of Darwin's work: one of
its central requirements is a demonstration that nothing in nature works

for anything but its own benefit and nothing in nature can provide evidence for what the natural theologians constantly saw in it, the power, goodness, and wisdom of God. Nature is not interested in mankind and it works, as Dennett puts it, like an affectless algorithm, not like a benevolent God. Not God, but causes now in operation created everything we know in nature, even us. Yet another of Darwin's central characteristics as writer and scientist is delight in that fundamentally material and mindless nature. Watching its astonishing phenomena and figuring them out provided Darwin with what consolation he could derive from a world not designed for him.

Still, he wasn't entirely happy with the mindlessness and human indifference of the world he delighted to observe, and throughout the *Origin* Darwin tried to think his way around the brutal strategies of natural selection. At the end of his chapter on the "Struggle for Existence," for example, he tries for a little more conventional consolation:

> When we reflect on this struggle we may console ourselves with the full belief, that the war of nature is not incessant, that no fear is felt, that death is generally prompt, and that the vigorous, the healthy, and the happy survive and multiply.

There's something a little feeble about this. Yet he always argued that nature and its organisms wouldn't flourish as they do if it were not for the fact that, as he put it, *on balance*, there is more happiness than suffering. Otherwise, why would any organism persist? But in his own life, reading pain against deep evolutionary time proved a rather weak consolation. What I would call his scientific imagination—although he would have called it reason—may have inured him to "the war of nature," but it did not harden him to a world in which that war seemed to be sanctioned by God, or to a world from which his beautiful and beloved daughter could be pointlessly removed. As John Bowlby has put it, "The suffering of others Darwin always found unbearable."

I want to look now at that episode in Darwin's life—the death of his daughter Annie—that seems at once to have confirmed him in his theory and to have embittered him in relation both to God and to poetry.

*   *   *

Darwin's second child, Anne Elizabeth, was a favorite from her birth in March of 1841, the year before he wrote the first draft of his famous theory. In an unpublished memorial he wrote of her shortly after her death, ten years later, Darwin talks of "her joyousness and animal spirits," which "radiated from her whole countenance & rendered every movement elastic & full of life & vigour." "Her dear face now rises before me," he wrote, "as she used sometimes to come running down stairs with a stolen pinch of snuff for me, her whole form radiant with the pleasure of giving pleasure." *   *   *

Annie, who had been as healthy and vital as Darwin's memorial suggests, and therefore one of those whom natural selection might have been thought to favor, suddenly became ill in the summer of 1850. For many months the condition worsened, marked by much vomiting of a sort characteristic of Darwin himself. With his wife Emma seven months pregnant (she seemed always to be pregnant in the first fifteen years of their marriage). Darwin decided to take Annie to his own doctor in relatively far-off Malvern, leaving Emma at home. For three weeks—during which Darwin returned to his extensive, almost unending work on barnacles—there seemed some possibility that Annie would be cured, but things suddenly turned worse, Darwin rushed back to Malvern, and he stayed by Annie's bedside until the end. From the seventeenth of April, when he arrived back at Malvern, until the twenty-third, he wrote to his wife at least eight times.

* * *

He tells Emma that he thinks it "best for you to know how every hour passes. It is a relief to me to tell you: for whilst writing to you, I can cry; tranquilly." And so he tells her about Annie's vomiting, her feeble attempts to eat, the bath he and his sister-in-law Fanny gave her with "vinegar and water," the reducing of the odor of vomit—"we keep her sweet with Chloride of Lime," and then, on April 23rd, "She went to her final sleep most tranquilly, most sweetly at 12 oclock today. Our poor dear child has had a very short life but I trust happy, & God only knows what miseries might have been in store for her." Here, movingly, is the not quite convincing consolatory voice of the *Origin*. Emma responded, talking of her longing for Annie and her immediate indifference to the other children, and telling Charles, "You must remember that you are my prime treasure (& always have been) my only hope of consolation is to have you safe home to weep together."

* * *

In the *Autobiography*, there is a telling passage that Emma and the rest of the family decided to excise from the original publication:

> That there is much suffering in the world no one disputes. Some have attempted to explain this in reference to man by imagining that it serves for his moral improvement. But the number of men in the world is as nothing compared with that of all other sentient beings, and these often suffer greatly without any moral improvement. A being so powerful and so full of knowledge as a God who could create the universe, is to our finite minds omnipotent and omniscient, and it revolts our understanding to suppose that his benevolence is not unbounded, for what advantage can there be in the sufferings of millions of the low animals throughout almost endless time? This very old argument from the existence of suffering against the existence of an intelligent first cause seems to me a strong one; whereas, as just remarked, the presence of much suffering agrees well with the view that all organic beings have been developed through variation and natural selection.

Natural selection tells a dirty story. And if it's not natural selection that is doing the dirty work, then it is God, and who, Darwin wondered, could worship a God like that? Remembering Annie's pinched, drawn face, he was revolted by the very thought.

Darwin's most extended and theoretically significant moral and intellectual impulse was against the argument from design. Although there is evidence in his notebooks that he had rejected Paley years before Annie's death, he could not have accepted the idea that Annie's death was part of some large, morally significant design.

* * *

I have been making two potentially opposed arguments about Darwin's resistance to poetry in his later years. On the one hand, I have tried to show that his reflections on his voyage led him to reject poetry as being too satisfying to the human, too much determined to make all of nature echo with human associations. In this respect, poetry simply falsified and was not consonant with the materialist understanding of nature to which his observations and reflections were driving him. Poetry seemed to share with natural theology an anthropocentric understanding of the natural world. On the other hand, I have argued that Darwin himself could not endure the pain of suffering, and particularly of suffering without meaning. Why then could he not turn to poetry as a resource against the brutal indifference of the material processes of nature and of causes now in operation?

Because poetry of the sort that Darwin didn't want to read any more, Shakespeare's poetry, did not inevitably offer the sorts of humanly satisfying narratives Darwin rejected in natural theology. Those kinds of narratives would have been, as he put it frequently in the *Origin*, "fatal to my theory." But what effect on his theory, and on his thoughts about his daughter, would there have been, say, if Darwin had forced himself to read the passage at the end of *King Lear*, in which Lear holds his dead daughter in his arms and watches her with Darwinian attentiveness? I simply can't imagine him doing it, and not because he would have found it dull.

> Howl, howl, howl! O, you are men of stones.
> Had I your tongues and eyes, I'd use them so
> That heaven's vault should crack. She's gone for ever!
> I know when one is dead, and when one lives.
> She's dead as earth. Lend me a looking glass.
> If that her breath will mist or stain the stone,
> Why, then she lives.
>
> This feather stirs; she lives! If it be so
> It is a chance which does redeem all sorrows
> That ever I have felt.

But of course, Annie and Cordelia are dead, and sorrows are not redeemed.

The unbearable pain of others was sufficiently widespread through the nature he discovered and described that he didn't want to confront it in poetry. Poetry either lied by giving nature a sympathy his science could not detect in it, or lied by redeeming and consoling for losses that were meaningless and unconsolable. And when it treated of those losses, it, like Annie's death, was unendurable.

Darwin was too much the poet to endure poetry or Shakespeare. He was too much the scientist to believe that he could make sense of the world by imposing on it his own, or his species' emotional needs. In the *Origin* he personifies Natural Selection as an intelligent being infinitely more perceptive than humanity; but he is careful in later editions to explain that he is only being poetic, or rather metaphorical, and he strips nature of its human analogy: "I mean by Nature, only the aggregate action and product of many natural laws, and by laws the sequence of events as ascertained by us."

Stripping nature of the meaning his inescapable metaphors imposed on it—even "natural selection" is a metaphor, of course—was a crucial last step for the too-poetic Darwin. Only by removing natural selection from the world of poetry could Darwin live with it. A "natural selection" which worked its deadly salvation intentionally would be an unendurable conception.

So of course it wasn't science itself that made Shakespeare nauseating to Darwin. He never would have imagined that science and literature are incompatible and his own career shows a mutual shaping of those forces. Science made literature unendurable because science was already deeply informed by the moral implications and the emotional intensities of literature.

Yet, as James Moore and Adrian Desmond emphasize, Darwin is buried in Westminster Abbey: "Getting a freethinker into the Abbey was not easy." Darwin's increasing disaffection from religion, which grew, as I have been arguing, as his discomfort with poetry grew, derived from the same source: the facts are not consonant either with poetry or religion, and it is positively immoral to lean on untruths, to evade or deny the pain in the interests of either esthetic or spiritual pleasure. Darwin wanted to love poetry as he wanted to be religious, and indeed his outward public life remained pious and conformist: he was a true friend of the Church in his home town of Downe. But honest engagement with his own feelings made it impossible to figure out how to take pleasure from poetry, that relentlessly human and imaginative mode, or how to achieve faith when he saw the world and his own life brutally and mindlessly afflicted. He could not find a way. One can argue, finally, that he belongs at last in the Abbey precisely because he resisted both religion and poetry on moral grounds in the name of the truth he valued above both.

* * *

GILLIAN BEER

Darwin's Plots (1983)†

* * *

In the M notebook one of Darwin's most extended discussions of the imagination at work describes the train of thought most full of pleasure to a botanist:

> the botanist might so view plants and animals. —I am sure I remember my pleasure in Kensington Gardens has often been greatly excited by looking at trees as great compound animals united by wonderful and mysterious manner.

This sense of the resourcefulness of life in trees, their analogical likeness to 'great compound animals', articulates one strand in Darwin's use of the tree image as part of a complex scheme of reference in *The Origin of Species*.

Darwin's problem in relation to the theology of his age is expressed in the image of two contrasted trees—life versus knowledge. In his argument and its expression he found a means of condensing this image so that the two opposed trees could prove to be one.

He knew well that there are still tracts of forbidden knowledge but he did not allow himself to be deflected from the implications of his 'System'. Amid the noble trees of Paradise stood the Tree of Life:

> High eminent, blooming Ambrosial Fruit
> Of vegetable Gold.

In the Notebooks and later in *The Origin* Darwin fastens on the image of the *tree* to express evolutionary organisation. In doing this he rebuts the Lamarckian idea of a chain of progression—and with it the older hierarchical organisation of the 'great chain of being', its ascending orders of existence each working like a substitute, a more earthbound version of its own platonic idea. The idea of the great chain places forms of life in fixed positions which are permanent and immobile. Quintessential to its organisation is the idea of degree.

Darwin needed a metaphor in which degree gives way to change and potential, and in which form changes through time. He did not simply adopt the image of a tree as a similitude or as a polemical counter to other organisations. He *came upon it* as he cast his argument in the form of diagram. This 'materialisation' of the image is important in understanding its force for him. It was substantial, a condensation of real events, rather than a metaphor. Here we come back to the problems he faced in adapting the language available to him (a language so steeped in natural theological

† From *Darwin's Plots* (London, 1983). Reprinted by permission of Routledge. Gillian Beer (b. 1935) is a lecturer at Girton College, Cambridge.

suggestions) to a world of material history in which things must find their explanations, their analogies, and their metaphors, within the material order.

The multivocality of Darwin's language reaches its furthest extent in the first edition of *The Origin of Species*. His language is expressive rather than rigorous. He accepts the variability within words, their tendency to dilate and contract across related senses, or to oscillate between significations. He is less interested in singleness than in mobility. In his use of words he is more preoccupied with relations and transformations than with limits. Thus his language practice and his scientific theory coincide.

Once *The Origin* was published Darwin became far more aware of the range of implications carried by this generous semantic practice. It was brought home to him that many of his terms could mean more and other than he could control. He defended his theory in succeeding editions by paring away multiple significations, trying at points of difficulty to make his key terms mean one thing and one thing only, as in the case of Natural Selection. Such labour came hard to him. The exuberantly metaphorical drive of the language of *The Origin* was proper to its topic. The need to establish more parsimonious definitions and to combat misunderstanding may help to account for that dimming of his imaginative powers which he so deeply regretted.

* * *

Darwin's is not an austere Descartian style. There are few lean sentences in *The Origin of Species*. According to his son Francis he often laughed at himself 'for the difficulty which he found in writing English, saying, for instance, that if a bad arrangement of a sentence was possible, he should be sure to adopt it'. He felt the problems of obscurity—the over-rapid condensation of argument and insight which dwells at length on inessential features because the deep connections are already so evident to the writer that they scarcely bear re-formulation. His son remarks that his style is 'direct and clear'. Though there is some truth in this, the effect does not derive from actual ordering of the sentences, which is often tortuous. Rather it derives from the frequent intervention of the first person and from what Francis Darwin calls the 'courteous and conciliatory tone towards his reader'. 'The tone of such a book as *The Origin* is charming, and almost pathetic . . . The reader is never scorned for any amount of doubt which he may be imagined to feel, and his scepticism is treated with patient respect.'

The book seeks to persuade, not by any attempt to 'force belief' but through a more and more intricate taking in of possible causes of disbelief and the elaboration of doubts. It has in that sense the fullness of a Utopian text, much of whose pleasure comes from the marshalling of insight and detail (a kind of ethnography of his ideal world) rather than from a simply ideological extrapolation from facts. Darwin's description of 'the polity of nature' is thorough and warm, giving an impression of benign fullness even while it points out loss, failure, and struggle.

* * *

The unruly superfluity of Darwin's material at first gives an impression of superfecundity without design. Only gradually and retrospectively does the force of the argument emerge from the profusion of example. Such profusion indeed, *is*, as in Dickens, the argument: variability, struggle, the power of generation and of generations, the 'broken and failing groups of organic beings' are exemplified abundantly. In Darwin this takes place through evidences drawn from geology, biology, botany and in a language generatively charged, always dwelling on the particular case, rich in intensitives, expostulation, and case histories ransacked for implications. It is with a sense both of surprise and recognition, I think, that the reader comes to the opening of the final chapter 'Recapitulation and Conclusion' which runs: 'As this whole volume is one long argument, it may be convenient to the reader to have the leading facts and inferences briefly recapitulated'.

It is true that the book is one long argument, but it proceeds by a strange intermingling of acquisition, concretion, analogy and prophecy. For a book thematically preoccupied with the past, the present tense is extraordinarily predominant. This reinforces the effect of *discovery*, of being on the brink of finding out, rather than sharing an already formulated and arrested discovery, a 'luminous and orderly presentation'. * * * Darwin shares with Carlyle and Dickens that use of the prophetic present which leaves no space between us and the future and poises us on the edge of the unknown.

* * *

Darwin faced four major problems in precipitating his theory as language. Two of them were intrinsic to all discourse. First, language is anthropocentric. It places man at the centre of signification. Even symbol is defined by its referential value and the Symbolist movement of the later nineteenth century might therefore be seen as the last humanist enterprise. Symbols, despite their appearance of independence, take their point of reference from human interpretative power and depend upon their own functions of reference to human concerns.

Second, language always includes agency, and agency and intention are frequently impossible to distinguish in language. Darwin's *theory* depended on the idea of production. The natural order produces itself, and through reproduction it produces both its own continuance and its diversity. His theory had no place for an initiating nor intervening creator. Nor for an initiating or intervening author. Yet terms like 'selection' and 'preservation' raise the question 'By whom or what selected or preserved?' And in his own writing Darwin was to discover the difficulty of distinguishing between description and invention.

Third, he faced a more particular problem concerned with the natural historical discourse he inherited. Natural history was still imbued with natural theology, and salient terms such as 'contrivance' and 'design' were freighted with presumptions of godhead and of pre-emptive patterning. Darwin was therefore obliged to dramatise his struggle with natural theological assumptions within a language weighted towards natural theology. He must write against the grain of his discourse.

We can see the problem of escaping from creationist language very exactly in the changes Darwin made through several editions to passages in which the question of originating forces is unavoidable. Sometimes he makes small emendations which shift into a more openly metaphoric, even misfitting, language: 'since the first creature . . . was created' becomes 'since the first organic beings appeared on the stage'. In the conclusion one sentence in the first edition runs thus: 'Therefore I should infer from analogy that probably all the organic beings which have ever lived on this earth have descended from some one primordial form, into which life was first breathed.' The passive 'was breathed' evades the problem. In the second edition he briefly and somewhat surprisingly reinstates the Creator. The sentence now ends, 'into which life was first breathed by the Creator'. In the third edition he changes the whole sentence considerably:

> Therefore, on the principle of natural selection with divergence of character, it does not seem incredible that, from some such low and intermediate form, both animals and plants may have been developed: and, if we admit this, we must admit that all the organic beings which have ever lived on this earth may have descended from some one primordial form.

The sentence ends without raising the question of the beginning of life itself. It is concerned with descent and it specifies and privileges the explanatory and active powers of 'the principle of natural selection with divergence of character'. As he had earlier written, 'It is so easy to hide our ignorance under such expressions as the "plan of creation", "unity of design", etc, and to think that we have given an explanation when we have only restated a fact.' In such examples we see Darwin's persisting struggle to reach explanations which can extend the scope of enquiry, rather than resting within the circle of assumption.

The fourth problem of language that Darwin faced was that of addressing himself towards a general readership as well as to his confraternity of scientists. * * *

One of Darwin's own concerns was to demonstrate as far as possible the accord between scientific usage and common speech. His interest in etymology established language-history as a more than metaphorical instance of kinships hidden through descent and dissemination. An aspect of his insistence on congruities, and branchings, was his desire to substantise or substantiate metaphor wherever this could be done. He needs to establish ways in which language may be authenticated by natural order, so that his own discourse and argumentation may be 'naturalised', and so moved beyond dispute: 'Our classifications will come to be, as far as they can be so made, genealogies; and will then truly give what may be called the plan of creation.' 'The terms used by naturalists of affinity, relationship, community of type, paternity, morphology, adaptive characters, rudimentary and aborted organs, etc., will cease to be metaphorical, and will have a plain signification.' This search for 'plain signification', as for 'one primordial form', is the counter-ideal which leads him into a labyrinth of connection, interrelation, and extension.

* * *

One of the major questions raised by *The Origin* is how far metaphors may overturn the bounds of meaning assigned to them, sometimes even reversing the overt implications of the argument. Seemingly stable terms may come gradually to operate as generative metaphors, revealing inherent heterogeneity of meaning and of ideology. Darwin's use of the concept of 'struggle' is one well-known example to which I shall return. But there are others, less remarked, such as *generation*, which yields the tree, the great family, the lost parent, the 'changing dialect' of life. Each of these consequent ideas extends some element in the initiating one of generation, and itself establishes a further range of incipient meanings.

Sometimes we can watch Darwin seeking to contain implications, as in the more directly political example of the master-slave dialectic. Darwin's own revulsion against slavery, inherited through his family's concern with emancipation and reinforced by his own early experiences of slave-owning societies in South America when on the voyage of the *Beagle*, is an element in his insistence that natural selection—unlike the selection of man—is concerned only with the usefulness of characteristics to the organism which possesses them, and not with their usefulness to any other species: 'natural selection can act only through and for the good of each being'.

Having seen the genocidal wars waged upon the Indians by the Spaniards in South America, Darwin knew that the concept of 'environment' must include that of the invader. A being may be in accord with its environment until that environment is invaded from without. When Darwin uses a term like 'natives' he directs it within natural-historical terms: 'Man keeps the natives of many climates in one country; he seldom exercises each selected character in some peculiar and fitting manner; he feeds a long and short beaked pigeon on the same food'. But in the paragraph before *that*, he introduced the topic through the term 'inhabitant' and then 'native inhabitant' balanced against 'foreigners'.

> For as all the inhabitants of each country are struggling together with nicely balanced forces, extremely slight modifications in the structure or habits of one inhabitant would often give it an advantage over others; and still further modifications of the same kind would often still further increase the advantage. No country can be named in which all the native inhabitants are now so perfectly adapted to each other and to the physical conditions under which they live, that none of them could anyhow be improved; for in all countries, the natives have been so far conquered by naturalised productions, that they have allowed foreigners to take firm possession of the land. And as foreigners have thus everywhere beaten some of the natives, we may safely conclude that the natives might have been modified with advantage, so as to have better resisted such intruders.

Since this paragraph opens the discussion, the non-technical range of senses for 'inhabitant', 'native', and 'foreigner' can thrive before the more precise use is established later. Darwin's argument in that initiating discussion allows room for contrary readings; native inhabitants are not fully developed and thus will inevitably be taken over by colonisers; native inhabitants lack perfection only *in that* they do not have the means to resist foreign intruders.

Darwin does not directly resolve the potential contradiction but turns to the metaphor of selective breeding and sets man's handiwork beside that of Nature, denigrating man's procedures in opposition to 'nature's productions' which are far 'truer in character', thus demurring at man's exploitative procedures. But the contrary implication that colonisation is inevitable (or even 'right' in evolutionary terms) also survives, precisely because it is never brought sharply into the focus of attention.

Despite the attacks on Darwin's biological anthropomorphism later it may be his *disregard* of the potential sociological applications of many of his terms which makes them so uninhibitedly available for application. But this position should not be misunderstood. Darwin worked from the assumption that his theories applied to man equally with all other species and not from any separation. So though the absence of specification in his language may be seen as undesigned or unaware, it is based on the assumed congruity of man with all other forms of life.

*   *   *

One extreme view of analogy is that it is a rhetorical trick, unstable in its implications and distorting in its procedures, asserting only specious, temporary, or accidental similarities. At the other extreme, it is seen as an instrument of discovery which reveals grounded congruities and makes manifest the actual though concealed coherences of a stable world order. The question of whether the perception of analogies was fickle and momentary or whether there were stable analogies in nature which we could discover and then retain as a means of explanation, was a topic much discussed in the middle of the nineteenth century: Comte's view was austere. He preferred, for example, the term 'gravitation' to 'attraction', because it expresses a fact without any reference to the nature or cause of this occurrence. He inherited consciously from Descartes an emphasis upon the necessary univocality of scientific language and an avoidance of metaphor because of its uncontrollable element. Metaphor creates proliferation of meaning by means of its never thoroughly parallel terms. The fashionable view in the period when Darwin was writing was to deplore the evasions and transferences of metaphor, and to seek a declarative directness for scientific or philosophical language.

*   *   *

The drive in metaphor towards merging, towards the single domain, is a search for an ideal wholeness which its disjunct nature persistently counters. First and second terms are interactive. But because of the possibility always of *further description*, the drive towards divergence and diversification survives through metaphor, only a little less powerful than the drive towards stable equivalence, and persistently subverting it. The polysemism of metaphor means that it is hard to control its implications: it may be argued, for example, that Darwin's metaphor of the tree is a formal analogy whose function is purely diagrammatic, describing a shape not an experience. Its initial value for Darwin lay undoubtedly in the fact that the diagram *declared* itself as tree, rather than being foreknowingly designed to represent a tree-like shape for descent. On the page, however, it could as well be interpreted by the eye as shrub, branching coral, or seaweed. But Darwin saw not only the explanatory but the mythic potentiality of this diagram, its congruity with past orders of descent, and extended these in a form which is experimental rather than formal at the conclusion of the same chapter 'Natural Selection'. The tree discovered in the diagram is not only Arbor Vitae but the Arbor Scientiae. Darwin establishes so close a connection between representation and actuality that he can claim 'truth' for it. The prose succession imitates the order it describes, branching out into further and further similitudes:

> The affinities of all the beings of the same class have sometimes been represented by a great tree. I believe this simile largely speaks the truth. The green and budding twigs may represent existing species; and those produced during each former year may represent the long succession of extinct species. At each period of growth all the growing twigs have tried to branch out on all sides, and to overtop and kill the surrounding twigs and branches, in the same manner as species and groups of species have tried to overmaster other species in the great battle for life. The limbs divided into great branches, and these into lesser and lesser branches, were themselves once, when the tree was small, budding twigs; and this connexion of the former and present buds by ramifying branches may well represent the classification of all extinct and living species in groups subordinate to groups. Of the many twigs which flourished when the tree was a mere bush, only two or three, now grown into great branches, yet survive and bear all the other branches; so with the species which lived during long-past geological periods, very few now have living and modified descendants. From the first growth of the tree, many a limb and branch has decayed and dropped off; and these lost branches of various sizes may represent those whole orders, families, and genera which have now no living representatives, and which are known to us only from having been found in a fossil state. As we here and there see a thin straggling branch springing from a fork low down in a tree, and which by some chance has been favoured and is still alive on its summit, so we occasionally see an animal like the Ornithorhynchus or Lepidosiren, which in some small degree connects by its affinities two large branches of life, and which has apparently been saved from fatal competition by having inhabited a protected station. As buds give rise by growth to fresh buds, and these, if vigorous, branch out and overtop on all sides many a feebler branch, so by generation I believe it has been with the great Tree of Life, which fills with its dead and broken branches the crust of the earth, and covers the surface with its ever branching and beautiful ramifications.

The sanguine profusion of comparisons makes for a fantastic comprehensiveness which is both truth-affirming and self-confirming. And so the chapter on 'Natural Selection' ends, with an image that lays claim on a succession of metaphors from deep antiquity.

* * *

Darwin's Influence on Literature

LIONEL STEVENSON

Darwin among the Poets (1932)†

* * *

What the Poets Thought of Darwinism

In its simplest terms, the result of the evolutionary theory was the supplanting of the idea of permanence by the idea of relativity. Of course, the change had been imminent ever since science began to investigate the universe; but so long as the doctrines of orthodox religion were formally respected, most people rested secure. All the evil in the world was attributed to the original sin by which man had forfeited his primal perfection. One had only to live according to the precepts of religion and one could be confident of eternal happiness. Good or wicked deeds would be suitably rewarded or punished in the next world, and self-denial in earthly desires led to compensation by heavenly luxuries. On this solid basis of accepted fact, men established their view of life in which the human race was the pivot of the universe. When microscope and telescope began to reveal infinities surpassing the powers of imagination, man for a time tried to accept them as showing that God had been all the more generous in providing a wonderland for human occupancy; but more and more he became aware of his own insignificance, bounded by inefficient senses and "moving about in worlds not realized." And then the evolutionary theory completed the disruption of the old order. The definite act of creation was replaced by indeterminately long natural processes; the intelligent controlling deity succumbed to blind forces functioning mechanically. Since man was of one essence with the beasts, how could he have an immortal soul, destined for reward or punishment? Human life became a mysterious and melancholy thing, a brief struggle of consciousness against overwhelming and irrational external forces. Mankind appeared as an incidental and fortuitous episode in the age-long history of the stars.

This was the vast shift in human values which gradually revealed itself to the poets. Tennyson, a keen amateur of science, began to perceive the

† From chapter 1 of *Darwin among the Poets* (New York, 1963; first published 1932), New York: Russell & Russell, 1963. Reprinted by permission of the publisher. Lionel Stevenson (1902–1973) was James B. Duke Professor of English at Duke University.

653

problem about 1830; he recognized the immediate necessity of adapting the idea of God to keep pace with the new outlook. *In Memoriam*, written between 1833 and 1850, is a discussion of the doubts and difficulties involved, an exaltation of human intuition as transcending rational science, and—on that basis—a definition of God as a loving being who directs evolution toward beneficent ends. The other leading poet of the time, Browning, with less attention to scientific arguments, also preached a God of Love, and aligned himself with evolution by finding in human imperfection a promise of development still to come.

The appearance of the Darwinian theory made the problem acute. One of the most painful elements to the poetic mind was the revelation of cruelty in nature. The ruthless struggle for survival, the wasteful fecundity that entailed inevitable destruction, went counter to the belief in beneficence which had colored all previous poetry about nature. If any god existed, he could not be endowed with both omnipotence and benevolence—one or other attribute must be discarded. And if no god existed, nature was but a vast machine indifferent to the sufferings of living beings. Tennyson had to be content with the unsatisfactory conclusion that the world is as yet in the "red dawn" which will eventually develop into a golden noon. Browning dismissed the dilemma more summarily by declaring that suffering and dissatisfaction are necessary concomitants of progress: "Irks care the cropfull bird, frets doubt the maw-crammed beast?" Both Tennyson and Browning were convinced that progress was primarily a matter of the soul, in which earthly life was but an episode.

There were other poets who could not convince themselves of this encouraging possibility. In particular, Matthew Arnold and his friend Arthur Hugh Clough perceived the depressing aspect, and their work was colored with a melancholy fatalistic mood. In *Dover Beach* and *Stanzas in Memory of the Author of Obermann* Arnold spoke regretfully of the loss of faith which left the human spirit unsheltered and oppressed; he looked back to the period when Christianity was unquestioningly accepted, as to a golden age of security and happiness which was irrevocably fled. The fullest expression of his opinions is to be seen in *Empedocles on Etna* (1852)—it is significant that he took the first evolutionist as a mouthpiece to express the fatalism of the nineteenth-century rationalists. He preaches acquiescent endurance of fate and self-reliant defiance of weakness. After surveying the decay of orthodox belief in a benevolent deity who has prearranged man's happiness, he declares that man is conditioned by environment and heredity; his life is but a trivial repetition of an endless recurrent process; he deceives himself with illusions about life, while the world moves on indifferently. Nature has no special regard for humankind:

> Nature, with equal mind,
> Sees all her sons at play;
> Sees man control the wind,
> The wind sweep man away;
> Allows the proudly riding and the founder'd bark.

Whether a man be good or evil, he is similarly the prey to fate; but instead of facing his lot fairly, "to fight as best he can," he has invented supernatural forces, finding it easier to suffer when he can rail at God and Fate for his ills. If any invisible power exists at all, it must be essentially identical with the phenomena and forces of nature, and therefore cannot be omnipotent:

> All things the world which fill
> Of but one stuff are spun,
> That we who rail are still
> With what we rail at, one;
> One with the o'erlabour'd power that through the breadth and length
>
> Of earth, and air, and sea,
> In men, and plants, and stones,
> Hath toil perpetually,
> And travails, pants, and moans;
> Fain would do all things well, but sometimes fails in strength.

This immanent life-force, creating and sustaining all nature with incomplete success, is the only God and Fate that can be rationally conceived, "this only *is*—is everywhere"; but man insisted on originating a more personal power to blame for his suffering. The next step of the anthropomorphic process comes when man believes that the gods, whom he first created to curse, are beneficent and will "perfect what man vainly tries." As man comes to realize his insignificance, he tends to impute to God the omniscience which he lacks in himself; but Empedocles scorns the argument as illogical. He sees the dream of immortality as a cowardly pretext by which men comfort themselves in the disappointments of life, and he declares that the only true and certain bliss is in making the most of what earthly life offers:

> Is it so small a thing
> To have enjoy'd the sun. . . .
>
> That we must fain a bliss
> Of doubtful future date,
> And, while we dream on this,
> Lose all our present state,
> And relegate to worlds yet distant our repose?

In closing, Empedocles counsels a temperate happiness, neither despair because the orthodox faith is discountenanced by reason nor extravagant hope, but a determination to make the best of life.

This poem expresses all that was abhorrent to Tennyson and Browning. Its materialistic disbelief in a beneficent God and an immortal life, its fatalistic hedonism, are typical of what the new generation was deducing from the evolutionary theory. In Arnold an innate ethical tendency fostered the austere creed of defying fate's blows; but other poets were more blatantly materialistic. In the very year of *The Origin of Species*, Edward Fitzgerald published his version of the *Rubáiyát*. Although the poem did not refer directly to modern science, it won its popularity because it voiced exactly the pessimistic hedonism that so many people drew from evolution.

Since an after-life was uncertain, and since man was powerless to over-come the blind fate in which he was enmeshed, life seemed to offer nothing better than self-indulgence.

Fitzgerald displayed this mood as world-weary and disillusioned; Swinburne, a few years later, endowed it with more virility. He combined it with praises of the Greek pantheon, and derived immense glee from his assaults upon the anthropocentric Christian god and the orthodox morality. However, he was not always the epicurean. His most significant evolutionary poems are the *Hymn of Man* and *Hertha*, in which a new creed is shaped—a pantheistic creed in which the human race is deified as the highest manifestation of nature. In the *Hymn of Man* he arraigns the orthodox creed for its selfishness:

> Therefore the God that ye made you is grievous, and gives not aid,
> Because it is but for your sake that the God of your making is made.
> Thou and I and he are not gods made man for a span,
> But God, if a God there be, is the substance of men, which is man.
> Our lives are as pulses or pores of his manifold body and breath;
> As waves of his sea on the shores where birth is the beacon of death.

He goes on to elaborate this concept of a god who is the sum total of mankind, "A God with the world inwound whose clay to his footsole clings." The evolutionary source of such an idea is obvious: man, as the final result of the creative process, is the most perfect embodiment of the life-force; the only spiritual element in the universe is that which has developed within the human species; and religion should be of service to the cause of the race's further development rather than the selfish hope of individual salvation. It is true, Swinburne admits, that man is physically helpless and vulnerable, a servant of Change, but the spirit can overcome the cruel blind forces which hinder him. Man has made himself chains and blinded himself by creating an external god, thereby incurring the evils of dogma and priestcraft. As a result, man has suffered dread and doubt and contrition, has delayed his progress, and only now awakens to the tyranny he suffered. Man's mind has conquered space and comprehended the law of the universe; though the individual perish, the race is immortal:

> Men perish, but Man shall endure; lives die, but the life is not dead.
> He hath sight of the secrets of season, the roots of the years and the
>   fruits,
> His soul is at one with the reason of things that is sap to the roots.
> He can hear in their changes a sound as the conscience of consonant
>   spheres.
> He can see through the years flowing round him the law lying under
>   the years.

Exulting that man is free from superstition, Swinburne proclaims that the anthropomorphic God is dead, and the poem closes with "the love-song of earth": "Glory to man in the highest! for Man is the master of things."

This is the positivist "religion of humanity" imbued with the fervor of a fanatic. Translated into analytic prose, it is unmistakably derived from scientific rationalism; but Swinburne's abundant emotion and imagery endow it with prophetic extravagance. *Hertha* is in the same mood, using the Teutonic earth-goddess as a symbol of the primordial force whence all life flows:

> I am that which began;
>   Out of me the years roll;
> Out of me God and man;
>   I am equal and whole;
> God changes, and man, and the form of them bodily; I am the soul.
>
> First life on my sources
>   First drifted and swam;
> Out of me are the forces
>   That save it or damn;
> Out of me man and woman, and wild-beast and bird; before God was,
>   I am.

The poem goes on to illustrate the ubiquity of the force, after the usual mystical manner. Then we are told that men are reaching "the morning of manhood" and casting off "the Gods of their fashion"; being responsible for all things, it was this life-spirit that "set the shadow called God in your skies to give light," but now man is evolving beyond it. As component parts of the great life-tree, men are immortal; but the gods are worms in the bark, and perish. The great process of growth, going on eternally, is the sole "guerdon" of existence. Man's part is to further this growth by independence: "the lives of my children made perfect with freedom of soul were my fruits." Man need not pray to Hertha, he need only be free. The parasitic God that man made is stricken, and truth and love prevail. Man is at one with the universal spirit that brought him forth.

Inspired by precisely the same fact, Arnold and Swinburne reacted in diametrically opposite manners. In the discarding of orthodox faith, Arnold saw uncertainty, futility, and loss of confidence in supernatural protection; Swinburne saw progress, emancipation, and escape from fear of supernatural vengeance. Science had set the mind free in the vastitudes of space; Arnold felt that it revealed man's impotence, and Swinburne that it revealed his omnipotence. Both conclusions, being based on materialistic assumptions, were unsatisfactory to Tennyson and Browning, who clung to belief in God and immortality.

In the foregoing poems of Arnold and Swinburne may be found seminally most of the ideas which were expanded by the next important poets of the evolutionary theme, George Meredith and Thomas Hardy. As in the case of Arnold and Swinburne, the two poets, owing to temperamental differences, move from identical premises to incompatible conclusions. Both saw that the old supernaturalism was inadequate to explain evolution, and both saw that some metaphysical system of explanation was necessary. Meredith agreed with Arnold that the orthodox God was a product of man's selfish desire for an external power to blame or entreat; Hardy agreed with Swinburne that the orthodox God was defunct. To replace him, they both undertook to develop a system out of the evolutionary theory itself.

Meredith accepted the idea of *Hertha*, that the cause of the human race is the highest thing in life, and that in the survival of the race the individual finds his immortality. Being essentially a nature poet, Meredith believed in an indwelling power in nature which made for progress, with man's assistance. Hardy accepted the idea of *Empedocles on Etna*, that if there is an invisible power it is a blind and limited one which cannot successfully carry out its designs. Being essentially a poet of fatalism, Hardy believed that progress was an illusion and that the primal force was merely a ceaseless craving for change in manifestation, unconscious of direction. Thus the two moods of Arnold and Swinburne, loosely labeled "pessimism" and "optimism," are reproduced in Hardy and Meredith.

By the nineties the period of evolutionary excitement in English poetry was at an end. Tennyson's late poems expressed a pantheistic creed in which the fact of evolution was accepted, with the corollary that its cruelties would be recompensed in a future spiritual development, and that progress was directed by God. Browning had died in his belief that the onward struggle was the greatest thing in this life and would continue in the next. Arnold had long abandoned poetry, and Swinburne had gradually modified the violence of his opinions until they practically vanished. Meredith and Hardy had given definite form to their systems in which the evolutionary theory was fundamental, and were merely elaborating them. The younger poets either adopted the Tennysonian pantheism or took the evolutionary principle for granted as an accepted phenomenon needing no discussion. The great shift in poetic outlook had been accomplished, and the poets were free to go back to some of the other topics of poetry which had been virtually neglected for a season. The mantle of prophecy and exegesis was laid aside, and the confraternity rather ostentatiously returned to the cultivation of its garden.

Thus the assimilating of the evolutionary idea appears as one of the chief currents of poetic thought during the Victorian era. Nowhere else, probably, can be found a more interesting illustration of the connection between poetic thought and contemporaneous developments in other spheres. * * *

GEORGE LEVINE

Darwin among the Novelists (1988)†

Of the great nineteenth-century scientists, Darwin is the one whose impact on nonscientific culture is best known, or at least most widely discussed. *The Origin of Species* and *The Descent of Man* have revolutionized the ways we imagine ourselves within the natural world and have raised

† From *Darwin and the Novelists* (Cambridge, Mass.: Harvard University Press, 1988). George Levine (b. 1931) is Kenneth Burke Professor of English and director of the Center for the Critical Analysis of Contemporary Culture at Rutgers University.

fundamental questions about the nature of self, society, history, and religion; and it did not take a scientist to know that this was happening. Obviously, Darwin's revolution was not single-handed, but he can be taken as the figure through whom the full implications of the developing authority of scientific thought began to be felt by modern nonscientific culture. Darwin's theory thrust the human into nature and time, and subjected it to the same dispassionate and material investigations hitherto reserved for rocks and stars. His history of the development of species gave authoritative form to a new narrative—or set of narratives—that has permanently reshaped the Western imagination. Darwin has transformed reality for us and, as Gillian Beer has put it, "We pay Darwin the homage of our assumptions."[1]

* * *

What I am after is a sort of gestalt of the Darwinian imagination, a gestalt detectable in novels as well as in science; and no simple list of "Darwinian" ideas will quite suffice to evoke it. Nevertheless, the Darwinian gestalt includes several clearly identifiable ideas, whose presence might be recognized anywhere, and certain fundamental attitudes toward science and toward the study of life that, if not exclusively Darwinian, were essential to Darwin's project. These ideas recur throughout the arguments of this book, and it will be useful here briefly to intimate what they are, how they work within Darwin's argument, and how they manifest themselves in the fiction.

The human subject. Part of the Darwinian enterprise was to create a theory that would be recognized as "scientific" within already acceptable terms for science, which Darwin had found most attractively formulated in John Herschel's *Preliminary Discourse on the Study of Natural Philosophy* (1830). What made Darwin's work problematic both for lay and scientific culture at the time was the attempt to apply scientific procedures appropriate to stars and chemicals to biological phenomena, and particularly to the "human": "Precisely because he was extending science into an area that his contemporaries thought unsuitable," writes Peter Bowler, "he was determined to minimize the risk of being criticized on grounds of inadequate methodology."[2] That is, the very attempt to be scientifically conservative was a radical act, and this doubleness is characteristic of the Darwinian imagination, and is implicit in even the most conservative nineteenth-century narrative. The patient, ostensibly detached registration of human character and behavior is an aspect of the Darwinian ethos central to the experience of the Victorian novel; it is part of a movement describing a new place for man in nature and tends to imply an ultimately material explanation for human behavior. As is evident in George Eliot's self-conscious commitment to the "natural history" of agrarian life, it is

1. Gillian Beer, *Darwin's Plots: Evolutionary Narrative in Darwin, George Eliot, and Nineteenth-Century Fiction* (London, 1983), 5. Beer's study is the classic consideration of Darwin as writer and as disseminator of literary myths.
2. Peter Bowler, *Evolution: The History of an Idea* (Berkeley: University of California Press, 1984), p. 160.

potentially disruptive of established social and moral categories.[3] * * *

Observation. The authority of science and its extension from natural phenomena to human was both a condition of Darwin's enterprise, and its consequence. The Baconian shift from traditional authority to the authority of experience (qualified by the self-conscious purgation of the idols that distort experience) was almost official dogma in the early nineteenth century, not least for Darwin himself. While recent study of Darwin makes clear that he was anything but a true Baconian in practice—"his entire scientific accomplishment must be attributed not to the collection of facts, but to the development of theory"[4]—Darwin expressly insisted on the accumulation of facts, most notoriously in his *Autobiography*. His work, with its sometimes disingenuous style of patient and plodding detail, helped foster the illusion that the power of science, and hence its authority, lay in its self-denying surrender to observed fact.

Only the establishment of an authority alternative to religious tradition made it rhetorically possible to extend the rule of science to the human. And that authority was a rigorously defined "experience" to be achieved through disinterested observation and experiment. Observation is the power that opens up the fact and subdues it into knowledge, and the disinterested observer is the true scientist. In nineteenth-century realist narrative not only is observation the primary source of the materials of the story, but the observer and the act of observation become increasingly the focus as much as the means of attention. The omniscient author convention—with its apparently unself-conscious directness of representation—does not inevitably treat the novelist's and narrator's activity of observation as unproblematic, and even when it seems to, it raises the problems of observation by filling narratives with unreliable spectators. It has become a commonplace of modern thought that the capacity to know is a form of power, as is evident in Fanny's story in *Mansfield Park* and in figures like Dickens's Jaggers and Tulkinghorn. The trick, as Darwin's own self-effacing strategies attest, is to avoid the exposure and thus the vulnerability that the act of observing normally if ironically entails. The peculiar Darwinian wrinkle in the scientific preoccupation with observation is that the observer becomes vulnerable, particularly because—as Darwin extends the rule of science from inorganic to organic phenomena—the observer also becomes the observed.

Uniformitarianism. I have already discussed briefly some aspects of this idea in its crossover from science to fiction. Novels as much as geology depended on the apparent plausibility conferred by the idea that all events

---

3. But in her famous essay "The Natural History of German Life," an important theoretical locus for these ideas, George Eliot is still looking to scientific detachment to provide moral sympathy by making us aware of the other. Here connections among art, social science, and evolutionary science are formulated, and here the ideal of a nontheoretical inductive approach to the phenomena of social life is adumbrated in ways that obviously influenced her novel writing: "The thing for mankind to know is, not what are the motives and influences which the moralist thinks *ought* to act on the labourer or the artisan, but what are the motives and influences which *do* act on him" (*Essays of George Eliot*, ed. Thomas Pinney, New York: Columbia University Press, 1963, p. 271). The tradition of "natural history" in Riehl's sense is part of the ethos that fed into Darwinian theory and assimilated it quickly to anthropology.
4. Michael Ghiselin, *The Triumph of the Darwinian Method* (Chicago: University of Chicago Press, 1969; repr., 1984), p. 4.

can be explained causally, and by causes now in operation, and that extremes are to be regarded as the consequence of the gradual accumulation of the ordinary. Lyell's uniformitarianism was meant as a sanction for secular scientific explanation against biblical authority. In its purest form, Darwinism broke from Lyell's essentially antihistorical position and implied development but without teleology. The central tradition of Victorian realism—as we can see it in such different writers as Eliot and Trollope—adopts that form, although the pressure of teleological thinking can be detected in that tradition, just as it can in Darwin's own writing. Dickens tended to find thoroughgoing gradualism inadequate and often implied through his narratives the possibility of causes outside the secular. His complex relation to this idea is an important register of the culture's ambivalence about Darwinism and about the extension of scientific study to human history; and it suggests some of the limitations and contradictions within the realist project.

*   *   *

Change and history. Obviously, the theme of change did not need Darwin to invent it. But in his world *everything* is always or potentially changing, and nothing can be understood without its history. Species, which had been conceived as permanent, transform into other species or are extinguished. The earth and all of its local ecological conditions are shifting. Traditionally, the more things change, the less "real"—that is, ideal —they are, the more corrupt and corrupting. But in submitting all things to time, Darwin challenged the ideals of a permanent substratum of nature and of permanent categories of thought. Categories become fictions, historical and conventional constructions, mere stopgaps subject to the empirical. In realist narrative change and development become both subject and moral necessity, and they tend to be as well a condition of plausibility; character can only be understood fully if its history is known because character, as George Eliot wrote, is not "cut in marble," and it is intricately embedded in "plot." Moreover, closure is perceived as artificial and inadequate because it implies an end to history and is incapable of resolving the problems raised by the narrative. Conventional comic marriages are subjected to ironies of time and are often explicitly treated, as by Thackeray, as mere conveniences that allow books to end. The alternative tradition, as in a novel like *Jane Eyre* or in some of Dickens, provides closure and appropriate resolution to what has preceded. Here again, the most obvious and "natural" aspects of fiction turn out to belong to a particular historical formation, and one that operates with great force theoretically and substantively in Darwin's theory.

Blurring of boundaries. The continuum of time is, in Darwin's world, an aspect of the continuum of life itself and of all other sharply defined categories. The boundaries between species and varieties blur, and the further Darwin carries his investigations the more this is the case. All living things in Darwin's world are quite literally related, and, as he will say in a variety of ways, graduate into each other. Isolated perfection is impossible, and science and fiction both concern themselves with mixed conditions. Fiction's emphasis on the ordinary and the everyday, its aversion to traditional forms of heroism and to earlier traditions of character "types," all reflect the tendency obvious in Darwin's world to deny permanent identities or sharply defined categories—even of good and evil. Note how rarely in Trollope or, more programatically, in Eliot, genuinely evil characters appear. Typical stories are of decline or of development; the case in Dickens, of course, is quite different. Character tends increasingly to be a condition of time and circumstance rather than of "nature." In Dickens, the tension between these two ways of imagining is reflected in his attempts to move in his later novels from characters whose natures are fixed to characters who, like Pip, appear to develop. Change, in Dickens's world, nevertheless tends to be radical and "catastrophic," rather than gradual; like Dombey, rather than like Pip.

   Connections—ecological and geneaolgical. Darwin's world is, as the famous last extended metaphor of the *Origin* puts it, a "tangled bank." All living things are related in intricate and often subtle patterns of inheritance, cousinship, mutual dependence. Adaptation of organism to environment is not, as in natural theology, a consequence of a divine fiat, but a result of history—of organic and environmental changes. To discuss the life and nature of any organism requires discussion of the many others with whom it struggles, on whom it depends, in seemingly endless chains of connection. Victorian realist narratives equally entail complex and intricately inwoven stories of many figures so that it is often difficult to determine which characters are the true protagonists, which the subordinate ones. The Victorian multiplot novel is a fictional manifestation of the attitudes implicit in the metaphor of entanglement in Darwin. Such entanglement is an aspect of the gradualism discussed earlier and reflects a distrust of abrupt intrusions from outside the system such as one might find in "metaphysical" fictions like *Jane Eyre* or *Wuthering Heights*, whose narratives are also sharply focused on a small, defined set of characters.

   Abundance. The ecological vision is connected with a view of a world bursting with life, always threatening overpopulation. In Darwin's world survival ultimately depends on variation and diversification, multiplicity of life and of kinds, some of which, from the vast and continuing waste and competition, will survive. Absence of diversity means vulnerability to change, and change is similarly a condition of life. The overpopulated worlds of the Victorian novel, those "large, loose baggy monsters," as James called them, are narrative equivalents of Darwin's "endless forms, most beautiful, most wonderful." Like Darwin's theory itself, they reflect the Victorian taste for excess in ornamentation, the Victorian sense of a newly crowded and complicated life in which there were new opportunities for variety in possessions, art, relationships.

   Denial of design and teleology. The Darwinian narrative unfolds "naturally," that is, without external intrusion. It is, as it were, self-propelled, unfolding according to laws of nature with no initiating intention and no ultimate objective. Adaptation, a key element in Darwinian as in natural-theological thought, seemed to imply design and intention, but Darwin had to show that it was merely "natural." His rejection of the natural-theological assumption of teleology fundamentally undercut the basis of most Western narrative. In the realist novel itself, certain conventional elements continue, willy-nilly, to imply teleology, but the movement is very clearly away from "plot"; and the Trollopean determination to focus on characters and to let the plot emerge from their encounters is a characteristically Darwinian way to deal with narrative and change. The characters, like Darwinian organisms, learn to adapt to their environments. The explanation of that adaptation is not metaphysical but "natural," and the emphasis on psychology is a means to explanation.[5] In character-oriented narrative, the events appear "natural"; they grow from the posited conditions of the fictional world and do not seem to be imposed by the author. This Jamesian ideal was implicit in the realistic narratives James often criticized, and it disguised well the romance or mythic elements that Northrop Frye suggests are the ultimate source of all literary narrative. The growing nineteenth-century dissatisfactions with closure—the most marked and inevitable feature of "plotting"—are further reflections of this Darwinian movement away from teleology and, as I have suggested, toward a new kind of emphasis on continuing change.

Mystery and order. In the multitudinous and entangled Darwinian world, order is not usually detectable on the surface, but the apparent disorder of nature is explicable to the keen observer in terms of general laws that can be inferred from phenomena. Similarly, the world of the realistic novel tends to be explanatory and analytic, showing that behavior is psychologically explicable and that events are "probable," that is, consistent with what might be regarded as empirical law, even if not strictly logical. Darwin's science aspired to the regularity of physics and astronomy, but in its biological preoccupation with individual differences could not achieve that. Nevertheless, Darwin demonstrates the regularity and comprehensibility of phenomena without reducing them to the strict form of logic and mathematics. On the contrary, "metaphysical" fiction, corresponding to the modes of natural theology, tends to be very strictly and rationally ordered. (The symmetries of *Wuthering Heights* are perhaps the most obvious example.) But no rational explanation can account for the order. Some force beyond nature is required. Full evidence for Darwin's theory is not immediately available, but the mysteries can be filled in by induction and extrapolation from the observable. In realistic fiction, similarly, mystery is merely a temporary gap in knowledge (despised by Trollope), but in metaphysical fiction, as in natural theology, mystery is the effect of a spiritual and inexplicable intrusion or initiation from outside of nature.

Chance. Darwin abjured chance but required it for his argument. Minute chance transformations are the source of all variations (Darwin could not explain the mechanism although he ventured a distinctly unsuccessful theory of "gemmules" later in his career), which are the first steps in speciation. Realism is programatically antagonistic to chance, but like Darwin almost inevitably must use it to resolve its narrative problems. The complications of chance in Darwin's theory and in narrative will require

5. J. Hillis Miller, in *The Forms of Victorian Fiction* (South Bend, Ind.: University of Notre Dame, 1968), talks about the way "intersubjectivity" displaces divine ordering in the Victorian novel. Psychology is the secular-scientific alternative to religious explanation of the human social and moral condition.

extensive discussion (and speculation), but it is important to note that like Darwinian theory, realism tends to depend on the smallest of events and on psychological minutiae for its stories and for change within those stories. Moreover, chance encounters seem like intrusions from another mode when they occur in realistic narratives. By contrast, in "metaphysical" fiction chance and coincidence play important roles, though almost invariably they seem not an intrusion from another mode but evidence of design and meaning in the world.

* * *

Darwin was more complex, more prodigiously inventive as a thinker than could ever be detected in a discussion that isolates some of his ideas and transplants them into other forms. It is my aim to shadow forth a Darwin more disruptive, perhaps, than even the greatest of his literary followers can suggest, a Darwin who, if fully absorbed by his contemporary novelists, might well have led to other kinds of narratives. In any case, the discussion of Darwin should make it possible to sustain in the readings that follow something of a double vision—of the Darwin whose imagination could not be contained in conventional narrative form, and of the Darwin who helped shape late-century narrative form and became a conservative political and literary force.

* * *

Either way, within the more comforting terms of mid-Victorian realism or the increasingly disruptive forms of the later century, the two Darwins have, whether we like it or not, transformed the way we can think about reality, about the way we exist in time, about what, after all, is possible. However bleakly Darwin's vision settled on a culture unprepared for the supremacy of natural explanation, he offered us—still offers—a vision of abundance, possibility, and life in which, as he says, there is "grandeur." Darwin provides the framework for a way of thinking about life in time that is still the primary antagonist to modern and Foucauldian views that argue for discontinuity and disruption (although, as will become clear, Darwinian thought is partly responsible for the development of those views).

JOSEPH WOOD KRUTCH

The Tragic Fallacy (1929)†

* * *

Three centuries lay between the promulgation of the Copernican theory and the publication of the *Origin of Species*, but in sixty-odd years which have elapsed since that latter event the blows have fallen with a rapidity

---

† From "The Tragic Fallacy" and "The Genesis of a Mood" in *The Modern Temper: A Study and a Confession.* Copyright © 1929 by Harcourt, Inc. and renewed 1956 by Joseph Wood Krutch. Reprinted by permission of the publisher. Joseph Wood Krutch (1893–1970) was a naturalist and literary critic.

which left no interval for recovery. The structures which are variously known as mythology, religion, and philosophy, and which are alike in that each has as its function the interpretation of experience in terms which have human values, have collapsed under the force of successive attacks and shown themselves utterly incapable of assimilating the new stores of experience which have been dumped upon the world. With increasing completeness science maps out the pattern of nature, but the latter has no relation to the pattern of human needs and feelings.

Consider, for example, the plight of ethics. Historical criticism having destroyed what used to be called by people of learning and intelligence "Christian Evidences," and biology having shown how unlikely it is that man is the recipient of any transcendental knowledge, there remains no foundation in authority for ideas of right and wrong; and if, on the other hand, we turn to the traditions of the human race, anthropology is ready to prove that no consistent human tradition has ever existed. Custom has furnished the only basis which ethics have ever had, and there is no conceivable human action which custom has not at one time justified and at another condemned. Standards are imaginary things, and yet it is extremely doubtful if man can live well, either spiritually or physically, without the belief that they are somehow real. Without them society lapses into anarchy and the individual becomes aware of an intolerable disharmony between himself and the universe. Instinctively and emotionally he is an ethical animal. No known race is so low in the scale of civilization that it has not attributed a moral order to the world, because no known race is so little human as not to suppose a moral order so innately desirable as to have an inevitable existence. It is man's most fundamental myth, and life seems meaningless to him without it. Yet, as that systematized and cumulative experience which is called science displaces one after another the myths which have been generated by need, it grows more and more likely that he must remain an ethical animal in a universe which contains no ethical element. * * *

And yet, nevertheless, the idea of nobility is inseparable from the idea of tragedy, which cannot exist without it. If tragedy is not the imitation or even the modified representation of noble actions it is certainly a representation of actions *considered* as noble, and herein lies its essential nature, since no man can conceive it unless he is capable of believing in the greatness and importance of man. Its action is usually, if not always, calamitous, because it is only in calamity that the human spirit has the opportunity to reveal itself triumphant over the outward universe which fails to conquer it; but this calamity in tragedy is only a means to an end and the essential thing which distinguishes real tragedy from those distressing modern works sometimes called by its name is the fact that it is in the former alone that the artist has found himself capable of considering and of making us consider that his people and his actions have that amplitude and importance which make them noble. Tragedy arises then when, as in Periclean Greece or Elizabethan England, a people fully aware of the calamities of life is nevertheless serenely confident of the greatness of man, whose mighty passions and supreme fortitude are revealed when one of these calamities overtakes him.

To those who mistakenly think of it as something gloomy or depressing, who are incapable of recognizing the elation which its celebration of human greatness inspires, and who, therefore, confuse it with things merely miserable or pathetic, it must be a paradox that the happiest, most vigorous, and most confident ages which the world has ever known—the Periclean and the Elizabethan—should be exactly those which created and which most relished the mightiest tragedies; but the paradox is, of course, resolved by the fact that tragedy is essentially an expression, not of despair, but of the triumph over despair and of confidence in the value of human life. If Shakespeare himself ever had that "dark period" which his critics and biographers have imagined for him, it was at least no darkness like that bleak and arid despair which sometimes settles over modern spirits. In the midst of it he created both the elemental grandeur of Othello and the pensive majesty of Hamlet and, holding them up to his contemporaries, he said in the words of his own Miranda, "Oh, rare new world that hath *such* creatures in it." * * *

It is, indeed, only at a certain stage in the development of the realistic intelligence of a people that the tragic faith can exist. A naïver people may have, as the ancient men of the north had, a body of legends which are essentially tragic, or it may have only (and need only) its happy and child-like mythology which arrives inevitably at its happy end, where the only ones who suffer "deserve" to do so and in which, therefore, life is represented as directly and easily acceptable. A too sophisticated society on the other hand—one which, like ours, has outgrown not merely the simple optimism of the child but also that vigorous, one might almost say adolescent, faith in the nobility of man which marks a Sophocles or a Shakespeare, has neither fairy tales to assure it that all is always right in the end nor tragedies to make it believe that it rises superior in soul to the outward calamities which befall it.

Distrusting its thought, despising its passions, realizing its impotent unimportance in the universe, it can tell itself no stories except those which make it still more acutely aware of its trivial miseries. When its heroes (sad misnomer for the pitiful creatures who people contemporary fiction) are struck down it is not, like Oedipus, by the gods that they are struck but only, like Oswald Alving, by syphilis, for they know that the gods, even if they existed, would not trouble with them, and they cannot attribute to themselves in art an importance in which they do not believe. Their so-called tragedies do not and cannot end with one of those splendid calamities which in Shakespeare seem to reverberate through the universe, because they cannot believe that the universe trembles when their love is, like Romeo's, cut off or when the place where they (small as they are) have gathered up their trivial treasure is, like Othello's sanctuary, defiled. Instead, mean misery piles on mean misery, petty misfortune follows petty misfortune, and despair becomes intolerable because it is no longer even significant or important. * * *

HERBERT J. MULLER

Modern Tragedy (1956)†

* * *

In *The Experimental Novel* Zola argued that the novelist should give fiction the validity of a scientific experiment by operating objectively on his characters in a given situation, just as scientists operated in the laboratory. Although we need not take this theory seriously, the early naturalists did adopt the method of close, impersonal observation and analysis—"the modern method," as Zola proclaimed—and with it the mechanistic, deterministic doctrine of nineteenth-century science. Habitually they demonstrated that men were victims of their heredity and environment.

The theory of naturalism is plainly disastrous for tragedy. If man is merely a creature of brute compulsion, in no sense a free, responsible agent, his story can have no dignity or ideal significance of any sort. It is not clear why the naturalists should have had such a passion for telling this story. But as their passion suggests, their practice was often inconsistent and impure. The mixed consequences of naturalism may be illustrated by two playwrights—August Strindberg and Gerhardt Hauptmann. * * *

Strindberg describes Miss Julia as a type of "man-hating half-woman" that may have existed in all ages, but has now come to the fore and begun to make a noise. In other plays, notably *The Father* and *The Dance of Death*, the battle of the sexes is still more desperate and elemental; man and wife fight to the death. Strindberg conceived this as Darwinian tragedy. To those who complained that it was too cruel and heartless he replied: "I find the joy of life in its violent and cruel struggles." A milder and perhaps fairer statement of his credo is this: "The true naturalism is that which seeks out those points in life where the great conflicts occur, which loves to see that which cannot be seen every day, rejoices in the battle of elemental powers, whether they be called love or hatred, revolt or sociability; which cares not whether a subject be beautiful or ugly, if only it is great." It was presumably the "greatness" of his conflicts that led Shaw to call Strindberg "the only genuinely Shakespearean modern dramatist."

For his distinctive purposes Strindberg originated a brilliant, if un-Shakespearean technique. Its essence is a fierce concentration. He reduced his cast to a minimum, usually three or four characters. He not only observed the unities but sought ideally a continuous action, without act intermissions. He confined himself to a single set on an almost bare stage, with the fewest possible props; in *The Father* he needed only a lamp and a strait jacket. Especially in this play he achieved a terrific intensity. In general, there is no denying the genius of Strindberg, and the unique power of his naturalistic drama. * * *

But we do not have a great tragic dramatist. Strindberg's naturalistic

† From chapter 6 of *The Spirit of Tragedy* (New York: Random House, 1956). Herbert J. Muller (1905–1980) was distinguished professor of English at Indiana University.

drama is the clearest illustration of Krutch's dismal thesis. The neurotic Miss Julia is much too mean to be a tragic figure; at most she stirs some pity—more than Strindberg intended, if we take him at his own word—in her utter bafflement. The heroes of his other tragedies are generally stronger, or at least fiercer, but no more admirable. They fight the battle of the sexes with an insane violence and mercilessness. Their madness is not, as with Hamlet and Lear, the result of their tragic experience—it is the mainspring of the tragedy. Though they illustrate the pathological extremes to which men are liable, the hell men can make of life, they are much too abnormal to represent the tragic fate of Man. * * *

At least the naturalists did not simply degrade man. Generally they tended to widen sympathies, create new values in literature. If the tragedy of low life has limited significance, high tragedy may also limit our awareness by accustoming us to an exalted realm where is enacted not the story of Man but of the heroic few. "As for our grand sorrows," remarked a simple woman in Santayana's *The Last Puritan*, "they are a parcel of our common humanity, like funerals; and the Lord designs them for our good to wean our hearts from this sad world. . . . And it's almost a pleasure to grieve, all hung in weeds, like a weeping willow. But the price of eggs, Mr. Oliver, the price of eggs!" Another reason why tragedy gives us pleasure is that it makes us forget the price of eggs, delivers us from all the petty, nagging, humiliating cares that we can never escape in life. No doubt this is all to the good, since we can count on having enough cares. But as Karl Jaspers observed in *Tragedy Is Not Enough*, the glamour of tragedy may obscure the appalling realities of human misery: the hopeless, helpless misery that the masses of men have always known; misery without greatness, without dignity, without any decent meaning whatever; misery that seems more intolerable because men have always tolerated it. We have no right to demand of artists that they treat such misery. As we value the tragic spirit and its essential humanity, we have no right either to condemn the naturalists who did treat it. * * *

Meanwhile most men in the West, including Christians, are still committed on principle as well as in practice to the humanistic belief in the value of life on earth, and of human enterprise to improve this life. They cannot accept the traditional Eastern wisdom of passivity, resignation, or renunciation, nor the traditional Christian view that the whole meaning and value of life derive from the life to come. They may agree with Reinhold Neibuhr that free reason, imagination, creativity—man's distinctive gifts and the source of his highest achievements—are also the source of all evil, which is therefore ineradicable; but like him they do not propose to cut the costs by discouraging the exercise of these gifts. In the democracies most are still committed, more specifically, to a belief in the values of freedom and individuality, the right of a man to a mind and a life of his own. And these distinctively Western beliefs, which gave rise to the tragic spirit, make it all the more relevant in a time of crisis.

To me, the tragic sense is the deepest sense of our humanity, and therefore spiritual enough. But all men may profit from it, whatever their faith. It is certainly valid as far as it goes, or this life goes. It sizes up the very reasons for religious faith, the awful realities that men must face up to if

their faith is to be firm, mature, and responsible. It also makes for sensi-
tiveness to the tragic excesses of all faiths, the inevitable corruptions of all
ideals—in the West, more particularly, to the rugged, irresponsible individualism that has battened on the ideal of freedom, and the bigotry and
self-righteousness that have flourished in the name of Jesus. It may deepen
the sense of community that has been one end of religion. The tragic
writer may most nearly realize the ideal mission of the artist stated by
Joseph Conrad:

> He speaks to our capacity for delight and wonder, to the sense of
> mystery surrounding our lives; to our sense of pity, and beauty, and
> pain; to the latent feeling of fellowship with all creation—and to the
> subtle but invincible conviction of solidarity that knits together the
> loneliness of innumerable hearts, to the solidarity in dreams, in joy,
> in sorrow, in aspirations, in illusions, in hope, in fear, which binds
> men to each other, which binds together all humanity—the dead to
> the living and the living to the unborn.

For the many who are unable to believe that man was specially created
in the image of God, and guaranteed that his earthly history will be con-
summated in eternity, herein may be the most available means—beyond
animal faith—to spiritual acceptance and order, in a society that has lost
its simple faith in progress but nevertheless remains committed to the
belief that "something ought to be done" about all our problems, and can
be. The tragic spirit can promote a saving irony, in the perception of the
naïve or absurd aspects of this belief; a spirit of compassion, through the
knowledge of irremediable evils and insoluble dilemmas; and a spirit of
reverence, for the idealism that keeps seeking truth, goodness, and beauty
even though human ideals are not everlasting. It is proof of the dignity of
man, which remains a basic tenet of Western democracy. It is now perhaps
the strongest proof because of the very realism, in modern thought and
art, that has commonly led to a devaluation of man and nature.

At its best, the realistic spirit is itself a value, and a source of further
values. It has meant tough-mindedness, the courage and honesty to admit
that we really do not know all that we would like to know, and that most
men have passionately claimed to know. In modern science it has meant
the admission that our most positive, reliable knowledge of the physical
universe is approximate, tentative, hypothetical, and that we cannot know
the final, absolute truth about it: a respect for both fact and mystery that
gives a pathetic air to the religious thinkers who have leaped to the odd
conclusion that this admission of ultimate uncertainty proves the certainty
of religious truth. In literature, realism as a technique has often meant
superficiality, meagerness, fragmentariness, confusion; but as a controlling
attitude it has also toughened the tragic faith. From Ibsen to Sartre, as
from Hardy to Malraux, many writers have not only reasserted the dignity
of the human spirit but proved its strength by holding fast in uncertainty,
or even in the conviction that there is no power not ourselves making for
righteousness. Although they cannot readily create heroes with the stature
and symbolical significance of the ancient heroes, they may exhibit or
exemplify a humbler, more difficult kind of heroism that may be more

significant for our living purposes. They no longer leave the worst enemy in the rear.

All this necessarily falls far short of any promise of salvation, and so brings us back to "reality." The spirit of tragedy can never deliver us from tragedy. It cannot take the place of religion. Even in literature it cannot give us the kind of exaltation that some critics now soar to under the spell of Myth. In *The Timeless Theme*, for instance, Colin Still argues that the Living Art of all humanity, like all "authentic" myth and true religion, has "but one essential theme, namely: the Fall of the human Soul and the means of its Redemption." In irony one may remark that he proves his thesis by the easy expedient of dismissing art that lacks this theme as not authentic or living (even though it happens to have lived for a thousand years or so), and that he makes it still easier by asserting that this timeless truth can be grasped only by the Spirit, which most scholars and critics lack. In reverence one should acknowledge that this has in fact been a major theme in Western literature, and that it is the most inspiring theme to many men of good will. In truthfulness one must add that tragedy has had no such uniform, timeless theme, beyond the realities of suffering and death. Modern tragedy is particularly deficient in Spirit; it seldom exhibits or promises Redemption. At most it may help to redeem us from fear or despair, or from the vanity of cheap hopes.

I can conclude on no more exalted note than a verse of Thomas Hardy: "If way to the Better there be, it exacts a full look at the Worst." Come the worst, the survivors of atomic war—if any—will have little stomach for tragedy. Come the better, in something like One World, there will still be sufficient reason for pity and terror, and many more men to experience it with more intensity. The East is now stirring with the willful Western spirit, demanding more of the goods of this world. Tragedy might at last become a universal form, and redeem all the critics who have written so solemnly about its universal and eternal truths. But if so, it will be because the rest of the world has taken a fuller look at the worst, and is no longer resigned to the eternal verities, no longer content to surrender to the will of its gods.

PHILIP APPLEMAN

Darwin-Sightings in Recent Literature (2000)†

1

Writers have been intrigued by science ever since Copernicus and Galileo stunned the seventeenth-century poets with the revelation that the sun and the earth had switched places—the sun at the center and the earth spinning around it—causing John Donne to lament:

> The Sun is lost, and th'earth, and no man's wit
> Can well direct him where to looke for it.

† First published in this Norton Critical Edition.

In the eighteenth century, Newton's *Opticks* prompted Alexander Pope to write:

> God said, "Let Newton be!" and all was light.

And in the early nineteenth century, Lyell's *Geology* inspired some of the most familiar lines of Tennyson's *In Memoriam*:

> The hills are shadows, and they flow
> From form to form, and nothing stands;
> They melt like mist, the solid lands,
> Like clouds they shape themselves and go.

Late nineteenth century authors were also captivated by science, as indicated in the other essays in this part. After the publication of the *Origin of Species* in 1859, evolution was recognized as a compelling new scientific idea that writers, like all Victorians, felt obliged to assimilate. And evolution has continued to inform fiction, poetry, and drama, ever since.

Darwin's complex personality has also proved intriguing to writers—the energetic, strapping young man who in midlife suffered from a mysterious, chronic, and debilitating illness; the respectable family man who toppled the sacred and established truths of his bourgeois society; the advocate of a strict "Baconian induction" who dared to risk speculating boldly about human origins, and then pinned his speculation firmly to fact. Altogether, Darwin has proved to be a literary subject too compelling to resist.

The *Beagle* voyage and the Galapagos experience have also intrigued writers of every genre, no doubt because they occasioned the most dramatic events in Darwin's life. Kurt Vonnegut's 1995 novel, *Galapagos*, for instance, is set there in 1986 but is narrated by a ghostly visitor from the distant future—by which time a few humans, the only survivors of a technological holocaust, and stranded forever on those inhospitable islands, have lived a life so "natural," for so long, that they have, by natural selection, shed their self-destructive "great big brains" and prehensile fingers and, like otters, have developed flippers and a contented life of underwater fishing. In a parody of Darwin's reasoning, Vonnegut's narrator tells us:

> It was the best fisherfolk who survived in the greatest numbers in the watery environment of the Galapagos Archipelago. Those with hands and feet most like flippers were the best swimmers. Prognathous jaws were better at catching and holding fish than hands could ever be. And any fisherperson, spending more and more time underwater, could surely catch more fish if he or she were more streamlined, more bulletlike—had a smaller skull.

And so the great big brains had to go, and human beings find themselves living unreflectively, like octopi. Which is all to the good, the narrator says, because "I have yet to see an octopus, or any sort of animal, for that matter, which wasn't entirely content to pass its time on earth as a food gatherer, to shun the experiment with unlimited greed and ambition performed by humankind." And thus, a "happy ending" to the human chronicle.

Another recent novel about the Galapagos is Cathleen Schine's *The

Evolution of Jane (1998), which takes place on a nature tour to those islands. Keeping the image of Darwin always hovering in the background, Schine accurately describes both the islands and the staggering scientific —and ultimately philosophical—revelations that were foreshadowed there. Jane, the central character, puts it this way:

> The frightening thing about Darwin is not nature red in tooth and claw. . . . The frightening thing about Darwin is . . . chaos. . . . There is no plan, there never was one. . . . Everyone knows this now. But Darwin knew it first. . . . Darwin met chaos head on. He saw it wandering aimlessly, meaninglessly, shifting and turning without warning through a world in which every creature considered itself the most important and not one of them mattered a whit. . . . Imagine realizing it for the first time, realizing it not just personally, but on behalf of the entire Western world.

Puzzling over a long and unexplained estrangement from Martha, her childhood friend and the guide on this Galapagos tour, Jane discusses it with her schoolteacher cabin mate, who tries to figure it out for her:

> I have my own theory about you and Martha. You see, organisms change over time, individual organisms, and some of the features that are useful to them when they are young are not of any use when they are older, and some features are only of use when they mature and must begin to court and find a mate. . . . That explains Martha. . . . Martha Barlow is a residual organ.

Pursuing such analogies, the novel uses evolution the way some authors use psychology: to investigate a character's personal problems.

Roger McDonald's novel *Mr. Darwin's Shooter* (1999) ranges widely across several continents and of course includes the Galapagos. In this story, Syms Covington, Darwin's assistant on the *Beagle* (who was, according to Janet Browne's detailed biography, "the unacknowledged shadow behind [Darwin's] every triumph"), retains his real name, but becomes a fictional character capable, under Darwin's tutelage, of tracking, shooting, and stuffing zoological specimens. Because of Covington's fundamentalist upbringing, he eventually comes to resent the threat of evolution to his religion. Darwin himself is constantly present in the novel, either in fictional scenes during the *Beagle* years or, later in the book, as a distant eminence casting a long shadow over Covington's life. An ironic twist comes after the voyage, when Covington's own private—and supposedly secret—collection of Galapagos finches is commandeered by the fictional Darwin to support his emerging ideas about speciation.

Andrea Barrett's story "Ship Fever" (from *Ship Fever and Other Stories*, 1996) is set in the present but also calls up the *Beagle* years, with anecdotes about Darwin's visit to Tierra del Fuego:

> Darwin had mused on the story of Jemmy Button [one of the Fuegians whom Captain FitzRoy had earlier brought to England and tried to Christianize]. Think of that. Jemmy Button: captured, exiled, re-educated; then returned, abused by his family, finally re-accepted.

Was he happy? Or was he saying that as a way to spite his captors? Darwin never knew.

Another story in the same volume, called "Soroche," places Alfred Russel Wallace in the Malay Archipelago, collecting specimens and pondering their seemingly infinite variety. Like Darwin twenty years earlier, he asks himself: "What is the method by which species undergo a natural process of gradual extinction and creation? There must be a *mechanism*." And in Barrett's 1998 novel, *The Voyage of the* Narwhal, set in the 1850s just before the *Origin of Species* appeared, she again suffuses the tale with portents of Darwinian thought and uses the name of Charles Darwin's grandfather, Erasmus, as the first name of her central character.

A. S. Byatt's "Morpho Eugenia," one of the novellas in her 1992 book *Angels and Insects*, is set in the early 1860s, just after the publication of the *Origin of Species*, and much is made of the shocking new revelations about human origins. For example, a distressed clergyman "could not abide arguments about male nipples and the rudimentary tail of the human embryo, which saw the [Divine] Creator as a fumbling craftsman who had changed his mind in mid-work." He asks a naturalist, "What do you make of the [religious] argument from beauty? . . . A man admiring a butterfly is more than a brute beast." He obviously expects an easy agreement that our sense of beauty distinguishes us from the other animals, thus indicating our supernatural creation. But instead, he is given this deflating scientific explanation: "Mr. Darwin believes the beauty of the butterfly exists to attract his mate, and the beauty of the orchid is designed to facilitate its fertilisation by the bee."

Naguib Mahfouz, in his 1991 novel, *Palace of Desire*—Part II of his Cairo Trilogy—traces the fundamentalist response to Darwin in a twentieth-century Islamic context. The protagonist, Kamal, an Egyptian college student, trained by his fundamentalist Muslim parents to read the Koran as literal truth, studies poets and philosophers, and eventually Darwin. When his father discovers this, he is outraged: "Darwin's certainly an atheist trapped by Satan's snares. If man's origin was an ape or any other animal, Adam was not the father of mankind. This is nothing but blatant atheism."

Kamal realizes that he has come to a significant passage in his education, and his life: "His faith had held firm over the past two years even when buffeted by gales coming from two of the great poets and skeptics of Islam. . . . But then science's iron fist had destroyed it once and for all."

Finally, however, Kamal manages to reconcile his new experience with his old aspirations.

> By freeing himself from religion he would be nearer to God than he was when he believed. For what was true religion except science? It was the key to the secrets of existence and to everything really exalted. If the prophets were sent back today, they would surely choose science as their divine message. Thus Kamal would awake from the dream of legends to confront the naked truth, leaving behind him this storm in which ignorance had fought to the death.

In my own 1989 novel, *Apes and Angels*, set in the Midwest in 1941, one of the plot lines involves a similar awakening in Paul Anderson, a high school student who has learned about Darwin and evolution in a biology class taught by Elaine Edelman, his most admired teacher. To his dismay, she is fired by the local school board for having discussed evolution in the classroom. Then she is denounced in Paul's church by the fundamentalist preacher, in a fiery sermon:

> "There is a time to gather stones, and a time to kill, Ecclesiastes Three, and when we are finally triumphant in the good fight, we can say to ourselves, in the very words of the Lord God himself, Exodus Twenty-Two: *Thou shalt not suffer a witch to live!*"
>
> Paul could hardly believe what he had seen and heard. As the verses of "Onward, Christian Soldiers" marched by, he tried to sort out his confused thoughts and feelings. What had he become? A dozen years of the Church Militant, Christian Soldiers, a Mighty Fortress, Soldiers of the Cross—what had he become? What might he yet become?
>
> Before the anthem was finished, he put down his hymnal, and as everyone stared, strode up the center aisle. He knew it was for the last time.

T. C. Boyle's "The Descent of Man" (the title story of his 1974 volume), develops the recurrent idea of a primate superior to humans. The narrator tells us he is living with a woman who begins to smell like an ape. "The room would fill with the stink of her, bestial and fetid." It turns out she has developed an intimate relationship with her colleague at the Primate Center, a genius chimpanzee named Konrad, who can communicate "the most esoteric ideas" in American Sign Language; knows English, French, German, and Chinese; is scoring his third opera; has translated Nietzsche; and is working on "a Yerkish[1] translation" of Darwin's *Descent of Man*.

A recent novel based on a similar conceit is Will Self's *Great Apes* (1997), in which, à la Kafka, an artist, Simon Dykes, wakes up to find that he has become a chimpanzee. Unlike Kafka's character, however, he discovers that everyone else is also a chimp. The only humans on earth, he is told, are denizens of the African savanna or are caged in the local zoo, because their habitats have been largely preempted by bonobos—and, according to an editorial preface (by a chimp), there are "as few as 200,000 wild humans left." Humans, he says, have always been fascinating for chimpanzees, adding:

> Early theorists positioned the human midway between the chimpanzee and "brute creation" in the Chain of Being. Latterly, in the wake of Darwin [who is, of course, a chimp], some supposed that the human might prove to be the "missing link."

Chimpanzees, we learn later in the story, have "always used the human as a clownish paradigm. Circus acts often incorporate chimps dressed up as humans, running around bashing into one another . . ." Simon Dykes's

---

1. A reference to the Yerkes Primate Center; see p. 511, n.

belief that he is human, his learned chimp observers assume, is simply "a bad psychotic interlude."

Taking this conceit in a different direction, the Danish novelist Peter Høeg sets his 1996 *The Woman and the Ape* in contemporary London; and the focal character, as in Barrett's *Narwhal*, is named Erasmus, obviously for Darwin's grandfather. Here, however, Erasmus is a super-chimpanzee weighing three hundred muscular pounds. As a rare zoological specimen, a "temperate-zone chimp," he has been captured and caged in a London biological research institute. Erasmus quickly learns to speak English and is secretly befriended by Madelene (the "Woman" of the title), who is the wife of the institute's director. They soon become lovers, then fugitives together when she helps him escape from the institute's deadly experimentation.

Erasmus, as it turns out, has deliberately come to England (with eleven other ape-apostles) on a civilizing mission from the wilds of Denmark— "the forests. Around the Baltic . . . that Danish island farthest to the east" — to try to help a humanity foundering in overpopulation, technological pollution, and greed. To explain how a chimp became such a progressive social thinker, a scientist tells Erasmus (and the reader):

> All things being equal, what one can say is that the more convoluted [the brain] is, the bigger the neocortex, the more intelligent the animal. Your brain . . . is the most convoluted ever seen. With the largest frontal lobe. The greatest volume. . . . Your ancestors, your race, after breaking away from us a million years ago on the shores of Lake Turkana, travelled northwards. And after that you outstripped us. . . . We thought we would learn something about one of those hominids which came before man. But you are not what went before. You are, rather, what comes afterwards.

In the end, all twelve of the apostle apes—with Madelene willingly joining them—go back where they came from, having given up on the hopeless job of saving a recalcitrant "civilization" from its self-destructive behavior.

Evolutionary themes also find their way into drama, in New York and London theaters. One such memorable play on Broadway was Jerome Lawrence and Robert E. Lee's *Inherit the Wind*, loosely based on the 1925 Scopes "monkey trial" (see p. 542); it has often been revived on stage and was also produced as a film. Another movie, the 1968 *Planet of the Apes* —which made its moral points by reversing our human/ape roles—has bred a multitude of film sequels, television series, and other spinoffs, indicating the popular appeal of this idea. In the 1990s, A. S. Byatt's novella "Morpho Eugenia" (see p. 673) was made into a film called *Angels and Insects*. And a number of television documentaries have looked closely at evolution, among them the British Broadcasting Company's mini-series called *The Voyage of Charles Darwin*. Using exotic settings and a host of notable characters, including Darwin and the *Beagle*'s Captain FitzRoy, this TV film effectively dramatized the five momentous years of the voyage, while incorporating Darwin's evolving ideas—thus uniting his physical adventure with his great adventure of the mind.

2

Poets have been as busy as fiction writers in exploring Darwin's life and work. Anne Becker, in her 1996 *The Transmutation Notebooks: Poems in the Voices of Charles and Emma Darwin*, transforms the letters of Darwin and his wife, Emma, into a book of narrative poems, reshaping the original Darwin materials by ellipsis, compression, and conflation. Like many of the Darwinian fiction writers, she finds the Galapagos irresistible. In "Galapagos Archipelago," using one of Darwin's letters home, she writes:

> It was as if in the night our ship had confounded
> ocean and sky, slipped from the surface of the earth,
> sailed out of this world and at dawn had anchored
> on the shore of the moon—the Galapagos. . . .
> Nothing could appear less inviting—but I felt
> I had come home—my chest hummed with a rough thrill
> at the sight of strange land: a broken field
> of black basaltic lava thrown in rugged waves
> like a dark frozen sea, the parched ground cracked
> and fissured, covered with sunburnt brushwood
> like the skeletons of stunted trees.[2]

Like Becker, Alfred Corn relives the experience of Darwin on the *Beagle*; and in a long poem called "Pages from a Voyage" (from *All Roads at Once*, 1976), he too finds poetry in Darwin's own words:

> . . . A journal entry
> From Cape Verde, his first port: "The scene,
> As beheld through the hazy atmosphere
> of this climate, is of great interest;
> If, indeed, a person, fresh from the sea,
> And who has just walked, for the first time,
> In a grove of cocoa-nut trees, can be a judge
> Of anything but his own happiness."[3]

Deborah Digges, watching an ancient tortoise, imagines, in her poem "Tartarchos" (from *Late in the Millennium*, 1989), how both Darwin and a later mariner, Herman Melville:

> . . . within ten years of each other on the Galapagos,
> herded the tortoises into the nets, used them for ballast,
> food for the long trip home, and filled their shells
> with earth, like planets halved . . .[4]

And in "Rock, Scissors, Paper" (from *Rough Music*, 1995), Digges sees a younger Darwin preoccupied with collecting beetles:

> It ended when he popped one of the three of the order
> coleoptera in his mouth. Two hands weren't enough for
> Darwin . . .

2. From *The Transmutation Notebooks*. Used by permission of Anne Becker.
3. From *All Roads at Once* (Counterpoint Press).
4. From *Lake in the Millennium* by Deborah Digges. Copyright © 1989 by Deborah Digges. Reprinted by permission of Alfred A. Knopf, a division of Random House, Inc.

> The beetle bit his tongue, and
>   like the dragon-
> angel Michael, who spit out the fallen world's new genus
> as he waded in an orchard through paradisiacal weeds,
> Darwin spat by a tree and laughed . . .[5]

James Harrison, in his poem "Darwin and the Galapagos" (from *Victorian Studies*, 1996), ponders the meaning of Darwin's visit to those strange shores:

> What was it you discovered
> On these enchanted islands . . .
> Could it have been the consoling
> Surf round these volcanic outbursts that
> Whispered to you nightly how all will be well
> Again and earth shall heal
> When man, hunted down like a forest fire
> By desolation of his own making
> And fast running out of trees,
> Takes up his last
> Stand?[6]

In Elizabeth Bishop's poem "A Miracle for Breakfast" (from *Complete Poems of Elizabeth Bishop*, 1979), an intricate Darwinian allusion occurs in these lines:

> A beautiful villa stood in the sun
> and from its doors came the smell of hot coffee.
> In front, a baroque white plaster balcony
> added by birds, who nest along the river,
> —I saw it with one eye close to the crumb—
> and galleries and marble chambers. My crumb
> my mansion, made for me by a miracle,
> through ages, by insects, birds, and the river
> working the stone.[7]

Interpretating this passage, the poet Anthony Hecht writes in his book *Obbligati* (1986):

> The miracle here I take to be engendered by the minute, close-up inspection of the crumb of bread. . . . The complex intricacies of the "architecture" of the risen dough, its baroque perforations, corridors, its struts, ribs and spans of support, all form the "beautiful villa" with its "white plaster balcony." And this bread, and the vision it provides, have come into existence by the miraculous and infinitely patient workings of that evolutionary process that Darwin (one of Miss Bishop's favorite writers) and other naturalists have so painstakingly recorded.

5. From *Rough Music* by Deborah Digges. Copyright © 1995 by Deborah Digges. Reprinted by permission of Alfred A. Knopf, a division of Random House, Inc.
6. Used by permission of James Harrison.
7. Excerpt from "A Miracle for Breakfast" from *The Complete Poems 1927–29* by Elizabeth Bishop. Copyright © 1979, 1983 by Alice Helen Methfessel. Reprinted by permission of Farrar, Straus and Giroux, LLC.

Philip Schultz returns Darwin to the Galapagos and draws parallels between the scientist's life and his own in a poem called "Darwin, Tortoises, Galapagos Archipelago, & New Hampshire" (from *Like Wings*, 1978):

> Darwin believed it his fate no sooner to discover
> what was most interesting than to leave it; in other words:
> to leave always before being left . . . .
> He pursued the male tortoise through swamps & hot rains
>   toward the female
> who welcomed him by drawing in her head & tail &
>   playing dead.
> He listened to the godawful bellowing that edged her into
>   the light
> & noted that the stench carried over the islands like a
>   sexual wind
> that drew buzzards ecstatic for the white spherical eggs . . .
>   He believed in the instincts of passion
> & the consequence of numbers. In the small act & the
> importance of buzzards; in other words: posterity.[8]

In Gjertrud Schnackenberg's "Darwin in 1881" (from *The Lamplit Answer*, 1985), the poet pictures the aged scientist in his last year, suffering from angina, knowing that death is imminent, but still immersed in the thoughts of a lifetime as he walks his property and returns:

> Up to their room: there
> Emma sleeps, moored
> In illusion, blown past the storm he conjured
> With his book, into a harbor
> Where it all comes clear,
> Where island beings leap from shape to shape
> As to escape
> Their terrifying turns to disappear.
> He lies down on the quilt,
> He lies down like a fabulous-headed
> Fossil in a vanished riverbed,
> In ocean drifts, in canyon floors, in silt,
> In lime, in deepening blue ice,
> In cliffs obscured as clouds gather and float;
> He lies down in his boots and overcoat,
> And shuts his eyes.[9]

Vince Clemente's poem "Darwin at St. Domingo" (from *Girl in the Yellow Caboose*, 1991) is set in a less celebrated area of Darwin's travels, the Cape Verde Islands, where the poet imagines Darwin in the first of his many exotic locales:

> he came upon a choir of black women
> who braided his path with indigo shawls

8. From *Like Wings* (New York: Viking, 1978).
9. Excerpt from "Darwin in 1881" from *Portraits and Elegies* by Gjertrud Schnackenberg. Copyright © 1986 by Gjertrud Schnackenberg. Reprinted by permission of Farrar, Straus and Giroux, LLC.

and then with great energy
droned a wild song
beating time with their hands . . .
I'm sure, though, he heard their song
again and again, and at night
unable to sleep, stars so low
he woke starbruised,
he saw the palms of their dancing hands
rise like forest birds
flushed out of hiding.[1]

Miller Williams, in "How Step by Step We Have Come to Understand" (1999), goes directly to the basic philosophical questions raised by Darwin's revelations:

In the sixteenth century Nicholas Copernicus
told us the earth was a ball and, what was worse,
was not the center of the universe.
"Well and so," we wanted to know,
"where does that leave us in the scheme of things?"

Wherever it left us,
we were just about learning to live with it,
when three centuries later Charles Darwin
grabbed our attention with the news
that we were cousins to the kangaroos.
"And so," we wanted to know,
"where does that leave us in the scheme of things?"[2]

Pursuing these same basic questions, Dorothy Sutton foreshortens Darwin's long and difficult trajectory from observation, to wild surmise, to theory, and finally to philosophical naturalism, in her poem "Darwin's Scope" (from *Startling Art: Darwin and Matisse*, 1999):

To get it right, he had to become an actor,
    listen
to the world's voices as if he had never heard
what they had to say. He saw all the way to the end
and beyond . . .
    transcended
mystery and wonder to what was more awesome still:
the way the earth came into being, facts,
conclusions he did not want to know, revealed,
fossils from an earlier life. He packed
them up and sent them home, crate after crate,
back to England—the bones of his dead faith.[3]

Sensitive to the social overtones of Darwin's work, David Ray, in his poem "Paradise at Dusk" (from *Kangaroo Paws*, 1994), evokes Thomas

1. Used by permission of Vince Clemente.
2. Used by permission of Miller Williams.
3. Used by permission of Dorothy Sutton.

Hobbes's savage state of nature, "the war of all against all." An American poet visiting Australia, Ray recalls the genocidal history of that nation (and, by implication, of the United States):

> These families under the gum trees
> are enjoying Eden, it seems,
> and yet there was a Holocaust here . . .
> Like wallabies, like rabbits,
> the Aborigines were hunted down . . .
> I see their faces now, haunting the town—
> a few standing for so many.
> Their eyes bug out with old fear . . .
> One massacre
> lasts thousands of years . . .
> Paradise
> still burns crimson,
> then the dark falls like a lid.
> Darwin's grasp did not reach so far.[4]

The Browningesque allusion in the final line ("a man's reach should exceed his grasp, / Or what's a heaven for?") pointedly reminds us of the many societal misuses of Darwinisticisms as justification for brutal behavior and ironically links that perennial brutality to the "Paradise" of the title.

Daniel Thomas Moran's poem "Some Call It Love" (from *Sheltered by Islands*, 1995) sets Darwin against tropical jungles that metamorphose into post-Freudian bars and discotheques, putting a contemporary gloss on Darwin's theory of sexual selection:

> In truth, it is only we humans who call it love,
> What the entirety of nature knows as propagation.
> Driven beyond control by endocrine eruptions
> To wild dances of courtship in the shadows
> Of deep green jungles and forests
> And discotheques with ten dollar covers.
> Exploding arrays of manes and plumage
> And pompadours glistening with perfumed lacquer
> Attempting under the over-wound strain of
> Desperate Darwinian overdrive
> To curry the attentions of the ever-reluctant female . . .
> Howling at the moonbeams dripping on the forest floor
> Each creature awaiting the evolution of the headache
> Stalking the bars for the two-martini conquest
> And a chance to find a piece of the happily ever after
> On the high seas aboard the *Beagle* with Darwin
> On a journey through time to a couch in Vienna.[5]

In their responses to Darwin, poets frequently reveal a strong personal identification with him—perhaps because in his writing, Darwin himself is always accessible and contemporary. For example, one of my own books

4. Used by permission of David Ray.
5. Used by permission of Daniel Thomas Moran.

of poetry, *Darwin's Ark*, consists entirely of poems about Darwin and evolution, a few of which serve as epigraphs to various parts of this book. Several show a distinct sense of identification with Darwin, partly because I went to sea in the Merchant Marine when I was twenty-two—coincidentally the same age as Darwin when he went to sea on the *Beagle*—and partly because on one long voyage, I read Darwin for the first time and was deeply affected by his work. One clear example of this personal identification is in my poem called "The Voyage Home" (from *New and Selected Poems, 1956–1996*, 1996). The epigraph to this poem is Darwin's remark, in *The Descent of Man*, that "The social instincts . . . naturally lead to the golden rule"; and the poem concludes with these passages:

> Alone
> on the fantail
> I hear the grind of rigging, and
> Darwin is beside me, leaning on the rail,
> watching the wake go phosphorescent.
> We've been out five years, have seen
> the coral islands, the dark skins
> of Tahiti; I have questions.
> "Darwin," I whisper, "tell me now,
> have you entered into the springs of the sea,
> or have you walked in search of the depth? . . .
> Who has put wisdom in the inward parts
> and given understanding to the heart?
> Answer me."
>
> The breeze is making eddies in the mist,
> and out of those small whirlwinds come the words:
> "I have walked along the bottom of the sea
> wrenched into the clouds at Valparaiso;
> I have seen the birth of islands and
> the build of continents; I
> know the rise and fall of mountain ranges,
> I understand the wings of pigeons,
> peacock feathers, finches: my mind creates
> general laws out of large
> collections of facts."
> The rigging sighs a little: God
> is slipping away without
> saying goodbye . . .
> "The activities of the mind,"
> Darwin murmurs, "are one of the bases of conscience."
>
> Astern the pious Spaniards go on praying
> and crushing the fingers of slaves; somewhere
> the Mylodon wanders away,
> out of the animal kingdom and
> into the empire of death.

For five billion years
we have seen the past, and
it works. . . .

So this is the final convoy
of the social instincts . . .
Now we ride the oceans of
imagination, all horizon
and no port. Darwin
will soon be home, his five-year
voyage on this little brig
all over; but when will I
be home, when will I arrive
at that special creation: a decent animal?

The land is failing the horizons, and
we only know to take the wheel
and test the ancient strength of human struggle,
remembering that we ourselves, the wonder
and glory of the universe, bear
in our lordly bones the indelible stamp
of our lowly
origin.[6]

As the twenty-first century unfolds, Darwin continues to inspire and instruct not only novelists and poets, but also science writers like Richard Dawkins, Stephen Jay Gould, and others, whose books and essays—like those of the late Loren Eiseley, Carl Sagan, and Lewis Thomas—engagingly clarify and amplify Darwinian ideas for a wide public. (See, for example, their several contributions to this volume.)

The profusion of recent literary works using Darwinian motifs and references demonstrates that evolution has become so much a part of our mental equipment that readers accept it as a given, and writers are eager to explore its implications in diverse and imaginative ways. Evolution continues to be a familiar theme in contemporary literature, and Darwin himself an abiding presence.

6. Used by permission of the University of Arkansas Press.

Selected Readings

•Indicates works excerpted in this Norton Critical Edition.

PART II. DARWIN'S LIFE

•Barlow, Nora, ed. *The Autobiography of Charles Darwin, 1809–1882*, (with original omissions restored). New York, 1969.
Bowlby, J. *Charles Darwin: A Biography*. London, 1990.
Brent, Peter. *Charles Darwin*. London, 1981.
Browne, Janet. *Charles Darwin, I: Voyaging*. New York, 1995.
Burckhardt, Frederick, Sydney Smith, and others, eds. *The Correspondence of Charles Darwin*, vols. 1–10. Cambridge, UK, 1985–.
Colp, Ralph, Jr. *To Be an Invalid: The Illness of Charles Darwin*. Chicago, 1977.
Darwin, Francis, ed. *The Life and Letters of Charles Darwin*. New York, 1959.
•DeBeer, Gavin. *Charles Darwin: A Scientific Biography*. New York, 1964.
Desmond, Adrian, and James Moore. *Darwin*. London, 1991.
Goldstein, Jared Haft. "Darwin, Chagas', Mind, and Body." *Perspectives in Biology and Medicine* 32 (1989): 586–601.
Gruber, Howard E. *Darwin on Man: A Psychological Study of Scientific Creativity*. Chicago, 1981.
Litchfield, H. E. *Emma Darwin: A Century of Family Letters, 1792–1896*. London, 1915.
Moore, James. *The Darwin Legend*. Grand Rapids, Mich., 1994.

PART III. SCIENTIFIC THOUGHT: JUST BEFORE DARWIN

Chambers, Robert. *Vestiges of the Natural History of Creation*. London, 1844.
•Herschel, John. *Preliminary Discourse on the Study of Natural Philosophy*. London, 1830.
•Lamarck, Jean Baptiste Pierre Antoine de Monet. *Zoological Philosophy*. Paris, 1809.
•Lyell, Charles. *Principles of Geology*. London, 1830–33.
•Malthus, Thomas Robert. *An Essay on the Principle of Population*. London, 1798; rev., 1803.
Mill, John Stuart. *A System of Logic, Ratiocination and Induction*. London, 1843.
•Paley, William. *Natural Theology: Or Evidences of the Existence and Attributes of the Deity Collected from the Appearances of Nature*. London, 1802.
•Wallace, Alfred Russel. "On the Tendency of Varieties to Depart Indefinitely from the Original Type." *Journal of the Proceedings of the Linnean Society, Zoology* III (August 20, 1858).
•Whewell, William. *Astronomy and General Physics Considered with Reference to Natural Theology*. London, 1833.

PART IV. SELECTIONS FROM DARWIN'S WORK

Barrett, Paul, and others, eds. *Charles Darwin's Notebooks, 1836–1844*. Cambridge, UK, 1985.
Burkhardt, Frederick, and others. *Darwin's Scientific Diaries, 1836–1842*. Cambridge, UK, 1987.
•Darwin, Charles. *Journal of Researches into the Geology and Natural History of the Various Countries Visited by H.M.S. "Beagle"* . . . London, 1839; 2nd ed., 1845.
———. *The Structure and Distribution of Coral Reefs*. London, 1842.
———. *A Monograph of the Sub-class Cirripedia* . . . London, 1851.
•———. "On the Tendency of Species to Form Varieties . . ." *Journal of the Proceedings of the Linnean Society, Zoology* III (August 20, 1858): 45–62.
•———. *On the Origin of Species by Means of Natural Selection* . . . London, 1859; facsimile edition, Cambridge, Mass., 1964.
———. *On the Various Contrivances by Which British and Foreign Orchids Are Fertilized by Insects, and on the Good Effects of Intercrossing*. London, 1862.
———. *The Variation of Animals and Plants under Domestication*. London, 1868.
•———. *The Descent of Man* . . . London, 1871.
———. *The Expression of the Emotions in Man and Animals*. London, 1872.
———. *Insectivorous Plants*. London, 1875.
———. *The Power of Movements in Plants*. London, 1880.
———. *The Formation of Vegetable Mould* . . . London, 1881.

Di Gregorio, Mario A., ed. *Charles Darwin's Marginalia, I.* 1990.
Keynes, Richard, ed. *Charles Darwin's "Beagle" Diary.* Cambridge, UK, 1988.
Stauffer, R. C., ed. *Charles Darwin's Natural Selection: Being the Second Part of His Big Species Book Written from 1856 to 1858.* Cambridge, UK, 1975.

PART V. DARWIN'S INFLUENCE ON SCIENCE

Ayala, Francisco J., ed. *Molecular Evolution.* New York, 1976.
Barkow, Jerome H., Leda Cosmides, and John Tooby. *The Adapted Mind: Evolutionary Psychology and the Generation of Culture.* New York, 1992.
Blinderman, Charles. *The Piltdown Inquest.* Buffalo, N.Y., 1986.
Bowler, Peter J. *Darwinism.* New York, 1993.
• ———. *Evolution: The History of an Idea.* Berkeley, Calif., 1984.
Clark, W. E. LeGros. *The Fossil Evidence for Human Evolution.* Chicago, 1978.
Corballis, Michael C. *The Lopsided Ape: Evolution of the Generative Mind.* New York, 1991.
Dawkins, Richard. *The Selfish Gene.* New York, 1976.
• ———. *The Blind Watchmaker.* London, 1986.
——. *Climbing Mount Improbable.* New York, 1996.
——. *Unweaving the Rainbow.* New York, 1998.
Depew, David J., and Bruce H. Weber. *Darwinism Evolving: Systems Dynamics and the Genealogy of Natural Selection.* Cambridge, Mass., 1995.
Desmond, Adrian. *Huxley.* Reading, Mass., 1997.
Dobzhansky, Theodosius. *Genetics and the Origin of Species.* New York, 1937.
Durant, John R., ed. *Human Origins.* New York, 1989.
Eibl-Eibesfeldt, Irenaus. *Human Ethology.* Hawthorne, N.Y., 1989.
Eiseley, Loren. *Darwin's Century.* New York, 1958.
• Eldredge, Niles. *Reinventing Darwin . . .* London, 1995.
• Endler, John A. *Natural Selection in the Wild.* Princeton, N.J., 1986.
Fisher, Ronald A. *The Genetical Theory of Natural Selection.* Oxford, UK, 1930.
Flanagan, Dennis, and others. *Evolution.* New York, 1978.
Fossey, Dian. *Gorillas in the Mist.* Boston, 1983.
Futuyma, D. J. *Evolutionary Biology.* Sunderland, Mass., 1979.
Ghiselin, Michael T. *The Triumph of the Darwinian Method.* Berkeley, Calif., 1969.
Gillespie, C. C. *Genesis and Geology.* Cambridge, Mass., 1959.
Goodall, Jane. *The Chimpanzees of Gombe.* Cambridge, Mass., 1986.
——. *In the Shadow of Man.* Boston, 1983.
• Gould, James L., and William T. Keeton, with Carol Grant Gould. *Biological Science.* New York, 1996.
• Gould, Stephen Jay. *Ever Since Darwin.* New York, 1977.
——. *Ontogeny and Phylogeny.* Cambridge, Mass., 1977.
——. *The Panda's Thumb.* New York, 1980.
——. *An Urchin in the Storm.* New York, 1987.
——. *Full House.* New York, 1996.
—— and Niles Eldredge. "Punctuated Equilibrium: An Alternative to Phyletic Gradualism." In T. J. M. Schopf, ed. *Models in Paleobiology.* San Francisco, 1972.
Grant, Peter R. *Ecology and Evolution of Darwin's Finches.* Princeton, N.J., 1986.
—— and Rosemary Grant. *Evolutionary Dynamics of a Natural Population: The Large Cactus Finch of the Galapagos.* Chicago, 1989.
Gruber, Howard. *Darwin on Man.* London, 1974.
Haraway, Donna. *Primate Visions.* New York, 1989.
Hennig, Willi. *Phylogenetic Systematics.* Trans. D. Dwight Davis and Rainer Zangerl. Urbana, Ill., 1966.
• Hull, David L. *Darwin and His Critics.* Chicago, 1973.
Huxley, Julian. *Evolution: The Modern Synthesis.* New York, 1963.
——. *Evolution in Action.* New York, 1953.
Jann, Rosemary. "Darwin and the Anthropologists: Sexual Selection and Its Discontents." *Victorian Studies* 37 (1984): 286–306.
Johanson, Donald C., and Maitland A. Edey. *Lucy: The Beginnings of Humankind.* New York, 1982.
——. *Lucy's Child: The Discovery of a Human Ancestor.* New York, 1989.
——. *Blueprints: Solving the Mystery of Evolution.* Boston, 1989.
—— and Greta Jones. *Social Darwinism and English Thought.* Brighton, UK, 1980.
• Koertge, Noretta. *A House Built on Sand.* New York, 1998.
• Kuper, Adam. *The Chosen Primate,* Cambridge, Mass., 1994.
Kohn, David, ed. *The Darwinian Heritage.* Princeton, N.J., 1985.
Lancaster, Jane B. *Primate Behavior and the Emergence of Human Culture.* New York, 1975.
Leakey, Louis S. B. *The Progress and Evolution of Man in Africa.* New York, 1961.
Leakey, Mary D. *Disclosing the Past: An Autobiography.* New York, 1985.
Leakey, Richard. *Origins Reconsidered: In Search of What Makes Us Human.* New York, 1992.
—— and Roger Lewin. *The Sixth Extinction: Patterns of Life and the Future of Humankind.* New York, 1995.

Lewin, Roger. *Thread of Life: The Smithsonian Looks at Evolution*. Washington, D.C., 1982.
Margulis, Lynn. *Symbiosis in Cell Evolution*. New York, 1993.
•Matsumara, Molleen, ed. *Voices for Evolution*. 2nd ed. Berkeley, Calif., 1995.
Mayr, Ernst. *The Growth of Biological Thought*. Cambridge, Mass., 1982.
•———. *One Long Argument: Charles Darwin and the Genesis of Evolutionary Thought*. Cambridge, Mass., 1991.
———. *This Is Biology: The Science of the Living World*. Cambridge, Mass., 1997.
Mead, Margaret. *Continuities in Cultural Evolution*. New Haven, Conn., 1964.
Montgomery, Sy. *Walking with the Great Apes: Jane Goodall, Dian Fossey, Birute Galdikas*. Boston, 1992.
Morgan, T. H. *Evolution and Genetics*. Princeton, N.J., 1925.
•National Academy of Sciences. *Teaching about Evolution and the Nature of Science*. Washington, D.C., 1998.
•———. *Science and Creationism*. Washington, D.C., 1999.
Oldroyd, David R. *Darwinian Impacts: An Introduction to the Darwinian Revolution*. Atlantic Highlands, N.J., 1980.
Ospovat, Dov. *The Development of Darwin's Theory: Natural History, Natural Theology, and Natural Selection*. Cambridge, UK, 1981.
Otte, Daniel, and John A. Endler, eds. *Speciation and Its Consequences*. Sunderland, Mass., 1989.
Pinker, Steven, *The Language Instinct: How the Mind Creates Language*. New York, 1994.
•———. *How the Mind Works*. New York, 1997.
Richards, Robert J. *The Meaning of Evolution*. Chicago, 1992.
Ruse, Michael. *The Darwinian Revolution*. Chicago, 1979.
———. *The Darwinian Paradigm: Essays on Its History, Philosophy, and Religious Implications*. London, 1989.
———. *Monad to Man: The Concept of Progress in Evolutionary Biology*. Cambridge, Mass., 1996.
Smith, Fred H., and Frank Spencer, eds. *The Origins of Modern Humans: A World Survey of the Fossil Evidence*. New York, 1984.
Smith, John Maynard. *The Theory of Evolution*. Harmondsworth, UK, 1975.
Simpson, George Gaylord. *The Meaning of Evolution*. New Haven, Conn., 1949.
Sober, Elliott. *Conceptual Issues in Evolutionary Biology*. Cambridge, Mass., 1984.
———. *The Nature of Selection*. Cambridge, Mass., 1985.
Smuts, Barbara B. *Sex and Friendship in Baboons*. New York, 1985.
Stringer, Christopher, and Robin McKie. *African Exodus: The Origins of Modern Humanity*. New York, 1997.
Tattersall, Ian. *Becoming Human*. New York, 1998.
———. *The Human Trail: How We Know What We Think We Know about Human Evolution*. New York, 1995.
———, Eric Delson, and John Van Couvering. *Encyclopedia of Human Evolution and Prehistory*. New York, 1988.
Tax, Sol. *Evolution after Darwin*. Chicago, 1960.
Weiner, Jonathan. *The Beak of the Finch*. New York, 1994.
•Wilson, Edward O. *Sociobiology*. Cambridge, Mass., 1975.
———. *Consilience*. New York, 1998.
Williams, George C. *Natural Selection: Domains, Levels, and Applications*. New York, 1992.

PART VI. DARWINIAN PATTERNS IN SOCIAL THOUGHT

Barlow, Connie. *Green Space, Green Time*. New York, 1997.
Birken, Lawrence. "Darwin and Gender." *Proteus* 6 (1989): 24–29.
Bowler, Peter J. *Biology and Social Thought, 1850–1914*. Berkeley, Calif., 1993.
Churchill, Frederick B. "Darwin and the Historians." In R. J. Berry, ed. *Charles Darwin: A Commemoration, 1882–1982*. London, 1982.
Degler, Carl N. *In Search of Human Nature: The Decline and Revival of Darwinism in American Social Thought*. New York, 1991.
•Carnegie, Andrew. *The Gospel of Wealth* . . . New York, 1900.
Diamond, Jared. *The Third Chimpanzee: The Evolution and Future of the Human Animal*. New York, 1992.
Ehrenreich, Barbara. *Blood Rites: Origins and History of the Passions of War*. New York, 1997.
•——— and Janet McIntosh. "The New Creationism: Biology under Attack." *The Nation* (June 9, 1997): 11–16.
Gordon, Scott. "Darwin and Political Economy: The Connection Reconsidered." *Journal of the History of Biology* 22 (1989): 437–59.
Gould, Stephen Jay. *The Mismeasure of Man*. New York, 1977.
Greene, John C. *The Death of Adam: Evolution and Its Impact on Western Thought*. New York, 1959.
Hrdy, Sarah Blaffer. *Mother Nature: A History of Mothers, Infants, and Natural Selection*. New York, 1999.
•Hofstadter, Richard. *Social Darwinism in American Thought*. Boston, 1955.
•Kropotkin Peter. *Mutual Aid*. London, 1902.

Lewontin, R. C., Steven Rose, and Leon J. Kamin. *Not in Our Genes.* New York, 1984.
Langs, Robert. *The Evolution of the Emotion-Processing Mind.* London, 1996.
Mayr, Ernst. *Evolution and the Diversity of Life.* Cambridge, Mass., 1976.
Nesse, Randolph, and George Williams. *Why We Get Sick: The New Science of Darwinian Medicine.* New York, 1994.
•Oldroyd, David, and Ian Langham. *The Wider Domain of Evolutionary Thought.* London, 1983.
•Stanton, Elizabeth Cady. *The Woman's Bible* (1895, 1898). See Annie Laurie Gaylor, ed. *Women without Superstition.* Madison, Wisc., 1997.
Tanner, Nancy M. *On Becoming Human.* Cambridge, UK, 1981.

PART VII. DARWINIAN INFLUENCES IN PHILOSOPHY AND ETHICS

Birx, H. James. *Theories of Evolution.* Springfield, Ill., 1984.
•Dennett, Daniel. *Darwin's Dangerous Idea: Evolution and the Meanings of Life.* London, 1995.
•DeWaal, Frans. *Good Natured.* Cambridge, Mass., 1996.
•Dewey, John. *The Influence of Darwin on Philosophy . . .* New York, 1910.
Gillispie, C. C. *Charles Darwin and the Problem of Creation.* Chicago, 1979.
Gorney, Roderic. *The Human Agenda.* Los Angeles, 1979.
Hull, David L. *Philosophy of Biological Science.* Englewood Cliffs, N.J., 1974.
•Huxley, Thomas Henry, and Julian Huxley. *Touchstone for Ethics.* New York, 1947.
Mayr, Ernst. "Darwin's Impact on Modern Thought." *Proceedings of the American Philosophical Society* 139 (1995): 317–25.
Rachels, James. *Created from Animals: The Moral Implications of Darwinism.* New York, 1990.
•Ridley, Matt. *The Origins of Virtue: Human Instincts and the Evolution of Cooperation.* New York, 1997.
Ruse, Michael. *Philosophy of Biology.* Buffalo, N.Y., 1998.
——. *Taking Darwin Seriously: A Naturalistic Approach to Philosophy.* Oxford, UK, 1987.
Waddington, C. H. *The Ethical Animal.* London, 1960.
Wilson, James Q. *The Moral Sense.* New York, 1993.

PART VIII. EVOLUTIONARY THEORY AND RELIGIOUS THEORY

•Behe, Michael J. *Darwin's Black Box: The Biochemical Challenge to Evolution.* New York, 1996.
Birx, H. James. "Origin of Life and Unbelief." In Gordon Stein, ed. *Encyclopedia of Unbelief.* Buffalo, N.Y., 1985.
Edis, Taner. "Islamic Creationism in Turkey." *Creation/Evolution* 34 (1994): 1–4.
Eldredge, Niles. *The Monkey Business: A Scientist Looks at Creationism.* New York, 1982.
Eve, Raymond A., and Francis B. Harrold. *The Creationist Movement in Modern America.* Boston, 1991.
——, eds. *Cult Archaeology and Creationism: Understanding Pseudoscientific Beliefs about the Past.* Iowa City, 1987.
Frye, R. *Is God a Creationist? The Religious Case against Creation-Science.* New York, 1983.
Gish, Duane T. *Evolution: The Challenge of the Fossil Record.* El Cajon, Calif., 1985.
Godfrey, Laurie R. *Scientists Confront Creationism.* New York, 1983.
Gould, Stephen Jay. *Rocks of Ages: Science and Religion in the Fullness of Life.* New York, 1999.
•Hughes, Liz Rank. *Reviews of Creationist Books.* Berkeley, Calif., 1992.
•Johnson, Phillip. *Darwin on Trial.* Washington, D.C., 1991.
Kitcher, Philip. *Abusing Science: The Case against Creationism.* Cambridge, Mass., 1982.
Larson, Edward J. *Summer for the Gods.* New York, 1997.
——. *Trial and Error: The American Controversy over Evolution.* New York, 1985.
•Matsumura, Molleen. *Voices for Evolution.* Berkeley, Calif., 1995.
McIver, Tom. *Anti-Evolution: An Annotated Bibliography.* Jefferson, N.C., 1988.
——, *Anti-Evolution: A Reader's Guide to Literature Before and After Darwin.* Baltimore, 1992.
Moore, James R. *The Post-Darwinian Controversies.* Cambridge, UK, 1979.
Montagu, Ashley. *Science and Creationism.* New York, 1984.
•Morris, Henry M. *Scientific Creationism.* Green Forest, Ariz., 1985.
Nelkin, Dorothy. *The Creation Controversy: Science or Scripture in the Schools.* New York, 1982.
Pennock, Robert. *Tower of Babel: The Evidence against the New Creationism.* Cambridge, 1999.
Ruse, Michael. *Darwinism Defended: A Guide to the Evolution Controversies,* Reading, Mass., 1982.
——, ed. *But Is It Science: The Philosophical Question in the Creation/Evolution Controversy.* Amherst, N.Y., 1988.
Scott, Eugenie C. "Antievolutionism, Scientific Creationism, and Physical Anthropology." *Yearbook of Physical Anthropology* 30 (1987): 21–39.
•——. "Antievolutionism and Creationism in the United States." *Annual Review of Anthropology* 26 (1997): 263–89.
White, Andrew Dickson. *A History of the Warfare of Science with Theology in Christendom.* New York, 1896.

PART IX. DARWIN AND THE LITERARY MIND

•Adams, James E. "Woman Red in Tooth and Claw: Nature and the Feminine in Tennyson and Darwin." *Victorian Studies* 33 (1989): 7–27.
•Appleman, Philip. *Darwin's Ark*, Bloomington, Ind., 1984; in *New and Selected Poems, 1956–1996.* Fayetteville, Ark., 1996.
——. *Apes and Angels.* New York, 1989.
——, William A. Madden, and Michael Wolff, eds. *1859: Entering an Age of Crisis.* Bloomington, Ind., 1959.
Barzun, Jacques. *Darwin, Marx, Wagner: Critique of a Heritage.* New York, 1941.
Beach, Joseph Warren. *The Concept of Nature in Nineteenth-Century English Poetry.* New York, 1936.
•Becker, Anne. *The Transmutation Notebooks: Poems in the Voices of Charles and Emma Darwin.* Washington, D.C., 1996.
•Beer, Gillian. *Darwin's Plots: Evolutionary Narrative in Darwin, George Eliot, and Nineteenth-Century Fiction.* London, 1983; Cambridge, UK, 2000.
Blinderman, Charles S. "Huxley, Pater, and Protoplasm." *Journal of the History of Ideas* 42 (1982): 477–86.
Brantlinger, Patrick, ed. *Energy and Entropy: Science and Culture in Victorian Britain.* Bloomington, Ind., 1989.
Carroll, Joseph. *Evolution and Literary Theory.* Columbia, Mo., 1995.
Chapple, J. A. V. *Science and Literature in the Nineteenth Century.* London, 1996.
Culler, A. Dwight. "The Darwinian Revolution and Literary Form." In George Levine and William A. Madden, eds. *The Art of Victorian Prose.* New York, 1968.
Faggen, Robert. *Robert Frost and the Challenge of Darwin.* Ann Arbor, Mich., 1997.
Hyman, Stanley Edgar. *The Tangled Bank: Darwin, Marx, Frazer and Freud as Imaginative Writers.* New York, 1962.
Krasner, James. "A Chaos of Delight: Perception and Illusion in Darwin's Scientific Writing." *Representations* 31 (1990): 118–41.
•Krutch, Joseph Wood. *The Modern Temper.* New York, 1929.
•Levine, George. *Darwin and the Novelists: Patterns of Science in Victorian Fiction.* Cambridge, Mass., 1988.
——, ed. *One Culture: Essays in Science and Literature.* Madison, Wis., 1987.
——. "Darwin among the Critics." *Victorian Studies* 30 (1987): 253–60.
•——. "Darwin and Pain: Why Science Made Shakespeare Nauseating." *Raritan Quarterly* 15 (fall 1995): 97–144.
Morton, Peter. *The Vital Science: Biology and the Literary Imagination, 1860–1900.* London, 1984.
•Muller, Herbert J. *The Spirit of Tragedy.* New York, 1956.
•Stevens, L. Robert. "Darwin's Humane Reading: The Anaesthetic Man Reconsidered." *Victorian Studies* 26 (1982): 51–63.
•Stevenson, Lionel. *Darwin among the Poets.* Chicago, 1932.
Young, Robert. *Darwin's Metaphor: Nature's Place in Victorian Culture.* Cambridge, UK, 1985.

BIBLIOGRAPHIES

Eisen, Sydney, and Bernard V. Lightman. *Victorian Science and Religion: A Bibliography with Emphasis on Evolution, Belief, and Unbelief.* Hampden, Conn., 1984.
Freeman, R. B. *Charles Darwin: A Companion.* Folkestone, 1978.
Ruse, Michael. "The Darwin Industry: A Guide." *Victorian Studies* 39 (1996): 217–35.
Also consult the annual "Victorian Bibliography" in the summer issue of *Victorian Studies* and the annual MLA "International Bibliography" in *PMLA*.
A number of Darwin Web sites exist, some of which include bibliographical resources.

Index